D0209409

AIMEE SONG

WORLD OF STYLE

AIMEE SONG

WORLD OF STYLE

With Erin Weinger

ABRAMS IMAGE, NEW YORK

Editor: Rebecca Kaplan

Designer: Shira Chung

Production Manager: Anet Sirna-Bruder

Library of Congress Control Number:
2018944557

ISBN: 978-1-4197-3336-9
eISBN: 978-1-68335-419-2

Text and photographs copyright © 2018 Aimee Song, except as listed on page 352

Cover © 2018 Abrams

Published in 2018 by Abrams Image, an imprint of ABRAMS. All rights reserved. No portion of this book may be reproduced, stored in a retrieval system, or transmitted in any form or by any means, mechanical, electronic, photocopying, recording, or otherwise, without written permission from the publisher.

Printed and bound in the United States
10 9 8 7 6 5 4 3 2 1

Abrams Image books are available at special discounts when purchased in quantity for premiums and promotions as well as fundraising or educational use. Special editions can also be created to specification. For details, contact specialsales@abramsbooks.com or the address below.

Abrams Image® is a registered trademark of Harry N. Abrams, Inc.

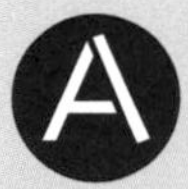

ABRAMS The Art of Books
195 Broadway, New York, NY 10007
abramsbooks.com

INTRODUCTION

Ten years ago, in October 2008, I was living in a small student apartment in San Francisco that faced a parking lot while studying interior architecture, which I was able to do after three years at a reception desk job and saving enough money for tuition. I was active on MySpace and Xanga—one of the earliest blogging platforms—and thought it would be cool to start a blog on Blogspot that shared my love of the perfectly appointed Kelly Wearstler rooms and majestic Victorian row houses that dotted my adopted city—aka the very things I was planning on making my living on one day very soon.

My first post was a video of an Adele performance on *Saturday Night Live* (non-interiors related, I realize, but never mind that), followed by some inspirational interior design photos. And then, as I was taking photos of myself in an outfit to see if it looked appropriate for an after-class job interview (on a point-and-shoot camera set up on a tripod, no less), I decided to do something different: post one of the outfit photos on my blog.

The picture was blurry and looked like it had a yellow filter. But people within the Blogspot community found it and responded—favorably, in fact. And I realized how much fun it was to create content that people seemed to like.

No matter how busy I was with my two jobs and full-time class load, I always made time to tend to my blog—hosting images on a third-party hosting service, journaling, writing random thoughts about school, and, yes, posting photos of the outfits I was actually wearing to work and class (with sensible school flats sometimes swapped out for platforms that were not S.F.-friendly in the least). I made it a mission to post five times per week; even on days when everything seemed to be going wrong and I didn't want to emerge from under the covers I would still take an outfit shot and post something new. Soon, other bloggers started reposting my photos. And before long *Song of Style* had an ever-growing following and some referral traffic.

Then, more people followed. And more referral traffic came my way. About a year after I began blogging it hit me that my words and photos were reaching thousands of people every month (150,000 people a month to be exact, according to Google Analytics). People started recognizing me at school, and complete strangers came up to me on the streets of San Francisco to say that they were a fan of my posts. More than once I was on the floor stacking boxes at the DSW Designer Shoe Warehouse where I worked and customers who were trying on shoes acknowledged me and

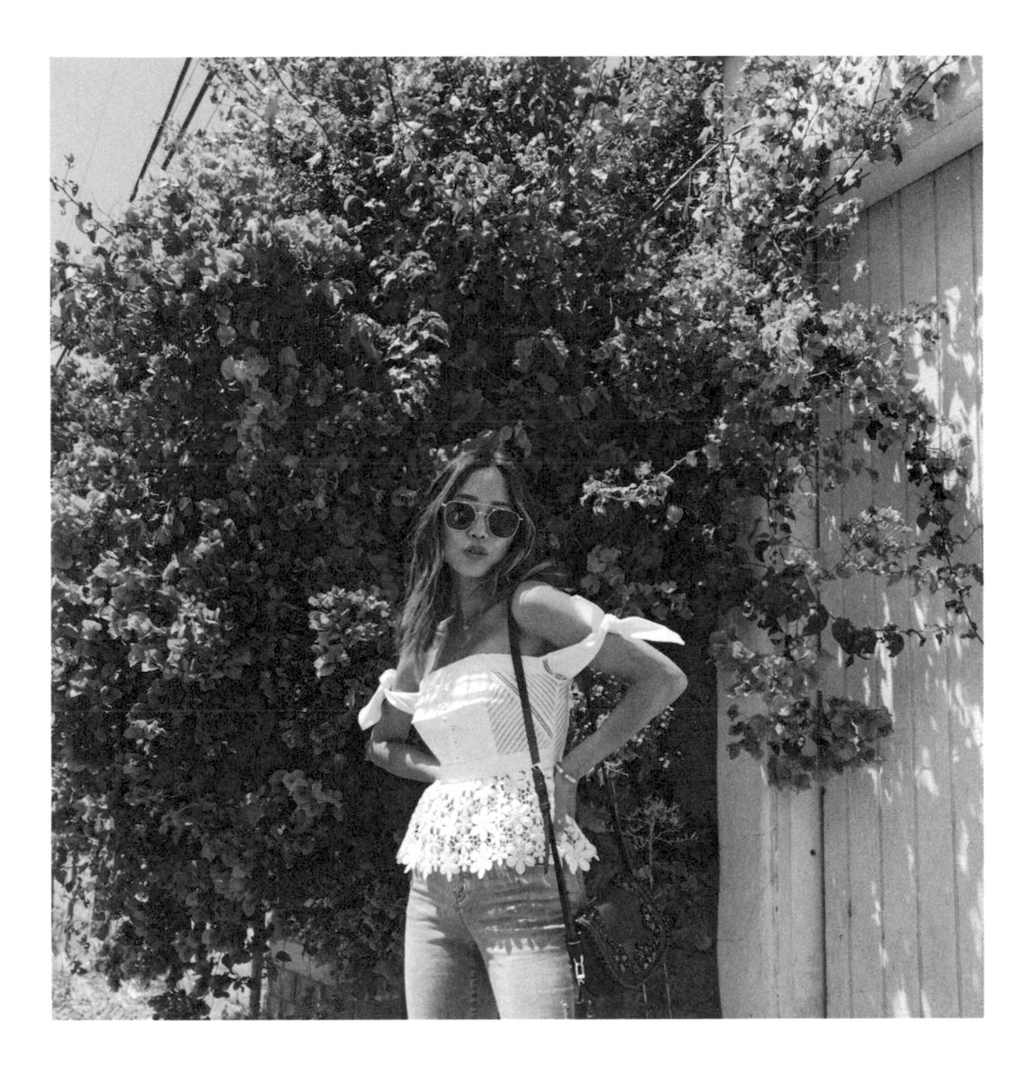

my blog. It was incredible. So incredible that I decided to invest in a better DSLR camera.

When *Song of Style* hit its two-year mark, small brands began reaching out and asking for my address so they could send me products, and I took the lead from other bloggers I followed and added small banner ads on my site so I could dip my toe in the advertising game. I had no idea what I was doing, but as they say, fake it till you make it. And I faked it hard.

Soon bigger brands began getting in touch with bigger opportunities. In 2010 Fossil flew me to Dallas so I could style and model pieces for a holiday campaign. It was my first paid partnership job that came as a result of *Song of Style*, and it still rates as one of the most important and meaningful moments in my professional life. I couldn't believe that I was able to get paid for doing something that I genuinely enjoyed so much.

After Fossil even more paid opportunities began to pop up. Then, around the time *Song of Style* turned three, I began getting invited to trips. And everything changed.

I grew up in Los Angeles and spent some time living in Japan and Korea as a child, not to mention we visited my grandma in Korea as a family. My parents split up when I was ten, so our family trips ended around that time, too (the family part being my favorite reason for traveling in the first place). Not to mention that my parents struggled financially, which meant that dreamy vacations were never a big part of our lives to begin with. When my classmates would come back from school breaks with tans and stories of their faraway adventures, I remember wishing to explore the world with my family and to make travel memories of my own.

Song of Style kept growing, and soon I was heading to New York with Charlotte Russe, and to Chicago, Florida, and Minnesota with Macy's. In 2012 famed Italian boutique Luisaviaroma invited me to Florence to partake in Firenze4Ever, the company's annual tech, fashion, music, and art festival. It was my first international trip that happened because of my blog, and I honestly couldn't believe that I was considered a big enough name to be included among the like of *The Blonde Salad* helmer Chiara Ferragni, an OG fashion blogger with an insanely huge following who I respected (and still respect) so much. After that trip it was official: I had caught the travel bug, and it wasn't going away anytime soon.

At that point *Song of Style* still felt like a hobby—an insanely fun and creative endeavor that I was incredibly passionate about working on as much as I could, even though I was still working at an architecture firm and moving toward my goal of becoming a full-time interior designer. But in 2011 I joined a new, small emerging platform called Instagram (you may have heard if it?) and things began to take off in a way that I never, ever in my wildest dreams could have expected.

Instagram opened my world up to a global audience, and I was getting comments and follows from people in countries that I'd only ever seen on a map. As my follower and engagement count went up, so did the amount of pinch-me opportunities that came my way. Luxury fashion and beauty brands, airlines, and even tourism boards wanted to work with me, and I got invitations to Morocco, Brazil, and others—again, places I'd only seen on a map and dreamed about visiting one day.

Today, with global fashion month happening twice a year, cruise shows in different cities each season, and photo shoots and partnership duties in places such as Dubai and Manila, I end up being on the road about eight months of the year. And I'm so incredibly fortunate to get to travel with people I love: my sister Dani, for one (who always makes everything better just by bringing her energy into a room), and my boyfriend Jacopo Moschin, one of the most talented photographers and smartest businessmen I know, who I met on a fateful trip to Morocco in 2014. While Jacopo has his own incredibly busy and burgeoning business and studio in New York, we try to collaborate as much as we can on shoots—which means many of our work trips to faraway locales end up being incredibly rich adventures that we get to share together. He's curious and takes the lead when we travel, and because of him I get to see a slice of the world that I never even knew existed.

I've met so many wonderful people that mean so much to me because of my travels, and I can truly say I have people I care about in every corner of the globe. Each trip I embark on ends up being an opportunity to learn about new cultures, ideas, and viewpoints. And I always come home feeing surer of myself, having a broader knowledge about a bevy of topics and a feeling of being more aware of my place on this planet—not to mention a heart full of immense appreciation for every opportunity I have been afforded.

I decided to organize this book—which at its heart is a tenth anniversary celebration of my blog—by the places I've visited as a result of it, because the perspective that global exploration has given me is one of the most invaluable rewards of *Song of Style*. Today, more than ever, it's so important to realize and understand the different angles and cultures that comprise our world, and I wanted to acknowledge that in this book.

You don't have to travel like a blogger or a baller to reap the benefits of leaving your comfort zone. You can do something as simple as taking a drive to a neighborhood in your city that you've never before explored, because if you do it with a curiosity and an open mind (two vital components of travel success) you'll come home richer and more fulfilled than when you left. I've never gone on a trip or adventure that I've regretted; even trips that have turned out completely different from what I had hoped still taught me unforgettable lessons and caused me to grow.

When I took my first outfit photo in my San Francisco apartment ten years ago, I never expected it to lead me to where I am today (travel pro tip #2,976: expect and embrace the unexpected). I wanted to work at an architecture firm, save enough money to buy a condo one day, and hopefully travel once a year when I was much, much older and settled. I couldn't afford to study abroad in college, so travel was something that always felt unattainable. Now I realize that absolutely nothing in this world is inaccessible with the right amount of hard work and an unwavering belief in yourself.

I have new dreams and plans today that include continuing to explore the world (Istanbul, Australia, and Sri Lanka are three places at the top of the current bucket list) and transforming my global brand into a media company that gives readers a new perspective and broader knowledge of our world. I wouldn't mind having a home to call my own in Italy, where my family can spend time creating cherished memories. And I want my Jacopo by my side for it all, of course.

Most importantly, I want you by my side, too—my readers and fans who have stayed with me as I've learned and grown throughout this process of turning a hobby into a business (complete with an ever-growing office and incredible team who make everything possible). We've all come up together, and so much of the joy I've been lucky enough to experience from *Song of Style* has happened as a direct result of you. There have been so many times that the hard work felt like too much and I didn't want to continue, but having you all with me for the journey has always been the guiding light that moves me forward.

A lot has changed in the last ten years, but my gratitude remains unwavering. It's a big, bold World of Style out there. I'm so excited to keep exploring it together.

Love,
Aimee

AMERICA

Austin

Chicago

Dallas

The Hamptons

Los Angeles

Miami

New York

Palm Springs

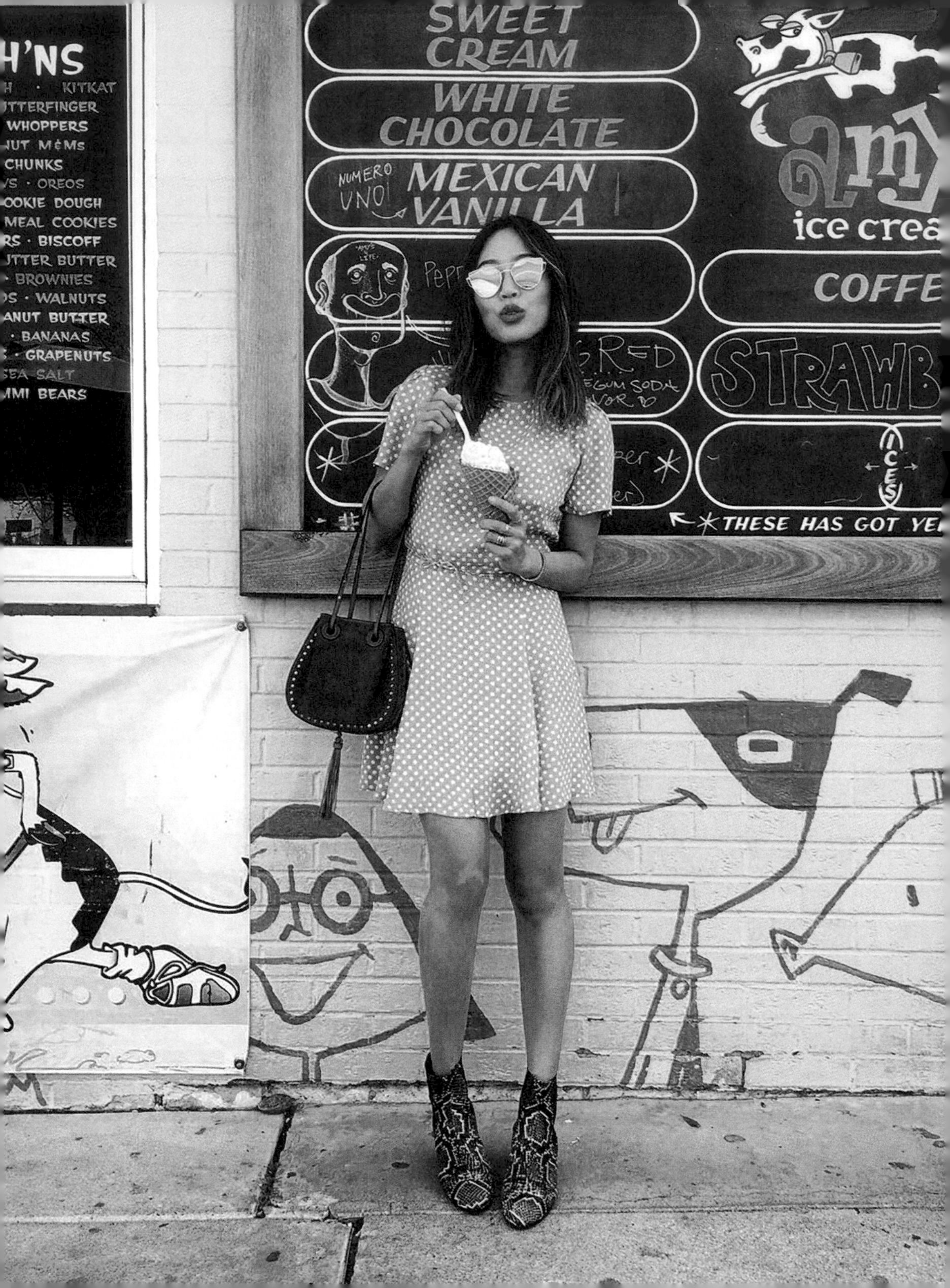

SWEET CREAM
WHITE CHOCOLATE
NUMERO UNO!
MEXICAN VANILLA
KITKAT
WHOPPERS
CHUNKS
OREOS
BISCOFF
BROWNIES
WALNUTS
BANANAS
GRAPENUTS
ICES

AUSTIN

I went to Austin for the first time in April 2016 with Revolve for South by Southwest (SXSW). I'd never heard a bad thing about the city and had always wanted to go, and that trip—which I went on with my sister Dani and one of my closest friends Camila (the first trip Camila and I ever took together!)—didn't disappoint. (How could a trip with your BFFs to an amazing, culturally progressive city with killer food ever be bad?) Think insane, creative comfort food, like cauliflower and mussels at a cool spot called Launderette, and roasted-beet-and-mint ice cream at Lick Honest Ice Creams, a parlor that my Instagram community recommended; amazing shopping (cowboy boots, anyone?); and a really trendy design and boutique hotel scene that feels upmarket but comfortable and unpretentious, aka my favorite aesthetic in the world.

OPPOSITE Getting ice cream—one of the best activities in the world. *Privacy Please dress; Isabel Marant boots.*

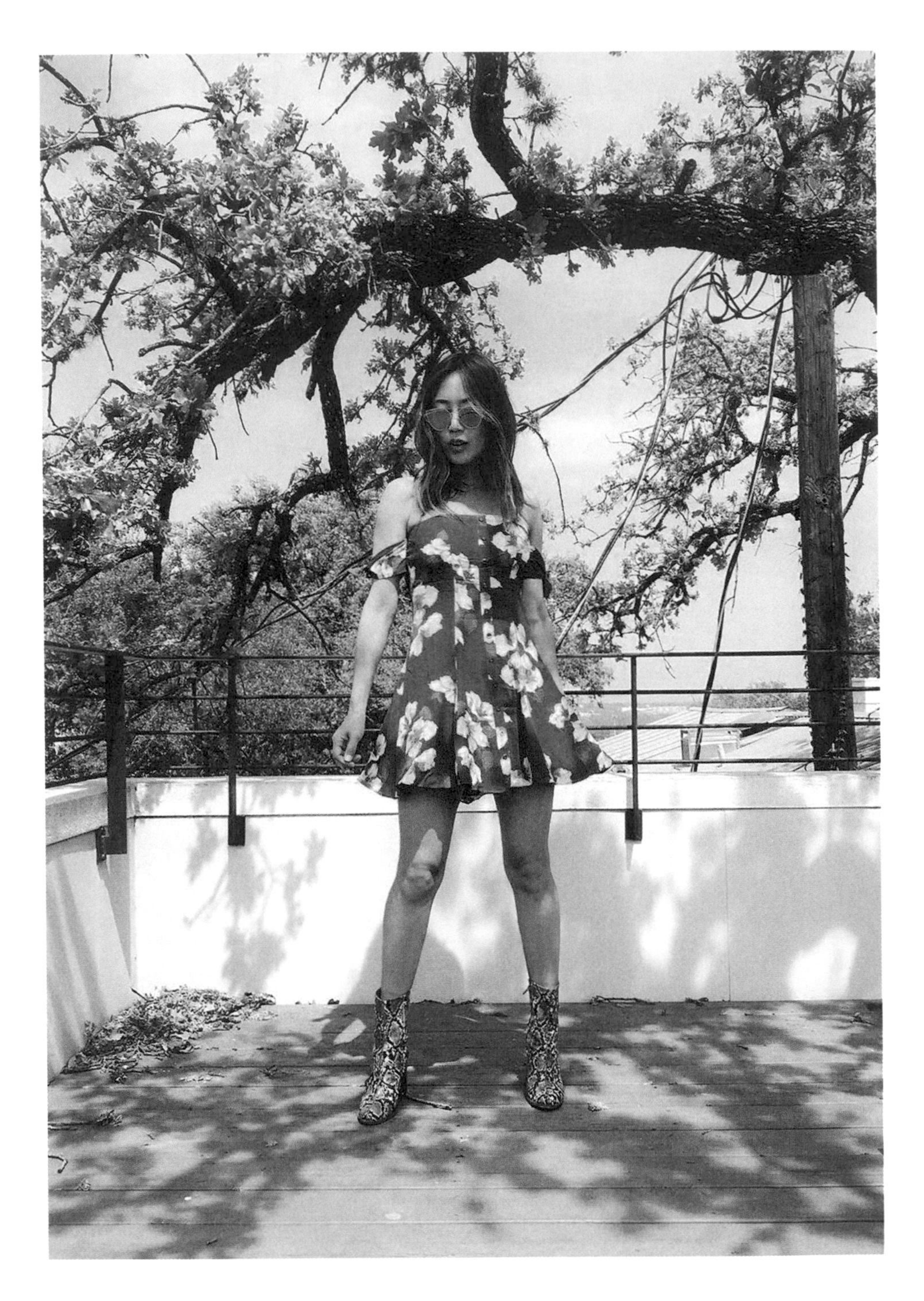

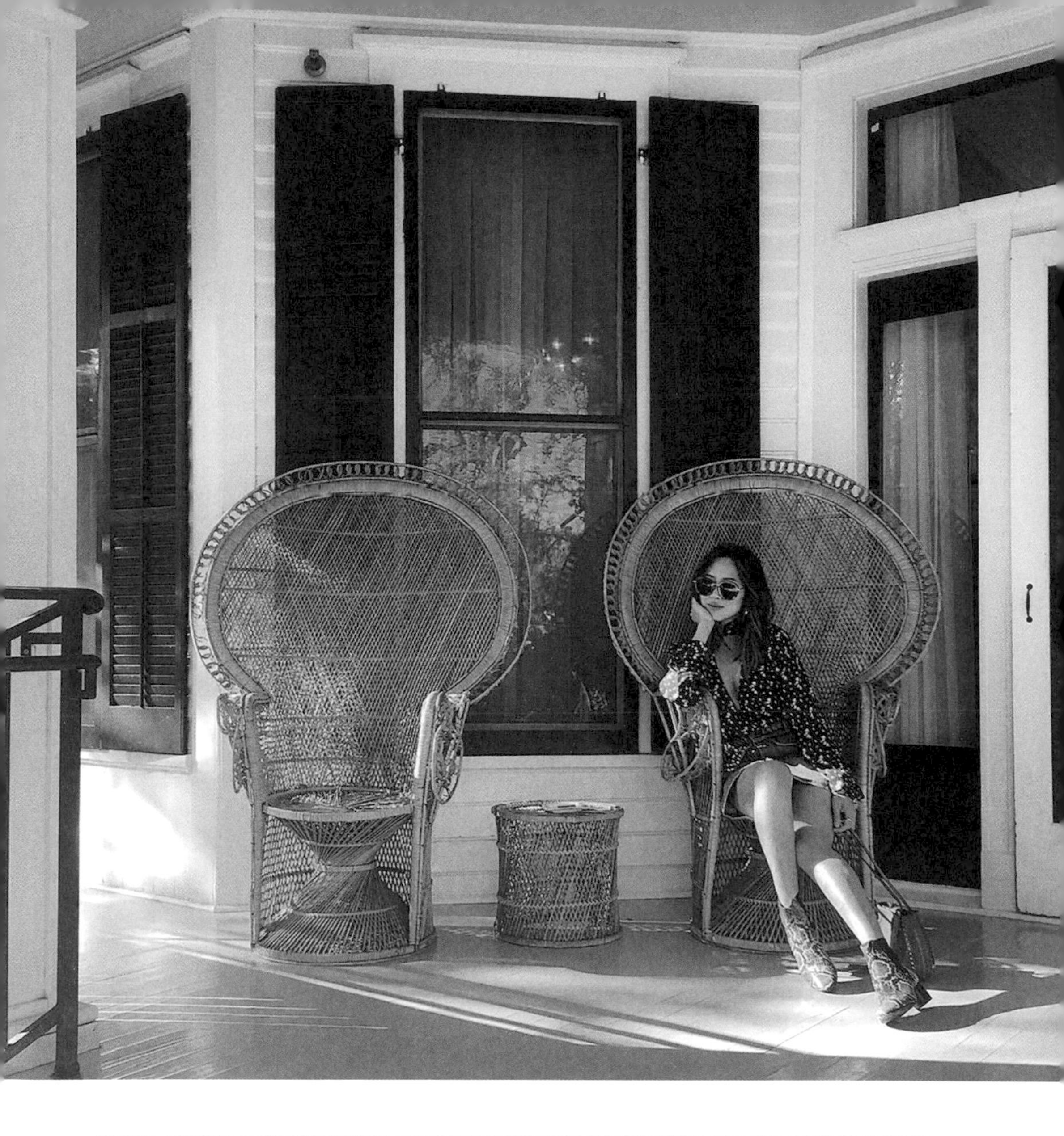

ABOVE When I saw these perfect Emmanuelle (peacock) rattan chairs in front of a hotel, I knew I had to have them for my house. I've since scored a very cool mini version that I found at the Rose Bowl Flea Market, but I'm still searching for the perfect original. Fun fact: Right after this, I saw Anthony Bourdain, one of my actual on-earth idols, sitting inside the hotel. I totally stared at him and didn't say hi and it was still one of the coolest celebrity sightings that has ever happened. *L'Academie blouse; Tularosa skirt.* **OPPOSITE** At our house. *Privacy Please dress.*

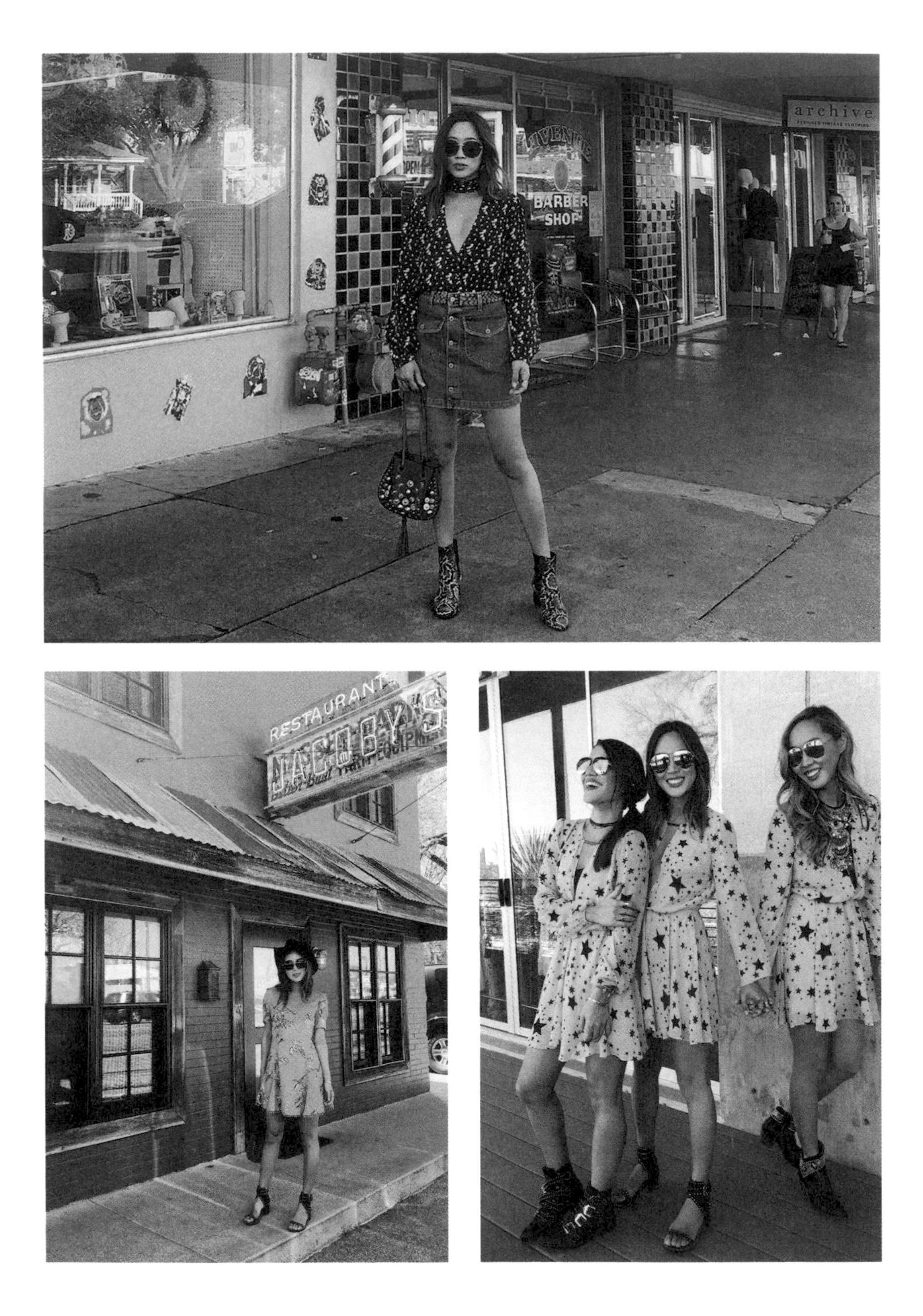
archive
BARBER
SHOP
RESTAURANT

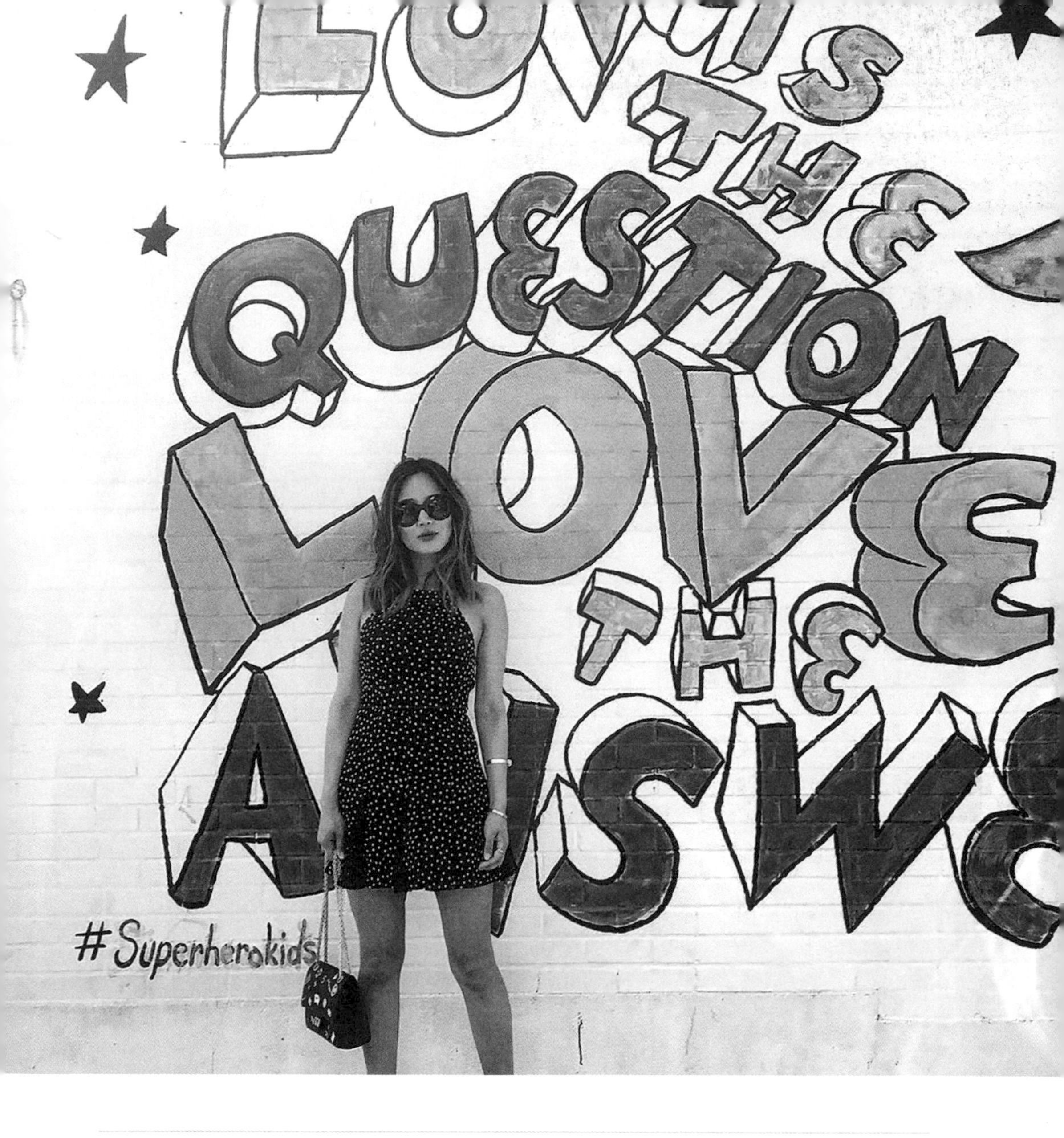

ABOVE Everyone was taking photos in front of this wall. When in Austin . . . *NBD dress; Chanel bag.* **OPPOSITE (CLOCKWISE FROM TOP)** *L'Academie blouse; Tularosa skirt; Isabel Marant boots* • Dani (far right) in her new cowboy boots, which I bought her as a gift on this trip. This was our twinning (tripleting?) moment with Camila. *All wearing Lovers and Friends; Dior sunglasses* • After eating at Jacoby's, a famous local spot where we didn't have a single bad meal. I bought the cowboy hat on this trip. Yee-haw. *Privacy Please dress; Isabel Marant shoes.*

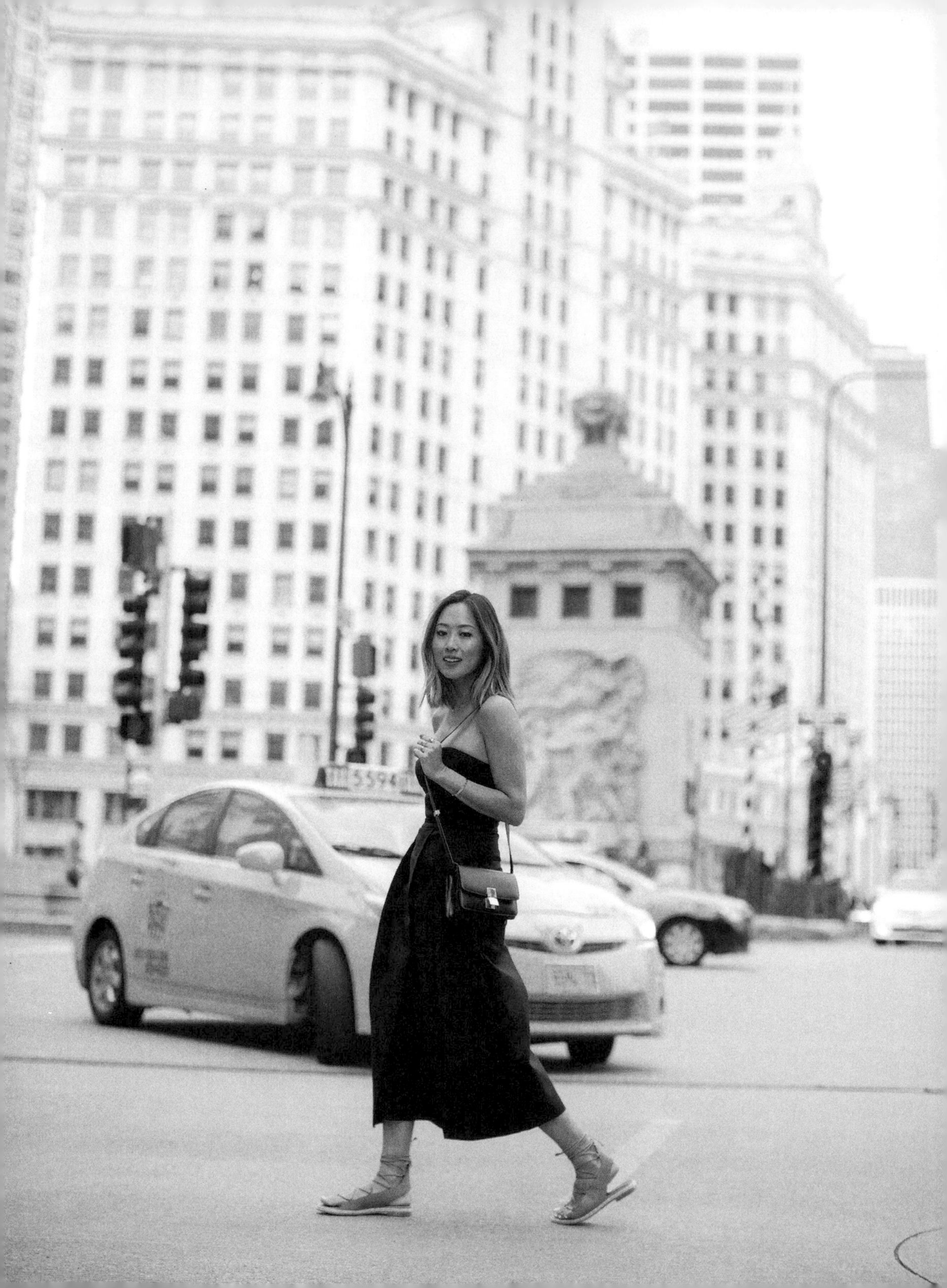
5594

CHICAGO

The first time I went to Chicago was in 2012 for a job with Macy's and its house line, Bar III. I instantly fell in love with the city—people had incredible midwestern manners and charm and were very nice. The weather happened to be perfect, which doesn't always happen in Chicago, and I went to the Randolph Street Flea Market, one of the best I've ever been to (think reasonably priced mid-century Herman Miller chairs that I still kick myself for leaving behind).

The second time I visited the Windy City was three years later, with my friend Jenny to help celebrate a Virgin Hotels opening. I took that trip to Instagram and started hitting up interesting people with great Chicago feeds—some of whom I still keep in touch with (that midwestern charm goes a long way in my book).

OPPOSITE *Tibi jumpsuit and sandals.*

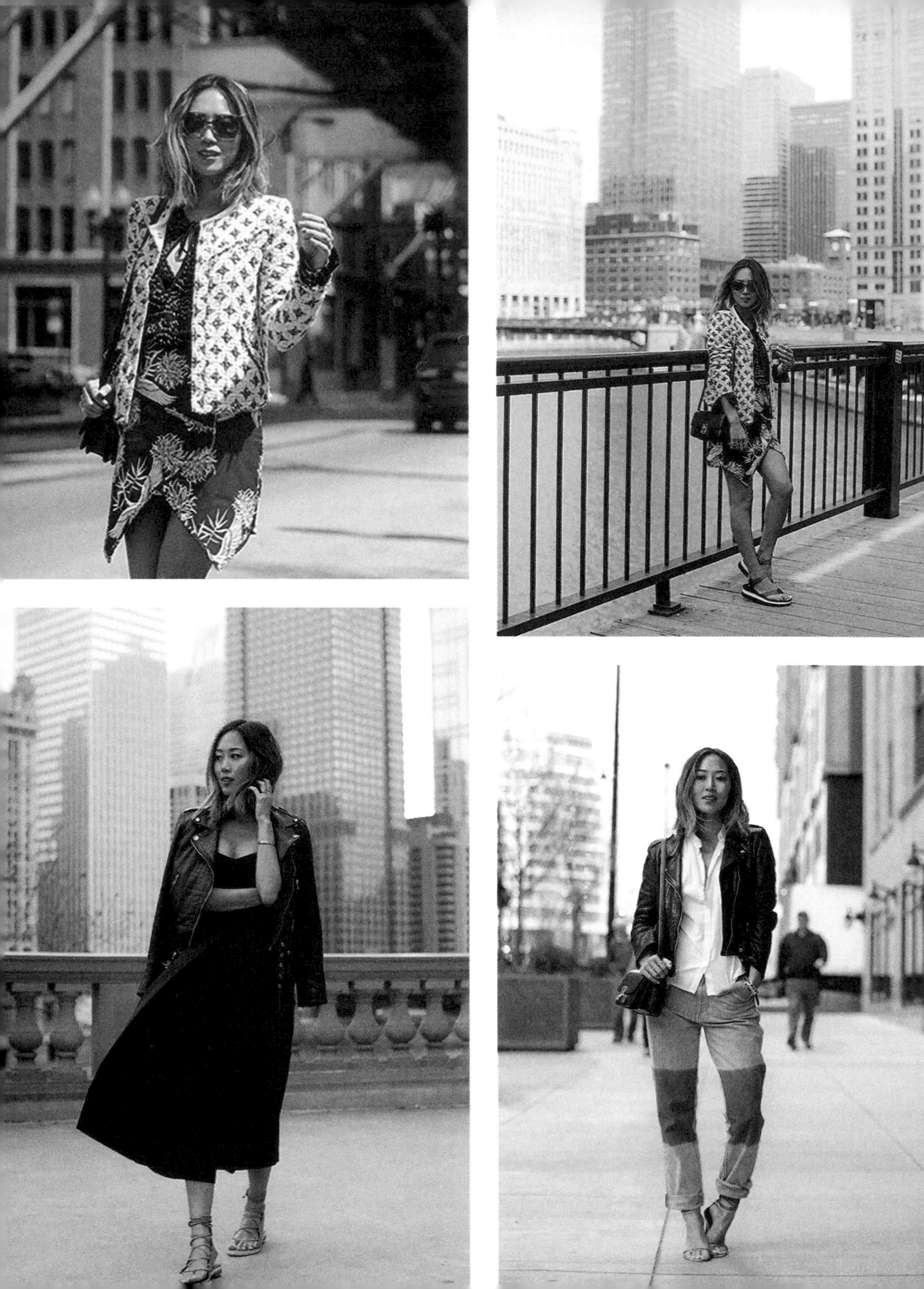

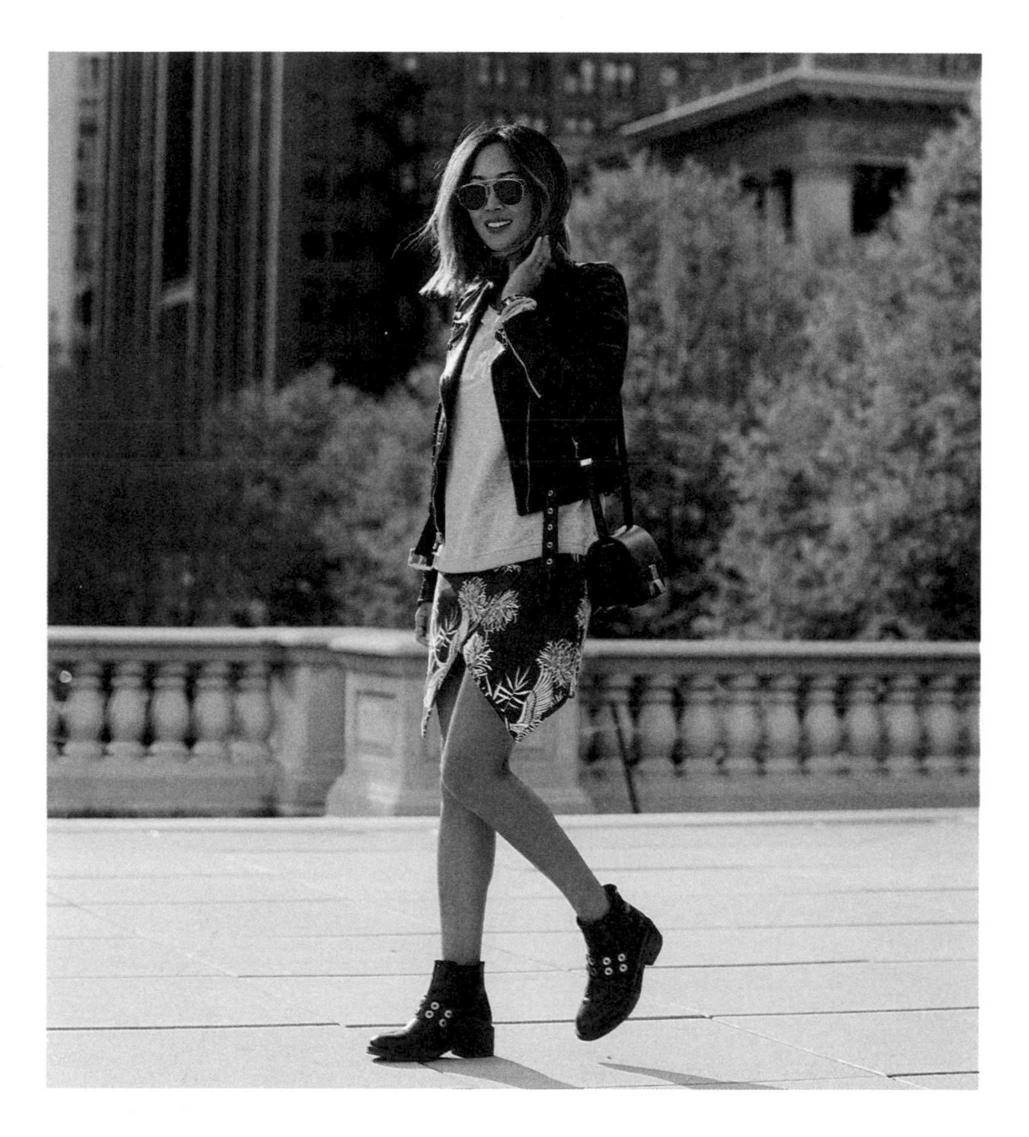

ABOVE *IRO boots; Dior sunglasses.* **OPPOSITE, TOP ROW** I got a blowout at a salon that was, uh, not great. I showed a picture of what I wanted based on how my usual stylist, Anh Co Tran, does my hair. I got very big, very round beauty pageant curls—very not me. Like, not at all. Despite having an SOS FaceTime with Anh, I still had trouble taming the blown-out beast. This is me exploring (and trying to flatten my hair). *Chloé sunglasses; IRO jacket; Celine bag; Teva sandals.* **OPPOSITE, BOTTOM RIGHT** *Laer leather jacket; Wildfox Couture jeans; Isabel Marant shoes.* **OPPOSITE, BOTTOM LEFT** *Laer leather jacket; Tibi jumpsuit; Tibi sandals.*

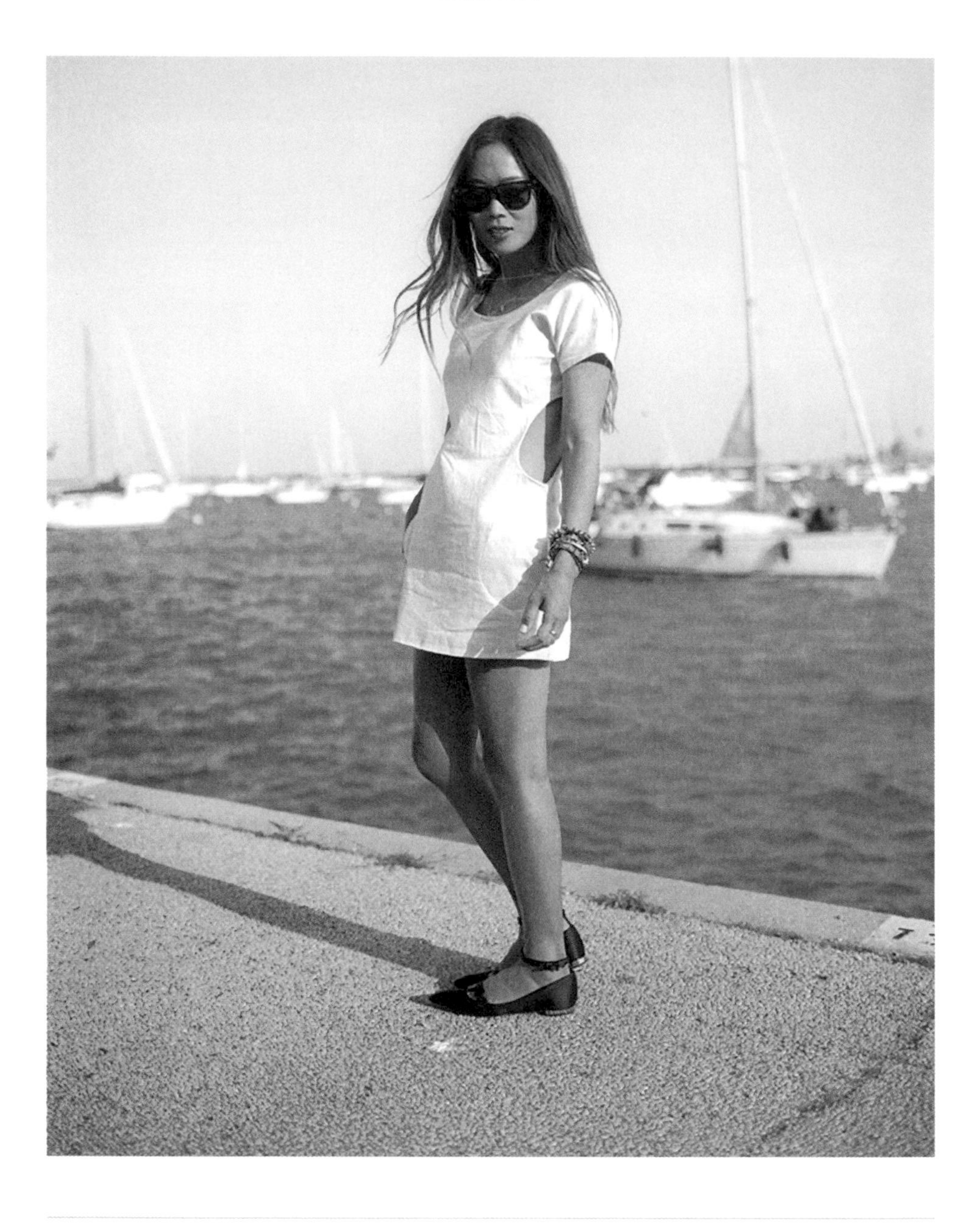

ABOVE *Local Celebrity dress; Tibi shoes.* **OPPOSITE (CLOCKWISE FROM TOP)** *Laer jacket; Two Songs sweatshirt; Keepsake skirt* • *Bar III sweater; Levi's; Botkier bag; Chanel espadrilles* • At the Macy's Bar III flea-market pop-up event. *Bar III romper and jacket; Sigerson Morrison shoes.*

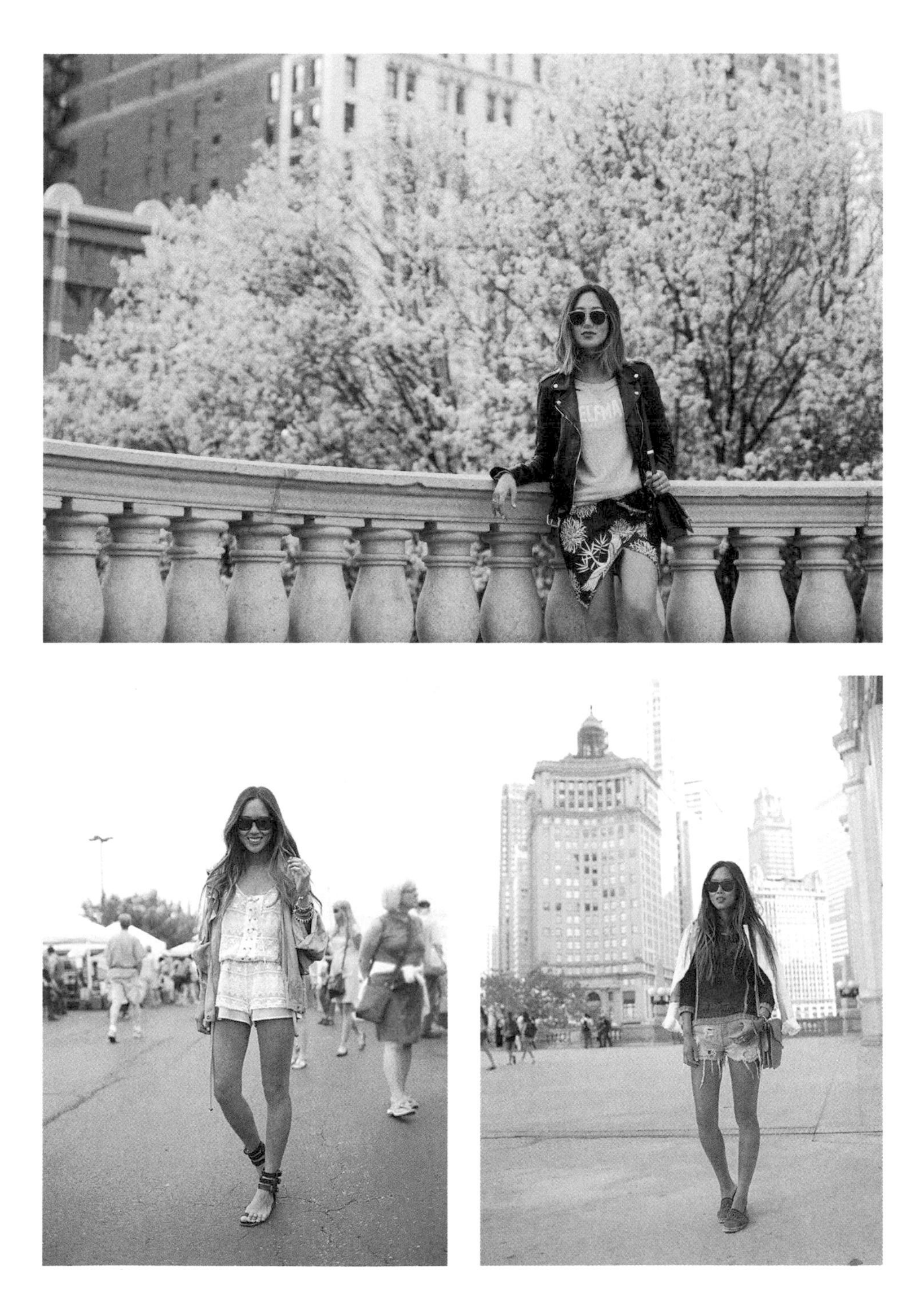

DALLAS

True story: The very first time I went to Dallas, I was in my mom's womb. My dad and his family ended up in Texas after they immigrated to the United States from South Korea, and my dad's sister (who we call "the Dallas aunt") lives there now. After that very early visit, I didn't go back to Dallas until 2010, when I was invited by Fossil to style and star in a holiday shoot, which ended up being my very first paid blogging job. (Kind of crazy, considering I used to wear Fossil watches growing up.)

Up until then, I'd worked with a small handful of brands who didn't pay me and made me feel like I was lucky to be associated with them. Fossil did exactly the opposite—they respected my time and treated me like an actual freelancer who made her living from partnerships, not a hobbyist blogger. They even booked my travel for me, which was a complete pinch-me moment; it was also a pinch-me moment when the brand sent me a W-9 form so I could get paid! (It wasn't a lot of money, but that job meant so much to me, and I was so incredibly grateful and excited for it, that it may as well have been a million dollars.)

Not only did I experience how a proper partnership should work, I also got to collaborate with an amazing group of talented bloggers who all talked about the things they wanted to do with their careers: Nadia Sarwar, a photographer who now shoots for *W* magazine; Connie Wang, who practically runs fashion editorial at Refinery29; and Taylor Sterling, who is the creative director of Glitter Guide. After meeting on that fateful first (or technically second, for me) trip to Dallas, we all came up together.

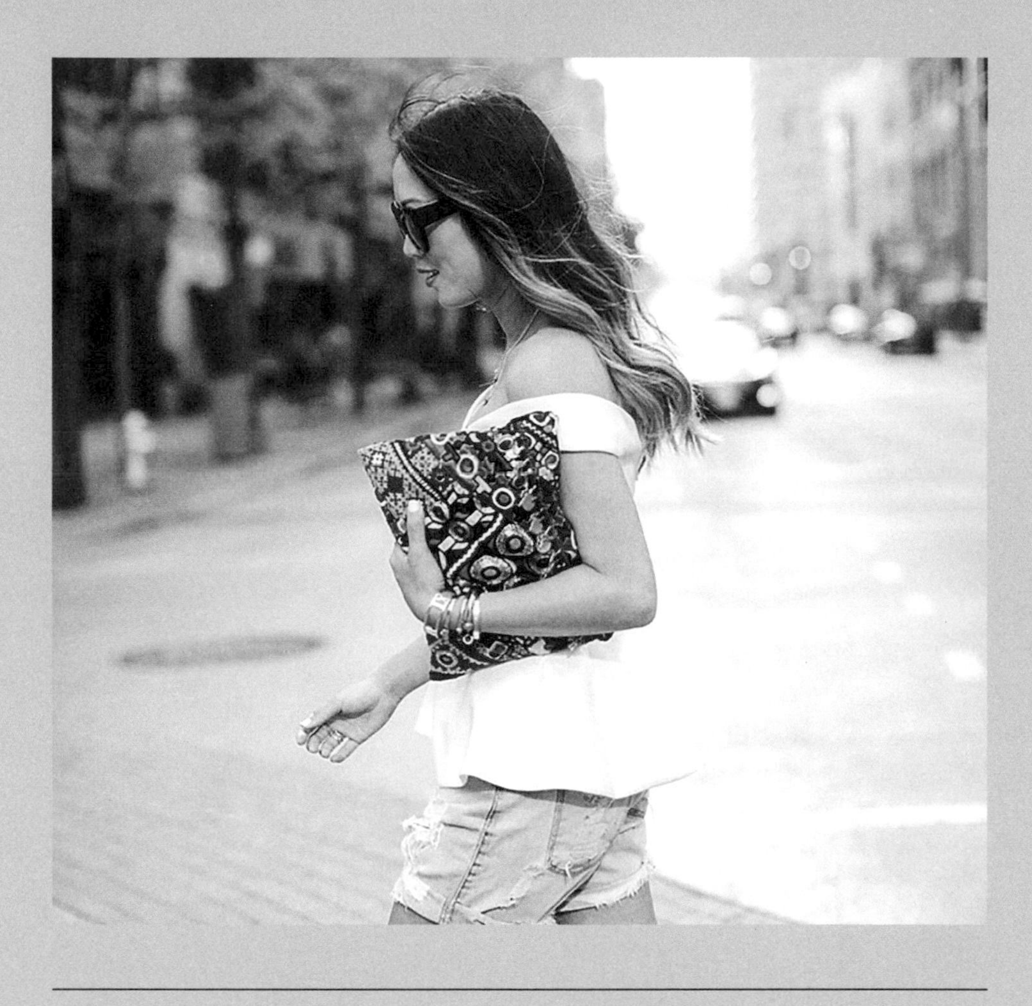

After that shoot I honestly never thought I would get a paid opportunity again; I couldn't have ever imagined what the next eight years would have in store for me. The fact that I genuinely loved what I was doing and made the money secondary is a huge reason why I believe I've been able to attract opportunities that both align with me and also help pay my bills (as they say, do what you love and the money will follow). The Fossil shoot images are still up on my blog today and they make me prouder than ever, for so many reasons.

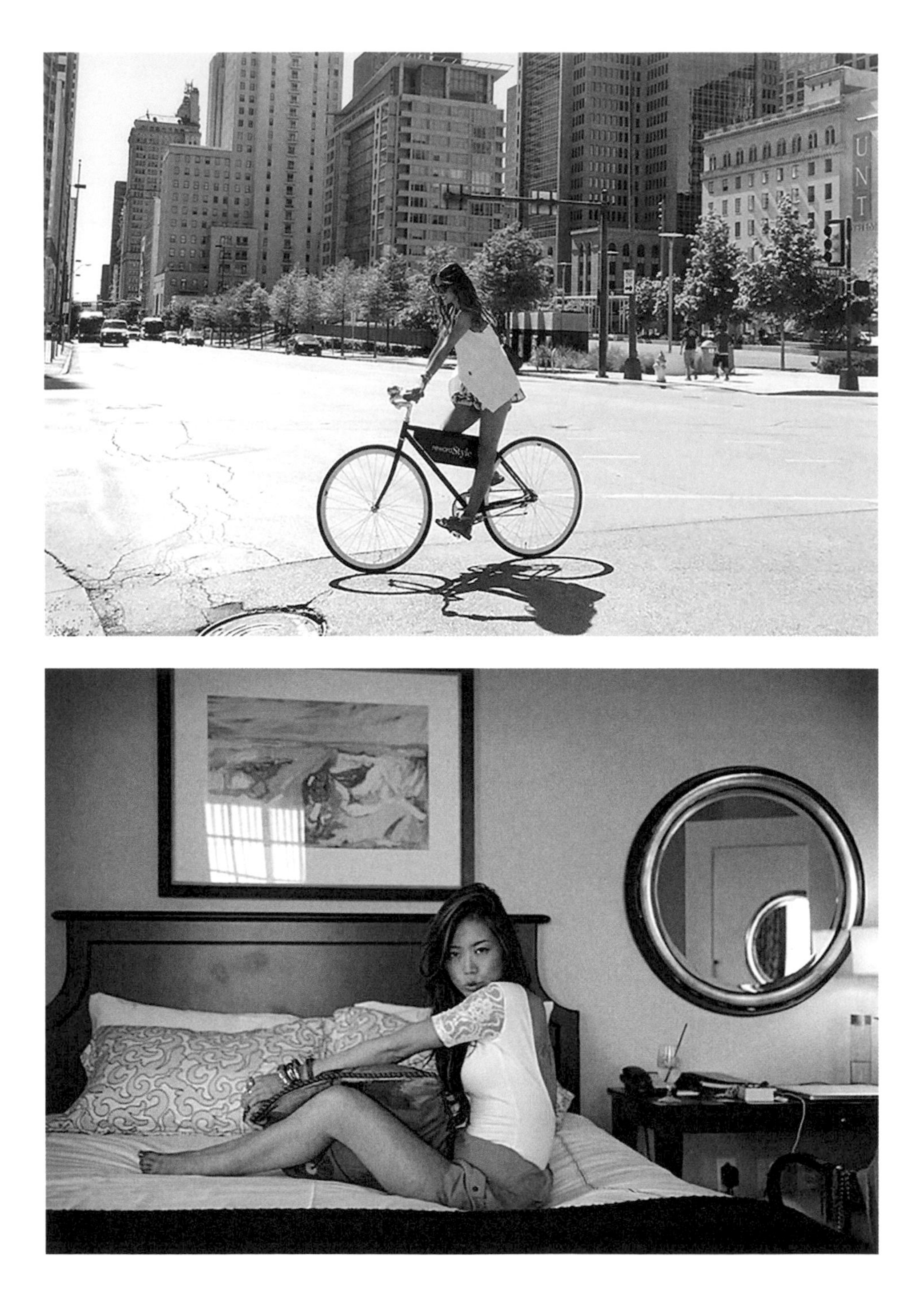

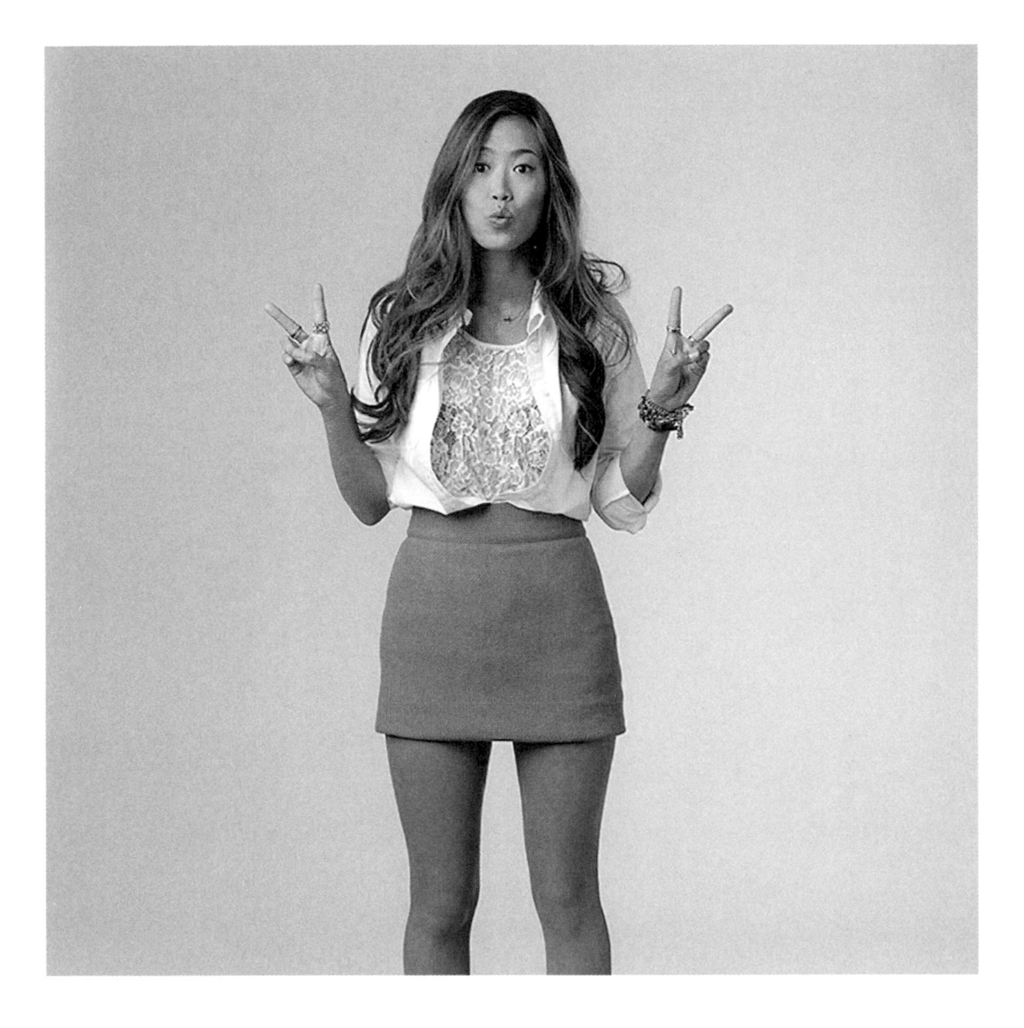

ABOVE This was a test photo that Fossil ultimately decided to use in the campaign. I was just being goofy and being myself—which I still try to do whenever I'm shooting. This campaign was so cool because Fossil let us style our own looks, and I felt like the outfits were really me. I also played tailor and had to get creative as the clothes were too big. I folded, tucked, and clipped my way to sartorial success. The campaign was so successful that I was asked to work with them as a model again two years later.

OPPOSITE (FROM TOP) In 2014 I went back to Dallas for a rewardStyle conference. When everybody was studying hard and learning about e-commerce and blogging, I thought it was the perfect time to duck out and take a bike ride. • Back in 2010 I was way too shy to ask other people to take my outfit photos (oh, how times have changed). This is me before the Fossil shoot setting up a self-timer in my hotel room so I could try on clothes.

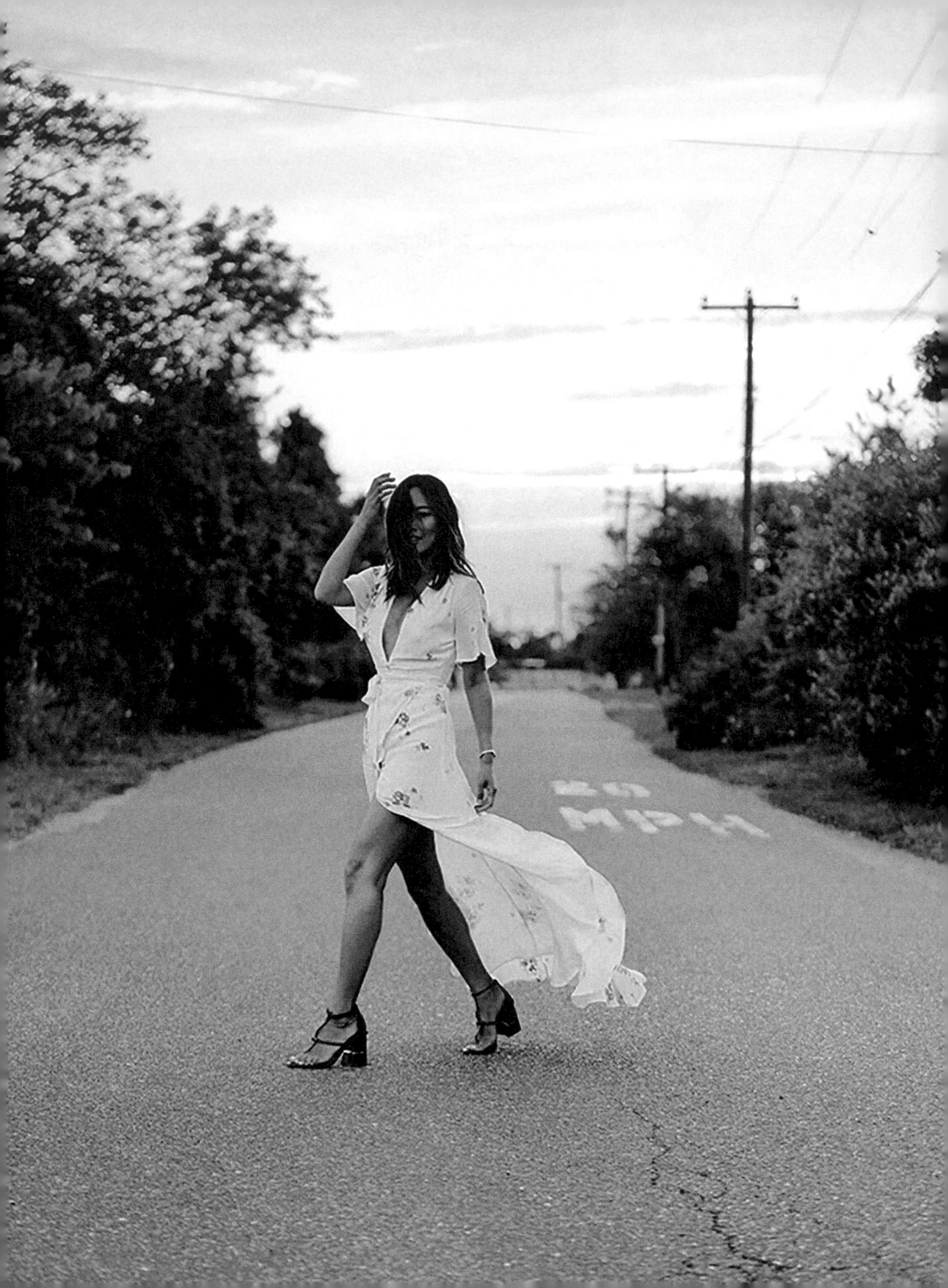
MPH

THE HAMPTONS

Because I'm from L.A., my version of summer is chill and carefree with major Malibu vibes. So the first time I went to the Hamptons with Revolve—who does the best summer house there every year, hosting press and influencers in a beautiful house and throwing parties and events—I didn't know what to expect. I quickly discovered that despite the Hamptons being a bit more polished and upscale than what I'm used to, it's impossible not to love them (and the French fries and lobster rolls to be had there). I've experienced things in the Hamptons that I'd never experienced before—for example, I took my first-ever private jet ride there and now can confidently say I know what it feels like to be P. Diddy. I also happened to get into a, shall we say, scuffle at a bar after a guy pushed my friend Rachel (don't mess with my friends, I will go gangster on you). I've been back to the Hamptons three other times with Revolve and once with Dani for a Brazilian brand called PatBo, and each time is truly special—nature, good seafood, great friends, and the smells of summer. I love it there, but every time I leave I am so happy to be going back to California. You can take the girl out of Cali, but you can't take the Cali out of the girl.

OPPOSITE A side-of-the-road shot in 2015. *Privacy Please dress.*

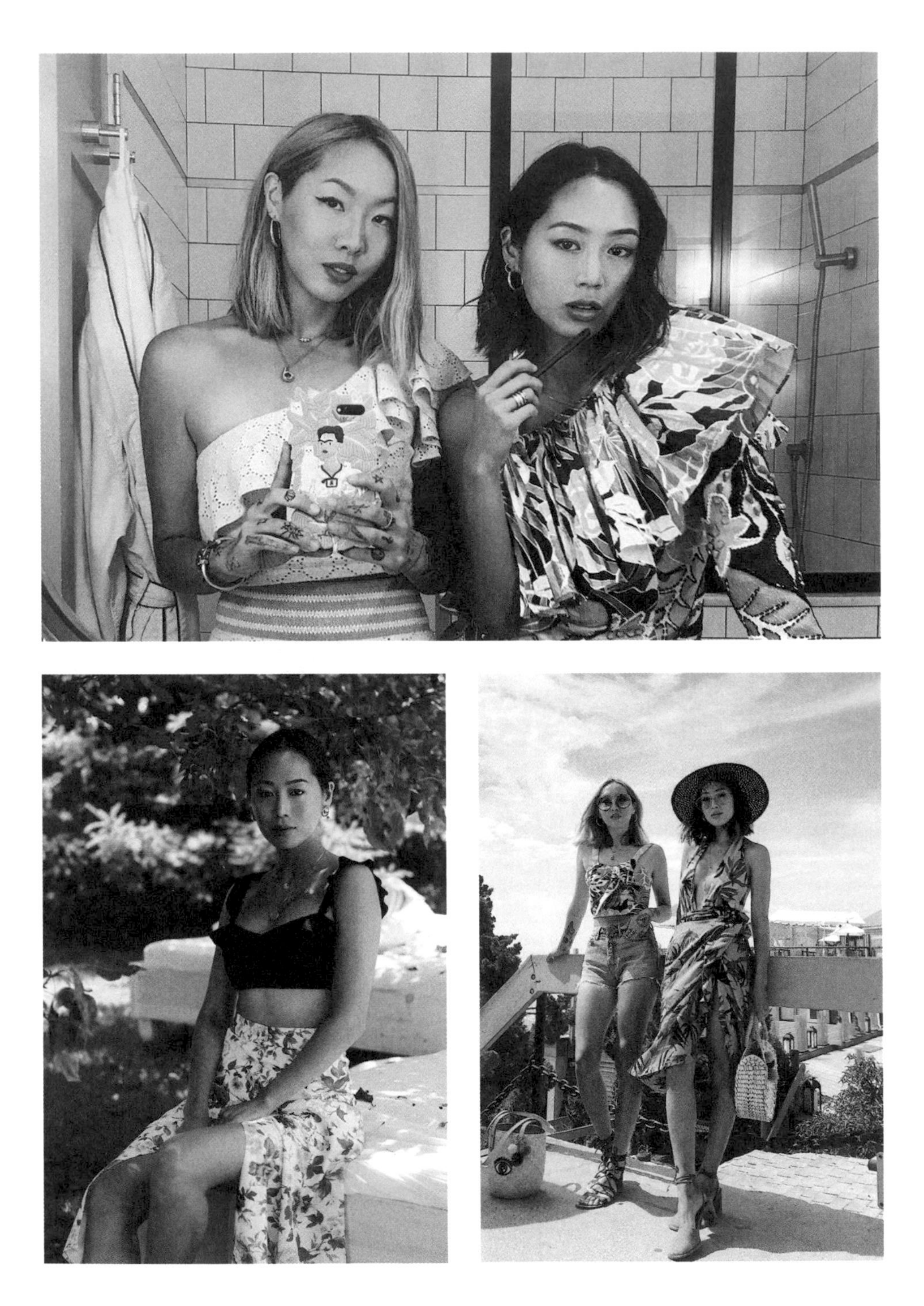

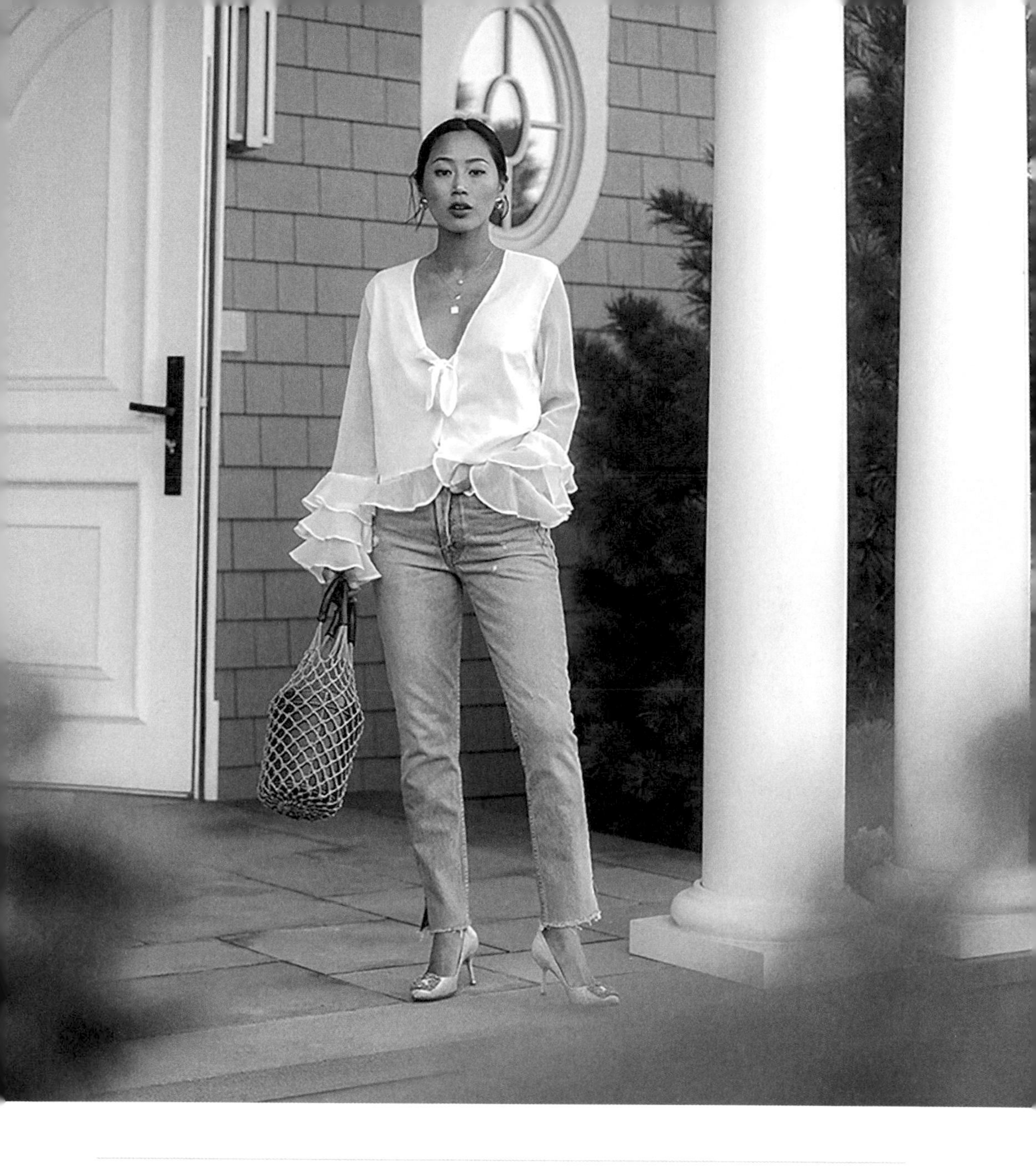

ABOVE Revolve always does a lunch or dinner with their in-house brands, and this was right before a dinner for their denim brand Grlfrnd. *Tularosa top; Grlfrnd jeans; Manolo Blahnik shoes.*

OPPOSITE (CLOCKWISE FROM TOP) Every trip I take with Dani is special, and this Hamptons visit was no exception. · The Revolve house backyard.

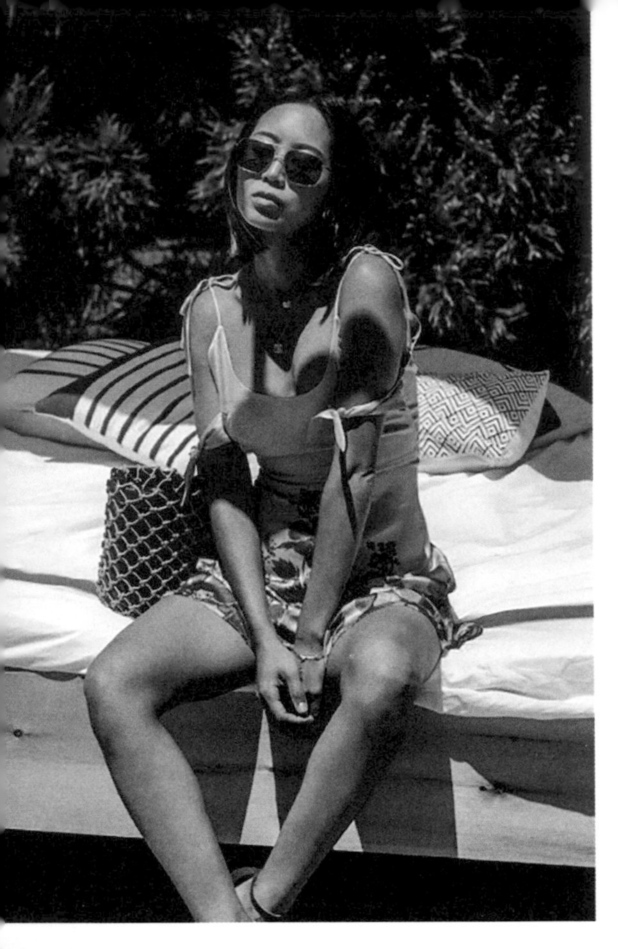

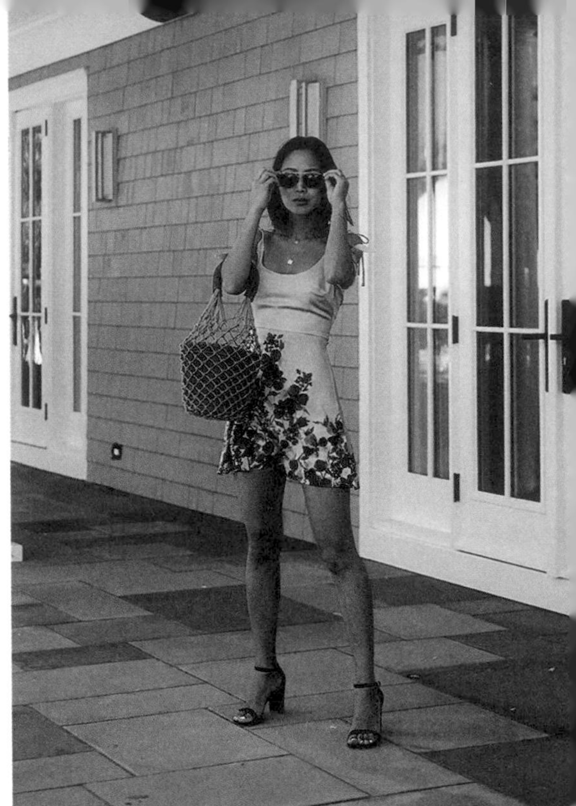

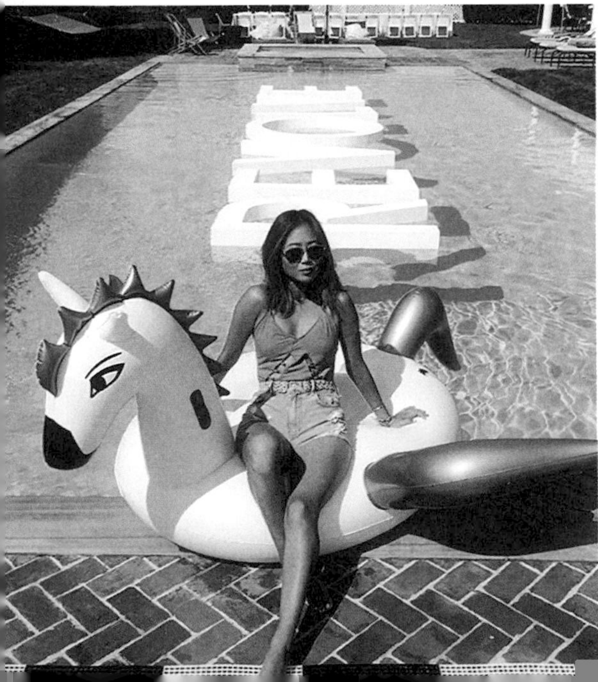

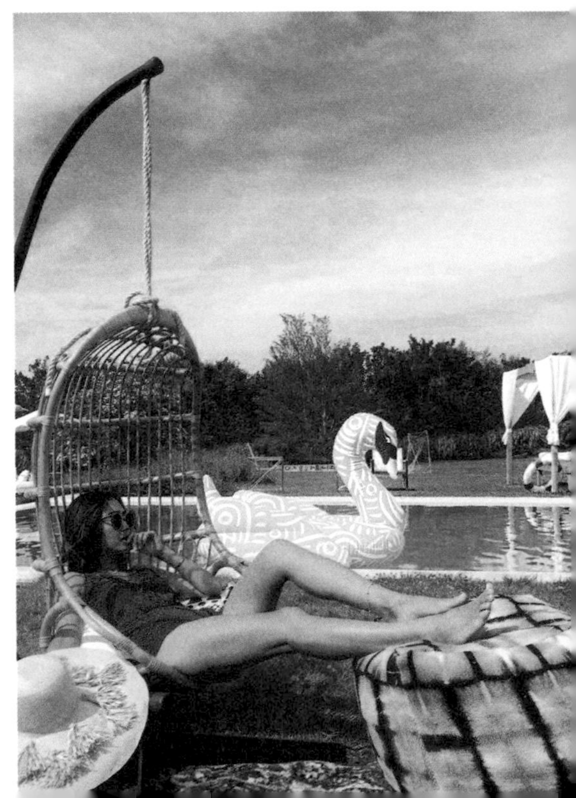

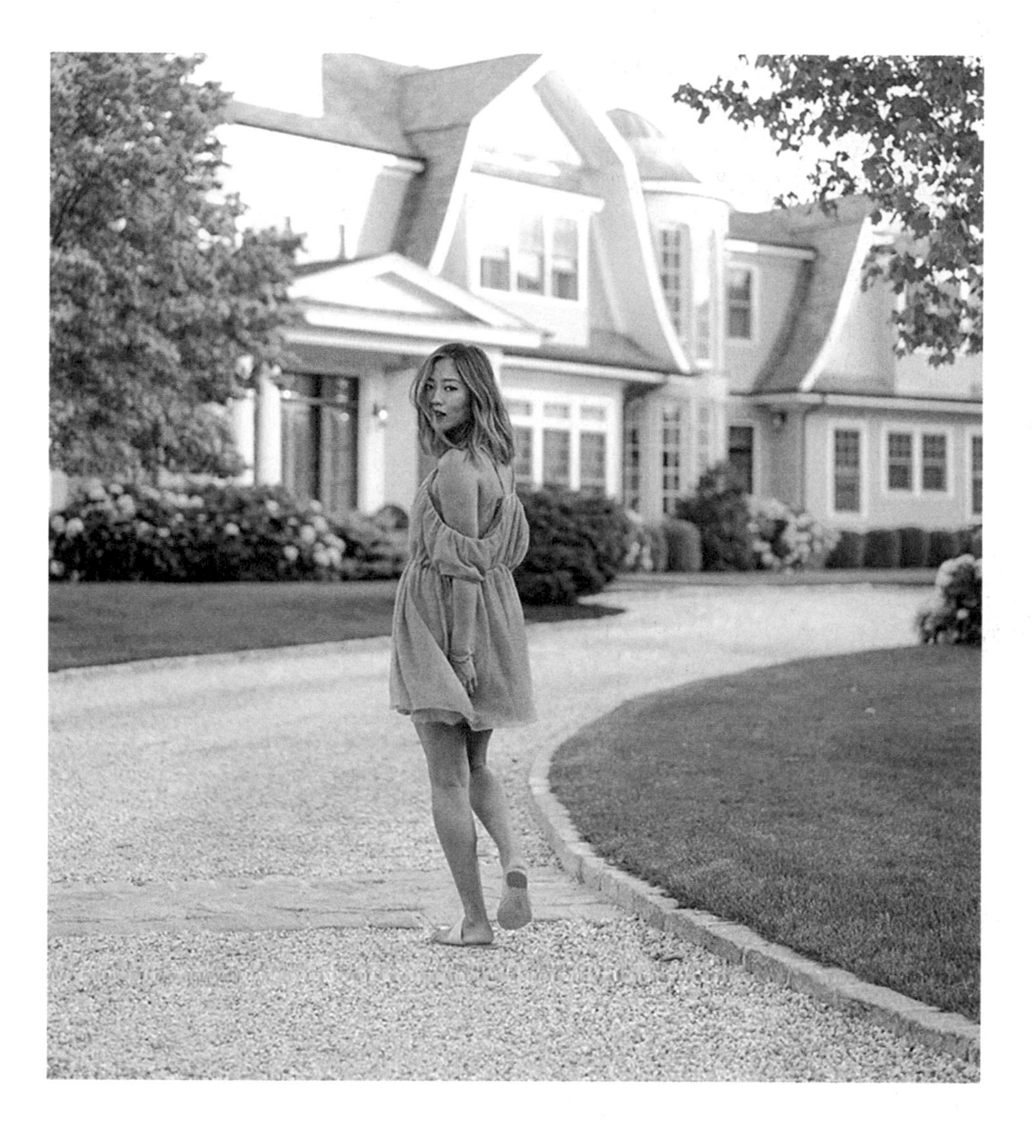

ABOVE Wearing a Majorelle dress designed by my friend Rachel Zeilic, who started the label Stylestalker in Australia a few years before. When I was a poor college student in San Francisco I was obsessed with her line, but Ross and TJ Maxx were more my speed. One day she emailed me and asked if she could send me clothes, and I was so excited that a brand I loved so much wanted to align with me. The resulting friendship between us is just icing on the cake. **OPPOSITE, TOP ROW** *LPA dress; Stuart Weitzman heels.* **OPPOSITE, BOTTOM ROW** At the Revolve house. The brand does a really good job of styling their events so everyone's Instagram feeds look beautiful.

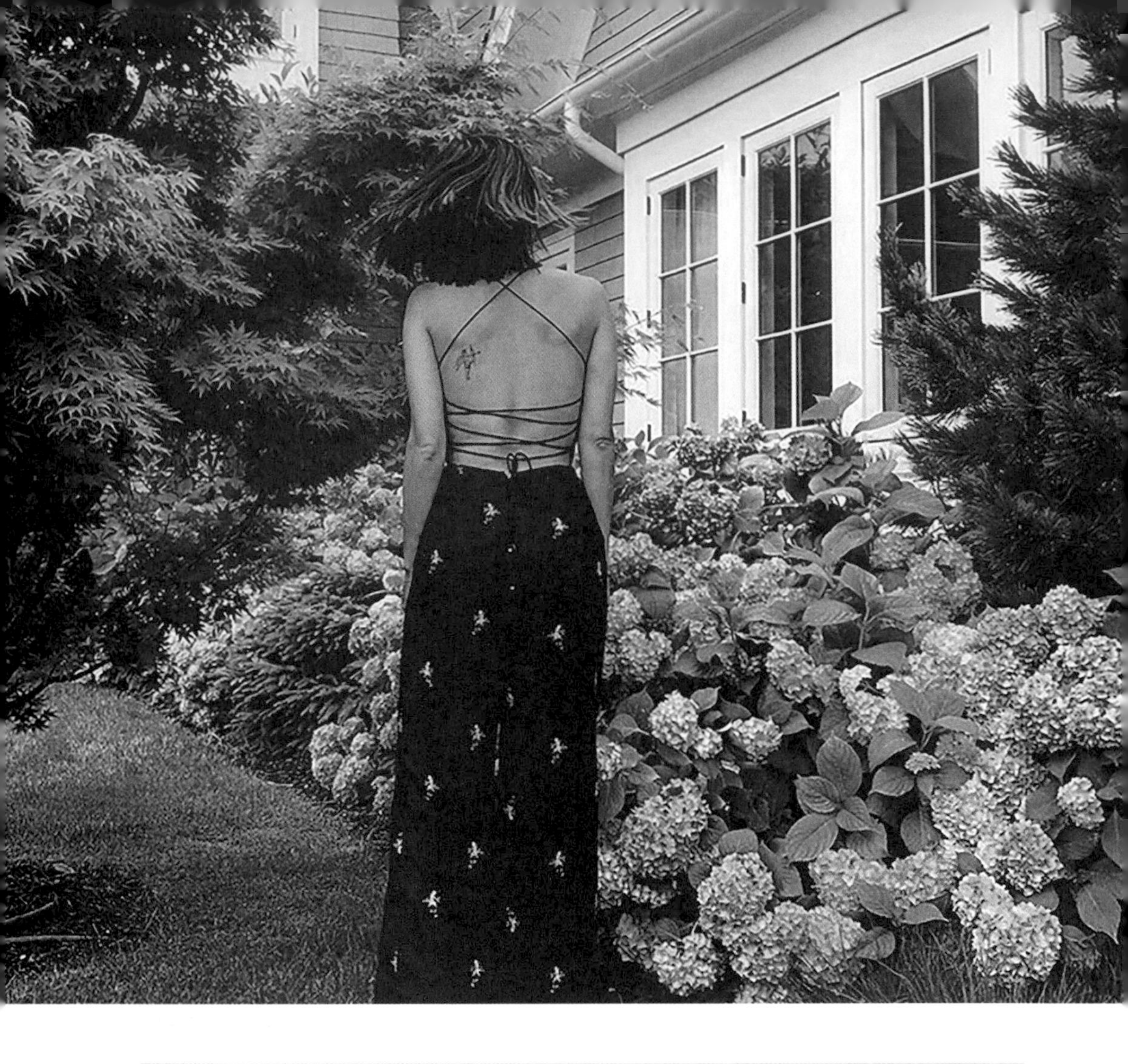

ABOVE My boyfriend Jacopo Moschin wasn't in the Hamptons yet and Jared—my best friend, who I love—is an unreliable photographer (he disappears and can usually be found dancing and eating far away from the shot I want). So I asked someone from the Revolve team to shoot the back of this jumpsuit. I positioned them, directed them, and told them to keep shooting. *House of Harlow jumpsuit.* **OPPOSITE (CLOCKWISE FROM TOP)** At the Surf Lodge in Montauk, where Jacopo and I ate lobster tacos and realized that this was our first public outing together as a couple. After this meal, we went from casually dating to being official. • They had bikes at the Revolve house in 2015. If I wasn't walking to get green juice, I was biking to get green juice. *Privacy Please dress* • In 2017 at the Revolve house, trying to get my outfit shot in. Jared joined me on this trip, and Jacopo was able to come meet us on the last day, so it was a very special trip with very special people. *Staud bag.*

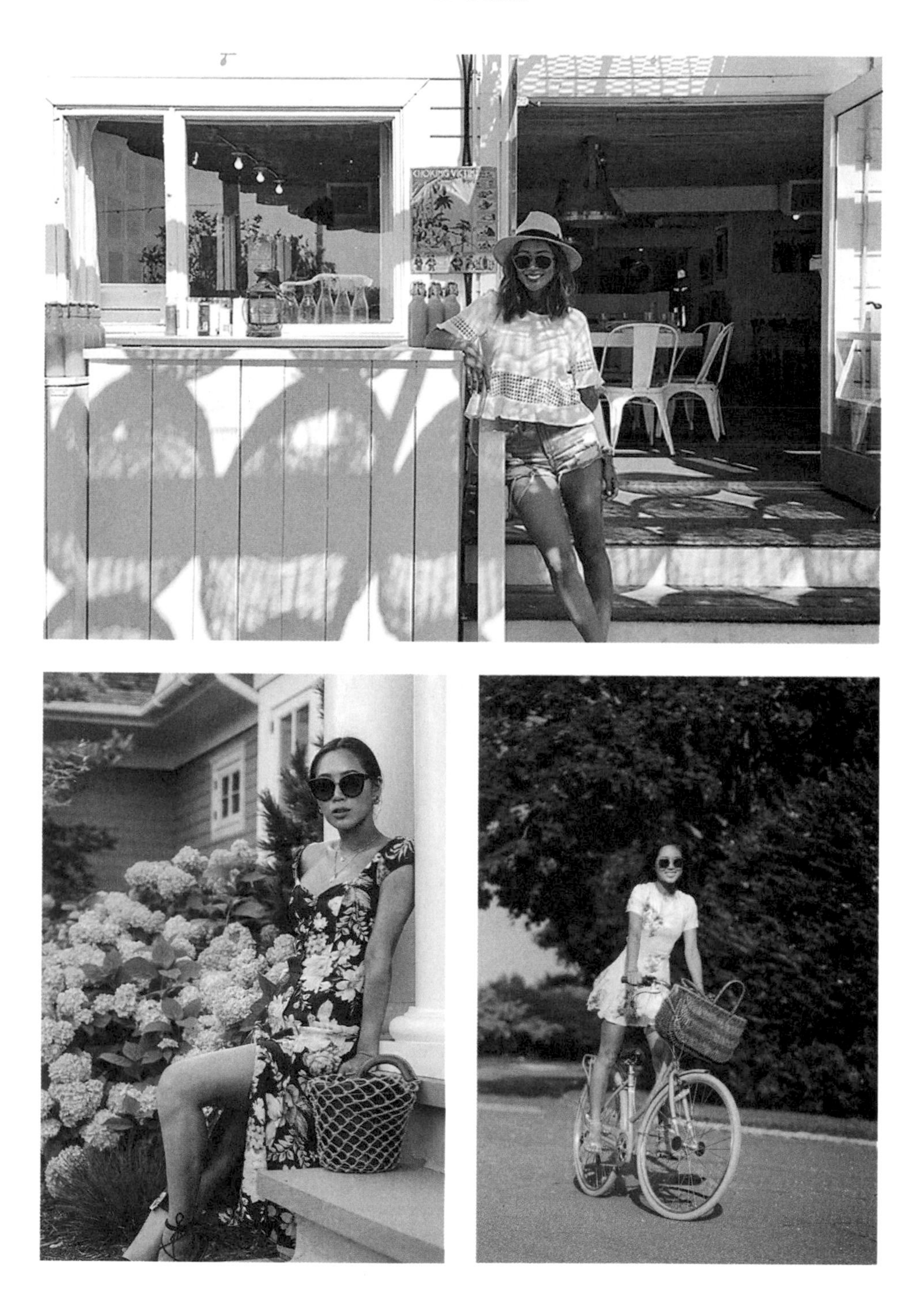

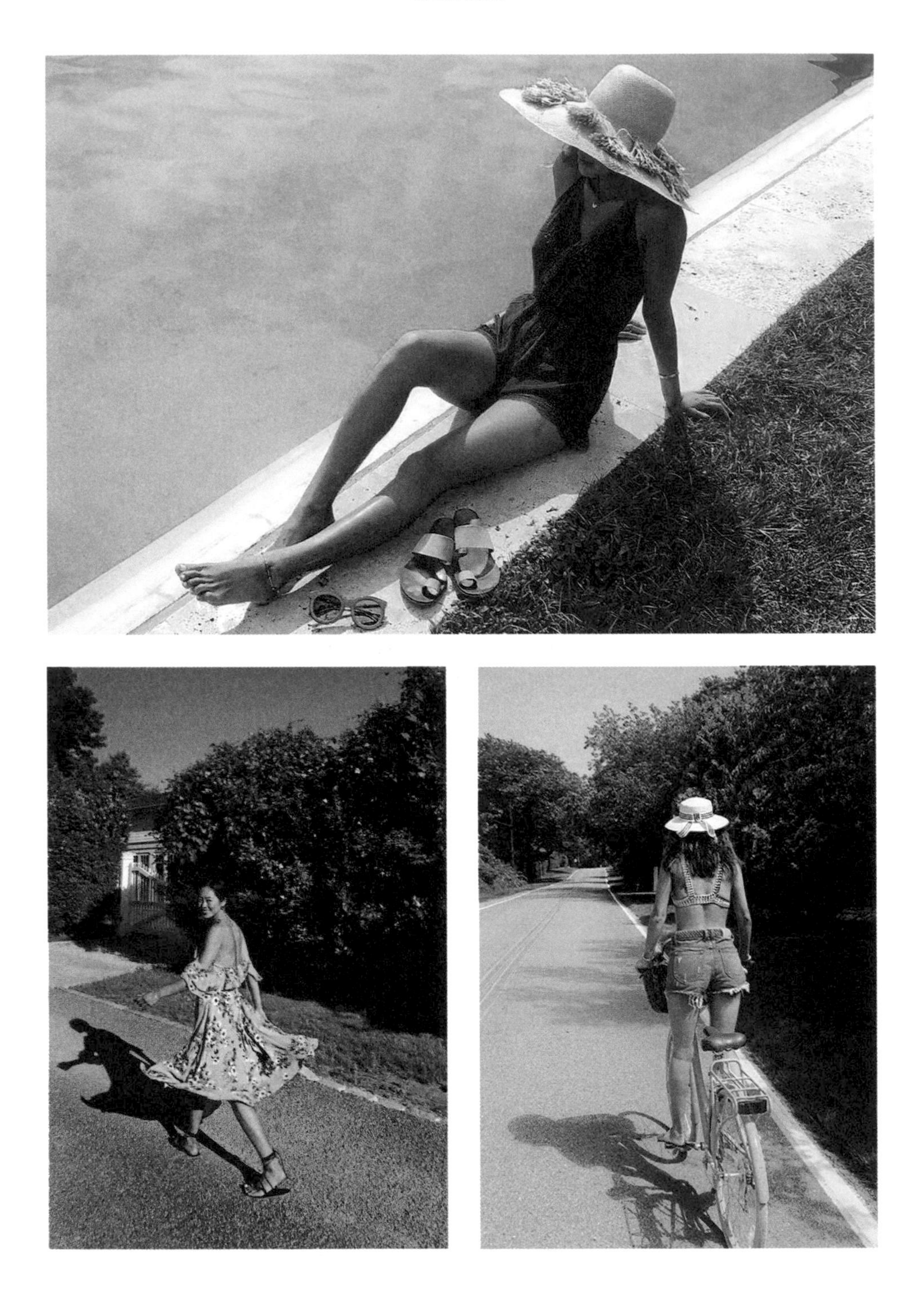

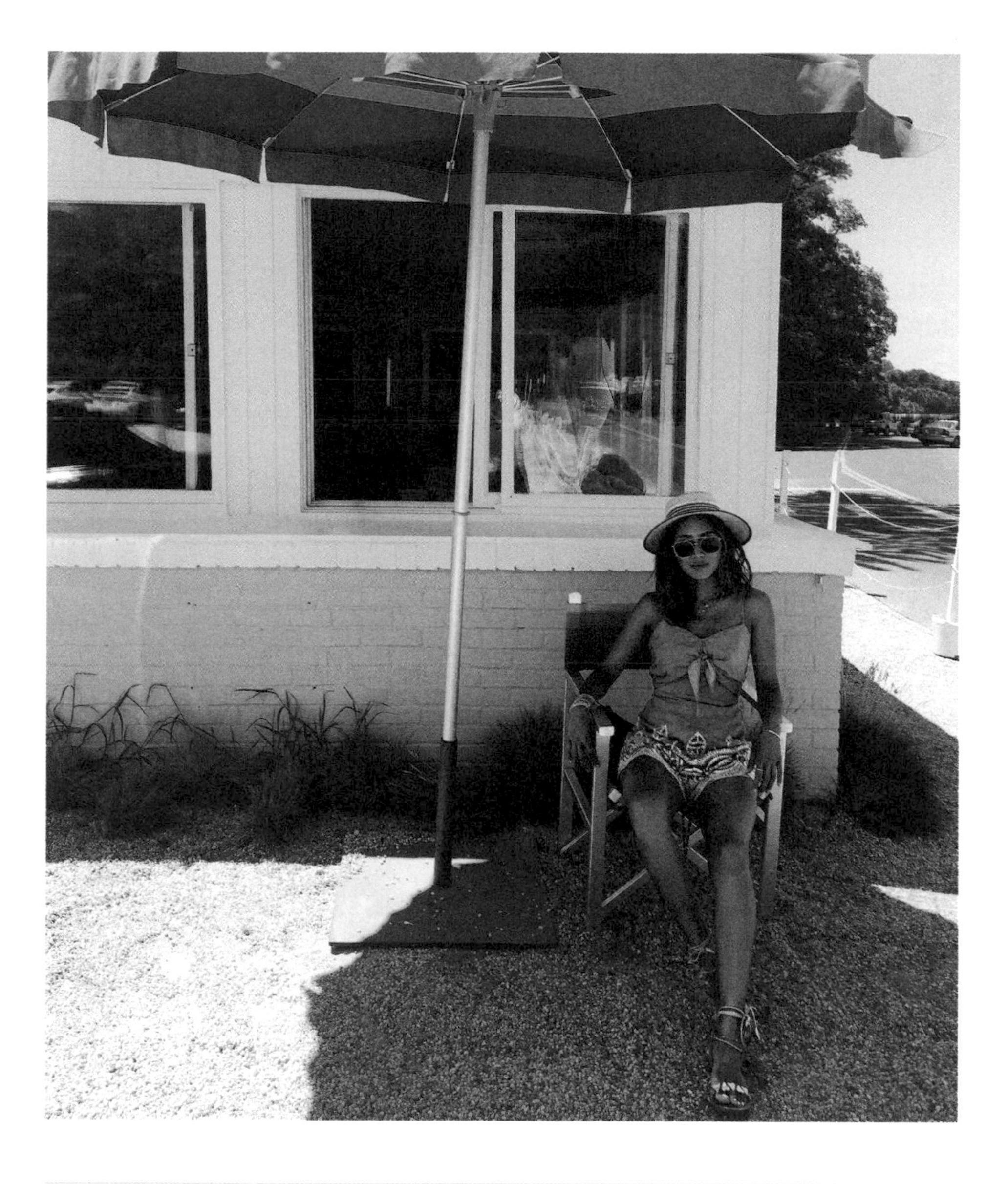

ABOVE Major Cinque Terre vibes at this roadside restaurant. *Tularosa romper.* **OPPOSITE (CLOCKWISE FROM TOP)** *Lovers and Friends romper; Raye shoes* • One of my first Hamptons trips. Wearing the straw hat I bought in Venice, Italy. *Kiini swimsuit; Tularosa shorts* • My daily morning green-juice run, which was a nice twenty-five-minute walk from the house (gotta get those steps in). *Asos dress.*

LOS ANGELES

I obviously love to travel—#jetset-Aimee is a pretty big thing, after all. But even when I find myself on the most beautiful black sand beach a million miles from home or sitting inside one of the finest fine dining restaurants in Paris, there's one thing that never, ever gets old, no matter how many frequent flier miles I rack up: landing in Los Angeles. My parents immigrated to L.A.—in my dad's case, by way of Dallas—from Busan, South Korea, in 1981 and 1984, respectively, and I was born and raised here. Despite a few stints out of town (Tokyo, for one) while I was growing up, I'm so incredibly proud to call Los Angeles home. Take away the fact that Dani, my parents, and some of my closest friends in the world are here (with more and more close friends from all corners of the globe seeming to pack up their cold-weather lives in favor of sunny, inspiring L.A. every single day), L.A. is a creative hotbed where individuality and creation are not only encouraged but demanded. This city is strong, resilient, and diverse (aka all the things that truly make America so special), and that diversity has allowed me to grow up as a Korean American who knew she could work really hard to make her wildest dreams come true.

Los Angeles has that rare but vital combination of polish and sheen mixed with grit and force, and those are the characteristic juxtapositions that inspire so much of my style and the style of the things I love here: hip-hop music and streetwear that's made its way from South L.A. to the designer mainstream; flavors found in the backs of hundreds of incredible taco trucks that

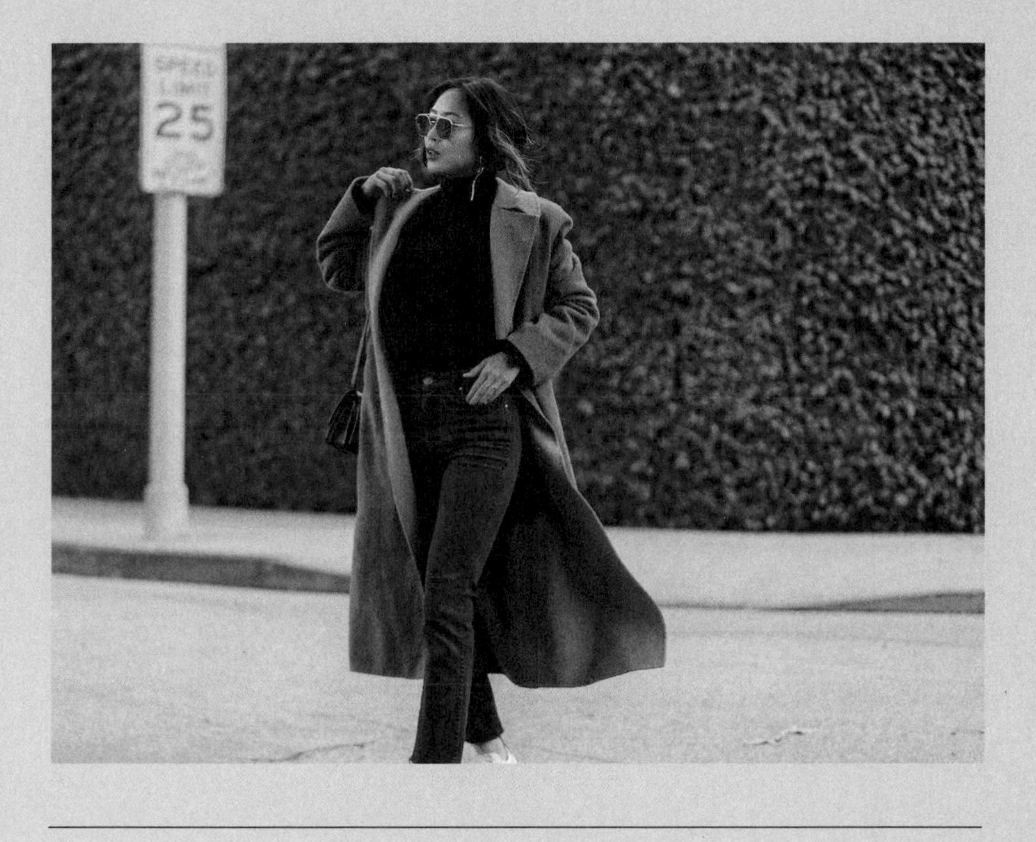

have landed on plates at the prettiest Insta-worthy restaurants in town; spray paint quite literally lifted from alleyways to become sold-out exhibits at the nation's foremost contemporary art institutions. Between our baller weather (which I will be the first to admit is a major factor in my usually upbeat mood), insane food, onslaught of culture, and anything-is-possible attitude (something especially displayed in the number of smart, strong women starting businesses here right now), I couldn't think of a better place to be. Though I'm a tried-and-true local, I still find so much joy in exploring my hometown like a tourist and discovering people, places, and things here (aka new places for perfect avocado toast) that constantly keep me on my toes. L.A., I heart you hard.

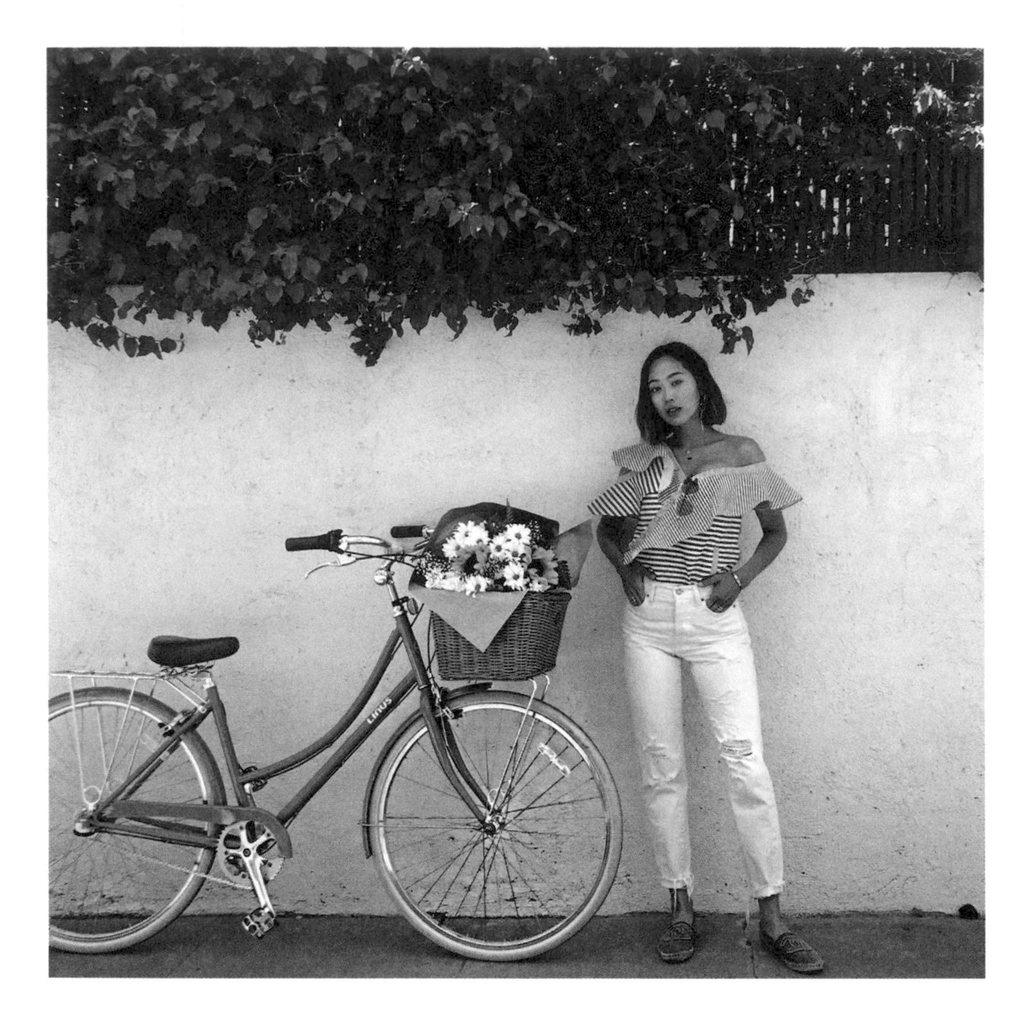

ABOVE In 2016 I decided to get rid of my car. Yes, this seems like a crazy decision in a driving city like L.A.; but I was traveling all the time and had a beach cruiser that needed using, so I went for it. Biking is my favorite thing ever—it's cheesy, but I'm seriously always smiling when I'm on a bike. I'm always riding around my new neighborhood, and my office is only fifteen minutes from my house (not that I bike to work as often as I should). **OPPOSITE (CLOCKWISE FROM TOP)** Because I travel so much for work it took me awhile to finish the master bedroom in my new house (I still can't believe I actually own a house). For the longest time I was sleeping in my newly upholstered bed in my guest bedroom. • I hadn't hung this mirror in the master bathroom so I'd always have to crouch or sit on the floor to get ready. • On the weekends you can usually find me on a bike. I keep a few at my house so my sister and my friends can ride with me (and have no excuse to meet me somewhere in their car).

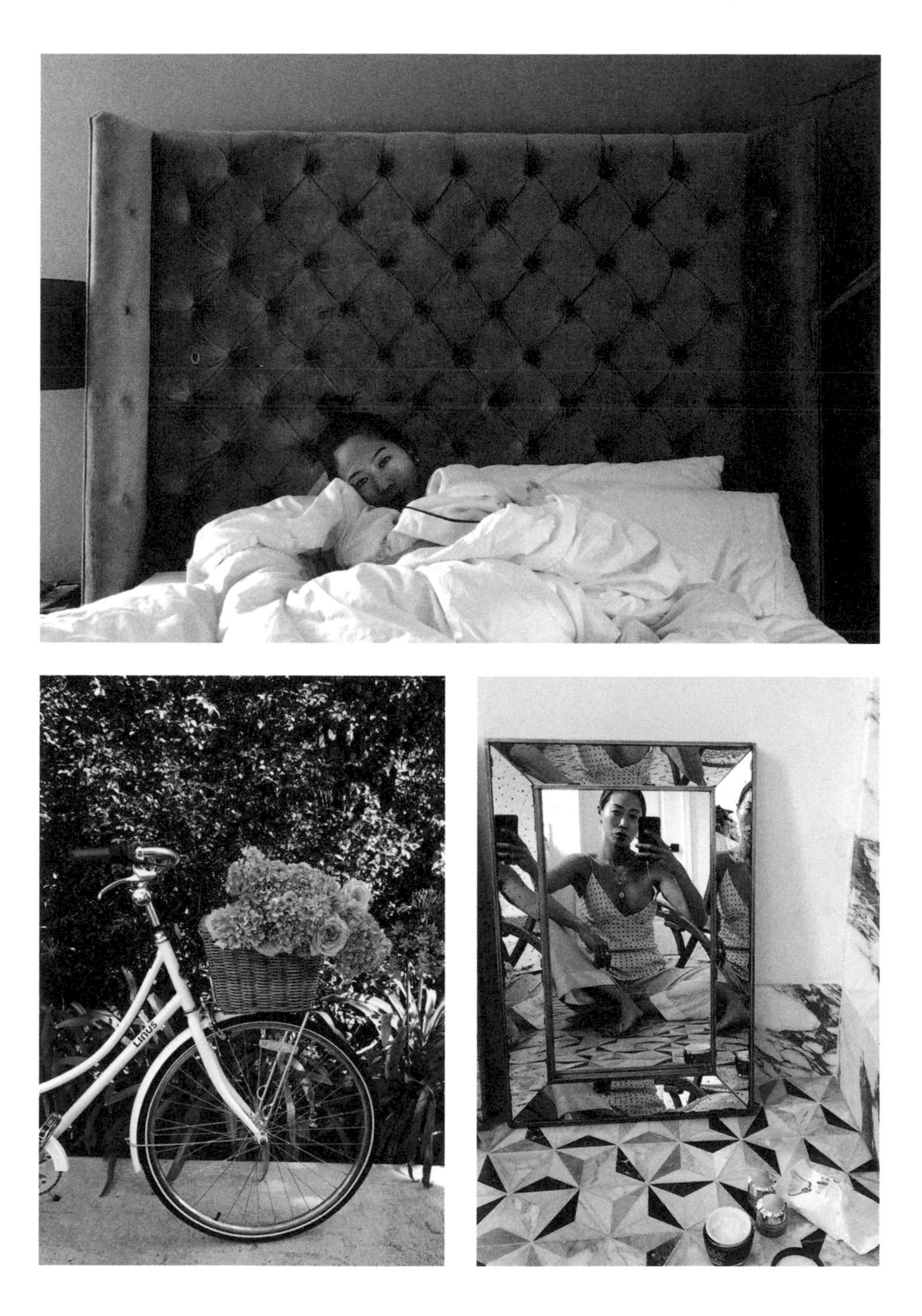
Linus

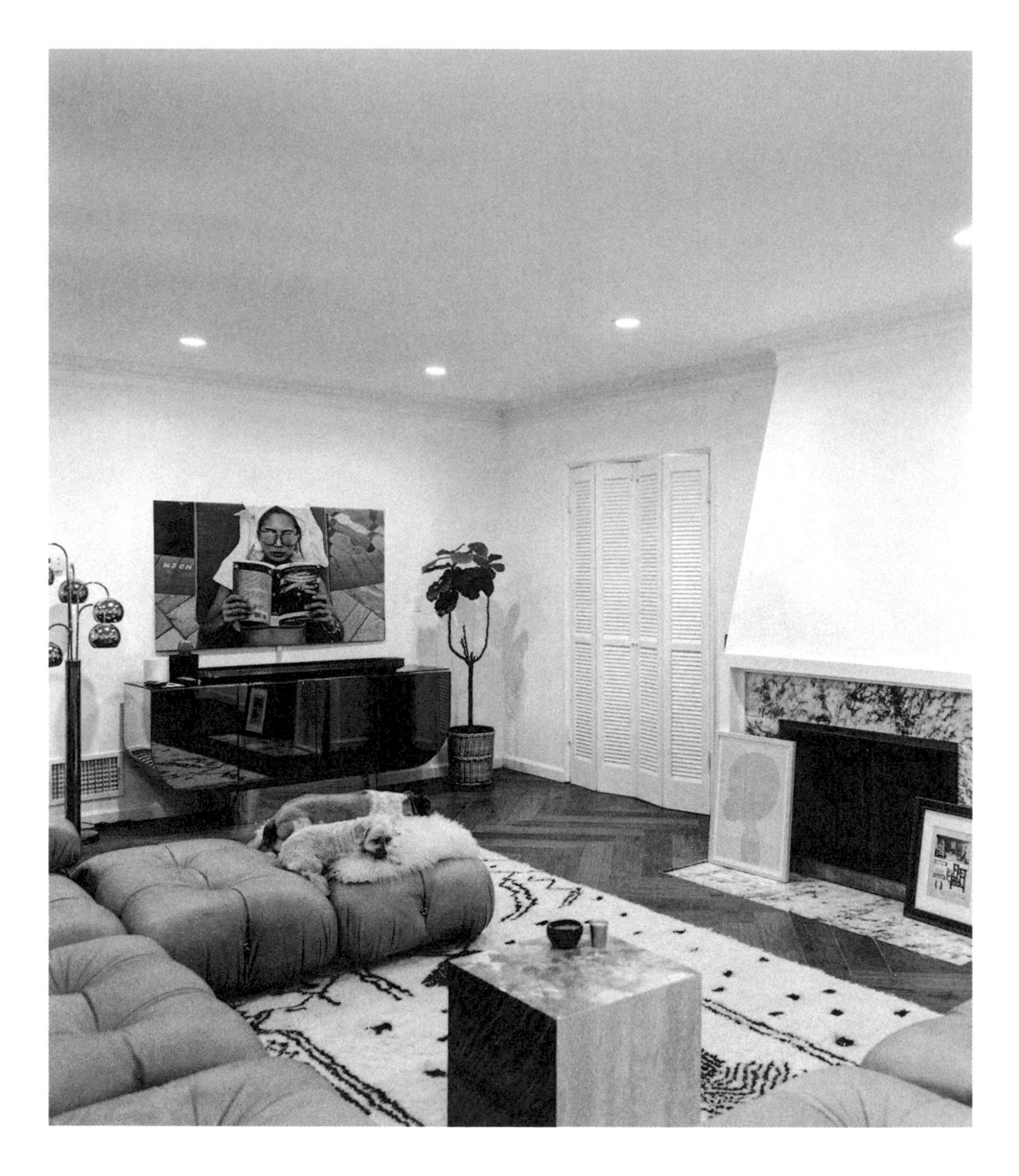

ABOVE My mostly finished living room, right after I had my new paper-thin TV installed. **OPPOSITE** In May 2017 Dior showed their cruise collection in Calabasas, a beautiful suburb about forty-five minutes outside L.A. (yes, where the Kardashians live). So many designers are doing such interesting, creative things in Los Angeles right now, which, as a native Angeleno, makes me so proud. *Christian Dior dress.*

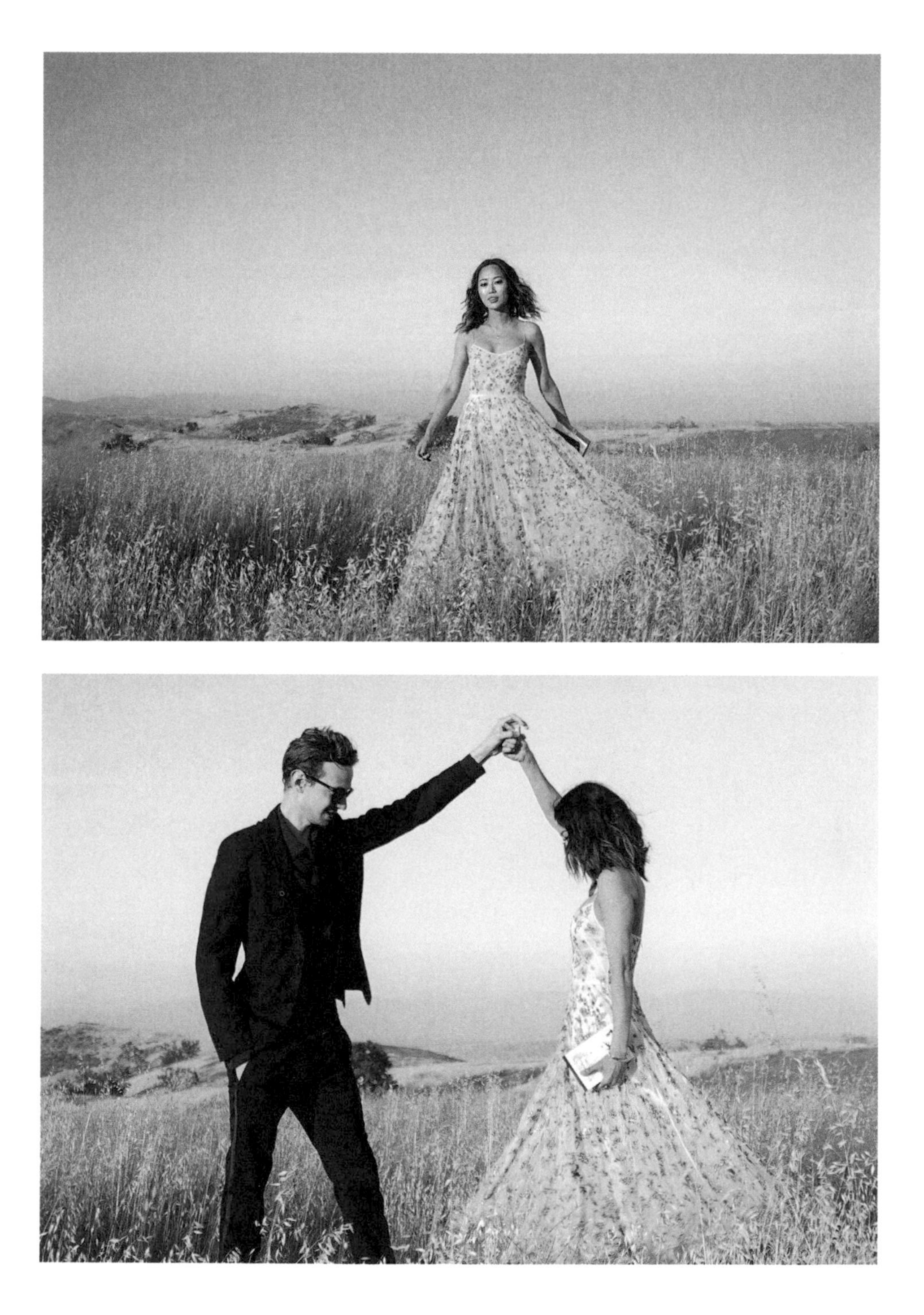

AVOCADO TOASTS IN THE U.S. WORTH TRAVELING FOR

We all know that I'm obsessed with anything avocado. (I once brought ten of them on a trip to Paris because I was so scared I wouldn't be able to find them there. True story.) That wasn't actually the case, and now Paris—along with many other typically non-avo cities—happens to have my favorite all-day food readily available. Of course being a California girl helps explain this deep-rooted need for the green, good-fat stuff, and I now pride myself on finding the best avo toasts in all corners of the globe (not to mention that they do indeed make for a lovely Insta opp). Below are a few of my favorite stateside options, which—in my experience—all have the proper avo-to-bread ratio (3:1, always) and a healthy dose of the chili flakes, salt, pepper, and olive oil (and, in extra-special cases, watermelon radish and/or a perfectly poached egg) that make avocado toast dreams come true.

AUSTIN

Irene's
@irenesaustin
irenesaustin.com

MIAMI

The Social Club at Surfcomber
@socialcubsobe
socialclubatsurfcomber.com

LOS ANGELES

The Hart and the Hunter
@handtheh
thehartandthehunter.com

Jon & Vinny's
@jonandvinnydelivery
jonandvinnys.com

Ostrich Farm
@ostrichfarmla
ostrichfarmla.com

NEW YORK

The Smith
@thesmithrestaurant
thesmithrestaurant.com

11 Howard
@11_howard
11howard.com

Dudley's
@dudleysnyc
dudleysnyc.com

PALM SPRINGS

The Pantry at Holiday House
@holidayhouseps
holidayhouseps.com

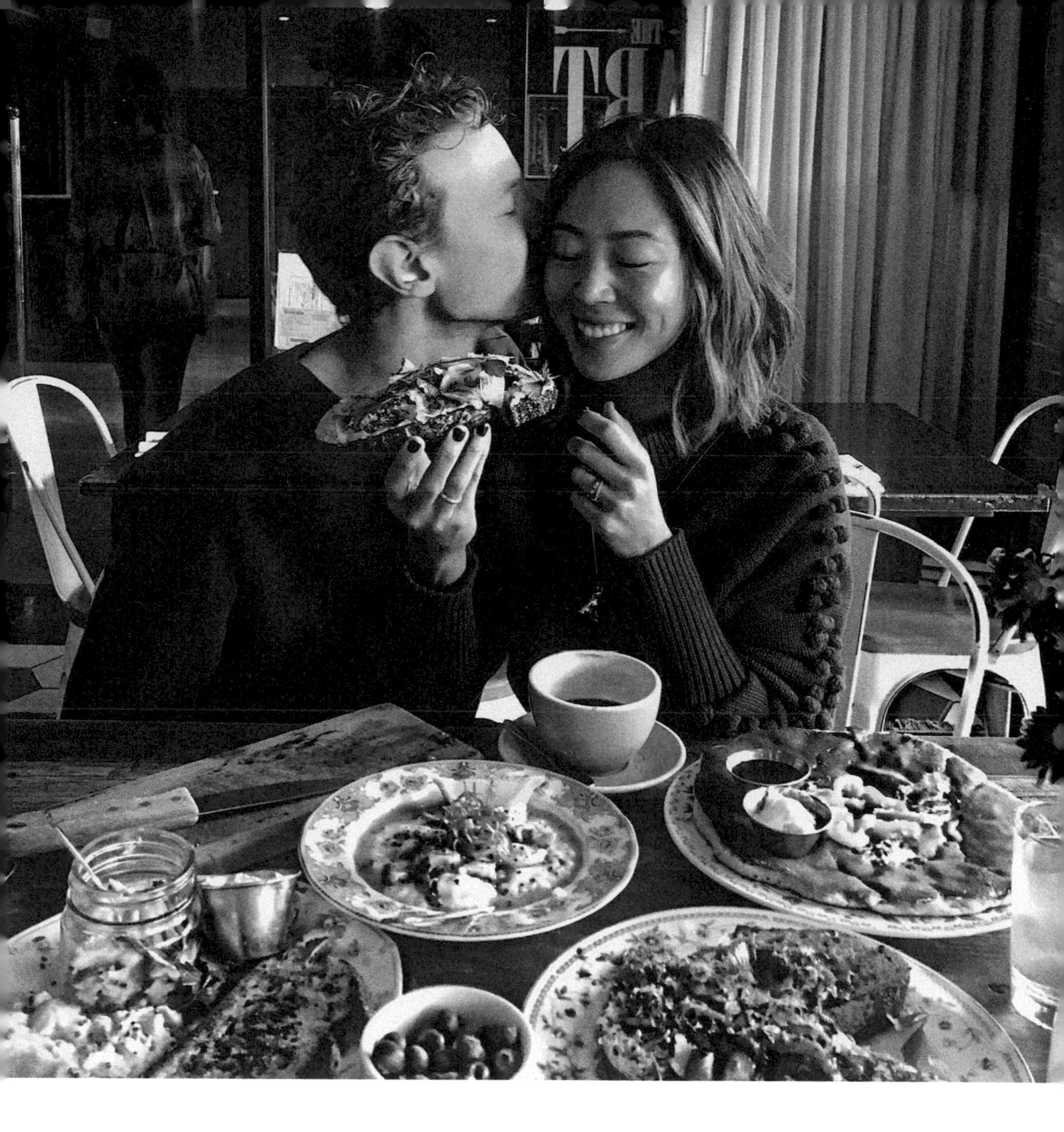

I make no secret of my deep love for avocado toast, so during one of Jacopo's visits from New York I made sure to make us a reservation at the Hart and the Hunter, one of our favorite brunch spots in town that happens to do a mean avo on bread. This was only one stop on our food tour, which continued well throughout the weekend (the fastest way to a man's heart really is through his stomach, and vice versa in our case!). *Chloé sweater.*

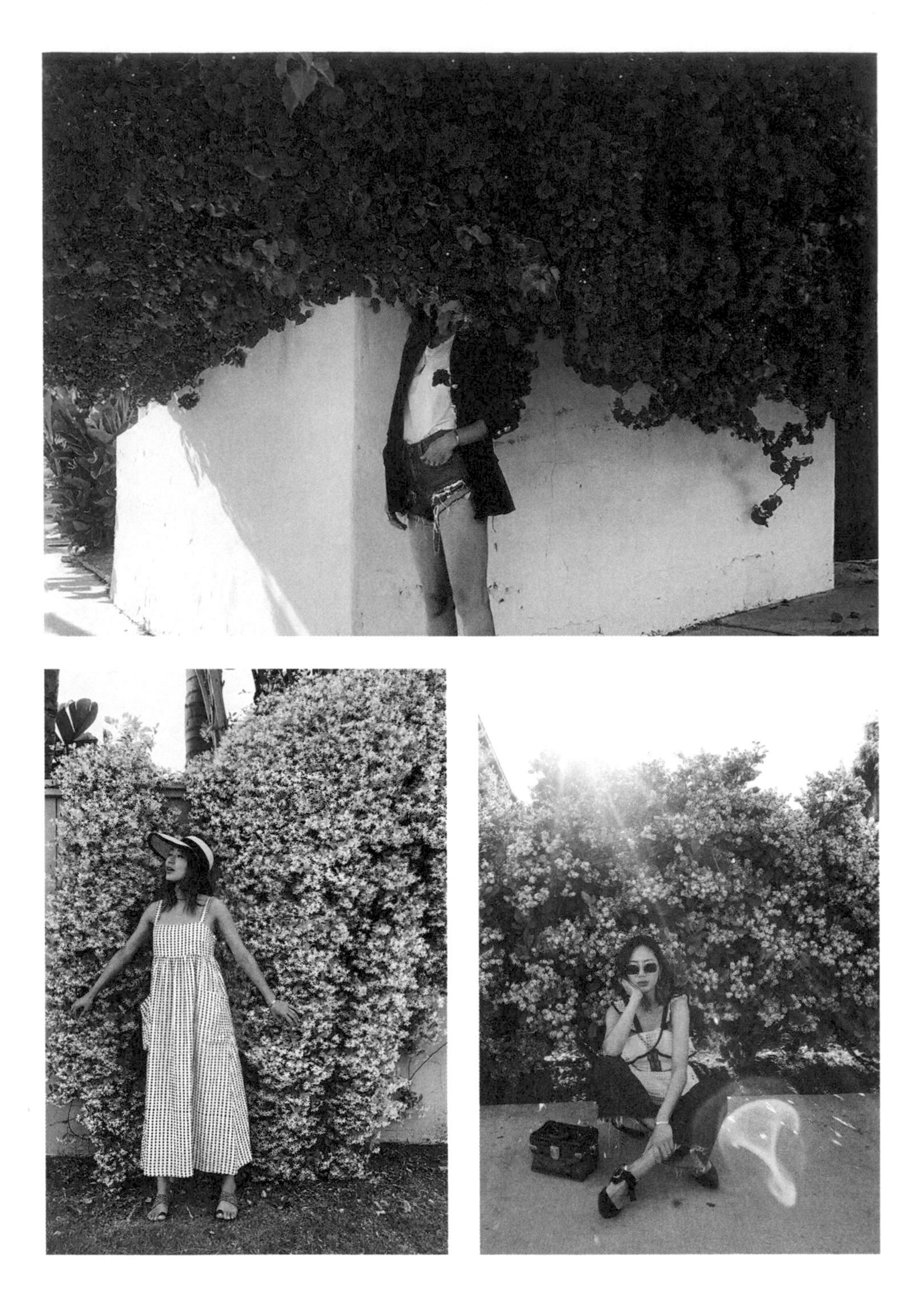

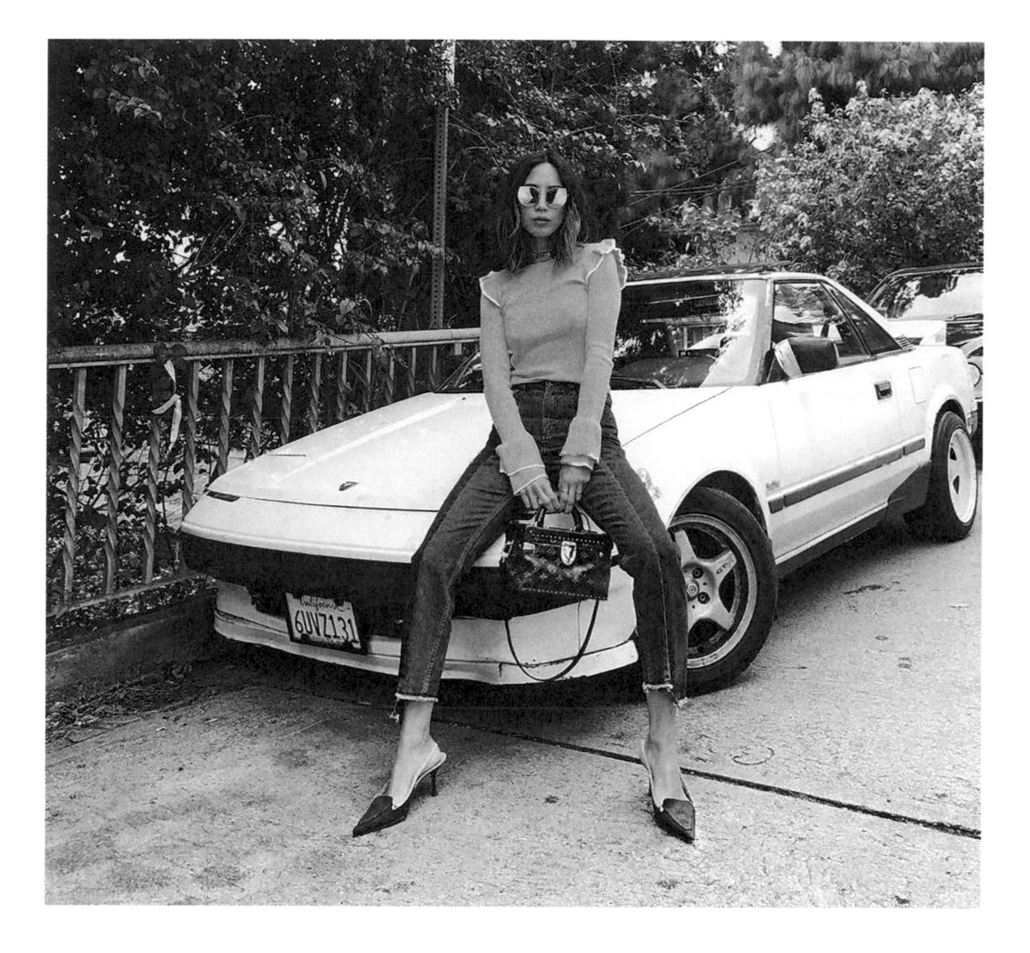

ABOVE As we know, I have many favorite things—a healthy smoothie, great conversation with friends, and my beach cruiser, included. Another one? Sitting on the hoods of stranger's cars (I know, it's weird). Cars—especially old ones with character—make such a cool backdrop for photos. And I'm always super careful to sit gently and to also choose vehicles that look like they can take it (let's just say I probably wouldn't do this on the hood of a brand-new Bentley). *Gentle Monster x Song of Style sunglasses; Topshop jeans; vintage Gucci kitten heels that belonged to my mom.* **OPPOSITE** It's warm all year in L.A. (to the point where we Angelenos sometimes beg for sweater weather), so there are always gorgeous flower walls to be found, especially in residential areas. And you know what that means: amazing photo backdrops. When I see one I love, I'll usually stop in front of the driveway (always on the public sidewalk and always without stepping on anyone's lawn or garden) to take a snap. Usually, if someone finds me taking pictures in front of their house they're super friendly. But one time, a less-than-pleasant homeowner yelled at me. Can't win 'em all—but I still got my shot.

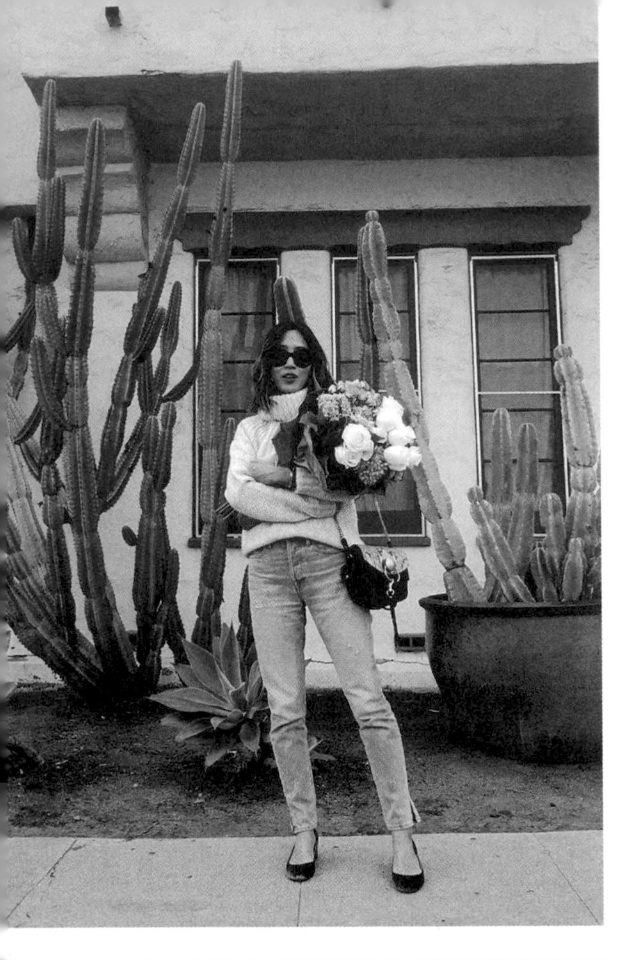
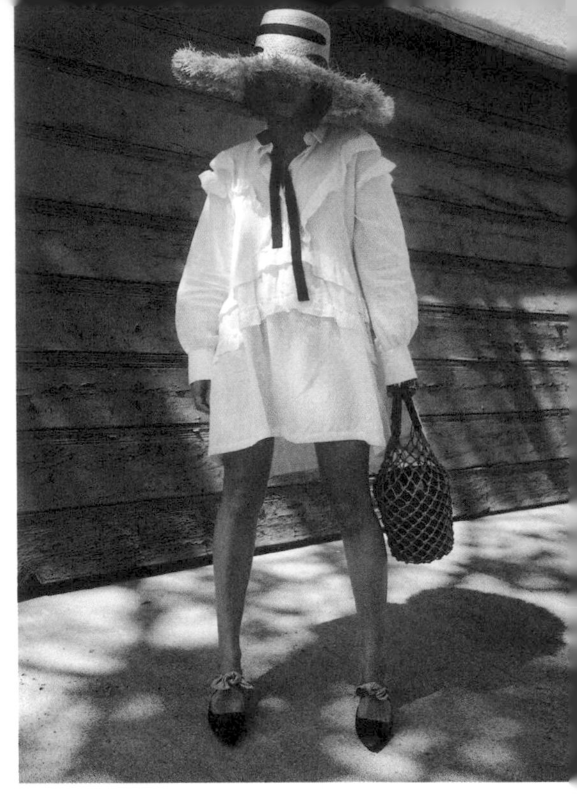
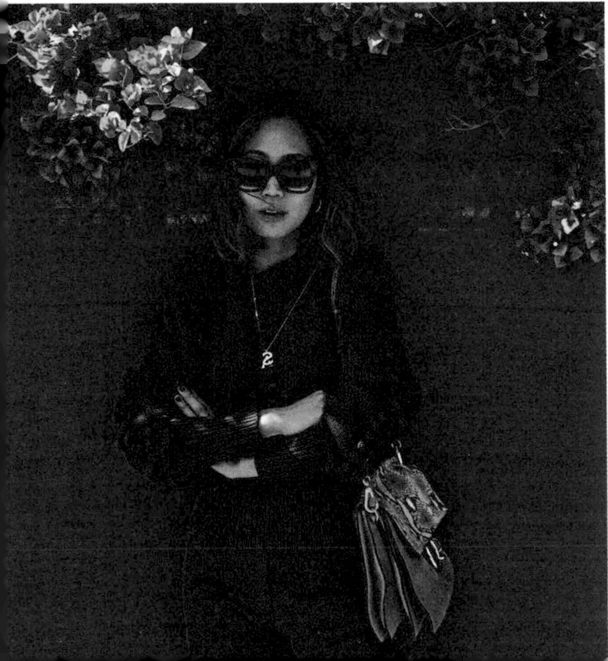
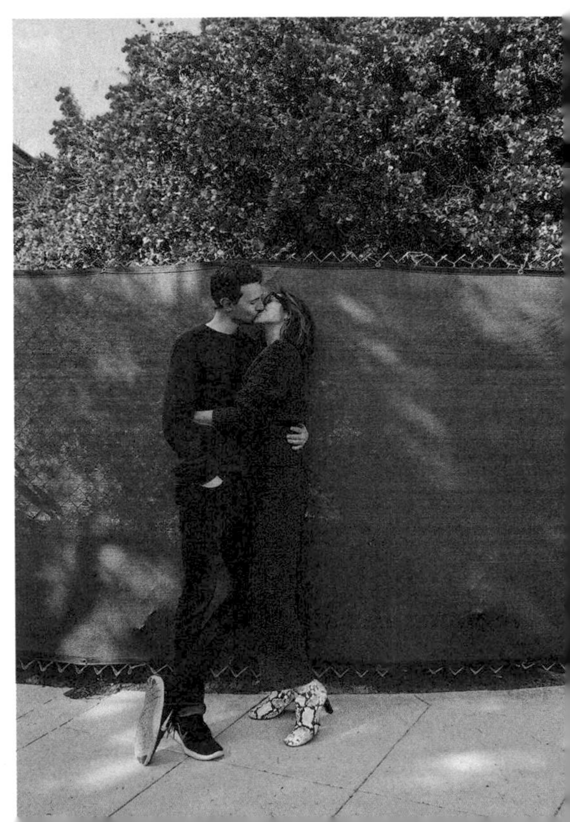

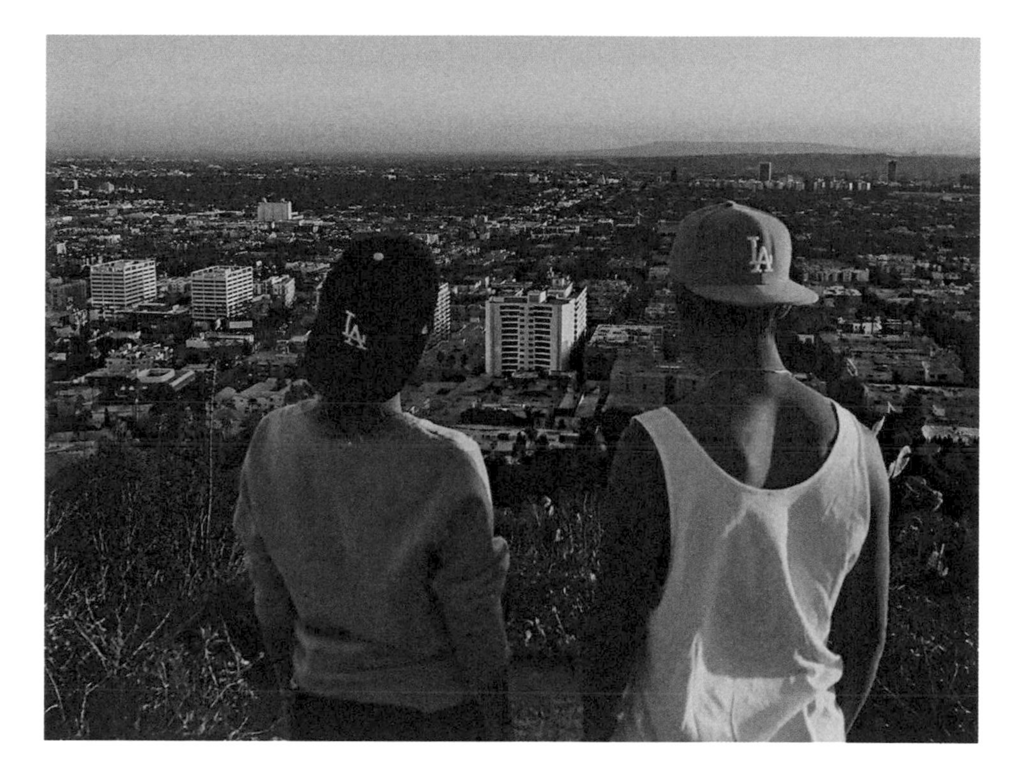

ABOVE Runyon Canyon has been a reliable hiking spot in L.A. for me for at least the last ten years. It's become a bit of a tourist trap now (you've definitely seen it all over Instagram) and makes you feel like you have to be wearing a full face of makeup to be there (a major #WorkoutFail in my book), but it still offers a great sweat if you can dodge all the people. Early morning and sunrise afford some of the best views you'll ever see. **OPPOSITE, TOP LEFT** This gorgeous flora is super close to my office, which I moved into in November 2016. I mean who can resist giant cacti? **OPPOSITE, TOP RIGHT** I love flea markets. Luckily, L.A. has some of the best ones in the world. My favorite is the Melrose Trading Post, a market that happens every Sunday in a high school parking lot on the corner of Melrose and Fairfax Avenues. My pro tip is to never wear labels or carry a designer bag when you're shopping unless you want the vendors to charge you more! I also love the Rose Bowl Flea Market in Pasadena, which is the second Sunday of every month, and the Long Beach Antique Market, which is the third Sunday of every month and has amazing furniture. **OPPOSITE, BOTTOM ROW** Jacopo and I can have fun anywhere—we love exploring and eating and hanging out and just roaming around spending time together. And I especially love when he visits L.A., because it gives me a chance to discover new things at home like weird museums, old bookstores, and neighborhoods I haven't visited. While we were exploring one weekend, we stopped to take a picture in front of some gorgeous bougainvillea because it matched my shirt. *Chloé sweater; Rachel Comey jeans; Chloé bag; Joseph boots.*

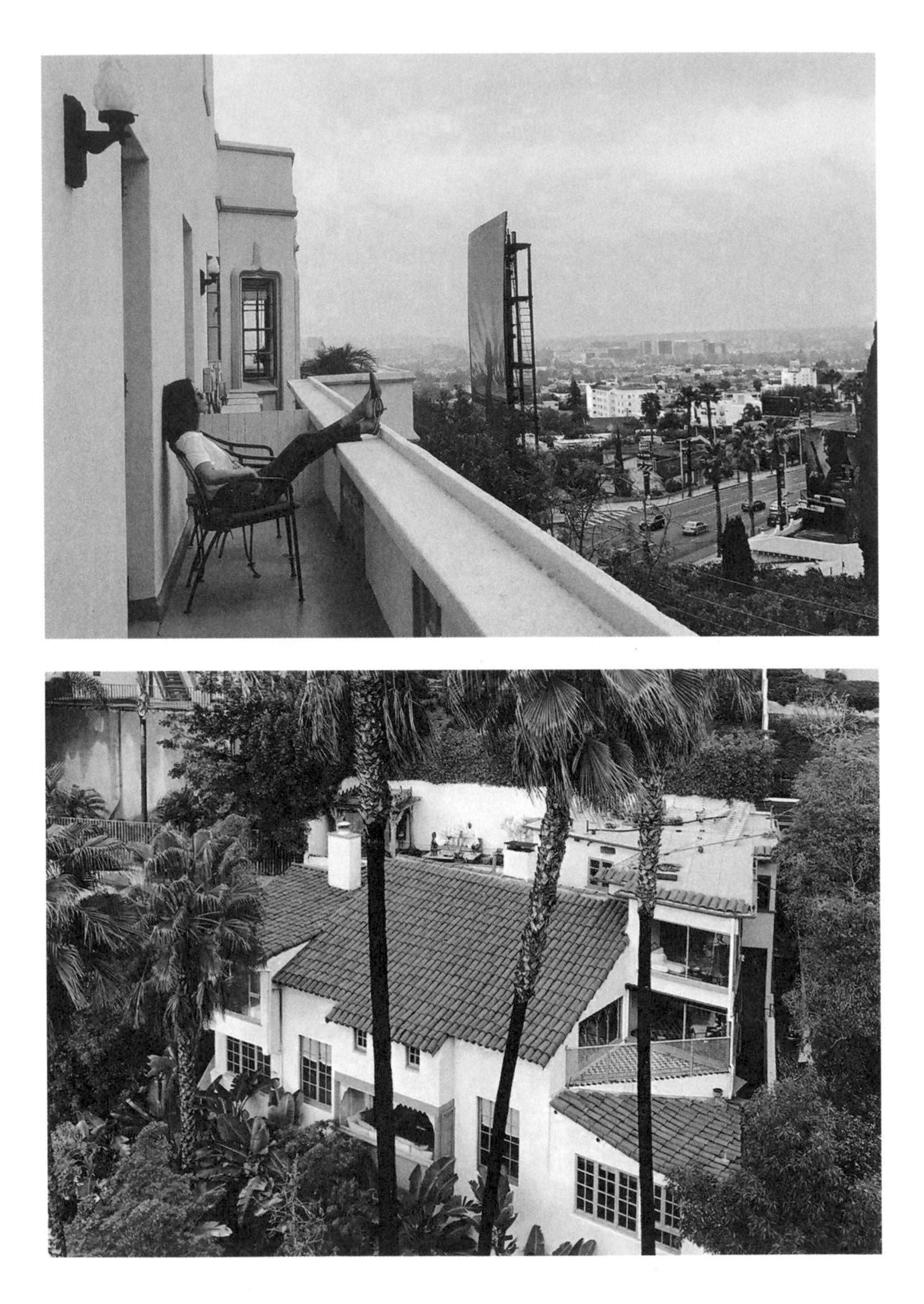

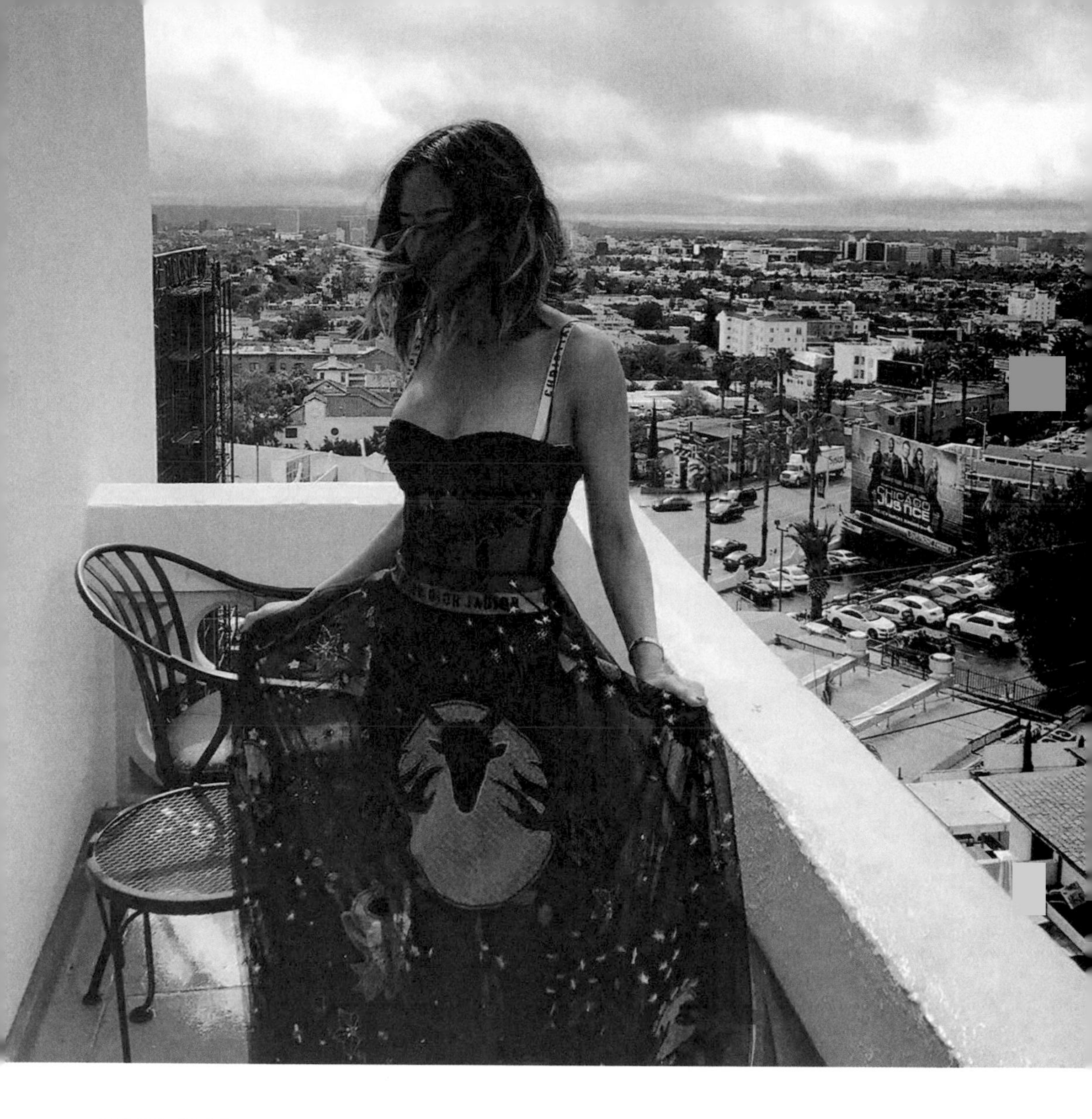

ABOVE I had a shoot with Dior and *Grazia* at the Chateau Marmont. Can you get more L.A. than that? I think not. **OPPOSITE, TOP** After a Tommy Hilfiger press preview at Chateau Marmont (tons of fashion events happen here!), I took the opportunity to soak up the view. **OPPOSITE, BOTTOM** Chateau Marmont is a super famous historic hotel set in a 1920s "castle" on Sunset Boulevard. It has a very "seen and be seen" vibe, with movie stars and musicians eating dinner outside on the patio every night of the week. It's so romantic and has so many Old Hollywood legends, and I always love attending fashion events here.

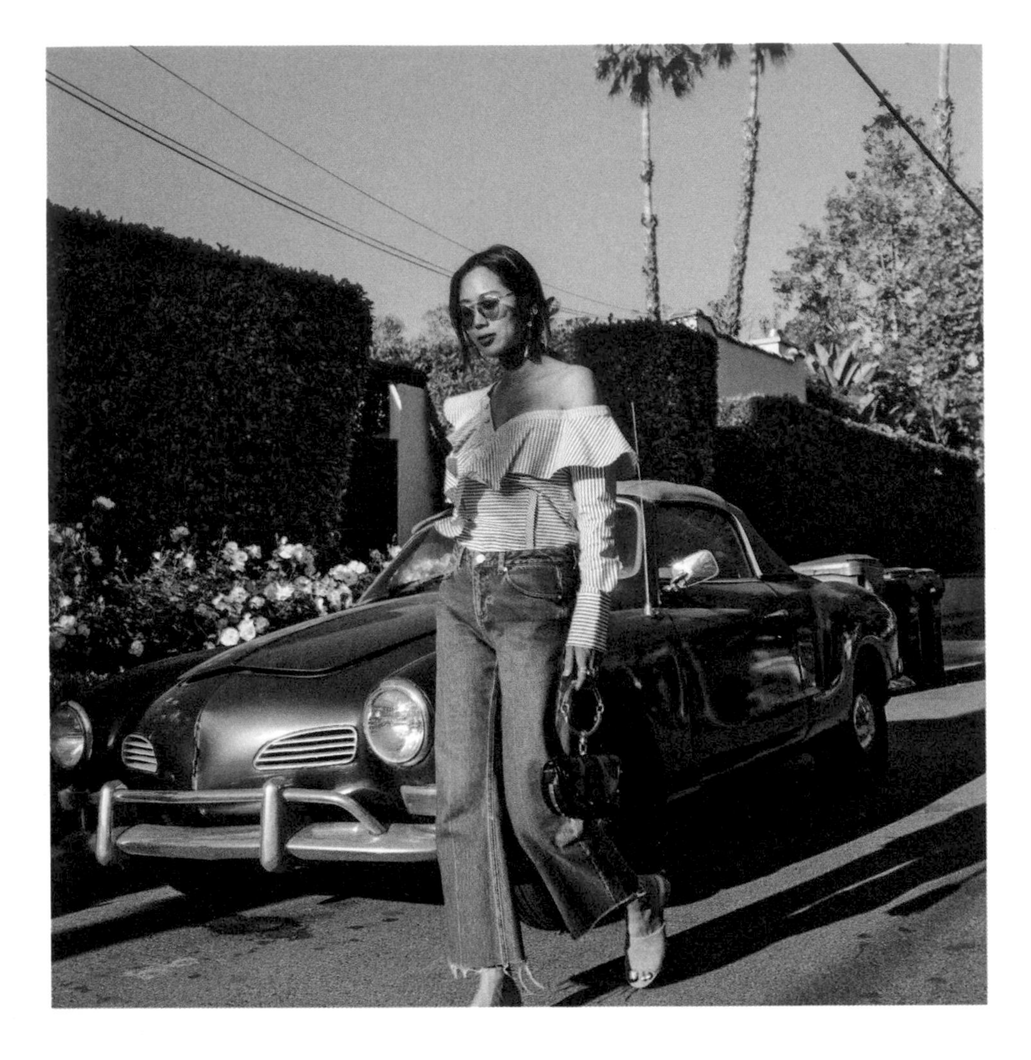

ABOVE This vintage car was parked near my office for three weeks straight, and every day there would be a new parking ticket on its windshield. My team and I never figured out who owned it, but it made for a really cute photo backdrop (especially since I was able to stand in a way that perfectly covered the parking ticket pile). *Dior sunglasses; Self-Portrait top; RAEY jeans; Chloé bracelet; Raye mules.*

OPPOSITE I grew up rollerblading (what nineties kid didn't?), but I hadn't taken a pair for a spin in forever. One day Nicholas, my old assistant, mentioned he was going rollerblading, and I kind of freaked out. We spent an entire Saturday blading around Venice, and I had the best time (and, unlike when I was a kid, I didn't steal my mom's maxi pads to use as knee pads. Very true story. Cue the see-no-evil monkey emoji).

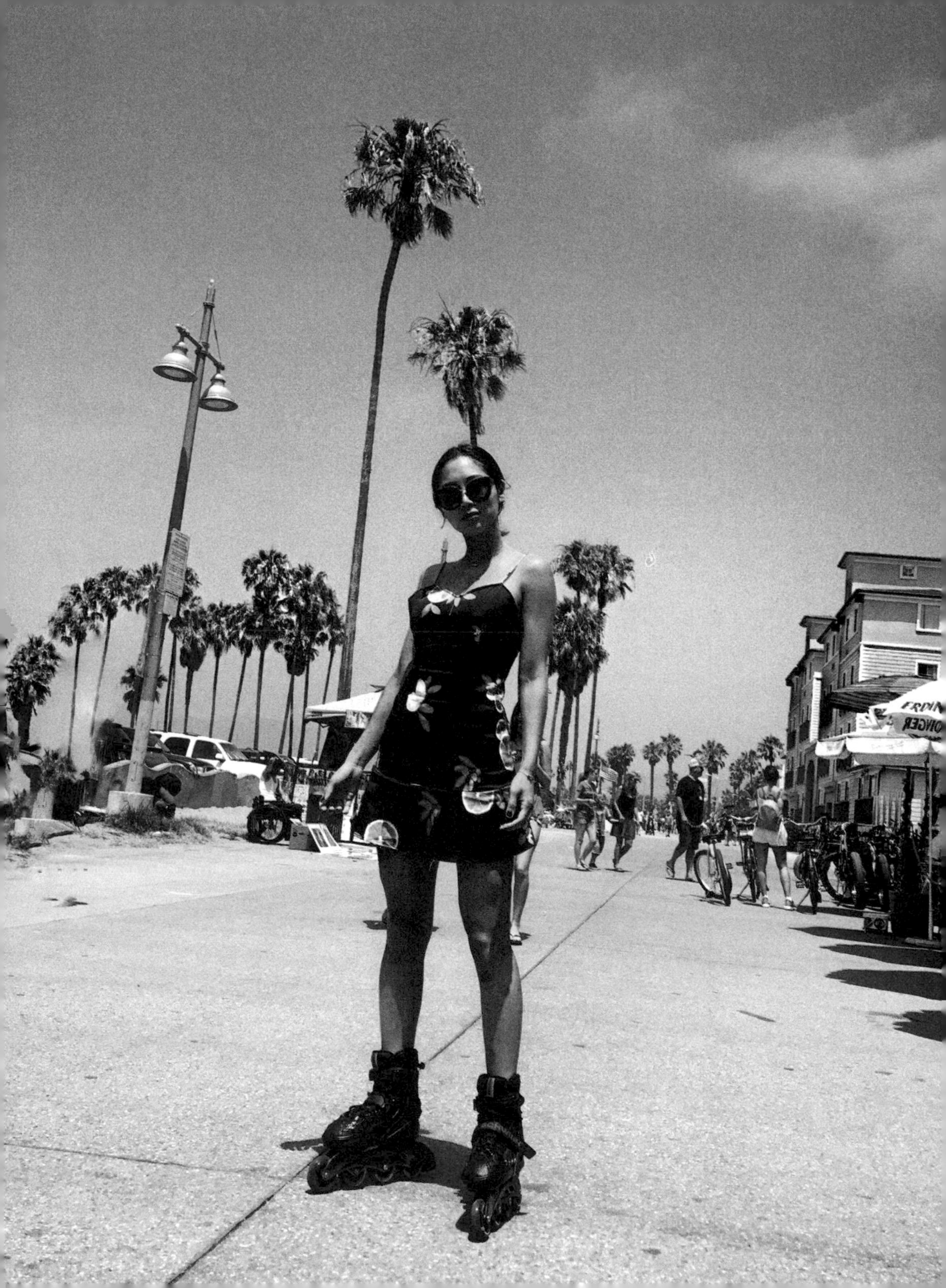

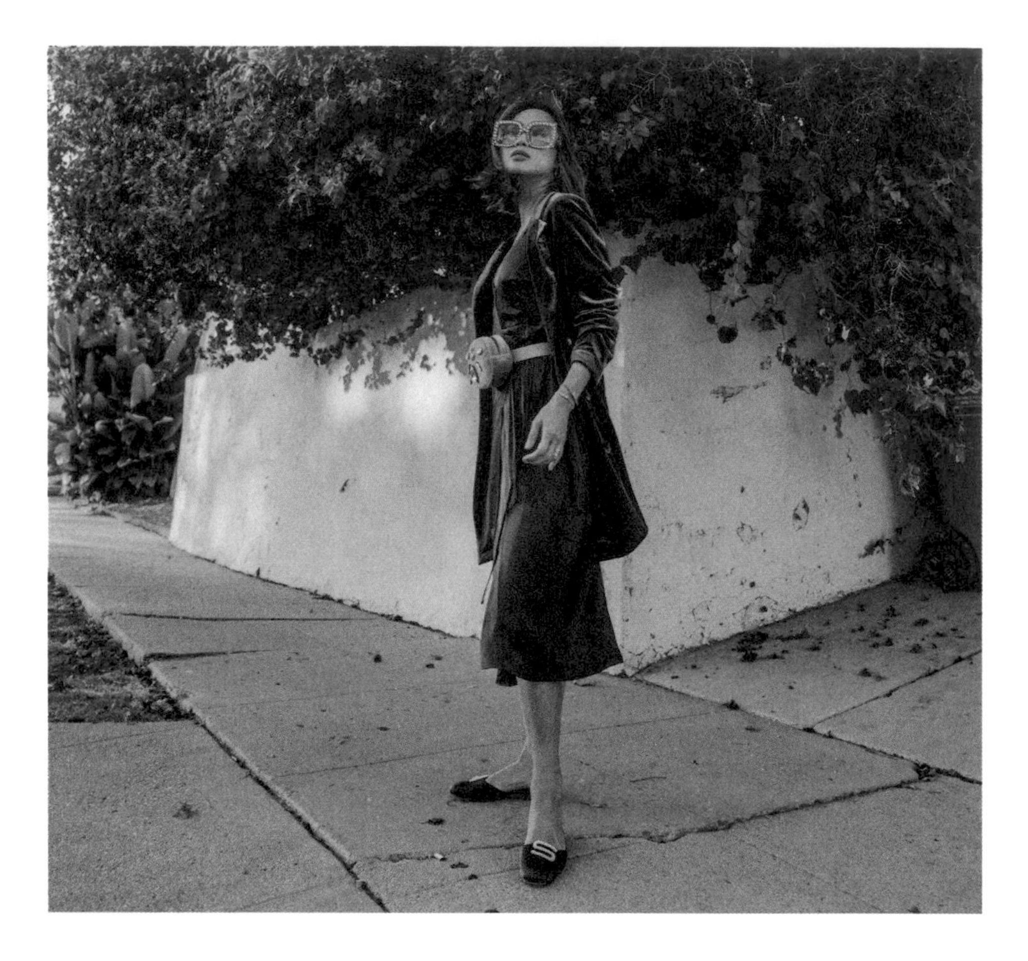

ABOVE Does this background look familiar? I've taken countless photos in front of this white wall that's festooned with bougainvillea. It's one of my favorite places to capture a shot. **OPPOSITE (FROM TOP)** What is Los Angeles (or anywhere in California, for that matter) without In-N-Out? It really is as good as everyone says, and I always order off menu—a grilled cheese without meat, with grilled minced onions. When we were shooting this, the boys in the background started posing, and when I posted it on Instagram some of them actually saw it and commented. The world really is connected, if only by fast food and social media! • When the Ace Hotel opened in downtown L.A. in early 2014 the entire surrounding area began a supersonic metamorphosis. Acne Studios, Gentle Monster, and Urban Outfitters followed nearby. There's also really cool food—famous L.A. chef Michael Cimarusti, who earned two Michelin stars at foodie-favored L.A. restaurant Providence a few years back, just opened a new restaurant called Best Girl at the hotel in October. I spend more time in New York than I do in downtown L.A., but when I do get downtown this is where I love to hang.

LOS ANGELES MUST-EATS

I'm definitely not home as much as I used to be these days, but when I am there's usually one thing on my mind: food. As in, where should I be spending my precious time in L.A. foraging for some. The food in my hometown is legitimately epic, with more taco trucks, Korean BBQ spots, and perfect avocado toasts than should be legally allowed. This list is just a small smattering of my favorites—I'd need an entire book devoted only to food to make it through all my favorites. But it's a start.

Angeleni Osteria
@angeliniosteria
angelinirestaurantgroup.com

Erewhon
@erewhonmarket
erewhonmarket.com

Jon & Vinny's
@jonandvinnydelivery
jonandvinnys.com

Earthbar
@earthbarweho
earthbarWeHo.com

Chosun Galbee
chosungalbee.com

Sweet Rose Creamery
@sweetrosecreamery
sweetrosecreamery.com

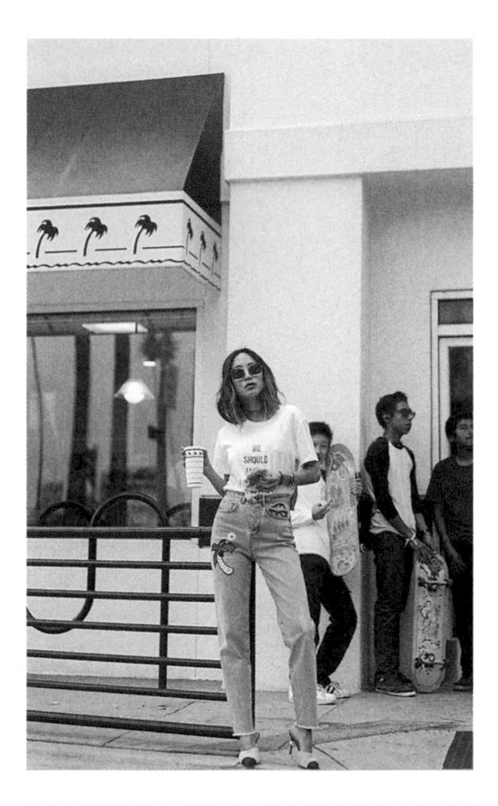

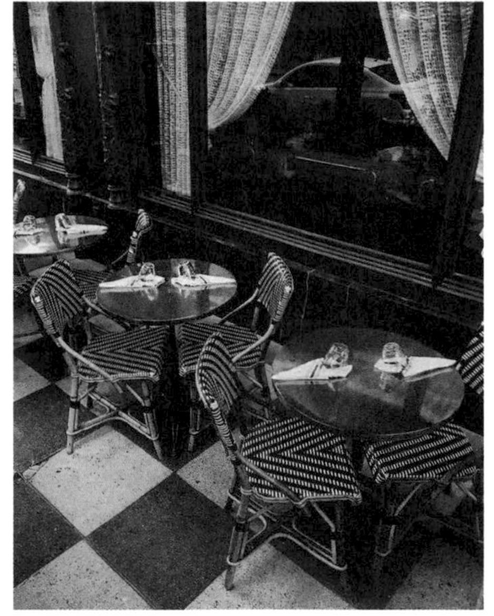

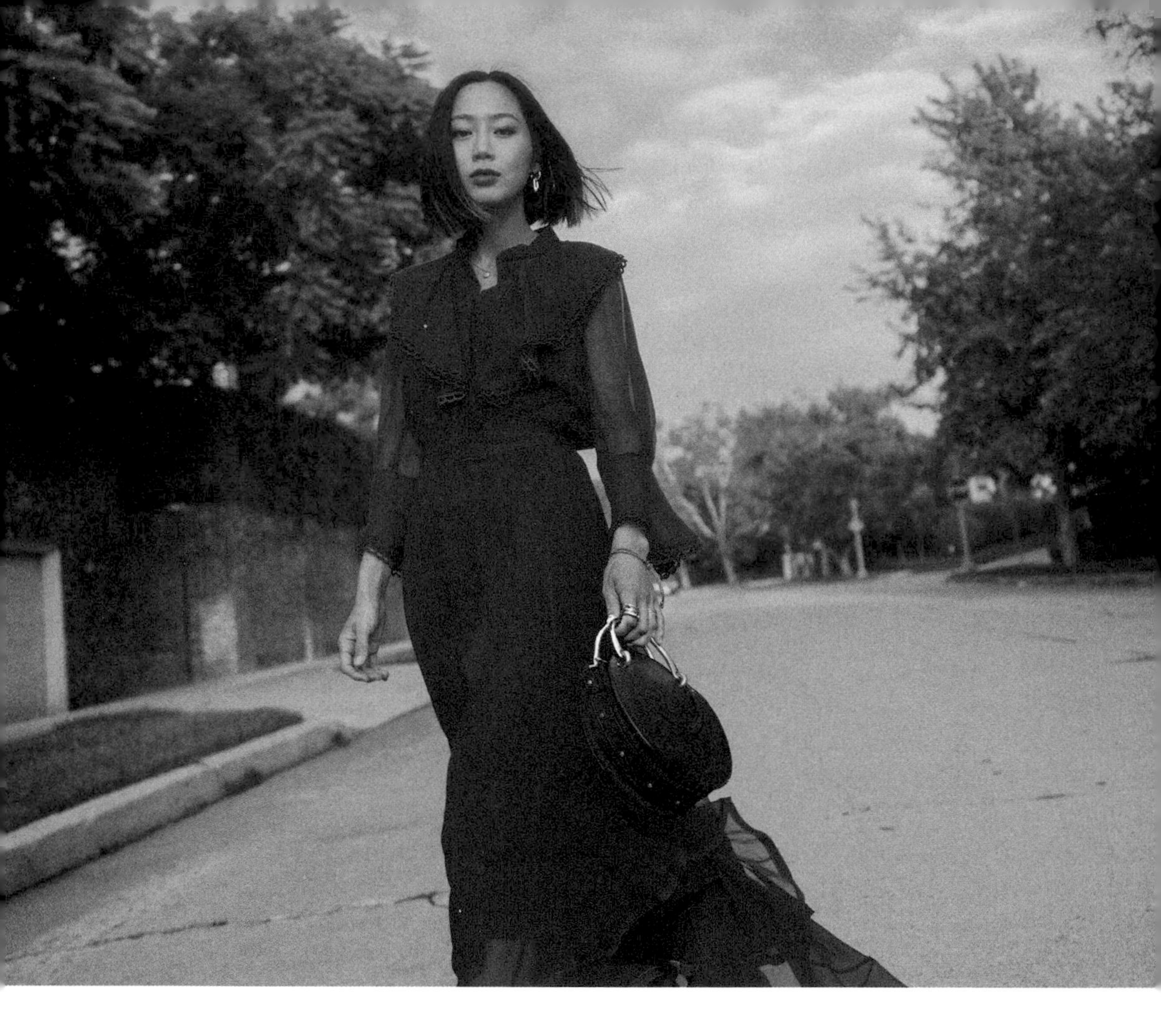

ABOVE AND OPPOSITE, TOP In September 2017 Chloé threw an event at MOCA, one of many contemporary art museums in downtown Los Angeles. The museum was about to open an exhibit featuring the work of Brazilian artist Anna Maria Maiolino, so we all experienced a pinch-me moment by getting a private tour. This is me, Emma Roberts, *Always Judging* blogger Courtney Trop, and Chloé public relations and communications director Arnaud Cauchois. *Chloé dress.* **OPPOSITE, BOTTOM RIGHT** The Broad museum, another downtown art gem, is another one of my favorite places in L.A. This was during Japanese contemporary artist Yayoi Kusama's exhibition there in 2017. **OPPOSITE, BOTTOM LEFT** I wanted to see some of Jean-Michel Basquiat's work at the Broad because one of his paintings had just sold for $110.5 million, and my mind was completely blown. Weirdly, I grew up in downtown L.A., just two blocks from where the Broad is now. We moved when I was in fourth grade so I missed the food and culture renaissance of the area, but it's so cool that I get to go back there now and witness just how much the area has changed.

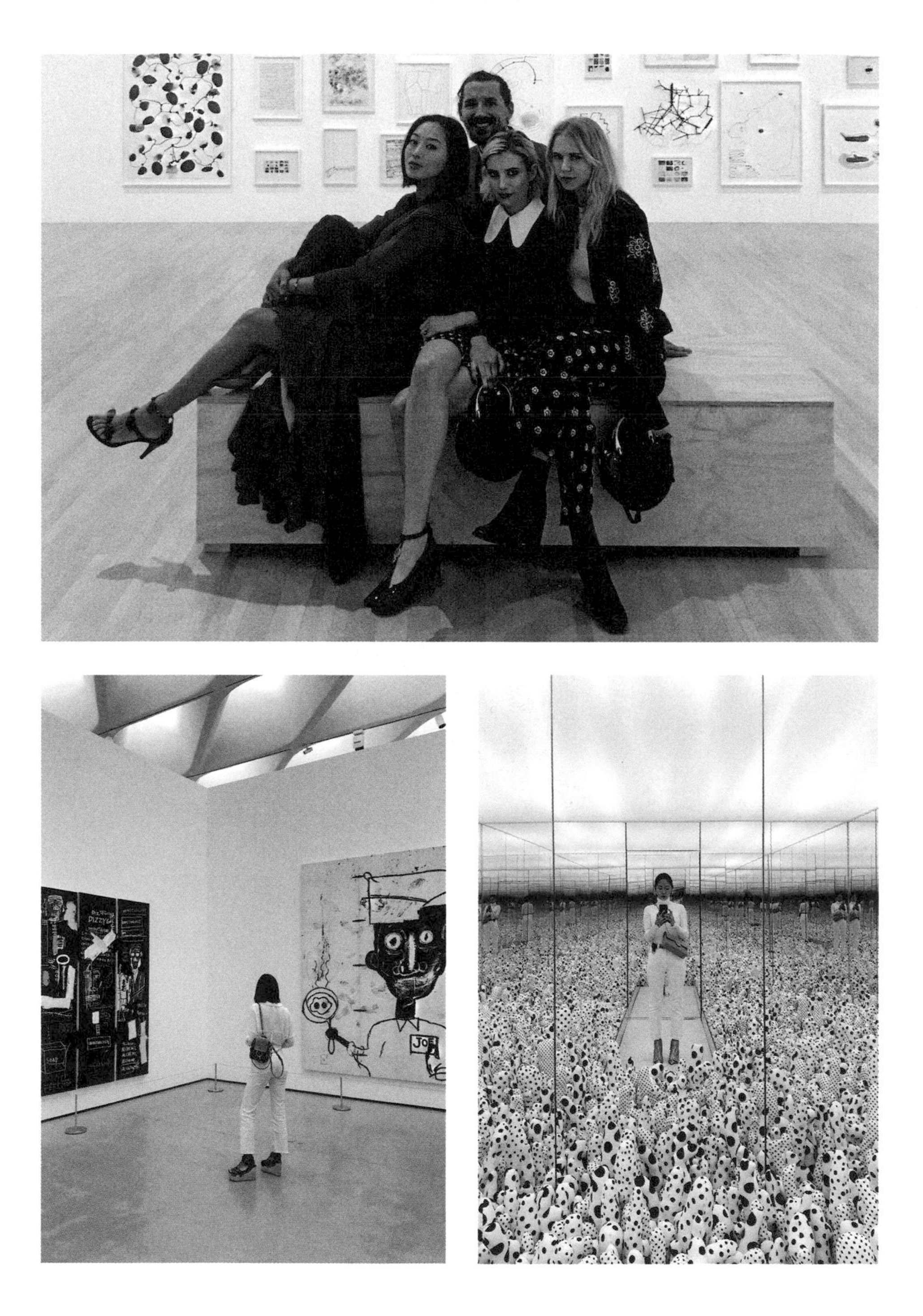
JOE

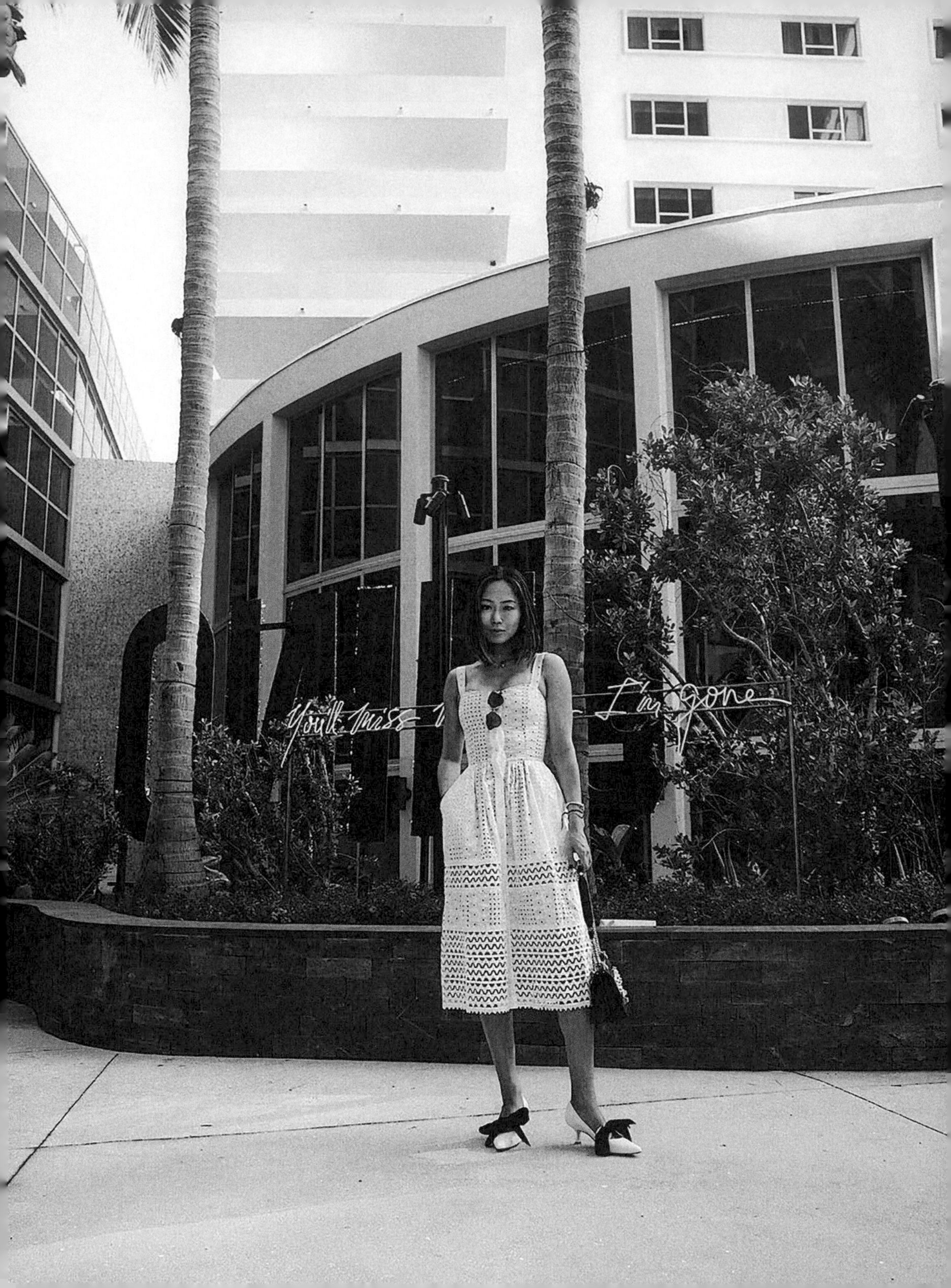
You'll miss
I'm gone

MIAMI

If I could live anywhere in America, besides California, I think I would live in Miami. Being an L.A. girl who craves perfect weather helps me fight that feeling of course, but every time I visit Miami there seems to be an even richer culture that's developed since the time before. I've gone for Art Basel the past five or six years and am always so pleasantly surprised when I land to see even more amazing boutiques, galleries, and cafés than I remembered from the last time. I always happen to meet up with incredibly interesting people in Miami who show me how to be a better storyteller—such as Scott Borrero, a photographer I knew from Instagram who I connected with at a dinner and ended up doing a shoot with in the city's Design District, and Craig Robins, a real estate developer and prominent contemporary art collector who founded the Design District and helped to cement Miami's place as a global arbiter of culture. There's so much life, vibrancy, and creativity in Miami, and I get really excited for my trips there.

OPPOSITE My most recent trip to Miami in December 2017 was for Art Basel, which was really nice because Jacopo was with me and he's like a walking art history textbook. Thanks to his perspective I saw everything with a fresh set of eyes, and learned so much walking the fairs and hearing about the artists from him. *PatBo dress; Manolo Blahnik shoes.*

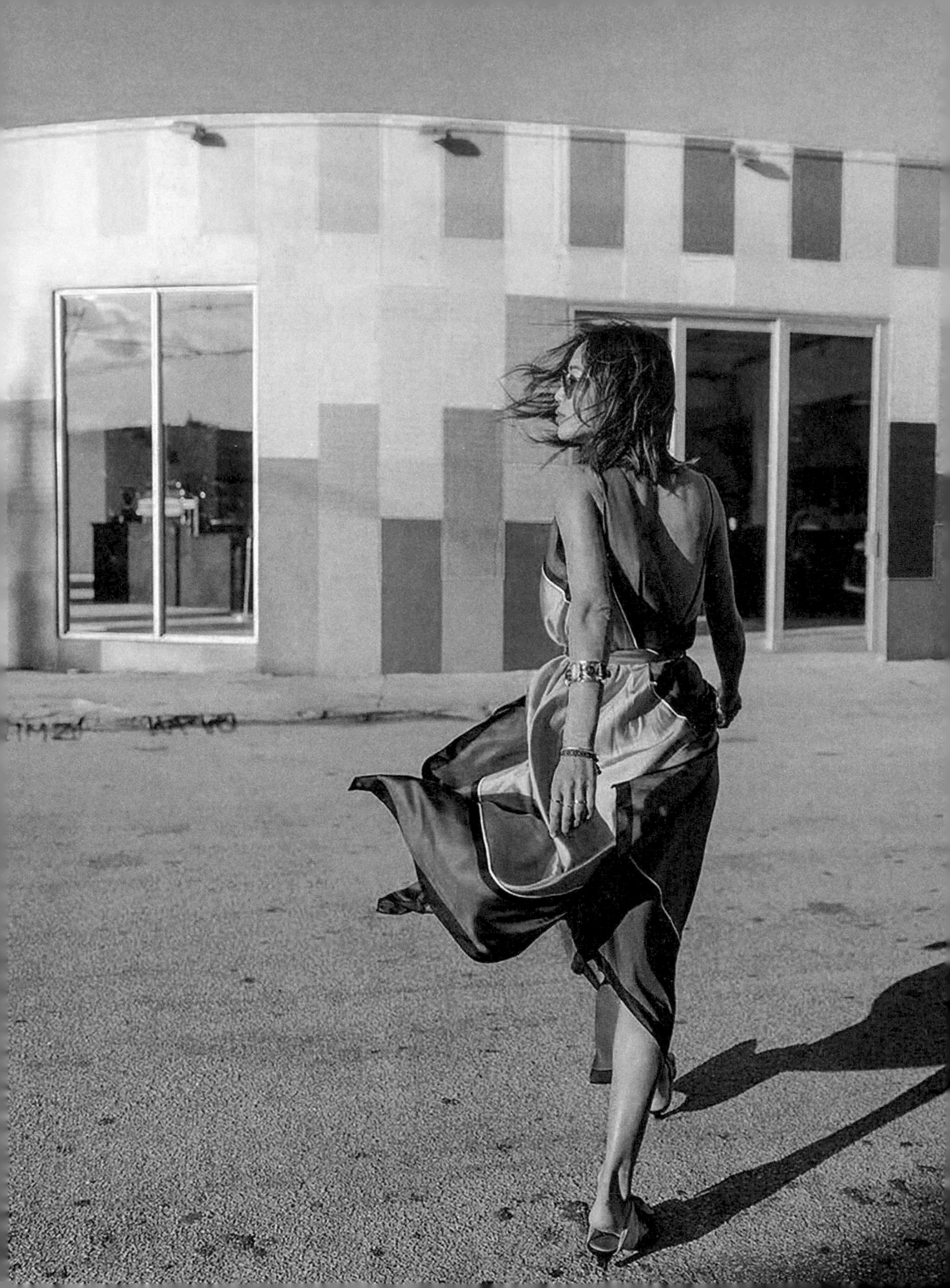

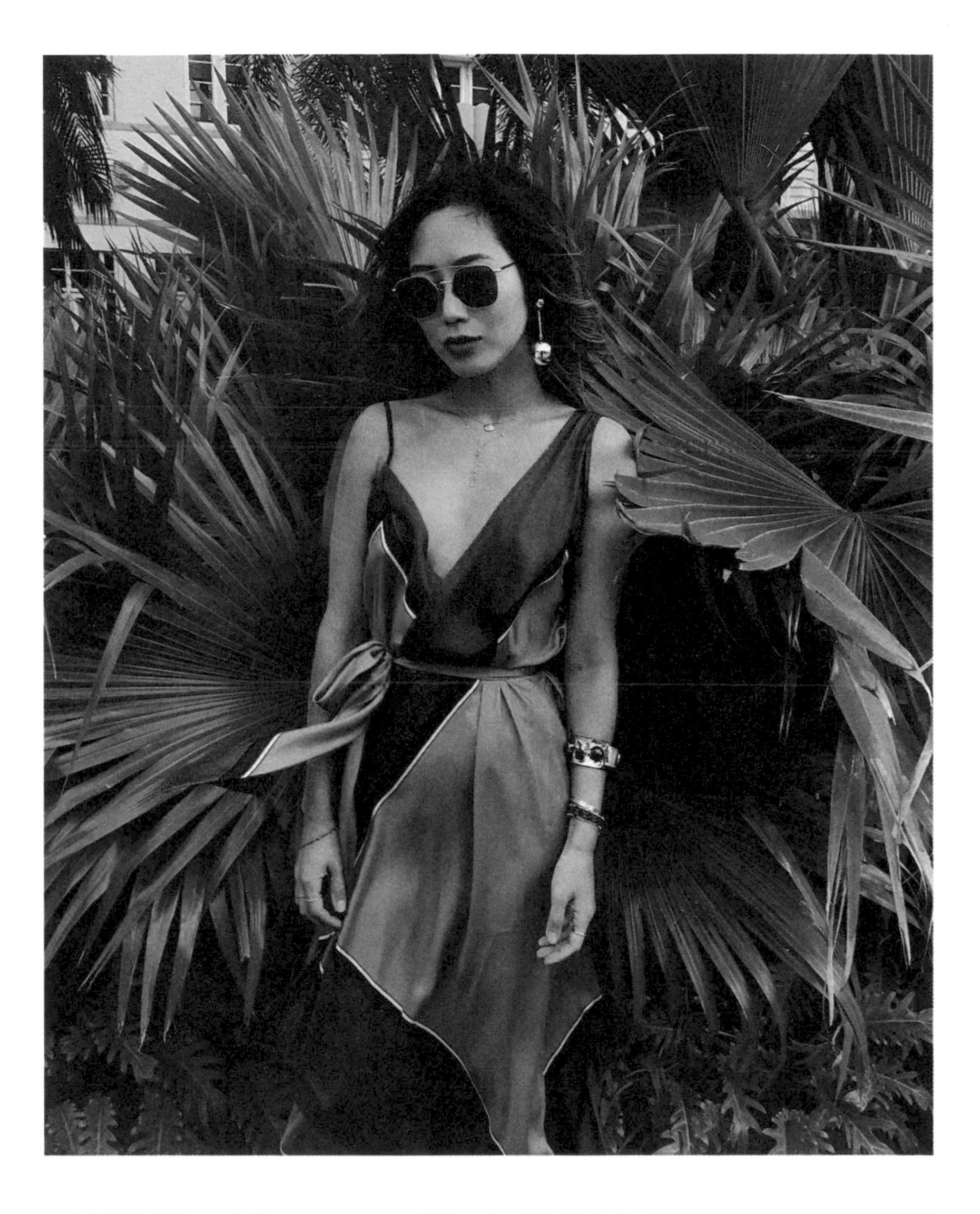

As I mentioned earlier, I met a photographer named Scott Borrero at a dinner in L.A., a year before Art Basel. And since we both happened to be in Miami at the same time and had hit it off at dinner, we decided to do a shoot in the Wynwood area of town.

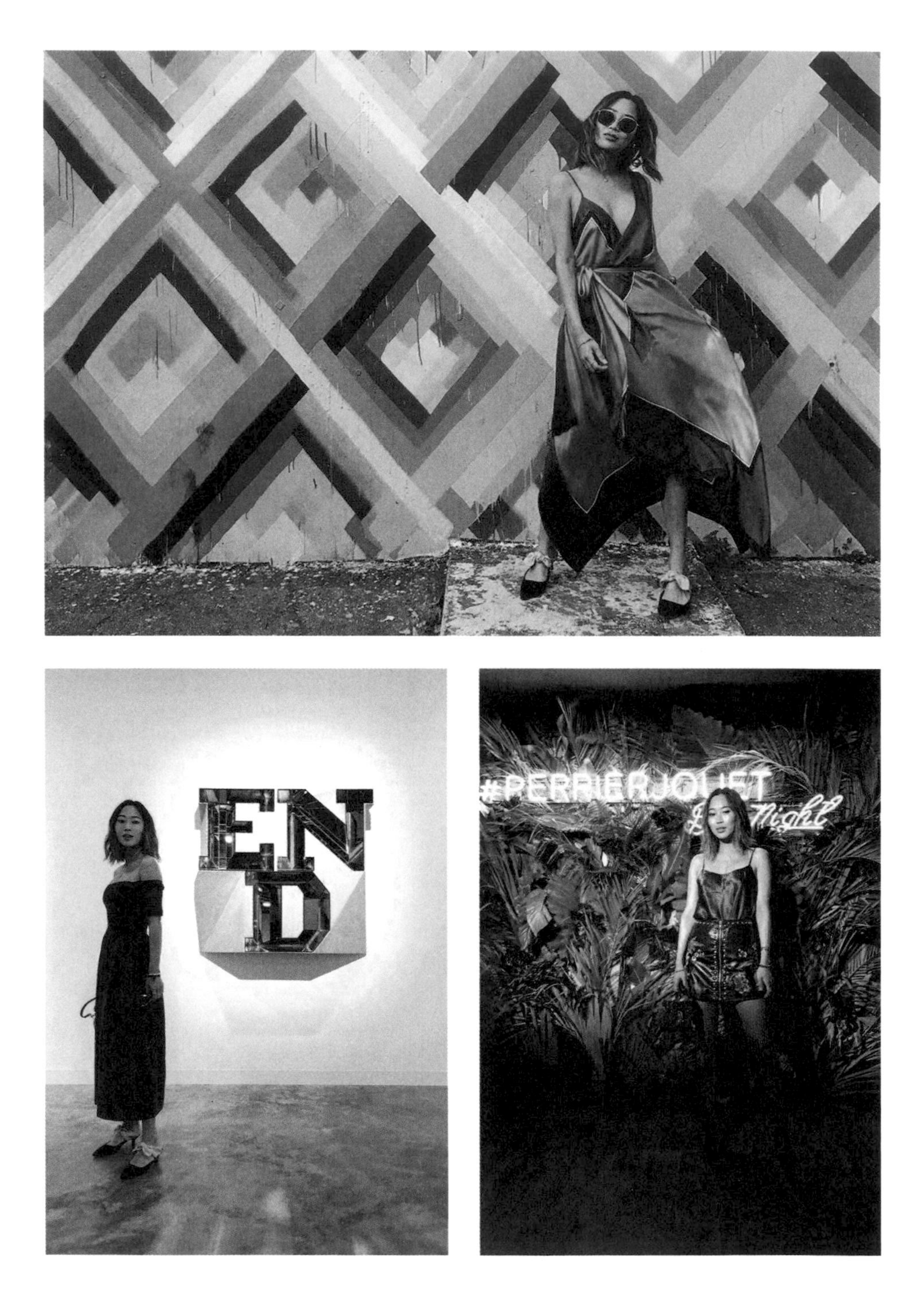
EN
D
#PERRIERJOUET
Night

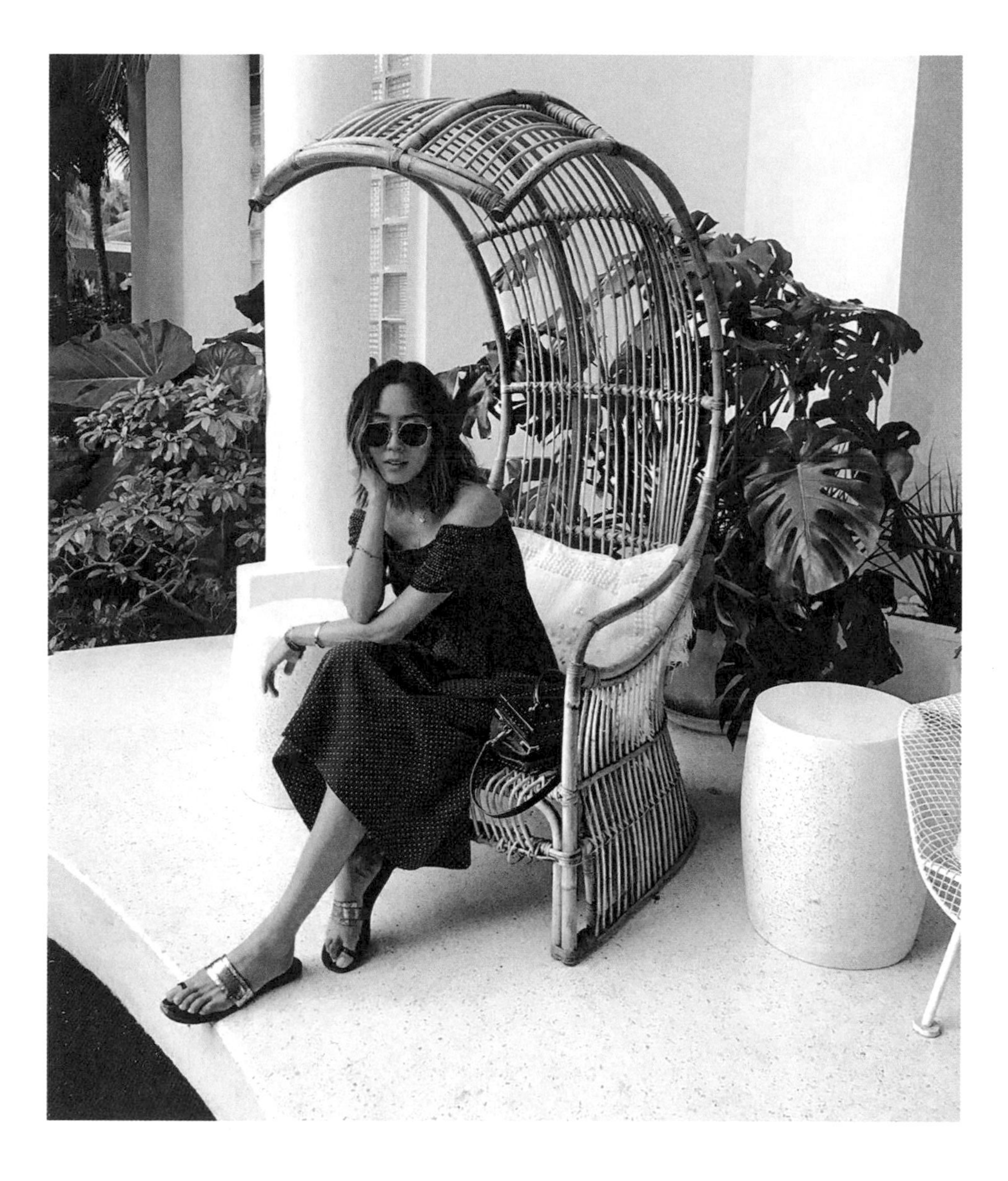

ABOVE *The Great dress.* **OPPOSITE (CLOCKWISE FROM TOP)** *Jonathan Saunders for DVF dress; The Row shoes* • *LPA skirt* • Art Basel. This is the year that I over-wore these slip-on mules from The Row—I wore them to death. I loved them so much that I got them in the black-and-white combo (which I realize isn't much different than the black-and-tan combo I'm sporting in this photo. But still.) *The Row shoes.*

MIAMI MUST-EATS

My love for Miami is real. And though I usually only get to go for Art Basel once every year, I always look forward to the culinary opportunities that await me there (#stonecrabsfordays). These are my MIA spots.

OTL
@otlmia
otlmia.com

Joe's Stone Crab
@joesstonecrab
joesstonecrab.com

Mandolin Aegean Bistro
@mandolinmiami
mandolinmiami.com

The Social Club at Surfcomber
@socialclubsobe
socialclubatsurfcomber.com

MC Kitchen
mckitchenmiami.com

Chef Chloe and the Vegan Cafe
@chefchloe
chefchloe.com

Plant Miami
@plantmiami
thesacredspacemiami.com/
plant-miami

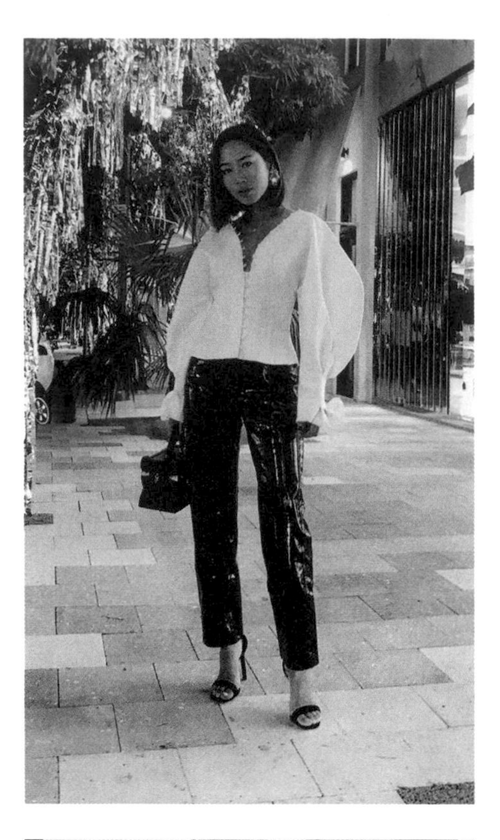

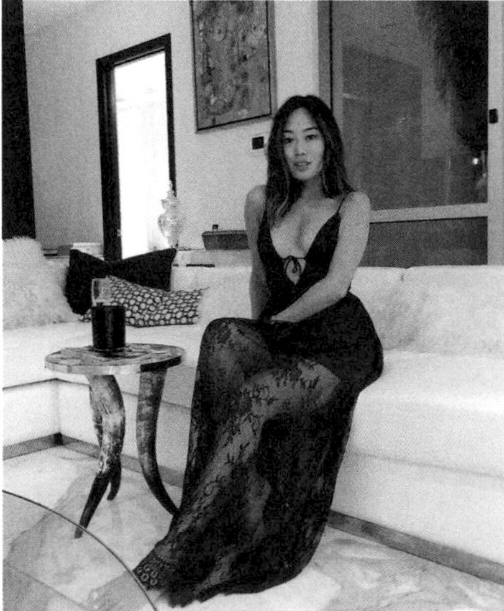

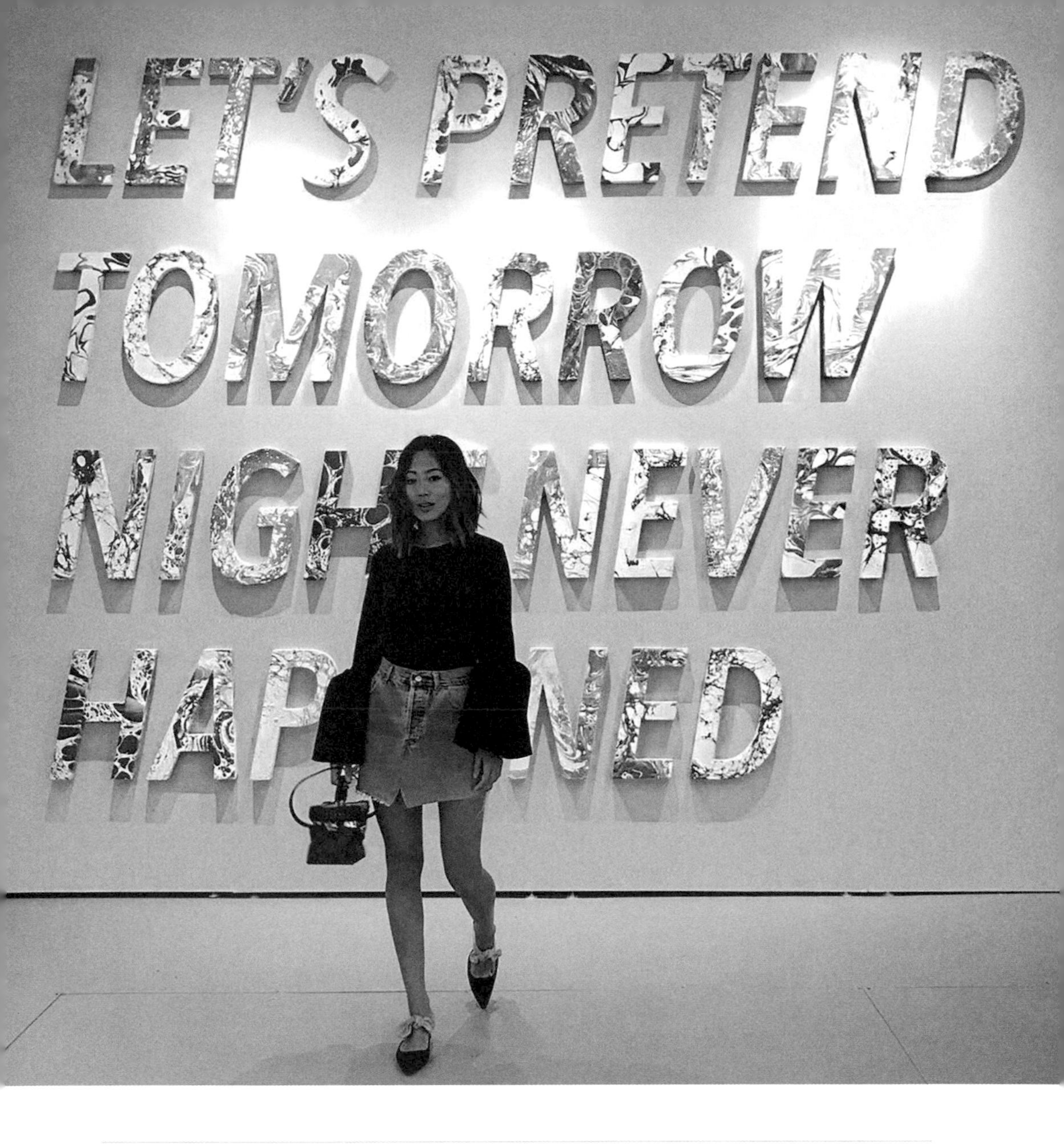

ABOVE At Art Basel wearing the same Row shoes, obviously. *Roksanda Ilincic top; Vetements denim skirt.* **OPPOSITE (FROM TOP)** The first night I got to Miami for Art Basel 2017 the stores in the Design District stayed open late and had events. Five minutes after this photo was taken, I saw Miuccia Prada and was rendered speechless (which of course never happens). *Jacquemus top; Self-Portrait pants* • Revolve did an Art Basel trip in 2015, and it rained the entire time (hence my picture inside our house).

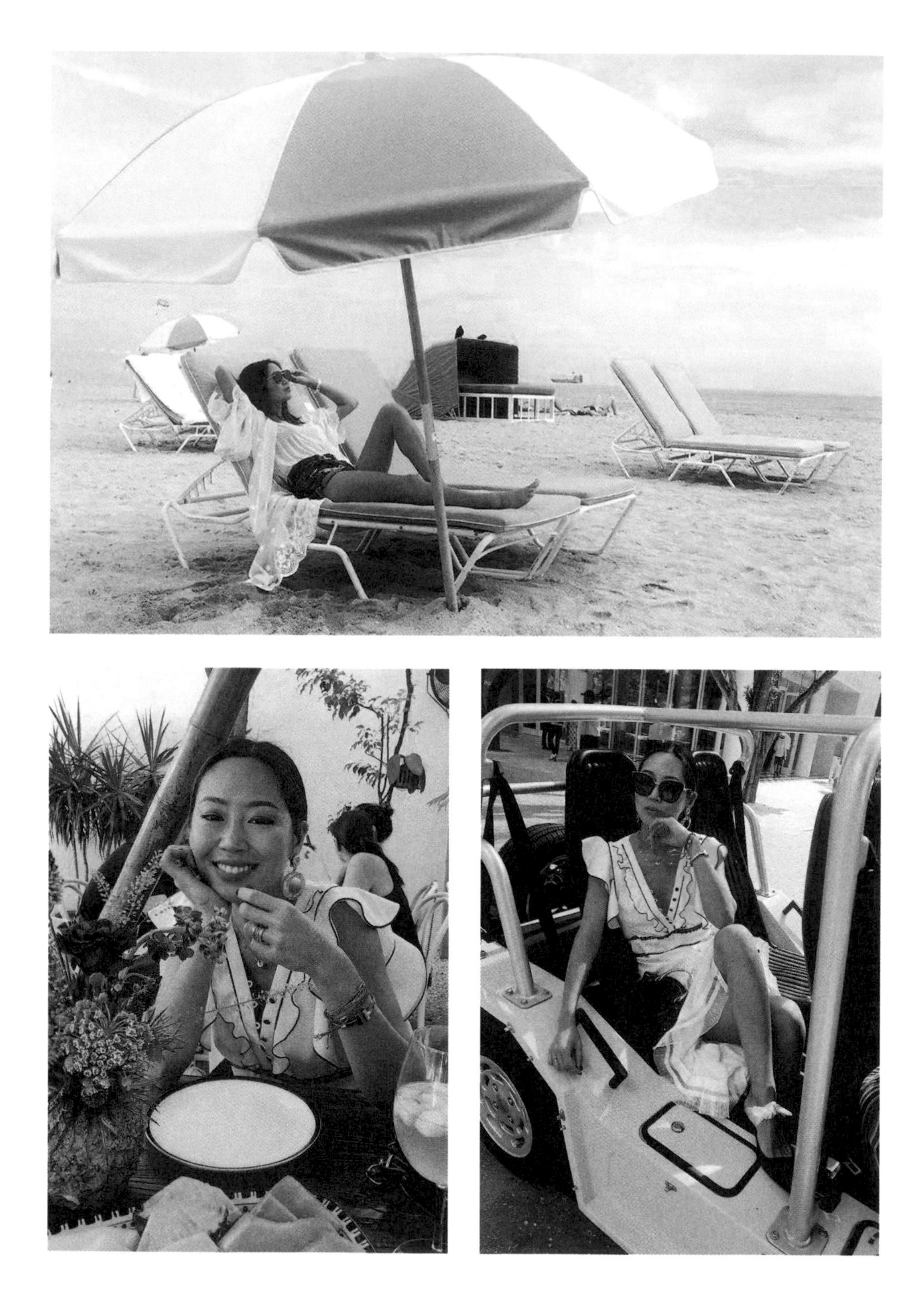

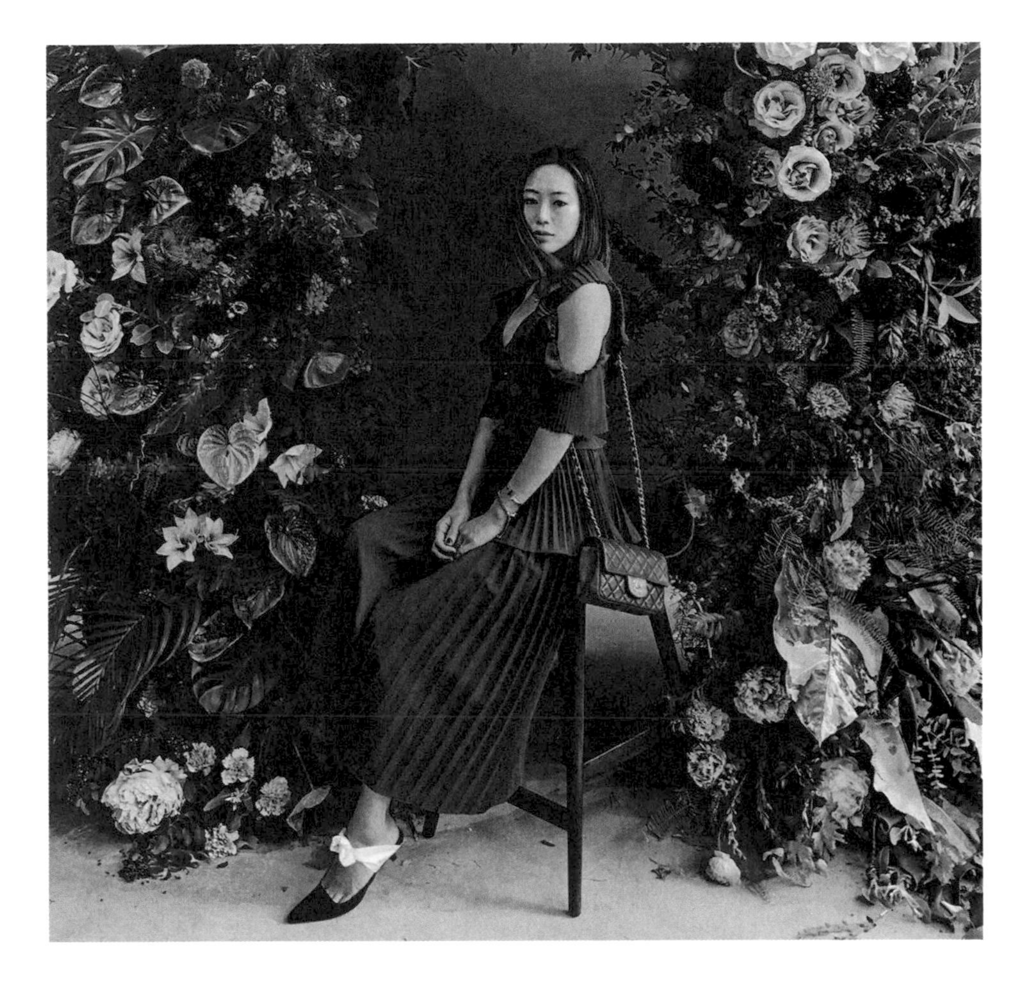

ABOVE At Art Basel in 2017. I went to Social Studies, an epic pop-up launched by former Supreme brand director Angelo Baque with Virgil Abloh and a slew of other streetwear creative heavy-weights. I didn't know who Angelo was until I met him at a dinner hosted by Craig Robins, the founder of Design Miami and the developer of the Miami Design District, and it took me a minute to put it together that Angelo was the man behind some of my favorite things happening in fashion right now. His pop-up benefited the Education Fund for Miami-Dade public schools, and I felt so inspired by him—and every other self-made person at that dinner. *Self-Portrait dress.* **OPPOSITE, TOP** With Revolve in 2015, the one morning it didn't rain. Life's a beach, indeed. **OPPOSITE, BOTTOM ROW** Being chauffeured around the Design District in a cute millennial-pink car, wearing Self-Portrait and those same Row shoes, of course.

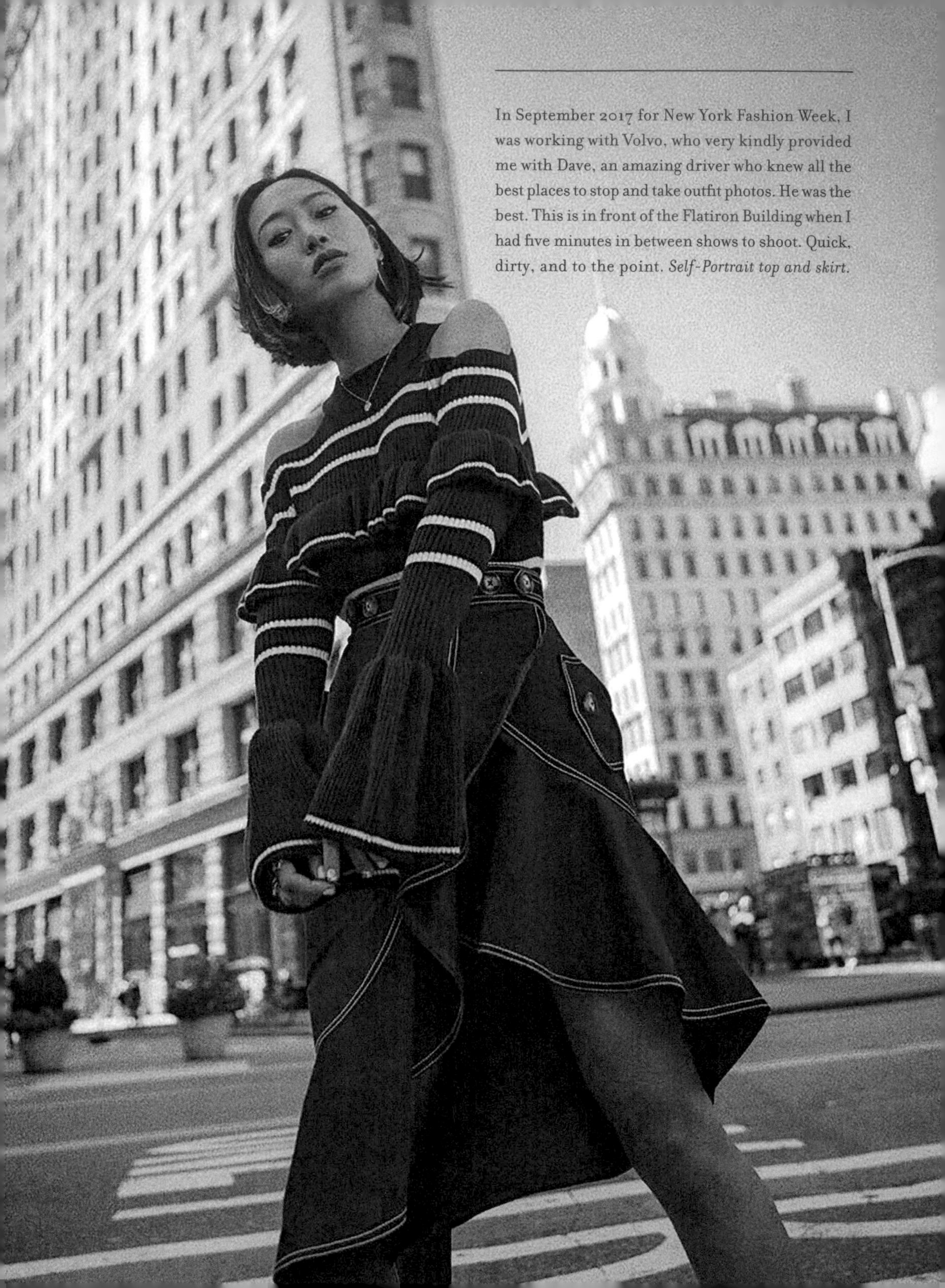

In September 2017 for New York Fashion Week, I was working with Volvo, who very kindly provided me with Dave, an amazing driver who knew all the best places to stop and take outfit photos. He was the best. This is in front of the Flatiron Building when I had five minutes in between shows to shoot. Quick, dirty, and to the point. *Self-Portrait top and skirt.*

NEW YORK

When I was growing up, my very smart multihyphenate mother owned a children's clothing shop called Cottontails in Beverly Hills, where the likes of Arnold Schwarzenegger would come in to buy baby clothes (true story!). She always went to New York on buying trips, but because I was so young I stayed home. She constantly talked about the trips and the lights and sounds of New York, and whenever I thought about fashion as a kid I would revert back to her stories and think about how I couldn't wait to visit the city when I was older. Once I started my blog, I got that chance.

In the early days of the blog, Charlotte Russe flew me out to do a styling challenge. I was a student at the time so I only had twenty-four hours to spare before I had to be back in San Francisco for class, and I couldn't sleep there because I'd forgotten contact solution and was scared to close my eyes. I think I was in the city for a total of twelve hours (thanks to the twelve hours of travel time), and after the shoot I ate at a Cuban restaurant called Café Habana where the only thing I could afford on the menu was corn on the cob—that was my dinner. I still eat there today (though my order is a bit different), as I now find myself traveling to New York for fashion week and meetings sometimes as often as once a month (it doesn't hurt that my Jacopo lives there, too). But I will always remember that very first trip and how hard I've worked to have the kind of New York visits I only dreamed about when I was a little kid, waiting for my mom to get home from the airport, stories in hand.

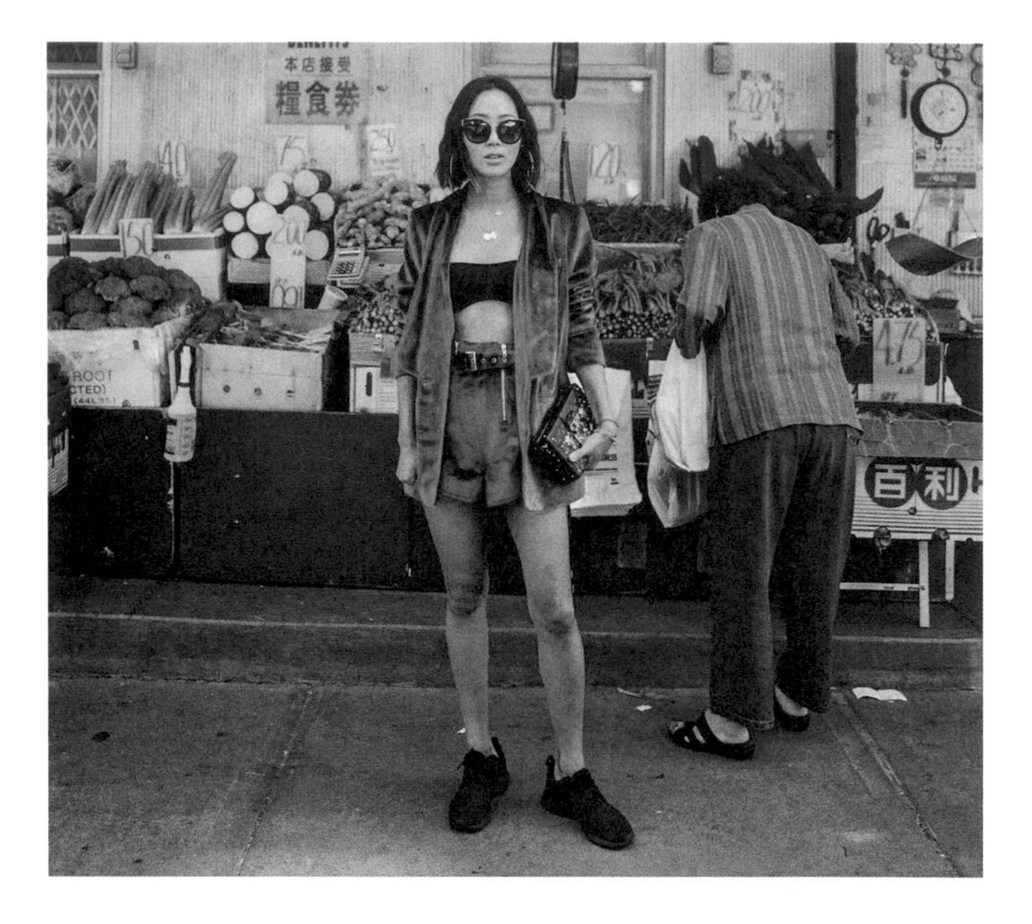

ABOVE During fashion week in 2017. I'm wearing a bra from The Line by K, blogger Karla Deras's collection. She's one of the coolest girls I know and never follows trends—she sets them by being herself and following her own unique vision, which I very much admire. Her stuff is made in L.A., too, and I couldn't not rep my hometown while in New York. *Self-Portrait jacket and shorts; The Line by K bra.* **OPPOSITE (CLOCKWISE FROM TOP LEFT)** After fashion week was over, I stayed in town for two more days because I had a shoot with a Korean beauty brand. That same day I was working with the tights company Hue and shooting looks for my blog. *Hue metallic tights* • Me and my friend Shiona Turini, who is a creative consultant and stylist from Bermuda, holding on to each other for dear life in the snow. We met on a trip to Morocco, and we've been close ever since. I learn so much about diversity from her. Whenever she works on a shoot she tries to cast girls who don't fit standard beauty stereotypes, and it's incredibly inspiring. *J Brand jeans* • I wore this reversible coat twice to 2016's fashion week (yes, that is allowed) because it works both indoors and out. I like functional clothing that does tricks. *Chloé coat* • Right after the Coach show. *Ganni top; Alexa Chung for AG Jeans; Chloé bag.*

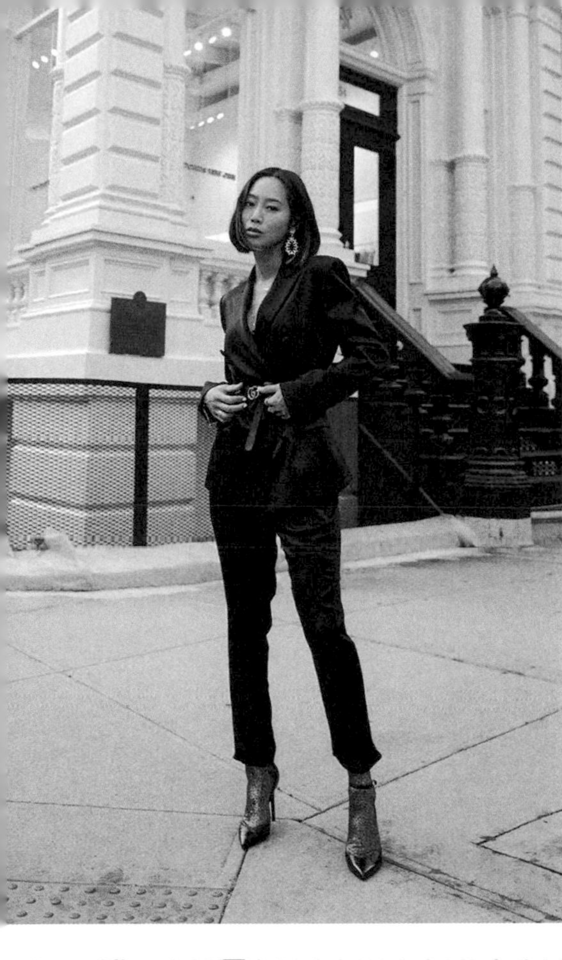

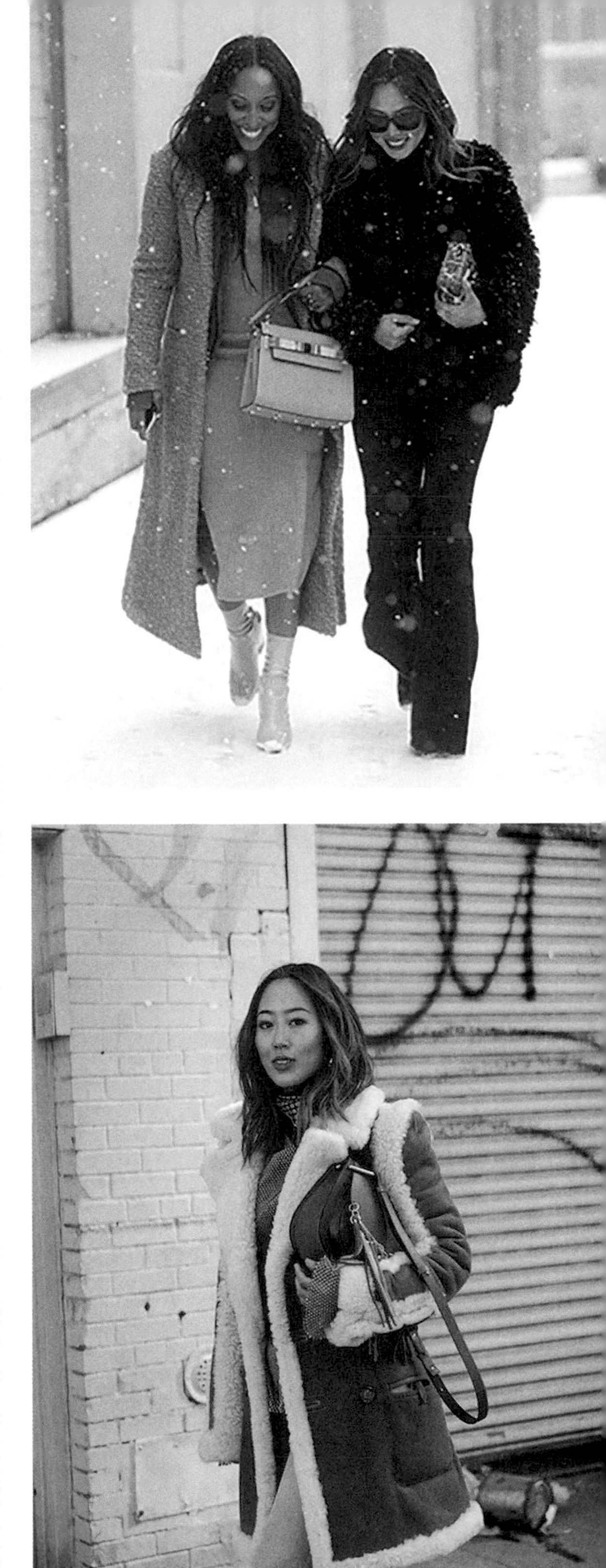

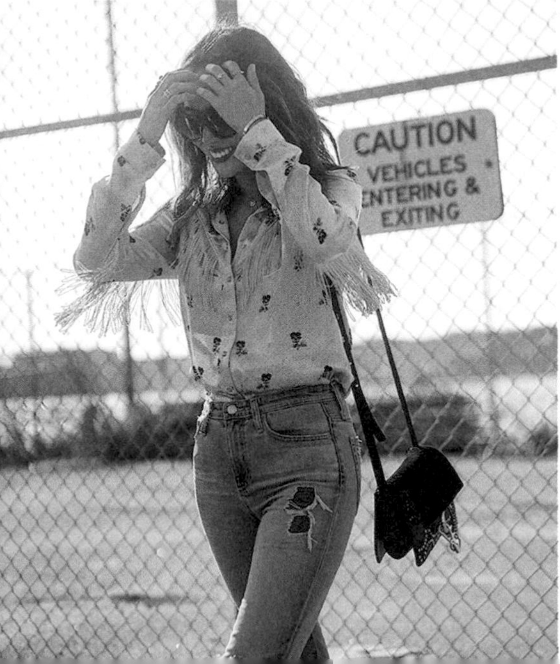
CAUTION
VEHICLES
ENTERING &
EXITING

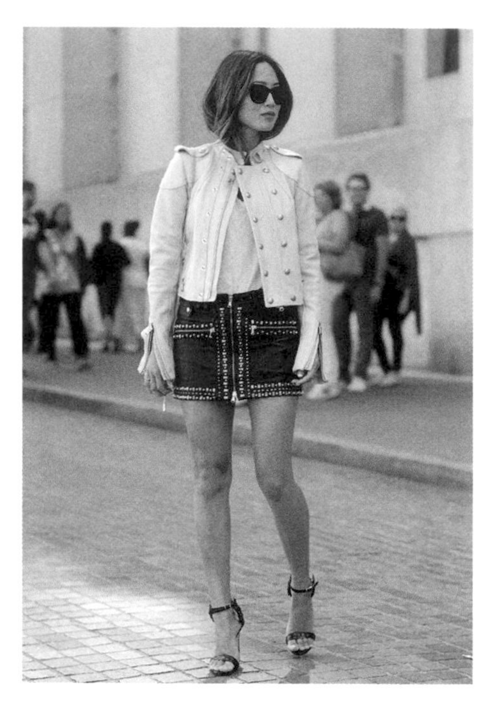

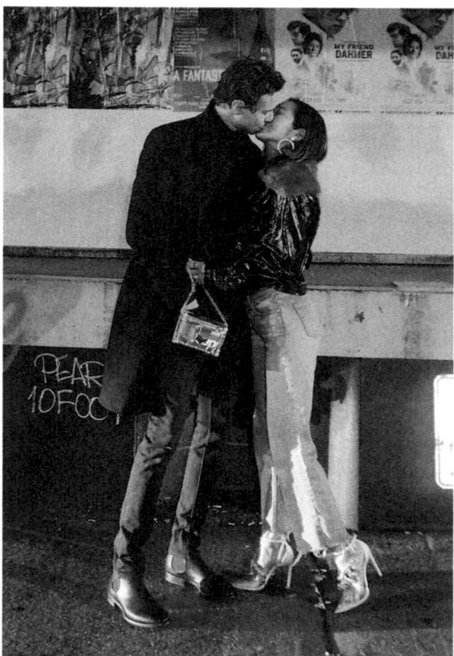

NEW YORK MUST-EATS

My trips to New York are usually hectic, to say the least. But regardless of how many meetings or shows I'm running to, a girl's gotta eat. These are my go-to picks for fresh, healthy(ish), and—in some cases—totally photogenic food spots perfect for noshing in New York.

ATLA
@atlanyc
atlanyc.com

Bo Càphé
@bocaphe
bocaphe.com

The Little Beet Table
@littlebeettable
thelittlebeettable.com

Estela
@estelanyc
estelanyc.com

Take 31
@take31NYC
mytake31.com

Fresco
@frescogelateria
frescogelateria.com

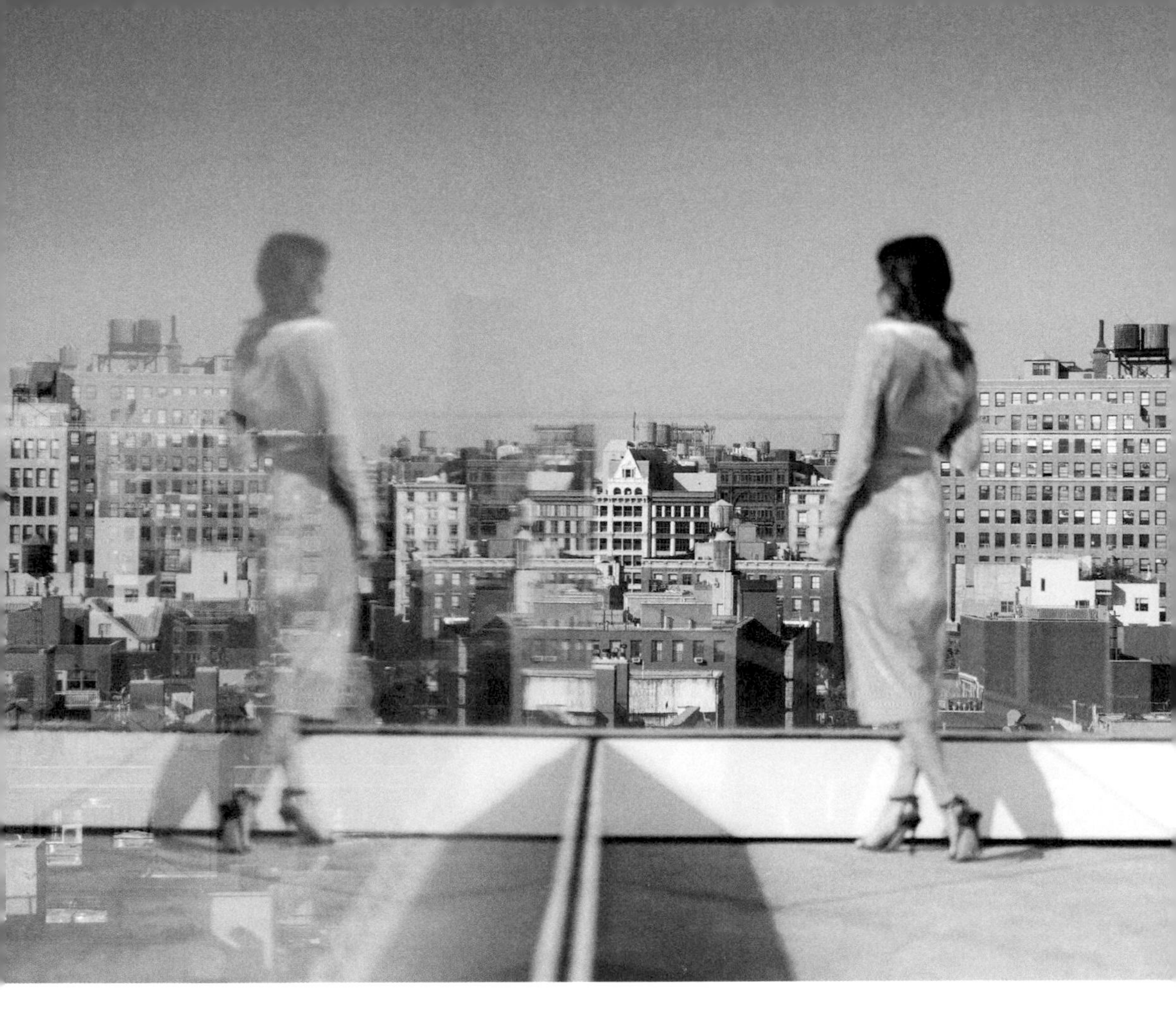

ABOVE In November 2016 I had the most insane opportunity to speak on a panel organized by Polimoda International Institute of Fashion Design and Marketing, a Florence-based fashion school that is considered one of the best in the world. The panel was called "Fashion Displacement" and focused on how education can adapt to the digital changes happening in the fashion industry—super interesting stuff. My fellow panelists were none other than the famed fashion critic Suzy Menkes, Barneys's former fashion director Julie Gilhart, and Burak Cakmak, the dean of fashion at Parsons, another renowned fashion school in New York. I couldn't believe that I was tapped for this as an expert—I'm normally speaking with my peers and other bloggers, but this was with so many fashion industry vets. It was such a cool experience, though, and one I was so honored to participate in. This is me on the balcony at the New Museum, where the panel was held, contemplating whether or not I did well. *Keepsake dress; Jimmy Choo shoes.* **OPPOSITE (FROM TOP)** At the Diesel Black Gold show, wearing a piece from the label that I lost while I was moving. It was one of my absolute favorites. Then, while I was working on this book, I happened to find it. Fate? It does exist. • Squeezing in date night with Jacopo during New York Fashion Week.

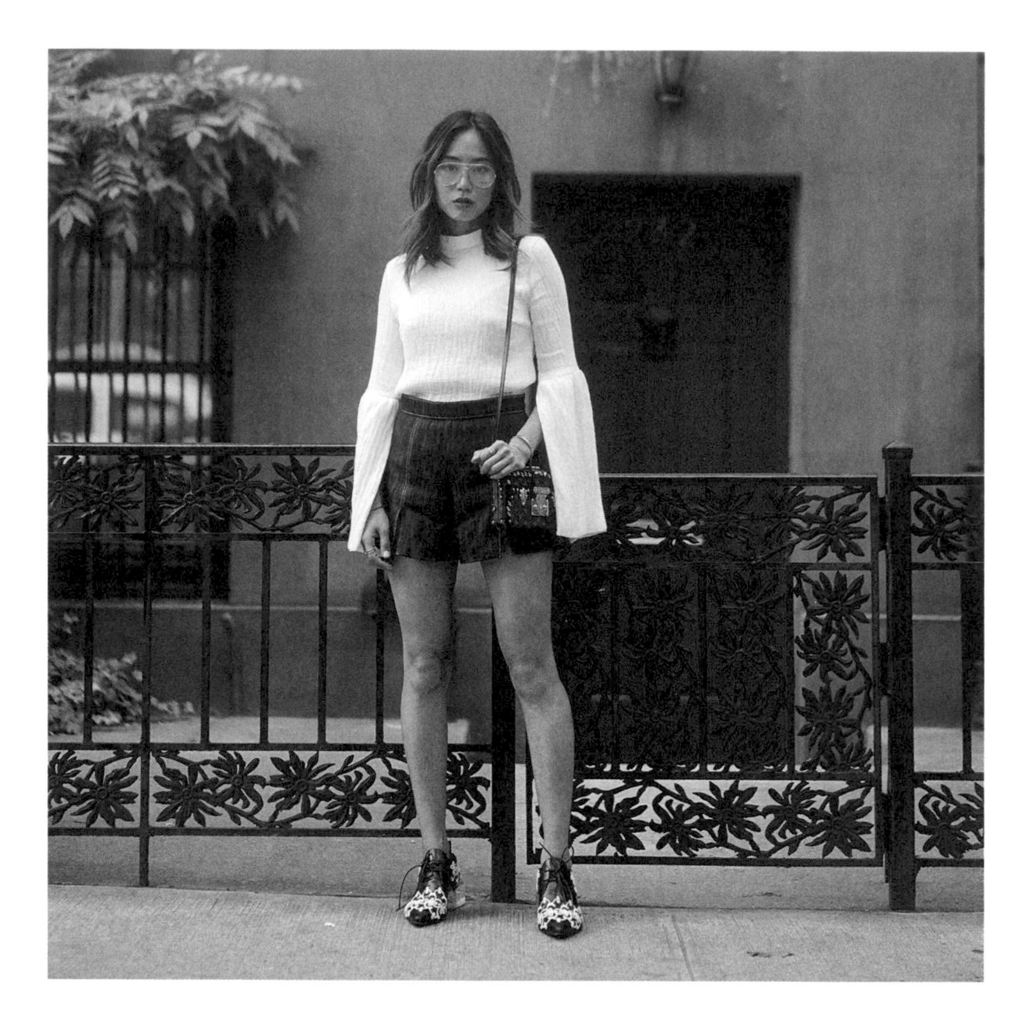

ABOVE AND OPPOSITE, TOP I love when Dani is with me in New York. I usually go to so many shows that I end up feeling like a robot and saying the exact same things to everyone at every show. But when I do it with Dani, we actually have real conversations with people. Everyone loves her because she has such a great energy and spirit, and she genuinely cares about people. Having her with me helps me relax, and because going to shows and working in fashion isn't Dani's life in the same way that it's mine, she reminds me to appreciate all of the moments that I tend to take for granted. She's my calming and grounding force. *Chloé glasses; Louis Vuitton bag and shoes.* **OPPOSITE, BOTTOM RIGHT** Skipping with joy after eating at my favorite vegan restaurant in the West Village. **OPPOSITE, BOTTOM LEFT** During New York Fashion Week 2018, when four people showed up wearing the same dress at the same show. *Tibi dress; Mansur Gavriel bag.*

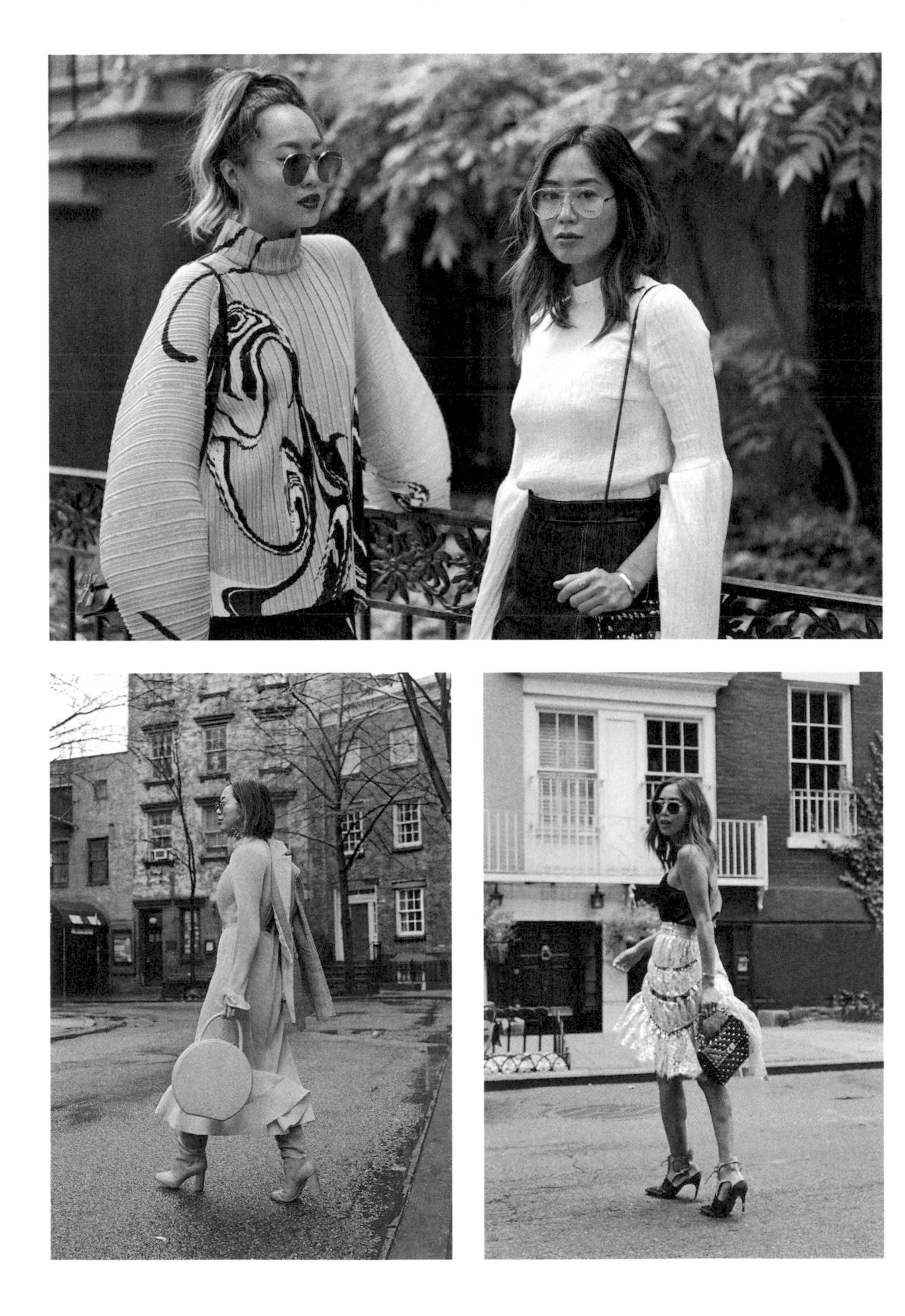

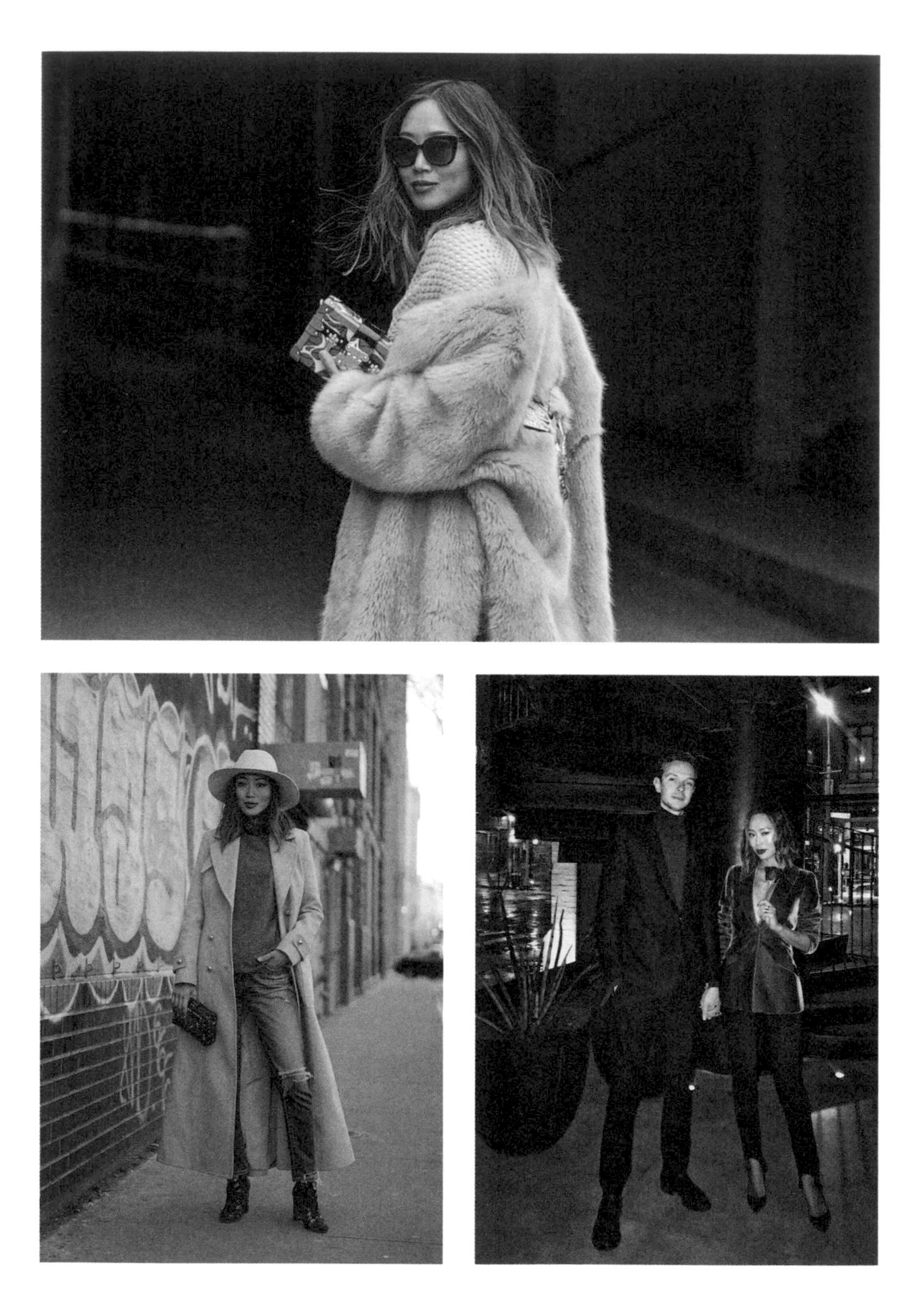

FAVORITE PLACES TO SWEAT IT OUT IN N.Y. AND L.A.

I'll be super real: I'm not obsessed with working out. If it didn't make me feel so strong and healthy, the chances of me moving my body on the regular would be slim to none. Add a layer of exhaustion on top of this laziness when I'm on the road, and the chances of me using the hotel gym are even smaller. Now, I always take a resistance band with me so I at least feel like I'm doing something (and I never don't pack my homemade raw bars, so I have healthy snacks on hand at all times). When I do go to a proper workout class, I like to engage in activities that don't feel like "work." That means fun, fast workouts that are more like dance parties and less like gym sessions. These are a few of my favorite ways to sweat in New York and L.A.

Barry's Bootcamp
@barrysbootcamp
barrysbootcamp.com

CruBox
@crubox
cruboxing.com

Playground LA
@theplaygroundla
playgroundla.dance

305 Fitness
@305fitness
305fitness.com

Shape House
@shapehouse
theshapehouse.com

OPPOSITE (CLOCKWISE FROM TOP) February 2016. This is one of my favorite fashion week outfits from that season, during which I had some major faux fur moments happening. I found the jacket through Instagram—the designers are Korean so we started talking via DM and the rest is history. *Wonder Sisters jacket* • Celebrating Jacopo's birthday. *Giorgio Armani blazer* • In a Zimmermann coat after the Zimmermann show. This was the year I decided to be comfortable—aka no more high heels in the snow. I finally felt comfortable enough with myself to stop suffering for fashion, which I always would do when dressed to impress at every show and event. It took me a few seasons to gain the perspective and wisdom that I could still look cute and feel great.

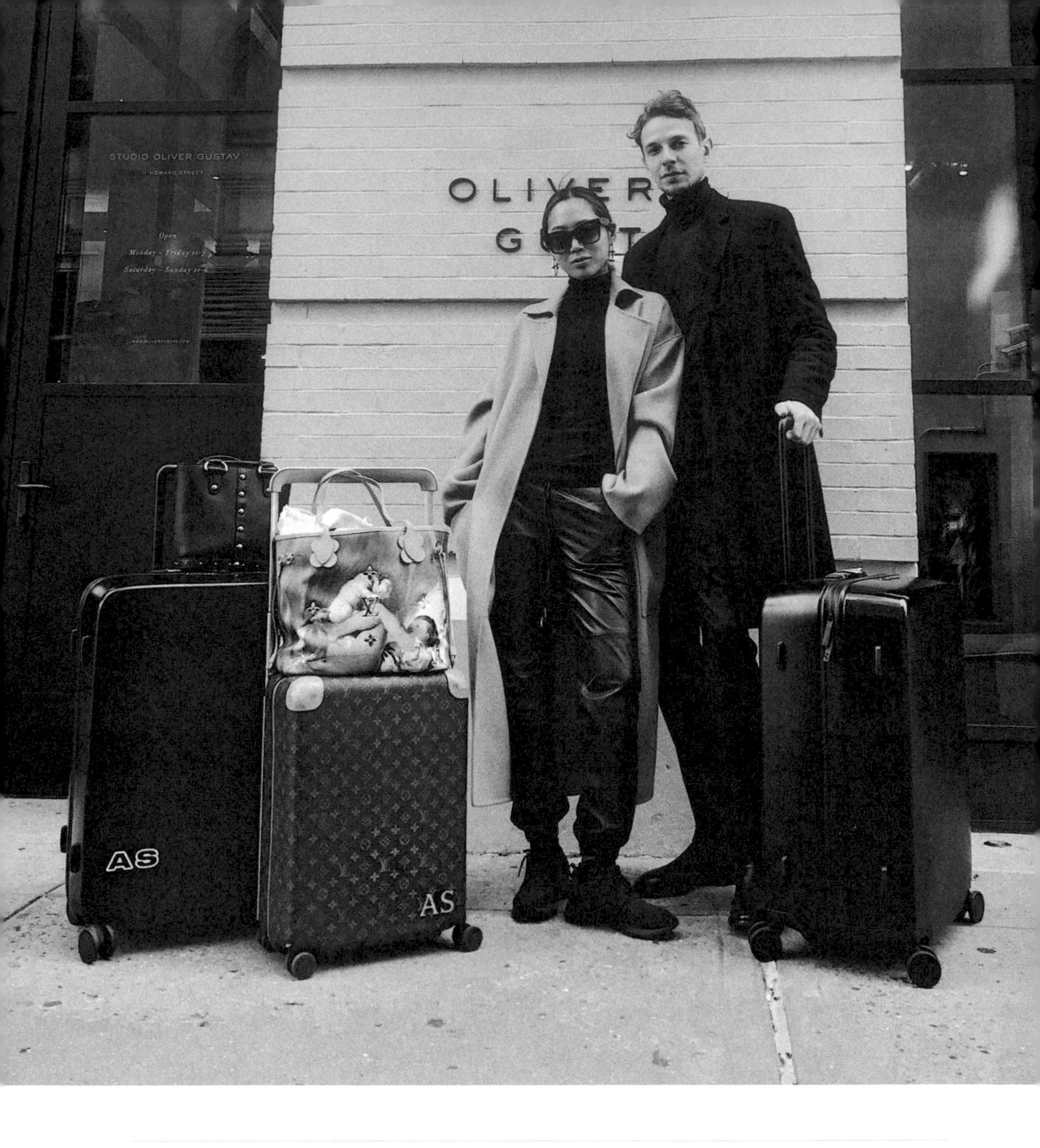

ABOVE How I roll. Jacopo was just there for effect, seeing as his apartment is actually only down the street from this hotel. **OPPOSITE (FROM TOP)** Infinity Aimee. At David Zwirner Gallery to see an exhibition featuring the work of Yayoi Kusama. • *Rebecca Taylor jacket; Céline sweater; Nanushka knit pants; Chloé bag.*

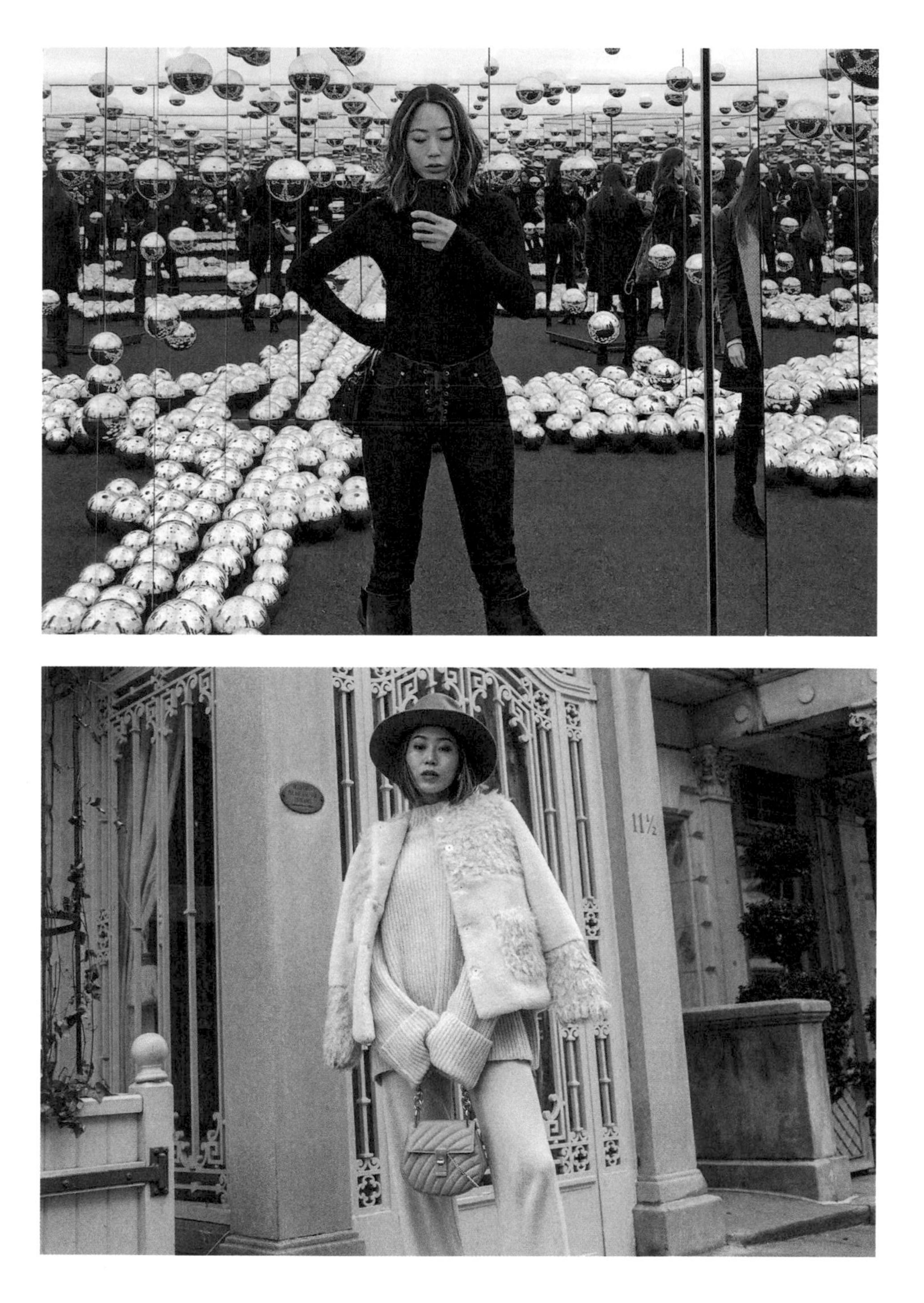
11½

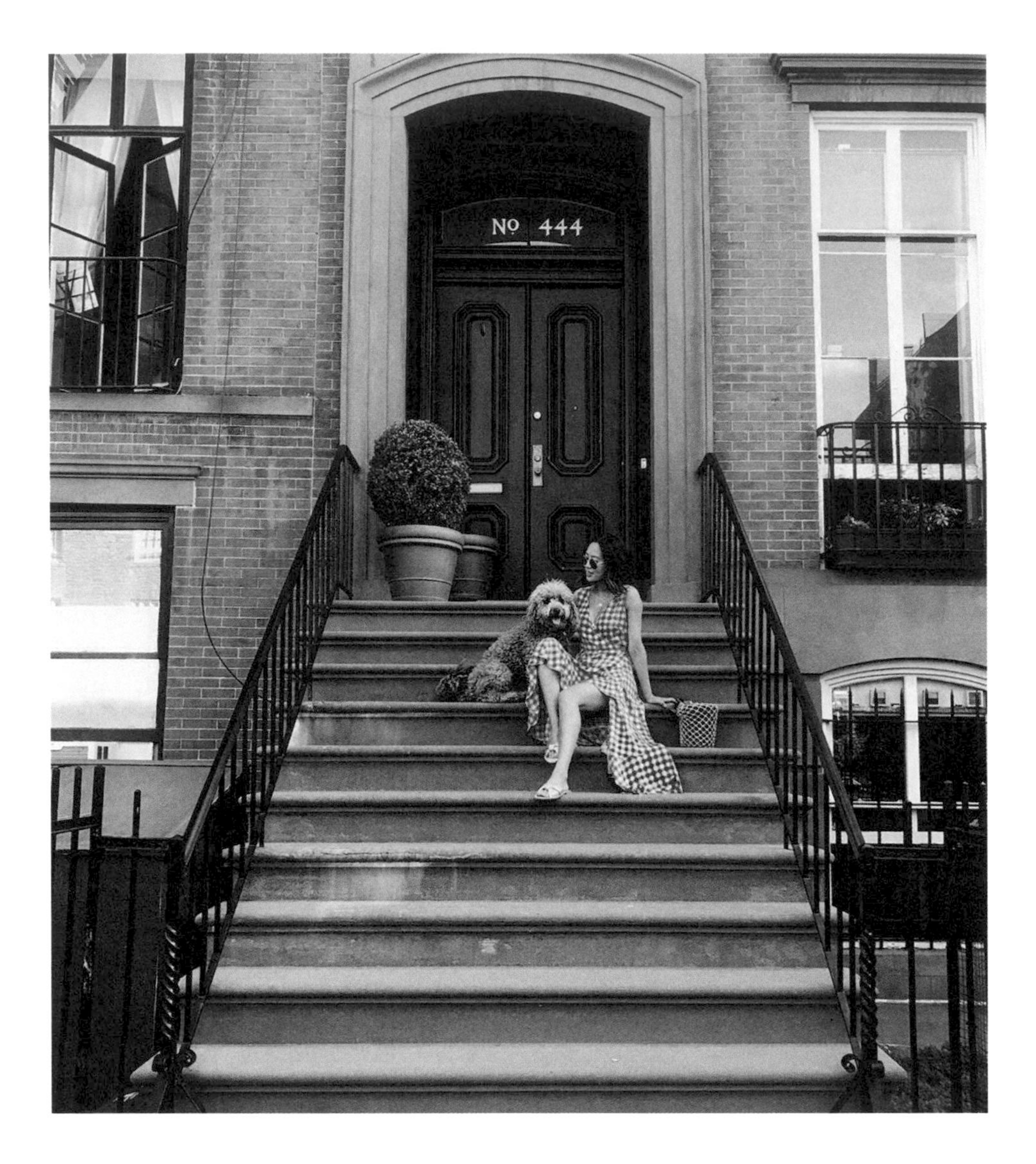

ABOVE There was a point in my life when I found myself following way too many animal accounts on Instagram (like more animal accounts than human ones). One of those accounts belonged to Samson, one of the cutest goldendoodles I've ever met in my life. He's one of the few animals I didn't unfollow, and we always comment on and like each other's photos. So when I was in New York shooting a Tiffany & Co. campaign, he hit me up and we went on a date (sorry, Jacopo). *DVF wrap dress; Loeffler Randall sandals.* **OPPOSITE** After my Samson date, Jacopo picked me up.

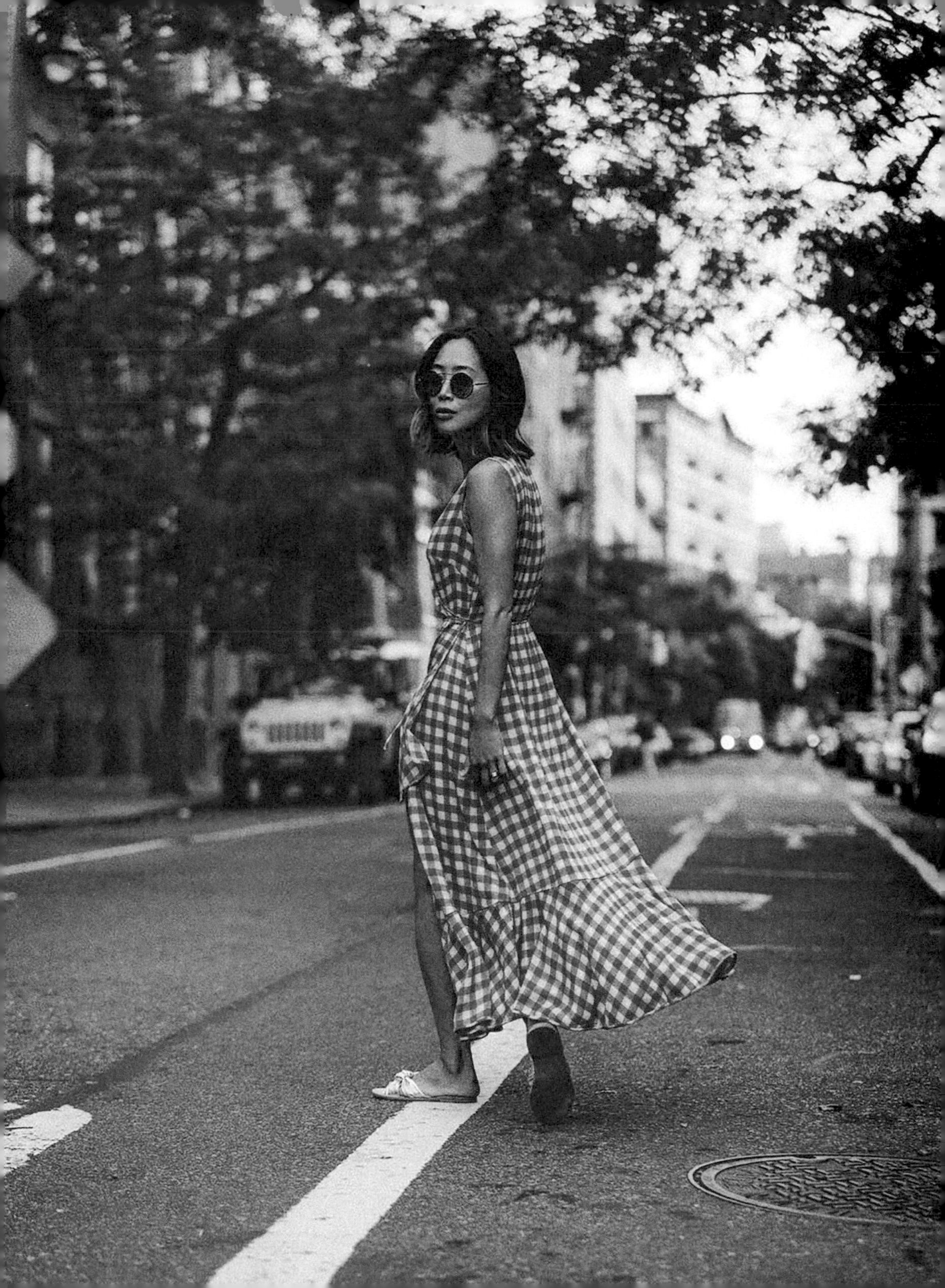

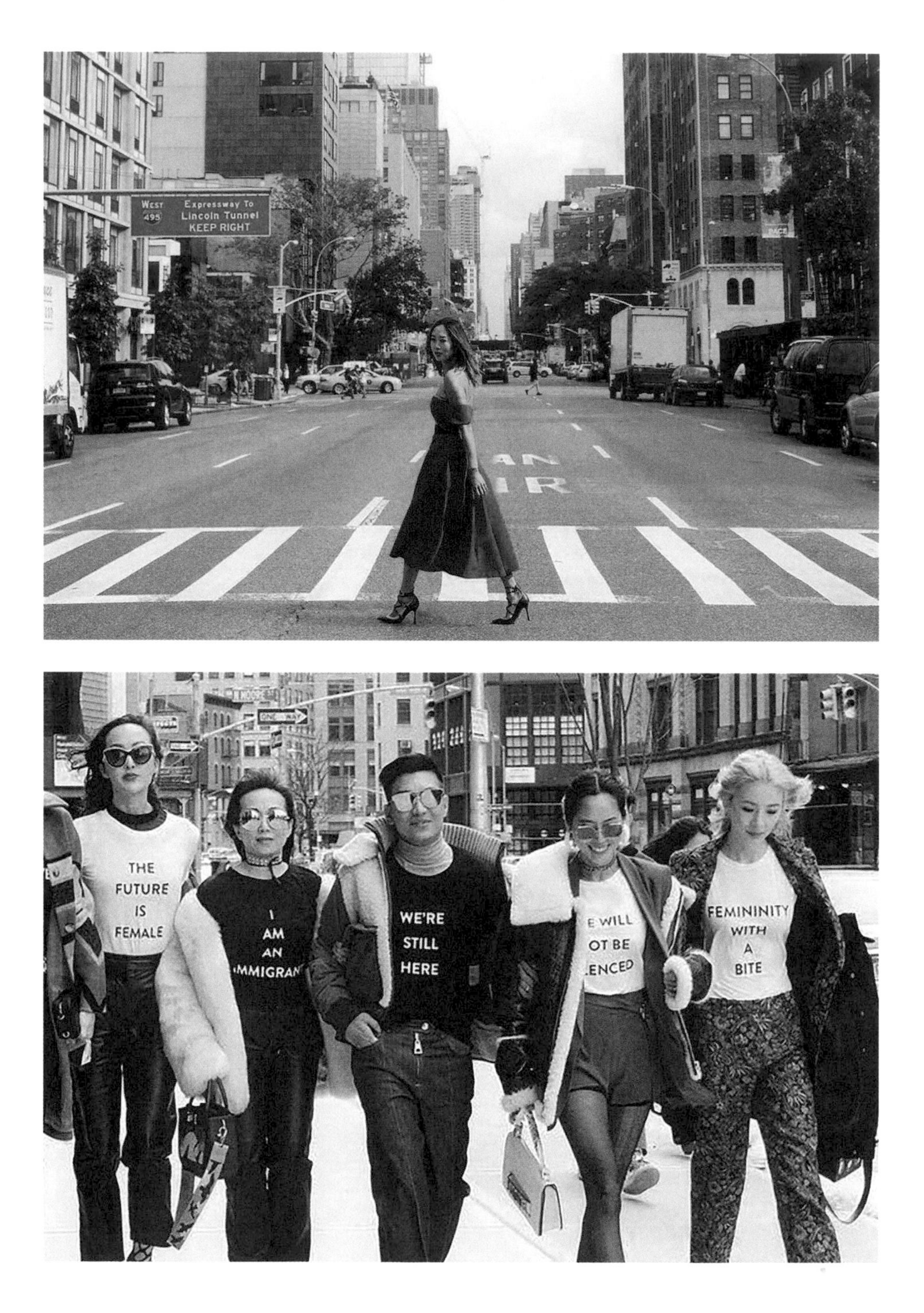
WEST 495
Expressway To
Lincoln Tunnel
KEEP RIGHT
THE FUTURE IS FEMALE
I AM AN
WE'RE STILL HERE
FEMININITY WITH A BITE

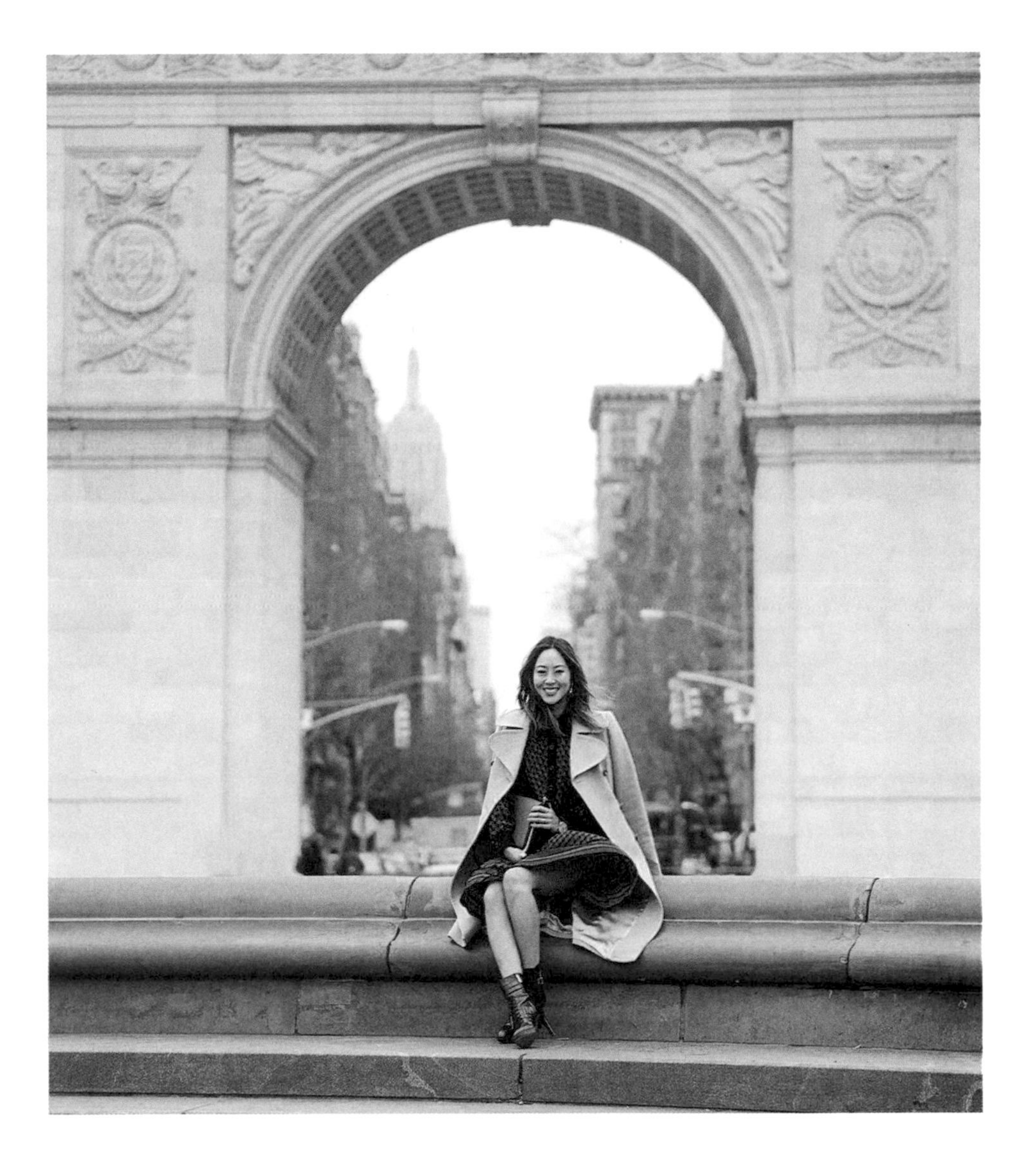

ABOVE It's always freezing during NYFW in February, but somehow the energy of a Michael Kors show makes everything feel warmer. *Michael Kors head to toe.* **OPPOSITE (FROM TOP)** Right after Self-Portrait's very first New York presentation in September 2015. *Self-Portrait dress* • In February 2017 Prabal Gurung showed "feminist" T-shirts on his runway, and Tina Craig, who cofounded Bag Snob, thought it would be amazing for a group of us to wear them at the same time so we could send a message across our channels.

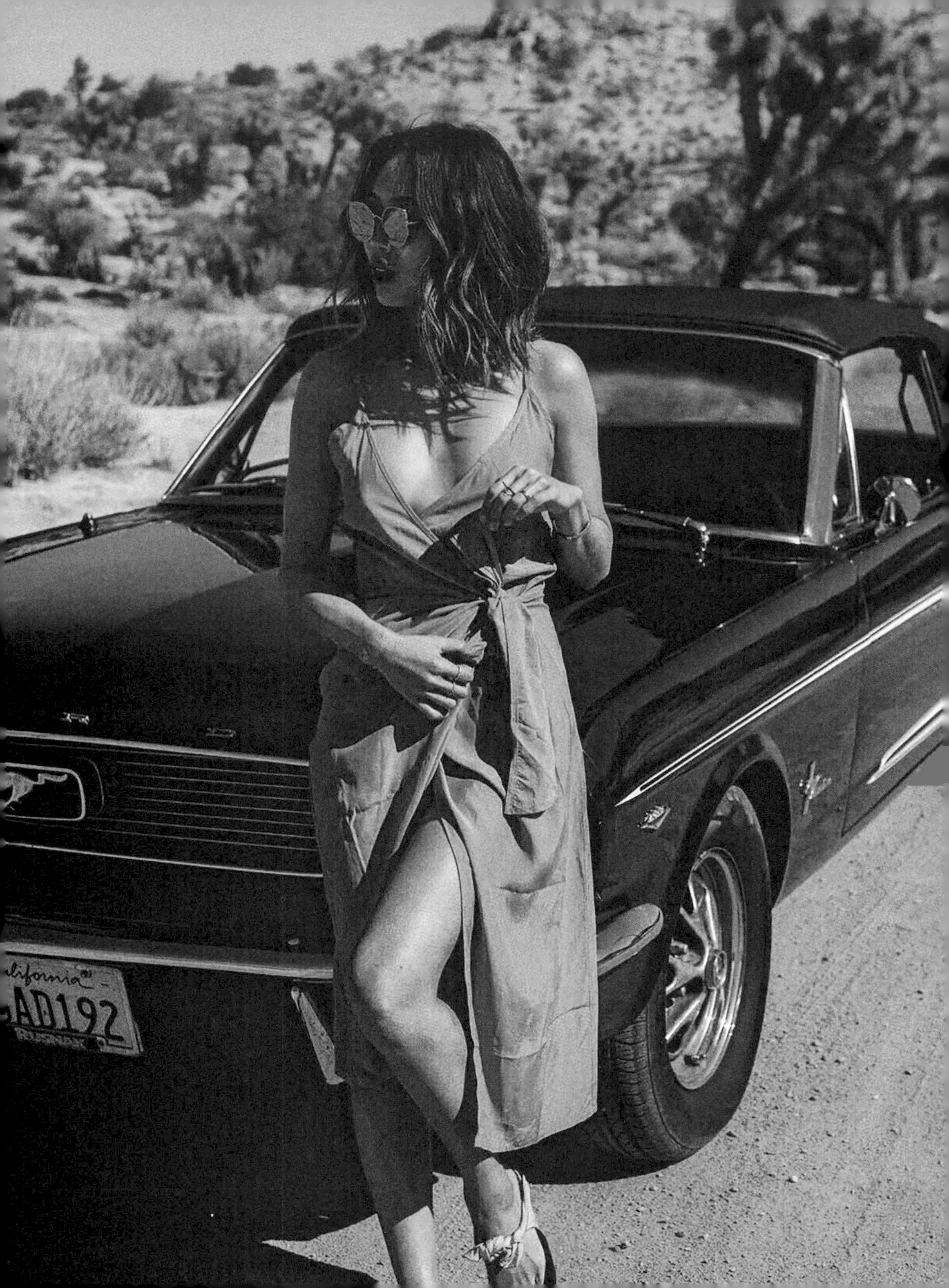
lifornia
AD192

PALM SPRINGS

Palm Springs is this incredible, relaxing desert oasis an hour and a half from L.A. It's such a special place, with amazing mid-century modern architecture, fun places to hang out at night, and really awesome boutique design hotels—which are worth going for alone. It's healing, and an amazing locale for an impromptu vacation. It's also near where Coachella happens, of course. The first time I ever visited Palm Springs was for that very music festival years and years ago—way before street style and brand brunches ever existed. When I was in high school, my friends and I would save up money to get tickets and then find someone with a car to drive us. I'd wear my Levi's cutoffs (yes, the same ones I still own), band T-shirts, and Chuck Taylors—maybe, only maybe would I wear boots if I felt like being "stylish." The festival has changed today, of course. But I still love to go. The desert really does make you feel like you're in a completely different place, yet it's so familiar to me because—as one does at music festivals—I grew up there.

OPPOSITE Jacopo was shooting me for an O&B shoe campaign in Joshua Tree. One problem: the shoes never came. We had to send hair and makeup home, lost all of the locations we had reserved, and Jacopo was nervous because he had to catch a flight for another job. On what was supposed to be the second day of the shoot, the shoes showed up at 4 P.M. after being held up in customs. Jacopo ended up shooting everything in an hour and rushing back to L.A. to catch his flight. Such is fashion. This photo was part of a desert shoot I did the day after my shoe job for Faithfull the Brand, shot by Grant Legan. *Faithfull the Brand dress.*

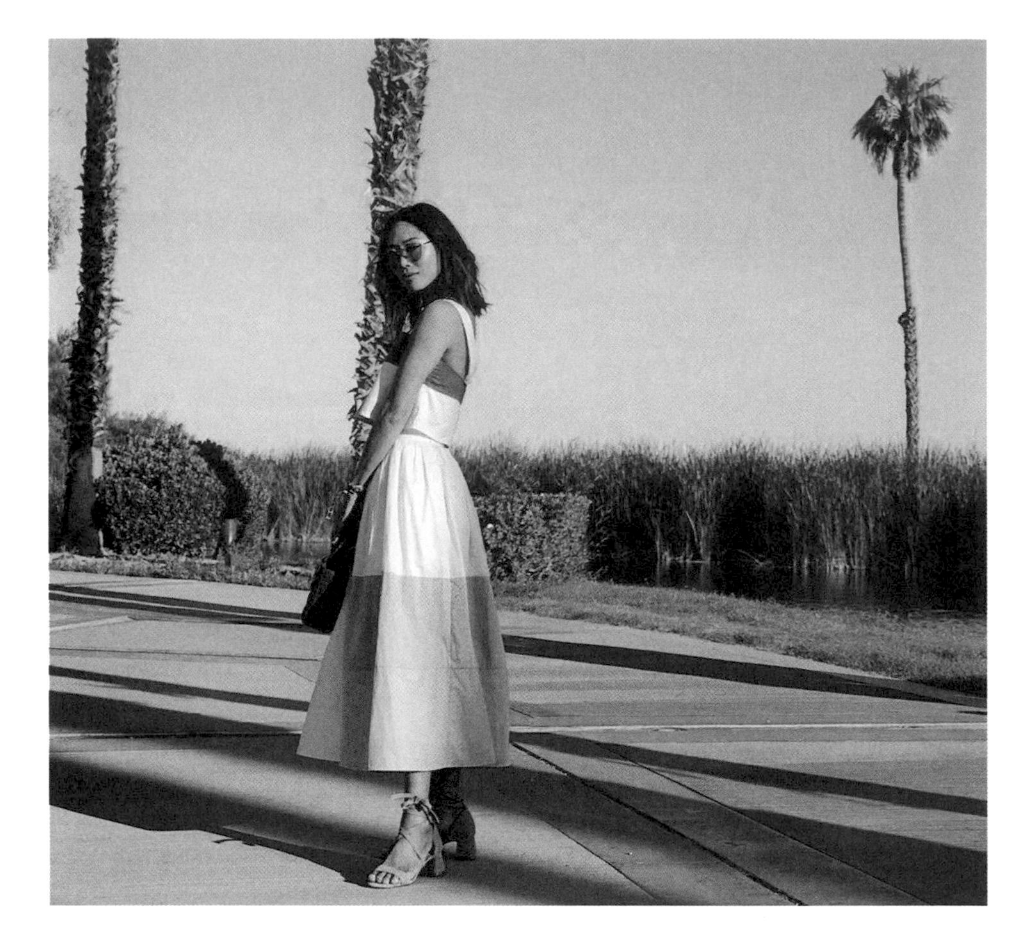

ABOVE Every Coachella, Revolve throws Revolve Festival, which is essentially a huge party where you can eat, drink, hang by the pool, listen to performances, and chill away from the actual music festival. I like to check out the events when headliners aren't performing during the day. *Mara Hoffman dress.* **OPPOSITE (CLOCKWISE FROM TOP LEFT)** I've been going to Coachella with Revolve since 2014, when it was just me and one other blogger with the Revolve team at a rented house. In 2017 they upped the game to create Revolve Festival, which is essentially a huge party within Coachella's already huge party. They rented out Arrive, a boutique hotel, to host half of Revolve Festival (the other half took place at late TV mastermind Merv Griffin's former estate in La Quinta nearby). And because we got to town a day before the festival started, we had a chance to relax. *Tommy Hilfiger boots* • *Chloé dress* • *LPA outfit; Dior sunglasses and bag; Art Youth Society jewelry* • At the polo fields in Indio, California, where the Coachella music happens. Wearing Prada that I picked up at an outlet on my very first trip to Italy. *Chloé backpack.*

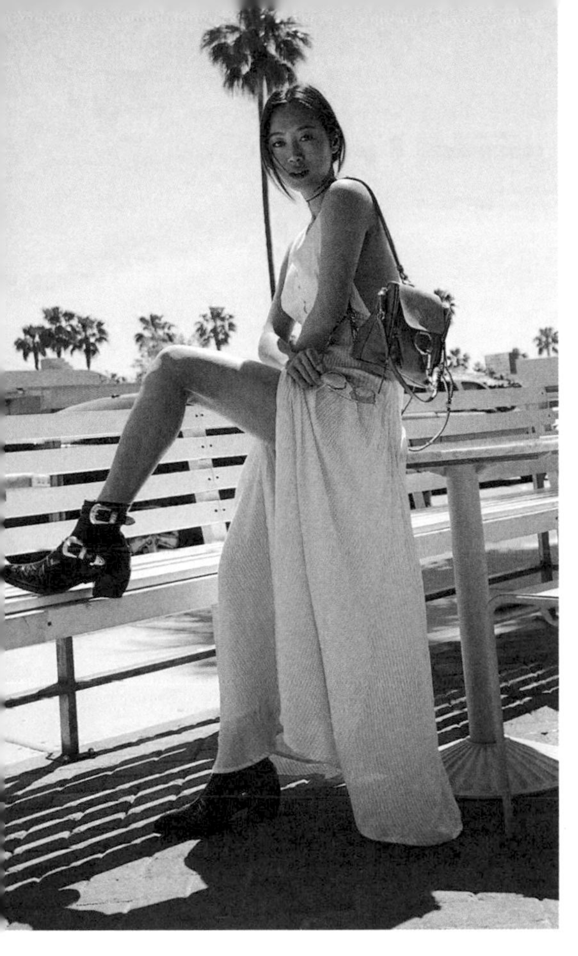

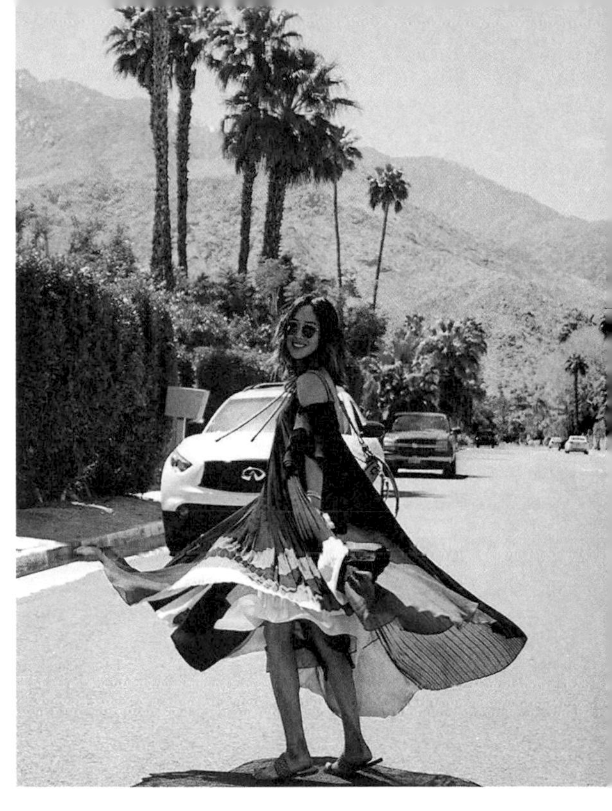

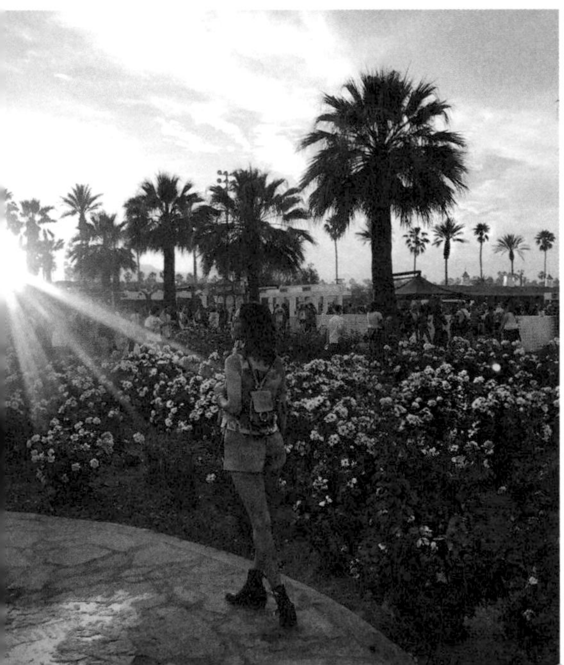

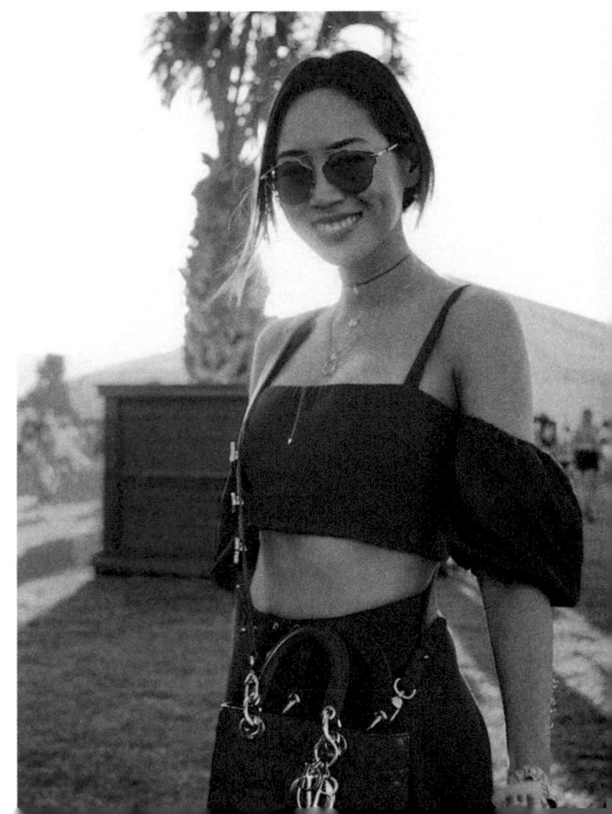

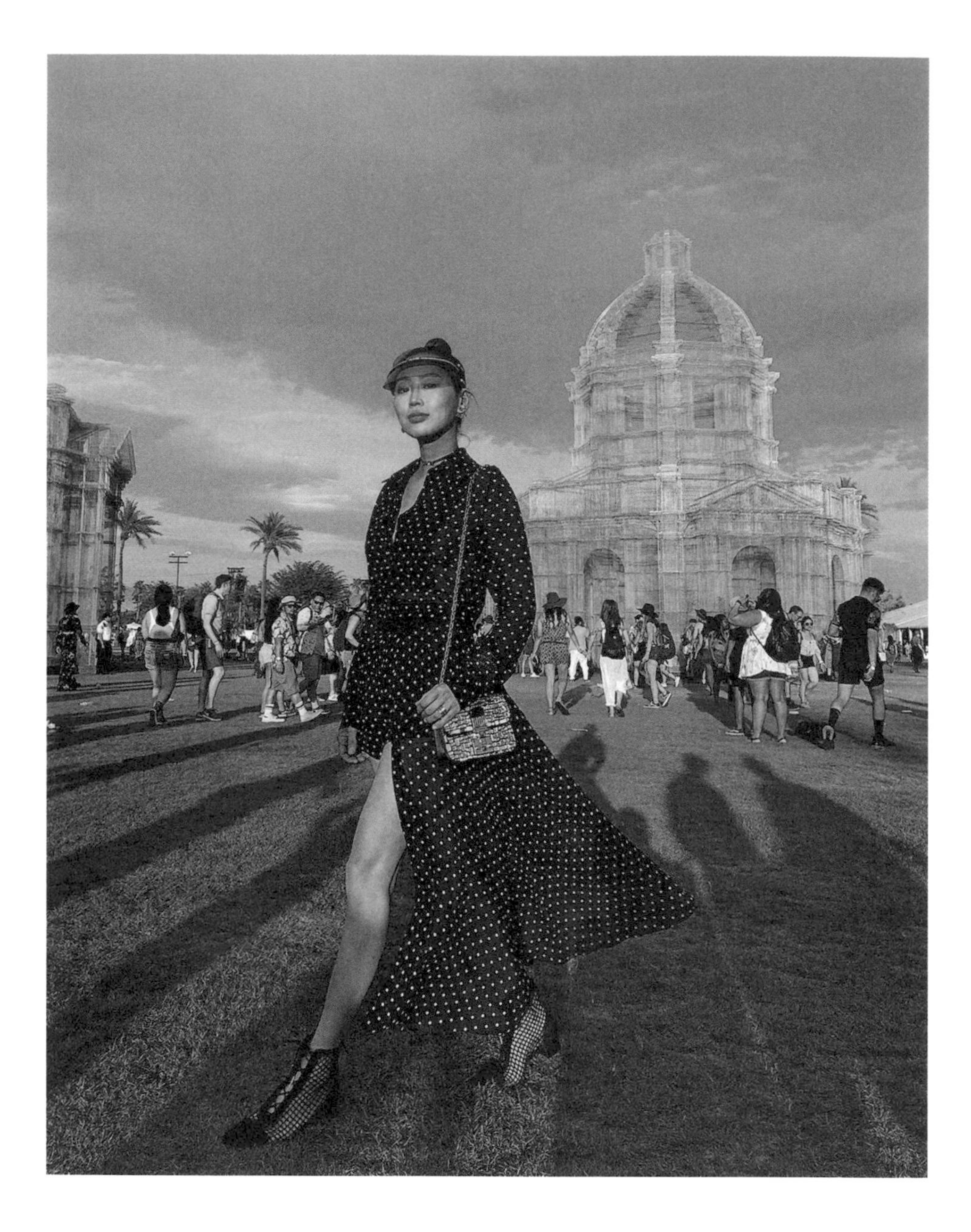

I love this photo that Jacopo took of me right after we saw Cardi B. *Dior head to toe.*

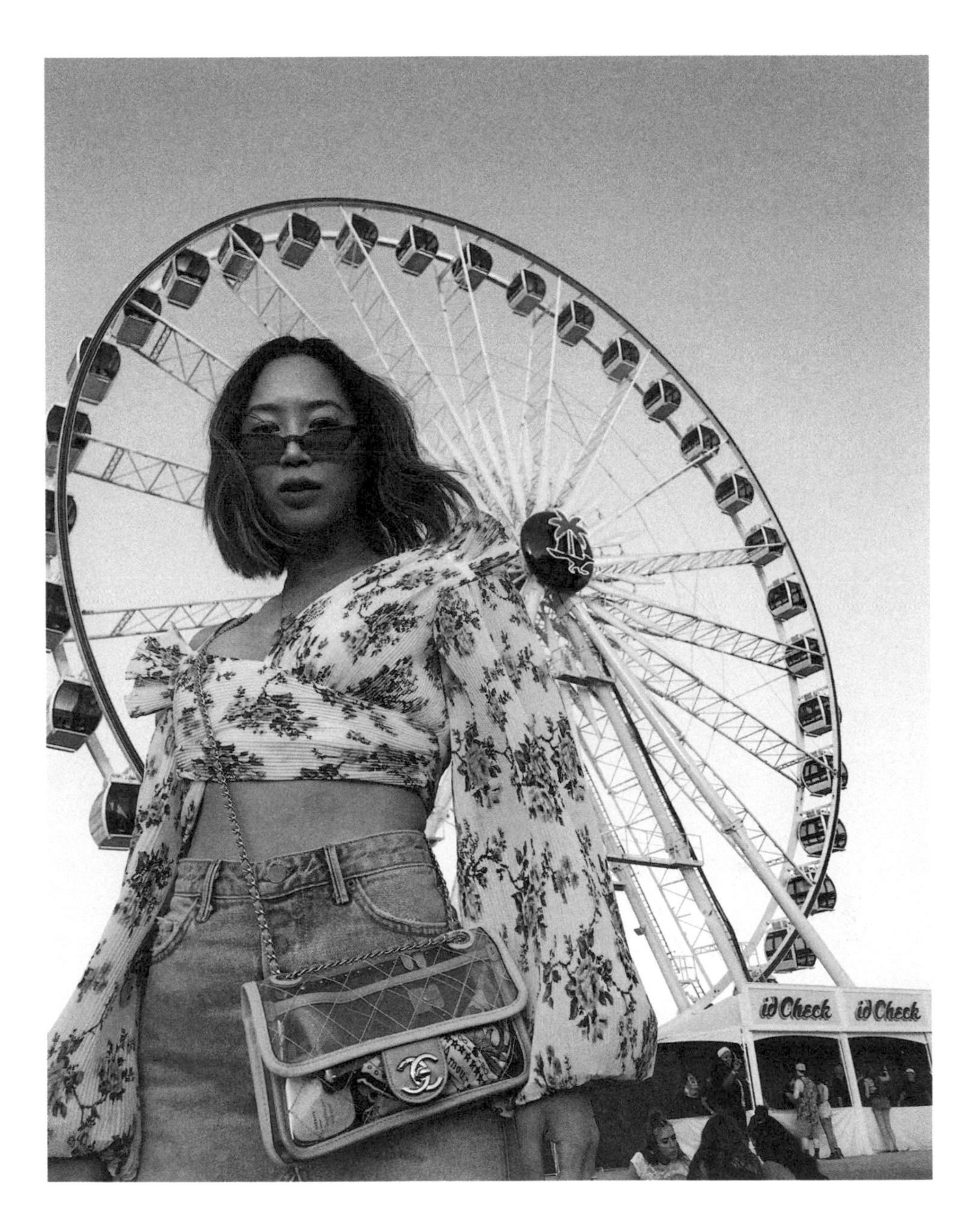

Coachella 2018. *Zimmermann top; Chanel bag.*

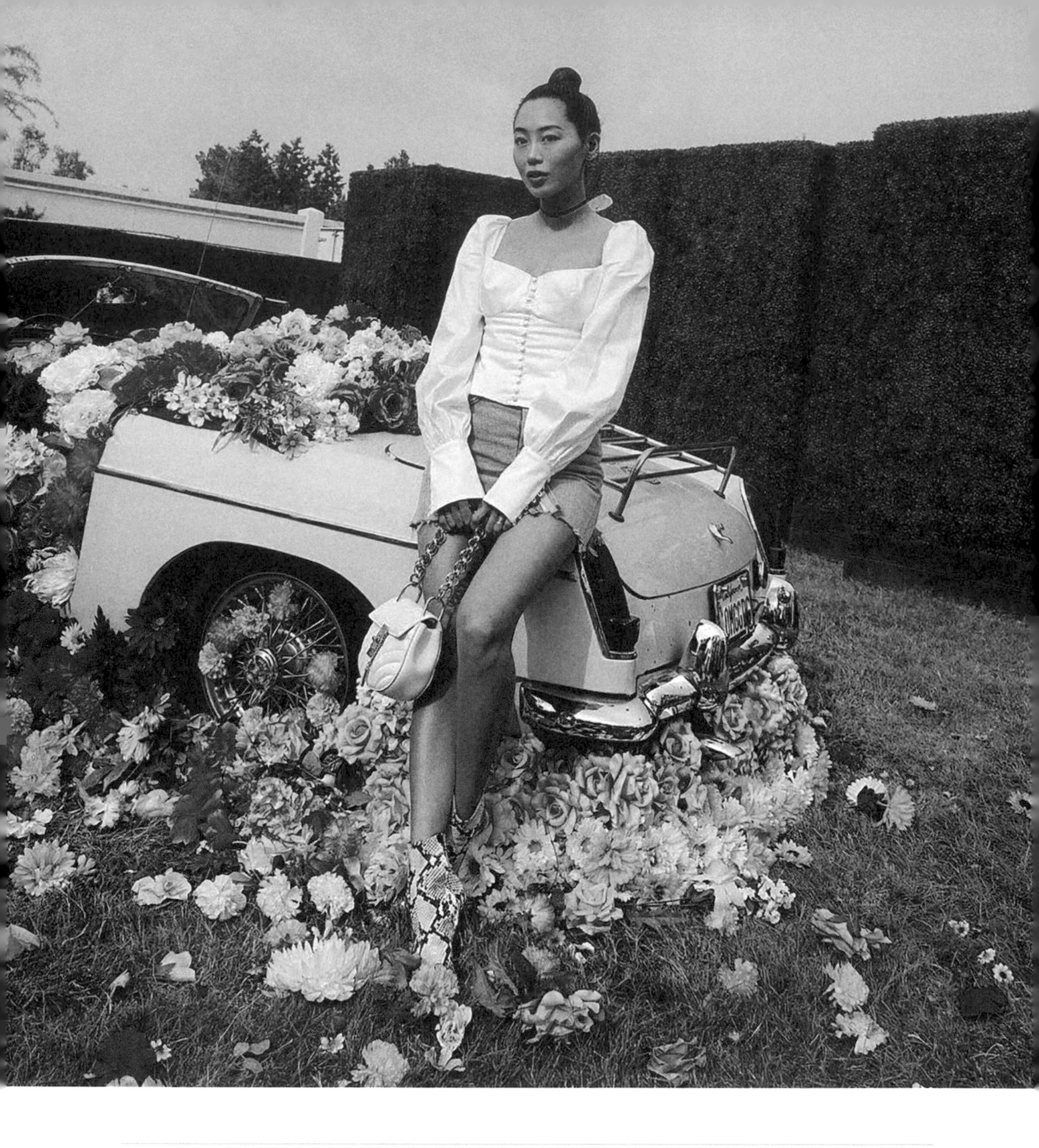

ABOVE Photo op at the #RevolveFestival, in front of a pretty vintage car filled with even prettier flowers. **OPPOSITE (CLOCKWISE FROM TOP)** Jacopo's first Coachella. I think he enjoyed it, no? • As usual, #RevolveFestival went all out, bringing in the Wave Swinger ride from Michael Jackson's Neverland Ranch. *LPA dress; Raye heels* • Coachella shenanigans. *Chloé head to toe.*

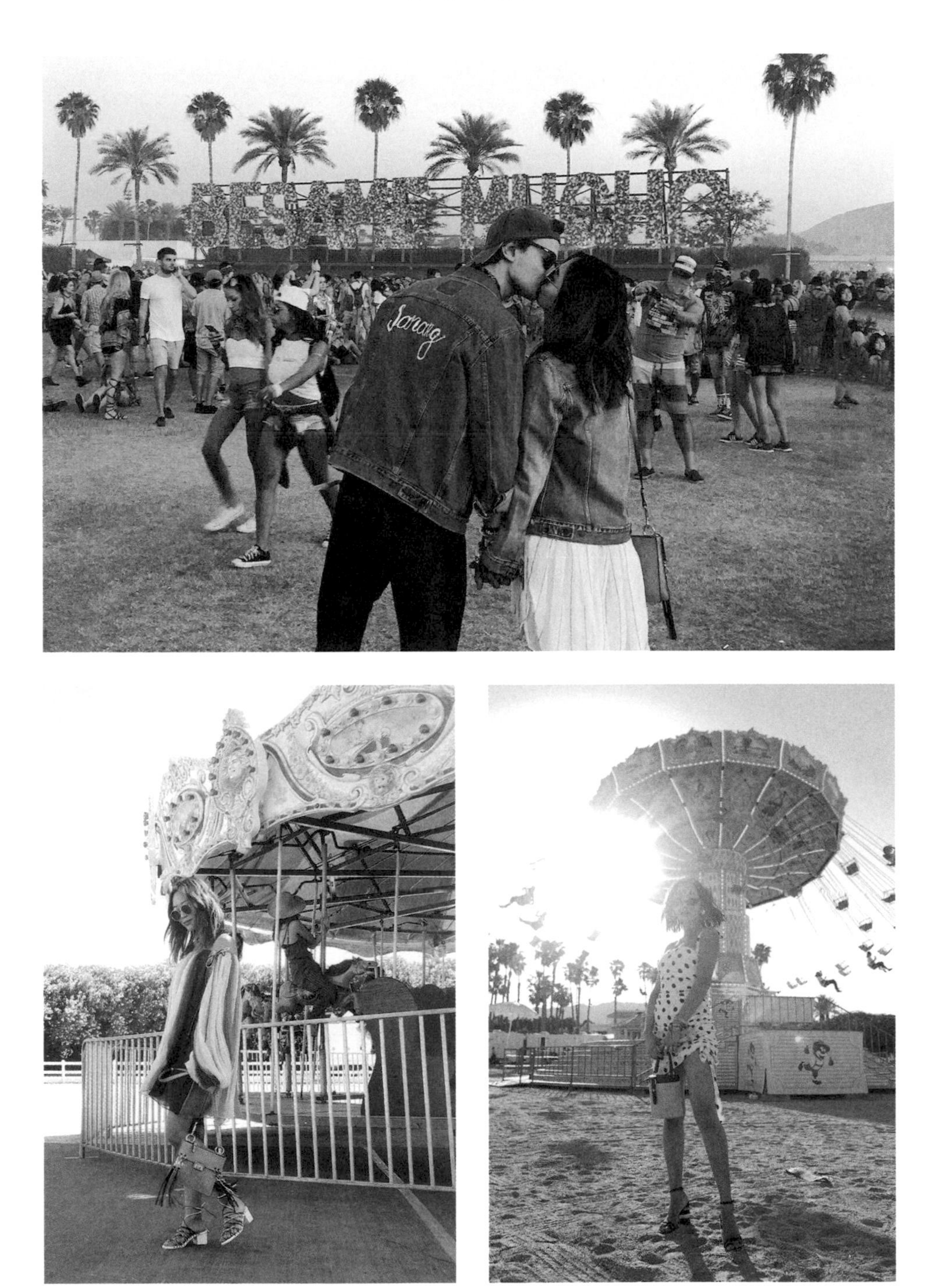

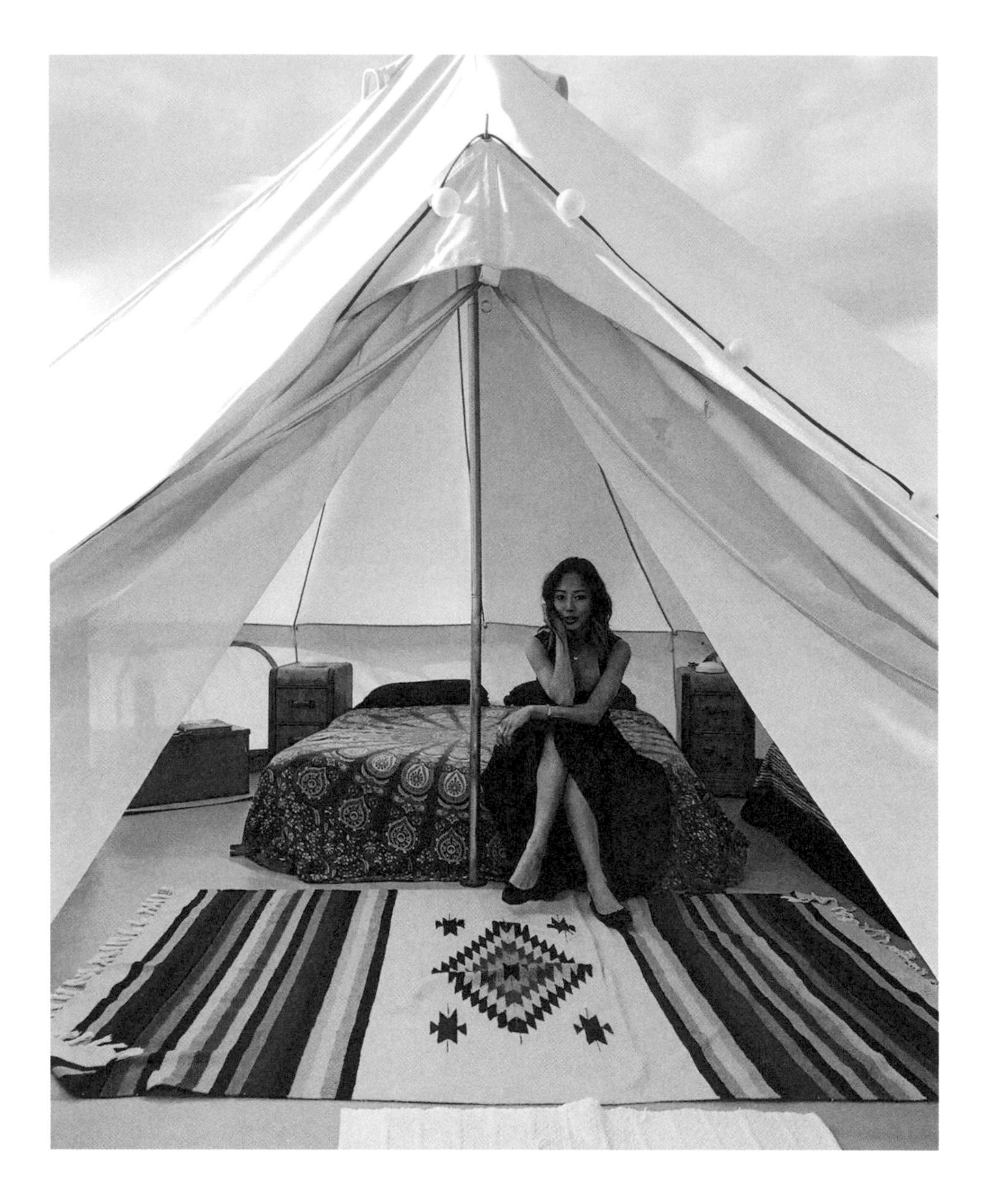

The day of that fateful shoe shoot, when Jacopo the miracle worker made it work despite everything going as wrong as it could. The space we rented was gone, and somehow he found a camp ground in Joshua Tree that we were able to turn dreamy in a matter of minutes. #MyHero.

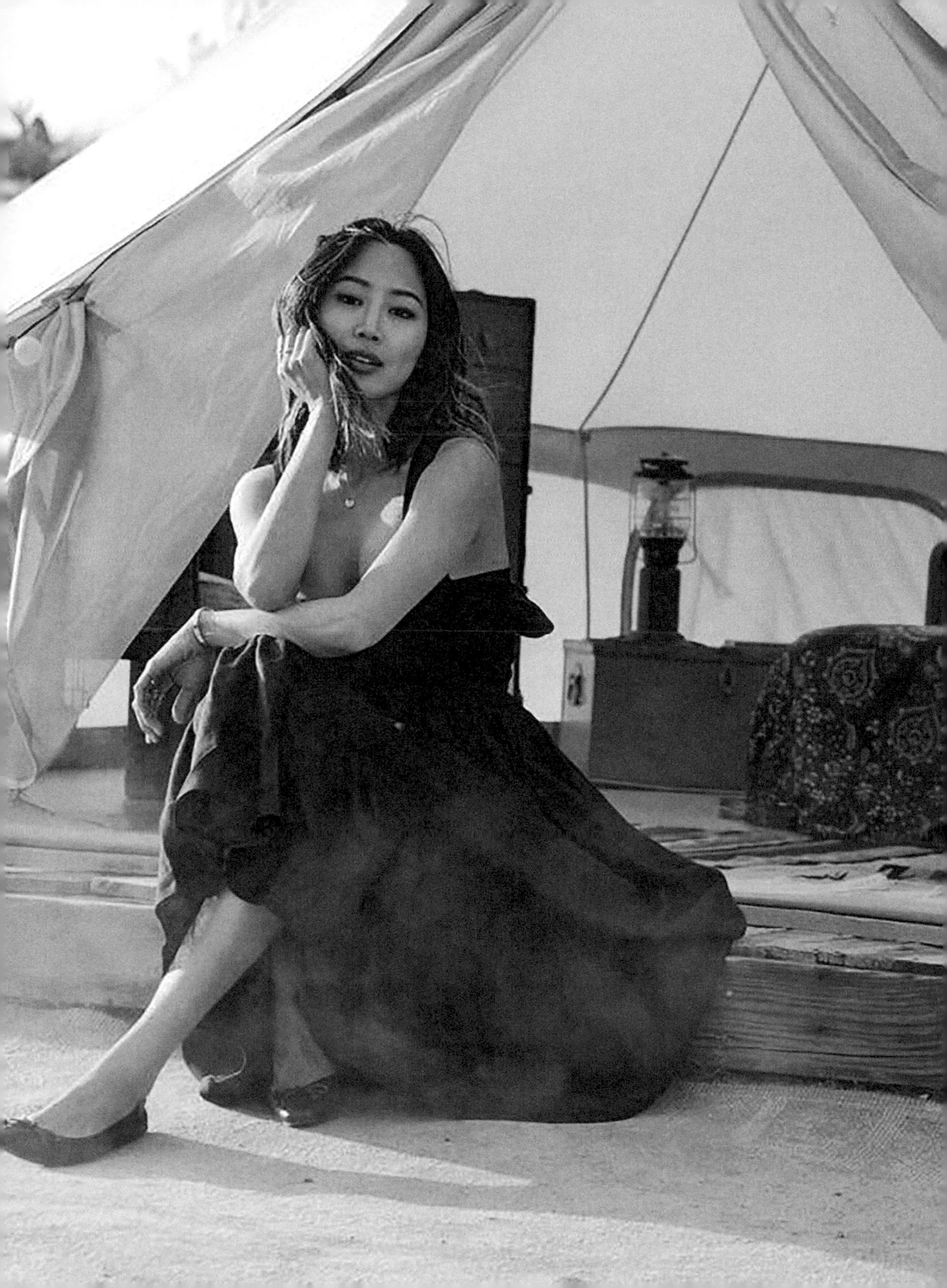

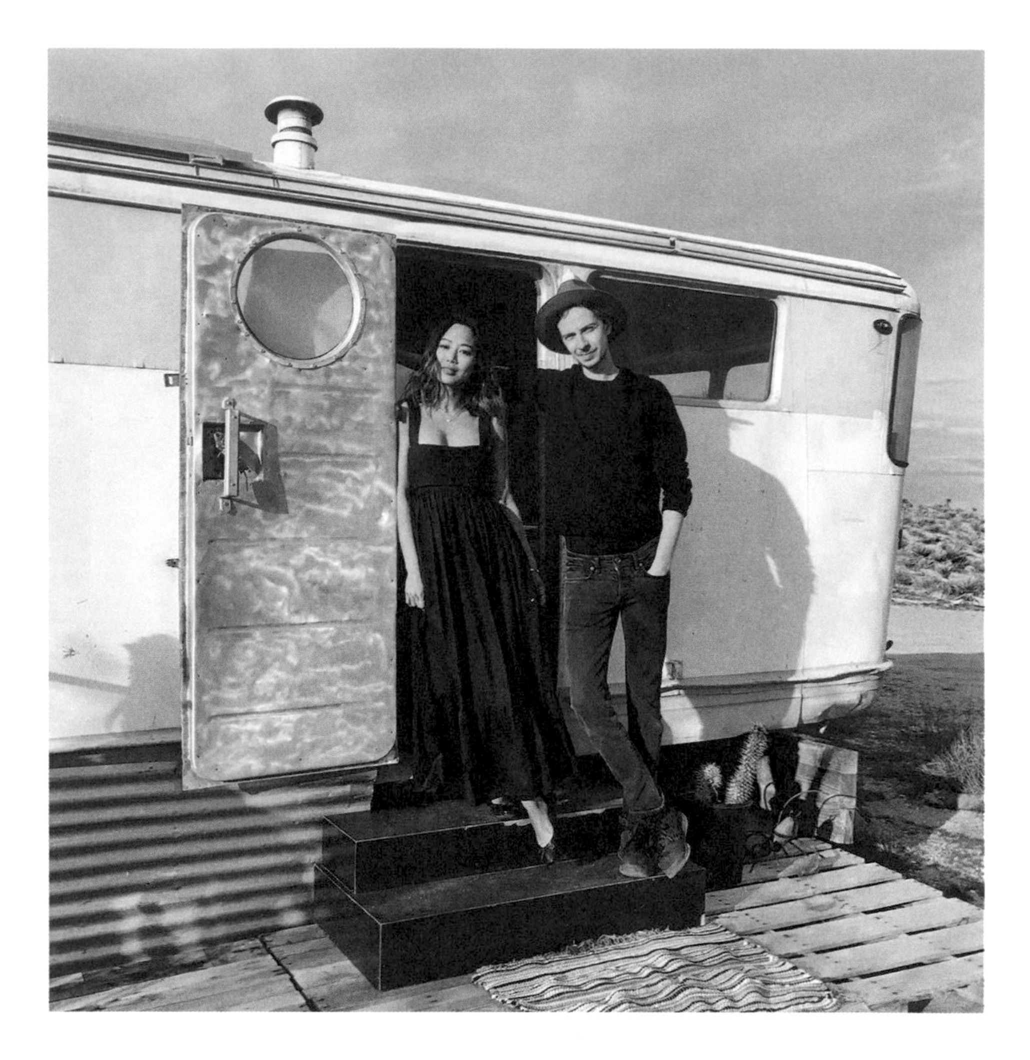

ABOVE Jacopo and I pretending that we lived in Joshua Tree. This shoot was hectic due to the, uh, things we were shooting not showing up, but because we were in such a serene place and so close to nature it somehow felt peaceful. The owners of this trailer ended up being Italian—Jacopo found them through a friend of a friend—so we waited there for the shoes to arrive (via Uber, no less) and talked about how nice it would be to have a place of our own off the grid, in the wild (but with really strong Wi-Fi, obviously). **OPPOSITE, TOP ROW** If building my very own media empire fails, I think Jacopo would be wise to hire me as his assistant. I listened intently while he told me what to do with the props. **OPPOSITE, BOTTOM ROW** The day after the shoe photo mishap, I had another shoot in Joshua Tree for Faithfull the Brand. These are more of the finished photos, shot by Grant Legan.

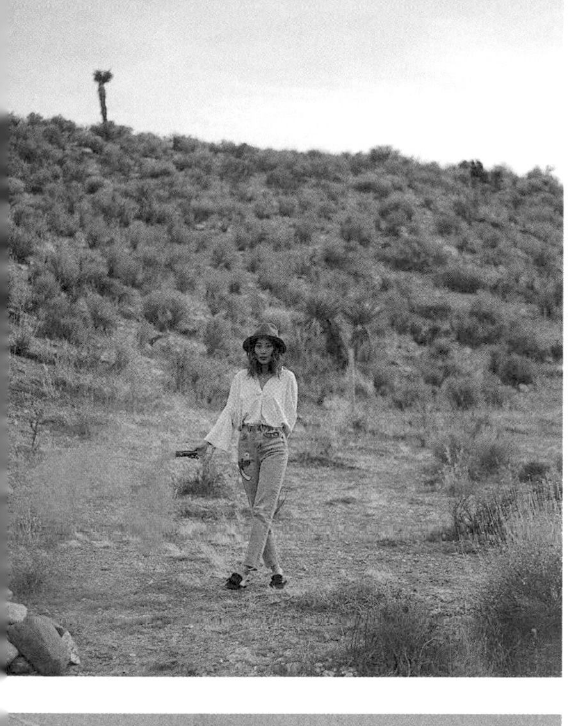

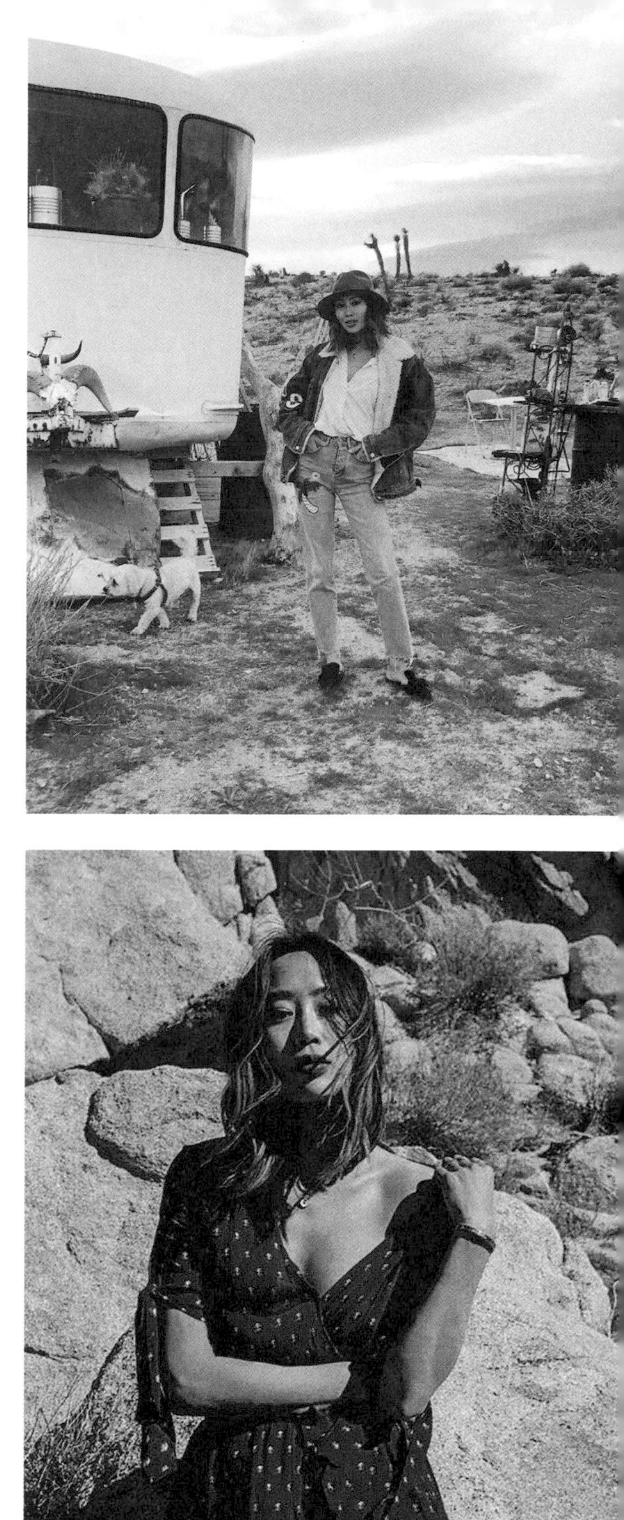

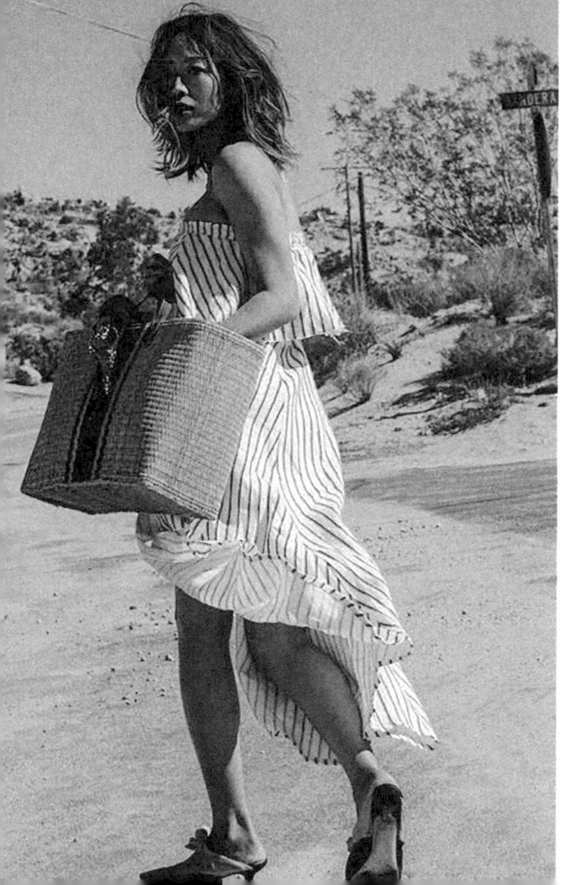

ASIA

Bali

Dubai

India

Jakarta

Kyoto

The Philippines

Phuket

Seoul & Busan

Singapore

Tokyo

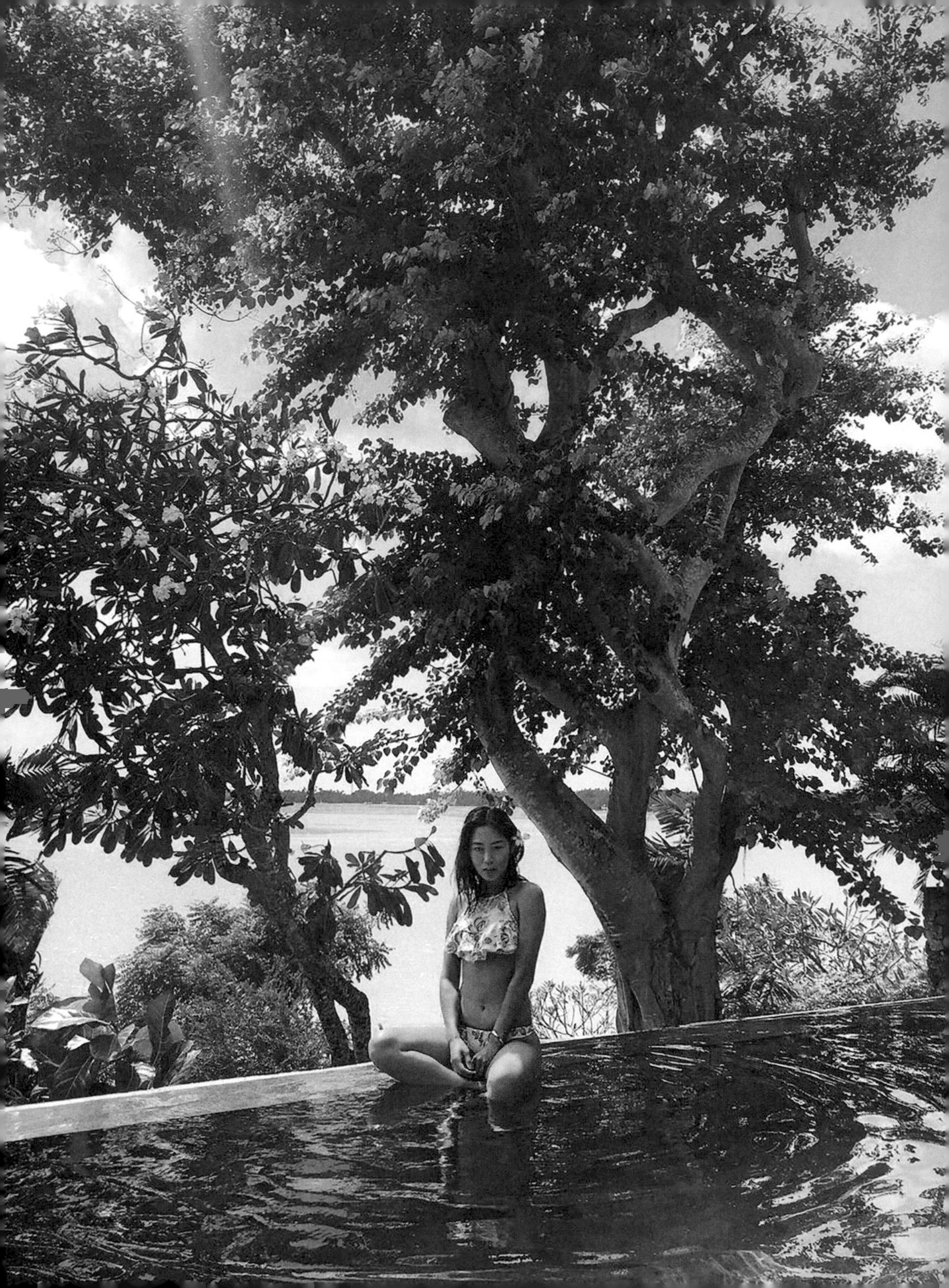

BALI

In August 2016 I had the opportunity to visit Bali for the first time ever with a shoe brand that asked me to shoot their pieces. The work portion of the trip was only four days, but I loved it there so much that Jacopo and I extended the trip and spent almost two weeks exploring various parts of the county. I even convinced my friends Gary and Edouard to spontaneously join me (not a very hard sell, shocker). I only brought one suitcase on this trip (a rare occurrence for me) and made Jacopo pack light (which he always does) so I could treasure-hunt at the markets and fit my finds in his bag. Outside of the friendly hospitality, I found amazing, healthy food, a huge emphasis on wellness (which the Balinese people have been organically focused on for years—something the rest of the world is just catching on to), and a very beautiful focus on spirituality, which reminded me to be present, mindful, and oh-so-grateful for the opportunity to experience such a wonderful time.

OPPOSITE Using flowers as a prop, obviously.
Zimmermann swimsuit.

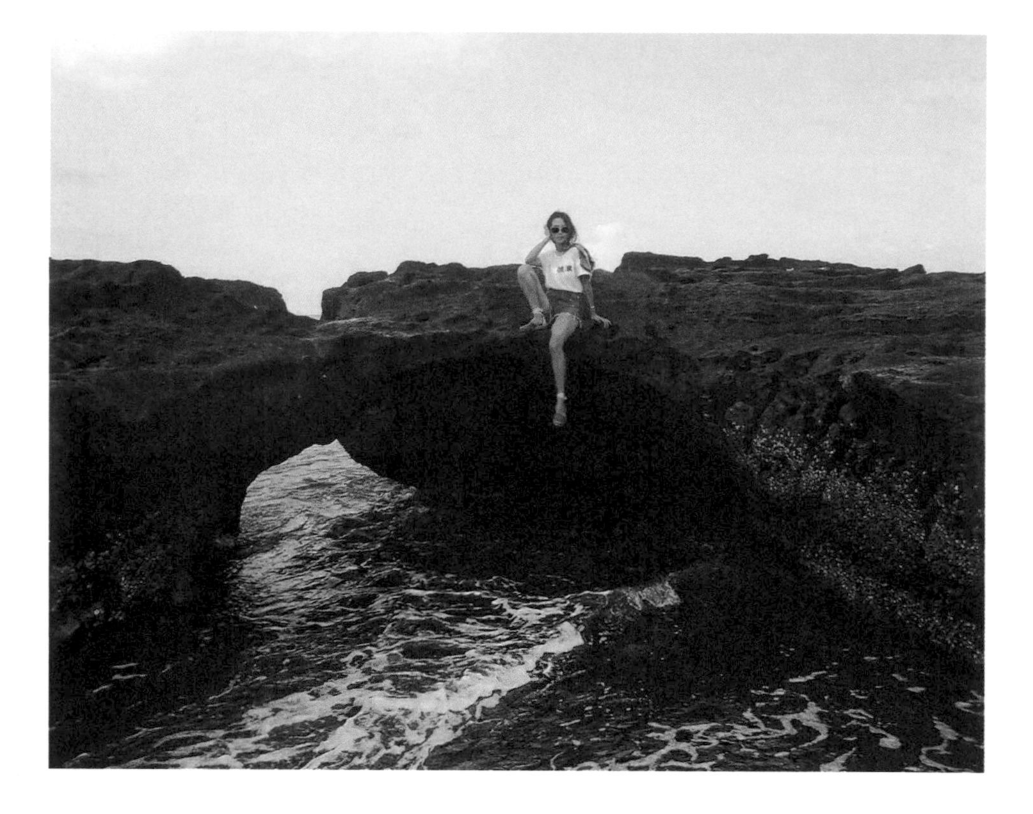

ABOVE After riding ATVs to a black sand beach, one of my favorite activities of this (or any) trip. This was later in the trip when my friends joined me, so we each had our own vehicle. But seeing as I was with three guys, we pushed them to the limit—something I most definitely didn't wear the right shoes for. (Espadrilles are not the correct choice of footwear for all-terrain vehicle riding . . . who knew?) We ventured into bat caves, went through mud, and got rained on—and I destroyed my shoes. **OPPOSITE, TOP LEFT** Most of the villas that we stayed at came with a beautiful private pool (which I couldn't believe and always got super excited to discover upon arrival). We'd come back from a day of activities and jump into the pool instead of the shower. *Marysia Swim swimsuit.*

OPPOSITE, TOP RIGHT We hiked to see a waterfall and—again—I wasn't wearing the right shoes. Everyone else around us was wearing swimsuits and flip flops or sneakers, and I was the girl decked out in the Ulla Johnson dress and espadrilles (eye-roll emoji). Jacopo was nursing a sprained ankle so my French friend Edouard took this shot and missed most of the waterfall (great travel companion; not-so-great photographer). **OPPOSITE, BOTTOM ROW** Catamaran day. I knew we'd be gone all day and going to a few beaches, so I packed a few different outfits—a swimsuit, denim shorts (my favorite pair of Levi's that I cut myself and have had for twelve years), and a top that I made by wrapping myself in a scarf and tying it with a hair tie (genius, no?).

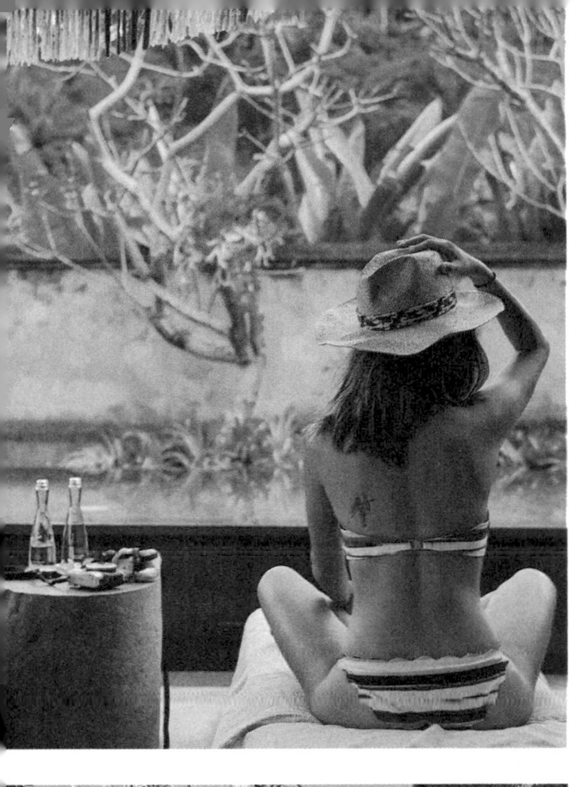

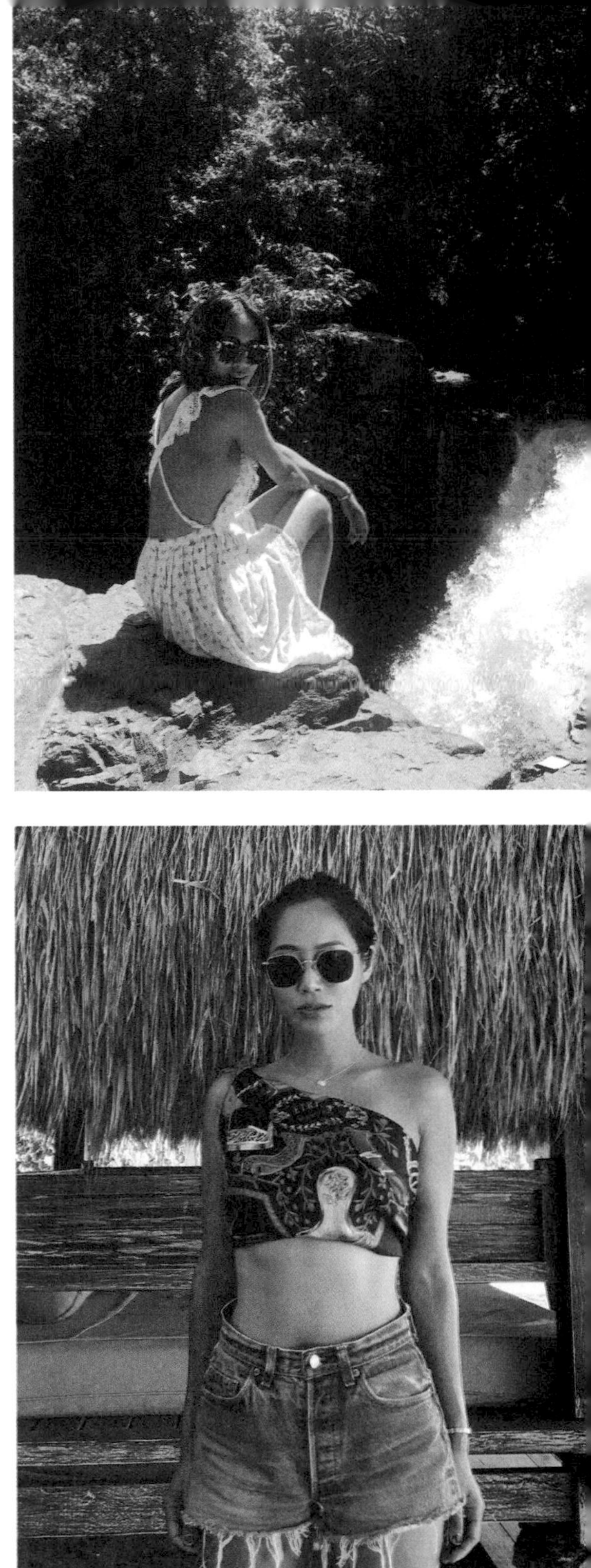

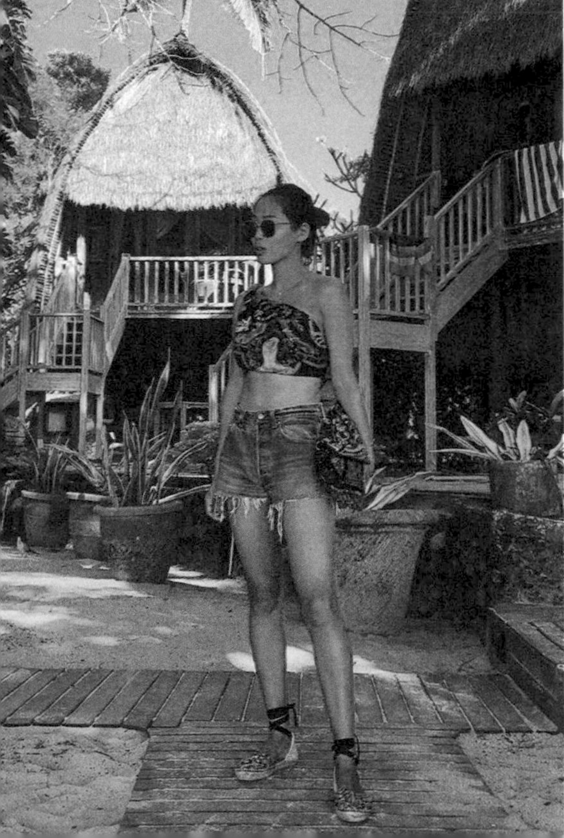

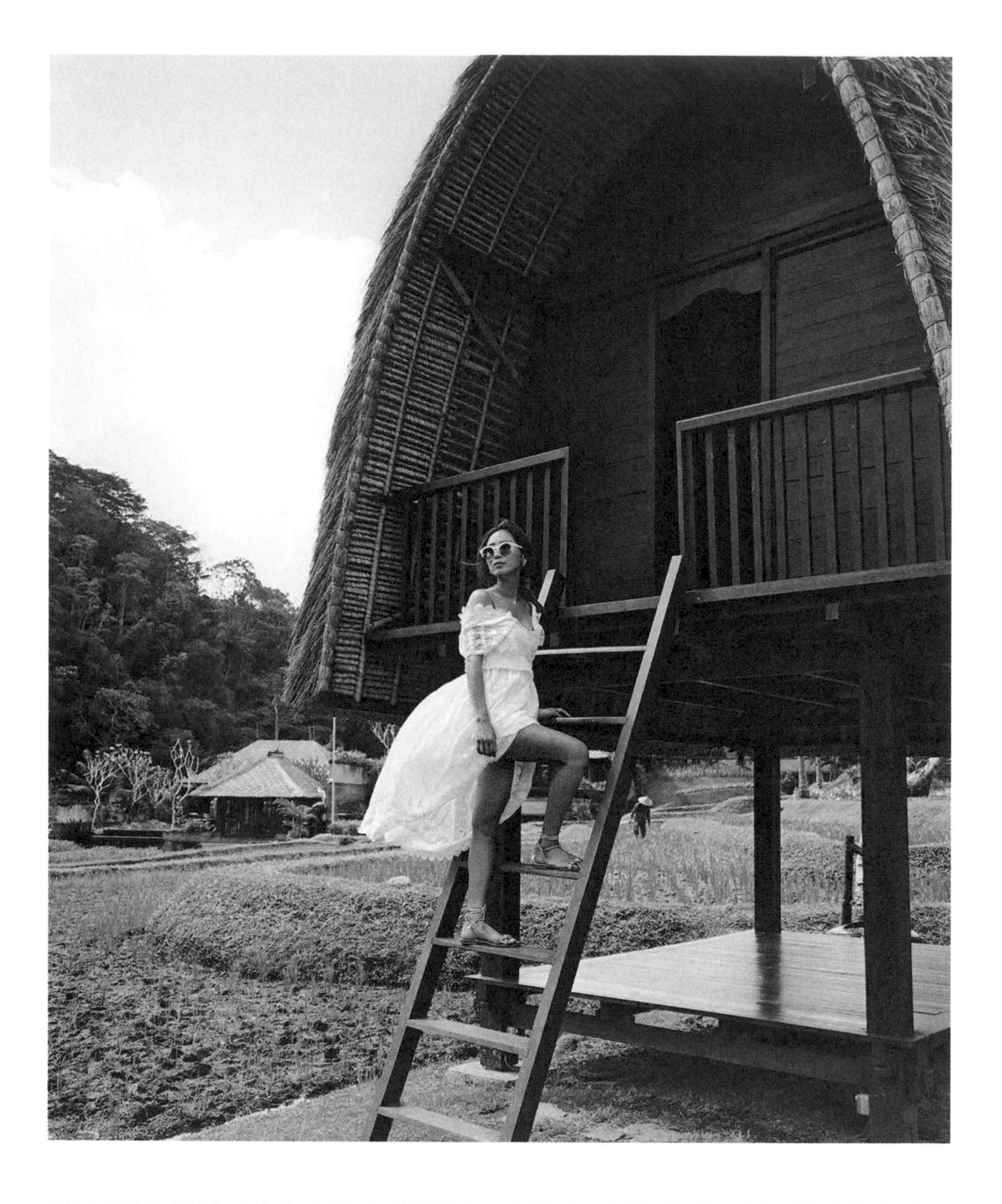

At the Four Seasons before touring rice fields. I Googled the weather before I left and packed a wardrobe of really simple, easy bohemian dresses that felt like they'd match the lush scenery of the country and seamlessly transfer between events and activities. I chose colorful accessories that popped with vibrancy—just like Bali itself. *Ulla Johnson dress; Cornetti shoes.*

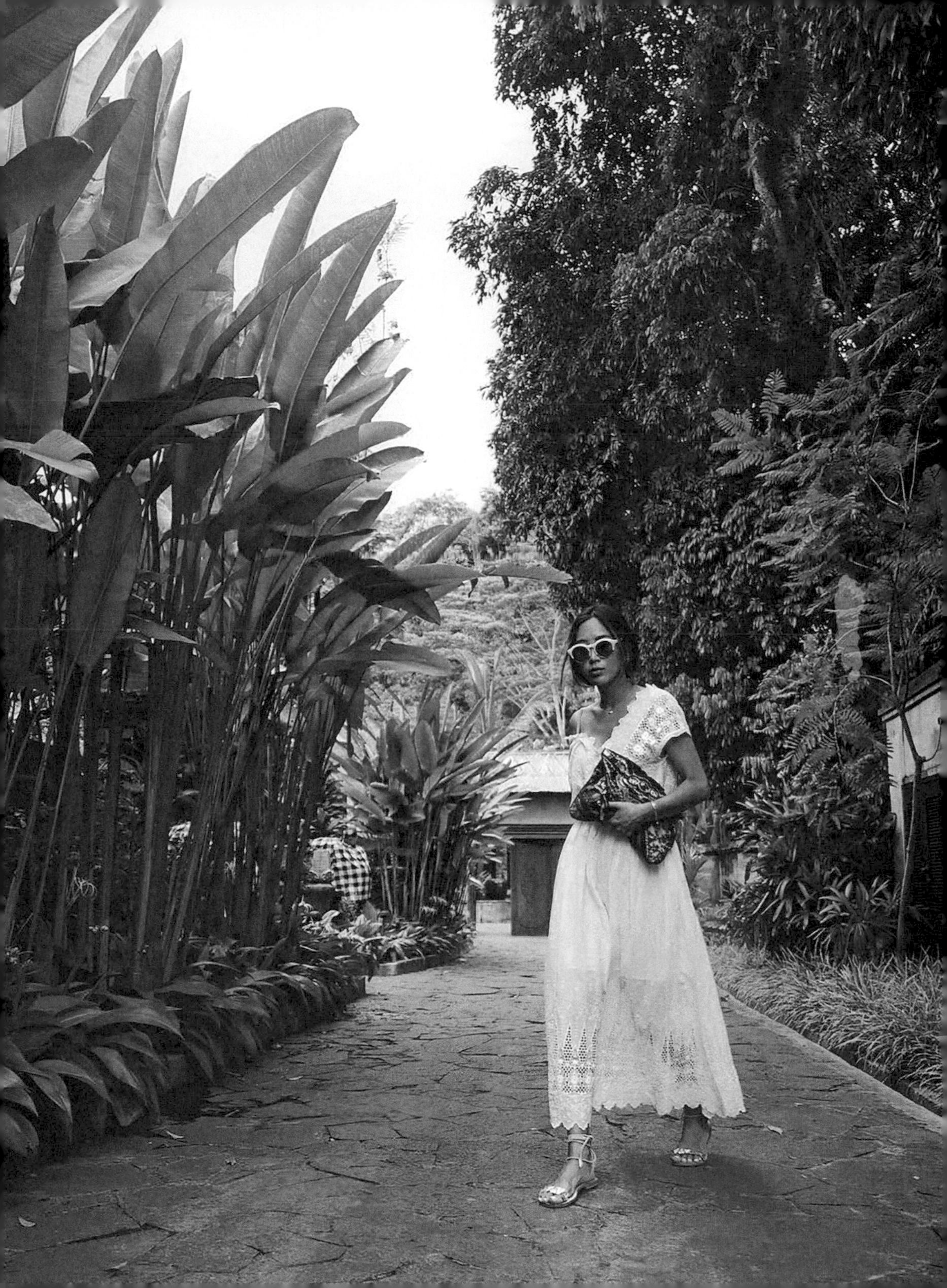

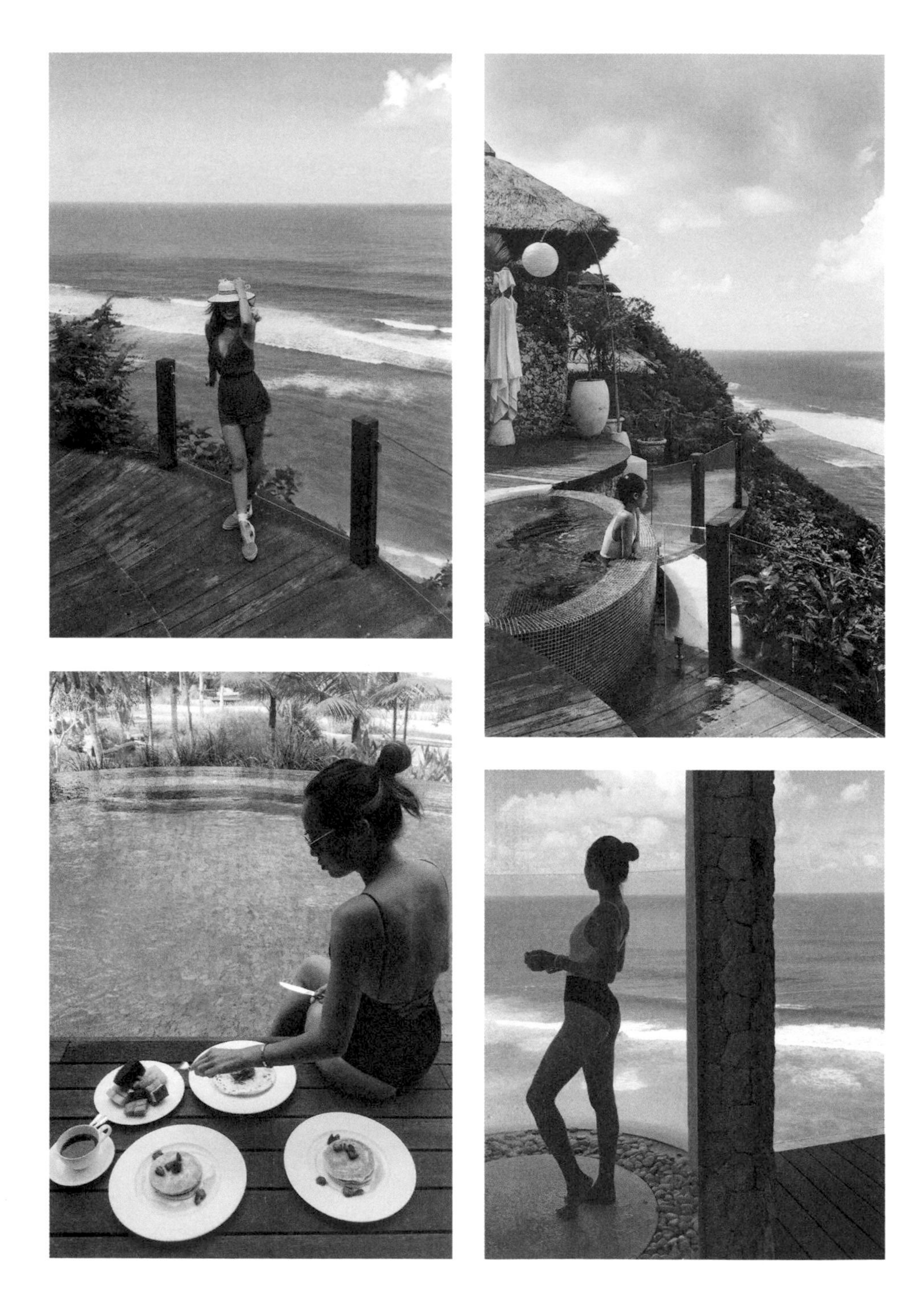

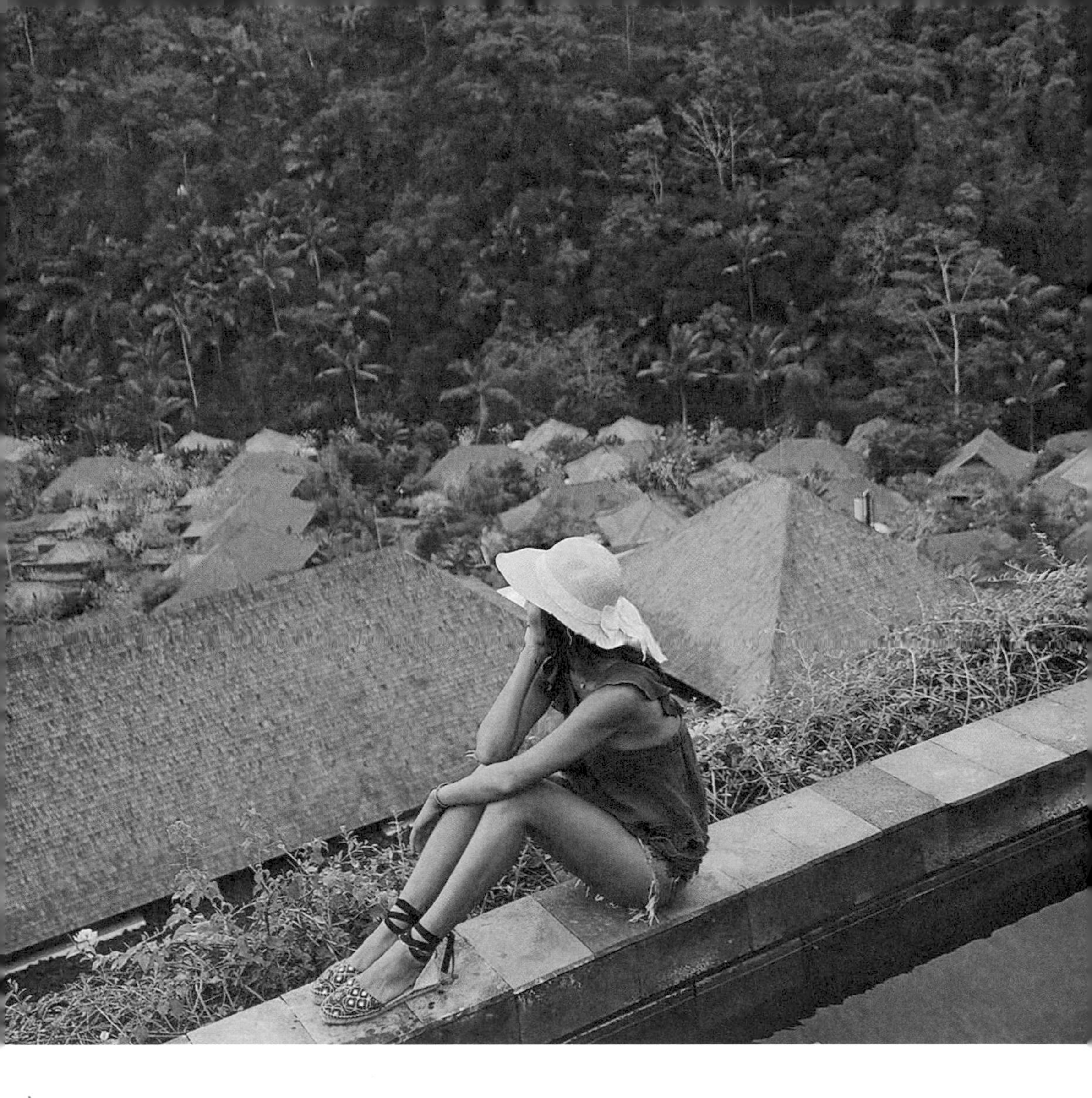

ABOVE Soaking up the nature-filled view at one of my hotels. This hat happened to be waiting for me inside my hotel room and happened to be super cute. Score. **OPPOSITE (CLOCKWISE FROM TOP LEFT)** *Lovers and Friends romper* • Right after a really nice couple's massage. I couldn't believe this insane view, so I forced Jacopo to take an iPhone photo—even though my art direction ruined the romance. • Another post-couple's massage shot against some of the bluest water I'd ever seen. • My morning ritual was breakfast by the pool and a swim. Breakfast in Bali includes lots of produce that's exotic in the United States—including dragon fruit—which I couldn't get enough of.

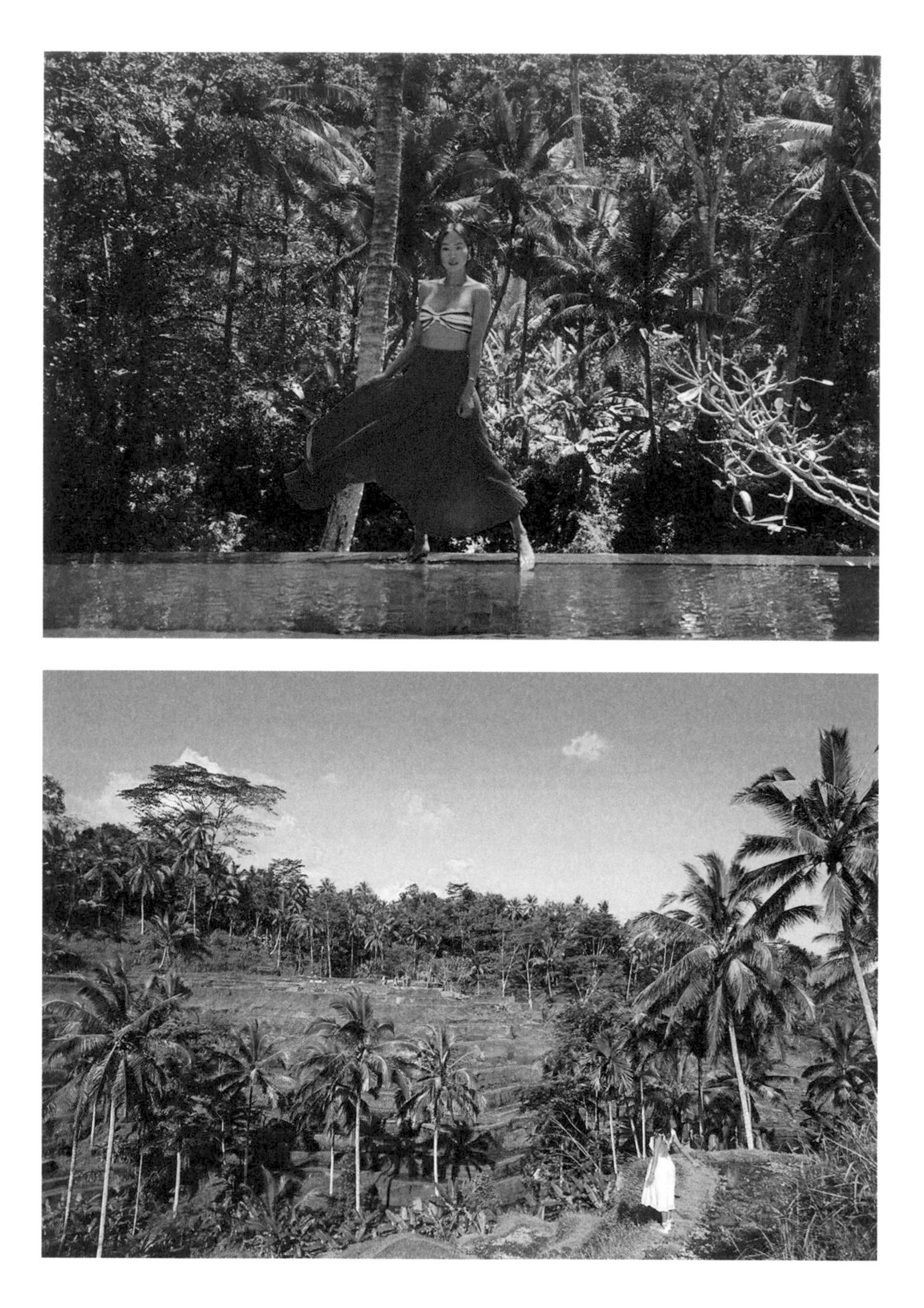

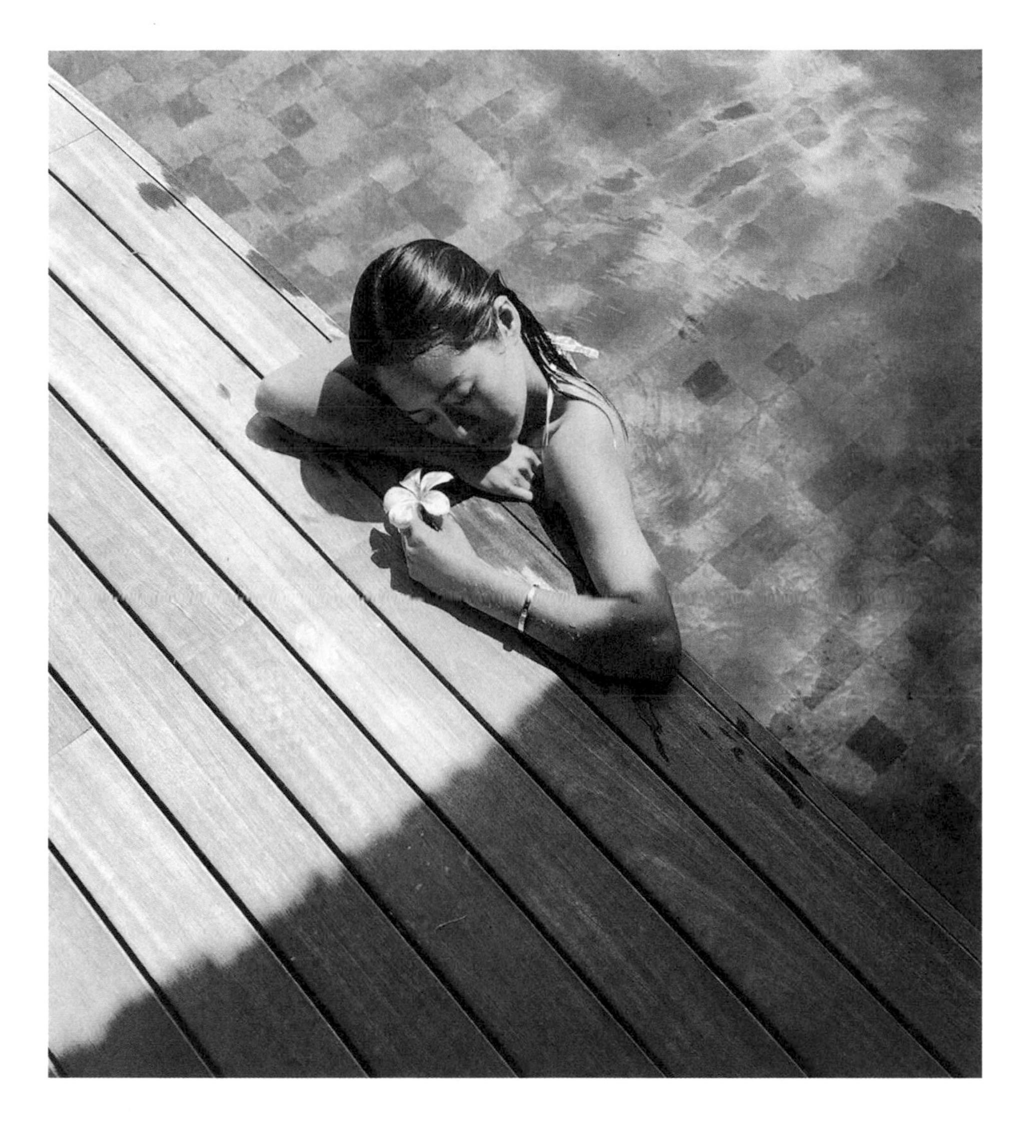

ABOVE Hanging in the pool. **OPPOSITE (FROM TOP)** Jacopo took this photo against the infinity pool by our villa, and I spent six minutes going back and forth and twirling the skirt to get the shot (believe it or not, six minutes is relatively quick to get a shot like this). I knew exactly what kind of shot I wanted and how I wanted to capture the skirt blowing in the wind—it just required Jacopo to click at exactly the right moment, which he always does. *Marysia Swim top; Alexis skirt* • At the rice fields, which are beautiful and a major tourist attraction. We got there right as a tour bus was pulling up so I had to run to get this shot before there would have been a bus full of strangers in the background.

We went to the desert in a jeep, which was so cool as I'd never been in a desert besides near Palm Springs before. I wasn't wearing appropriate footwear on the scorching hot sand, obviously.

DUBAI

The first time I went to Dubai was in 2014, for a Michael Kors store opening, which was a really cool experience as I got to hang out with local Dubai bloggers and really learn about the UAE—an experience made extra special as it was my first time in the Middle East. I obviously played the part of a tourist and went to the top of the Burj Khalifa—aka the tallest building in the world. And I happened to meet an amazing fellow Instagrammer named @shackette when he commented on one of my photos (this was the pre-DM days) and we ended up connecting. He was an amazing IRL tour guide; however, I made a major mistake in wearing clothes that weren't culturally appropriate: denim shorts and a really thin T-shirt (remember, this was the desert and it was super hot outside). I took my jacket off and my bra was visible, which I quickly learned was a big no. That experience taught me about the importance of learning about the cultural dress code of a place before getting there, and being respectful and mindful enough to plan accordingly. My second trip there for a speaking engagement the following year, I traded my shorts and tiny T-shirts for more modest options in line with the customs of the country. The more I travel the more my eyes are opened to various cultures around the world, and how as a global citizen it's incredibly important to be attentive to them whenever you leave home.

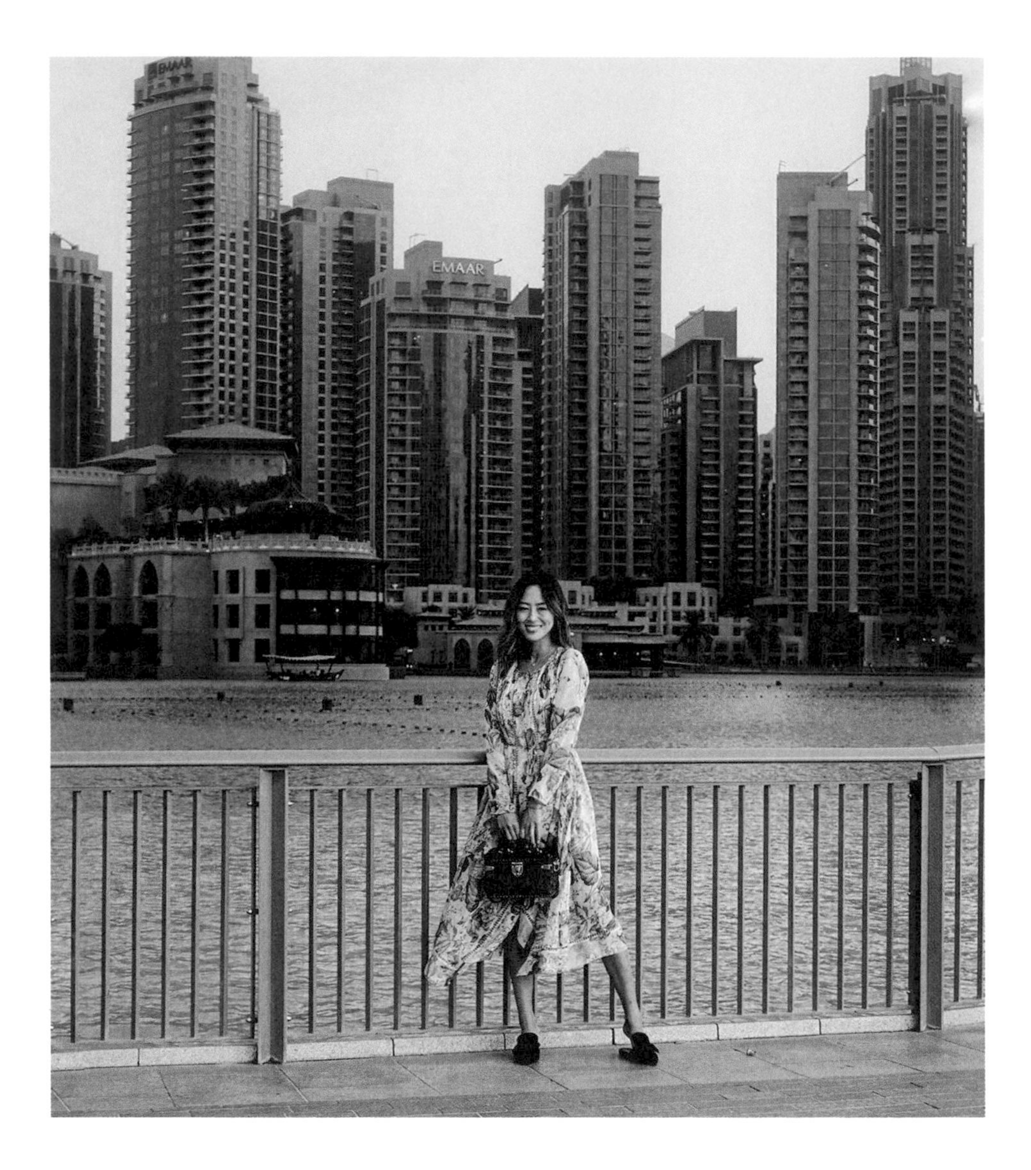

ABOVE Waiting to see the water fountain show across from the Burj Khalifa. *Zimmermann dress; Prada mules.* **OPPOSITE, TOP ROW** Right after working and doing interviews, I was looking for food, of course. *Vince tank top; L'Academie duster jacket; Current Elliott jeans; Prada mules.*

OPPOSITE, BOTTOM RIGHT Sitting at the top of the Burj Khalifa—literally on top of the world. **OPPOSITE, BOTTOM LEFT** On one of my free days we went to Abu Dhabi, and I wanted to tour the Sheikh Zayed Grand Mosque, where I borrowed an abaya to wear inside.

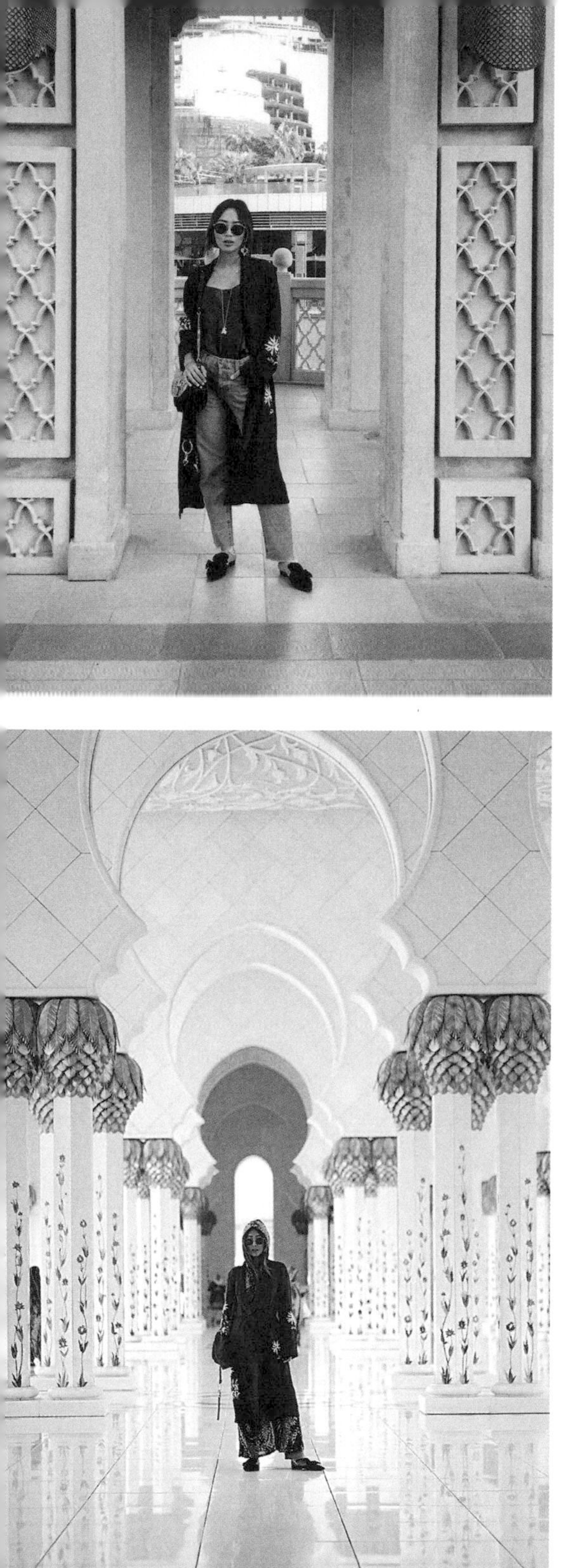

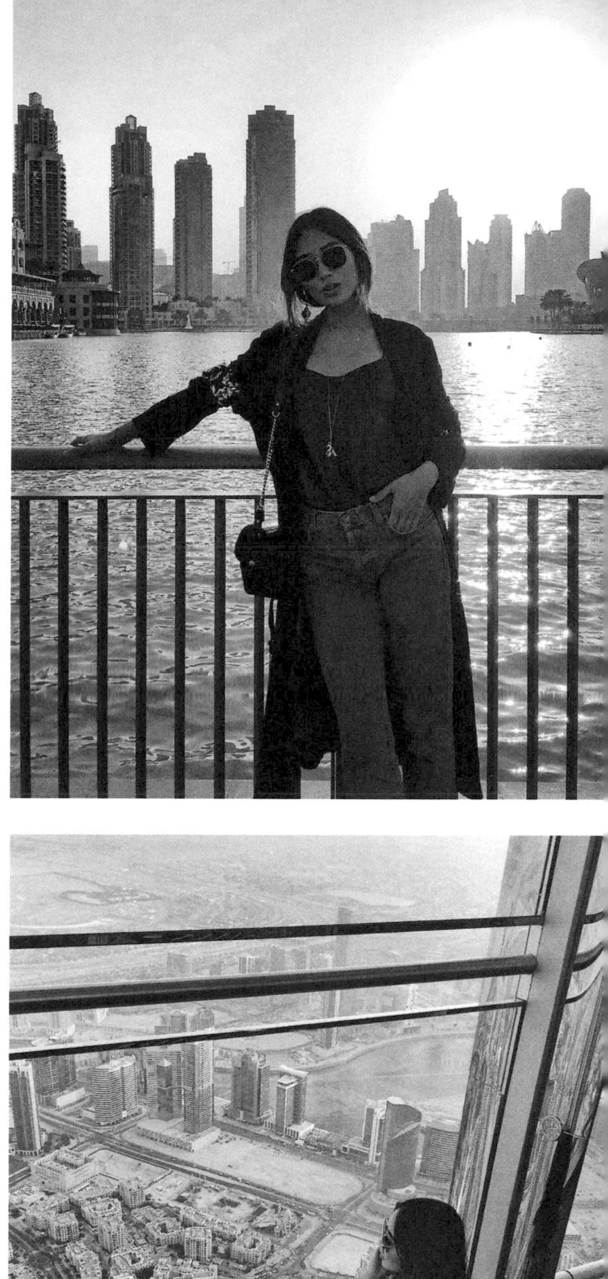

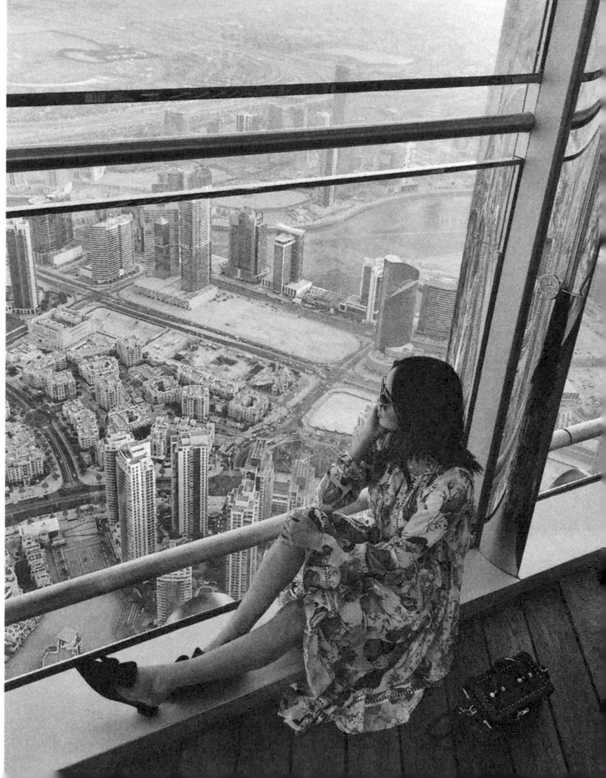

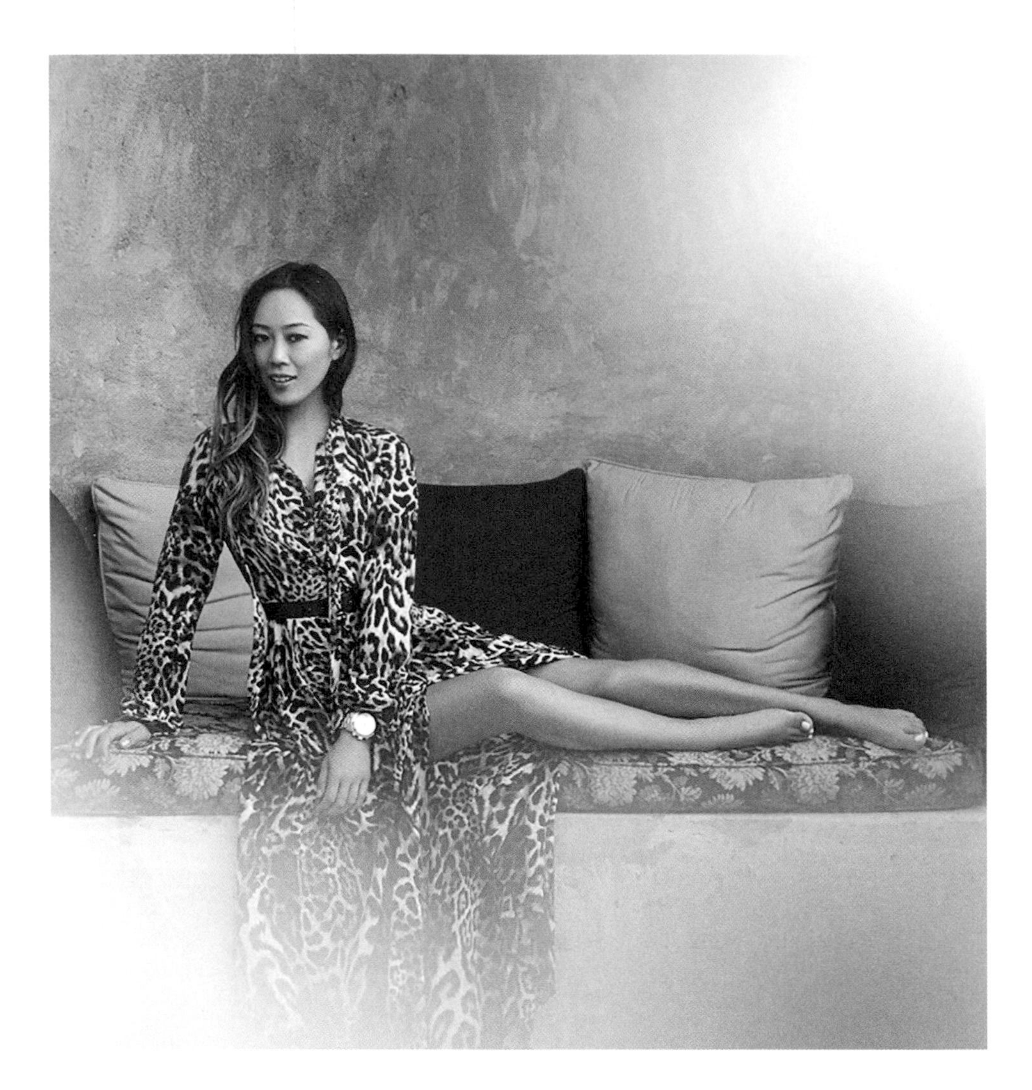

ABOVE With Michael Kors, shooting digital content for the brand. This was right after camel riding, so I packed this long dress because it was easy to roll and take with me all day. **OPPOSITE (CLOCKWISE FROM TOP)** *Michael Kors bag* • This is what I wore to speak about my experience as a blogger and how to build a brand. Fits the part, no? *Anna October dress; Chanel mules; Valentino bag* • The day I met local bloggers in Dubai. I wanted to look chic but also fun, and back then I loved showing off my legs. I also wore really ridiculous high heels that I no longer own—I can't wear heels that are that high anymore. Back then I always wanted to dress to impress, and now I prefer comfort over anything else.

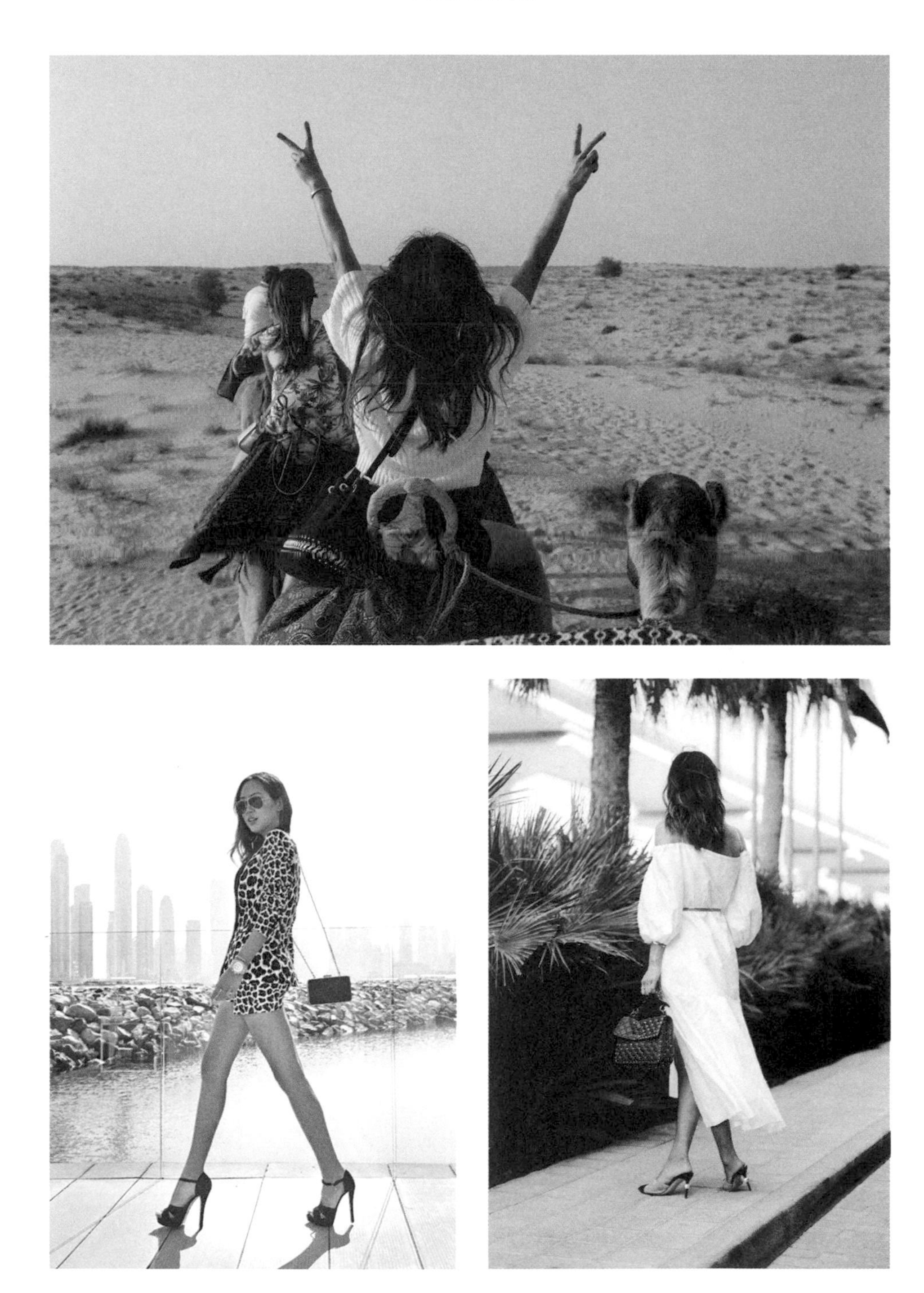

INDIA

My visit to Jaipur, India, in November 2016 is one of the most significant journeys I've ever been on. Not because the country is beautiful in a way that I hadn't before seen or filled with the kind of touching humanity I never knew existed, but because visiting here completely transformed the way I look at life.

Even before embarking on this trip with Jimmy Choo to help them create digital content, I always participated in giving, donating time and resources to those less fortunate. This trip touched me in ways that allowed me to understand just how much more I could be doing to give back.

After picture-perfect, magical days tirelessly arranged by the Jimmy Choo team, we'd drive back to our hotel and see all sides of Jaipur—especially those that typically don't make it onto Instagram. It was then that a fire was lit inside me to use my platform in an even more meaningful way, to help make a difference in the world and give back to those who aren't afforded basic necessities such as food, clean water, warm clothing, and safe housing—something you and I have the power to do, together.

I was completely present on this trip and soaked in every feeling and sound, so I could translate the experience into action the second I got home. Which I did in many ways, such as my humanitarian trip to Ethiopia for Charity: Water that allowed me to assist in raising more than $81,000 for water projects in Africa. If you're willing to open your eyes and your mind, travel has the power to change your life in ways you never imagined.

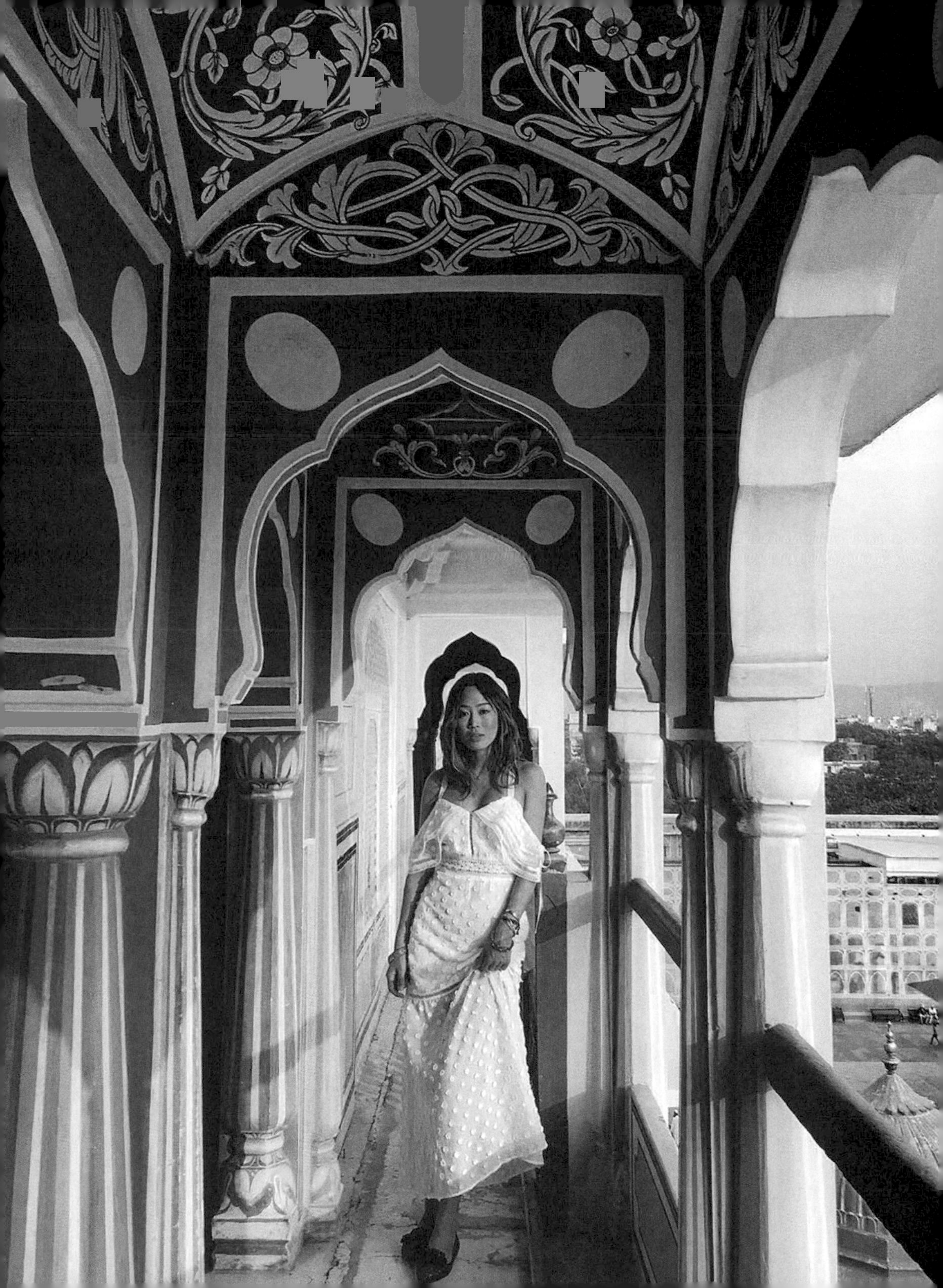

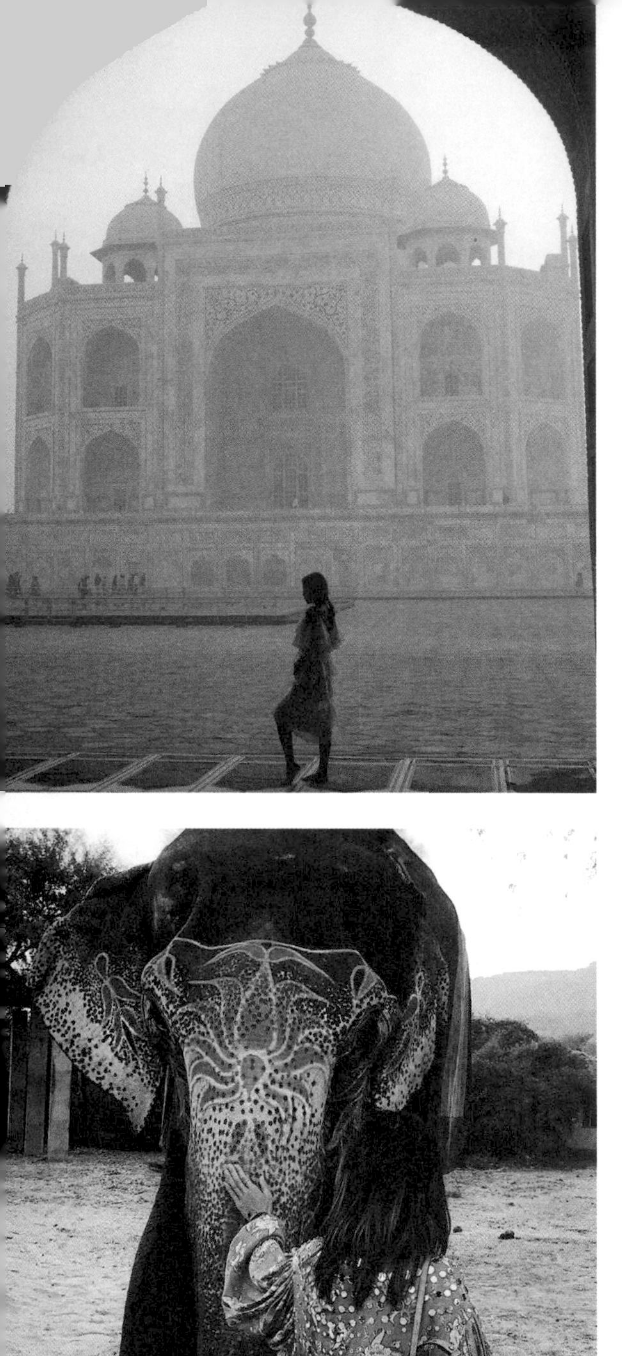
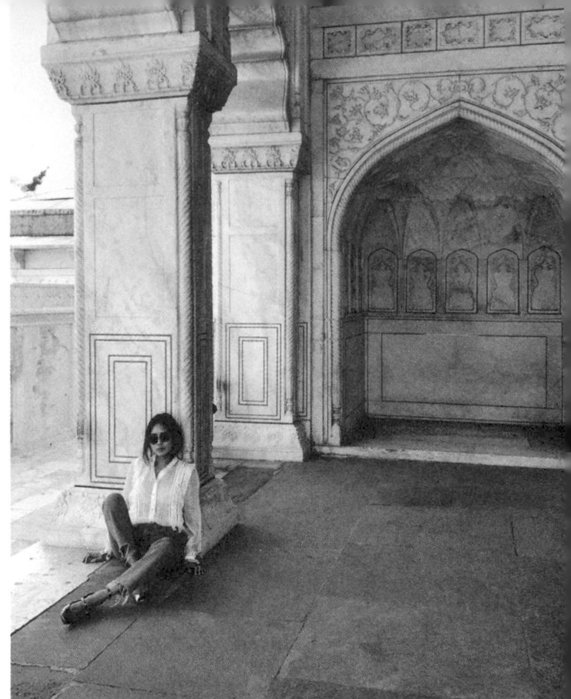
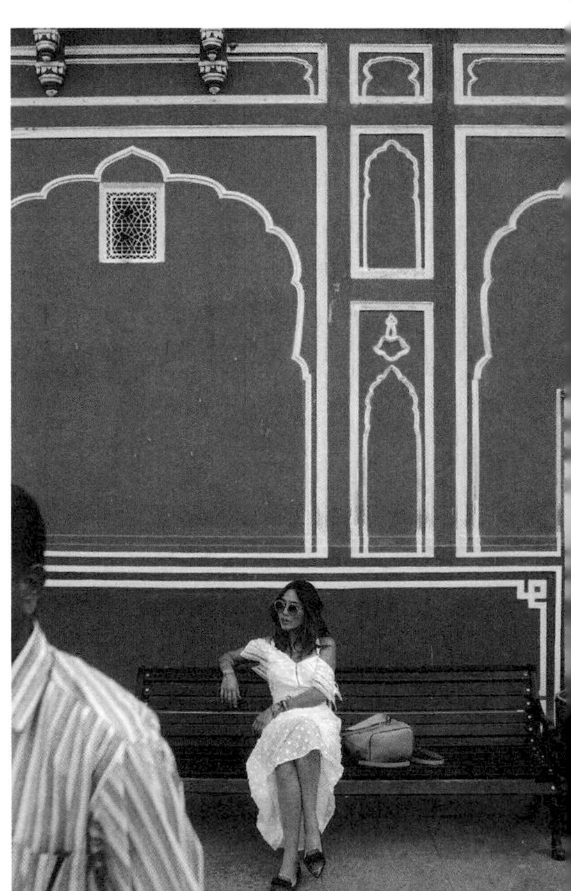

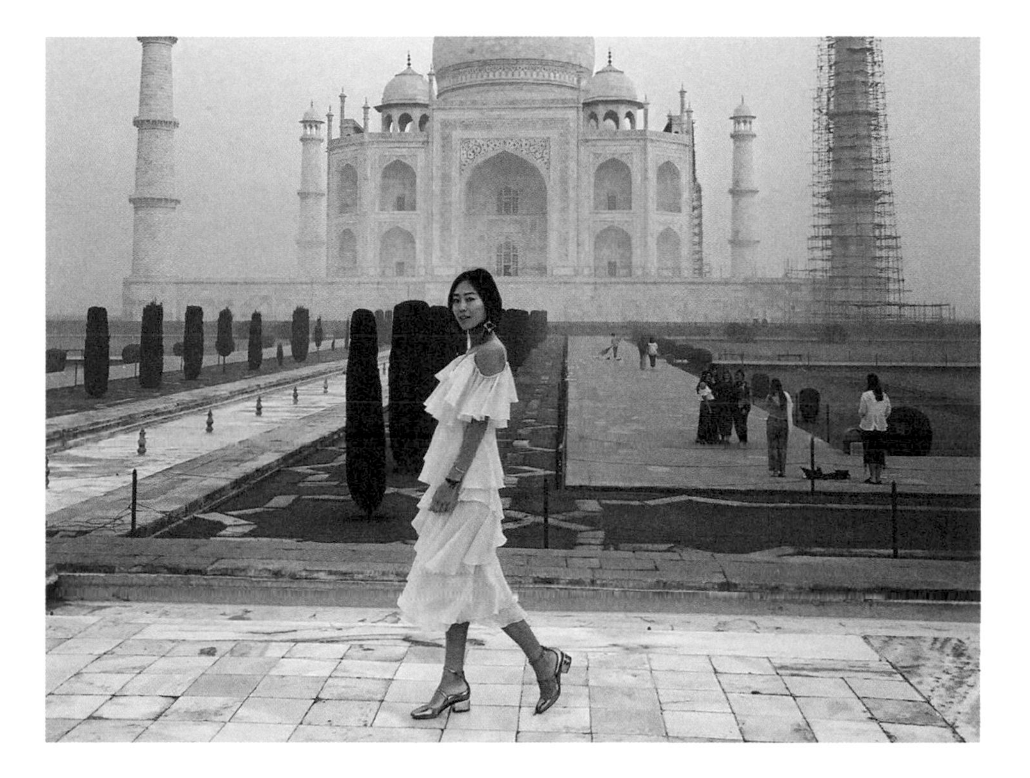

ABOVE The Taj Mahal I visited was very different from the Taj Mahal I had pictured in my mind, although still impressive. There was construction going on and the fountains were drained, but it was still a pretty epic sight to see. *Anna October dress; Jimmy Choo shoes.* **OPPOSITE (CLOCKWISE FROM TOP LEFT)** In this particular part of the Taj Mahal, visitors aren't allowed to wear shoes unless they're covered with paper booties (which obviously didn't go with this outfit). So I chose to ditch footwear altogether. The Taj Mahal is incredibly packed all the time. We arrived first thing in the morning before it opened to visitors and there was still an insane line, who all rushed inside the second the doors opened. It was impossible to take a shot without anyone else in the frame (and we know how I feel about that) so I tried to capture something with as few people as possible. • A theme of this trip: me trying to get a solo shot sans crowd. *Zimmermann blouse, Citizens of Humanity jeans, Jimmy Choo shoes* • Again, I don't like other people in my shots. But this guy happened to walk by as Jacopo was snapping and there was something about the movement and his presence that I loved. • I was completely unaware about the horrible treatment of elephants at tourist attractions when I took this shot. After I posted it, my Instagram community helped clue me in and educate me about the abuses that go on in this world. I felt so ashamed that I had been so ignorant, but thanks to the new knowledge I was able to take from this experience, I went to a proper elephant sanctuary in Thailand on a later trip where I actually got to help with conservation efforts. No mistakes, just growth—especially when traveling.

PACKING 101

There are so many ways to pack for a trip (rollers vs. folders—you know what I'm talking about). Not to mention that packing drastically differs based on the type of trip you're taking and the climate when you get there (I'm definitely not taking the same size bag to Switzerland for a week that I'm taking to San Francisco for a long weekend). But regardless of the trip, there are a few tried-and-true rules I follow that help make packing a snap. Because let's be real: no one loves doing it and doesn't just want to be there already.

1. **Choose a theme.** When I'm packing, I choose a general color story so I can easily mix and match my pieces on the ground.

2. **Preplan outfits.** Because I'm a blogger and travel extensively for work, I typically have to bring enough outfits to carry me through multiple changes each day. But regardless of my itinerary, I always make a detailed agenda for each day of my trip—even if "sitting by the hotel pool for six hours" is one of the major points—and break down what I need to wear for each activity, each day. For example, if I know I'm taking a workout class before a day of meetings that ends with a casual dinner with friends, I know I need gym shoes, a polished outfit for my day, and something to wear to dinner—or, at the very least, a change of jacket and/or jewelry to take my business look into something a bit lighter. Mixing and rewearing versatile pieces is encouraged, and knowing exactly what activities I have to dress for before I go helps me make sure I'm packing correctly and won't have to make any unforeseen Zara runs upon landing.

3. **Always pack a black blazer.** It goes with everything and can be worn dressed up or down, and you never know when you're going to sit next to your dream boss on an airplane and have a job interview upon landing (that happens, right?). It's just a good thing to bring. And here's a nifty, wrinkle-free trick: When you pack your blazer, turn it inside out, put one sleeve inside the other, and roll it up. Voilà—a perfectly packed blazer. Go get that dream job.

4. **Roll, don't fold.** I know that this is one of the most hotly debated topics in modern history. But for me, there's no question that rolling your clothes in your suitcase is the only way to go. It creates more space, keeps things

relatively wrinkle free, and takes less time. I consider the issue closed.

5. **Come prepared.** Irons are usually a given at hotels. But if you're staying at a private house or an Airbnb, where your hosts may not keep a de-wrinkling device, pack a small travel steamer. Trust. A crease-free outfit elevates and polishes your look, even if you're simply in jeans and a T-shirt.

6. **Organize your beauty.** I pack all my makeup and skin-care products in pouches from The Daily Edited—one for makeup, one for skin care—so I know that everything is together (and leak-proof) in one place. I also bring mini versions of my favorite full-size potions so I can carry them with me, unless I'm going on a long trip. If your luggage goes missing, there's nothing better than having your makeup with you!

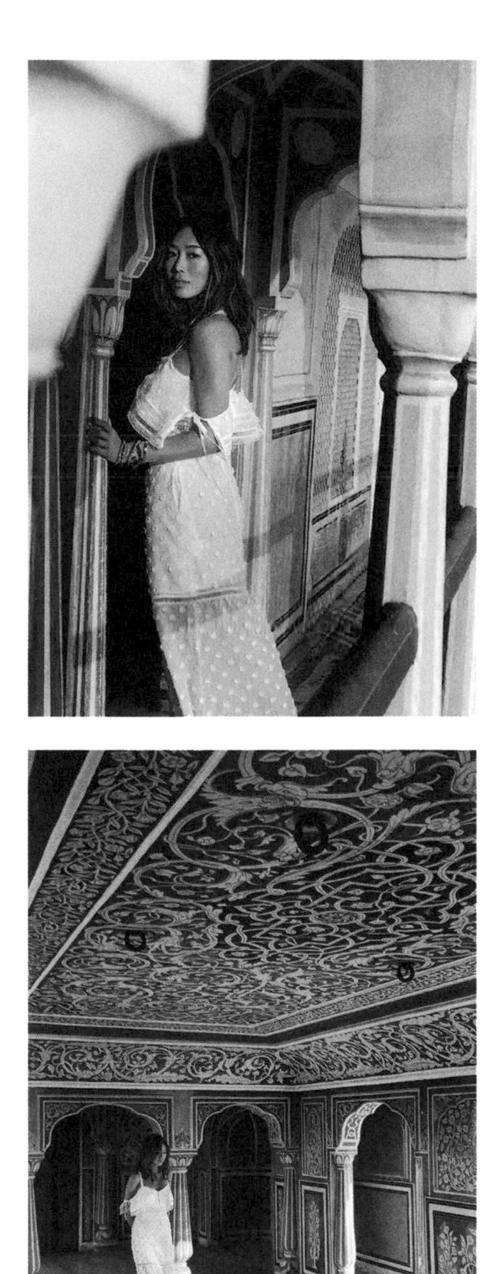

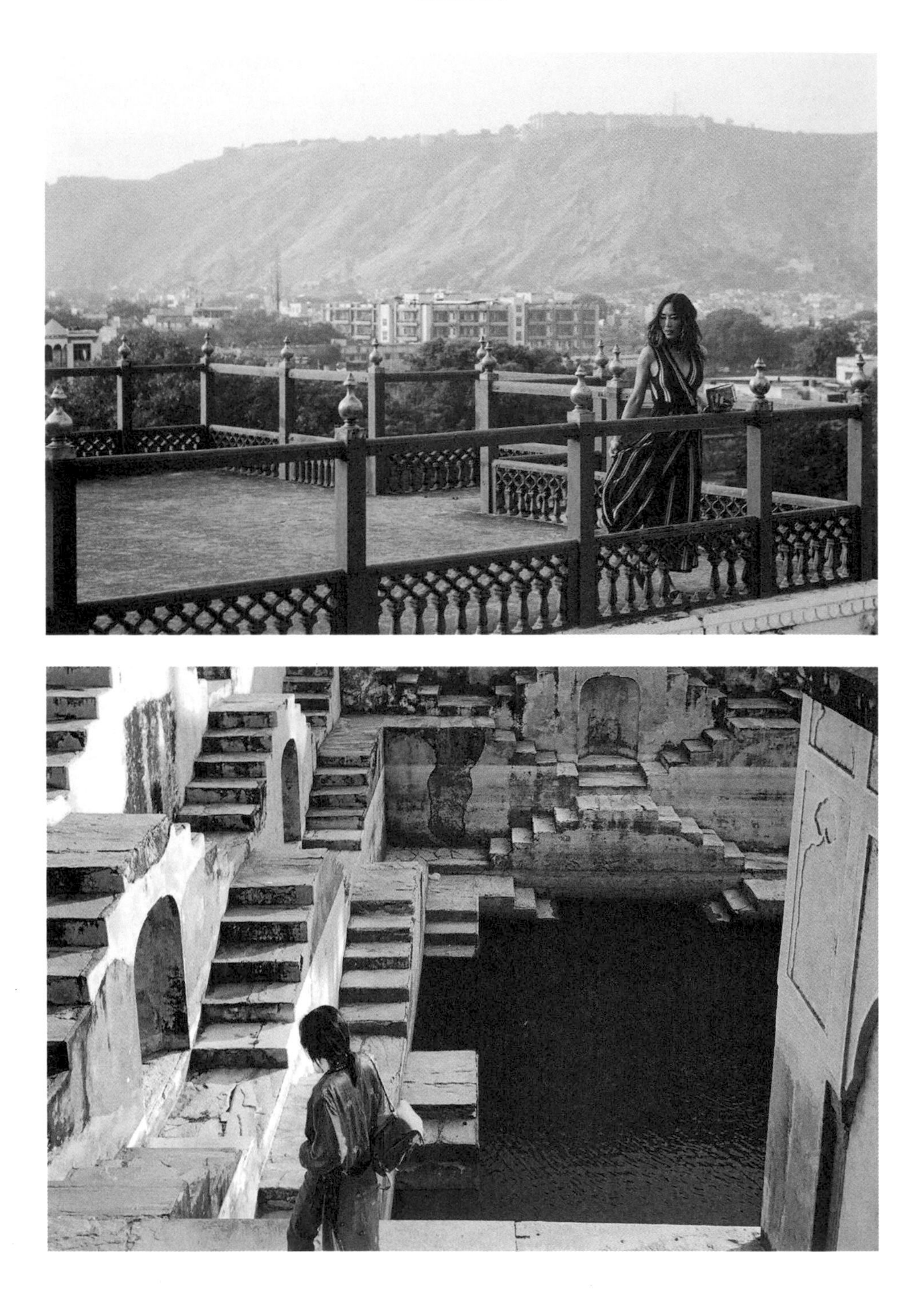

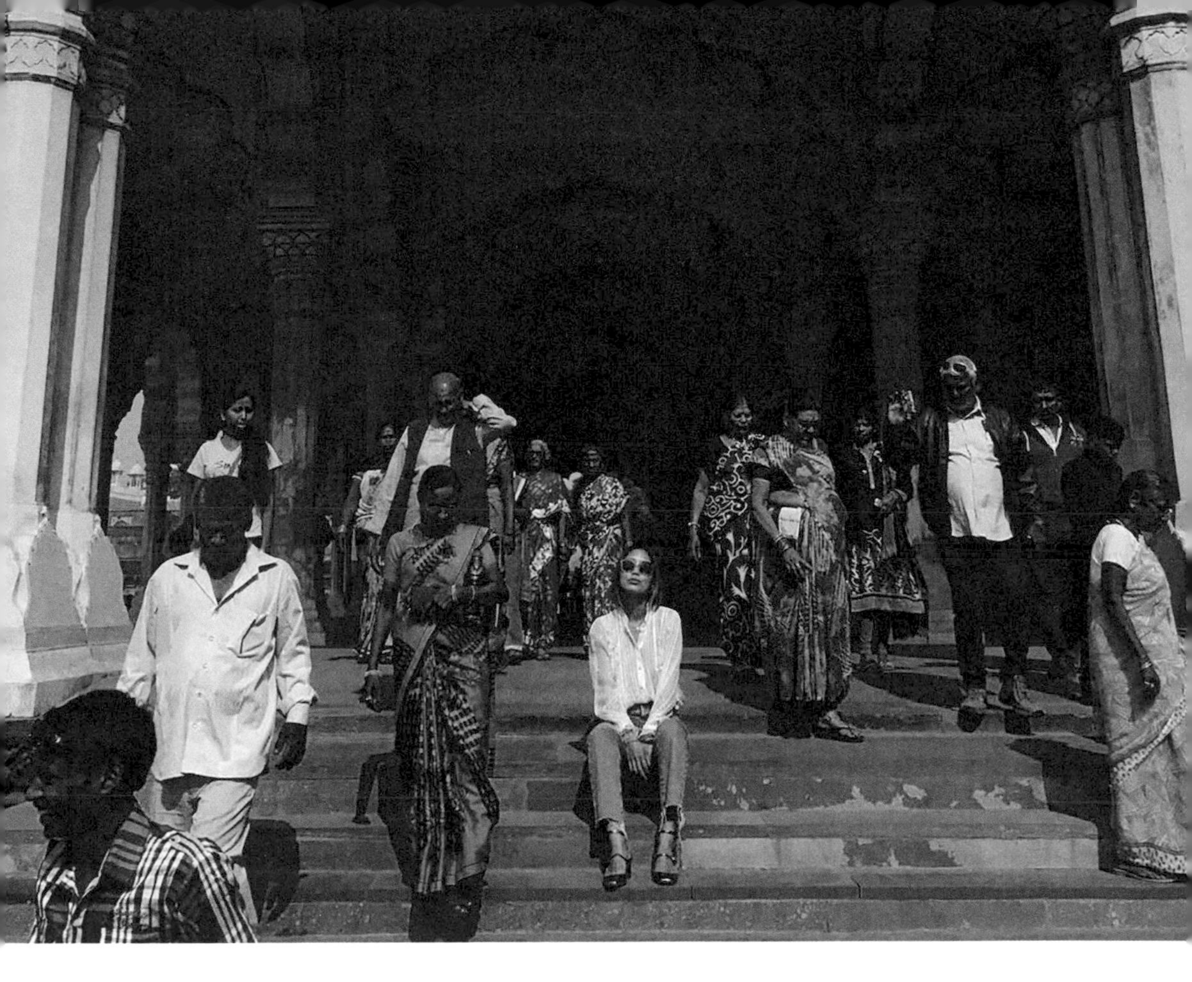

ABOVE The women in India were so beautiful and well-dressed, and I loved seeing the gorgeous, colorful saris and churidars they wore. In this shot, I was waiting for the crowd to disappear but Jacopo loved how striking this scene was with the crowd walking by and the way everyone juxtaposed with my casual outfit (when it comes to food and photography, that boy knows what's up). This is the photo I ended up using on my Instagram. **OPPOSITE (FROM TOP)** Toward the end of the City Palace day, when the sun was getting ready to set. I packed the DVF wrap dress I'm wearing in the shot because it rolls really well (that's how I pack—I roll). And I was able to roll it into a Chloé backpack and carry it with me all day. *DVF dress* • One of my favorite moments of this trip was making bespoke silk pajamas and a robe with a proper tailor. I picked out the fabric and they made the pieces by hand—for only $40 (you wouldn't even be able to find silk pajamas for that price at the Palm Springs outlets). I wanted to take my robe for a real-world test drive, and used a free morning to explore on my own. I had done research and knew I wanted to see these steps—at which I had to sweet-talk a security guard and convince him to let me walk around. He ended up being the one who took this iPhone shot (I guess I'm convincing when I need to be).

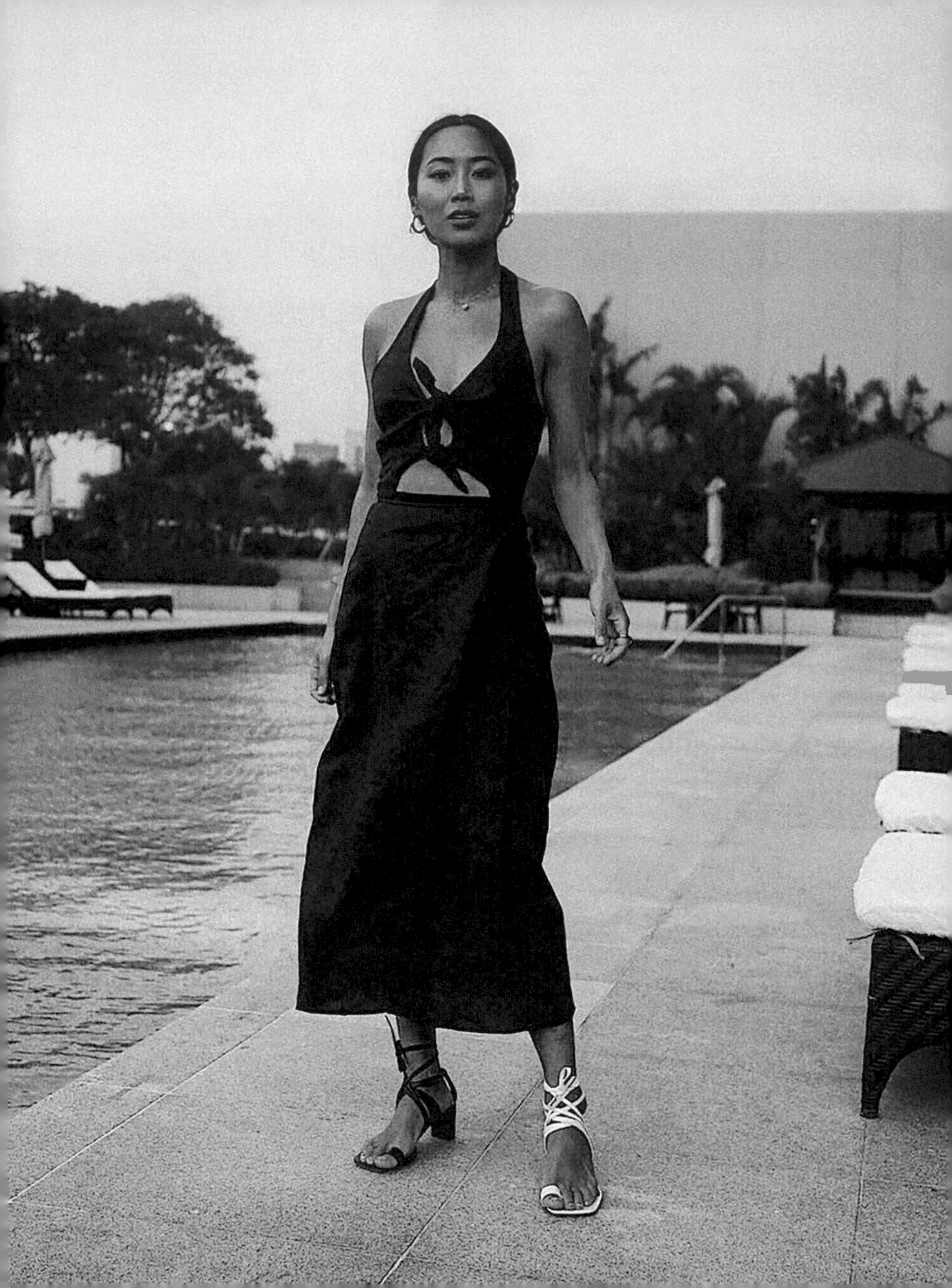

JAKARTA

When I started my blog in 2008, if someone had told me that one day I'd be gracing covers of fashion magazines I would have legitimately laughed in their face (and hugged them because the joke would have been so flattering). But fast-forward to 2017 and lo and behold, I found myself in Jakarta for three days to shoot a cover for *Harper's Bazaar Indonesia*—a tremendously cool experience, to say the least. As part of that same trip I also helped Dior open a store there. Needless to say, I was high-fiving my younger self the entire short time I was there—which I very much tried to make the most of with a healthy mix of work, exploration, and discovering interesting Indonesian snacks.

OPPOSITE My first day in Indonesia, before going out to dinner. *Reformation linen dress; Céline shoes.*

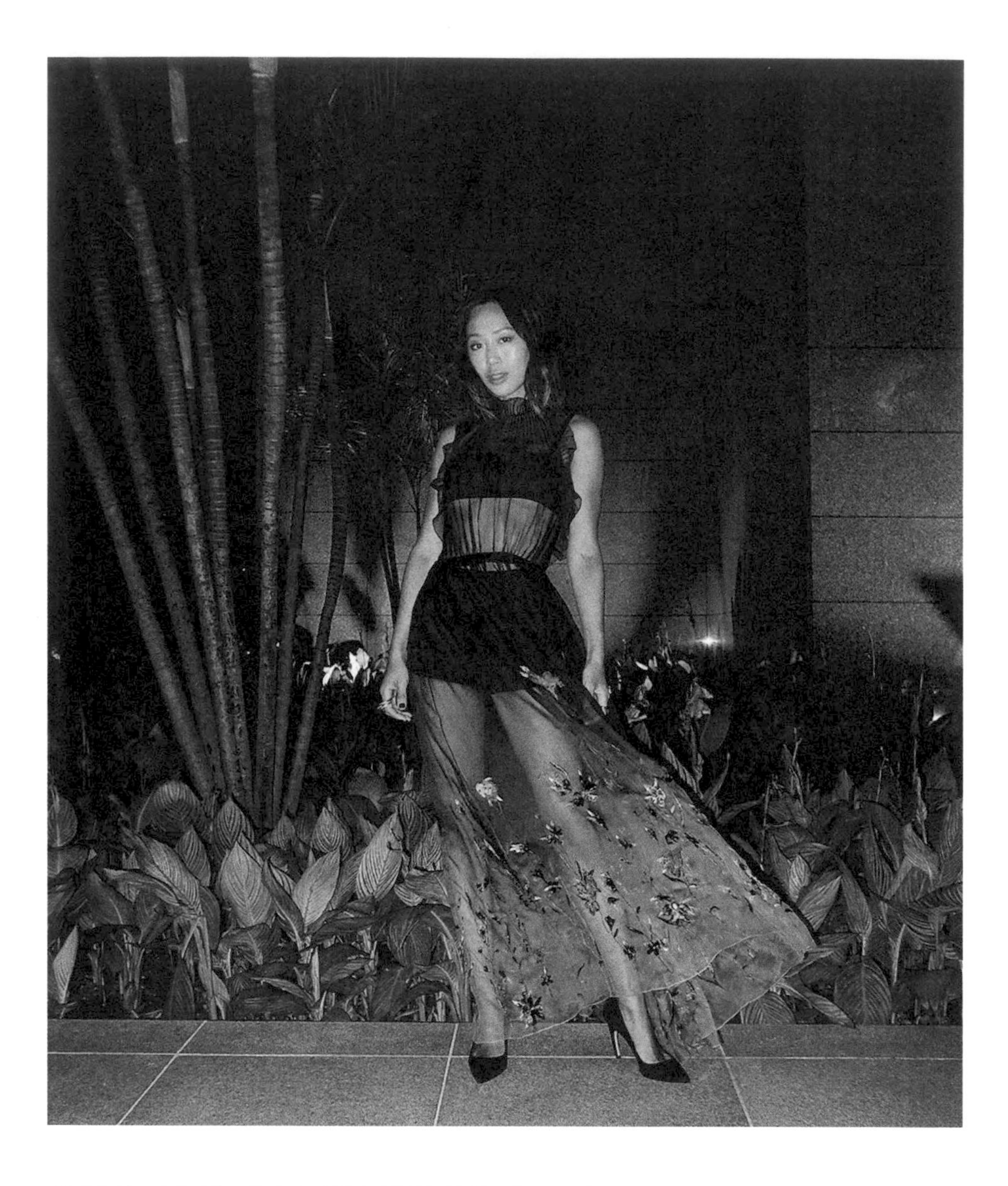

The evening of the Dior store opening, which was so incredibly packed with people. I did my own hair and makeup, and I couldn't wait to get a photo of this beautiful dress. *Dior dress.*

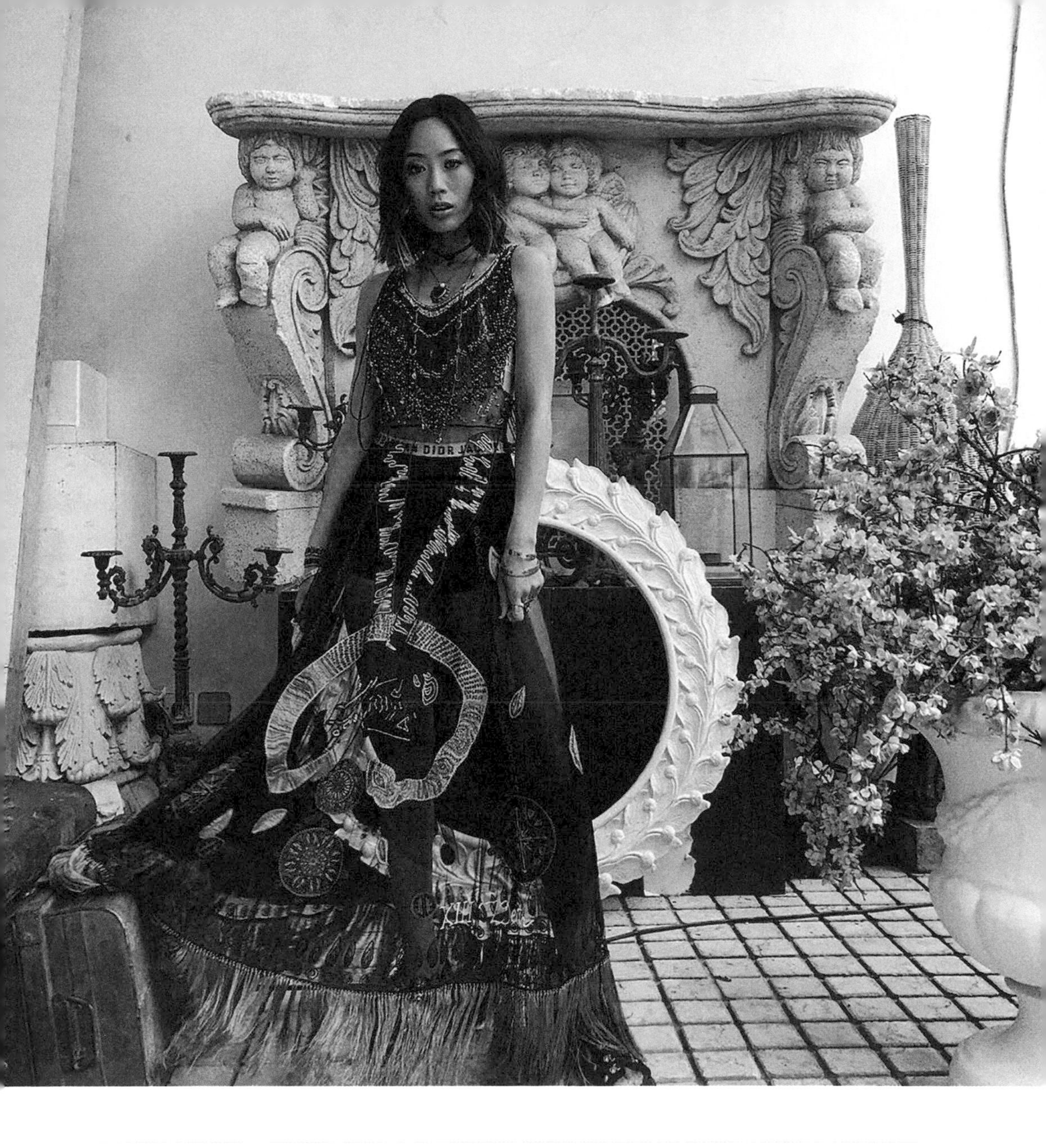

Between takes of my *Harper's Bazaar Indonesia* cover shoot, which included six or seven looks. A proper magazine shoot is so different than getting one of my Instagram outfit shots! This time I had hair and makeup, a video crew to get behind-the-scenes footage, and—because they did their homework and knew how much I love to try really cool foods that I've never experienced before—tons and tons of snacks on set. Mission accomplished. *Dior dress.*

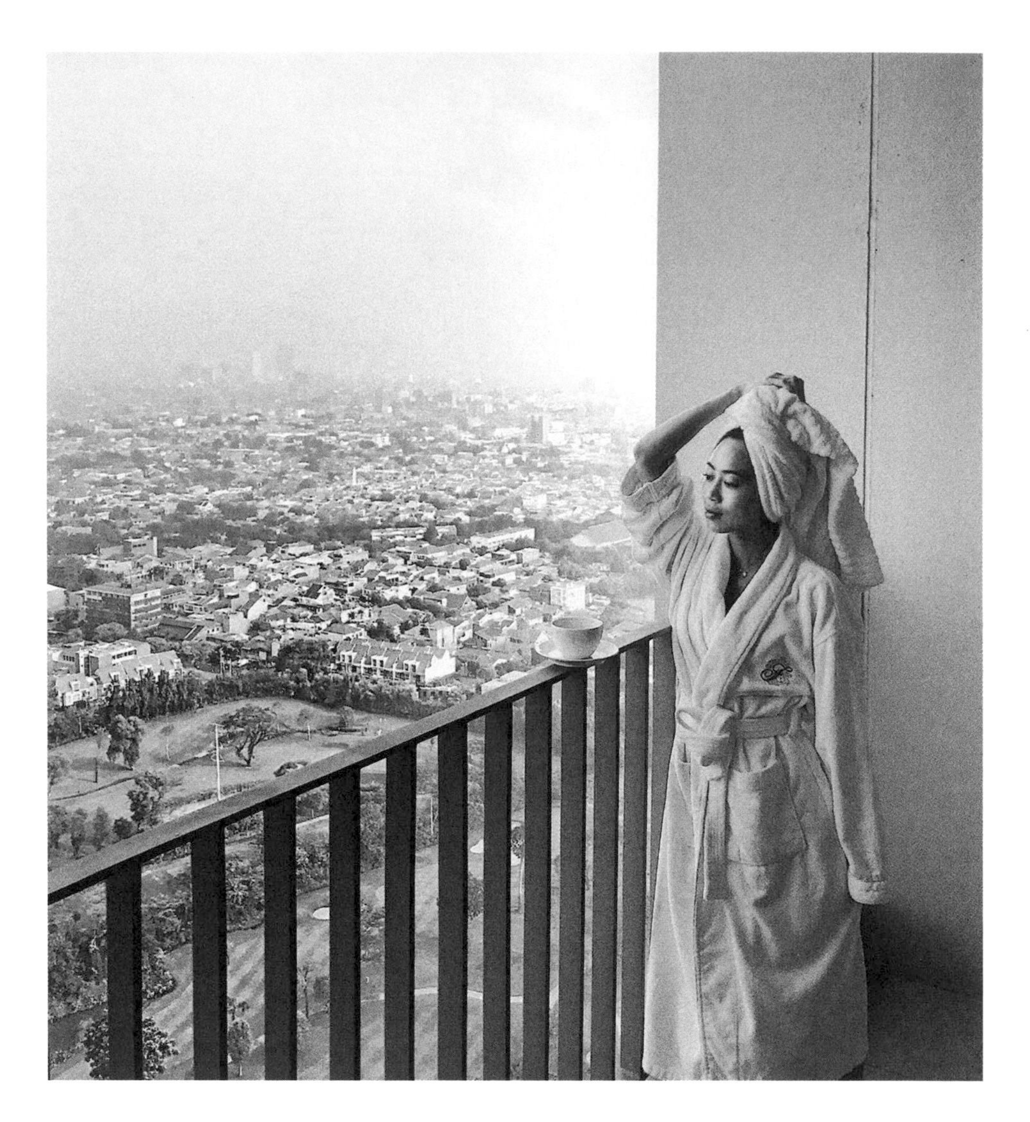

ABOVE The morning of the shoot. I woke up, soaked in the view from the hotel balcony, and tried to enjoy that #robelife as best I could. **OPPOSITE** Right after the cover shoot, completely exhausted. I normally don't buy souvenirs from all of my travels and instead only bring home really meaningful things, but I knew I wanted something from this trip. (The shoot was such a souvenir in itself, but I wanted to remember the experience in multiple ways.) So I bought some pottery and woven raffia baskets from artisans we happened to see on the side of the road—one of which is now holding a plant in my house. If I don't love something I don't buy it, and these things I loved. *Reformation dress.*

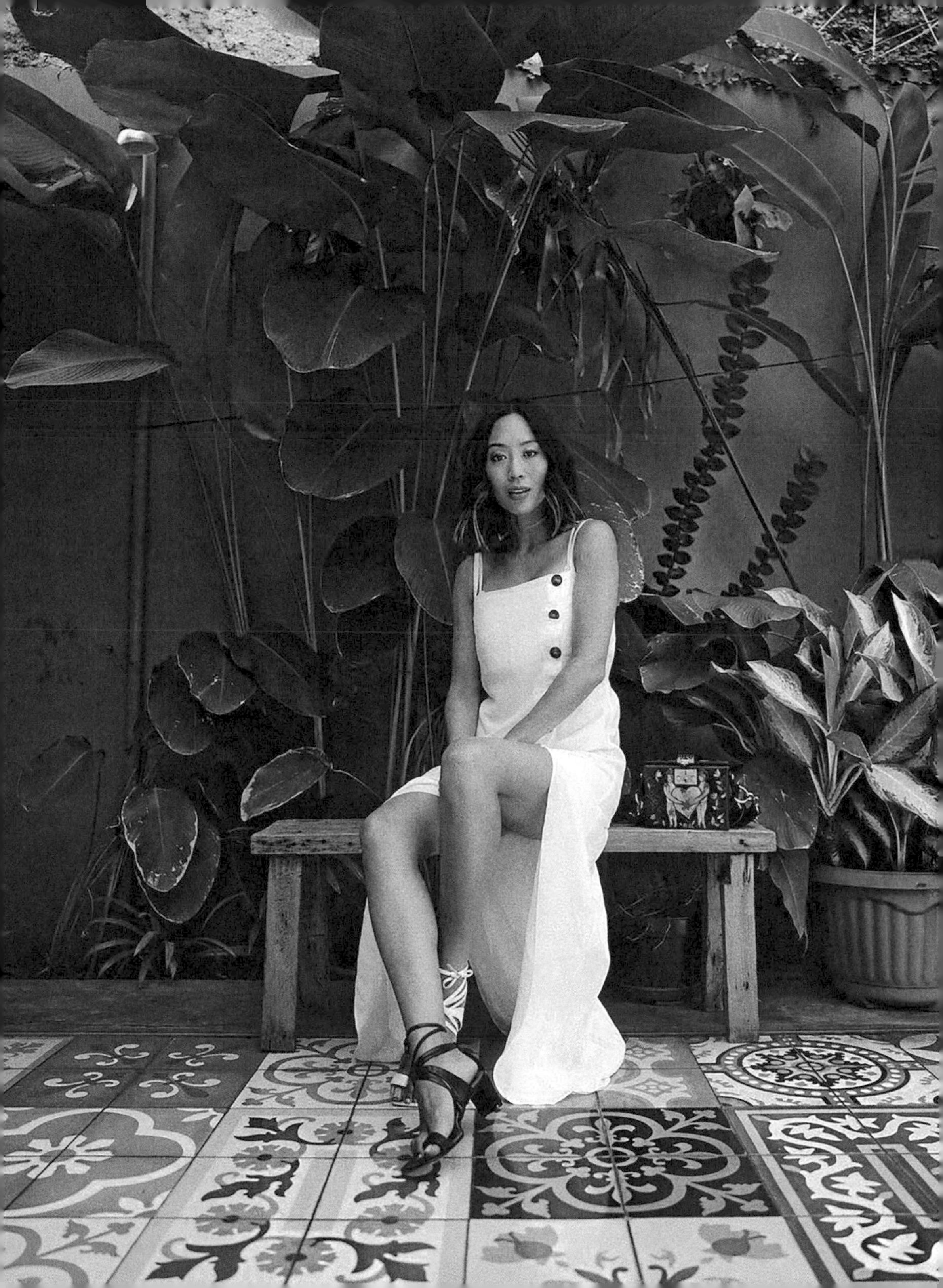

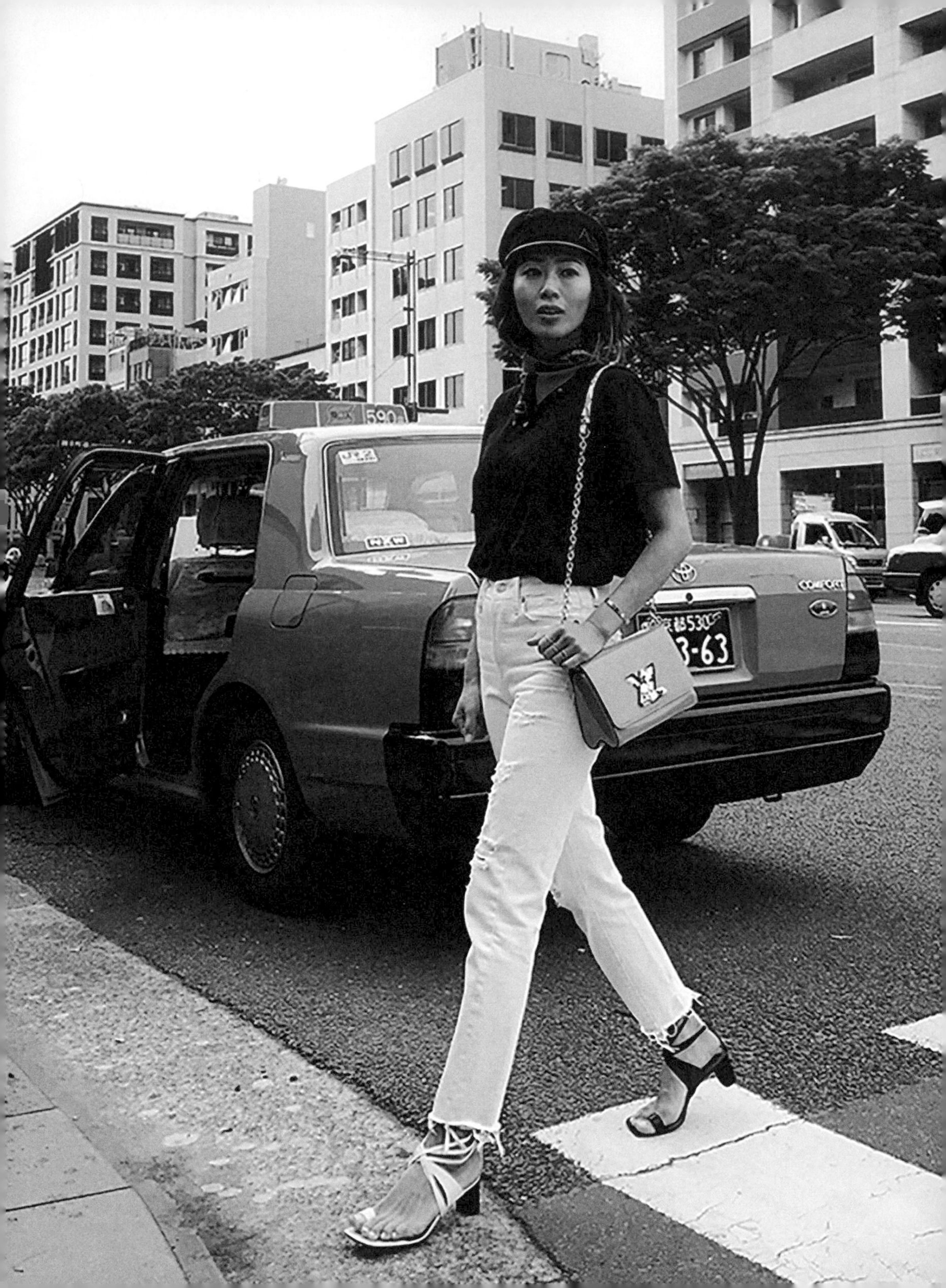
590
COMFORT

KYOTO

As I mentioned earlier, I lived in Japan for six months when I was fifteen. And though I've visited Tokyo many times, I'd never been to Kyoto until May 2017, when Louis Vuitton invited me to attend their cruise show. Kyoto is only a few hours from Tokyo but has a completely different vibe. It's slower and more serene, filled with gorgeous temples and amazing fresh food. Jacopo was with me on this trip and, being a major foodie, totally did his homework and led us to some of the best sushi I've ever experienced on this planet (Izu, I'm coming for you).

OPPOSITE Right outside of the Nishiki Market. Throughout the trip I tried to wear comfortable shoes (for once!), like these Céline heels—which were my summer go-to in 2017. Pro tip: When I pack hats, I stack them in my suitcase and stuff gym clothes and socks inside so they don't get crushed.

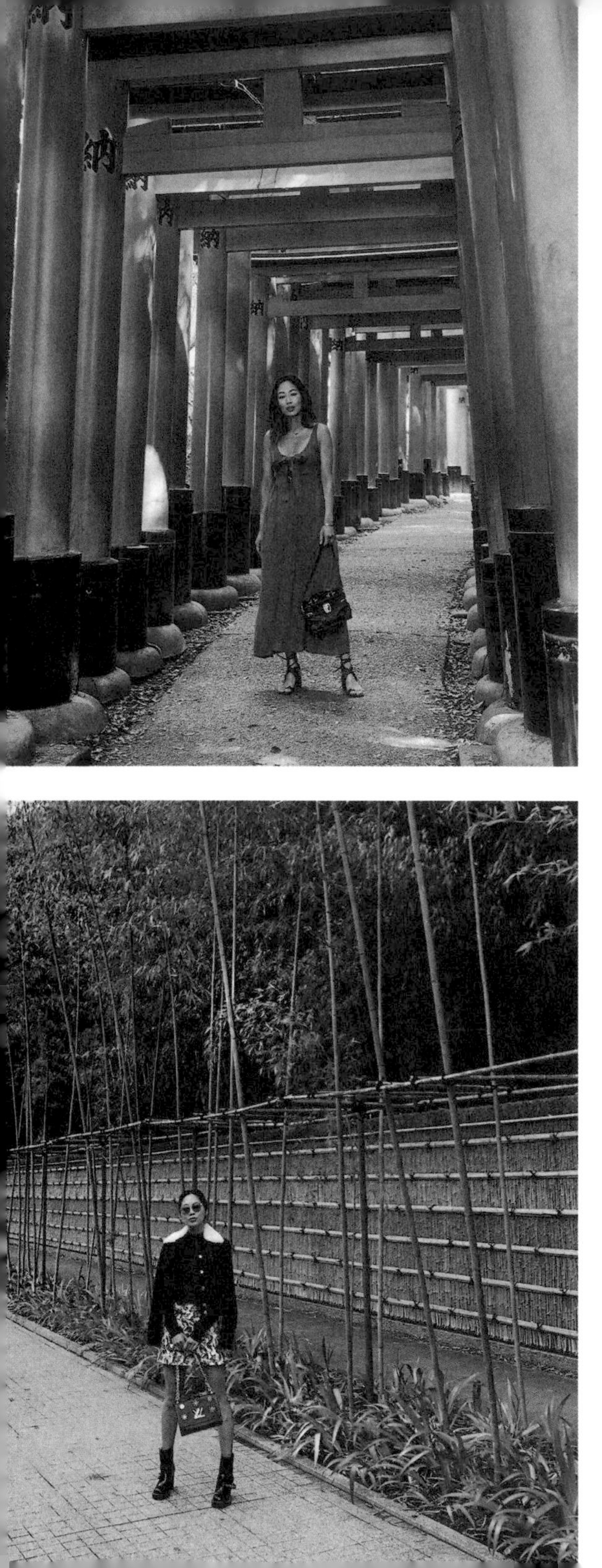
納

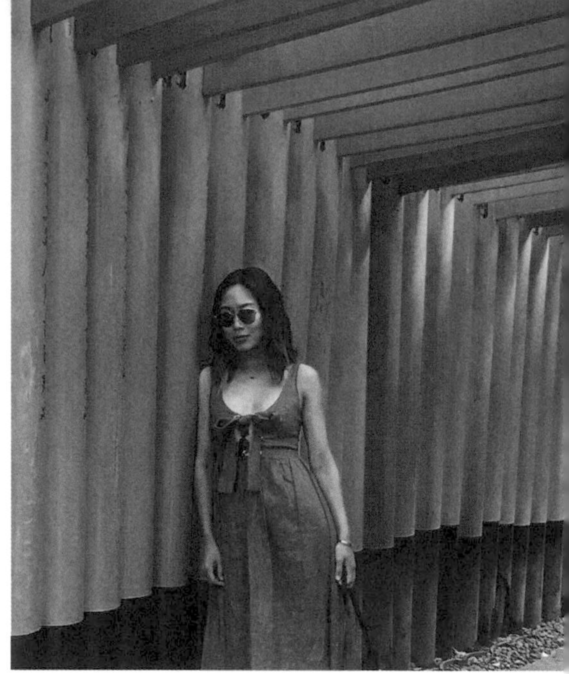

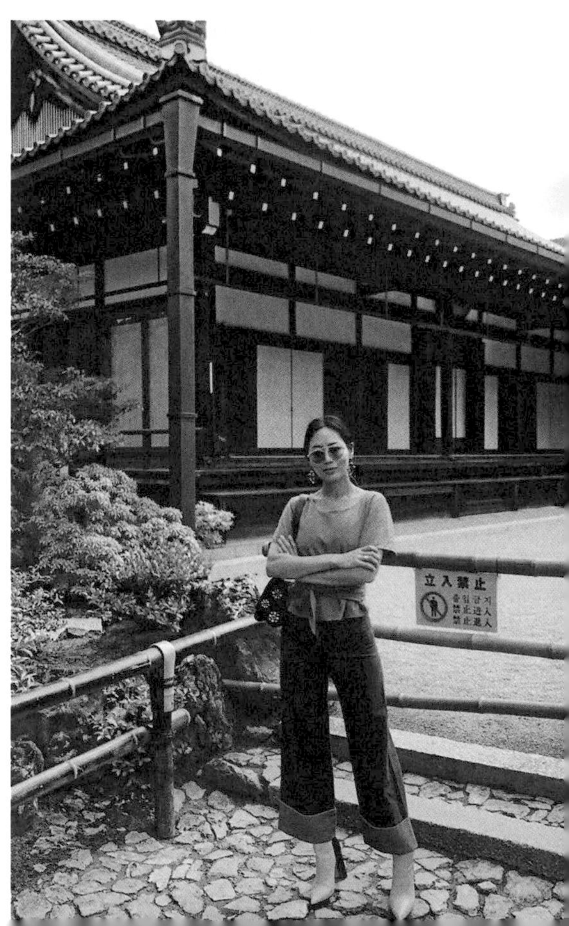
立入禁止
출입금지
禁止进入
禁止進入

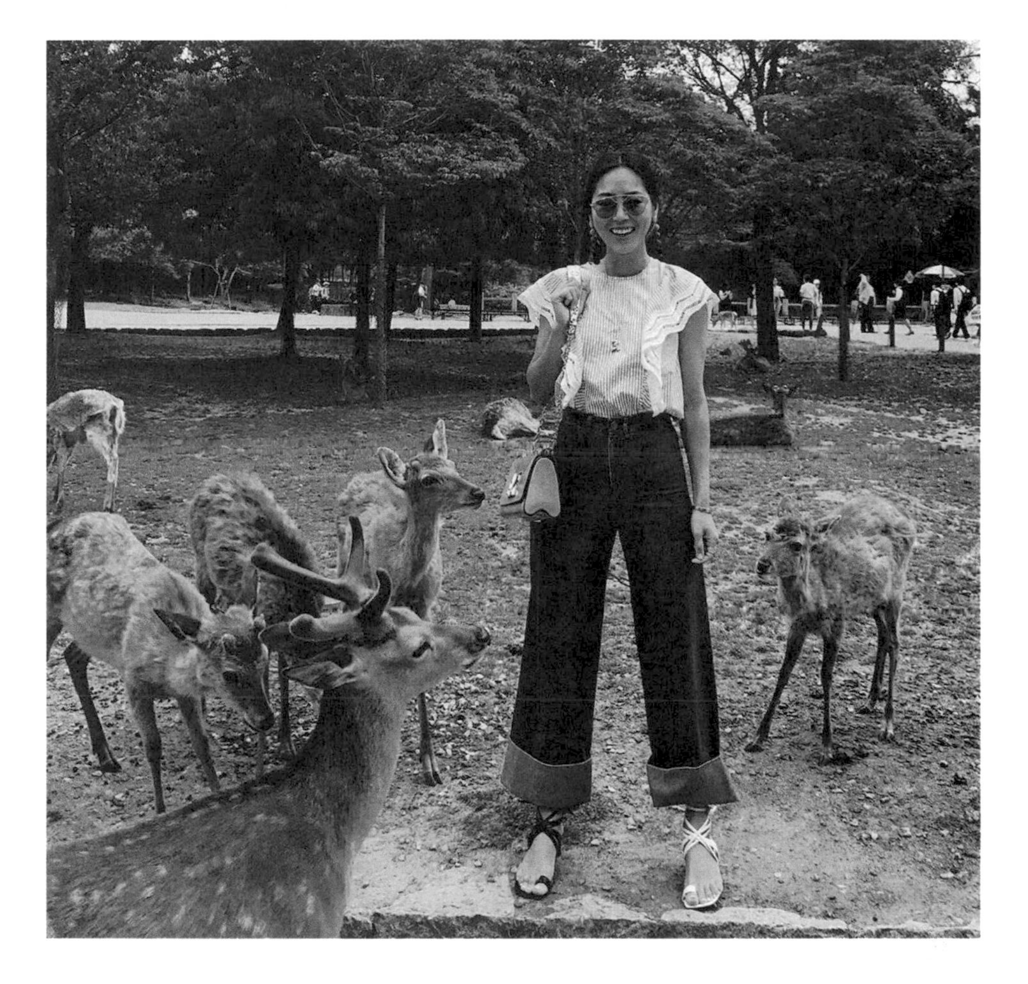

ABOVE In Nara, which is an hour away from Kyoto and features temples dating back to the eighth century. We spent a half day at Nara Park, which is a local park that was founded in the 1300s that has very friendly deer roaming freely. We bought treats to feed them, and I accidentally got head-butted by a hangry buck. Can you say #spiritanimal? *Sea pants and top; Céline shoes; Louis Vuitton bag.* **OPPOSITE, TOP ROW** I visited the Fushimi Inari shrine and was able to submit a prayer courtesy of some friendly Japanese high school students who offered me help. My blue Mara Hoffman dress stood out against the bright orange structure. **OPPOSITE, BOTTOM RIGHT** Kyoto is full of temples, and this one—the Kinkaku-ji temple—was gold. I didn't realize we'd be walking so much, so I was wearing high-heeled Louis Vuitton boots. My gorgeous-but-impractical footwear choice cut our visit short, sadly. *Sea top and bottom; Louis Vuitton bag and shoes.* **OPPOSITE, BOTTOM LEFT** Decked out in Louis Vuitton on my first night in Kyoto. I wore this to the welcome dinner.

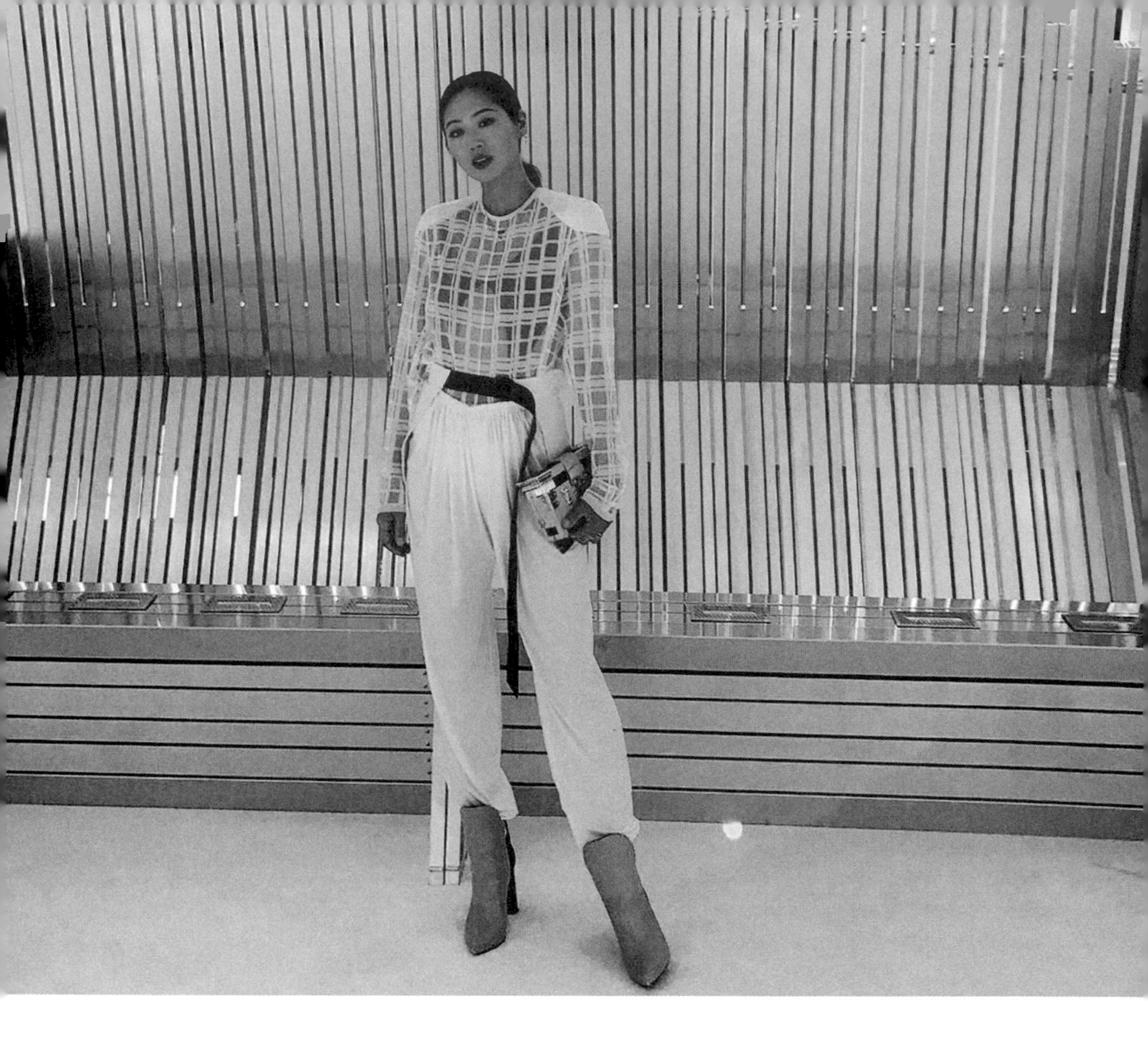

ABOVE The Louis Vuitton cruise show, which was held at the architecturally significant Miho Museum an hour outside of town and done in collaboration with contemporary Japanese designer Kansai Yamamoto. The production was insane and the collection was incredibly beautiful, and I couldn't believe I was actually getting the chance to watch this happen from atop a mountain in Japan. My outfit was from Louis Vuitton's previous season, and because the show was in a location outside of Paris, I wasn't able to get fitted beforehand for the show, as I usually do when I attend big fashion shows on behalf of a designer. These were the LV pieces that I absolutely loved and wanted to wear, and I felt strong and bold but sexy and feminine at the same time. **OPPOSITE** After the Louis Vuitton show, Jacopo and I had some free time to hang. This is Kiyomizu-dera Temple, one of the many temples we visited, which we saw before going to Nishiki Market for sticker photos and cool food. We loved the market so much that we went back a second time. *Janessa Leoné hat.*

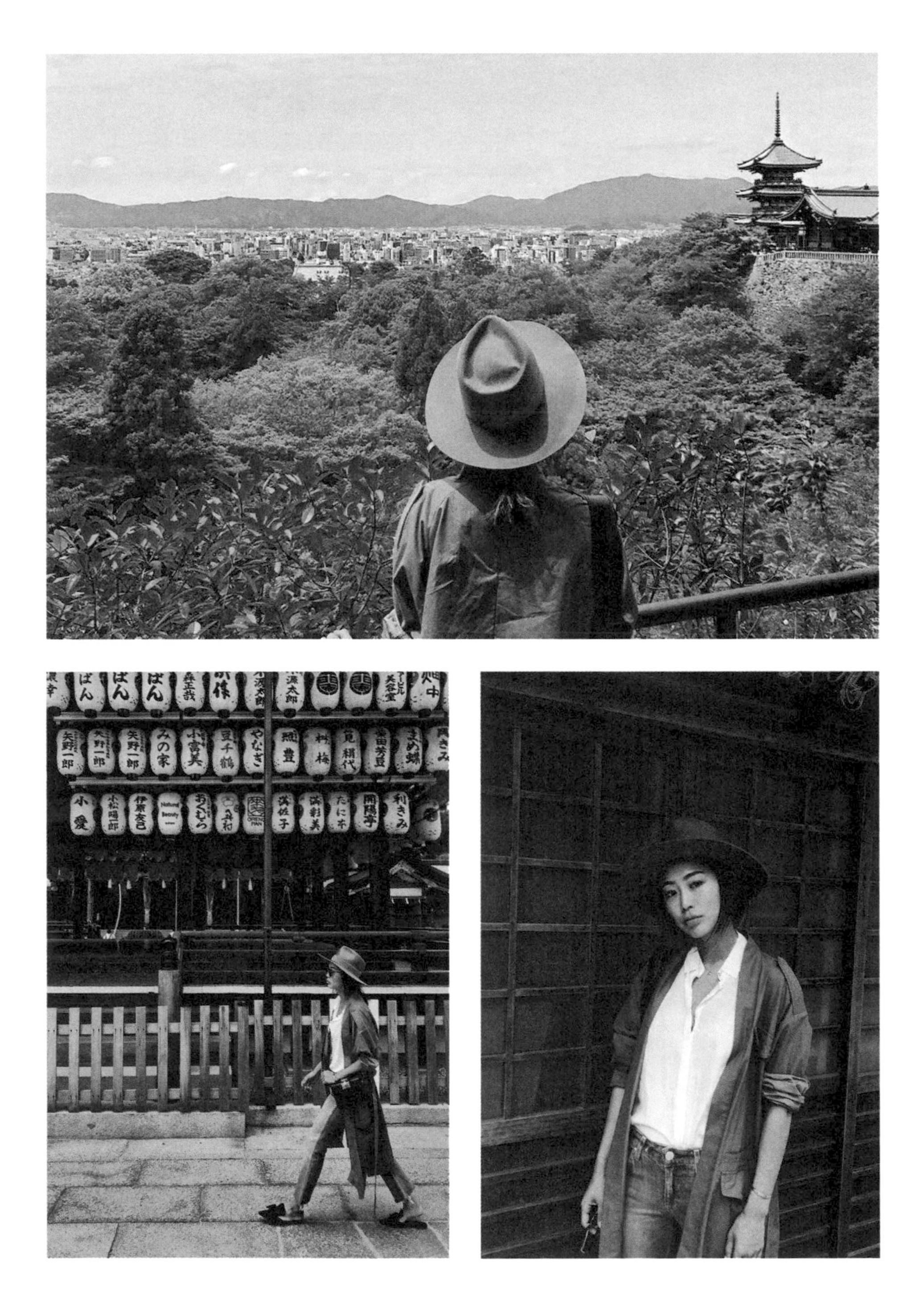
ばん
ばん
ばん
源太郎
美容室
矢野一郎
矢野一郎
矢野一郎
みの家
小富美
豆千鶴
やなぎ
小愛
小松陽一郎
伊原友己
Natural
Beauty
満佐子
たに本
利きみ

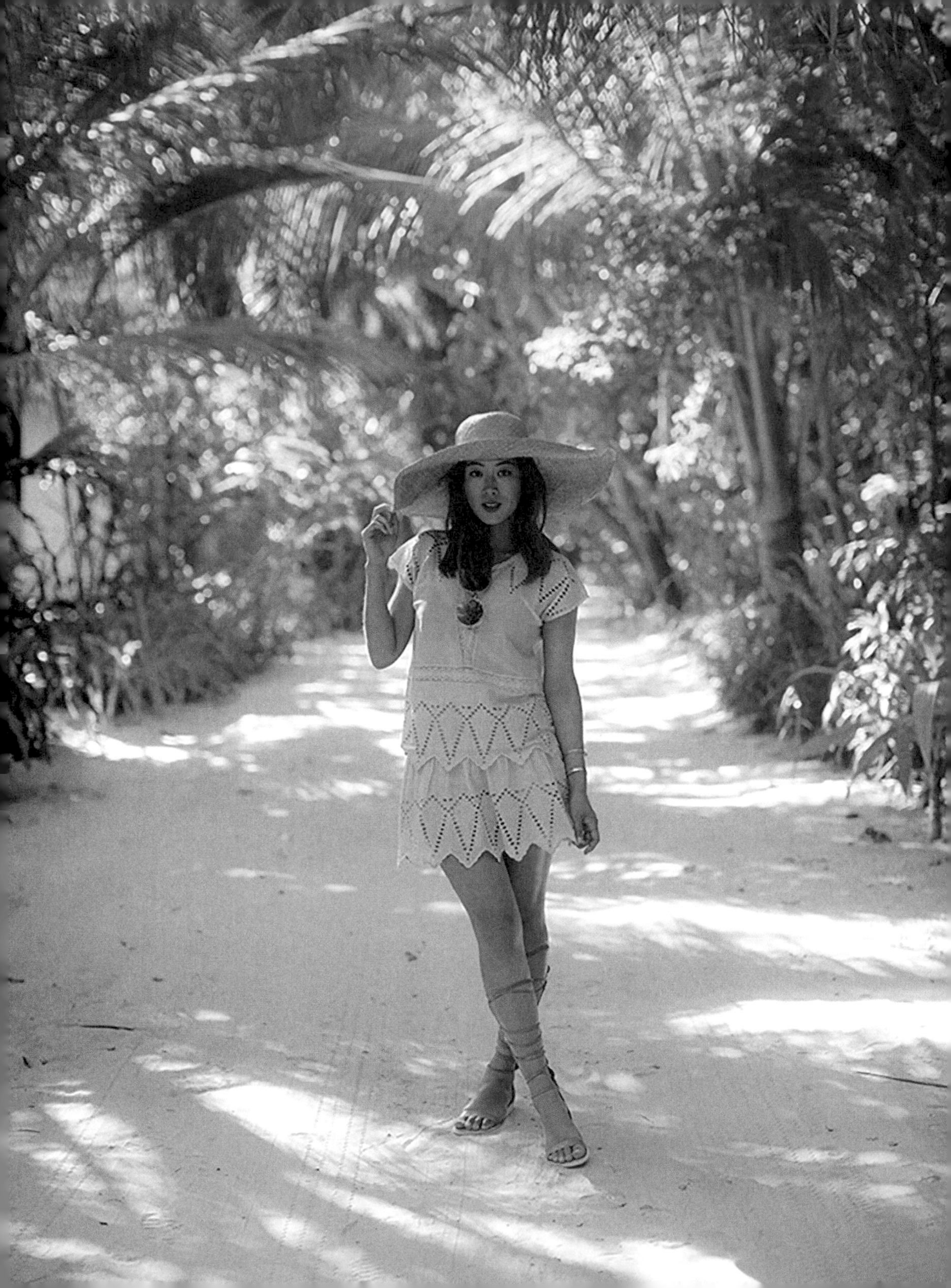

THE PHILIPPINES

There's really no one I'd rather travel with than Dani, even though we have crazy intense fights when we travel: We stop talking to each other, text our parents to complain, get food, and make up. The older we get, the better we are at fighting fair. We bicker over meaningless things such as someone moving the other one's makeup brush, but I'm mindful to use less hurtful words. That kind of fighting is exactly what happened in 2015, when Dani and I went to Manila and Palawan together before continuing on to Japan. It was epic.

The second time I visited the Philippines was in 2016, when I was with Jacopo shooting a campaign for SM Supermalls, a huge mall chain that tapped Carrie Bradshaw herself—Sarah Jessica Parker—as its face right before me (dying!). It was a huge deal for me and I was so excited to be there, despite it being a really intense trip filled with shoot days, press days, and super hot, humid weather. There was very little down time until the very end, when Jacopo and I got roughly forty-eight hours on a beach in Cebu, where all we did was eat dried mangoes and bliss out.

OPPOSITE Dani took this photo of me in my favorite hotel hat and an Ulla Johnson dress, right after I discovered her brand. Now, I rarely pack a bag for a warm-weather destination without some of her pieces inside.

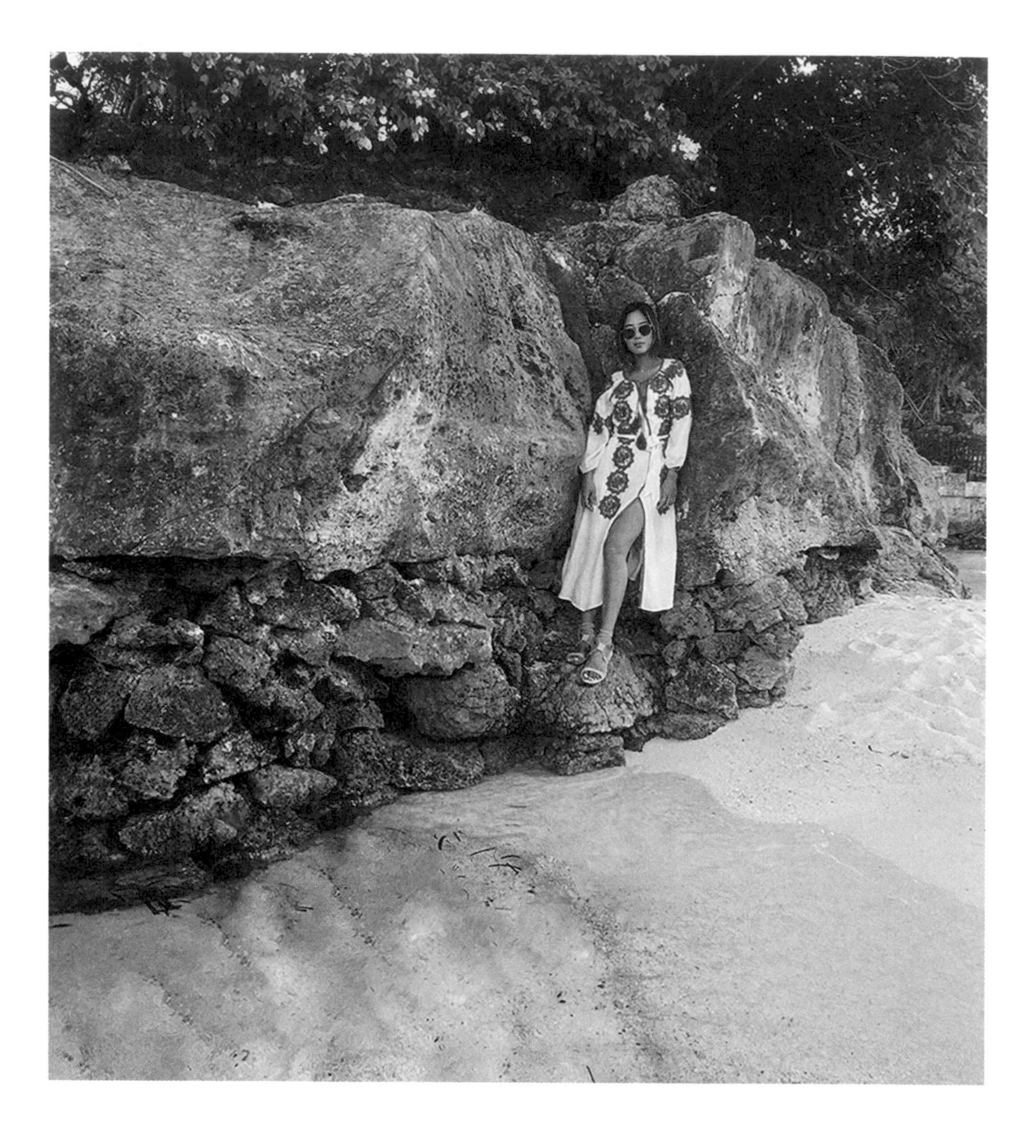

ABOVE *Line and Dot dress.* **OPPOSITE (CLOCKWISE FROM TOP LEFT)** Cebu with Jacopo, unwinding. There was a random inflatable flamingo right by the beach, so thinking it belonged to our hotel I grabbed it. Not so much—turns out I stole someone's flamingo. My bad. • Gorgeous blue water. • Our second—and last—free day in Cebu. Thankfully we stayed on the beach and had enough time to swim and lay out before heading out. *Marysia Swim swimsuit* • I remember walking into this property and feeling super cold—which is not something that happens in Manila. After we left, we were told that it's actually haunted. Cool. *Line and Dot dress; Gucci bag.*

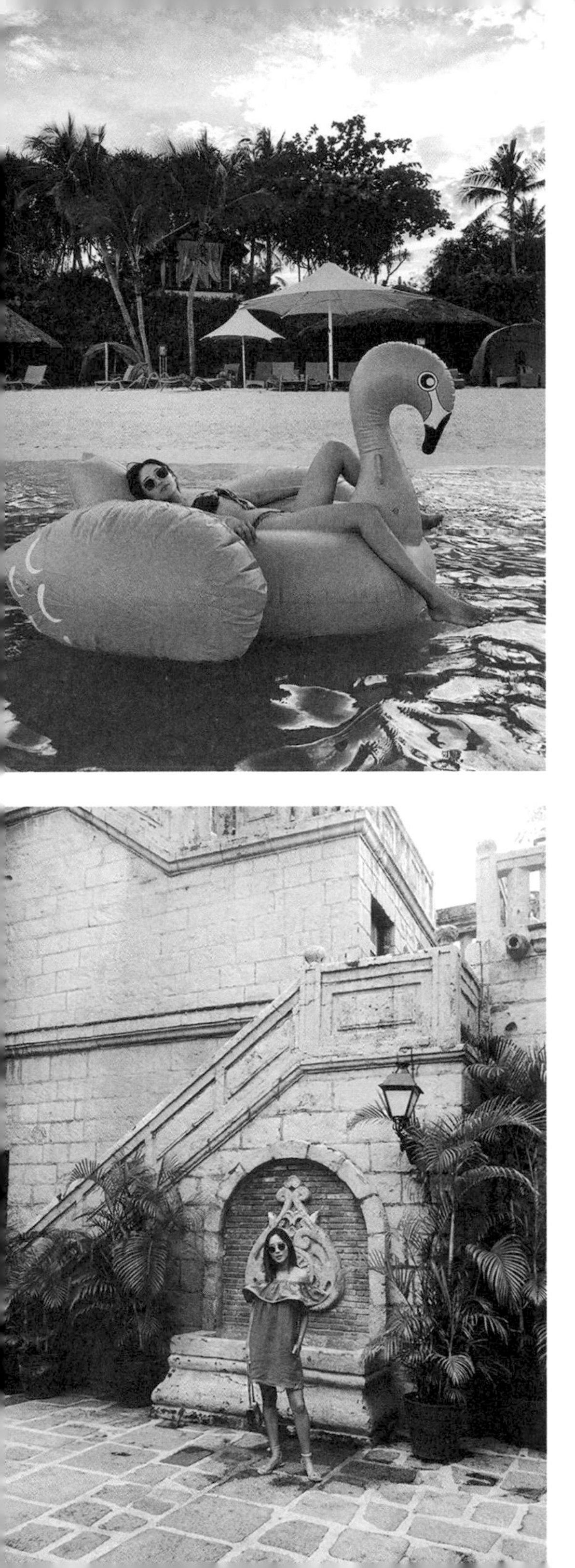

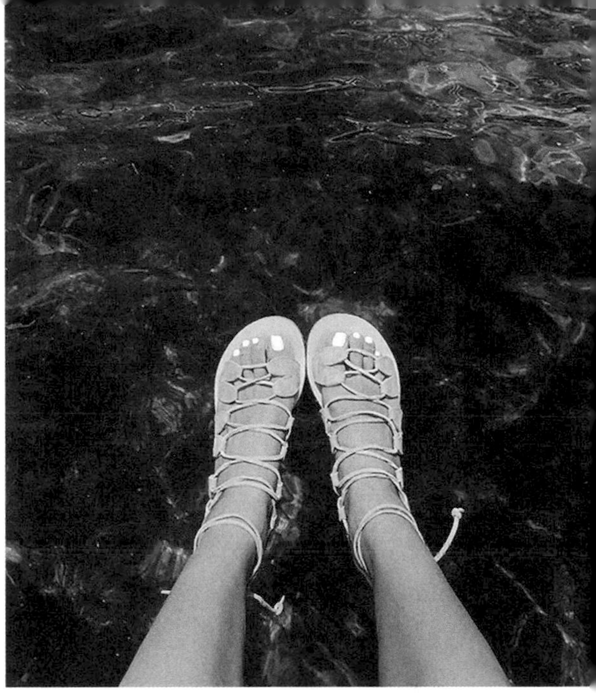

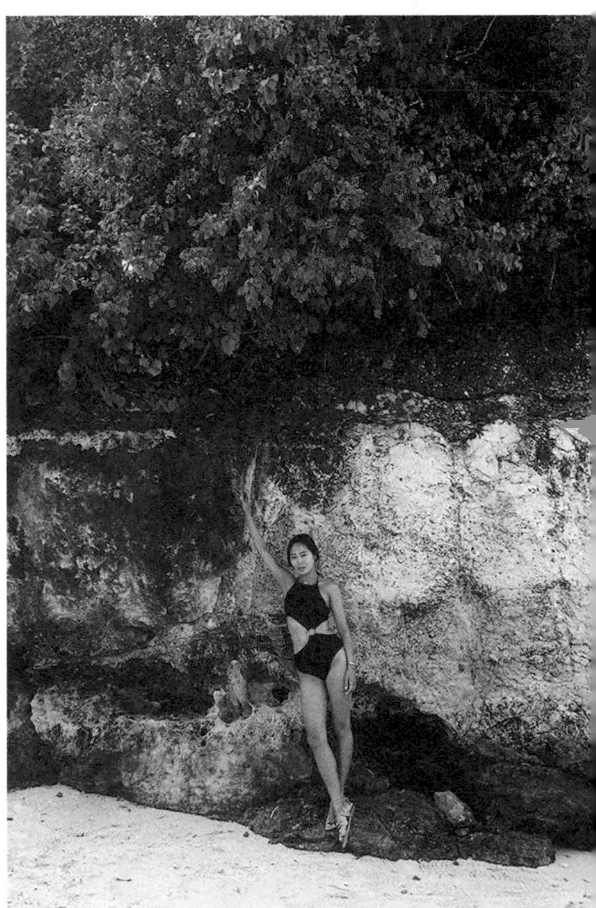

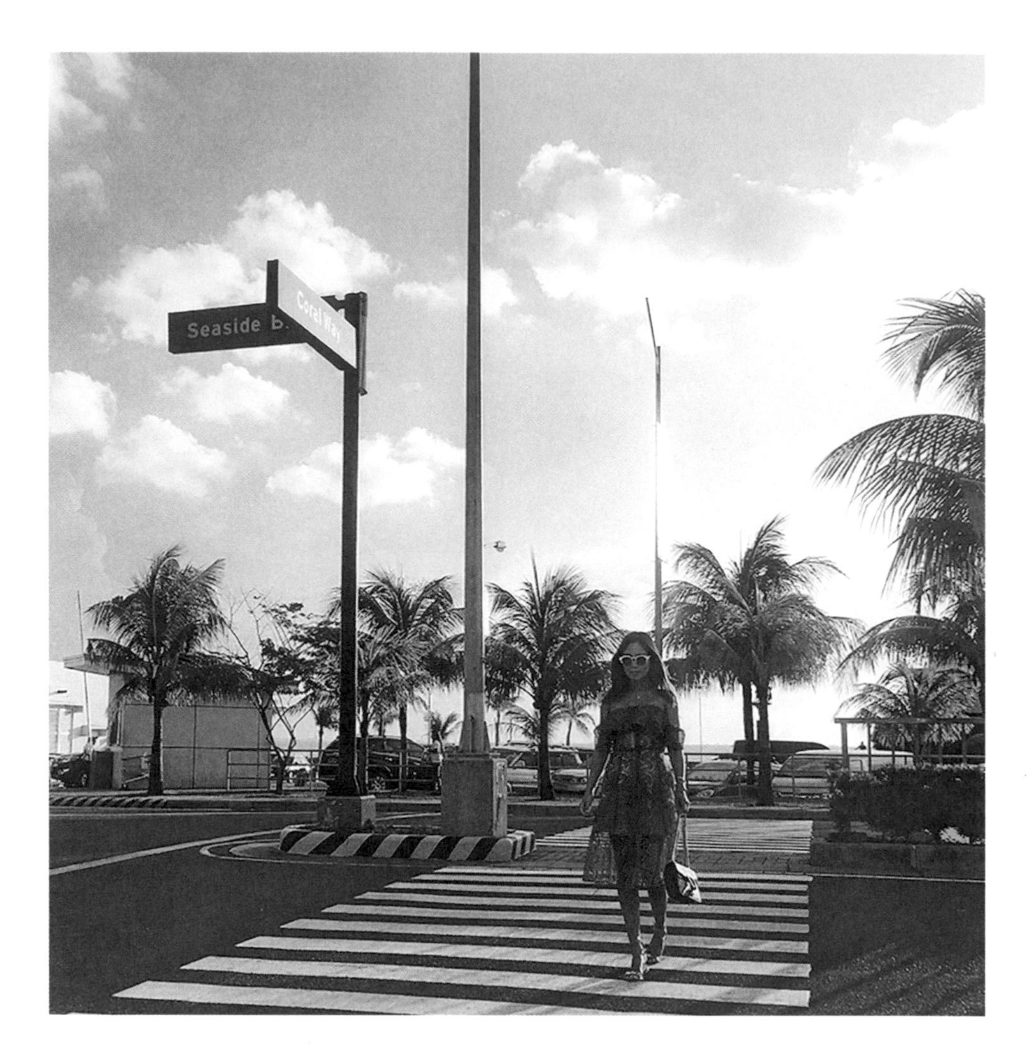

ABOVE At the beginning of the trip, before shooting the commercial. I met all the mall executives, got my schedule, and toured three different SM malls to prep. I was so busy that it was hard to find time for photos, so this is at the end of my workday in front of our hotel. I chose this dress because I needed something that looked nice enough to meet the president of SM, but was still young, comfortable, and "me." *Line and Dot dress; Cornetti sandals; Self-Portrait x Le Specs sunglasses.* **OPPOSITE** In Manila right after I was done shooting my SM commercial. It was super humid and hot there, and—like L.A.—no one walks. But I wanted to walk back to the hotel and explore. By the time I got to the hotel I was drenched in sweat. My hair looks perfect here because I happened to have a helmet of hairspray from the commercial to keep things down. *Topshop sandals.*

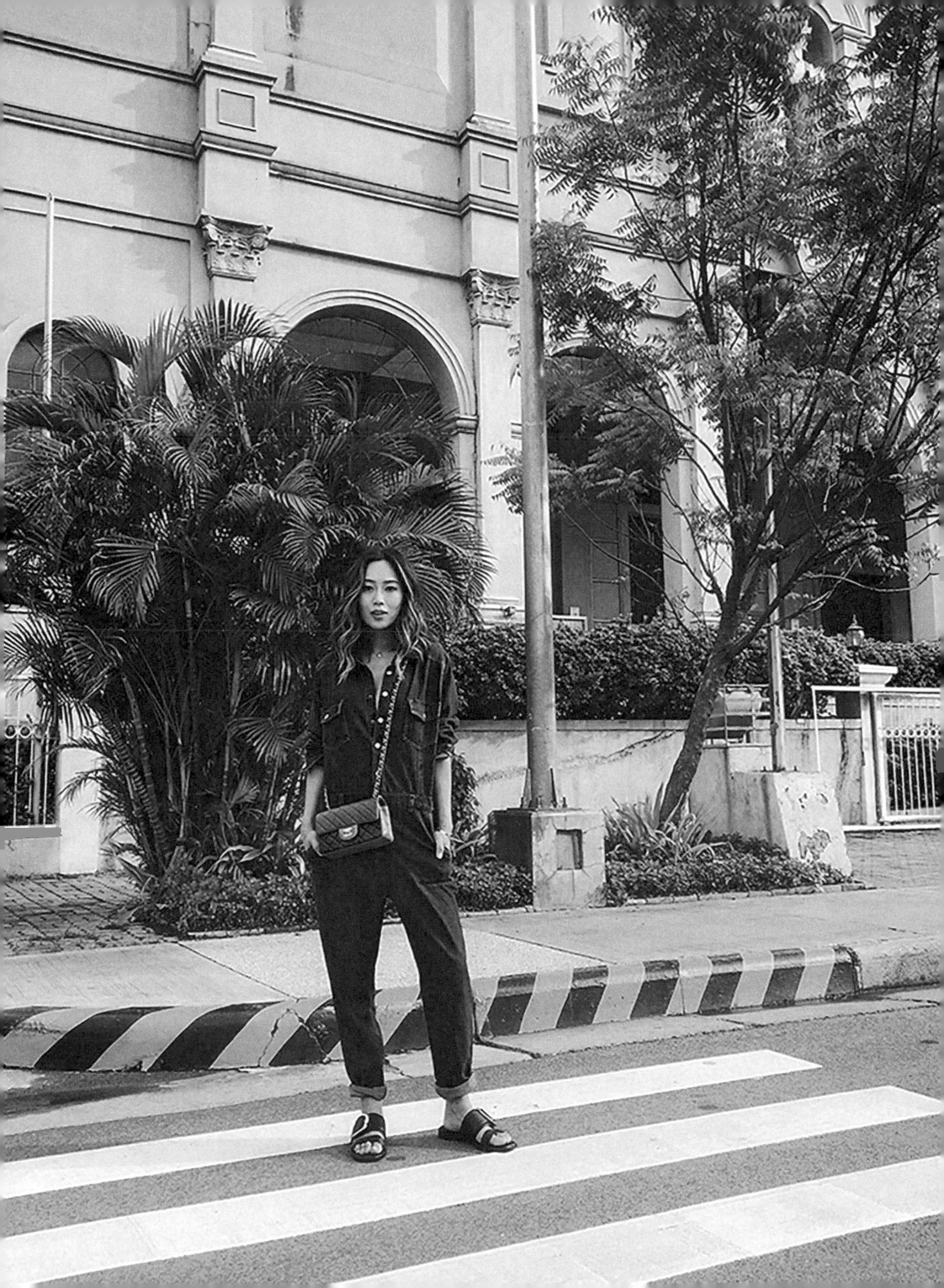

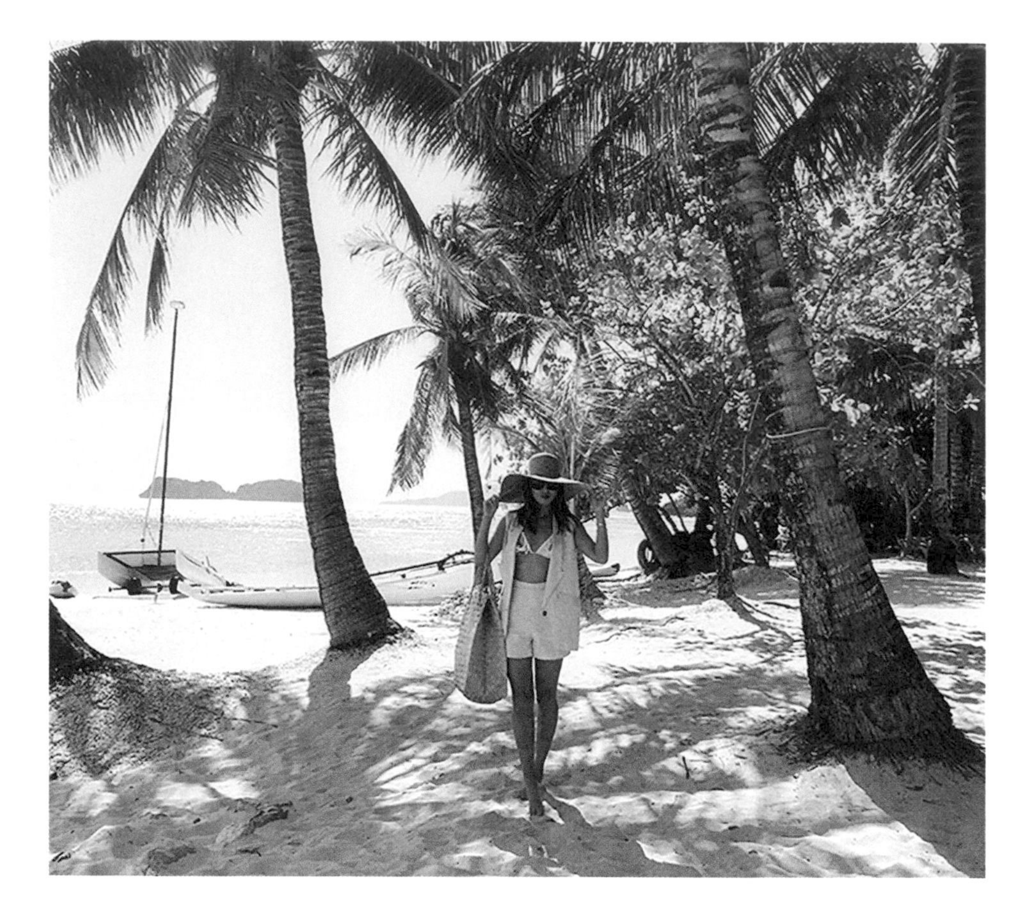

ABOVE My 2015 trip to Palawan at a resort called El Nido. Palawan is one of the most beautiful islands I've ever been to—the water is literally translucent light blue. Dani and I went snorkeling, ate amazing (and inexpensive!) food, and generally had such a good time. We stayed for three days and I'd do it again with my sister in a heartbeat. The hat and bag in this shot were in the hotel room, so I snagged them and used them the whole time. **OPPOSITE (CLOCKWISE FROM TOP LEFT)** *Mara Hoffman swimsuit* • Every day I drank at least two or three coconut waters. Every time I go to Asia, my skin is amazing when I come home (humidity plus coconut water is a tried-and-true beauty secret), and I'm always more plump from eating too much (happy plump but plump none the less). *Ulla Johnson dress* • Snorkeling at El Nido. A friend that I met during fashion week years ago, Ingrid Chua, was at the resort at the same time as us, and we went snorkeling together. She took this photo with her GoPro. She meant to take photos of the coral and I happened to be in the frame (the big fish she got was me). • In 2015 this type of beach flat lay wasn't done ad nauseam quite yet. The coconut was so fresh, the sand was so fine, and I really was having the time of my life.

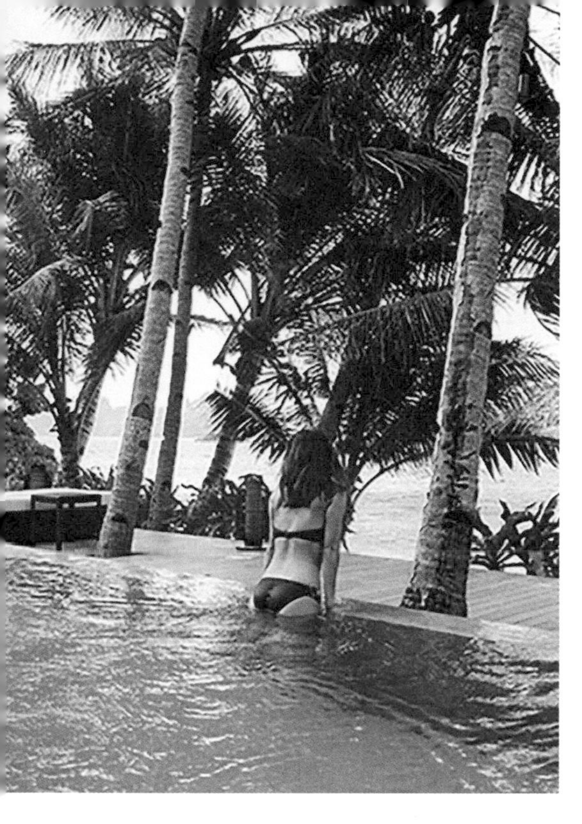
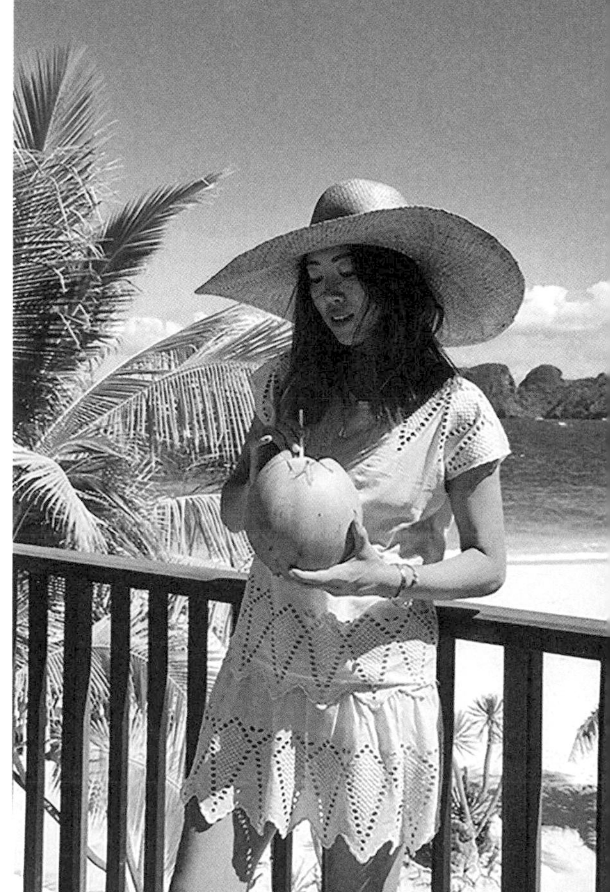
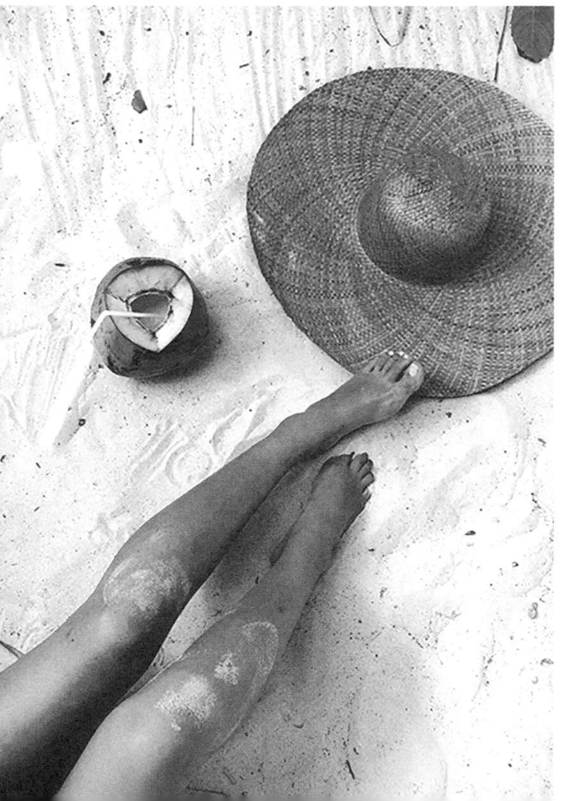
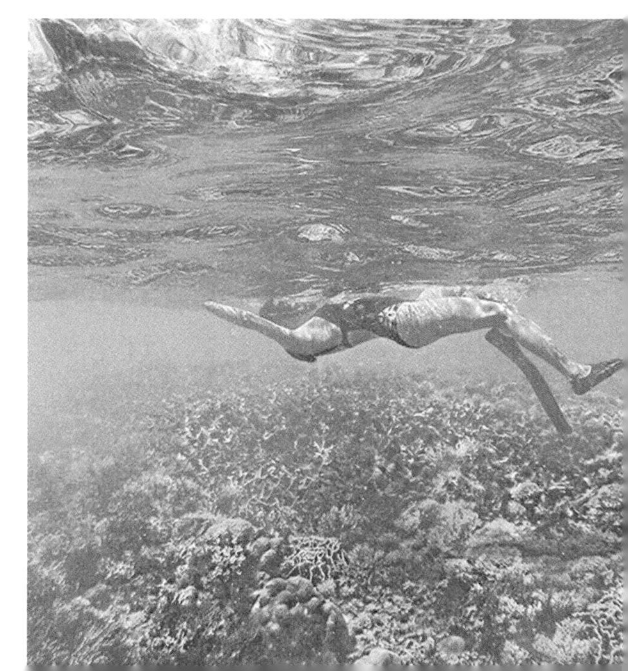

PHUKET

Phuket Province, Thailand, was my first trip of 2018 and one of Revolve's #RevolveAroundtheWorld getaways. Jacopo had to work over the holidays so we didn't get to spend New Year's Eve together—a con of being in a long-distance relationship is, well, the distance. But the upside is that we get to meet up in really fun places that we can explore together, such as Phuket. We stayed for almost a week with all of my Revolve friends—Raissa, Camila, Jules, Sara, and the rest of the team—all of whom I've become close to. I picked out pieces from Revolve so packing was super simple, and I ended up changing my ticket home ($150—big airline score) so I could stop in South Korea to see my ninety-year-old grandma.

On that trip, I found myself feeling really insecure and self-conscious around all of my beautiful friends—you can't help but compare yourself, even when you try really hard not to. I wasn't feeling my healthiest (I know how good I feel both mentally and physically when I'm eating really nutritious food and moving my body—two things that I hadn't been doing in this case). I gain more confidence with each Revolve trip I take, but I never feel like the fittest or the prettiest—something I know I'm not alone in feeling. Dani always says, "But you're the funniest!," which is such a wonderfully kind compliment to get from her. It is hard sometimes (we all see ourselves so differently than other people do, don't we?). By the end I got my confidence back and didn't care and ate extra pad thai and had all of the fun.

I couldn't think of a better way to start a new year.

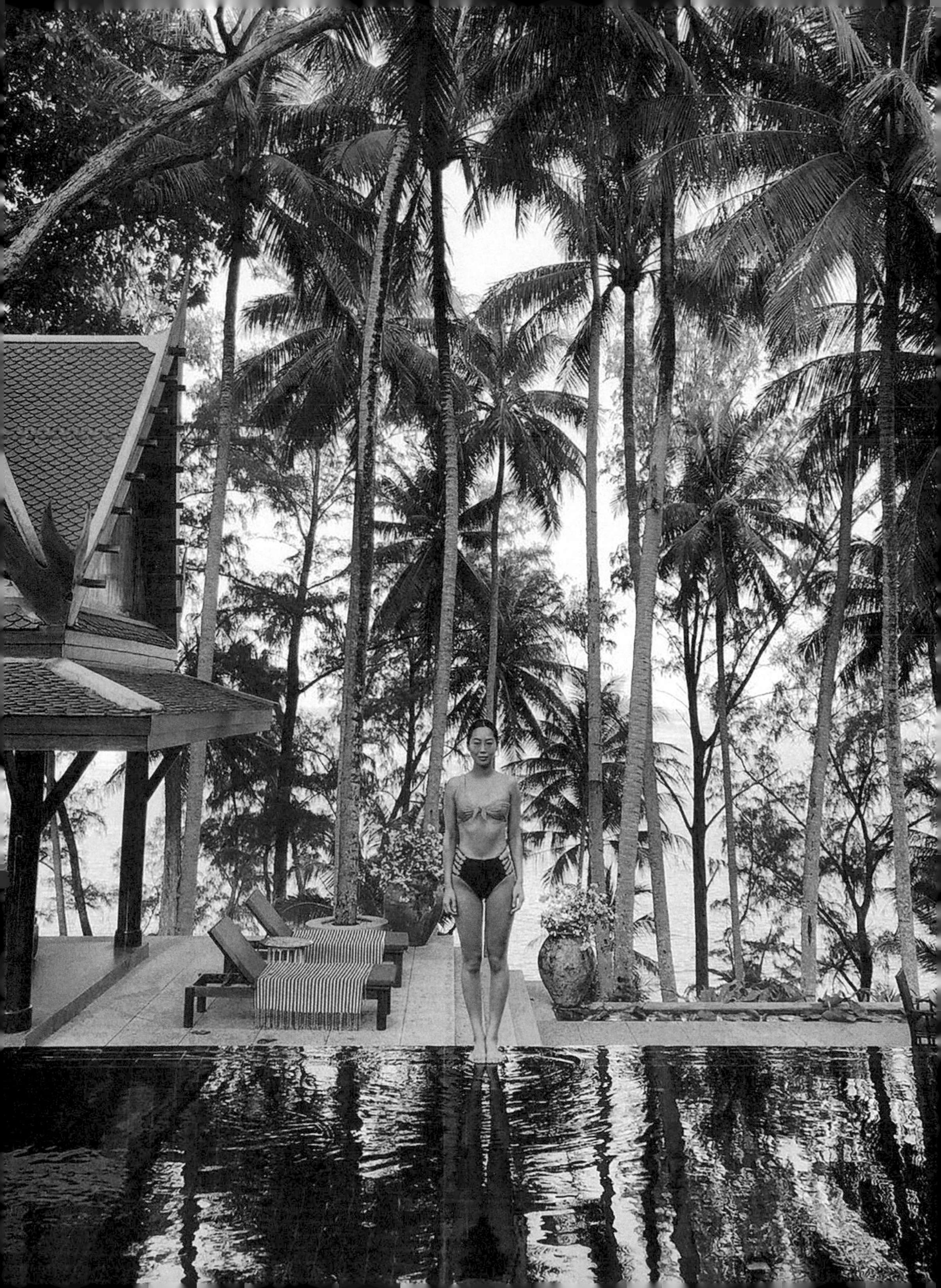

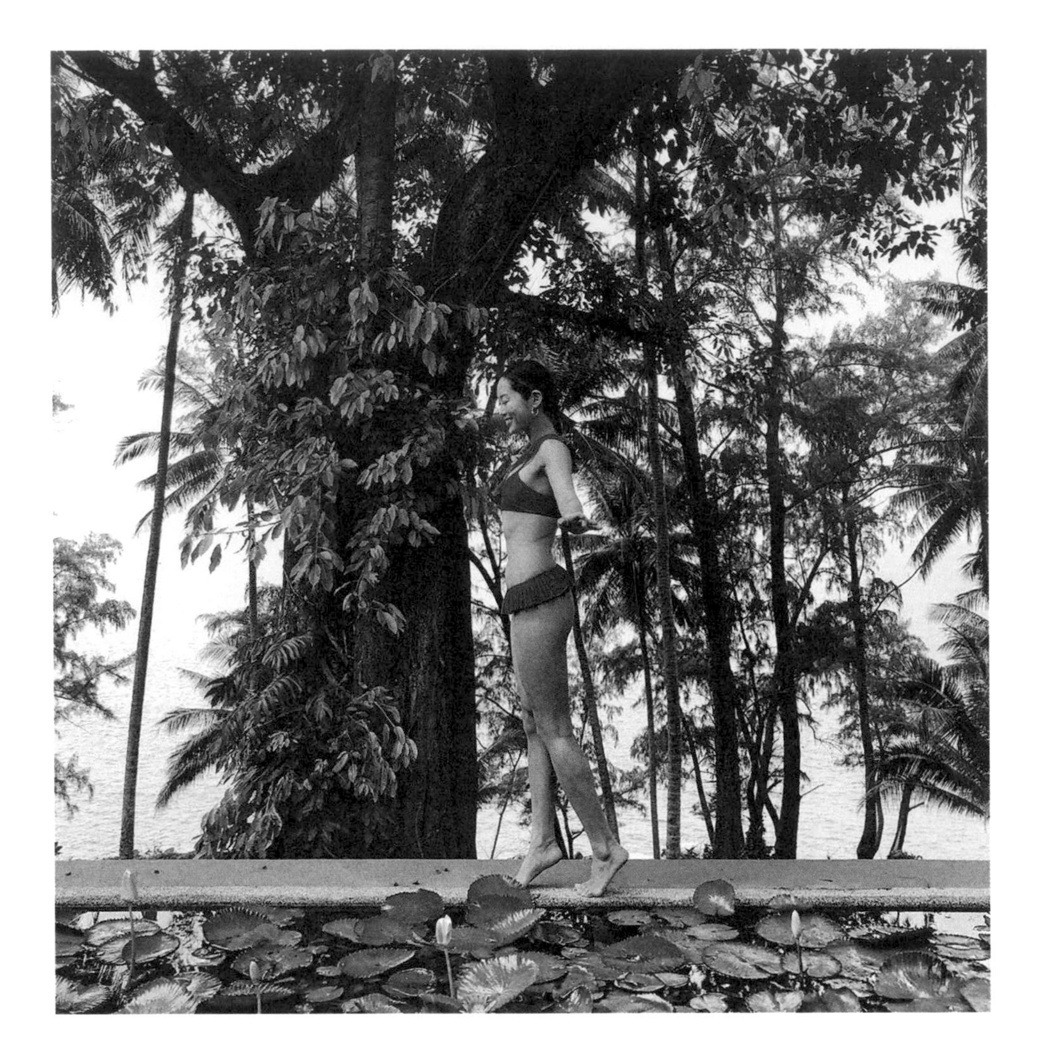

ABOVE One of the first days in Phuket. I also wore this out and about with a denim skirt because the ruffles on the bikini top make it look like a real top. *Lovers and Friends swimsuit.* **OPPOSITE (CLOCKWISE FROM TOP)** These sunglasses were $15 at the Phuket night market, and I later found out I could have negotiated down to $5. I love them and still have them. *Zimmermann swimsuit from FWRD* • We stayed at a resort called Amanpuri, which is truly one of the most gorgeous places I've ever been lucky enough to visit. Everything was on demand, including a Cali girl–perfect avocado-infused green juice (they made the best juice). I'm the happiest girl in the world with my juice, especially when it's bomb. • I packed a blouse in case I needed one for nice dinners, but I ended up wearing it during the day and dressing it down with shorts instead. *Self-Portrait blouse; Grlfrnd denim shorts.*

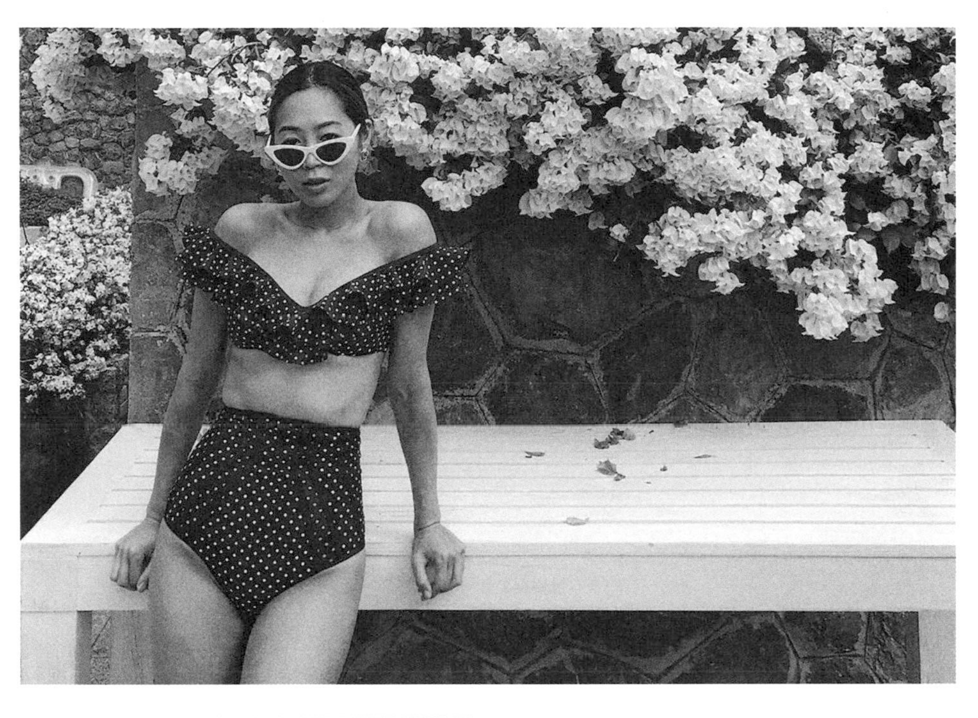

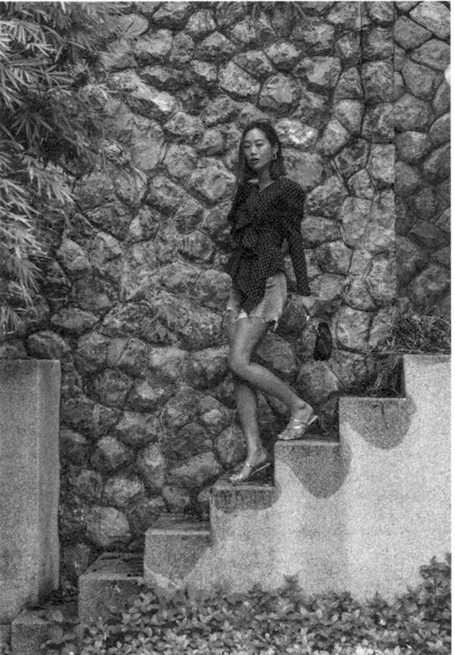

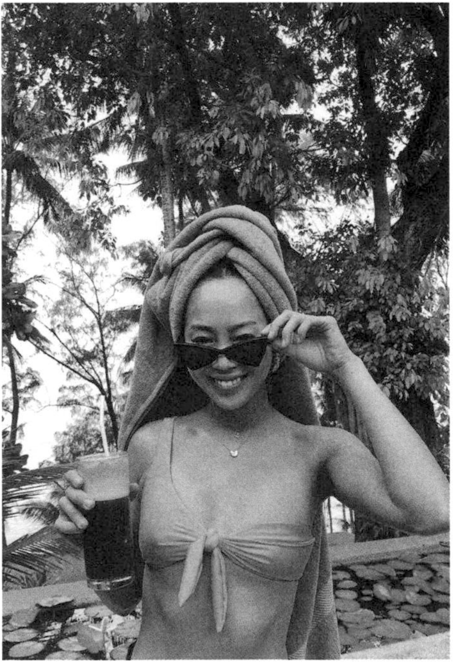

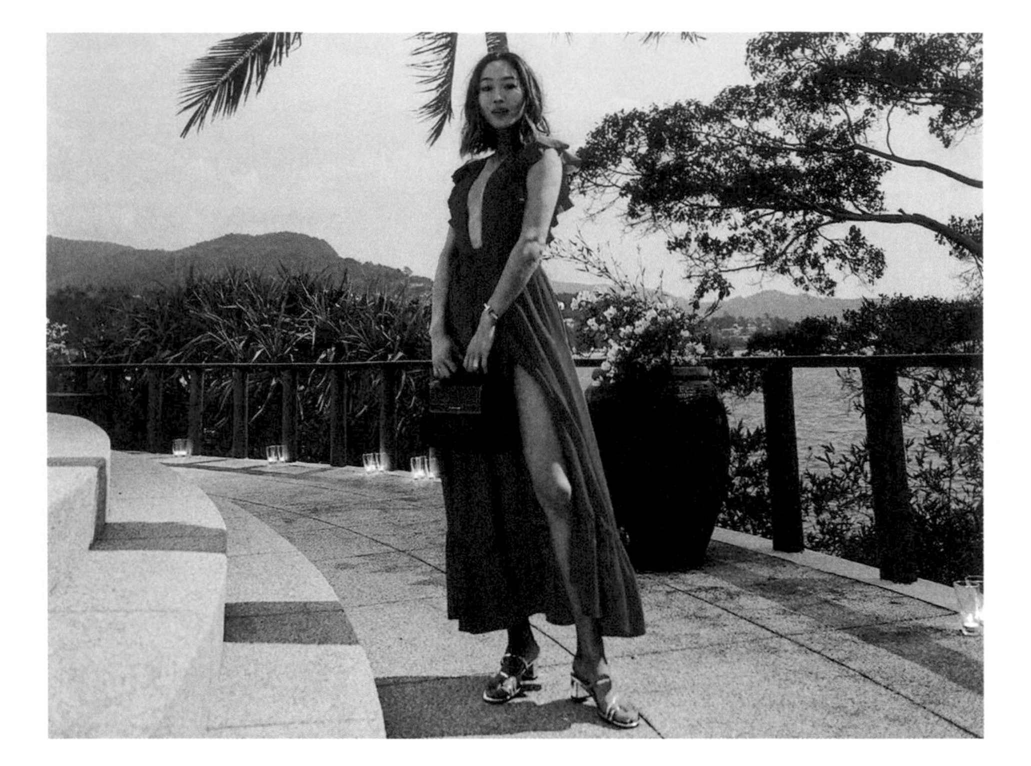

ABOVE The first night at the hotel, where we had dinner. My friend Rachel has a line called Majorelle, and I'm obsessed with her flowy, romantic dresses. This is also the night Jacopo was flying in from New York, and I really wanted to wear something that made me feel amazing. *Majorelle dress; Raye shoes.* **OPPOSITE, TOP ROW** The Phuket Elephant Sanctuary is an ethical elephant rescue that takes in and cares for older, overworked elephants. We spent the day there and learned about how the organization runs, and how typically if a sanctuary allows you to ride or interact with the animals, it isn't actually properly caring for the animals. It was so important for me to go here, especially after my India trip during which I rode elephants and later learned just how bad for the animals that is. The elephants were so amazing—and I have to think they took a liking to me for me, and not because I had a banana in my bag. *Lovers and Friends bustier and pants.* **OPPOSITE, BOTTOM RIGHT** After visiting the night market, I experienced one of the best Thai meals I think I've ever had in my life. I wanted to wear something appropriate for a long walk but still fun and dressy. Mission accomplished, no? *NBD body suit and pants.* **OPPOSITE, BOTTOM LEFT** Our group boat day. I brought extra outfits and wanted to shoot a few different looks. Jen Atkin (yes, THE Jen Atkin) did my hair. I had so many inspiring talks with so many people on this trip—especially Jen. She talked about her badass businesses and how she creates balance in her life. It was a gloomy-weather day, but it was one of my favorite days because I had such incredible, meaningful conversation with a woman I truly admire. *Nicholas dress.*

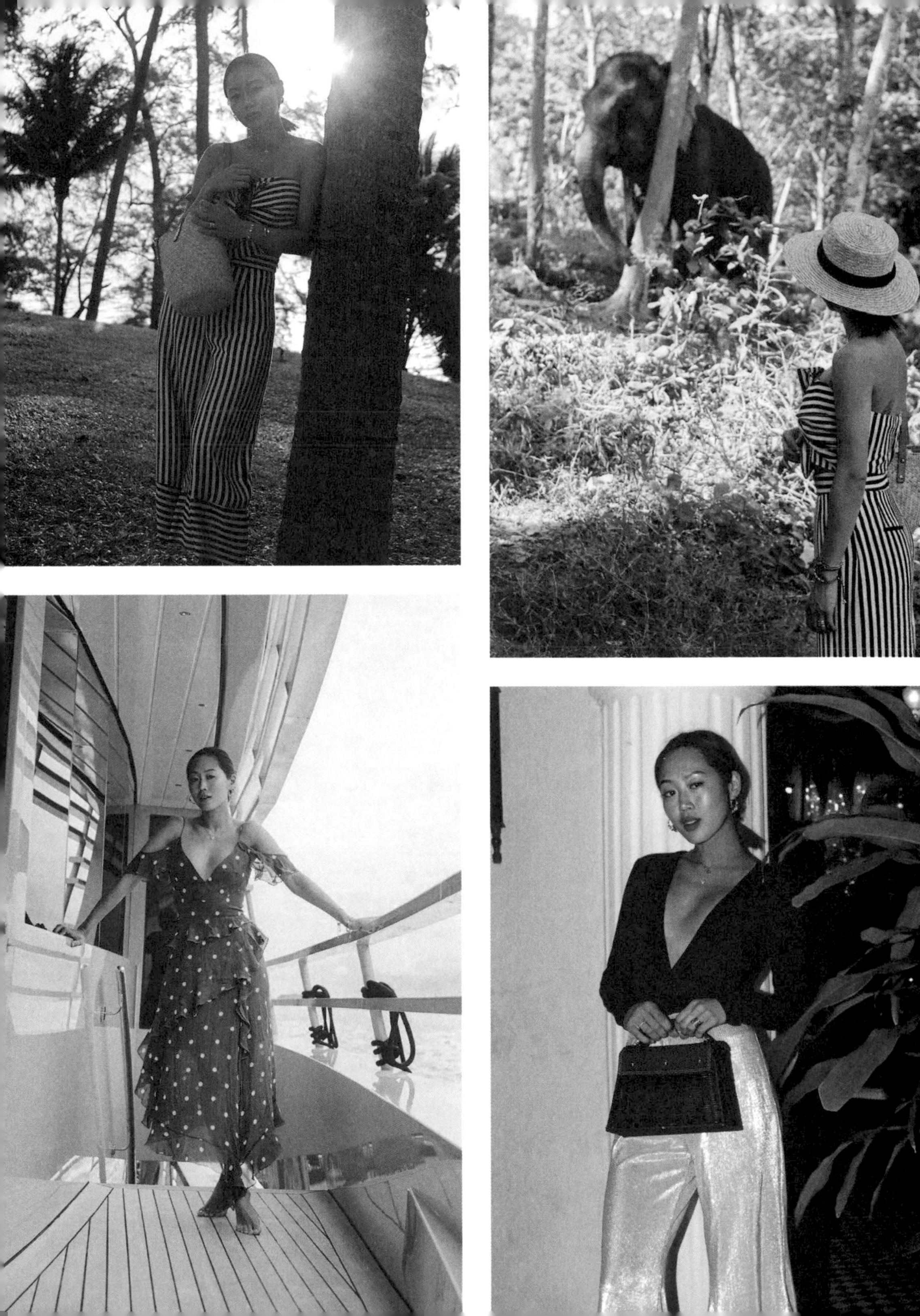

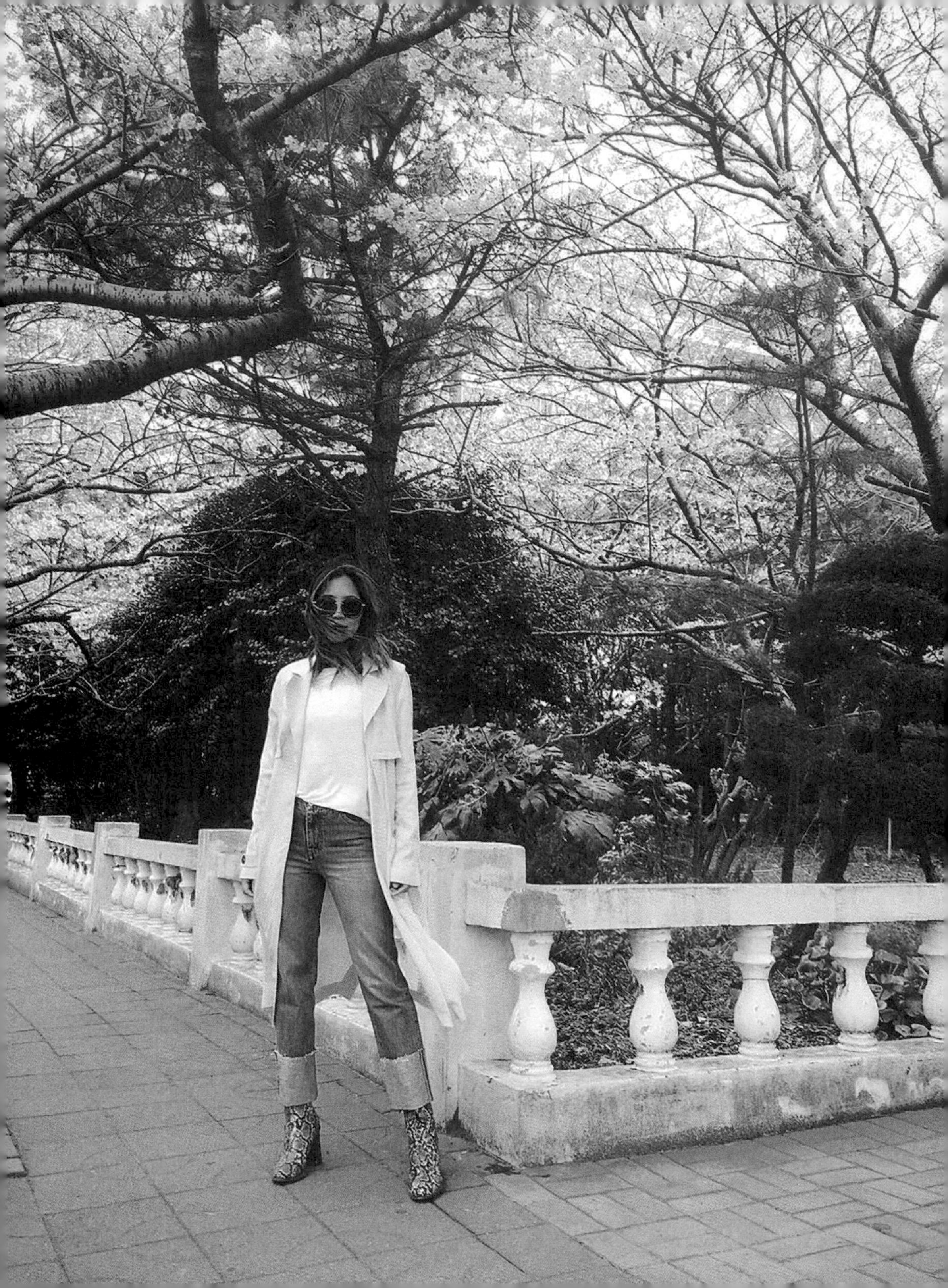

SEOUL & BUSAN

Weirdly, I barely spent any time in Seoul until I became a blogger—even though my parents are South Korean immigrants and my ninety-year-old grandma lives a short distance away in Busan. I'm obsessed with Korea and think it's so cool that I've been able to visit so many times for work; it's one of my favorite places to go, and I never miss up an opportunity to see my grandma. I could be away for as little as six months, and everything will feel different the next time I go back: the culture, trends, technology—all of it. I never feel like I have a full grasp of the city, and I have yet to find myself bored in Seoul.

Busan is only an hour flight, but I prefer the three-hour trip on the KTX bullet train. They have snacks—so. many. snacks. (Not to mention free Wi-Fi!) Every half hour or so, someone pushes a drink and snack cart through the aisle to offer boiled eggs (a very typically Korean thing to eat), dehydrated sweet potato sticks (at least two bags for me, please), regular potato sticks, and—the pièce de résistance—*kimbap*, which are Korean-style veggie, seaweed, and rice rolls. But better than the snacks is who greets me upon arrival in Busan: my grandma.

OPPOSITE In Busan. Jacopo took this photo for me. Some cherry blossom time in front of my grandma's apartment, where I stay every single time I'm there. If I'm ever in Asia—no matter where—I go see my grandma, even if it's only for two days. My grandma is one of the strongest women I've ever known, and she is such a role model for me. Growing up I took her strength, intelligence, and resilience (she raised three kids all by herself) as qualities I hoped to have one day, too. *Two Songs trench coat.*

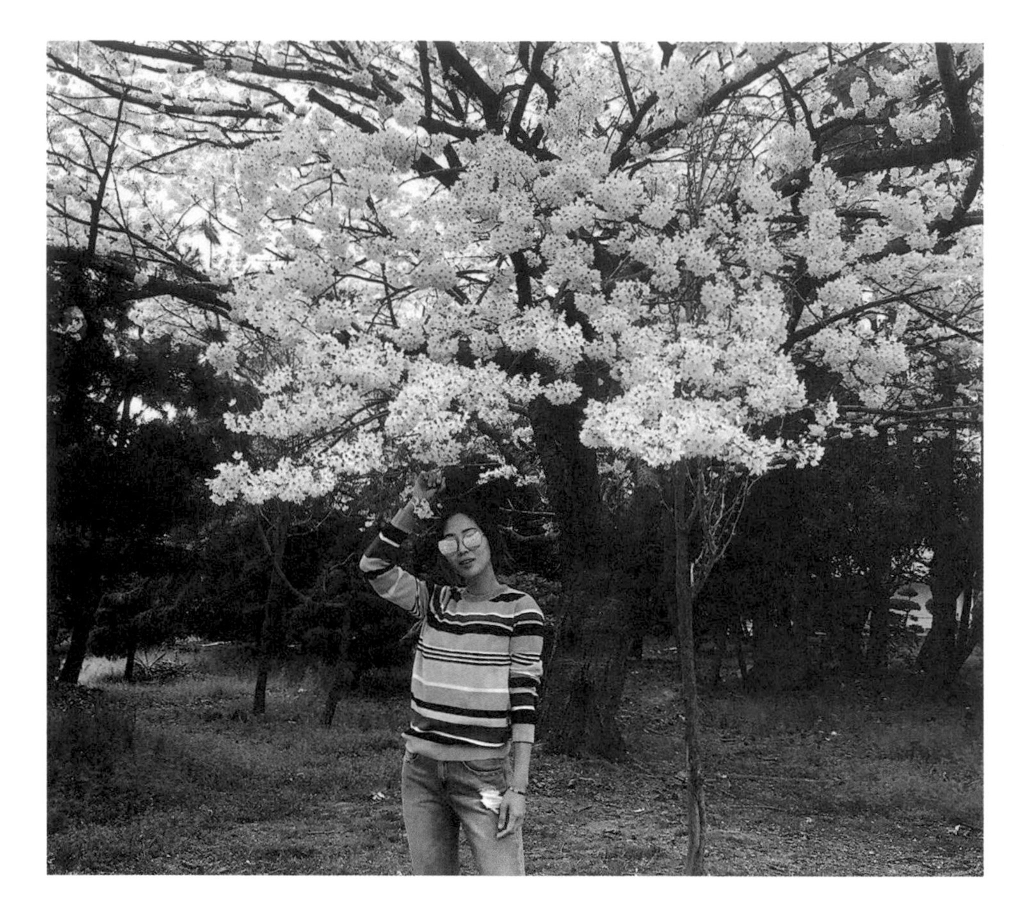

ABOVE I went to Busan by myself in March 2016. Jacopo had already left so I was visiting my grandma solo, and I asked a very kind Korean stranger to snap this photo. Tons of tourists were around taking pictures of the cherry blossoms anyway so it was really easy to find someone to help. And I ended up taking her picture, too. **OPPOSITE (CLOCKWISE FROM TOP LEFT)** The day Dani and I got to Seoul for Louis Vuitton. *Louis Vuitton head to toe* • In 2013 we went to Korea with my friend Chriselle Lim, who is also a blogger, before she had a baby and got married—it was a total girls' trip. We hung out with her grandma in Seoul and afterward I visited my grandma in Busan. This was a very hot summer day, so my hair was natural and straight because of the humidity. *Givenchy bag; Isabel Marant shoes* • One of my first magazine shoots in Korea was with *W Korea* in 2016, and this was the day of the shoot. My hair and makeup were so different from what I normally do—think straighter eyebrows and slicked-back hair. • I finally gave up on my hair. This is the day we hung out with Chriselle's grandma. I'm wearing boyfriend jeans (a staple back then), which I would always taper and pair with high heels. My 2013 go-tos were Giuseppe Zanotti.

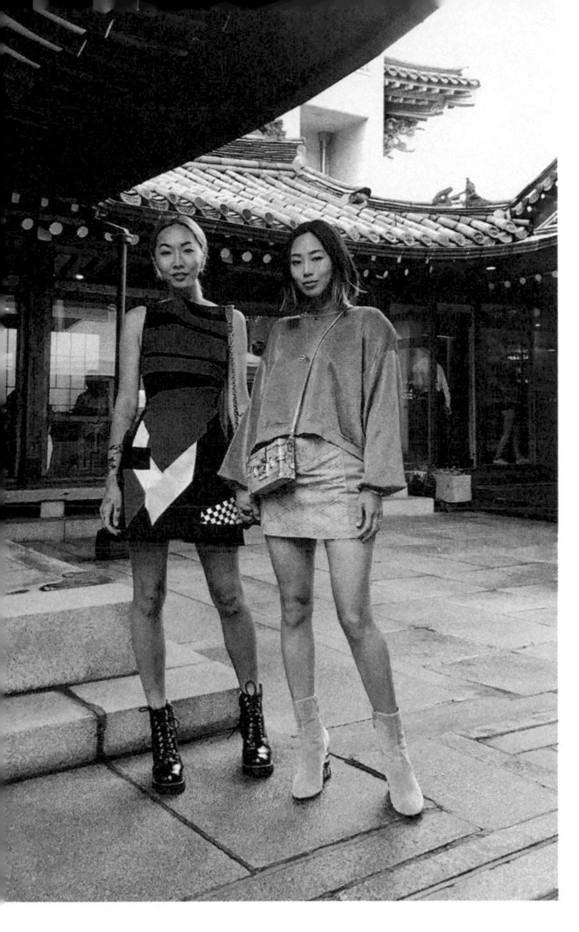

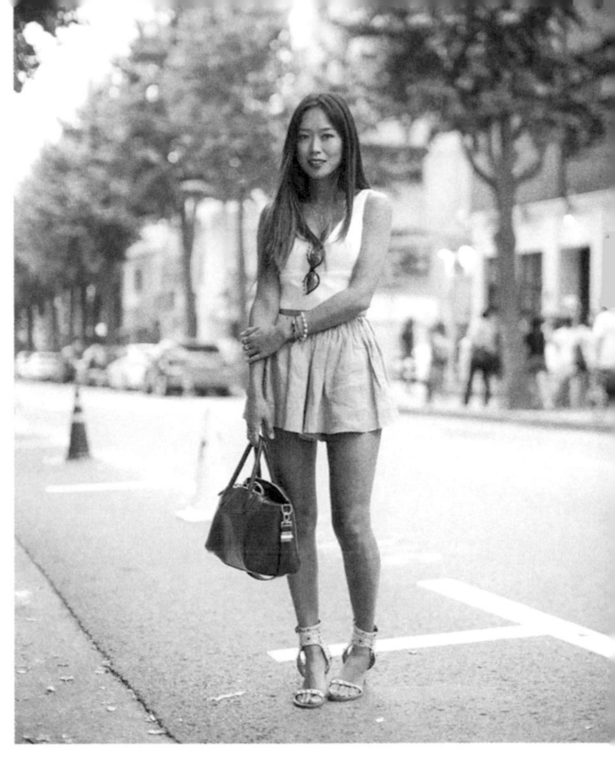

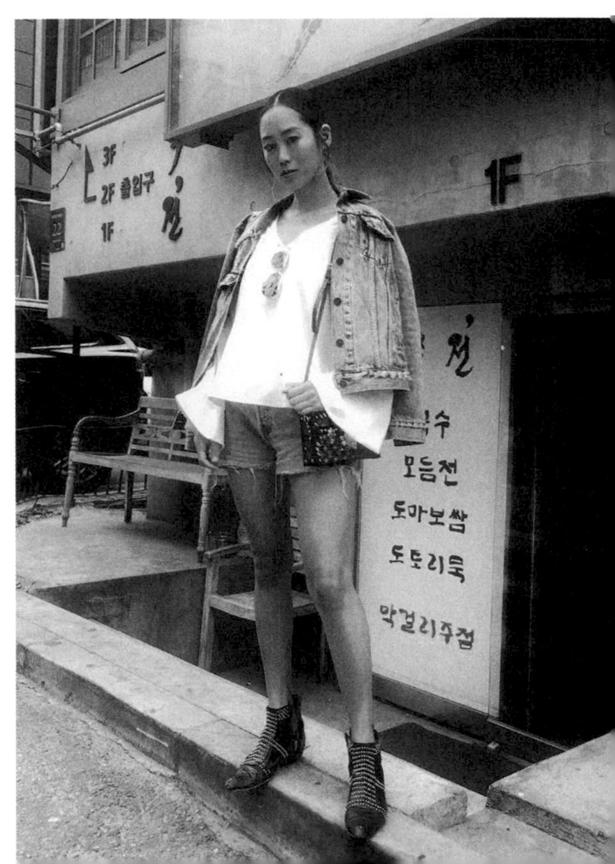
3F
2F 출입구
1F
1F
모듬전
도마보쌈
도토리묵
막걸리주점

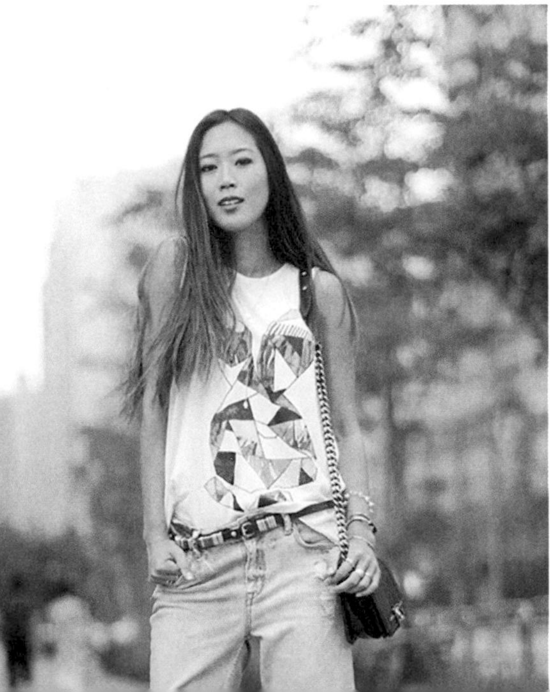

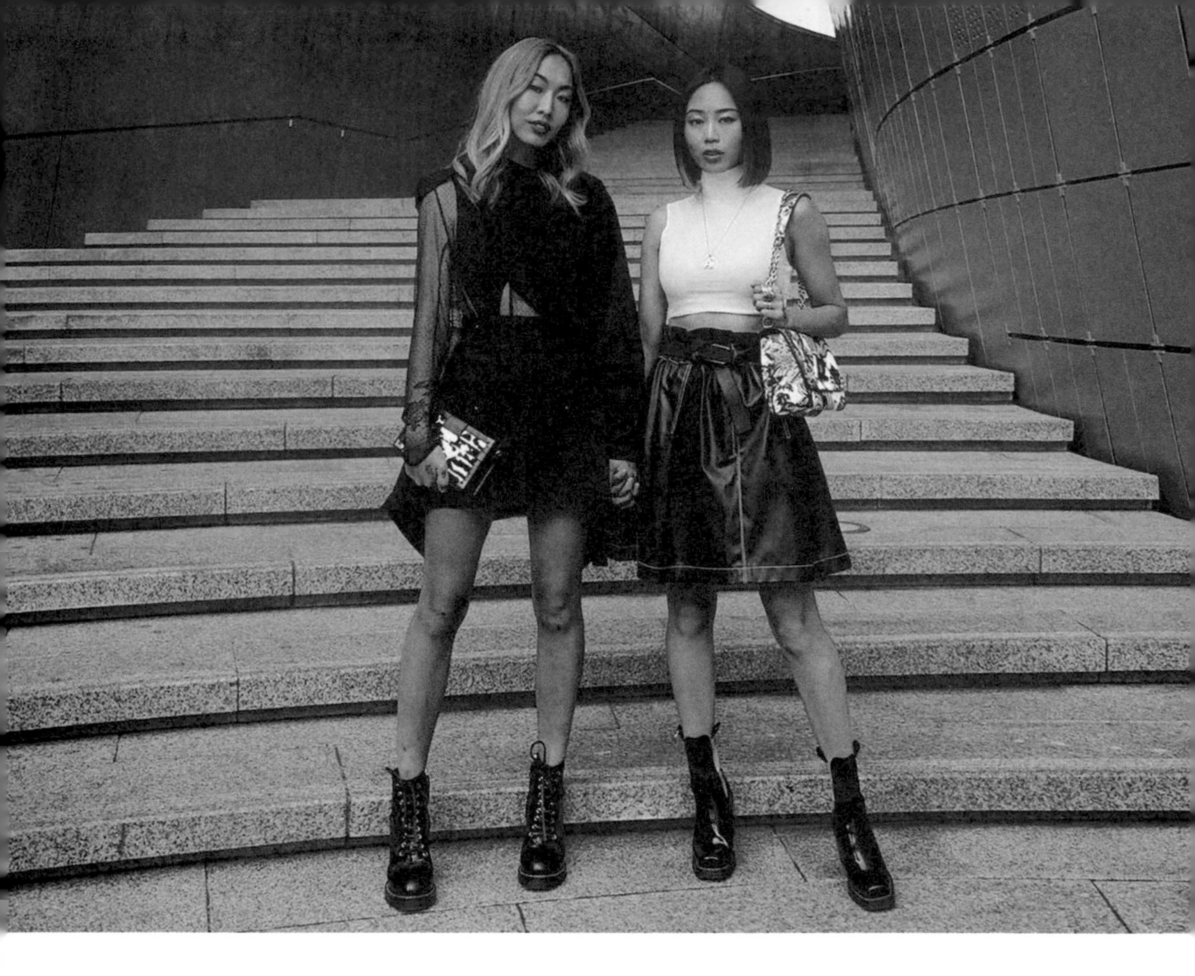

ABOVE At the Louis Vuitton exhibition with Dani. This trip was really special for us because this is the first trip Dani took after she broke up with her now ex-boyfriend, with whom she had a really unhealthy relationship. We hadn't traveled together for a year while she was in the relationship, so it was really nice to spend time with her. We're at the Dongdaemun Design Plaza, which is one of the last buildings that architect Zaha Hadid designed before she passed away. *Louis Vuitton head to toe.* **OPPOSITE (CLOCKWISE FROM TOP)** During the trip with Dani and my parents, we stopped at a Gentle Monster store. We love their sunglasses so much, and this was a year before I ever even met the Gentle Monster team to discuss designing my own pair. I manifested it! I had gotten offers to do sunglasses deals before but I didn't want to work with anyone but Gentle Monster. And it worked out. • On a 2013 visit, I attempted to put curls in my hair and they straightened out almost immediately because of the Seoul humidity. (It was so hot that we had to go eat shaved ice instead of shopping.) • With Dani and my friend Tiffany, who used to be in one of the biggest girl groups in Asia, called Girls' Generation. We were on our way to see Britney Spears perform in Seoul and had just eaten a huge Italian feast which has become a tradition for us every time we hang out. *Isabel Marant dress.*

SEOUL MUST-EATS

Growing up in L.A. never left me wanting for amazing Korean food, but that doesn't mean I'm not obsessed with eating my favorite bulgogi, mul mandoo, and barbequed short-rib dishes in the place where it—along with my parents—was born.

C. Through
@c.through

Hannam Boo-Uh Gook
Phone: 02 22971988

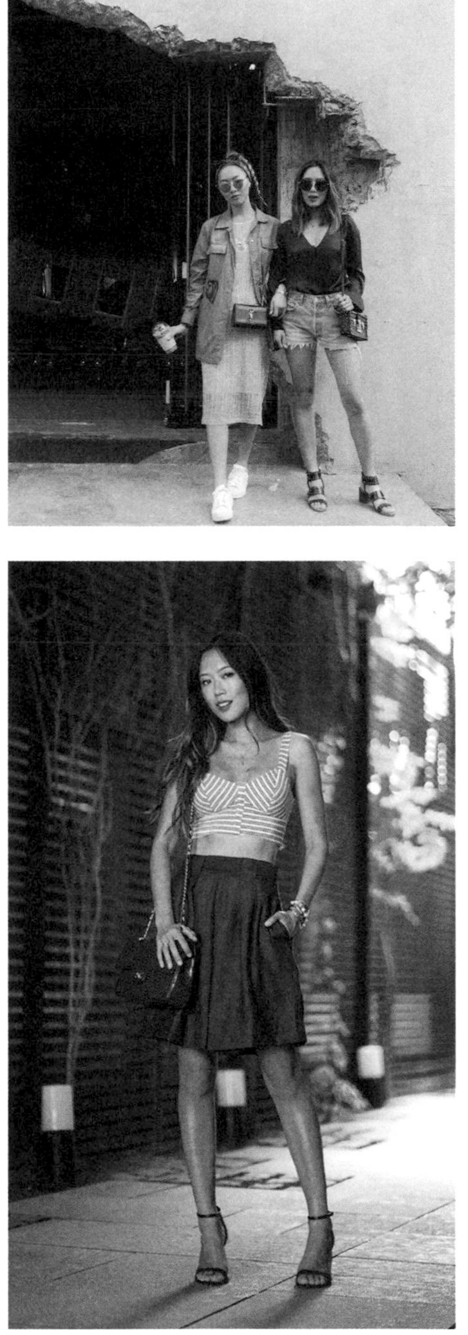

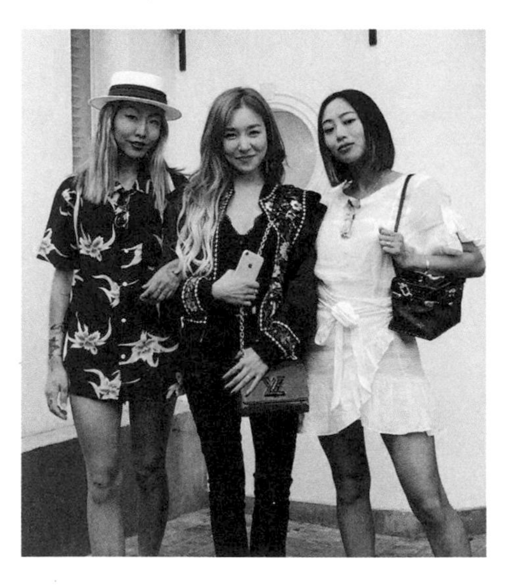

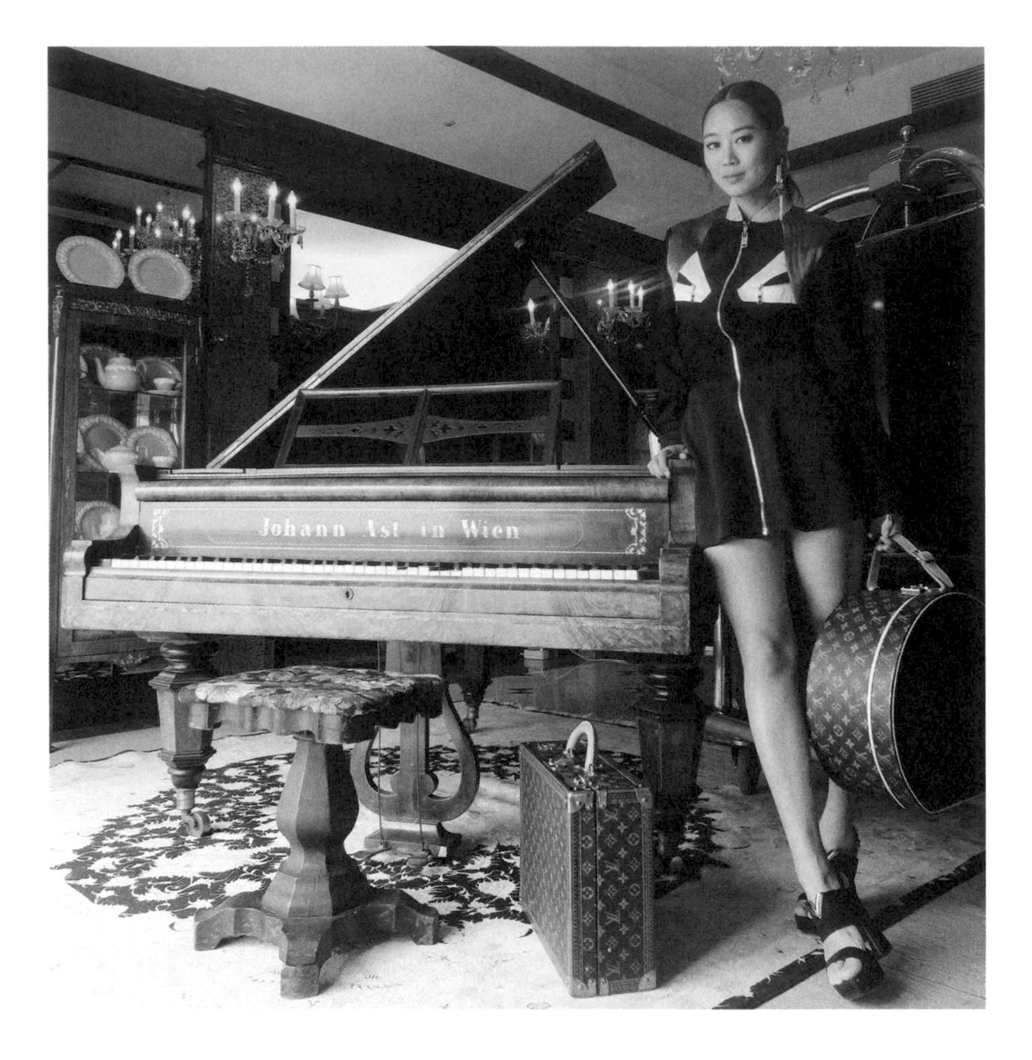

ABOVE During my first *W* magazine shoot. *Louis Vuitton head to toe.* **OPPOSITE, TOP AND BOTTOM RIGHT** This is from a trip in 2016 when my sister, mom, dad, and I went to Korea together as a family for the first time ever, so needless to say it was incredibly special. We spent a few days in Seoul before going to visit my grandma (who is my mom's mom) in Busan, and this is us browsing the shops in an area called Garosu-gil, which is like the Melrose Avenue of Seoul (complete with ginkgo tree–lined sidewalks), but a bit more wallet-friendly. My dad took the bottom right photo. *Levi's denim jacket; Chloé shoes.* **OPPOSITE, BOTTOM LEFT** When my sister and I visited our grandma in 2015 we walked to a huge grocery store, and I remember it being really hot even though it was autumn. Busan is typically warmer than Seoul, so I packed accordingly. *Vince turtleneck; Chloé bag.*

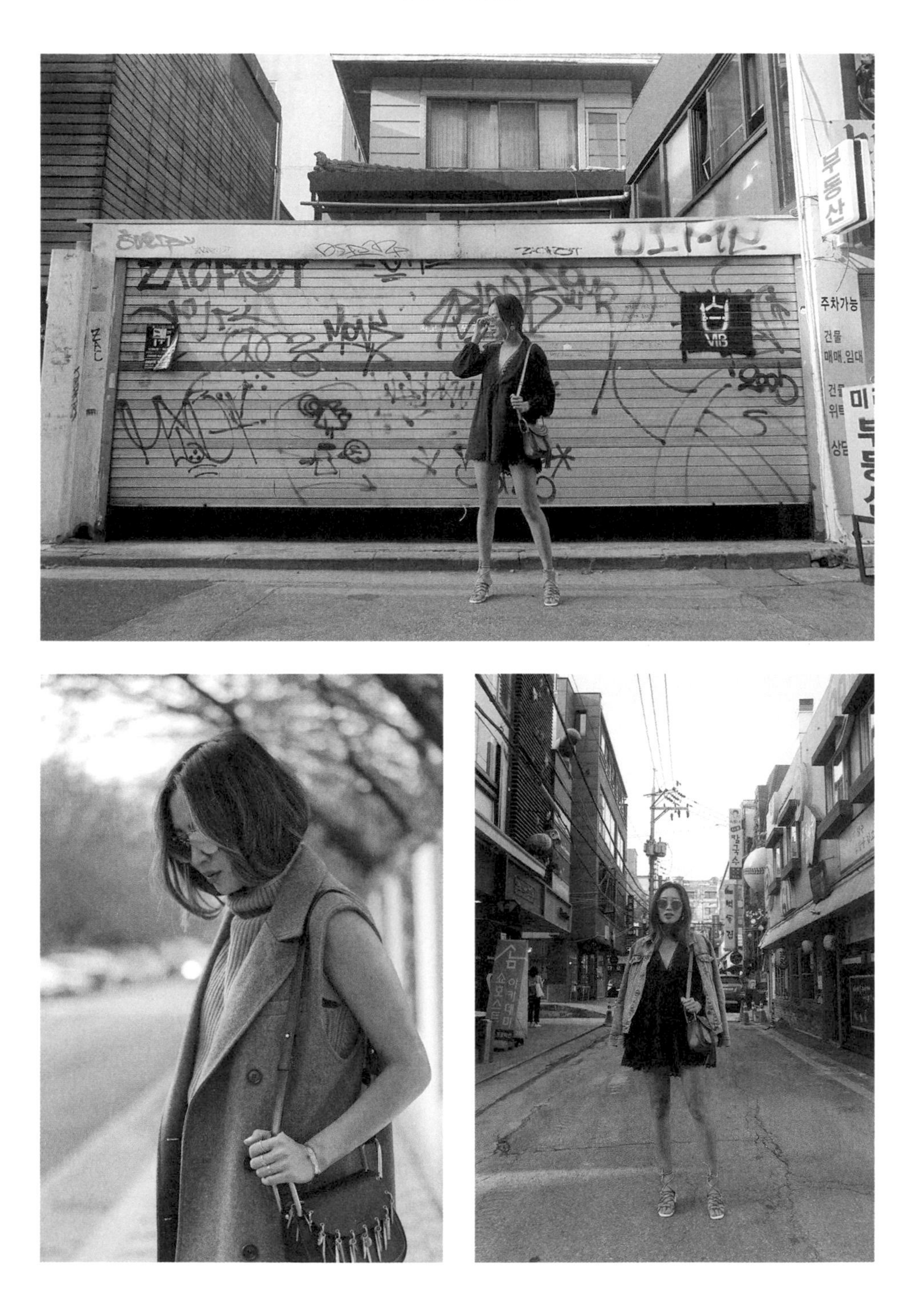
부동산
주차가능
건물
매매.임대

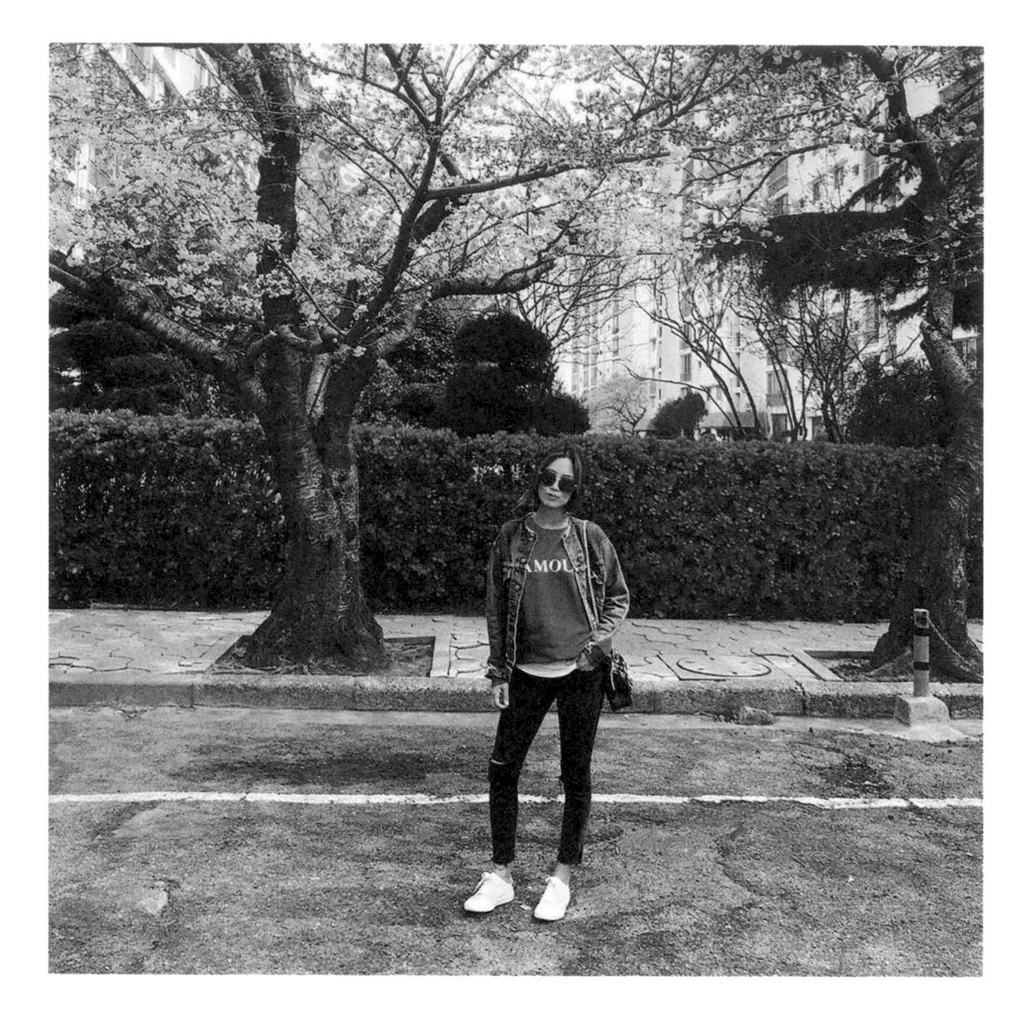

ABOVE Also in Busan. Dani took this photo. *Two Songs sweatshirt; J Brand jeans; Stella McCartney shoes.* **OPPOSITE (CLOCKWISE FROM TOP LEFT)** Right before my train ride to Busan, after my book signing in Seoul. *Chanel T-shirt; MCM bag; AG Jeans* • In Seoul, waiting for my friend's car at a parking lot, wearing almost all Korean designers. *Steve J and Yoni P trench coat; Plac jeans; Topshop boots; Gentle Monster sunglasses* • My airport travel outfit. My Tumi suitcase that I've had for four years has traveled more than a million miles with me (I swear!), and now that I have a piece of amazing and sturdy luggage I totally get why good luggage is expensive. It's so worth the splurge to get a great bag that won't fall apart. *French Connection kimono; J Brand skinny jeans; Louis Vuitton carry-on* • Shopping with Jacopo during Seoul Fashion Week in 2016. This is right before leaving for Busan to see my grandma. *A.L.C. jacket; Steve J and Yoni P denim; Topshop boots.*

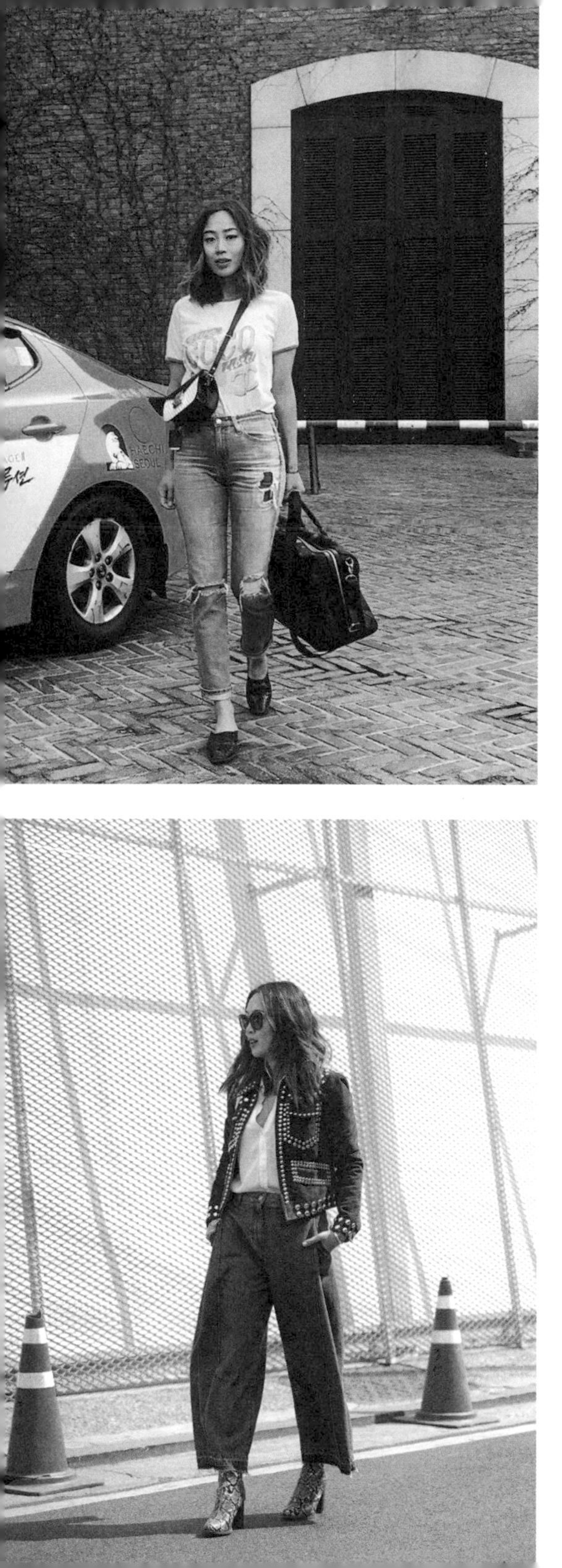
HAECHI
SEOUL

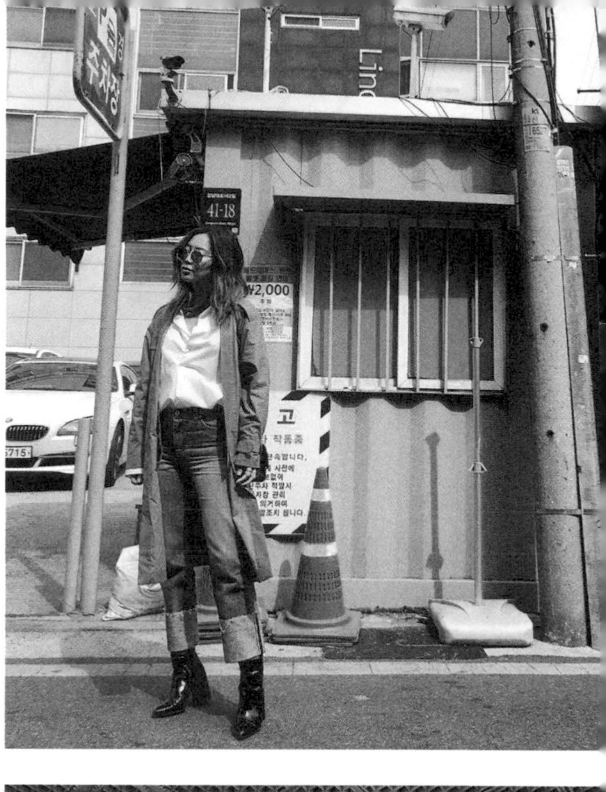
주차장
41-18
₩2,000

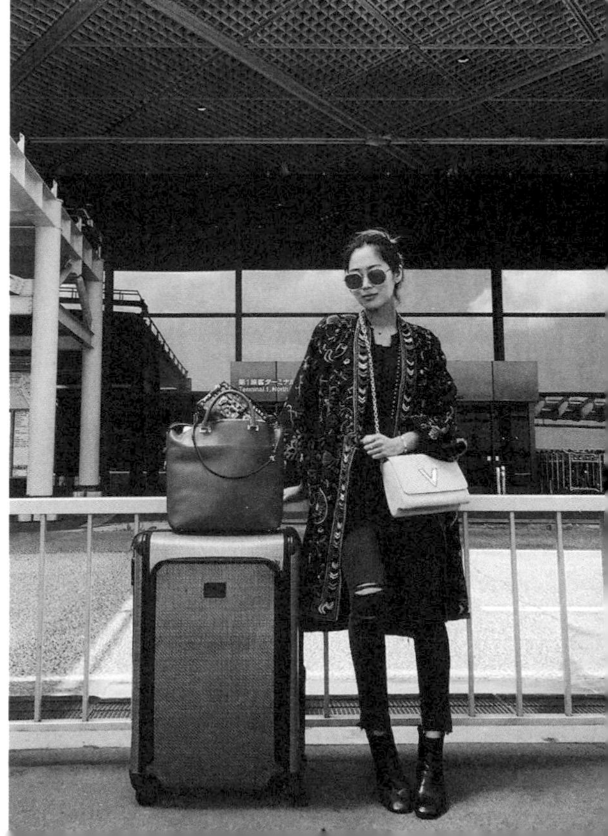

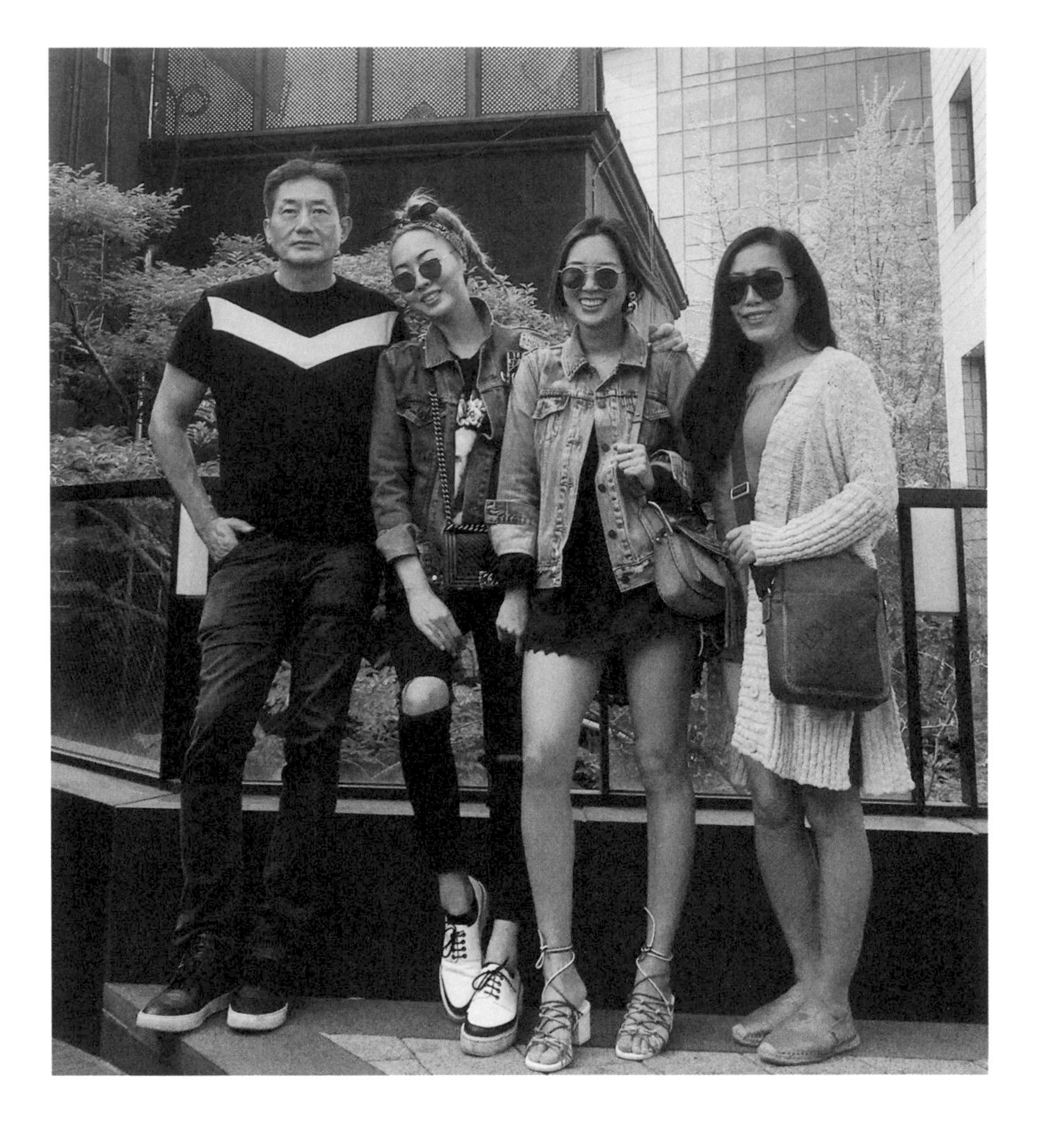

ABOVE Me, Dani on my right, and our mom and dad. This Seoul trip was extra special because we took it as a family. **OPPOSITE (FROM TOP)** In May 2017 Louis Vuitton held its traveling *Volez, Voguez, Voyagez* exhibition in Seoul, so I went for a week and took the opportunity to do a few other work things while I was there. This is an editorial shoot for *W Korea* wearing Louis Vuitton. The amazing boots had to go back to LV, sadly, and taking them off was so hard that the process required a helper. • For my *Capture Your Style* book launch in Seoul. *Gentle Monster x Song of Style sunglasses.*

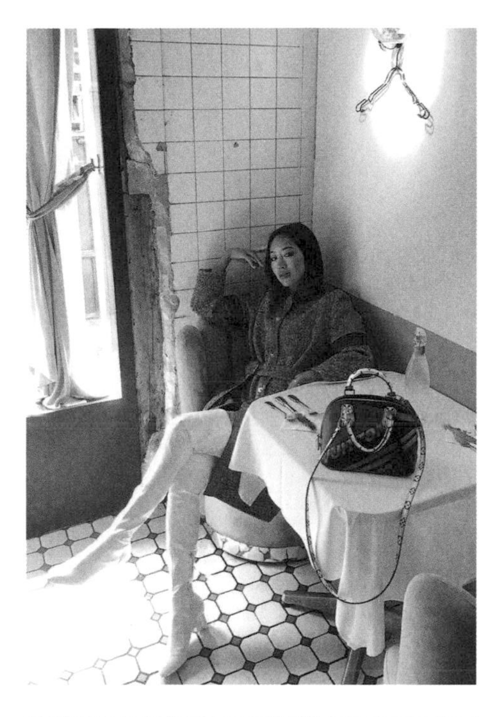

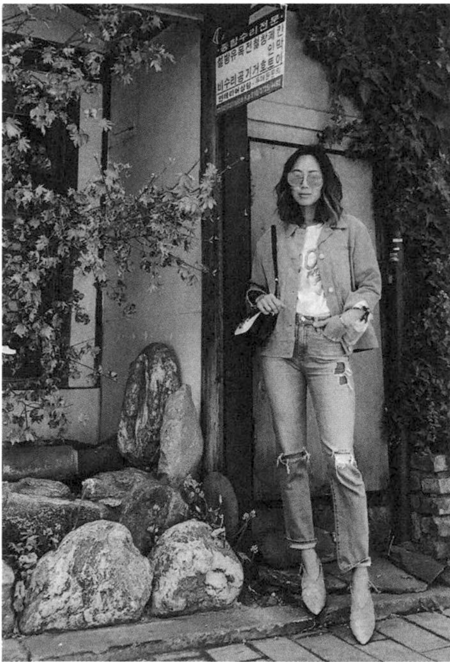

SEOUL SPAS & SKIN-CARE BRANDS TO KNOW

I love visiting Korea for so many reasons. My ninety-year-old grandma is at the top of that list, with the country's immense array of delicious snack food coming in a close second. But as a self-proclaimed beauty junkie, I also adore discovering the innovations in Korean skin care when I'm in Seoul—not to mention I always treat myself to interesting spa treatments and facials there, too (how can one not after a twelve-hour flight?). Here are a few places and brands I always pay attention to upon touchdown.

Shangpree
@shangpree
shangpree.com

Sulwhasoo
@sulwhasoo.us
us.sulwhasoo.com

Olive Young
@oliveyoung_official
oliveyoungstore.com

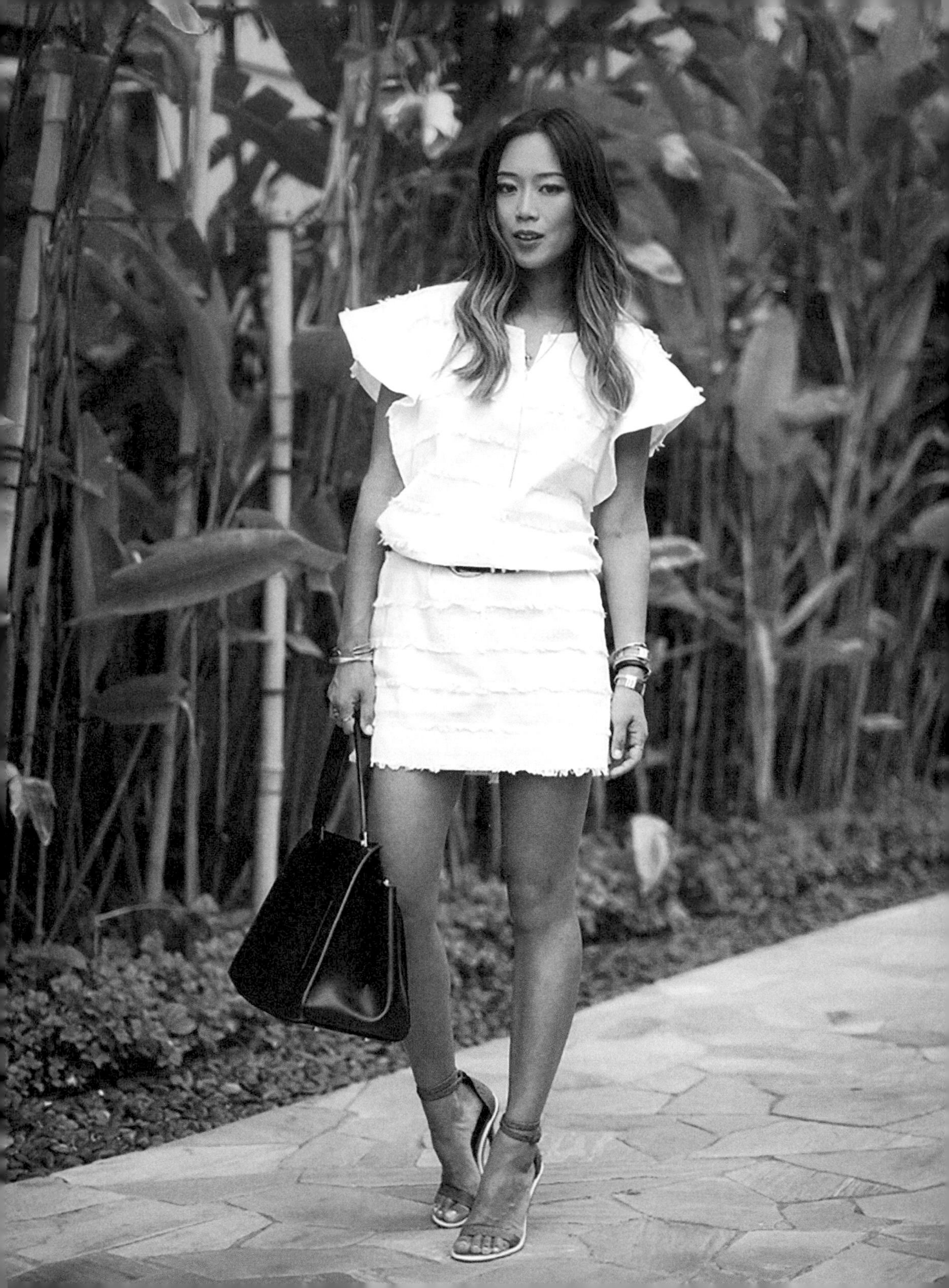

SINGAPORE

I've been to Singapore twice: once with Dani in 2014, and again with Jacopo in 2016. Both were crazy work trips—the first visit was with the skin-care brand Skin Inc., which I love, and the second time I was a keynote speaker at the Galboss Asia symposium along with Skin Inc. founder Sabrina Tan. It was such an amazing experience to speak to young women about starting businesses of their own. I also shot a cover for *Cleo* magazine, a women's lifestyle magazine based in Singapore—which was yet another pinch-me moment. I've never had a ton of time to explore Singapore because of all my work obligations there, but I can't wait to go back. The people there are stylish, kind, and business-minded all at once—aka my peeps!

OPPOSITE When I first started getting interview requests and being asked to do press events, I had absolutely no idea what they were, how to act, or what to wear. This photo is from my 2014 work trip, and I thought this was what was appropriate for a press moment—young and flirty. Now, I always try to look polished, sophisticated, and chic for these types of things. You live and you learn!

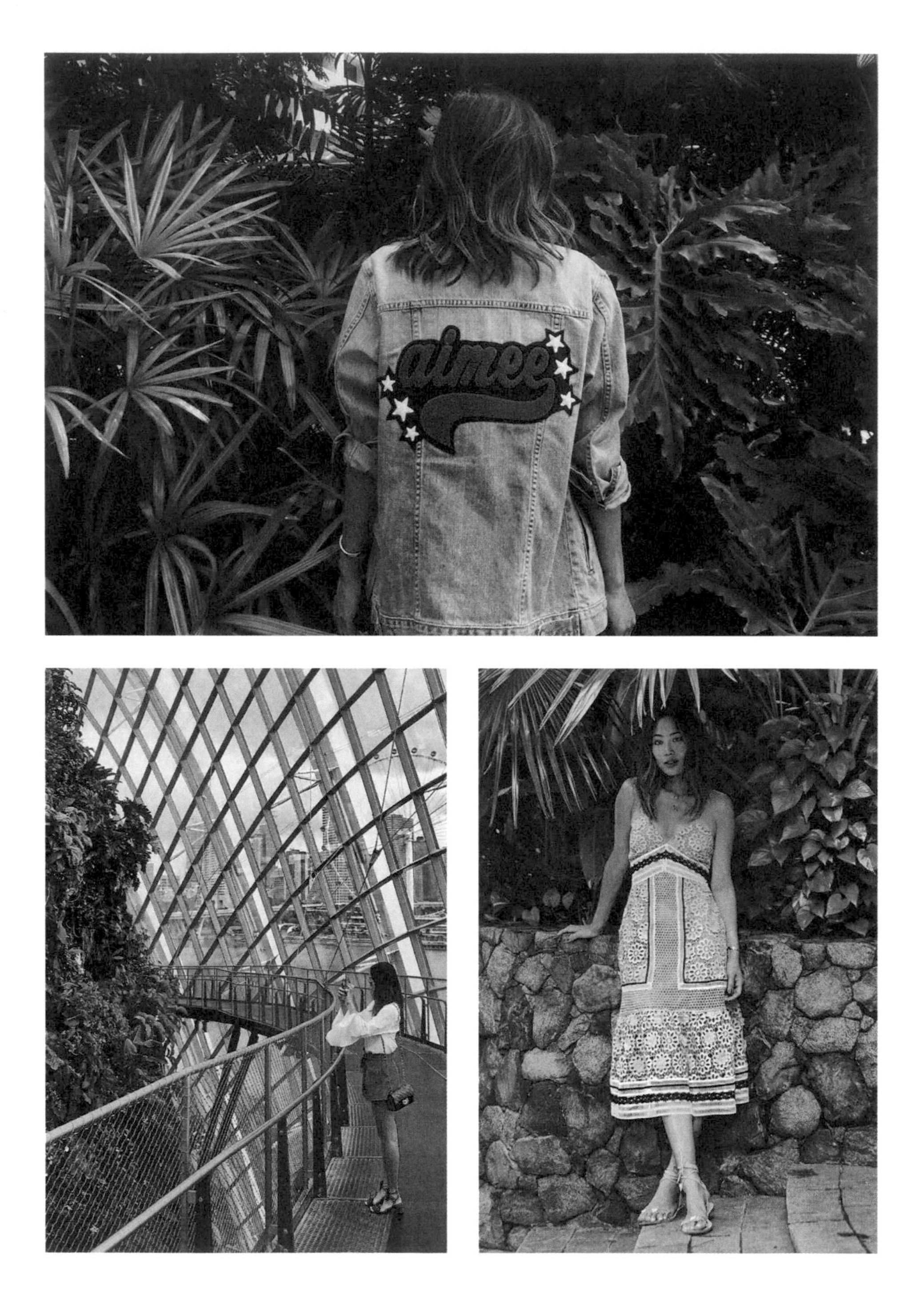
aimee

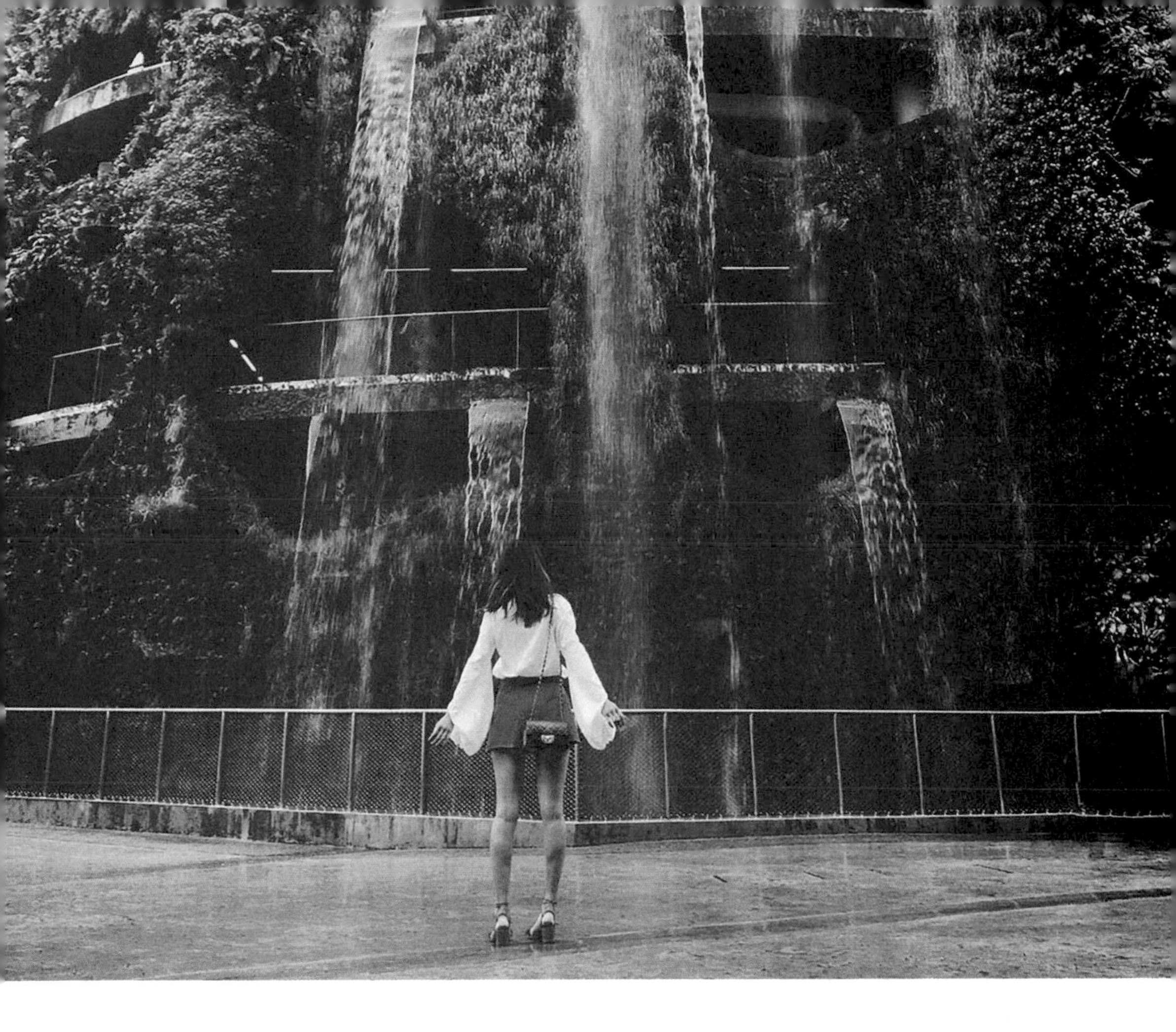

ABOVE At the Cloud Forest, which is an indoor mountain that features the world's largest indoor waterfall. It's my favorite place in Singapore—it feels like Jurassic Park and is just so cool. Right after this we ate some bomb boat noodles and a weird fruit called durian, which smells like feet. Of course I tried it, and I happened to love it (it's an acquired taste, I assume). *Alexis shorts, Aquazzura shoes.* **OPPOSITE (CLOCKWISE FROM TOP)** On trips to places that I know are going to be super hot and humid, I always pack a light denim jacket. *Rails custom denim jacket* • From my 2016 trip with Jacopo. Maddy from my management team was also with us, which was great because I was doing a lot of press and interviews. It was my first trip that I actually had someone from my management team with me, so I had help organizing my schedule and felt very taken care of (and forced to be on time, a rarity in my world). It was also really nice that Jacopo could just be my boyfriend and not have to deal with my work stuff, as he usually so kindly does. *Self-Portrait dress* • More time in the Cloud Forest. How cool does this place look?

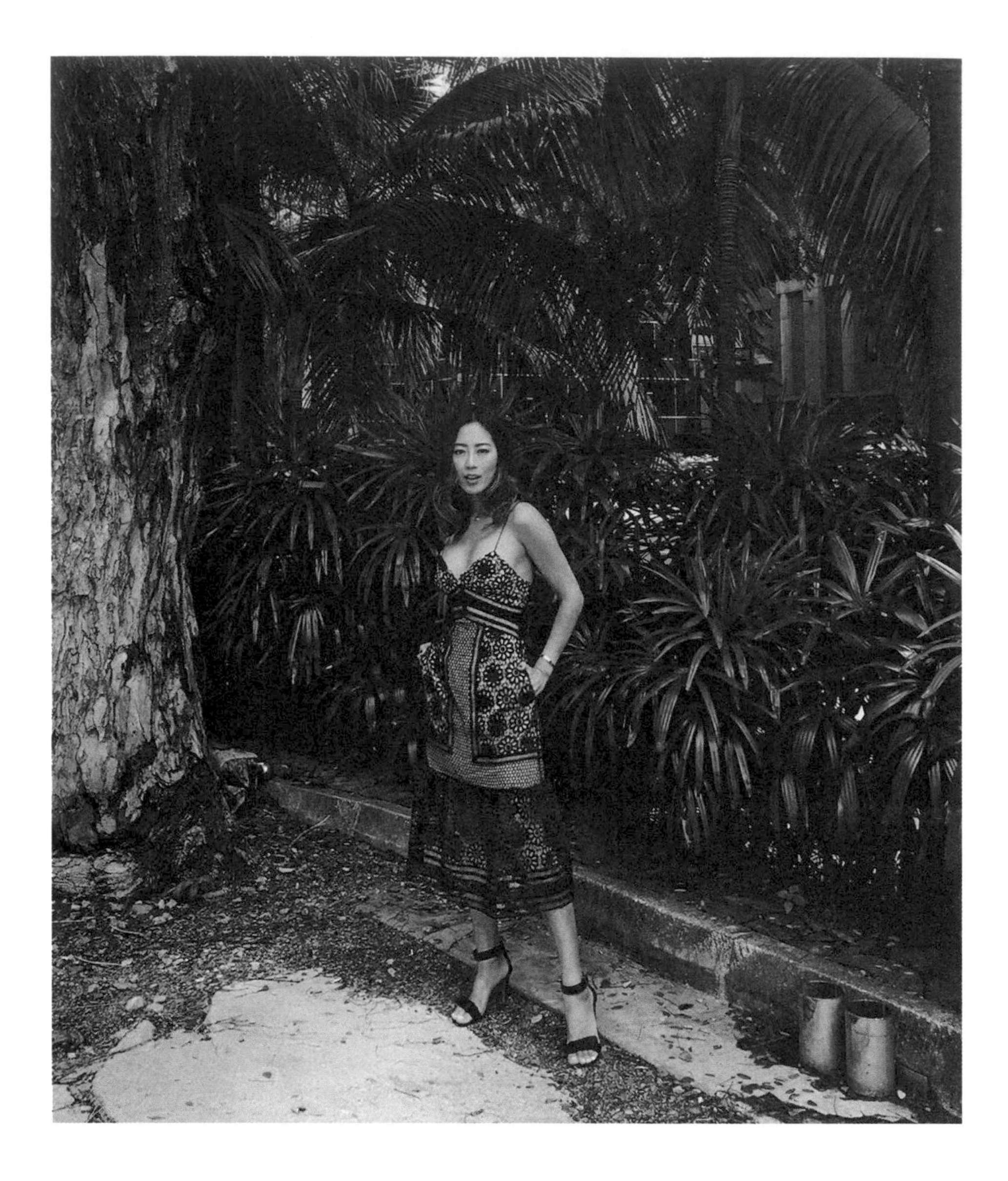

ABOVE After an interview with the BBC. *Self-Portrait dress.* **OPPOSITE (CLOCKWISE FROM TOP RIGHT)** Crossing one of Signapore's pristine, clean streets. • Sightseeing with Dani in 2014. • Someone sent these flowers to our hotel and they happened to match my outfit, so obviously I needed a picture. • I'm a Cali girl and always need my denim, even from 8,800 miles away. *J.Crew top; Topshop denim skirt.*

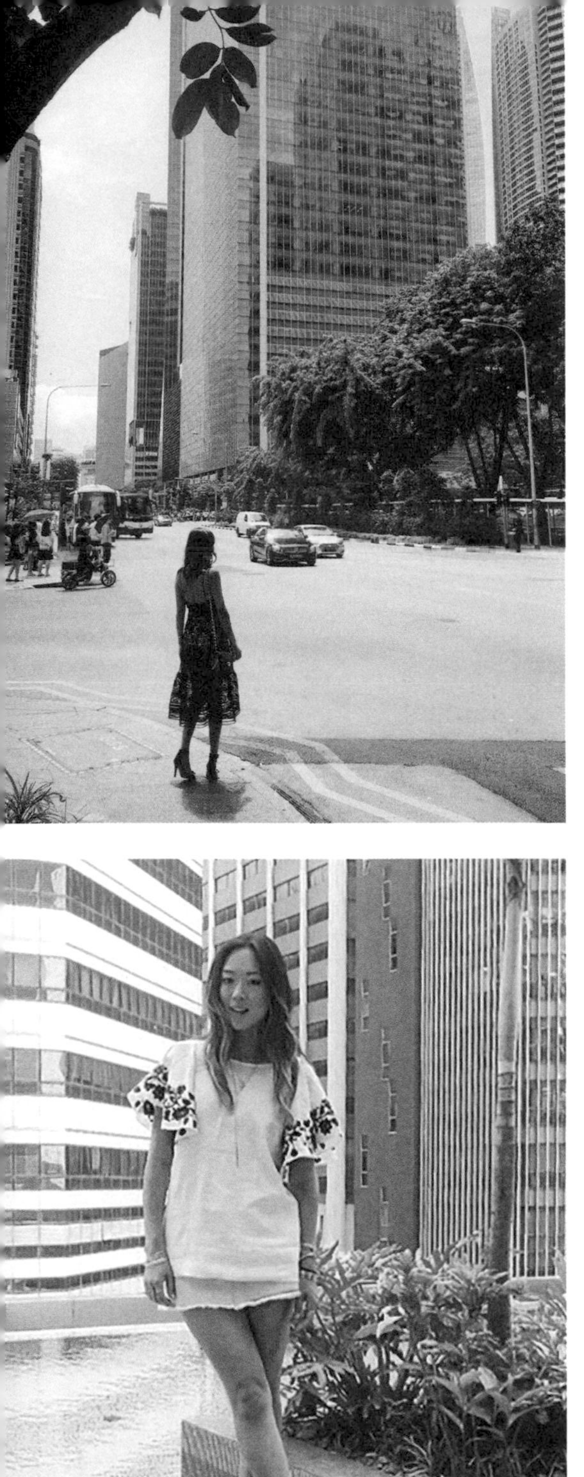

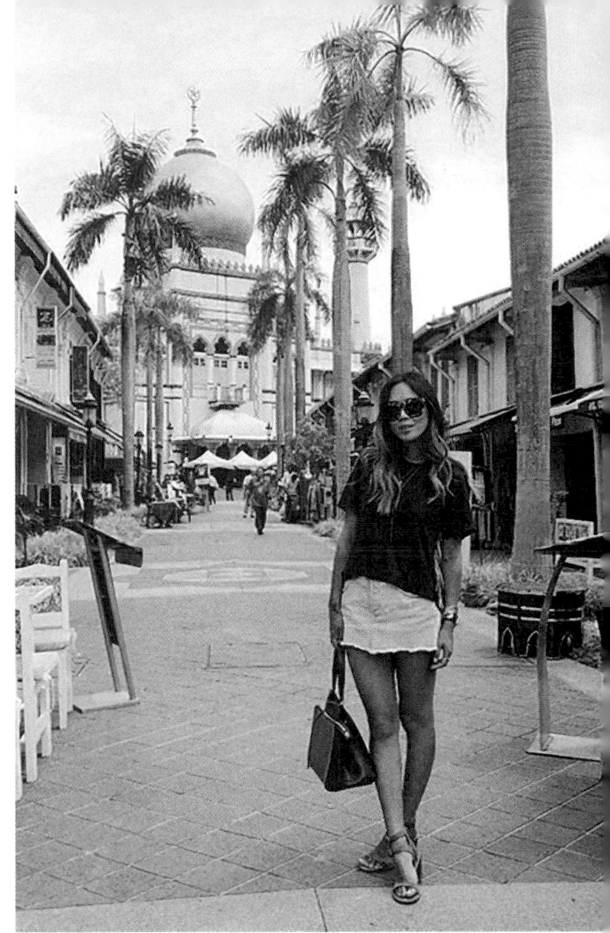

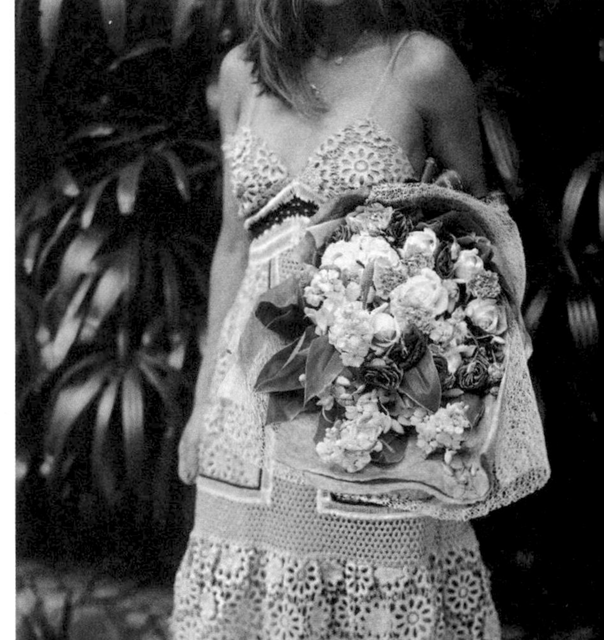

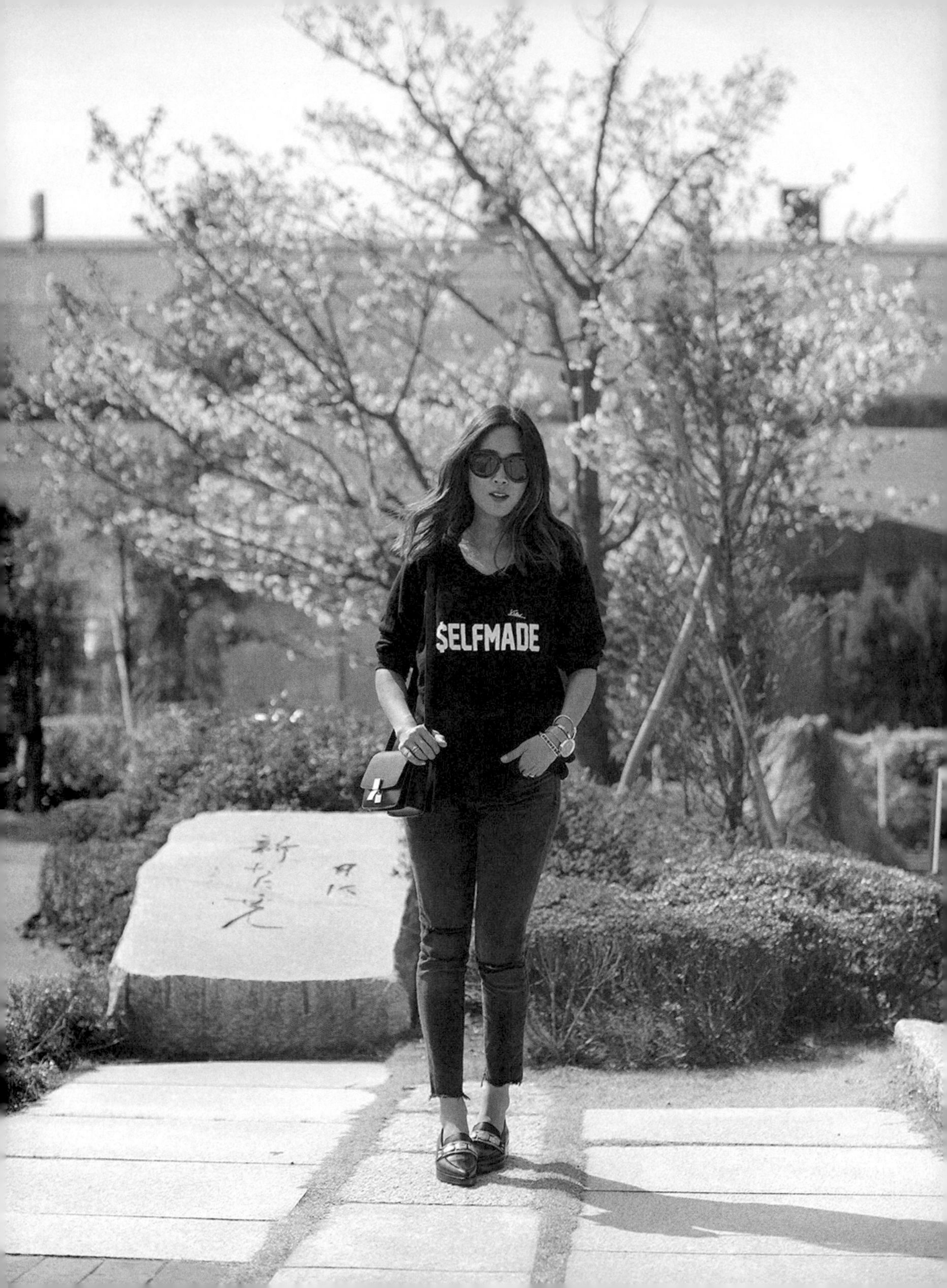
$ELFMADE

TOKYO

It wasn't until 2013 that I got to know Tokyo as an adult, when Michael Kors brought me there for a store opening. I was overwhelmed by the city—in a good way!—and found it all to be so energetic and interesting. Dani was with me, and we had such a good time that she and I came back around cherry blossom time in 2015 as a layover from Manila (put a layover in an amazing country on your bucket list, stat). Except we didn't plan correctly and every hotel in Tokyo was booked minus one—near Disneyland, an hour outside the city. (When in Tokyo, right?) We obviously went to the park and had the best time—that was something we didn't do as a family growing up near the original Disneyland, so it was really special to get to experience that with Dani as adults. Japan can be intimidating for travelers because there is very limited English being spoken (although I actually understand a bit of Japanese and very much enjoy getting the opportunity to practice my skills there and navigate the country's meticulous subway and train systems). But that's half the fun of it—going with the flow, getting lost, and feeling like a kid again who experiences everything for the first time.

OPPOSITE In 2015, after Disneyland and in front of the gorgeous cherry blossoms near our hotel. In my comfy go-to airplane outfit. *Two Songs T-shirt; J Brand jeans.*

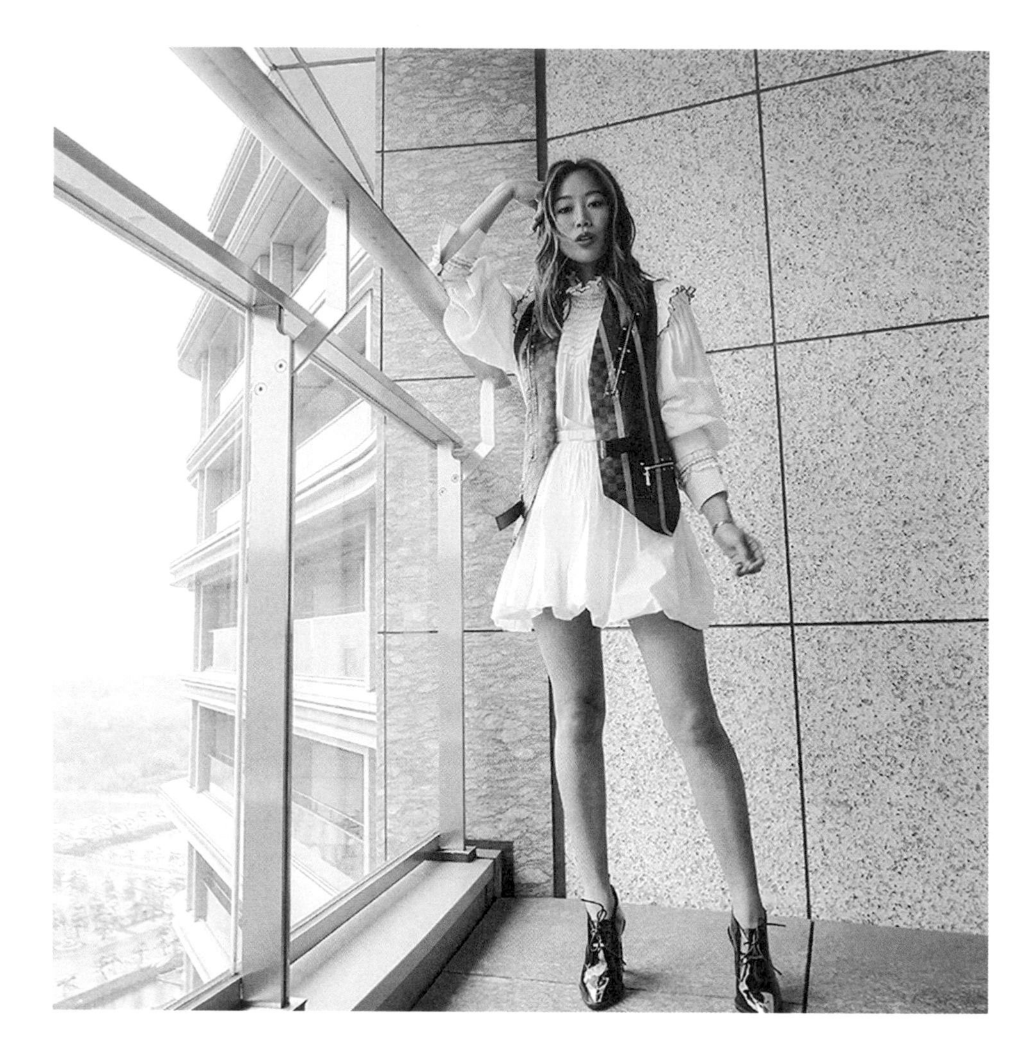

ABOVE In April 2016 Louis Vuitton invited me to see their *Volez, Voguez, Voyagez* exhibition in Tokyo, which featured vintage monogram trunks, past collaborations, and other interesting things they've done as a brand over the years. The great thing about traveling with LV is that their trips feel like their famous city guides come to life, which is an incredible, pinch-me way to travel. This photo is from a test series I did when I was deciding what to wear to the exhibition opening (I'm in head-to-toe LV, of course). I ended up loving the outfit so much that I did a mini photo shoot. **OPPOSITE (CLOCKWISE FROM TOP LEFT)** *Louis Vuitton head to toe* • Shooting with Chloé in Tokyo. Right after this we had udon, obviously. • Breakfast in Tokyo is my favorite non-avocado toast breakfast in the world. • At the famous Shibuya Crossing. *Chloé dress.*

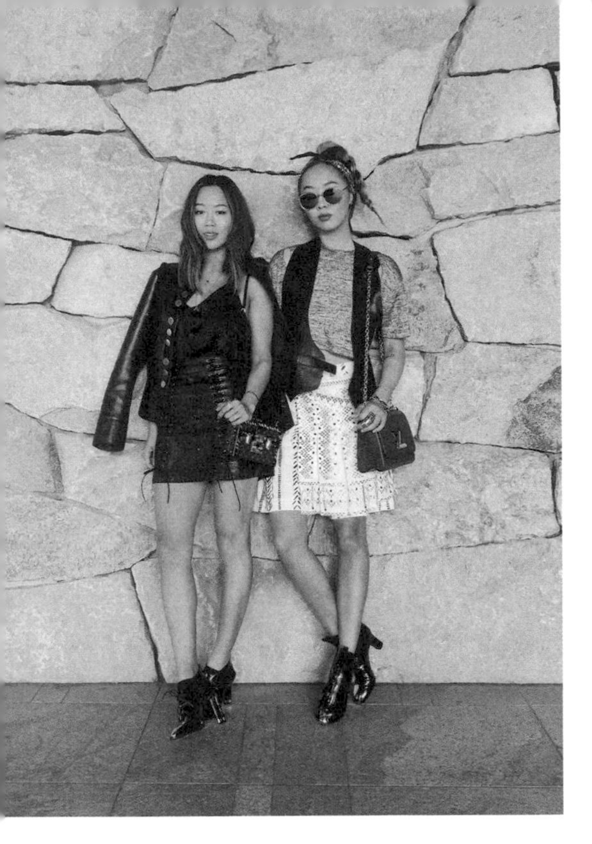

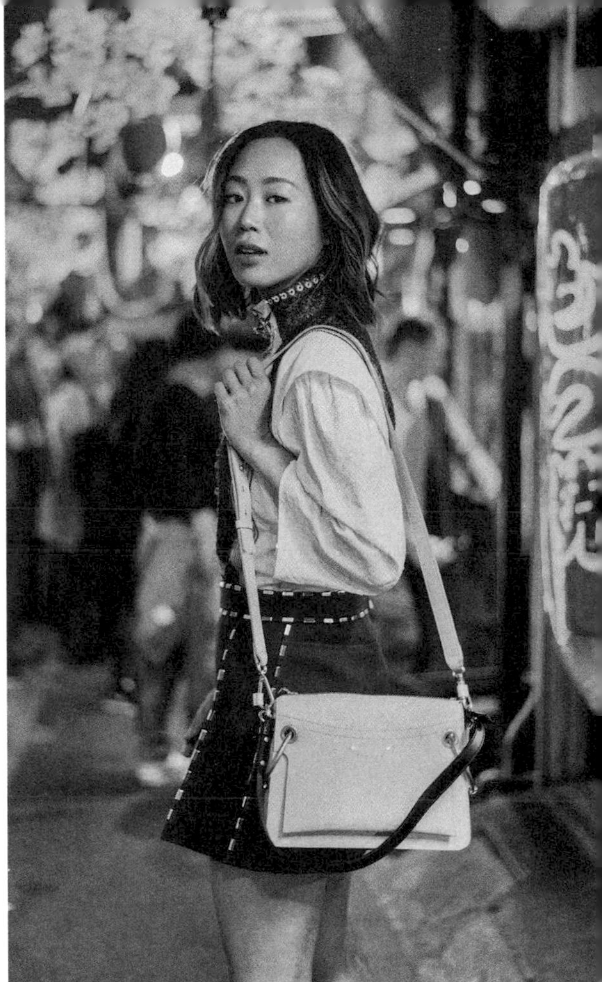

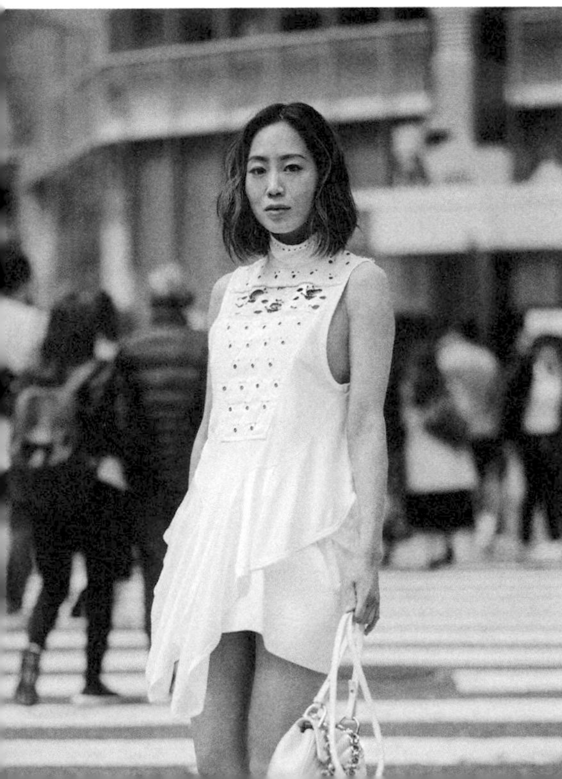

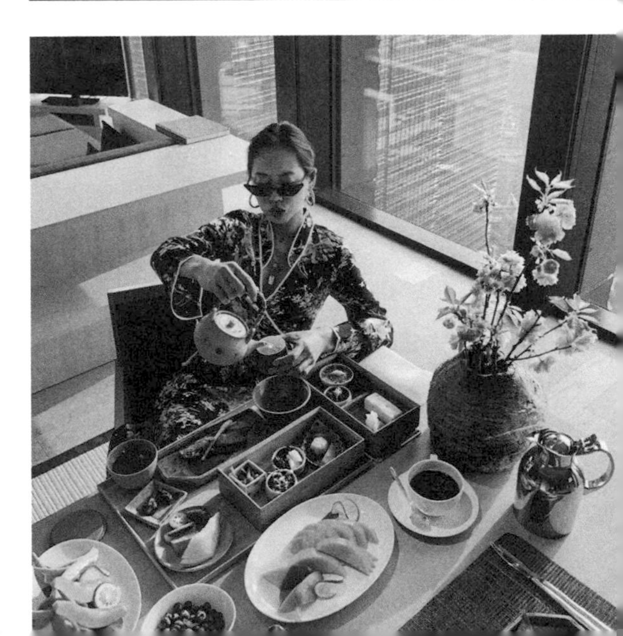

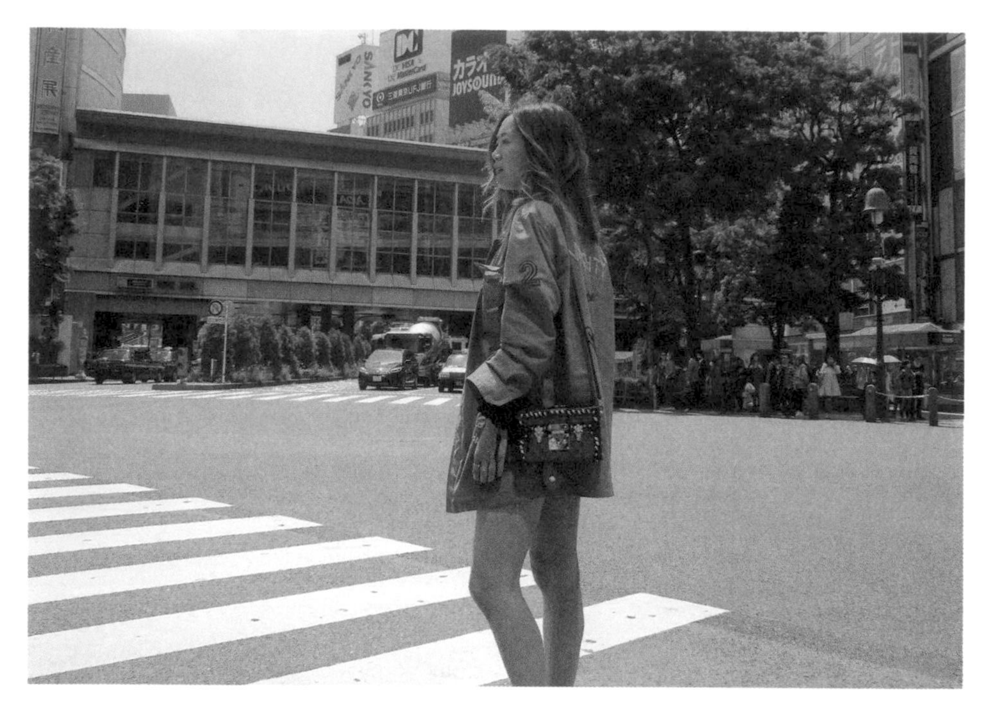
SANGYO
カラオ
JOYSOUND

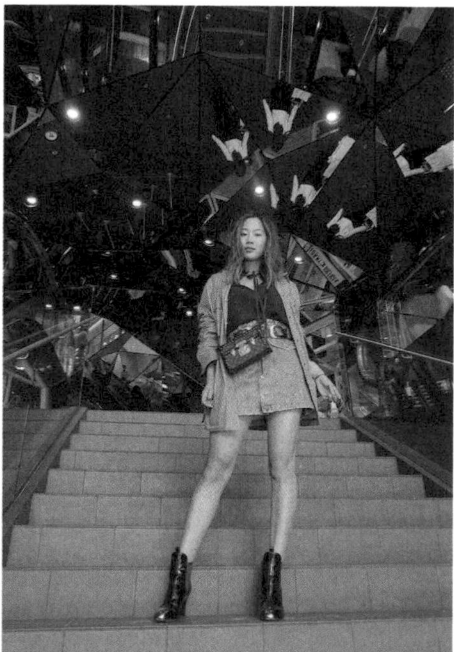

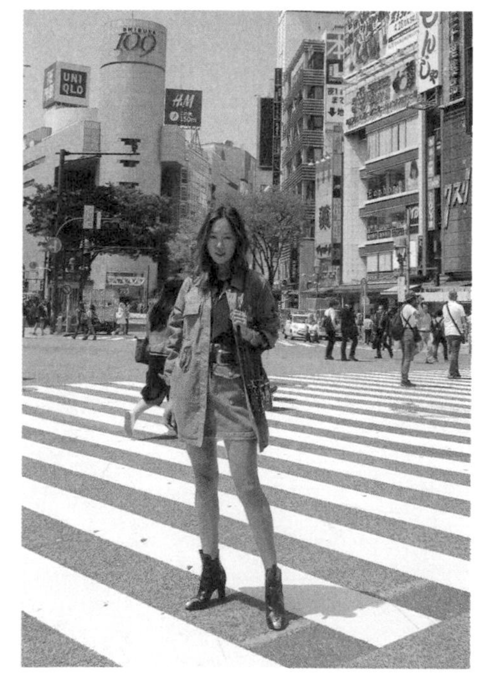
109
UNIQLO
H&M

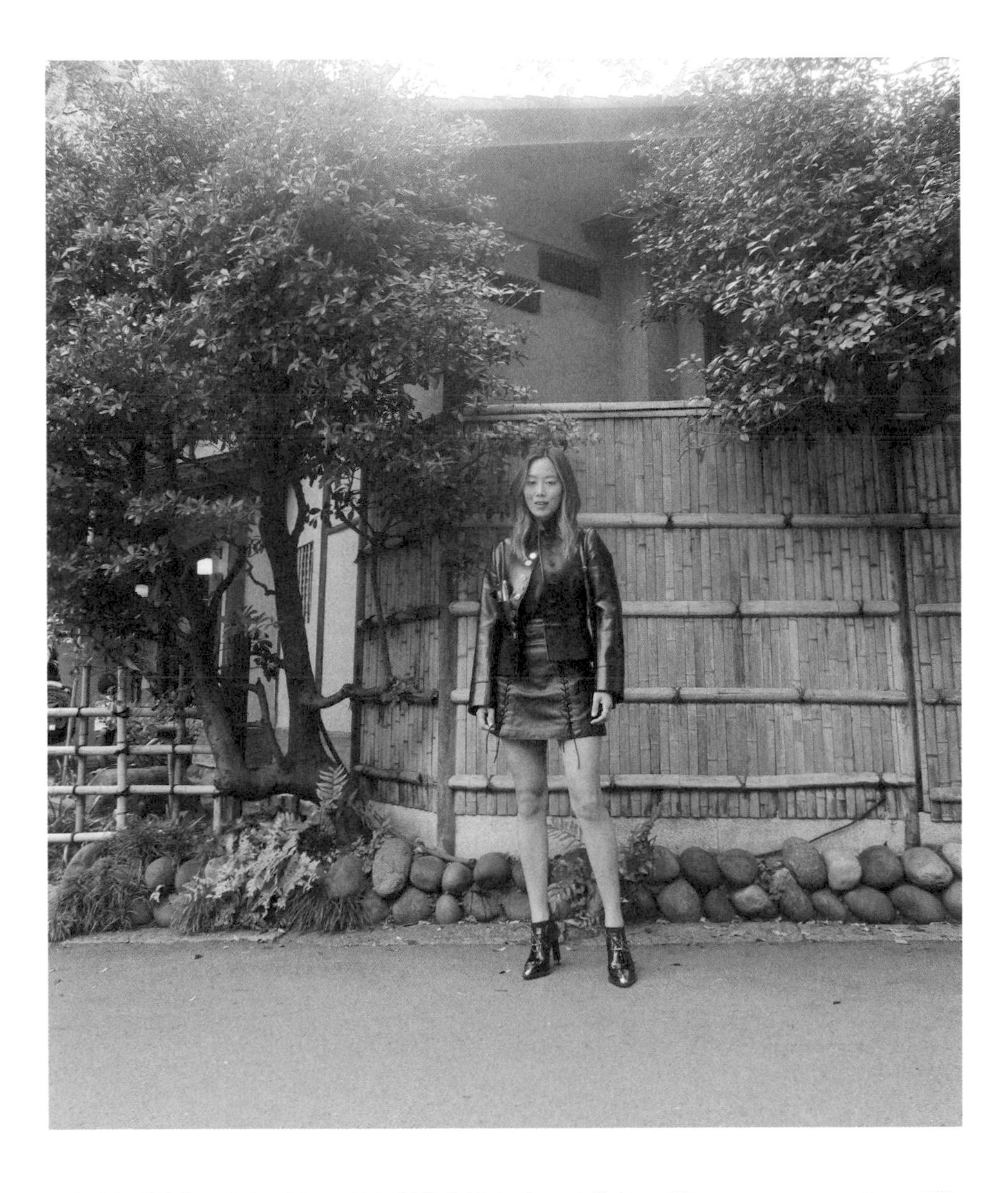

ABOVE One of my last days on LV's itinerary, in front of a tea garden. *Louis Vuitton head to toe.* **OPPOSITE** We stopped at Don Quijote in the Shibuya district, which is a market that sells really cheap things—beauty products, character socks, fake lashes. I stocked up on boob tape, Hello Kitty socks, funny pens, face masks, and fake lashes—you know, all the essentials. *Steve J and Yoni P military jacket; Topshop skirt; Louis Vuitton bag and shoes.*

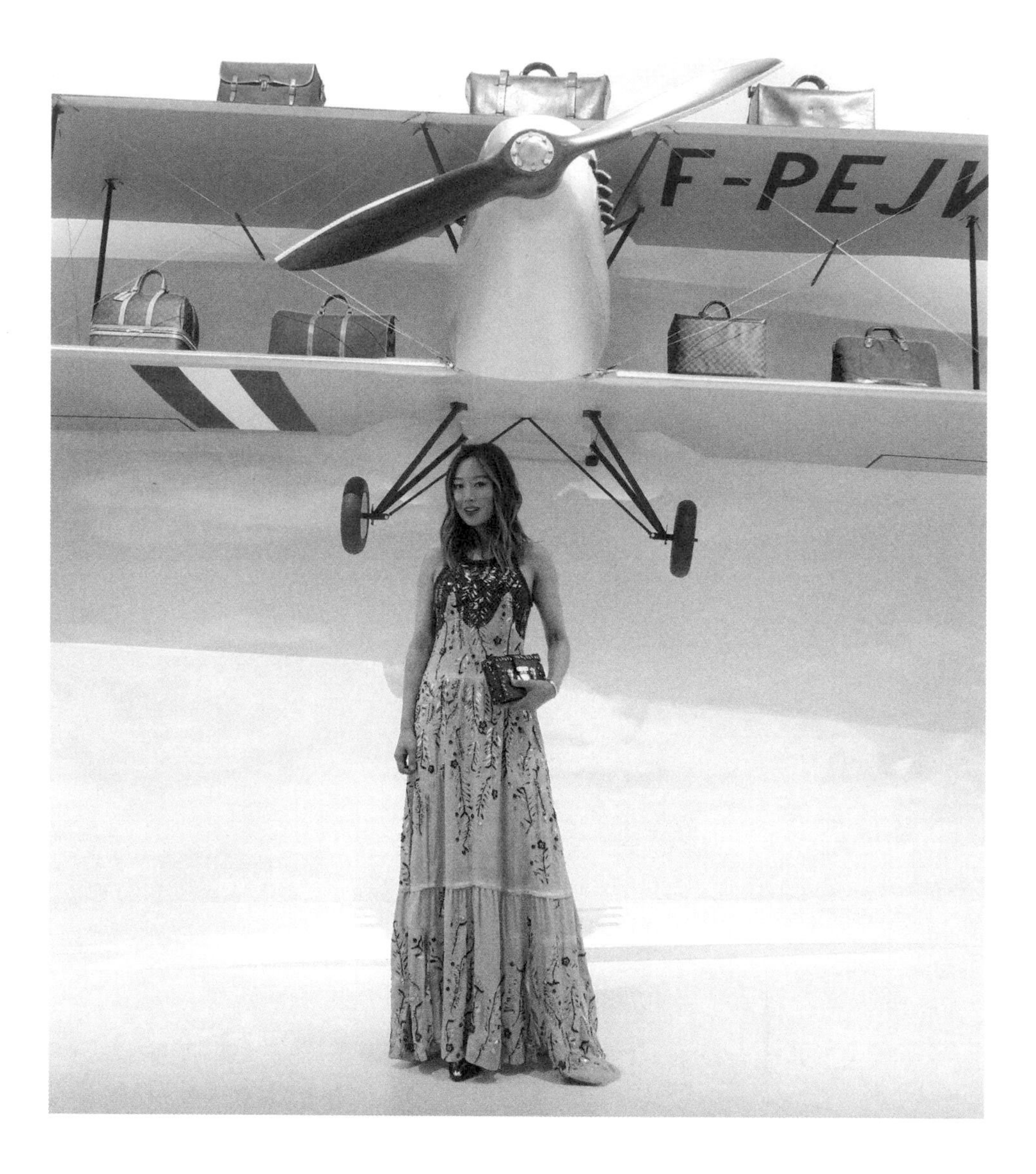

ABOVE AND OPPOSITE, TOP LEFT At the *Volez, Voguez, Voyagez* exhibition. My sister was my date. Her hair was so long back then! *Louis Vuitton dress.* **OPPOSITE, TOP RIGHT** The famous mirrored escalator at Tokyu Plaza Omotesando Harajuku in Shibuya. *Steve J and Yoni P military jacket; Topshop skirt; Louis Vuitton bag and shoes.* **OPPOSITE, BOTTOM ROW** Exploring Omotesando Hills, an area with different luxury stores, courtesy of LV's *Tokyo City Guide. Self Portrait top; Tibi trench; Levi's shorts.*

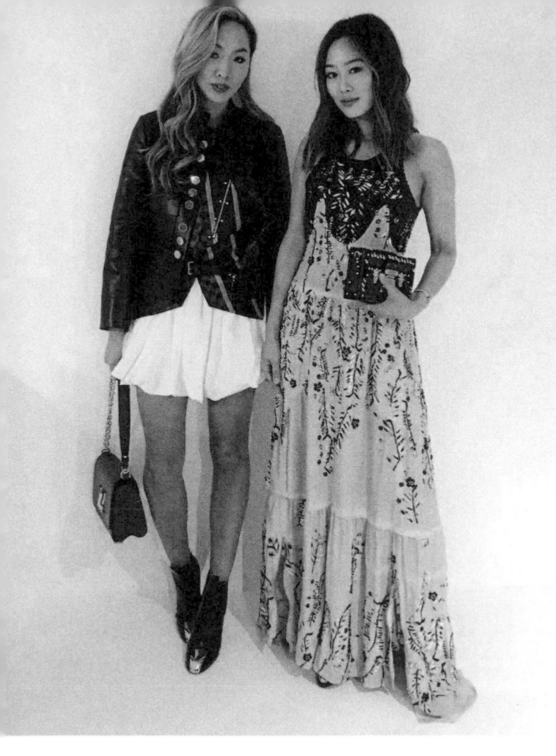

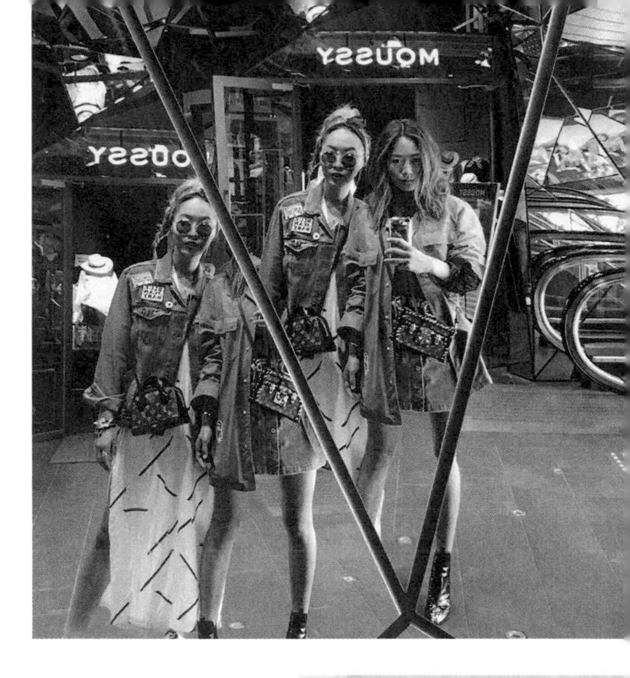

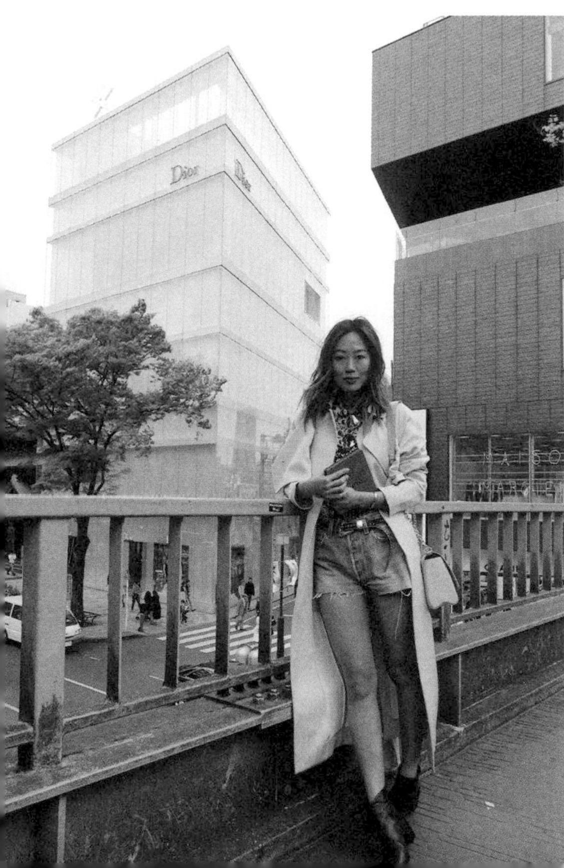
Dior
Dior

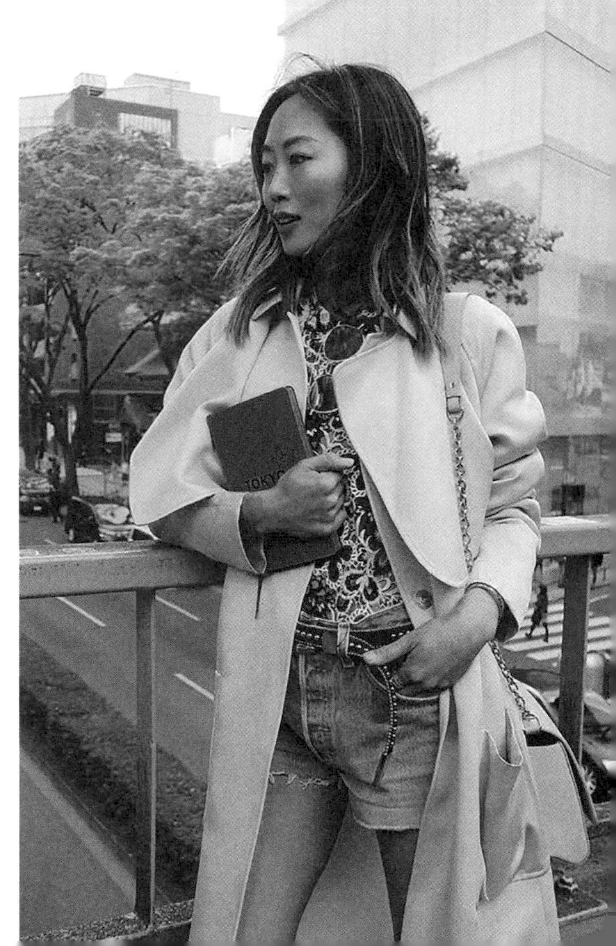
TOKYO

AFRICA

Mauritius

Morocco

South Africa

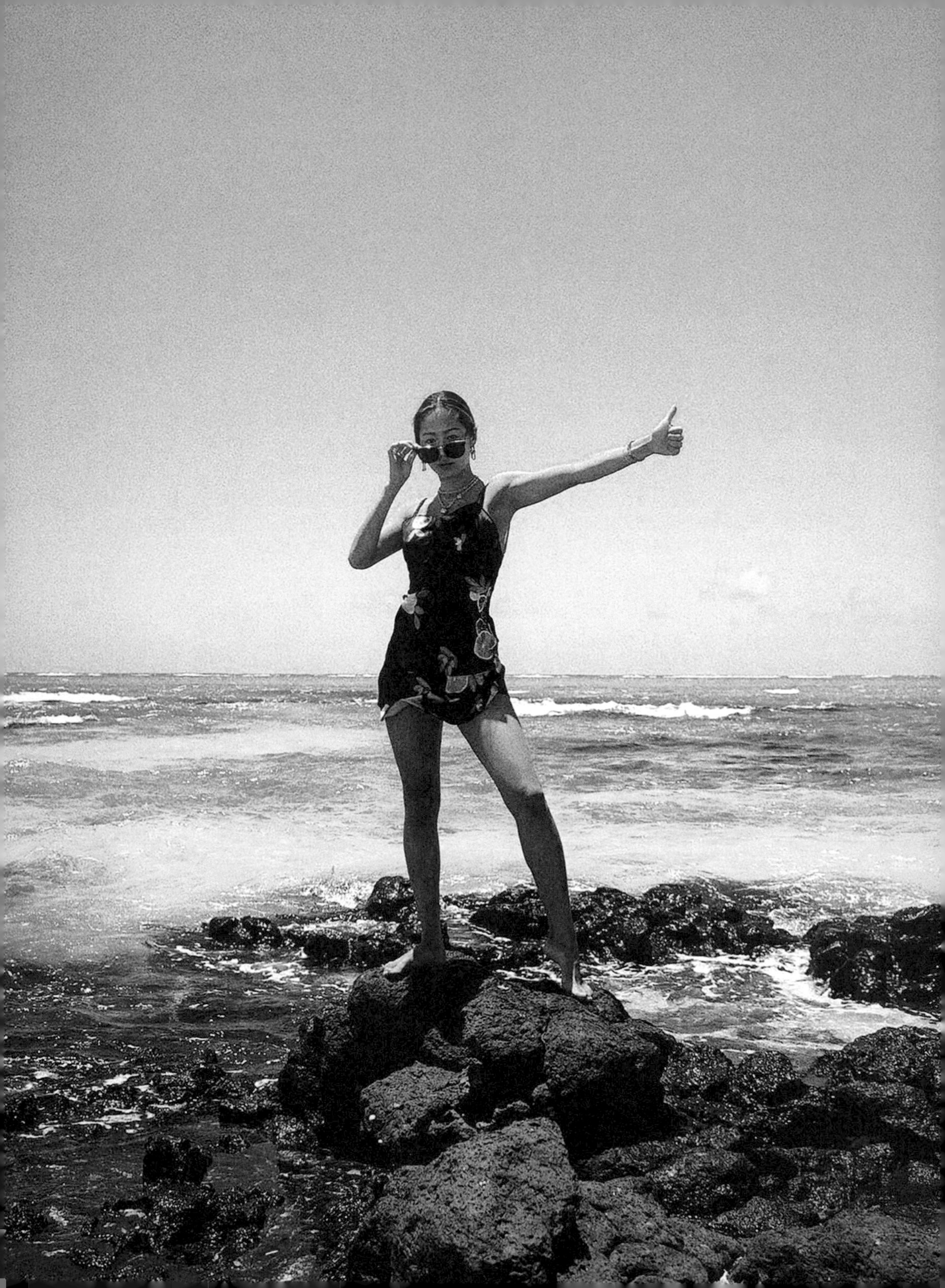

MAURITIUS

In October 2017 I had the opportunity to go on a diamond discovery trip with Tiffany & Co. to learn about the process of not only sourcing diamonds but also transforming them from their raw state to the gorgeous, sparkling finished products we see in Tiffany's windows. The trip started in Belgium—which is one of the leading diamond markets in the world (more on that later)—and continued to Mauritius, a small island in the Indian Ocean off the eastern coast of Africa that happens to be filled with immense natural beauty.

My favorite part of the trip was learning about the processes that Tiffany has in place to ensure that their stones are ethically sourced from known mines that are operated responsibly. I was also surprised to learn that the company owns its own workshops which means that local artisans are extensively trained (not to mention paid a living wage) to finish each stone which contributes to the local economy. Another eye-opening moment was when I found out that Tiffany rejects 99.96 percent of the gem-grade diamonds they mine. So it's safe to say that the one I got to actually polish myself likely didn't end up in a little blue box.

I was so fascinated by everything I learned, which was evident by the full notebook of notes that I took. The experience was only aided by Mauritius's friendly residents, just-caught seafood, and magical scenery.

OPPOSITE *Reformation dress.*

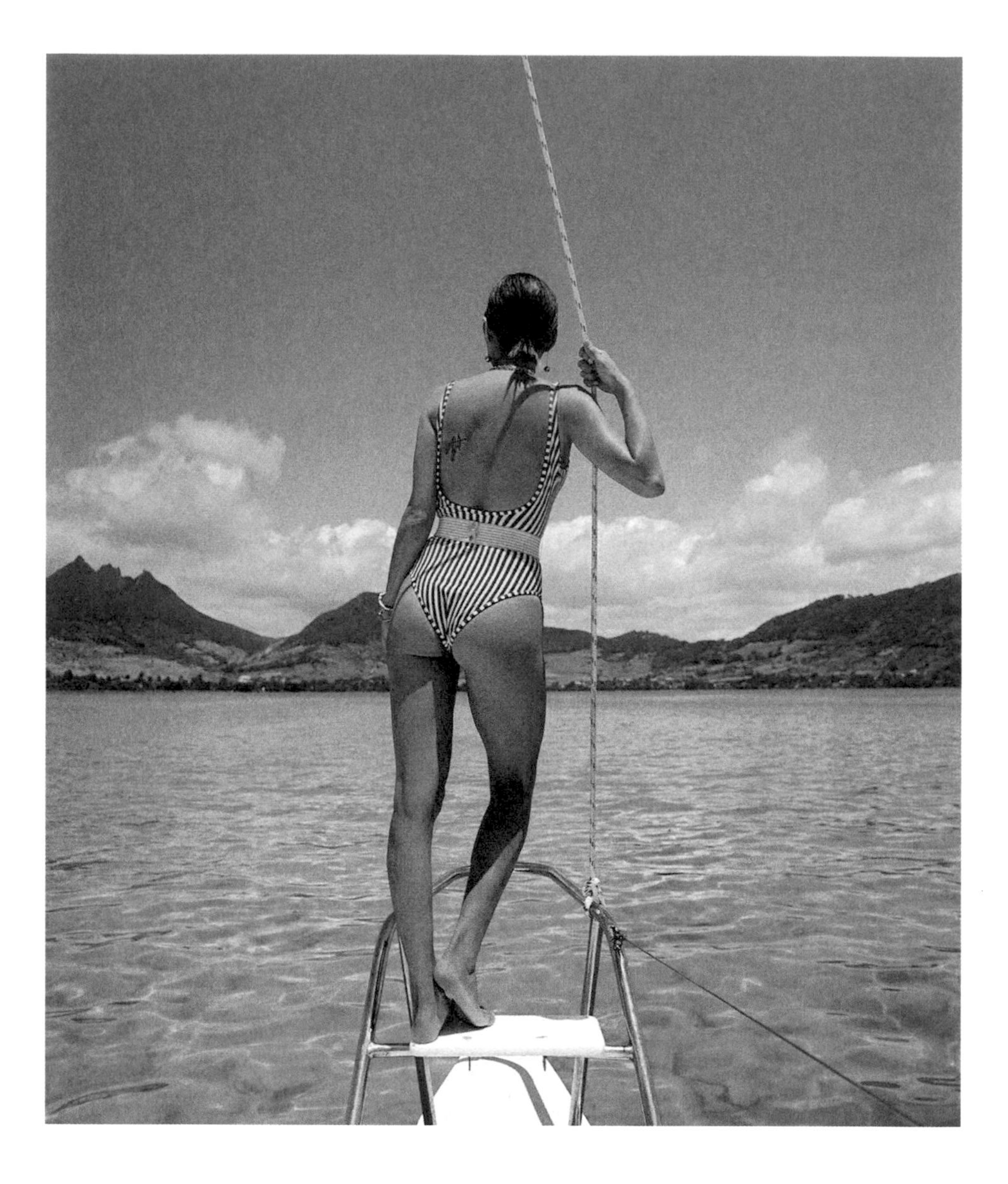

ABOVE *DVF swimsuit.* **OPPOSITE (CLOCKWISE FROM TOP)** *Sea NY top; Tiffany & Co. jewelry* • Mauritius transportation: taxi boats (take that, Lyft). *Jacopo's hat; Loeffler Randall sandal* • Tiffany loaned me jewelry for the trip, and I never took these pieces off—even while I was swimming. The button-down belongs to Jacopo. He always wears it, so I "borrowed" it to use as a cover up.

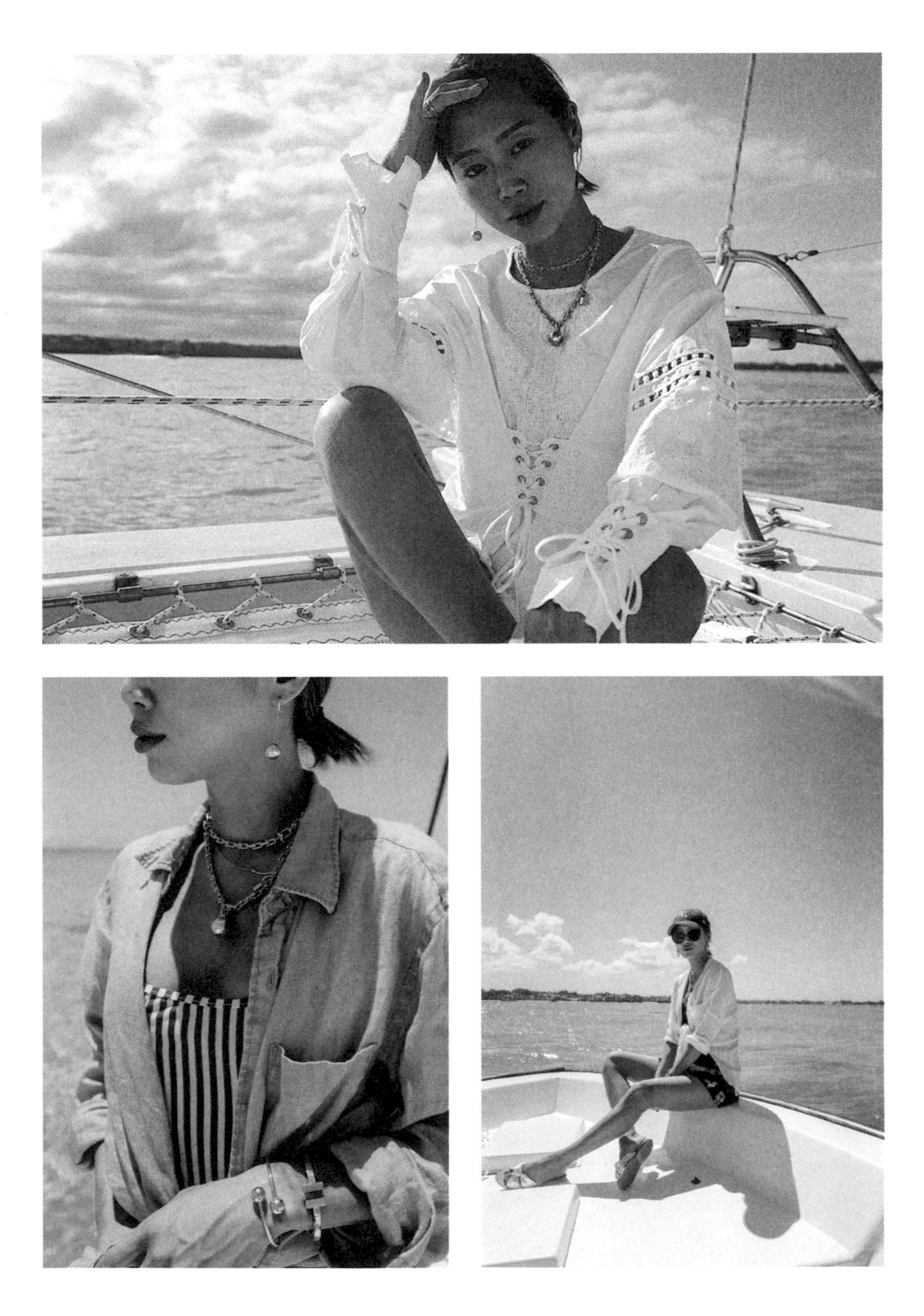

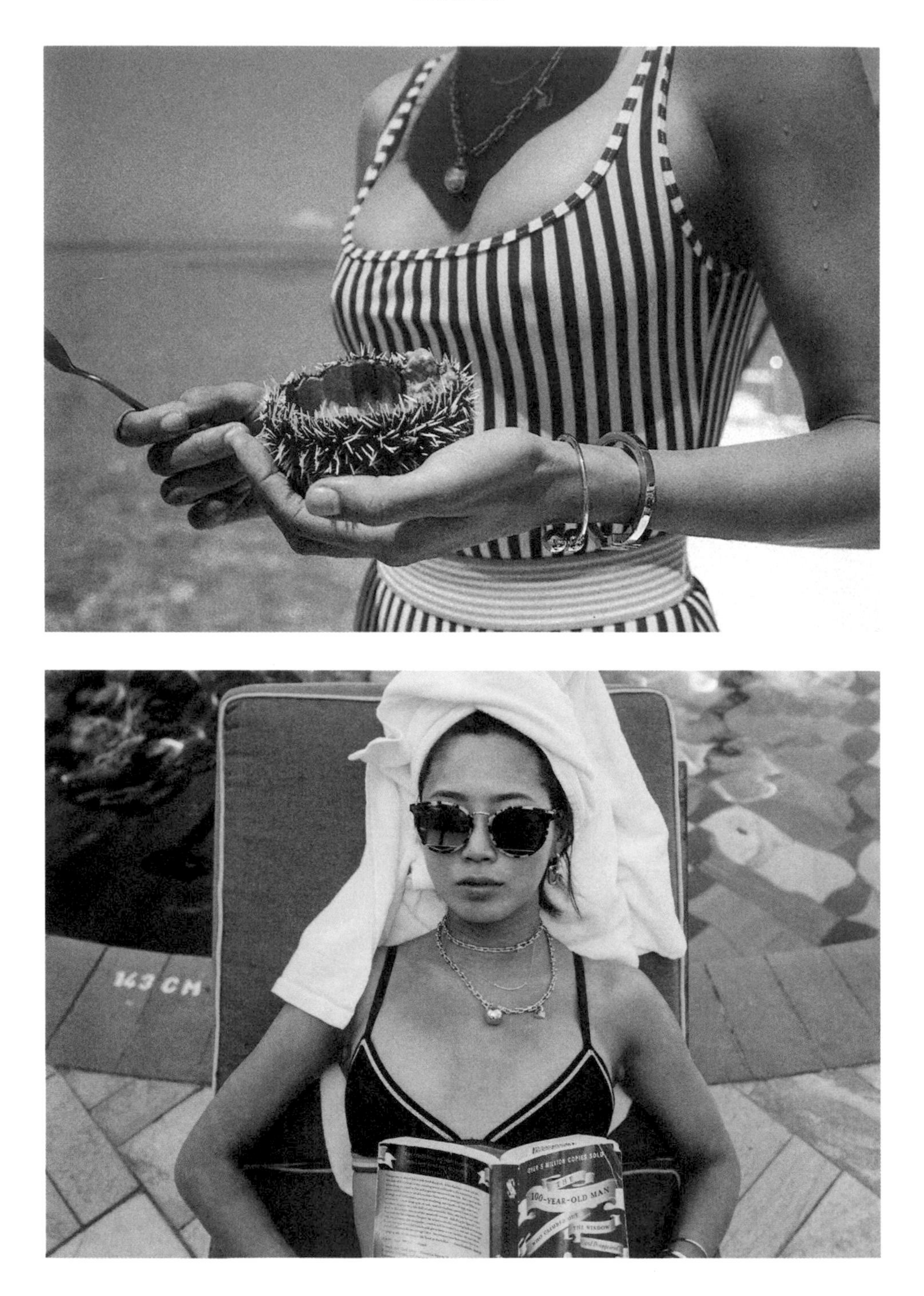
143 CM
OVER 5 MILLION COPIES SOLD
THE
100-YEAR-OLD MAN

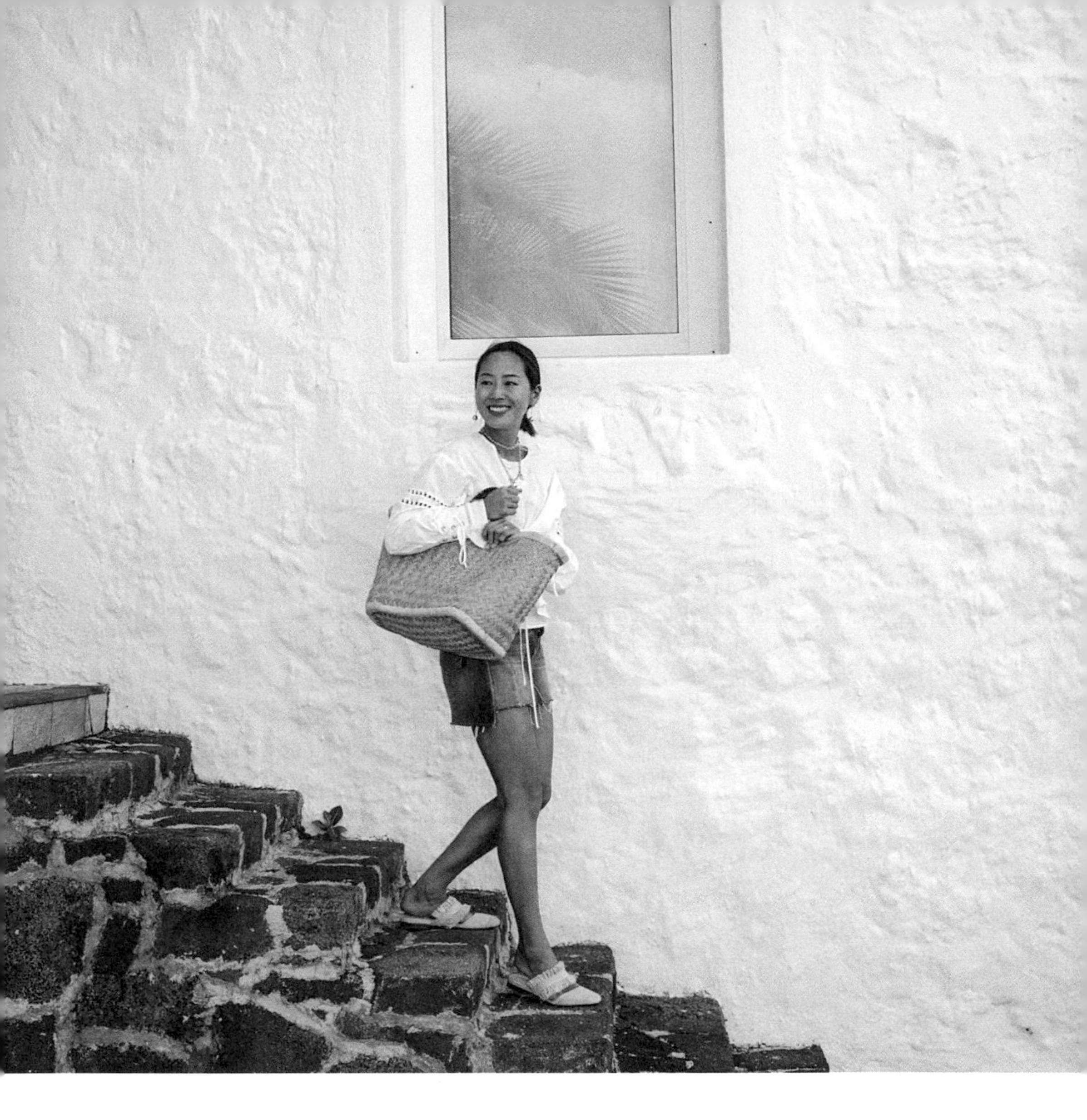

ABOVE *Grlfrnd denim skirt*. **OPPOSITE (FROM TOP)** My favorite activity in Mauritius outside of our diamond-polishing factory visit was a boat day where we ate sea urchin en masse. I'm obsessed with sea urchin—so much so that Jacopo got Santa Barbara sea urchin delivered for my birthday in 2017, and we had an amazing low-key night at home eating seafood with friends. I must have eaten seven of them on the boat. • I still haven't finished this book. I usually make it a mission to finish one book per trip, but I didn't have time to finish this one and haven't gone back to it yet (adding it to the to-do list). *Gentle Monster x Song of Style sunglasses.*

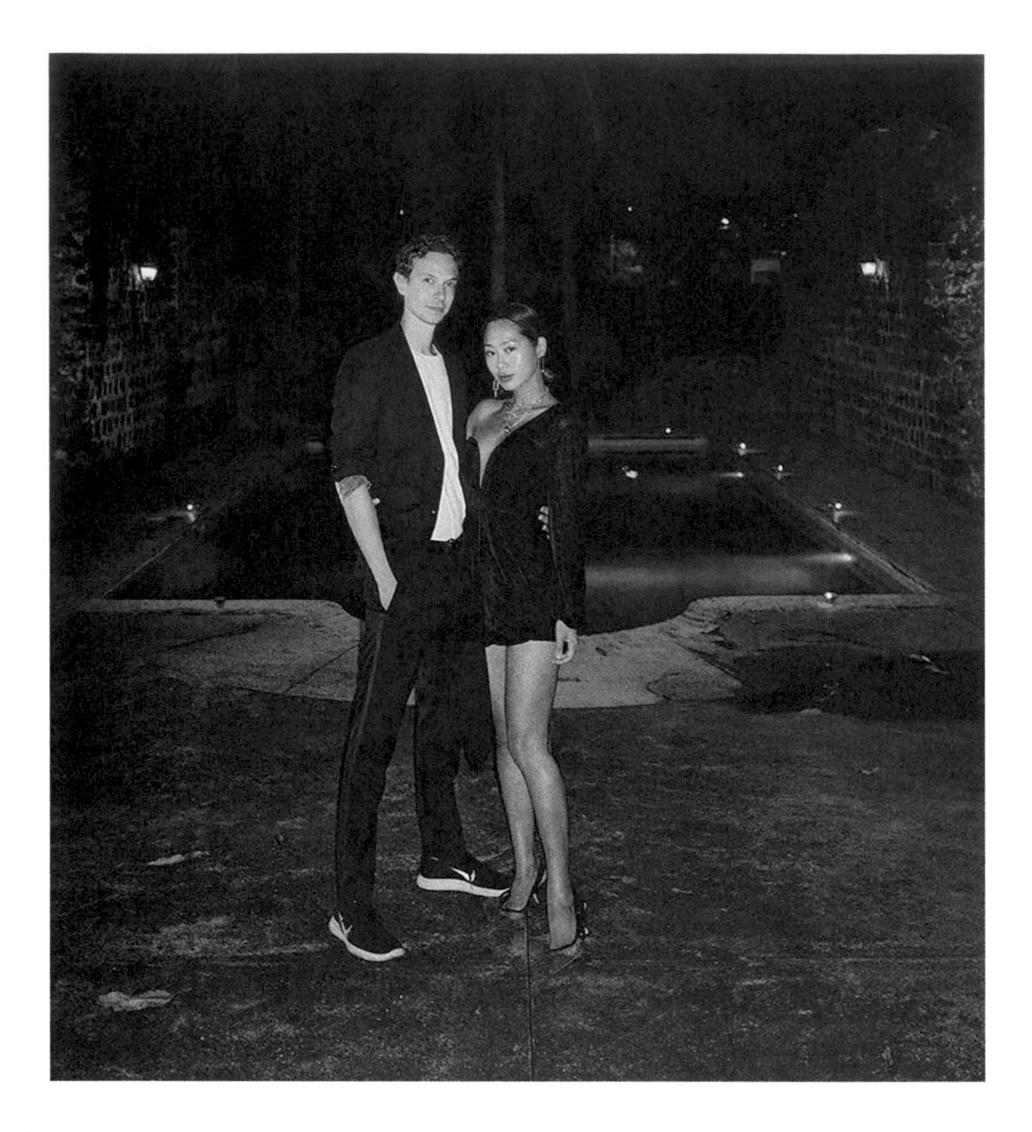

ABOVE Jacopo and I before dinner on our last night, which was at this incredible restaurant inside a historic mill called Le Café Des Arts. The owner's mother was an artist and a protégé of Matisse, so the space was filled with gorgeous paintings and art books—it felt like being in someone's house. Even the napkins were printed with line drawings done by the owner's mother (I may or may not have taken one home as a souvenir). *Michelle Mason dress; Dior pumps; Tiffany & Co. jewelry.* **OPPOSITE** Enjoying the tropical vibes. *Reformation dress; Tiffany & Co. jewelry; Gentle Monster x Song of Style sunglasses.*

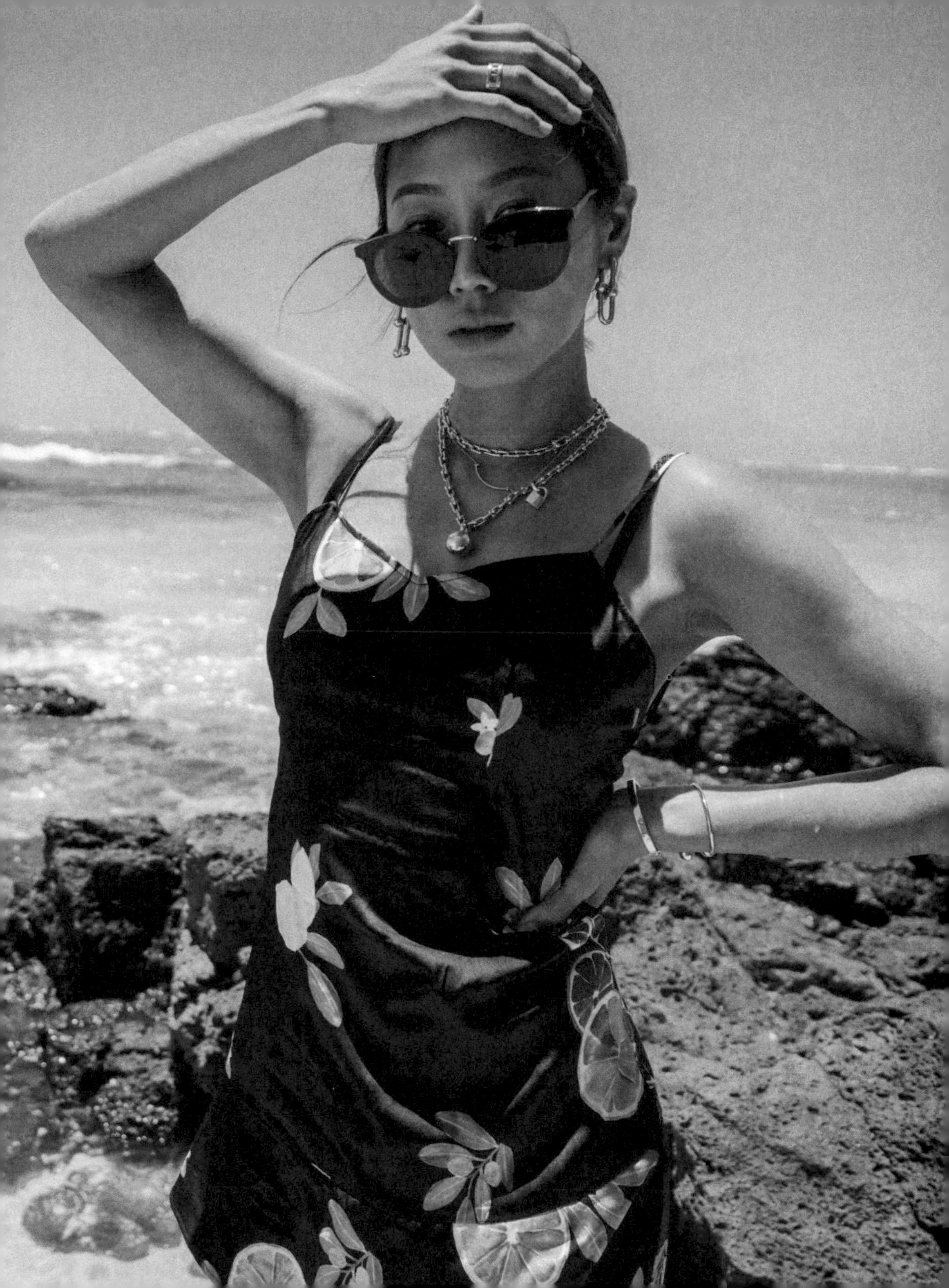

MOROCCO

Different trips serve different purposes for me. Beach vacations tend to fill a need to unplug, lie in the sun, and read a book, while visits to new cities turn me into an urban explorer whose curiosities are quenched with museums, art, new designers, and interesting food. And then there's Morocco—a cultural exchange so special and different from daily American life that it touches you in ways you never saw coming. I've been lucky enough to experience magical Morocco three times—in 2013 with Dani as part of a press trip with the Moroccan National Office of Tourism, and again in October 2017 after Paris Fashion Week. The most important memory I have of Morocco is that it's where Jacopo and I first met, on my second trip there in 2014.

It was another National Office of Tourism trip, and a few days into the visit I saw a boy sitting in my hotel lobby. It wasn't love at first sight; but he was sitting alone and, as is my personality, I sat next to him and decided to say hi—something I encourage you to do, as you never know where a friendly smile and simple "Hello" will lead. In my case that "Hello" has led to one of the most important relationships in my life.

I soon learned that the mystery man in the lobby was an Italian photographer named Jacopo, who was in town to shoot a sunglasses campaign, and he happened to be working with the publicist that my group was touring with. We all ended up going to lunch before serendipity (by way of someone else's bad case of food poisoning) saw Jacopo and me on an ATV ride together. The

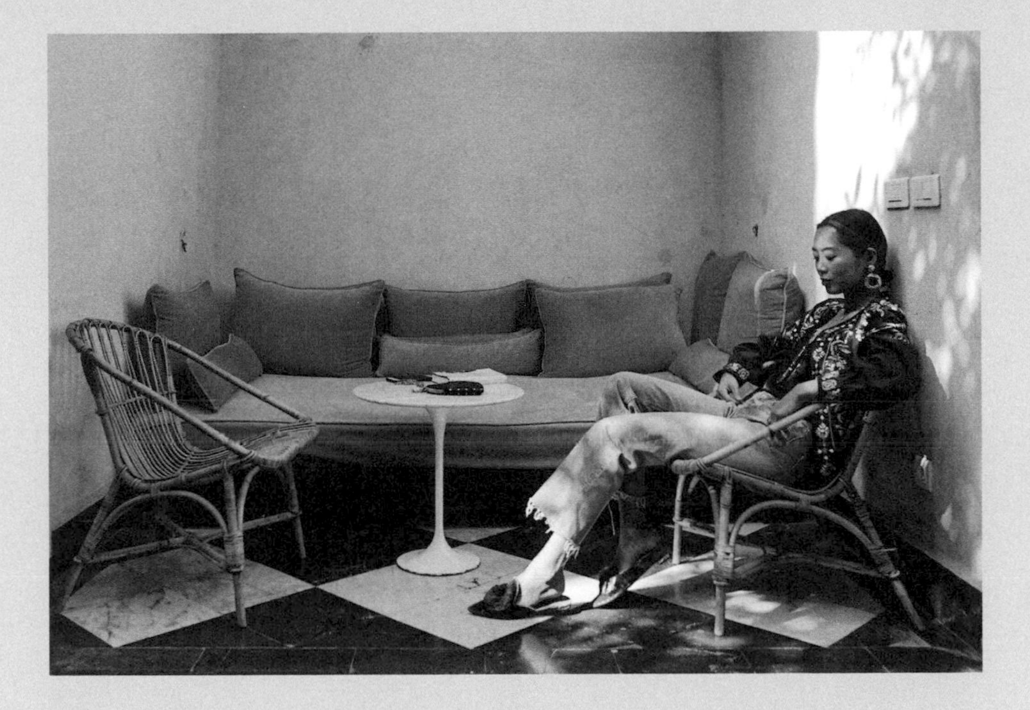

love connection had yet to reveal itself, but as our group explored the medina, Jacopo—who, having visited Morocco before, was practically a medina pro—took the lead and showed us around. He guided us from stall to stall and demonstrated patience, respect, and a quiet confidence as he negotiated with sellers on our behalf. His energy made an impression.

Later, there was an incident where two taxi drivers got into a fight over which one was going to drive our group. I was sure a fistfight was going to break out, but Jacopo calmly and coolly defused the situation with aplomb, and I was officially intrigued.

We exchanged Instagram handles and left things at that, with nothing officially developing between us until much later (plus I was in a relationship at the time). But I love thinking back to that trip and remembering how saying "Hello" to a stranger ended up being such a fateful milestone in my life.

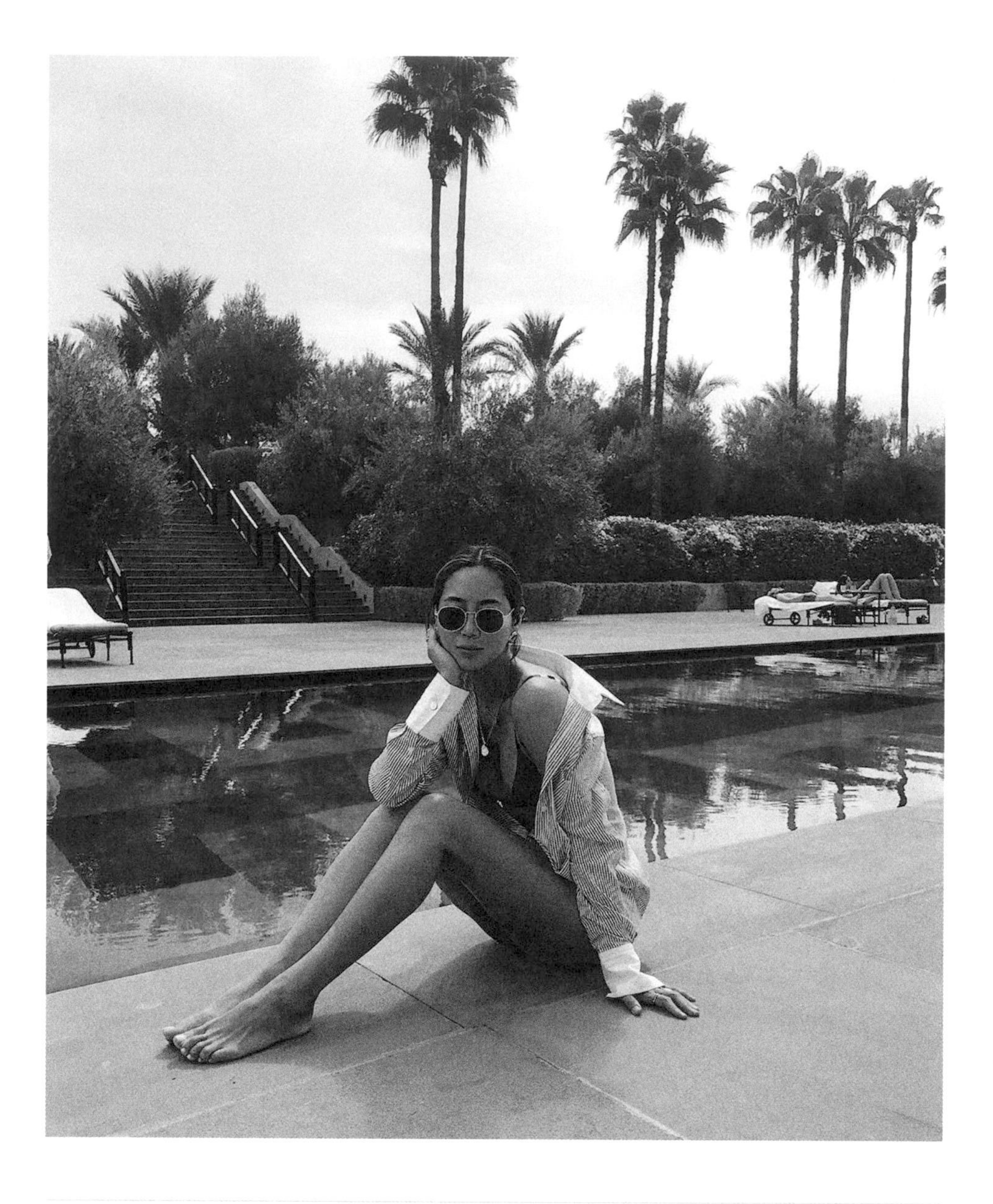

ABOVE On my recent trip in 2017, at the Selman Marrakech hotel. This trip was pretty chill compared to my others—Jacopo and I relaxed at the hotel, shopped, ate at some restaurants I wanted to try, and enjoyed quality time together. *SJYP shirt.* **OPPOSITE (FROM TOP)** One of my favorite riads, which is a typical Moroccan house built around a courtyard. • *For Love & Lemons dress; Lanvin earrings.*

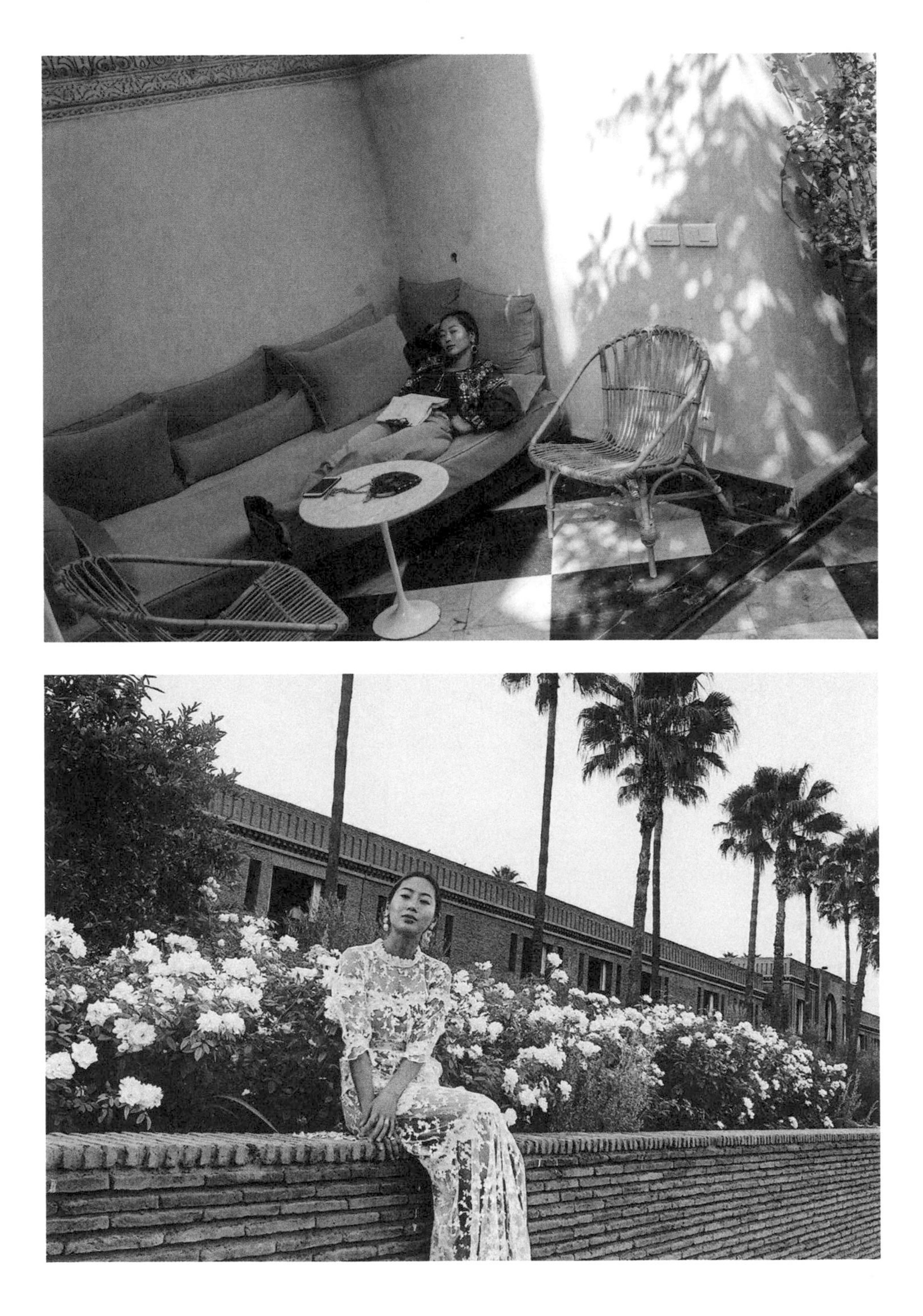

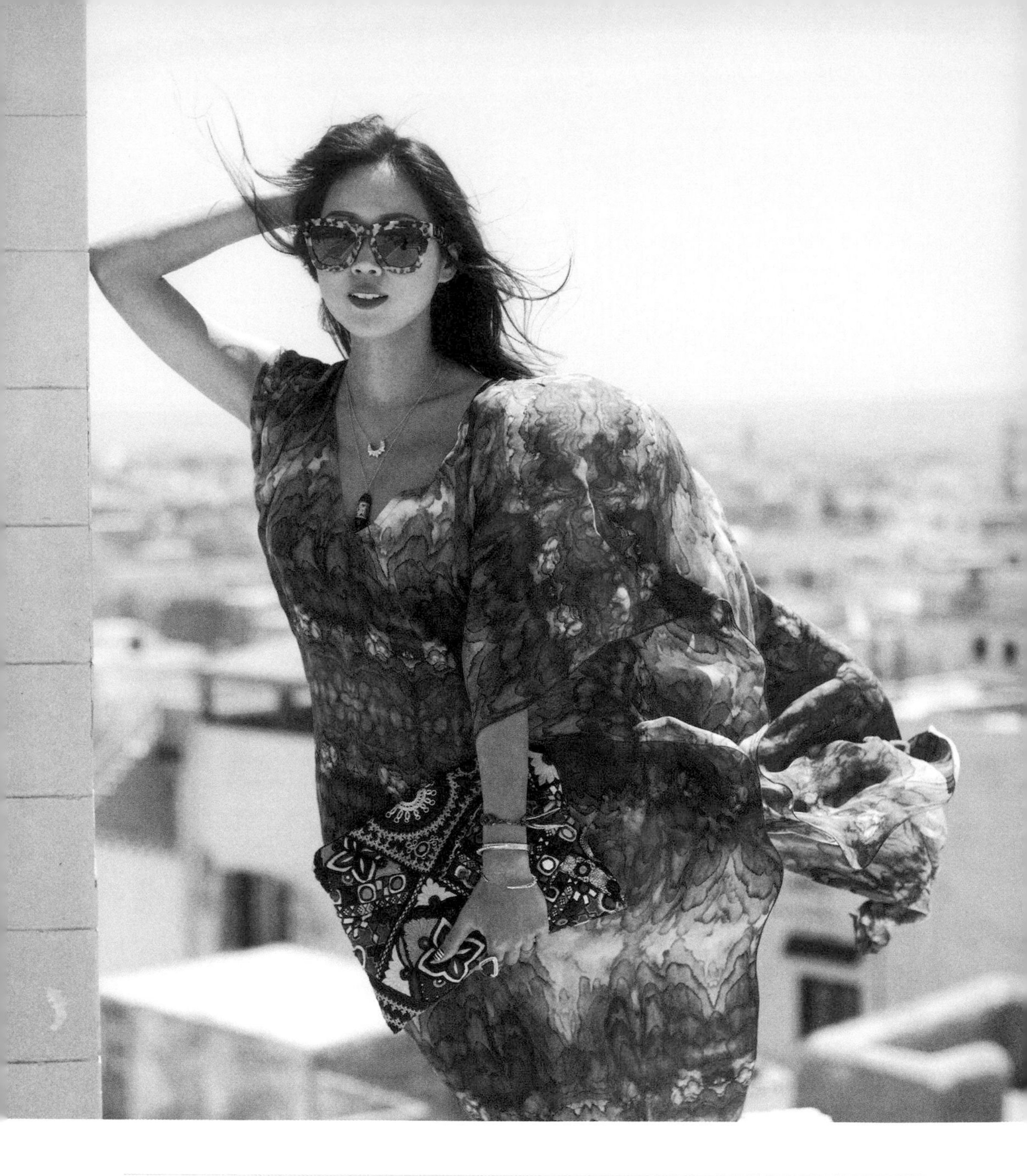

In 2014 I visited the port city of Essaouira, on the Atlantic coast. My best friend Jenny was with me and shot this. *Cheyann Benedict dress; Pamela Love jewelry.*

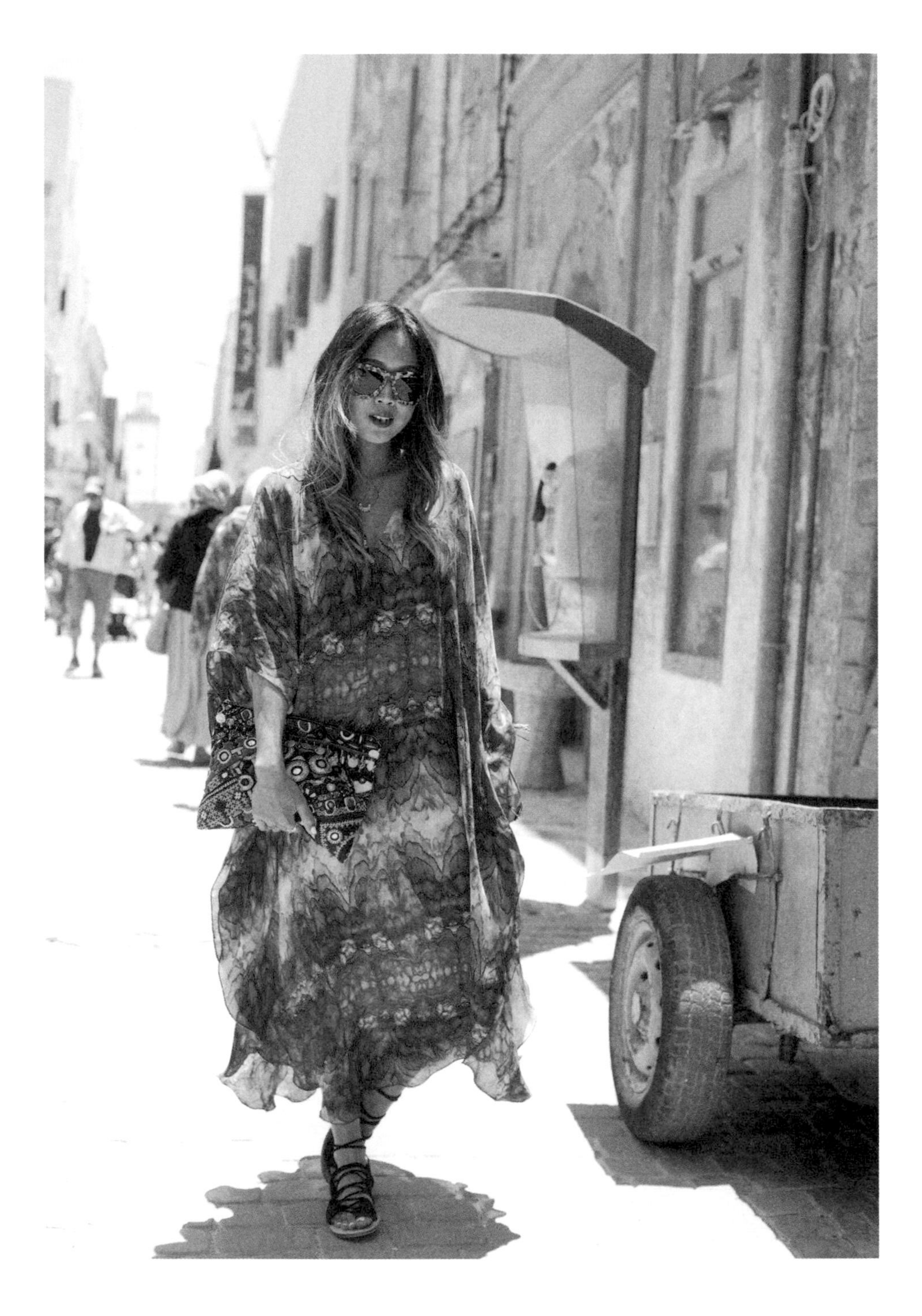

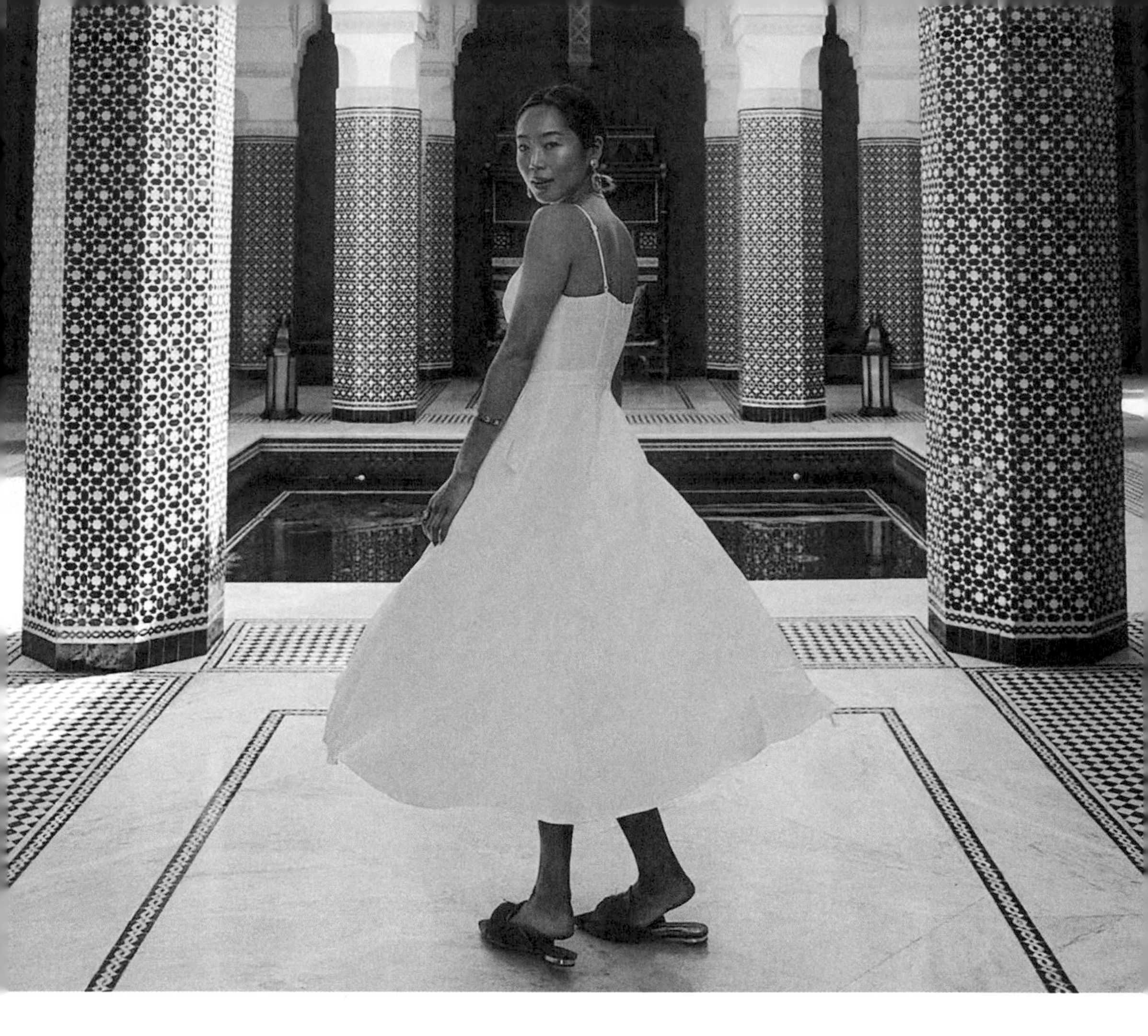

ABOVE Every single building and column in Morocco is more gorgeous than the next. This is inside one of the hotels we stayed at. *Yumi Kim dress; Aquazzura flats.* **OPPOSITE** On my 2017 trip, I had one goal: to buy a Moroccan rug. I bought a house last year and I knew I wanted to bring something back that would cover my living room. Jacopo and I went to a few rug places in Marrakech and found a seller I liked, where I must have sifted through at least fifty different options. I went in knowing what I wanted: a piece that was imperfect, asymmetrical, and looked more like art than a traditional floor covering. I knew I would know it when I found it (like so many things in life), and finally I did. Jacopo is the king of negotiating—he's patient, respectful, and reasonable (opposites attract, as they say). And four hours and a ton of talking later, he saved me thousands of euros and got me a piece I could actually afford. I love him so much for getting me that rug—among many other reasons, of course. *Caroline Constas top; The Volon bag.*

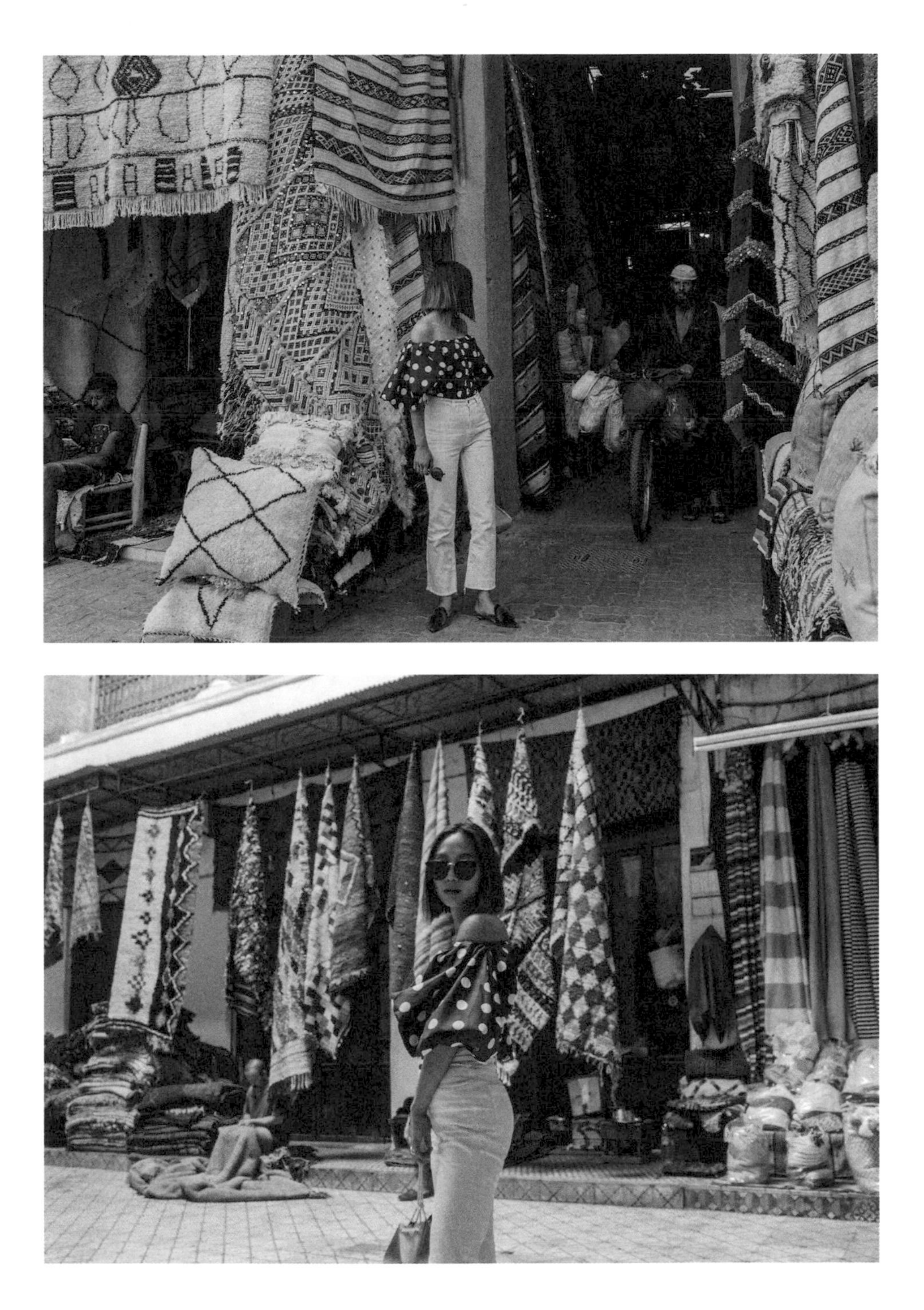

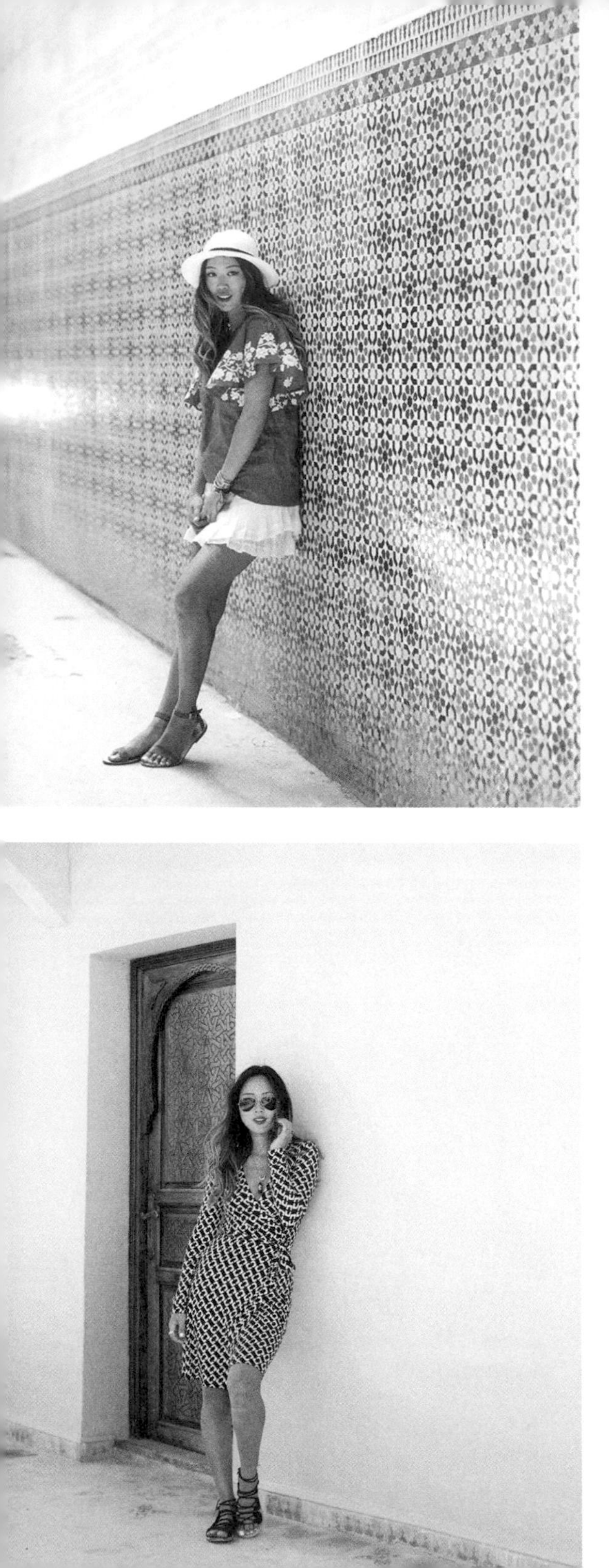

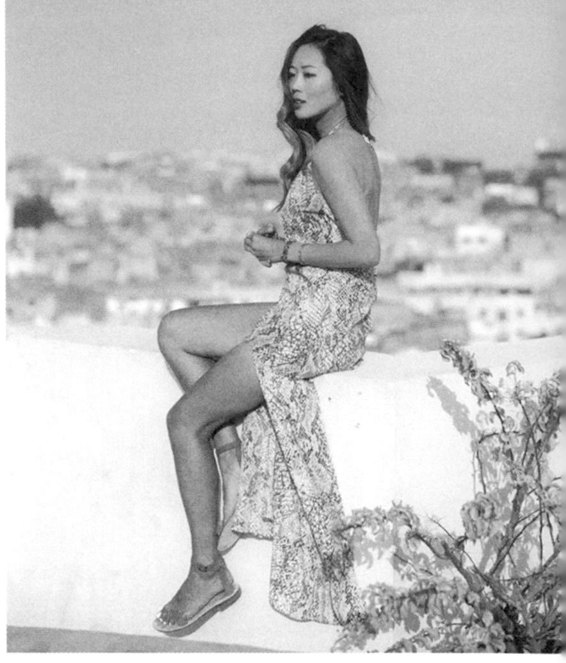

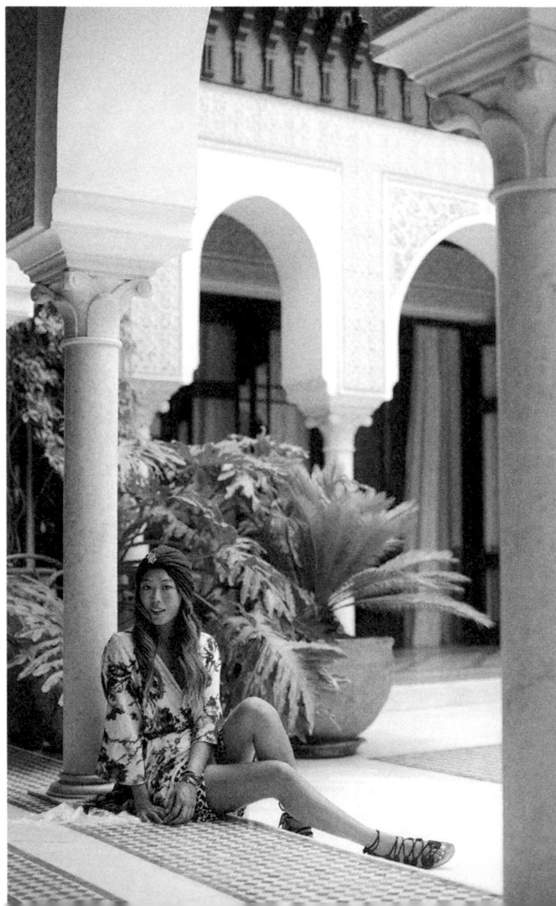

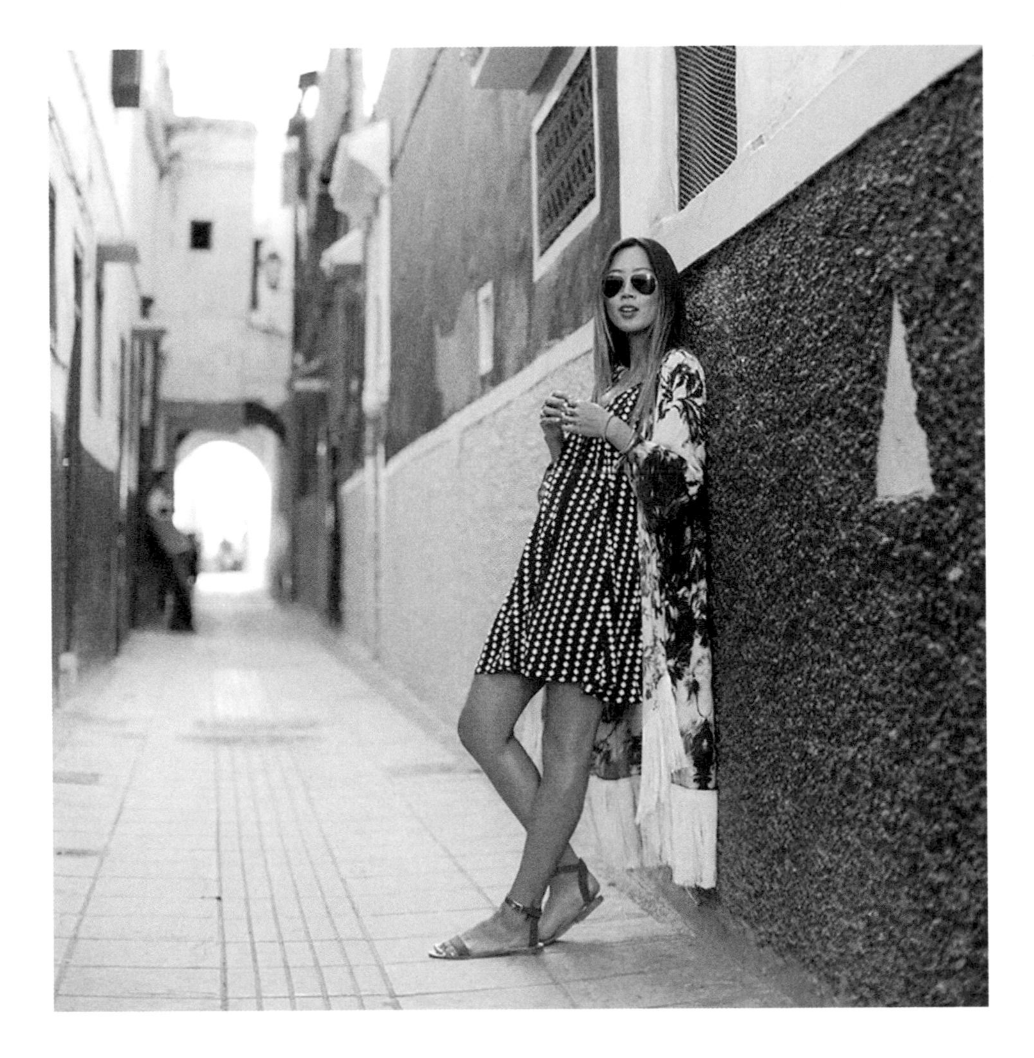

ABOVE In Rabat, Morocco's capital, where Dani and I saw Rihanna perform. She follows us on Instagram (like, what?), and after we each posted a picture from the show, she commented on both of our posts: "I was hoping to see you guys here—what are you doing after?" We legitimately freaked out. Sadly, in the pre-DM age we missed seeing her and still haven't met her, but Rih, if you're reading this, hit us up. We're here! *Athena Procopiou kimono.*

OPPOSITE (CLOCKWISE FROM TOP LEFT) We stopped in Fès, which is known for amazing leather goods. I didn't own a house at the time so I passed up gorgeous poufs that now haunt me. Talk about retail regret. *J.Crew top* • Also in Fès. On the rooftop of our hotel. *Lovers and Friends dress; Cornetti sandals* • My 2014 trip, right before meeting Jacopo. • *DVF wrap dress; Pamela Love jewelry.*

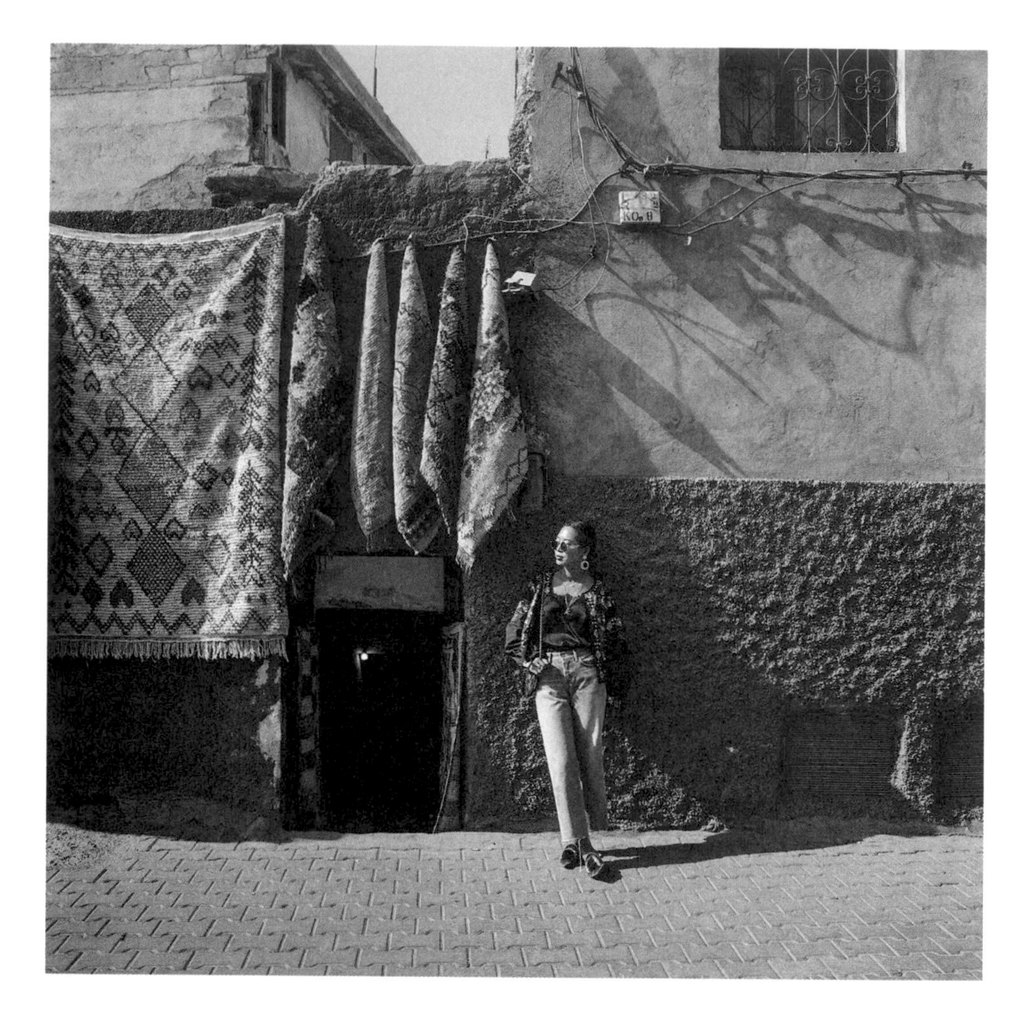

ABOVE Islam is the state religion of Morocco, so modest dress is appreciated—a fact that I didn't realize on my first visit, when I packed loads of mini dresses and shorts. My Instagram community commented on my posts to let me know that I should cover up, so I started talking to local people I was meeting and getting as much information as possible. That education helped me become much more mindful and respectful of my surroundings—in Morocco and on all the trips that have come after it. By the third trip in 2017, when this was taken, I knew how to dress like "me" while covering up. *Misa Los Angeles jacket; Michelle Mason top; Grlfrnd denim; Aquazzura shoes.* **OPPOSITE, TOP** My second visit, I also went rug shopping (though not for *the* rug) and ended up leaving the medina with a Moroccan wedding blanket and the colorful rug behind me. *DVF romper.* **OPPOSITE, BOTTOM ROW** *The Fifth Label top and skirt.*

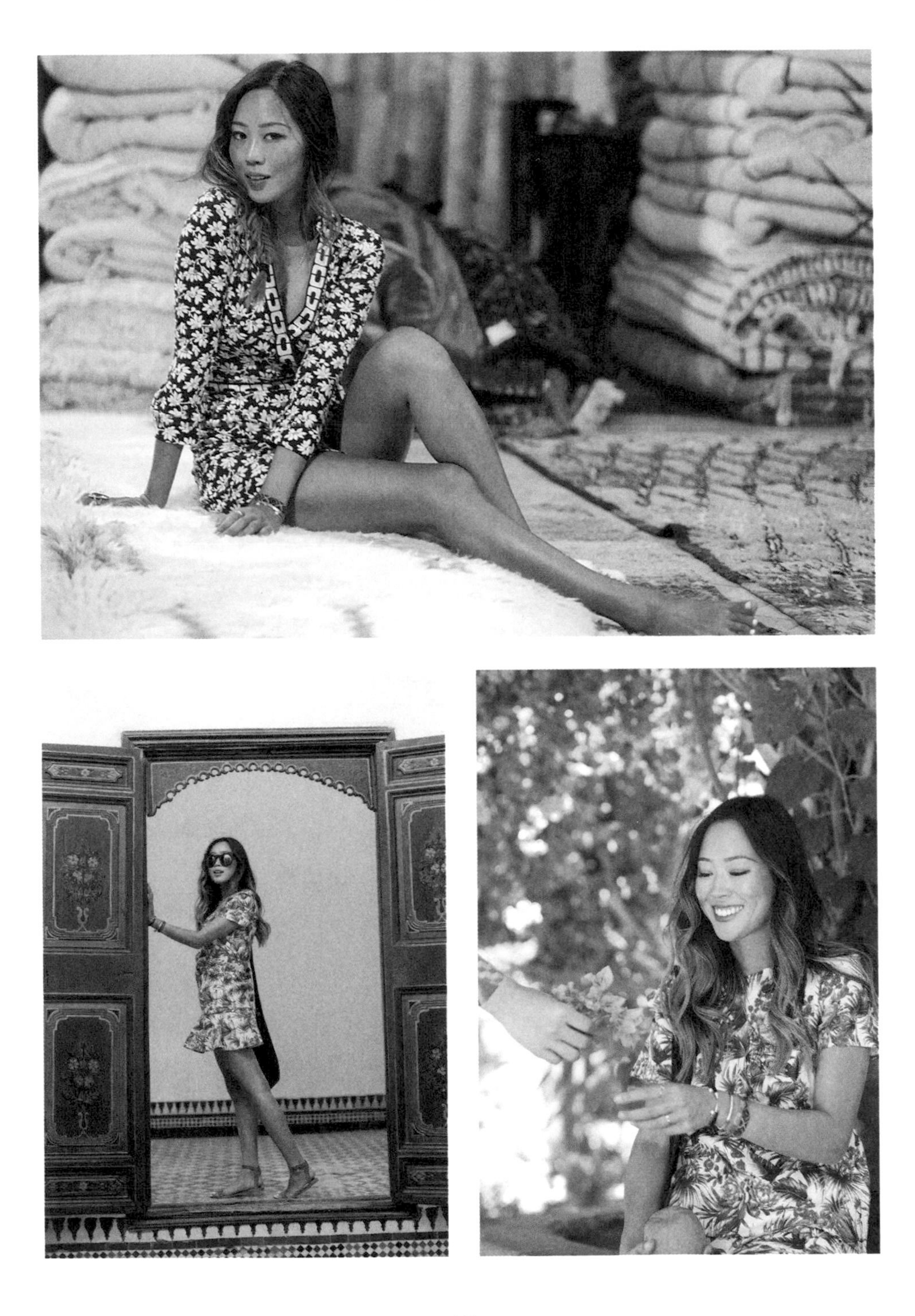

Beach day in Knysna. *Lolli Swim top; Levi's shorts.*

SOUTH AFRICA

South Africa pushes you out of your comfort zone and offers not only a cultural exchange, but also a look at the world that an American might not have had before. I've been twice—once in January 2014, when I visited the beautiful coastal town of Knysna with Dani, and again in November 2014, for South African Fashion Week in Johannesburg. On that first trip we were surrounded by nature and really tried to experience many facets of the country, which I always like to do when I travel. It was really important to me to absorb the history of the country and explore how race relations have shaped its history. We also visited a big-game reserve on that trip, an incredible experience that allowed me to see zebras, giraffes, and rhinos in the wild—animals that until then, I'd only seen in captivity and photographs. It's breathtaking to realize that those things actually exist on our planet.

My trip to Johannesburg was a bit different, but also familiar, since I was there for Mercedes-Benz Fashion Week. I had a packed show schedule and lots of work obligations, and my suitcase didn't get off the plane with me, so I was without any of my beauty products and had to do a last-minute Zara run. My suitcase eventually showed up—on the last day of the trip.

Pro tip: Now, I always take a few nice pieces in my carry-on just in case. I also carry travel-size beauty products in my carry-on, and I try to make sure my travel outfit is still somewhat chic so I can wear it with other pieces if I have to.

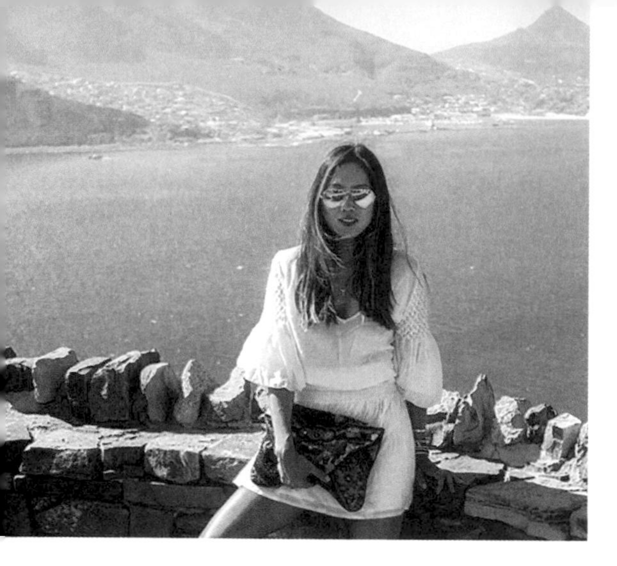
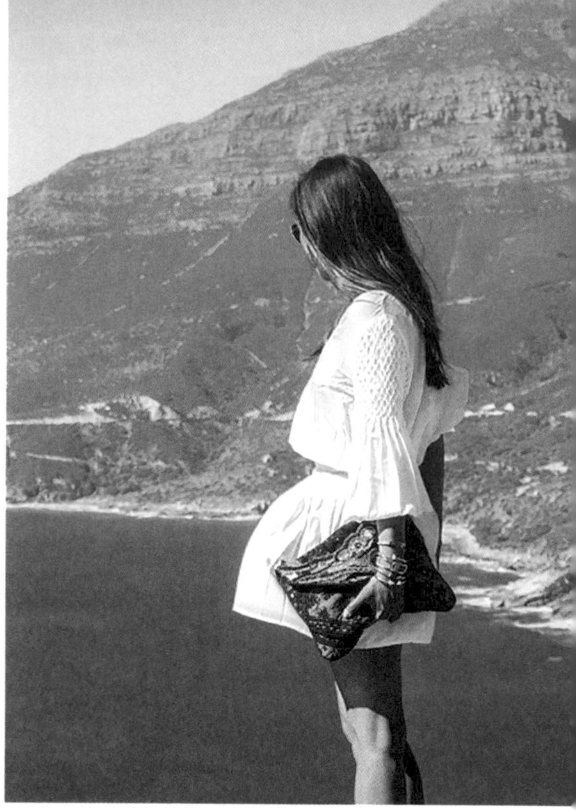
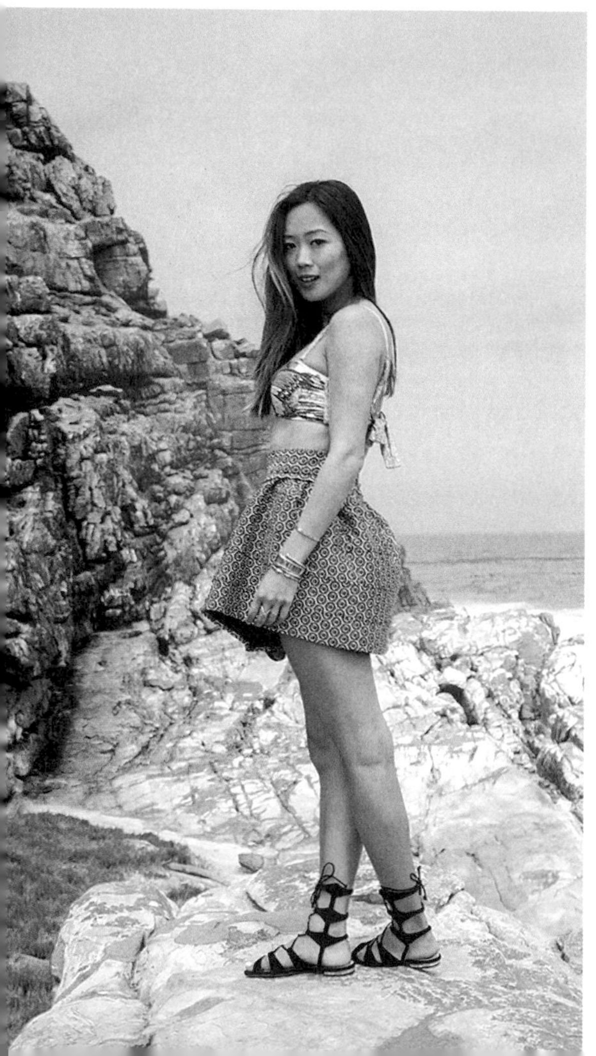
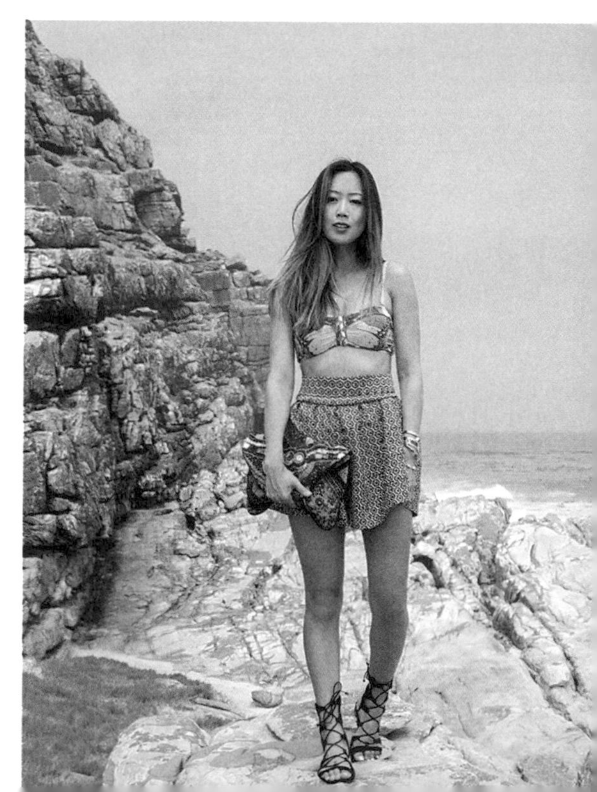

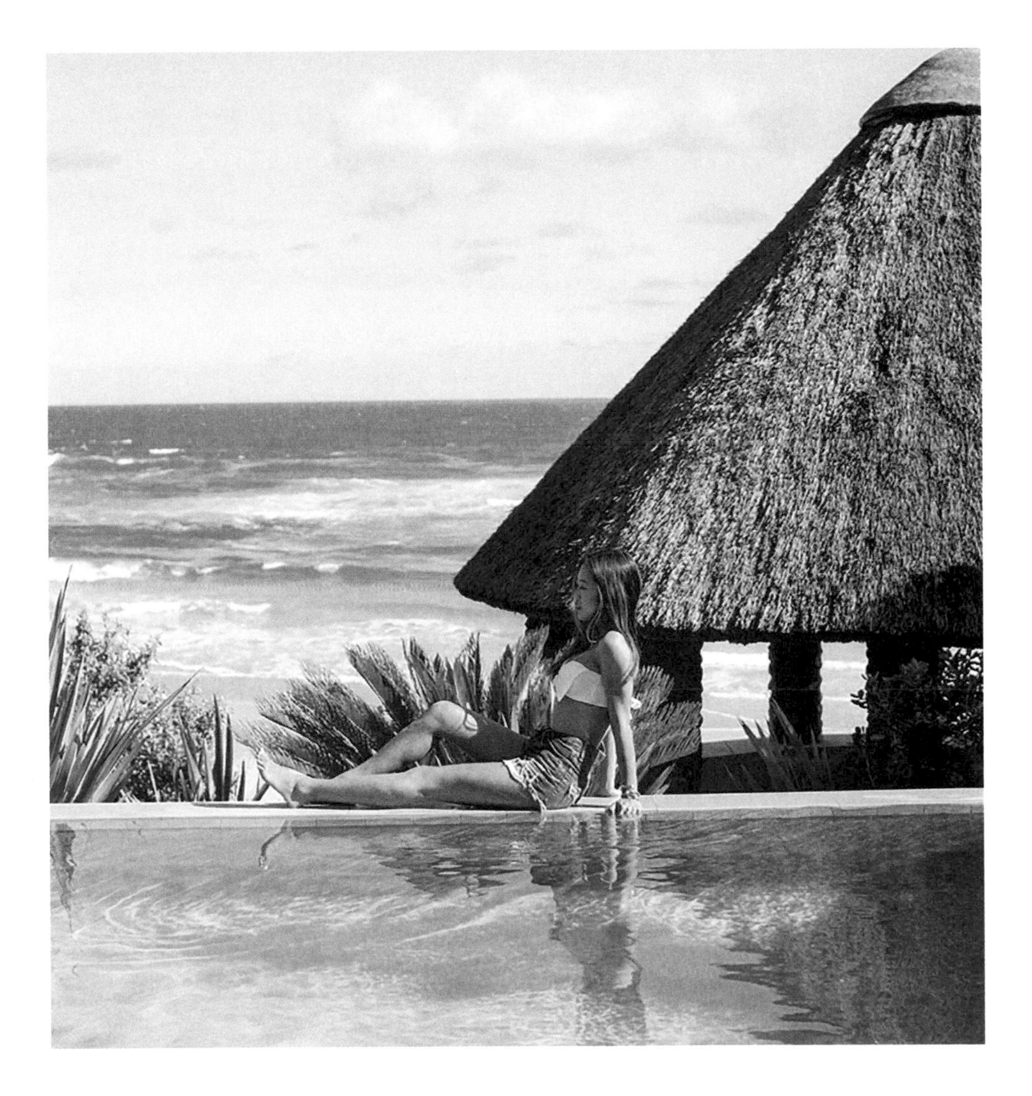

ABOVE Enjoying the architecture. **OPPOSITE, TOP LEFT** In Cape Town, where Dani and I went after Knysna. We were there for two days, and we rented a car through the hotel and saw a ton of the sites. When I only have a short amount of time in a location, I love booking a private car and a guide so I can really maximize my sightseeing—it's usually inexpensive and so worth it. *Lovers and Friends dress; Antik Batik bag; Ray-Ban sunglasses.* **OPPOSITE, TOP RIGHT** Checking out surfers, obviously. There's so much cool wildlife in South Africa. **OPPOSITE, BOTTOM ROW** This is on Boulders Beach near Cape Town, after seeing penguins on the beach. Right after this we went to the Cape of Good Hope and saw ostriches. Insane. *Maje bikini; T-Bags skirt; Antik Batik clutch; Schutz shoes.*

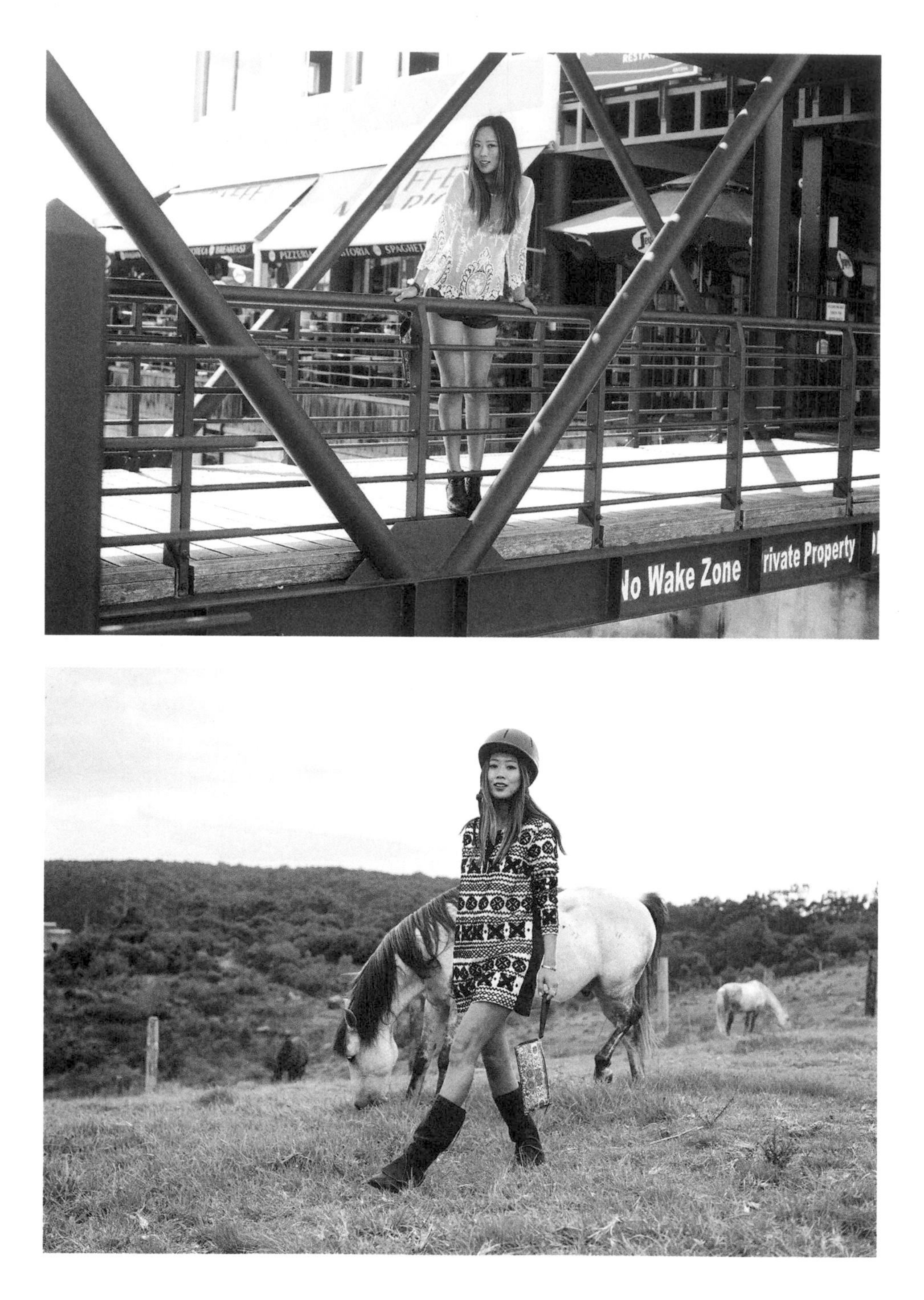
No Wake Zone
rivate Property

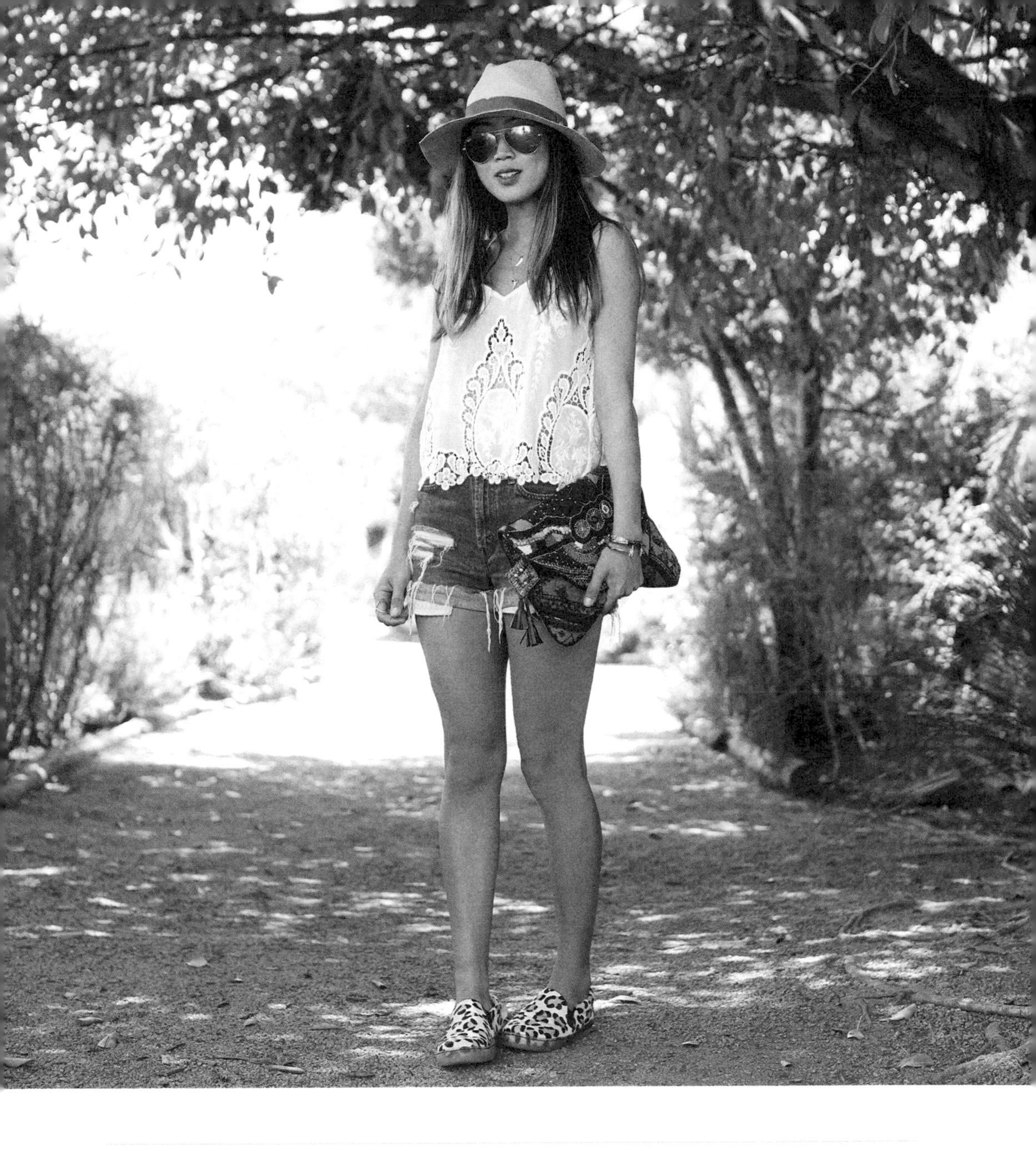

ABOVE This is the day we went on safari. I chose my outfit accordingly (all faux, of course!). *Dolce Vita top; Levi's shorts; Senso slip-ons*. **OPPOSITE (FROM TOP)** *Dolce Vita top, Lovers and Friends faux leather shorts, Senso boots* • Dani and I love riding horses—we actually grew up riding them because our dad owned a retired racehorse. It ended up being too expensive for him to keep the horse, so we didn't ride again until we grew up. *Antik Batik dress.*

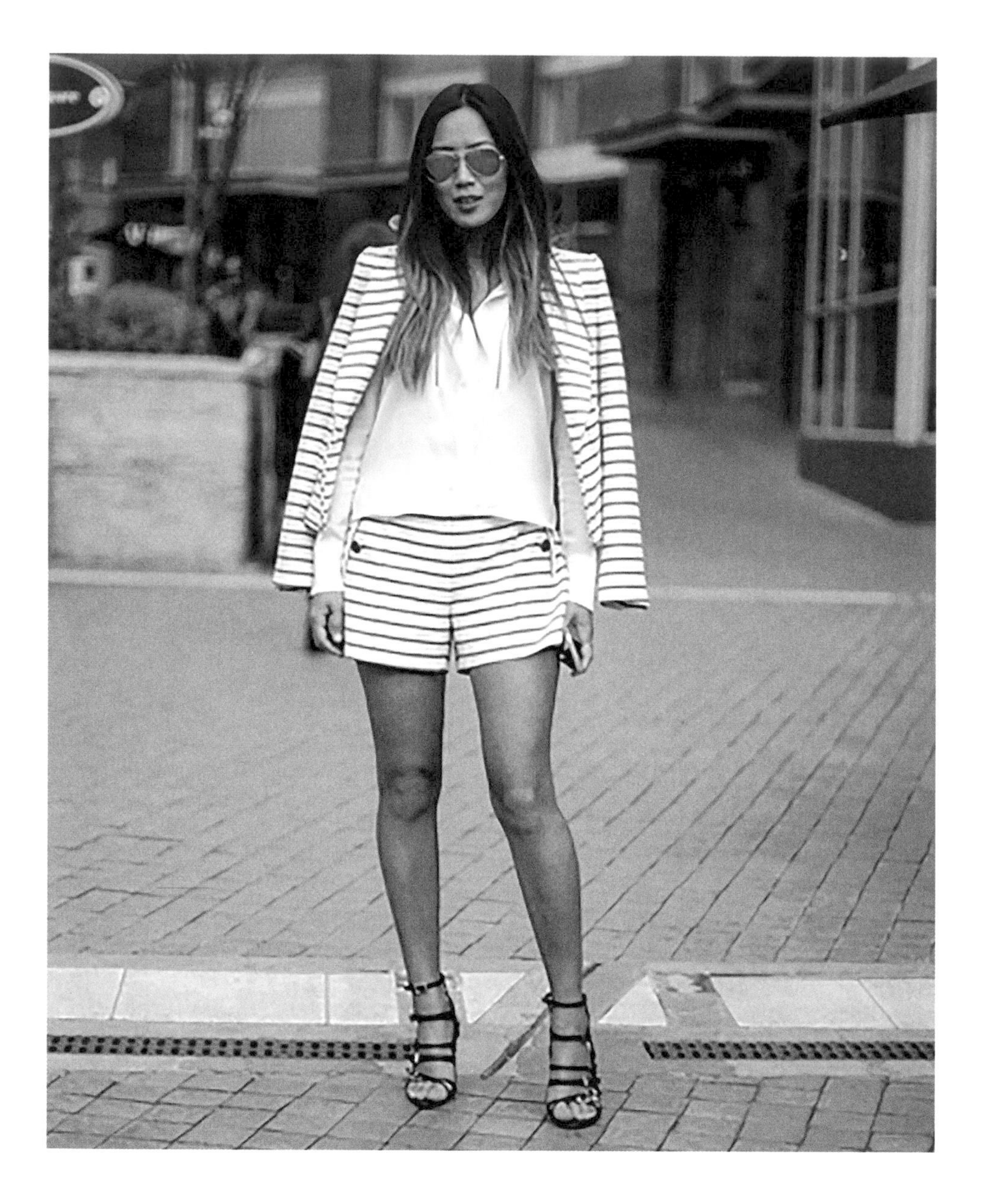

ABOVE Johannesburg in a Zara outfit that I had to buy after my suitcase didn't land.

OPPOSITE On my last day in Johannesburg after my suitcase finally came. *Two Songs sweatshirt; Céline shoes; Ray-Ban sunglasses.*

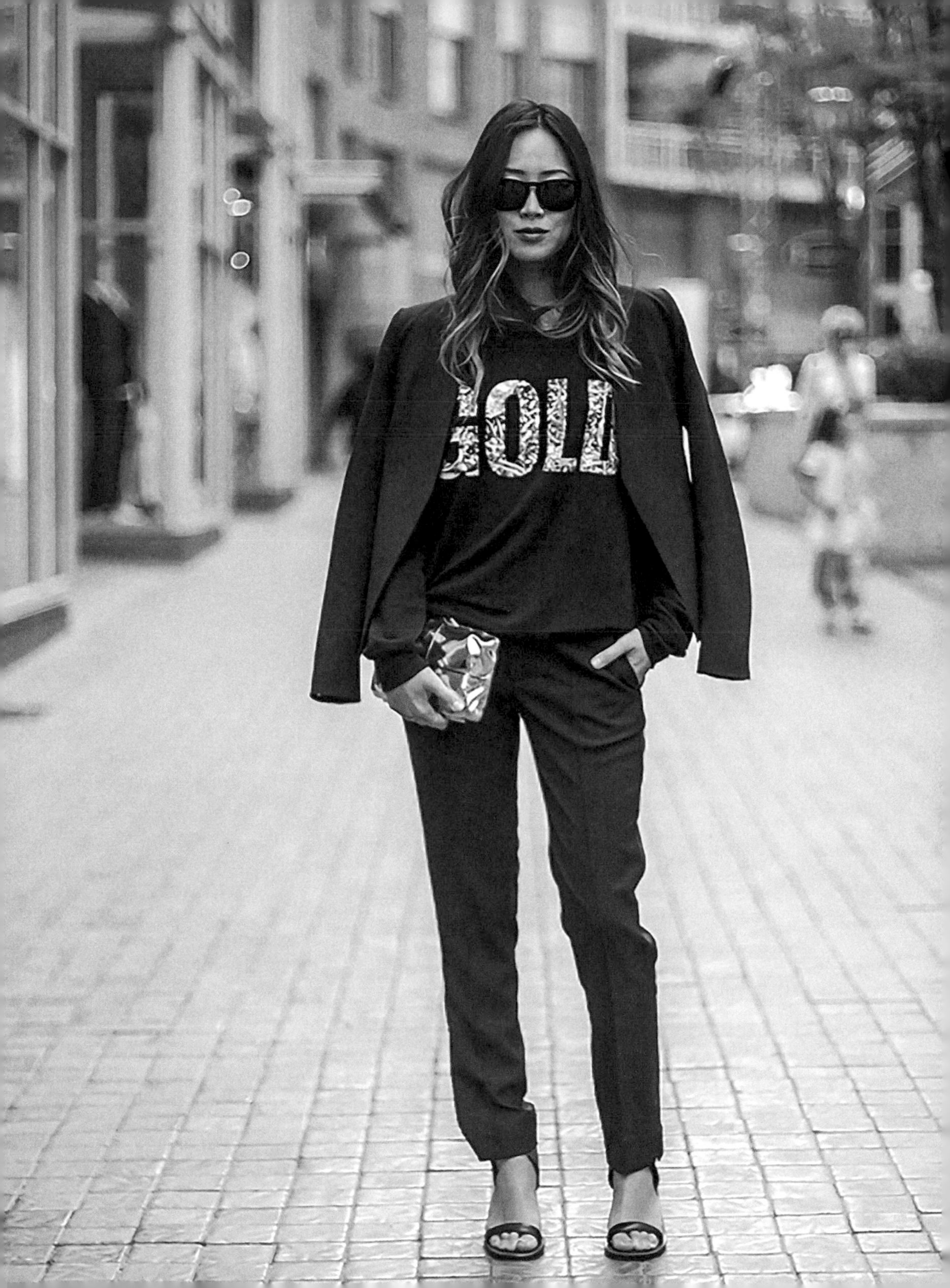

SOUTH AMERICA
LATIN AMERICA
MEXICO
THE CARIBBEAN

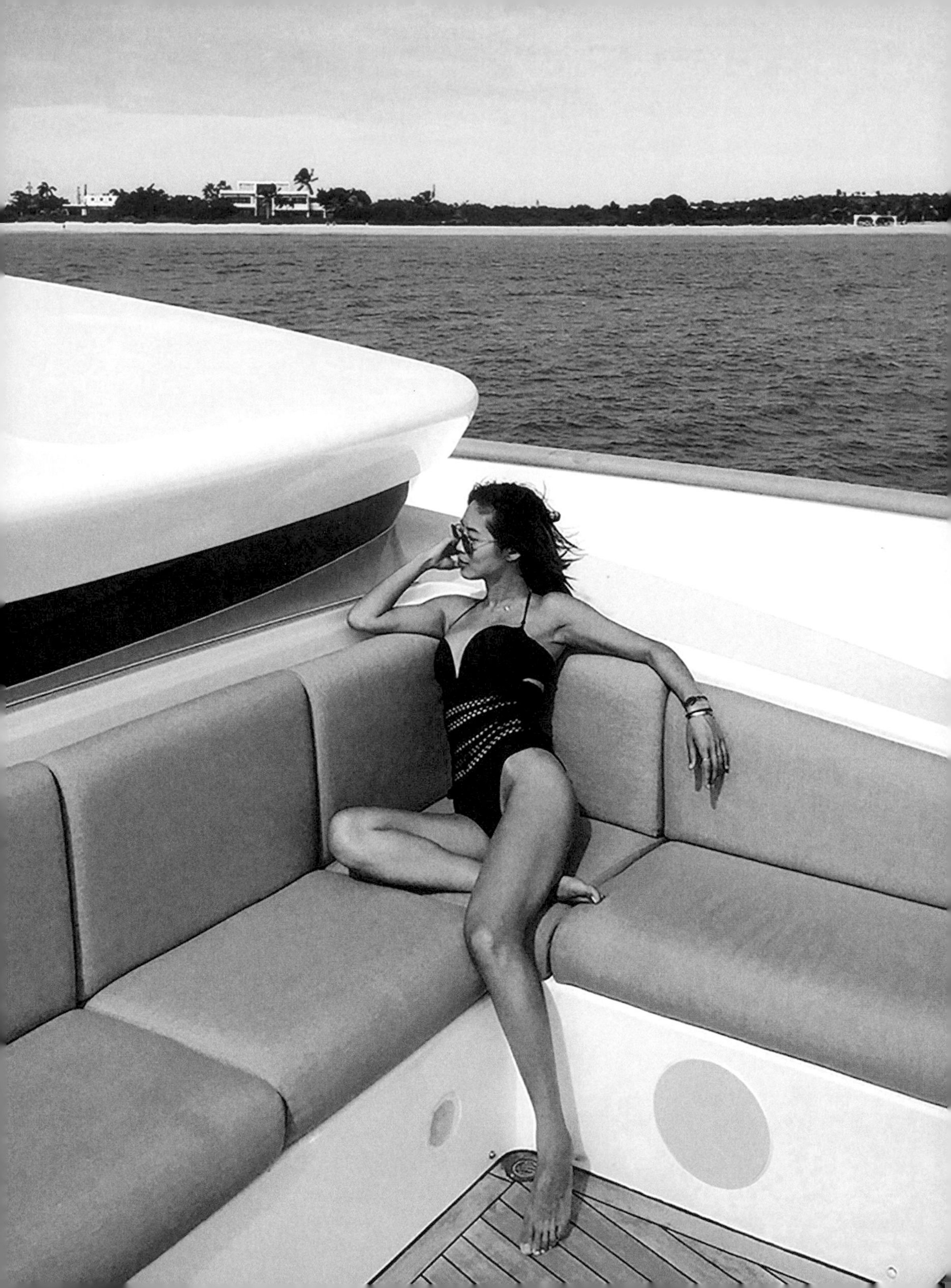

ANGUILLA & ST. BARTS

In January 2017 I went to Anguilla and St. Barts with Revolve for one of its #RevolveAroundTheWorld trips. I love all of my Revolve trips so much, but this one in particular has to be my favorite one yet because I got to hang out with girls I'd never met before and made a crop of new connections and friends. This also marked the first time that Revolve started using a defined itinerary—before we were left to plan our own days and dinners. There were all kinds of experiences that they planned—interesting restaurants and horseback riding included—and working off a schedule made me realize how much I love traveling with already planned activities. It's such a game changer to hire guides, make reservations, and plan certain activities in advance. Travel should have a degree of spontaneity to it, of course, but it's very helpful—especially when you're somewhere new for the first time—to have an idea of what you want to accomplish there.

OPPOSITE I love Tularosa because a lot of their swimsuits are a bit dressed up, so it's easy to go from swimming to a restaurant with a few simple (yet creative) styling tweaks.

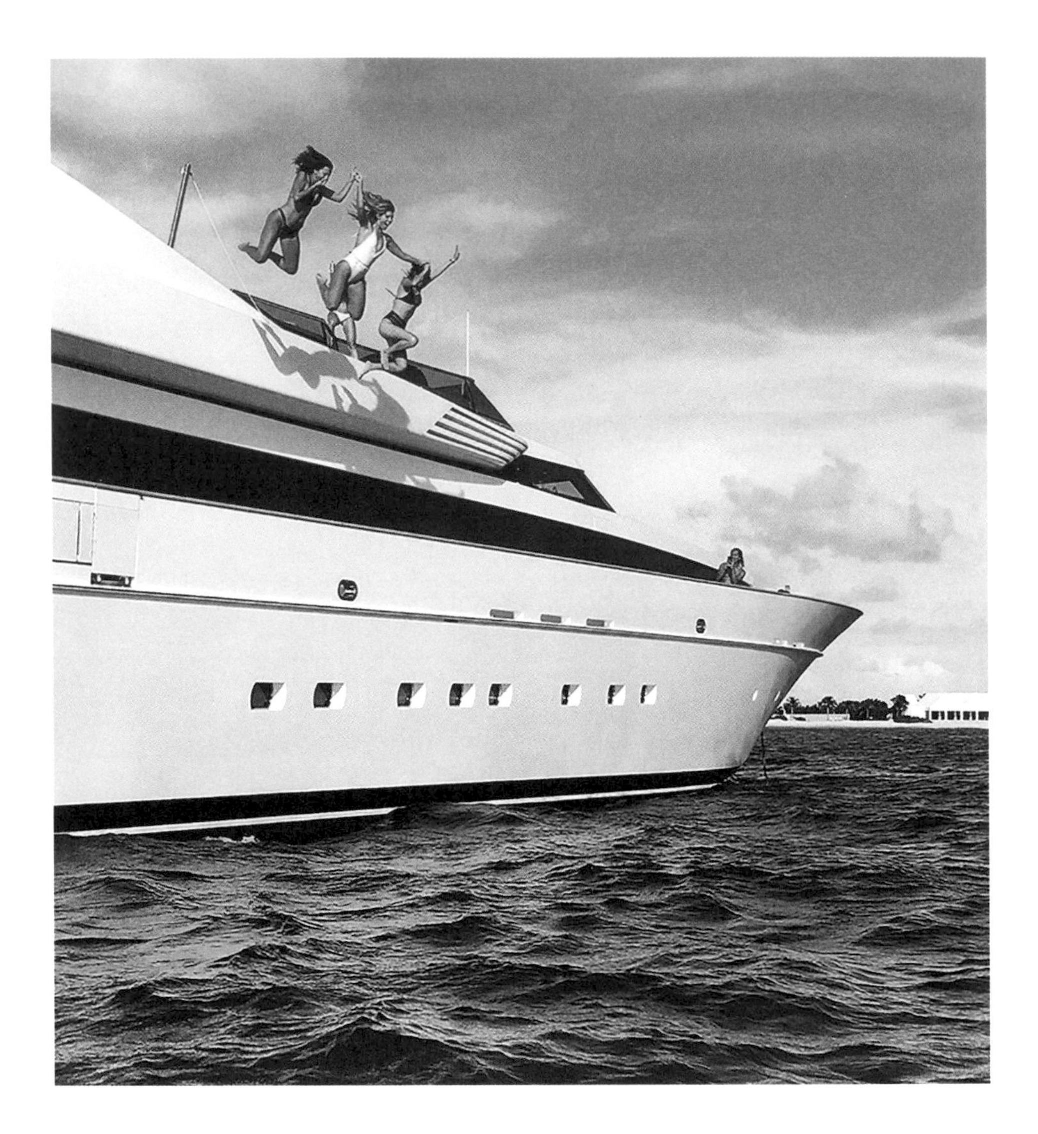

ABOVE I was so nervous to jump off the yacht with my new friends Tash Oakley and Devin Brugman, but it ended up being so much fun. Travel pro tip: Just say yes. **OPPOSITE (CLOCKWISE FROM TOP)** Exploring the town of St. Barts after getting ice cream (of course). Wearing Jacopo's shirt with a pair of Grlfrnd jeans. • I love pajama-inspired looks; they're so luxurious, and the tops and bottoms always look so cute both together and separately. *House of Harlow set* • We went horseback riding on the beach, which was a first for me. I felt like I was in a commercial (or, at the very least, the cover of a romance novel). *Hudson jeans.*

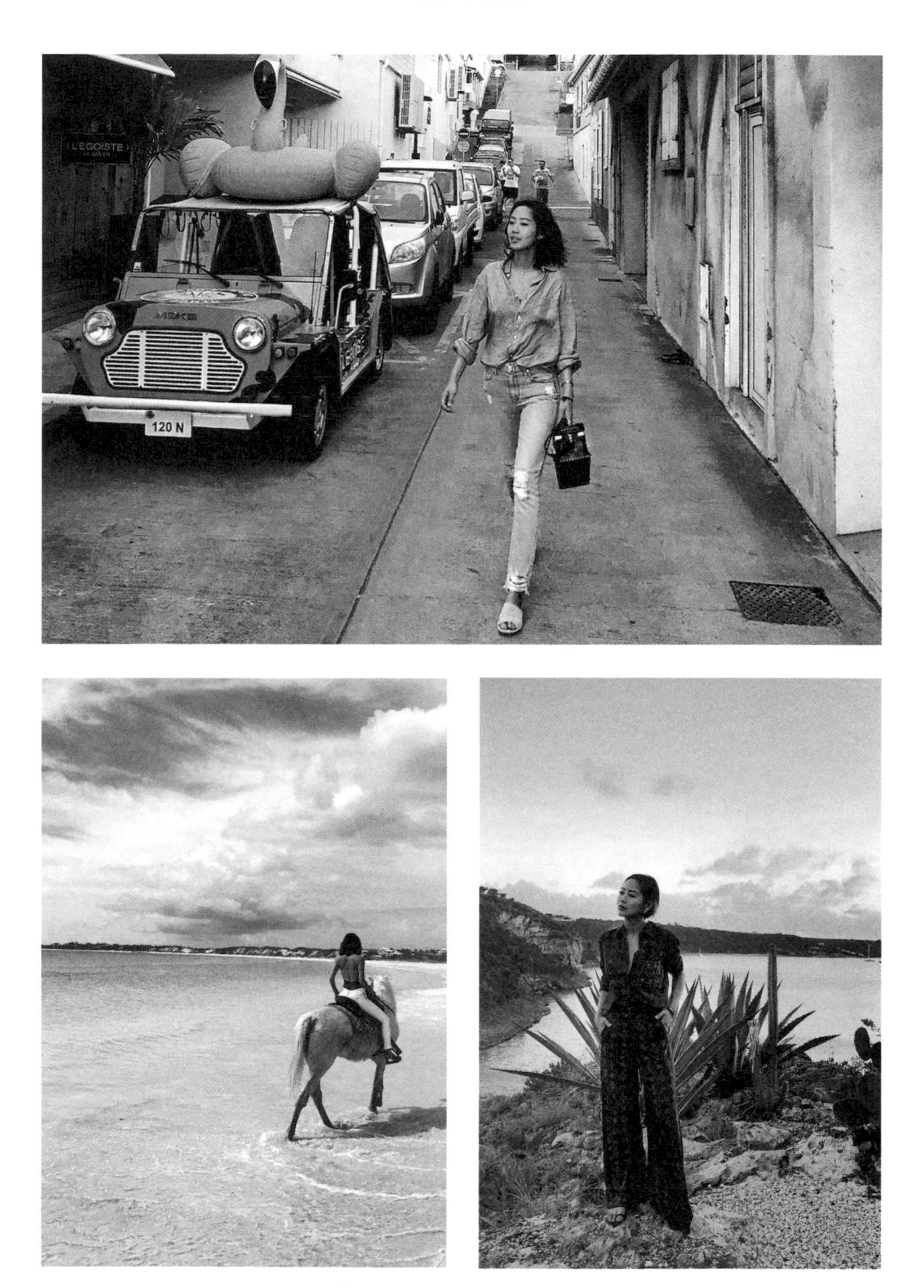
L'EGOISTE
120 N

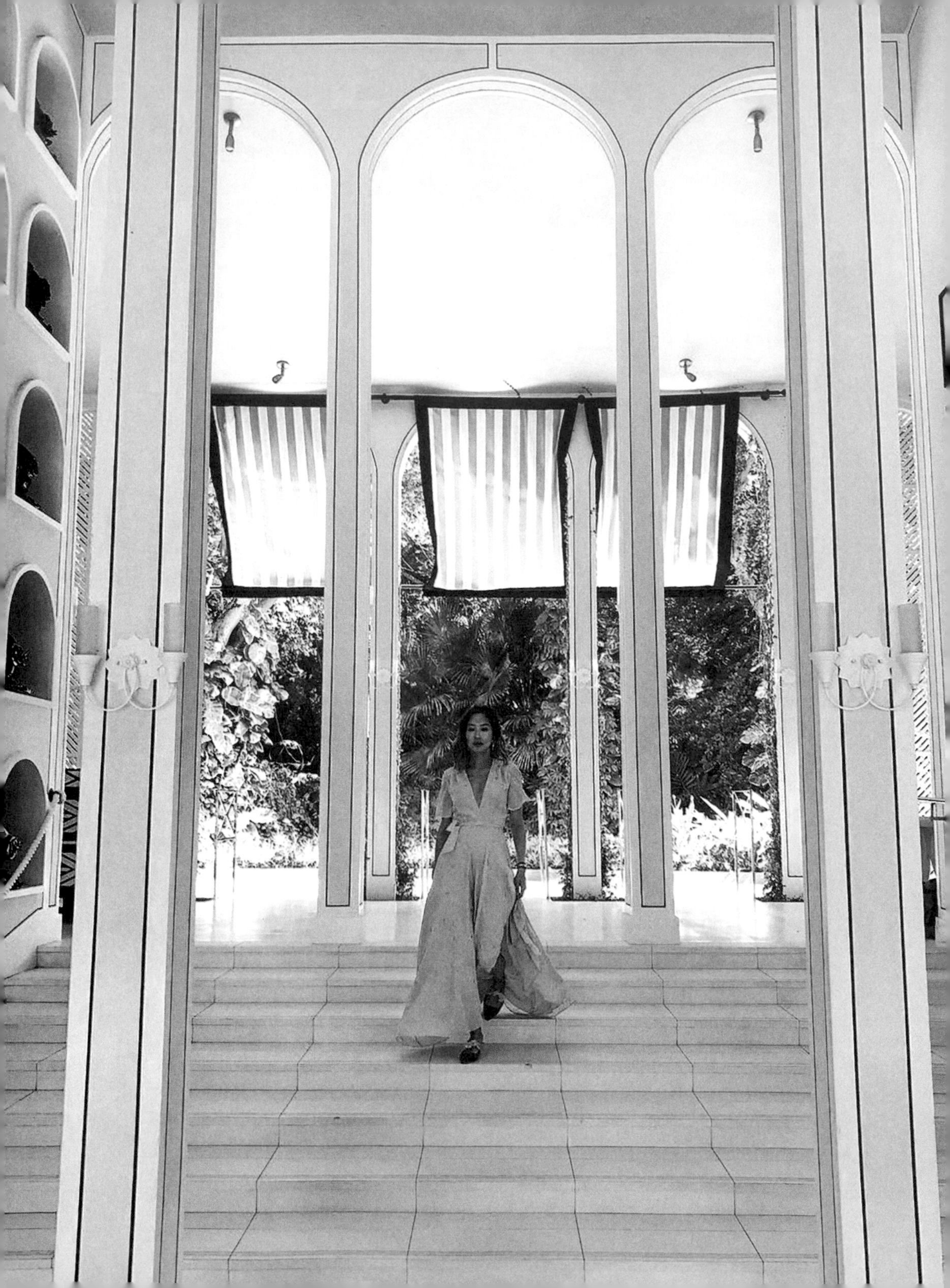

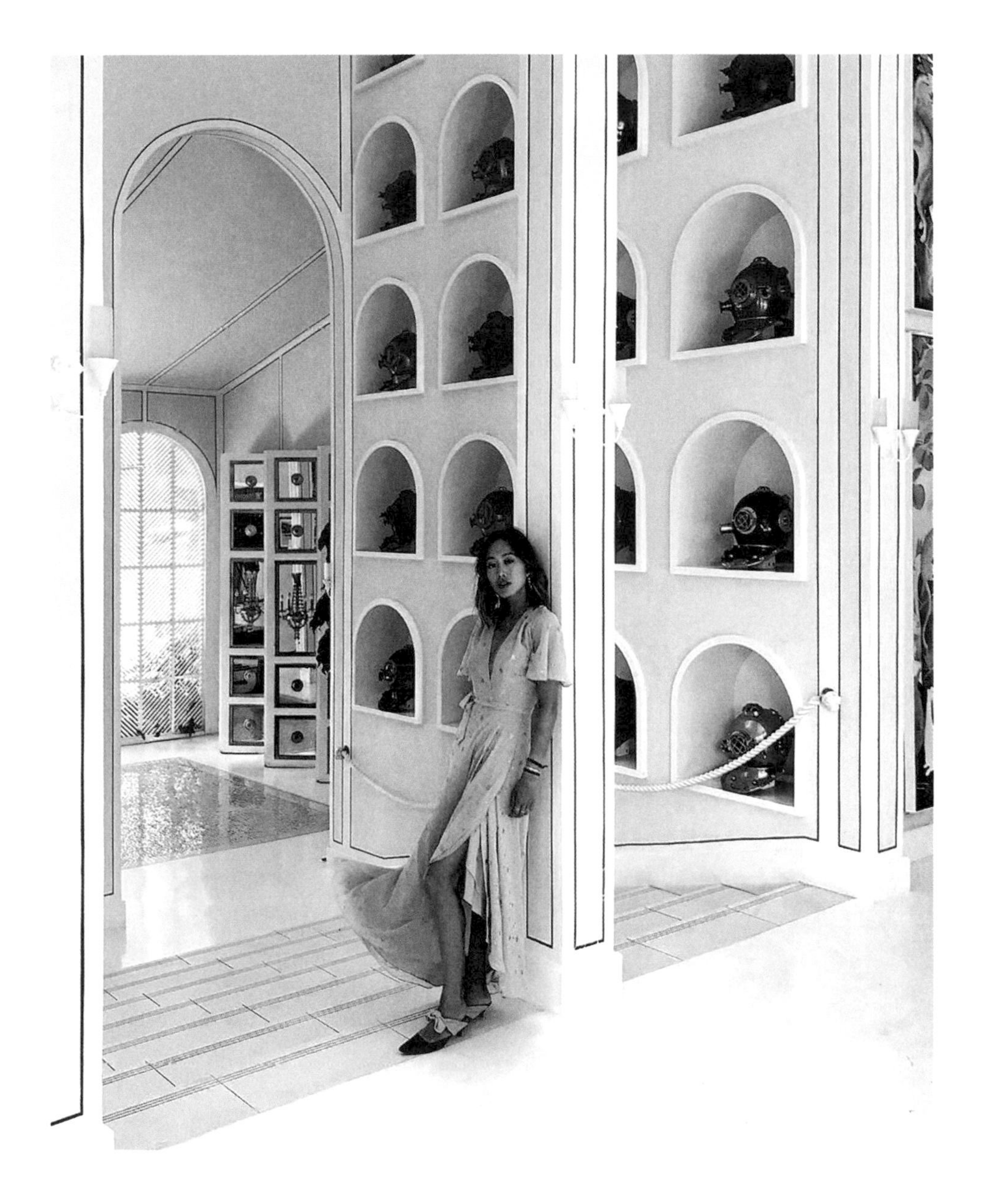

In Anguilla, we stayed at the Malliouhana Hotel, which felt like something out of a Wes Anderson movie because everything was styled so perfectly and thoughtfully. After I posted this dress on my Instagram, it sold out on Revolve's site. *Privacy Please dress; The Row shoes.*

SWIMSUIT SHOPPING 101

Like anything else in life, swimsuit shopping success depends on your outlook. Go into it with bad vibes and the experience will likely be less than pleasant. But approach your quest from a place of confidence and excitement about all of the amazing memories you'll make in said swimsuit (and the glorious Insta snaps you'll have to save those memories for posterity), and your swimsuit pursuit will be strong. Here are a few of my rules of thumb for choosing a suit that leaves me feeling like fire.

1. **Choose a style and colorway that make you feel amazing instead of following trends.** I feel good when I'm standing out, so I tend to choose suits with color and pattern. More of a landlubber who likes to keep it low-key? Opt for something more muted. Be honest in what makes you feel best instead of going for a suit that seems to be "popular."

2. **Choose a suit that accentuates the parts of your body you already love.** I happen to feel really comfortable in high-waist bikini bottoms because they highlight my legs (a part of my body I appreciate) and leave less of my stomach exposed (an area that I like to give extra TLC to in the gym to feel my best). The key is to feel comfortable, which in turn creates confidence.

3. **Multitasking is a must.** I love swimsuits that do double duty—something that can also be worn as a top and dressed up with accessories so you can easily go from the pool or the beach to dinner with the addition of a simple button-down shirt and jeans or a skirt.

OPPOSITE At our hotel in St. Barts. *Tularosa bikini.*

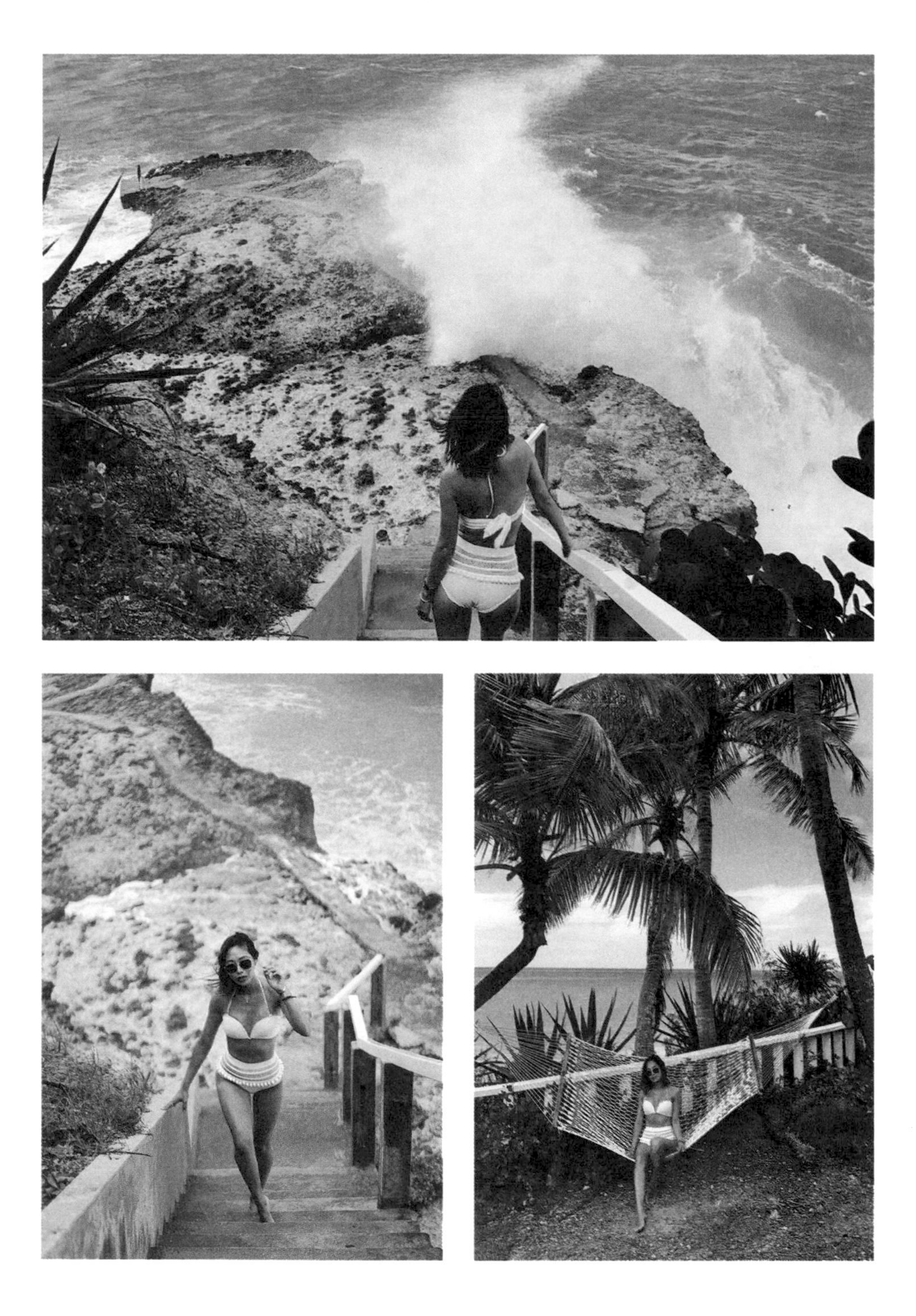

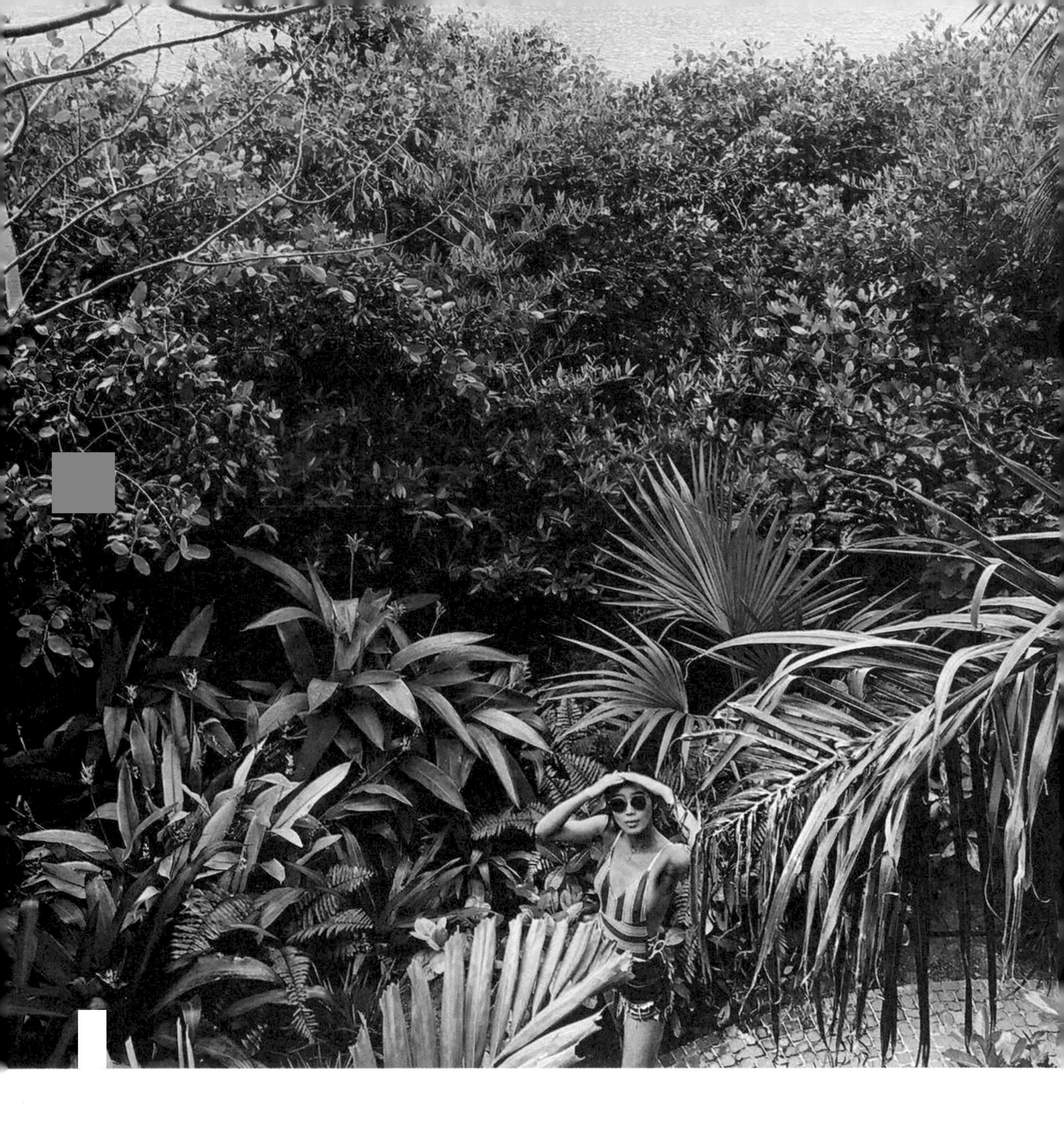

ABOVE An epic unplanned shot in St. Barts. I was heading back to my room from the pool and got lost, so I yelled for Jacopo and he not only found me, but snapped this shot, too. My hero, as always. **OPPOSITE (CLOCKWISE FROM TOP)** *Tularosa swimsuit; Privacy Please wrap skirt* • It was so cold toward the end of our yacht day that I had to wear a jacket over my swimsuit. • I loved this dress so much that I wore it again during the same trip (repeat offender, don't care). But I paired it with Jimmy Choos this time.

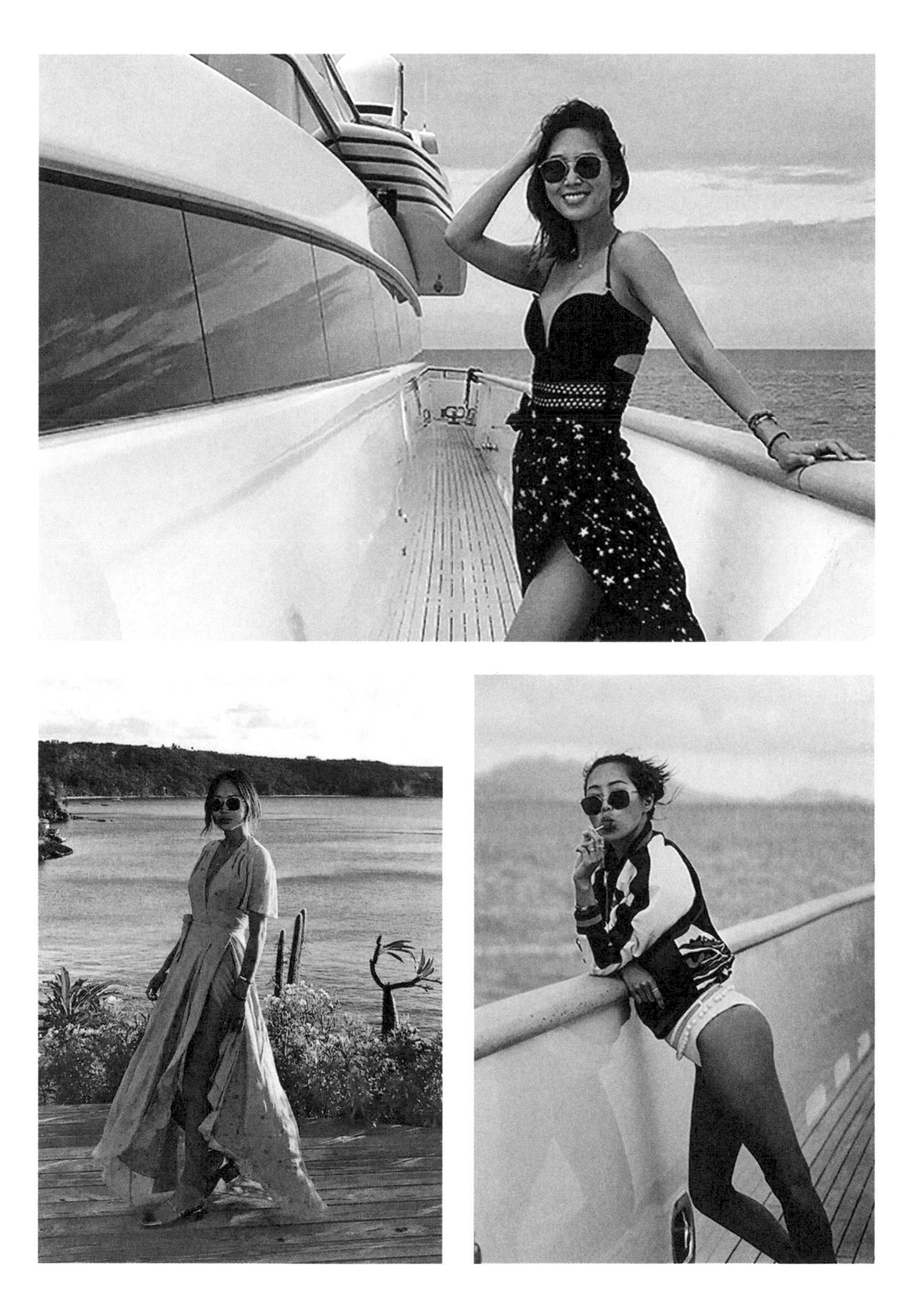

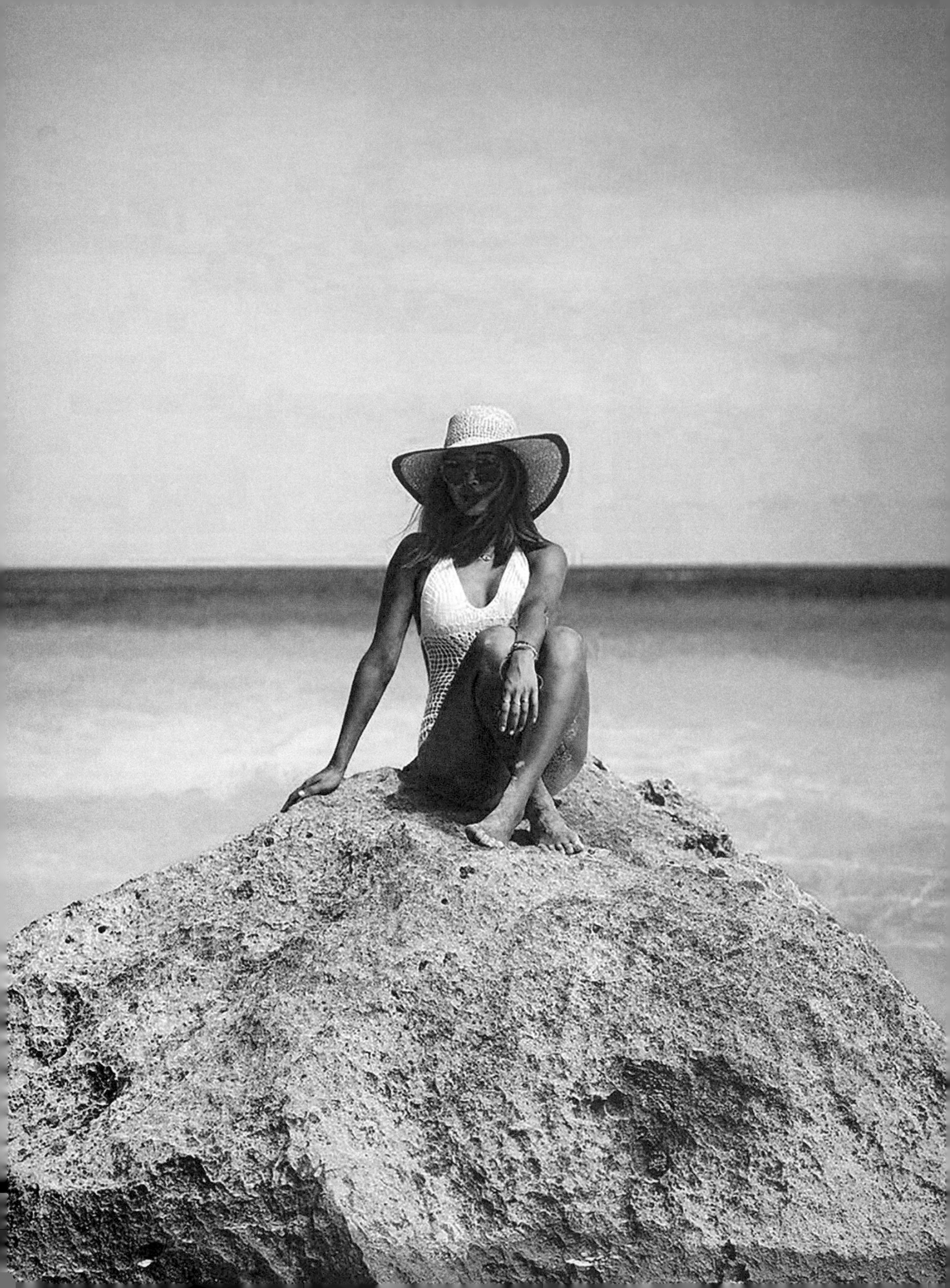

BERMUDA

A few years back, I met my friend, stylist and creative consultant Shiona Turini, on a trip to Morocco. Shiona—who is from Bermuda—is smart, strong, and incredibly stylish. So naturally I liked her right away. Fast-forward a year or so, and Shiona extended an invitation for Dani and me to visit her in Bermuda, which we obviously took her up on (she also invited Solange and Melina Matsoukas, who directs the HBO show *Insecure*. NBD.). Shiona wanted us to experience her home like a true vacation—relaxing on the beach, boating, and exploring. Which is exactly what we did (in addition to going to a local photographer's parents' house for dinner and, again, hanging out with Solange. Like, what?). It's such a beautiful, calming place. It's insane that Bermuda is only a two-hour flight from New York.

OPPOSITE At the pink sand beach. Dani shot this in front of our hotel. *BCBG hat.*

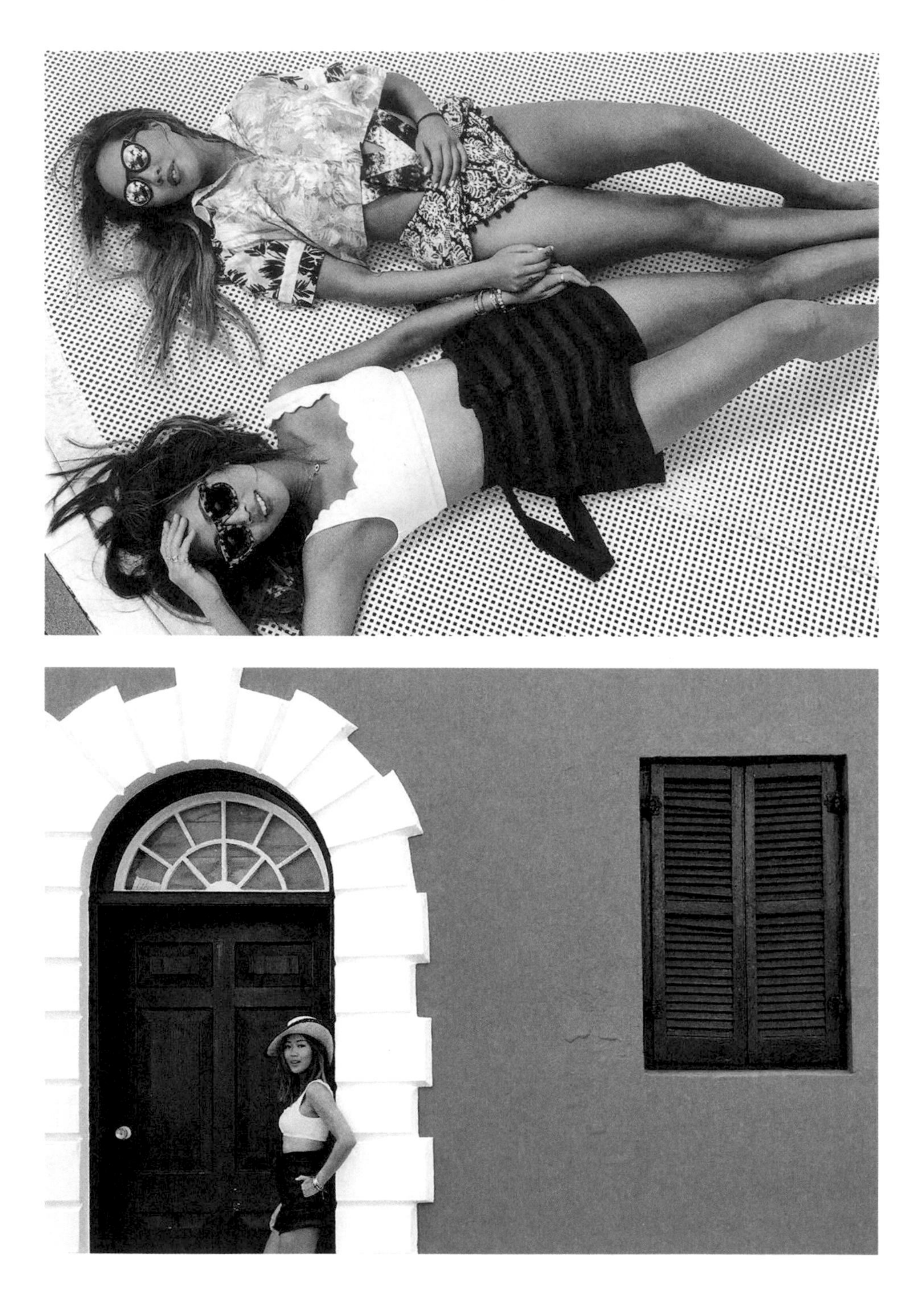

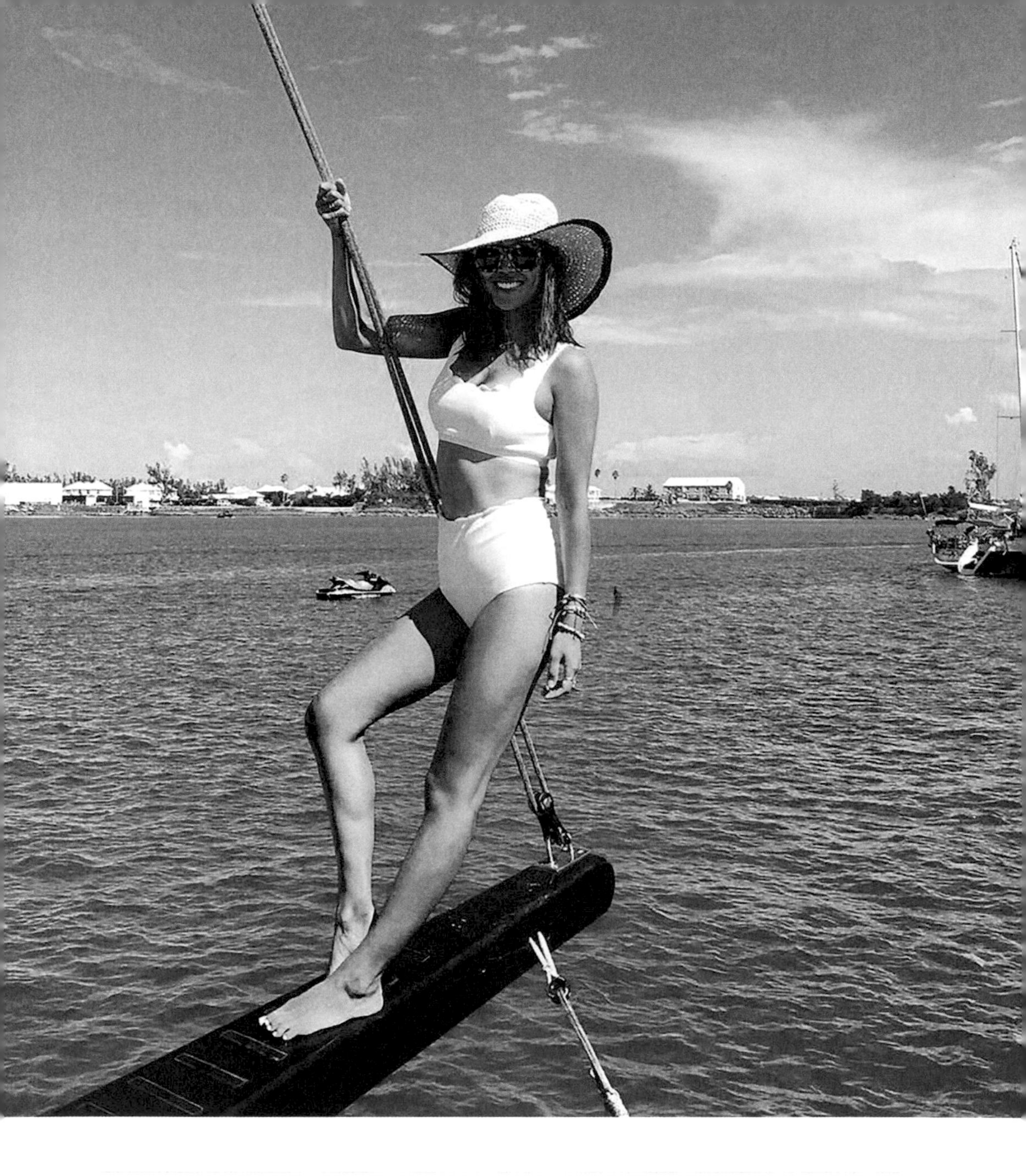

Yacht day. We spent the day boat-hopping—Somers Day, the day the English arrived in Bermuda. Like true Bermudians, we partied it up and made friends. My sister, Shiona, and I partied like crazy on this trip. I don't usually do that so it was fun to see how they live it up there. They had amazing music.

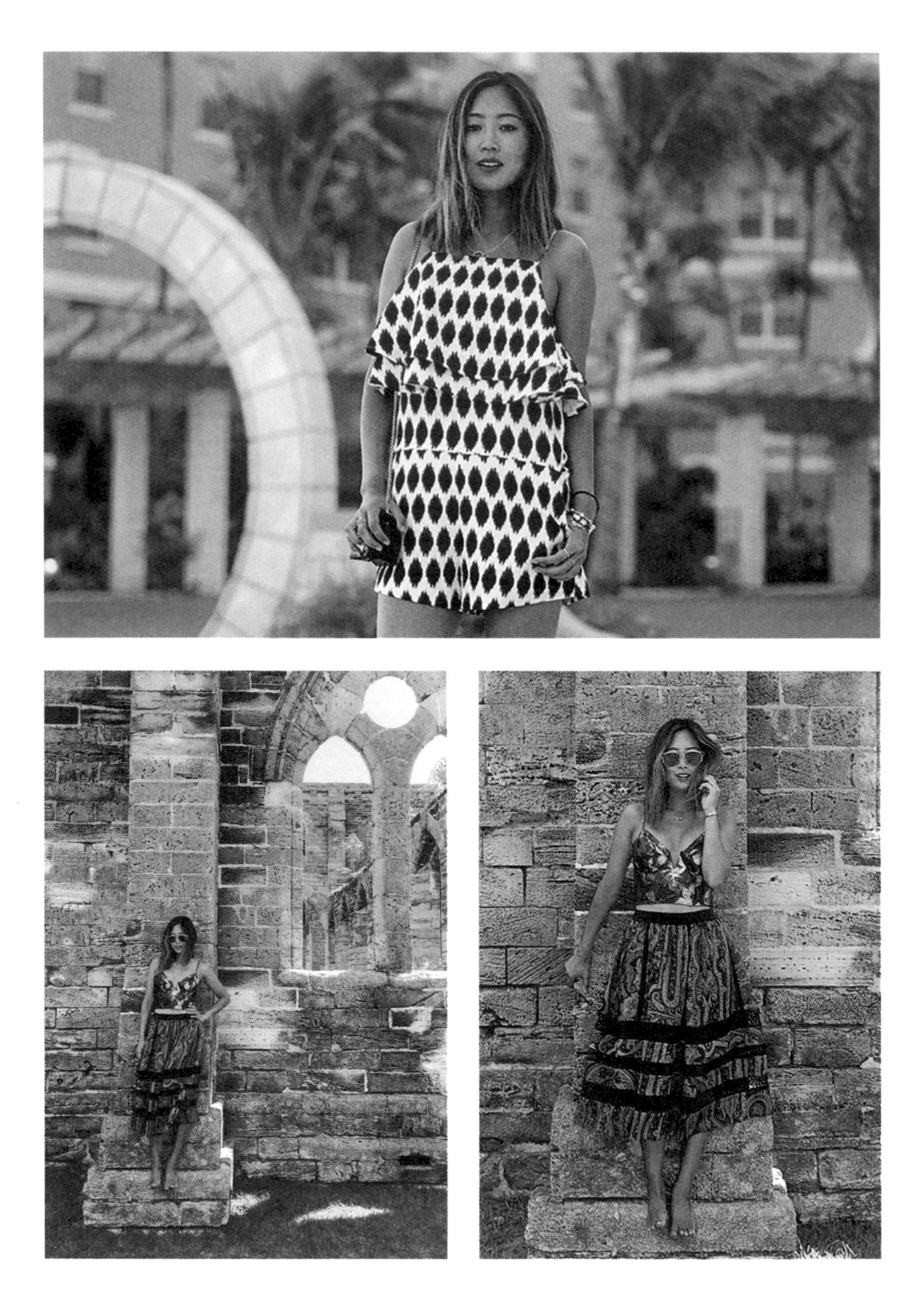

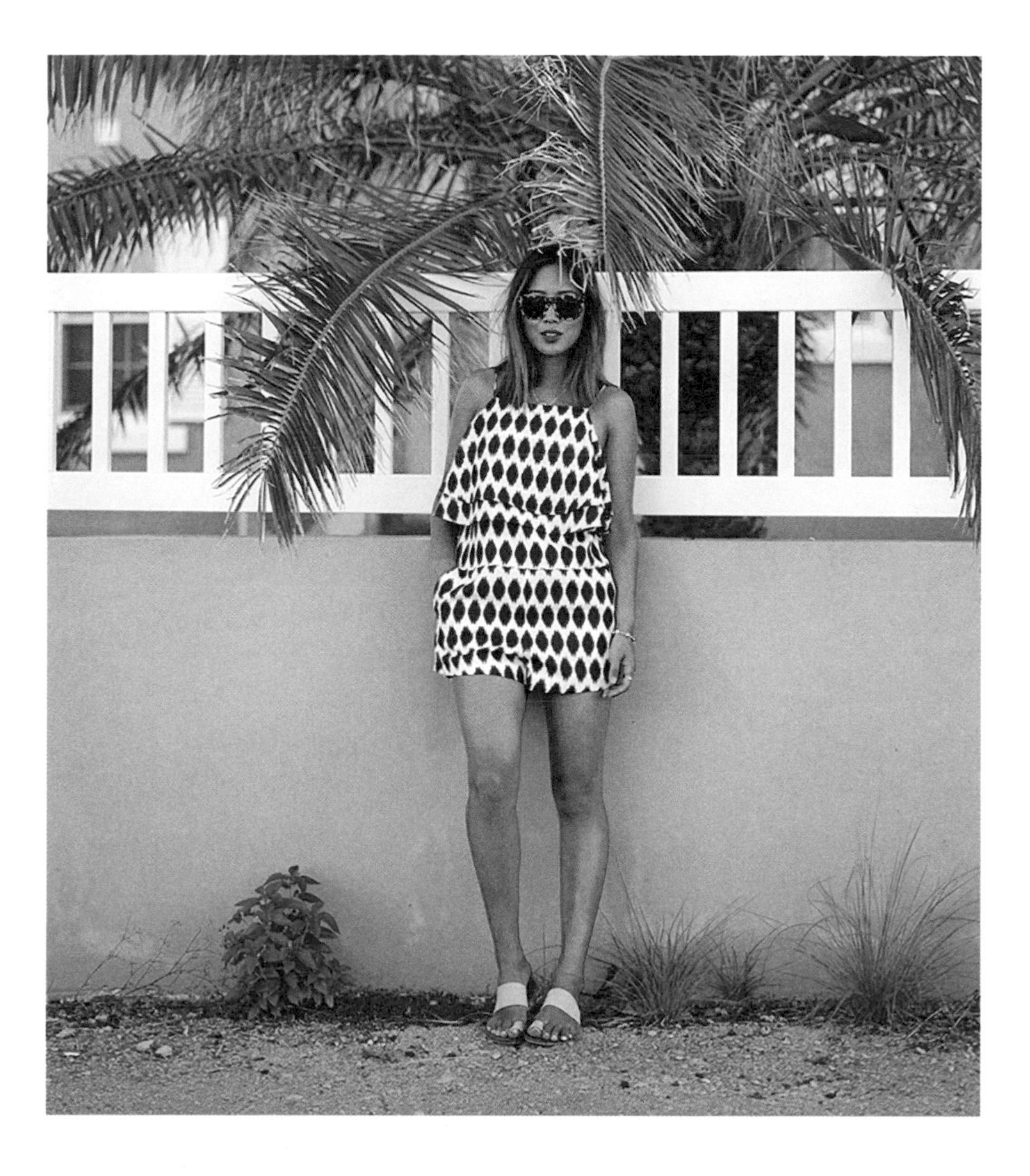

ABOVE AND OPPOSITE, TOP One of our first days in Bermuda, Dani and I drove to an Italian restaurant about thirty minutes away from our hotel. I purposely wore this forgiving romper because I was pretty sure I could predict the feeding that was to come—and sure enough, the pot of mussels we ate was so good that we ordered two more (always plan ahead, I say). **OPPOSITE, BOTTOM ROW** A gorgeous, unfinished church. I don't remember why I was barefoot, but I'm sure I had a good reason (like, not packing practical shoes, perhaps?). *Zimmermann top and skirt.*

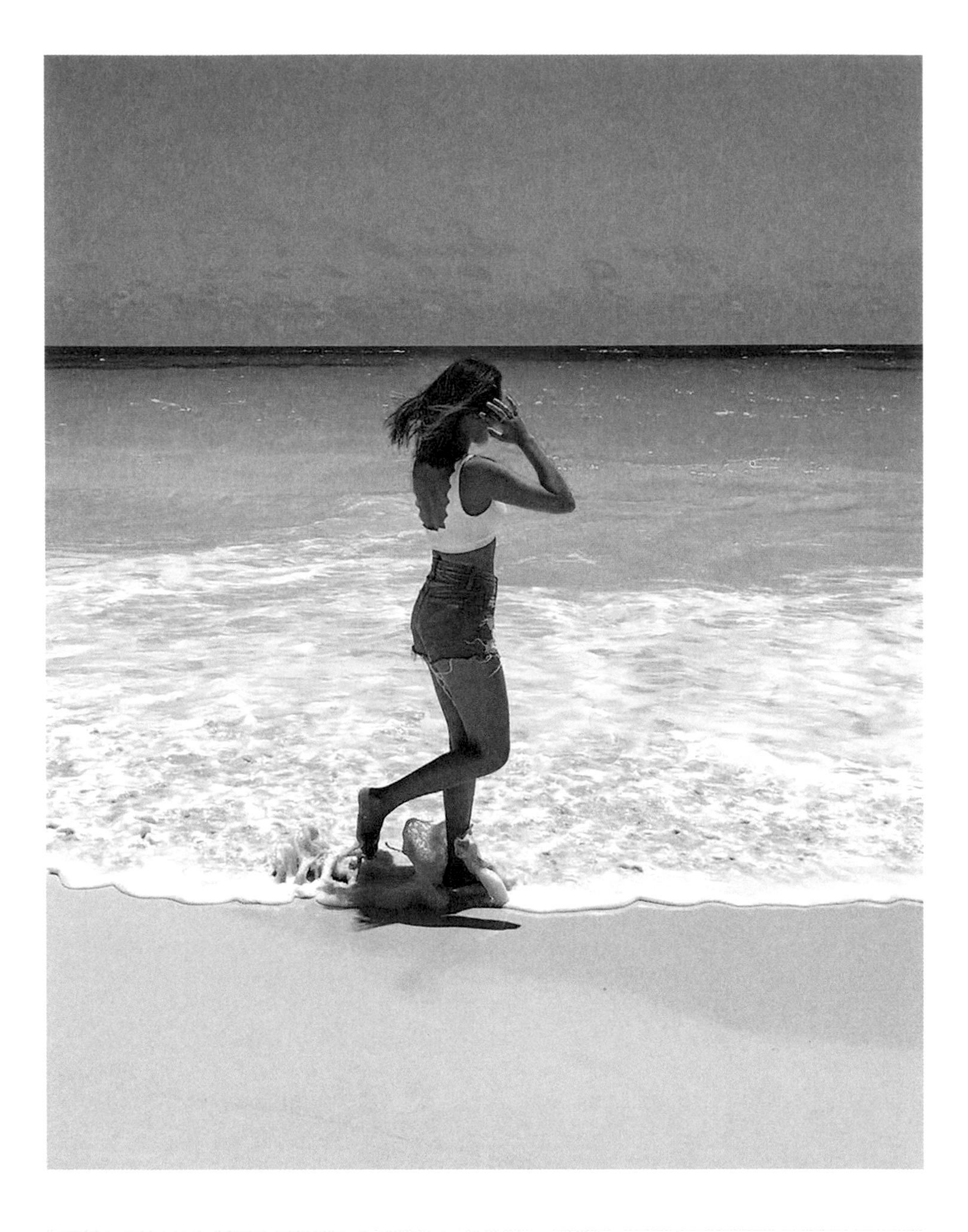

ABOVE A millennial-pink sand beach. Yes, this really exists.

OPPOSITE Exploring. *Keepsake outfit.*

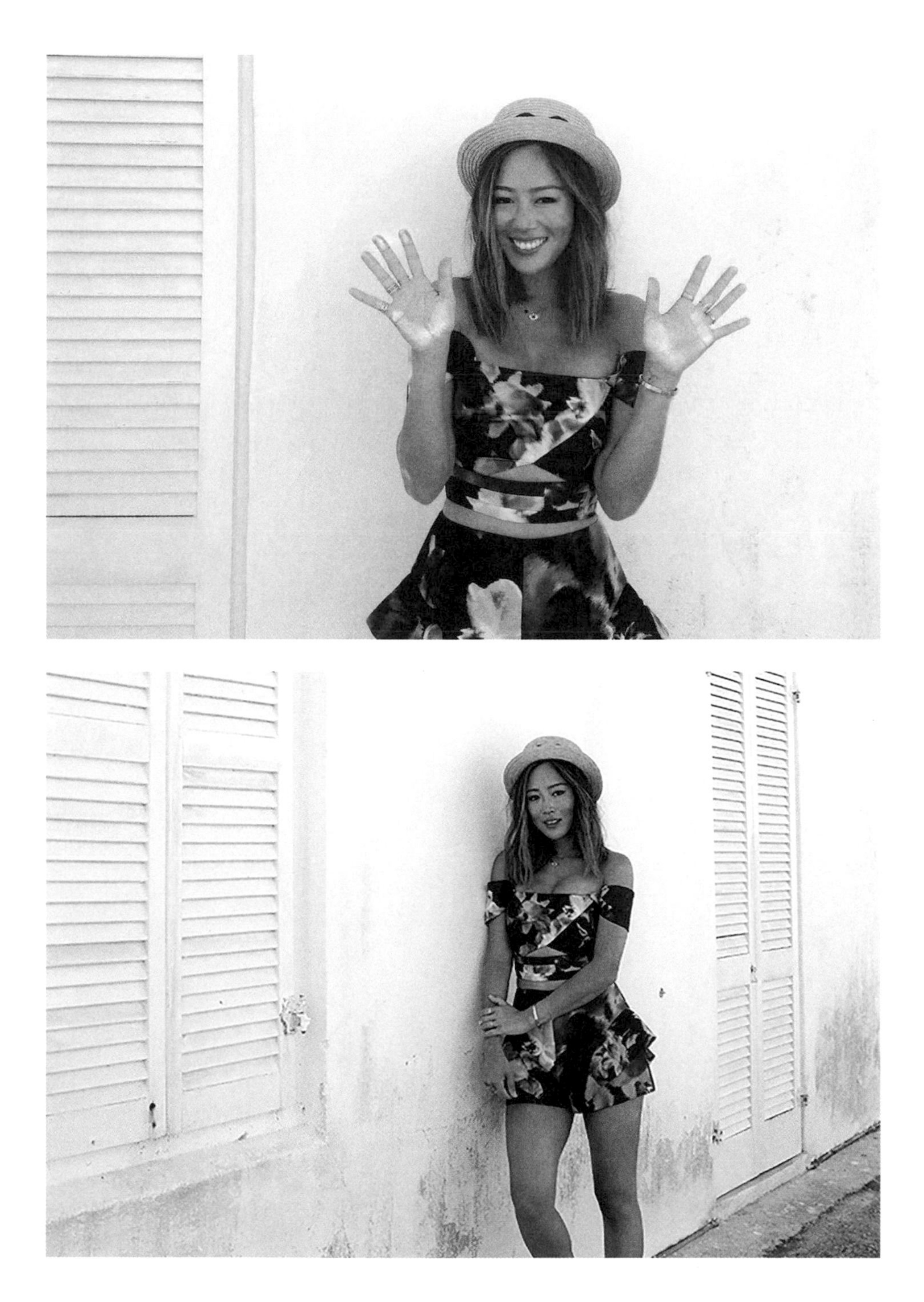

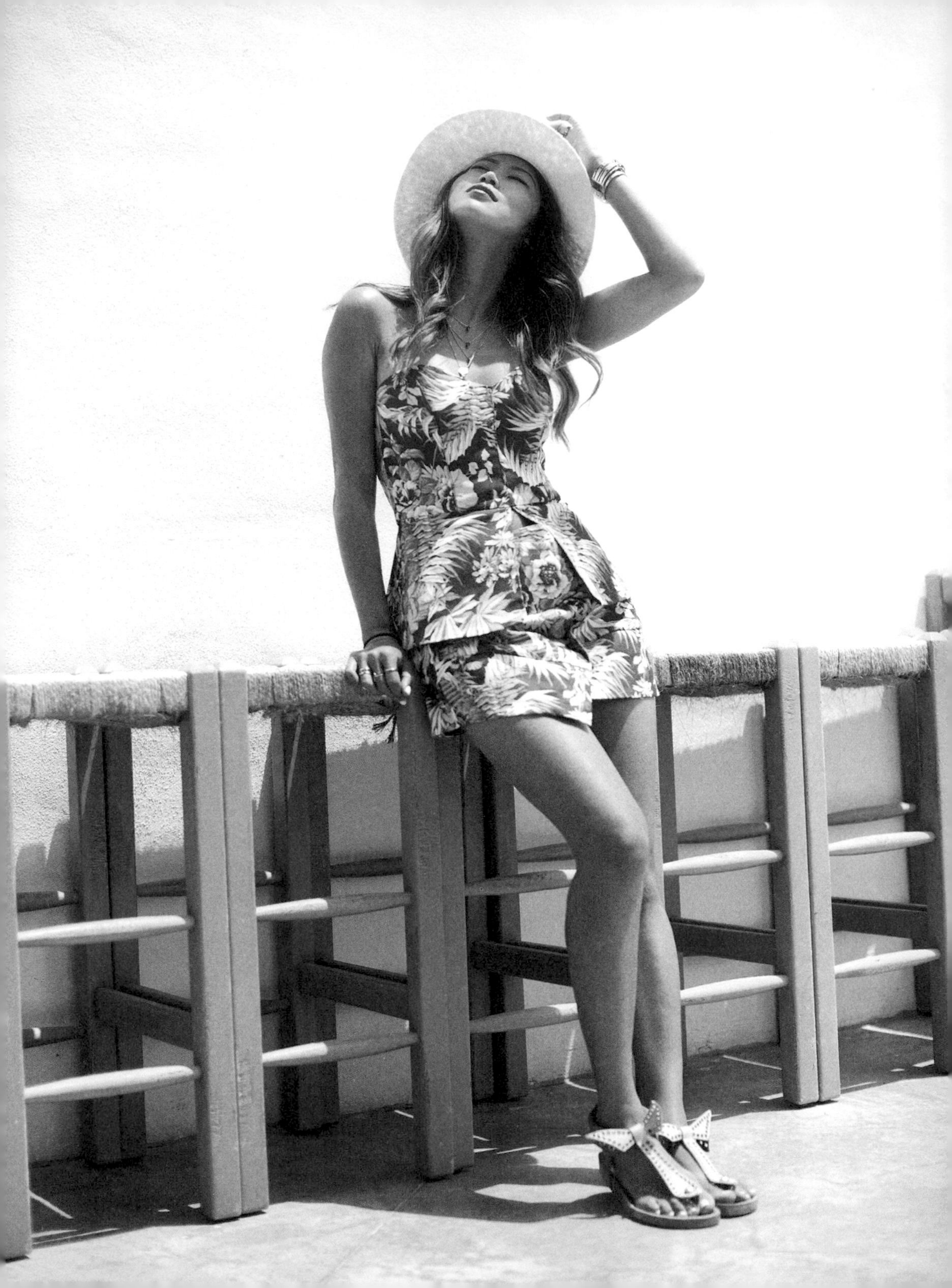

LOS CABOS

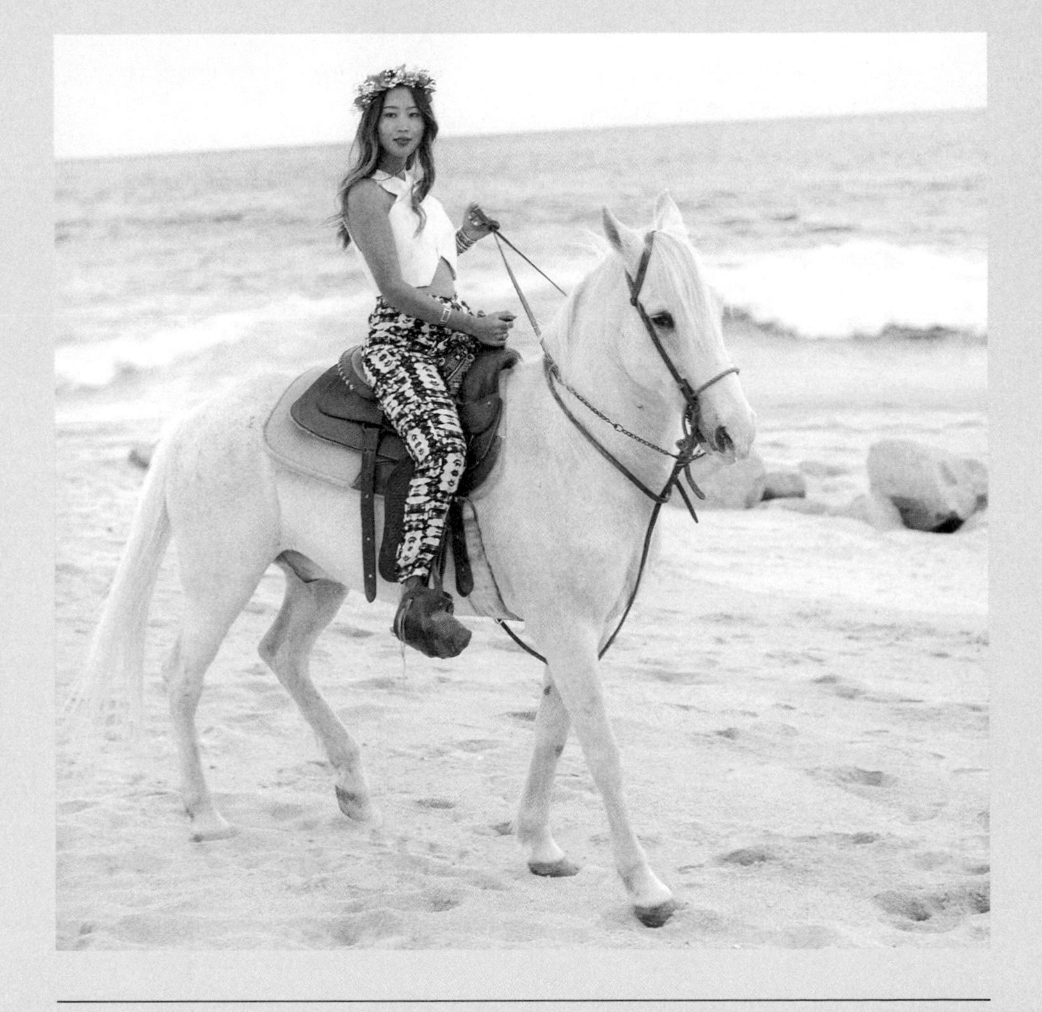

OPPOSITE In 2014 the trend was tropical prints—people loved banana leaf. This is my homage. Also, what am I looking at? *The Fifth Label dress.*

ABOVE Horseback riding on the beach. Danielle Steele novel cover, anyone? *C/MEO top.*

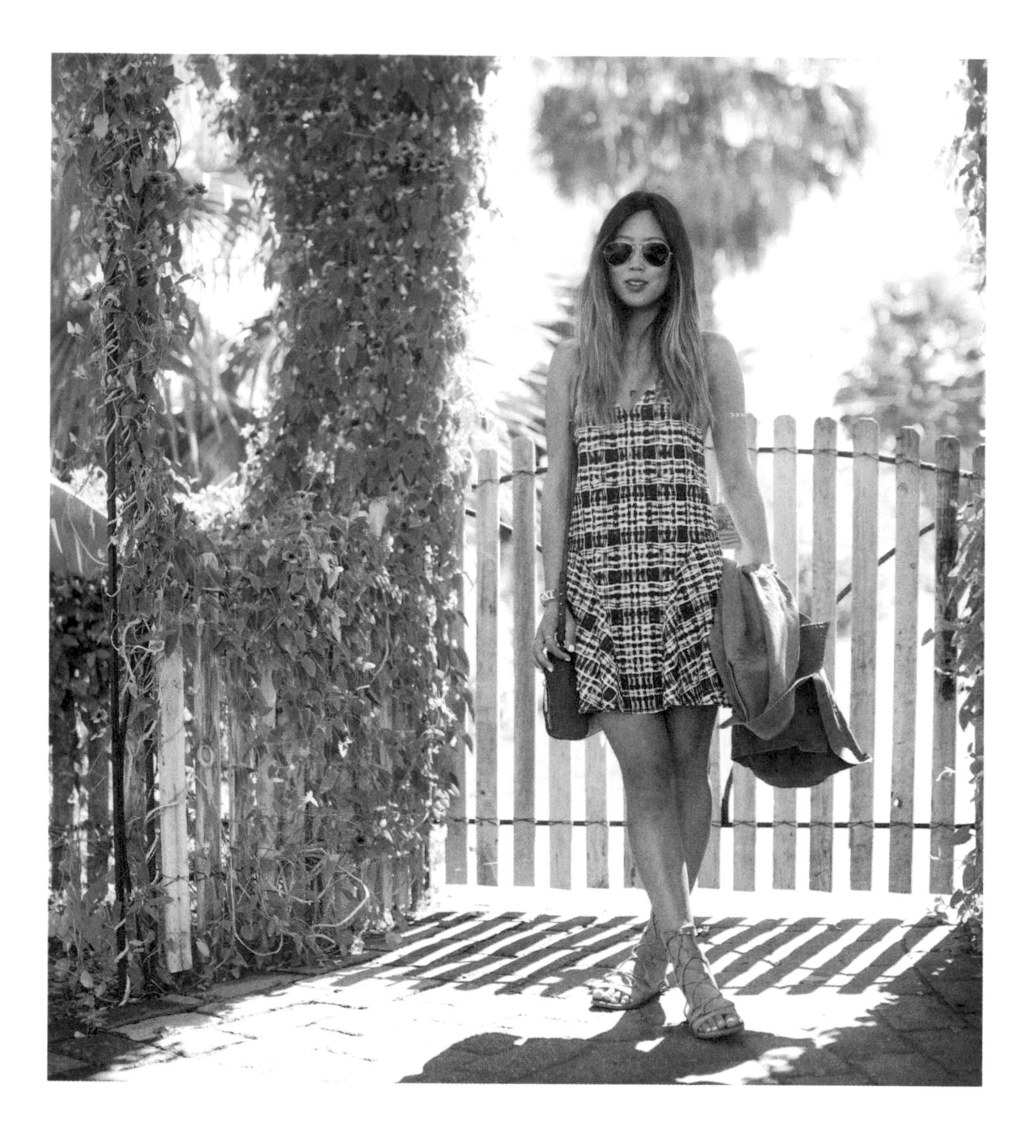

ABOVE Heading to Flora Farms, this incredible working farm with an on-site restaurant, cooking school, and spa. I had lunch and hung out with dogs that live on the property, so you could call this my perfect day. *Finders Keepers dress; Schutz sandals; Botkier bag.* **OPPOSITE, TOP** Flora Farms. **OPPOSITE, BOTTOM ROW** I had just filmed a tutorial on how to take good Instagram scenery shots for my YouTube channel and wanted to put it into practice. Back in 2014 I was obsessed with all my lines being straight (I also loved overalls—still kind of do—and mirrored aviators). These days, those glasses would have been left at home. *Isabel Marant thongs.*

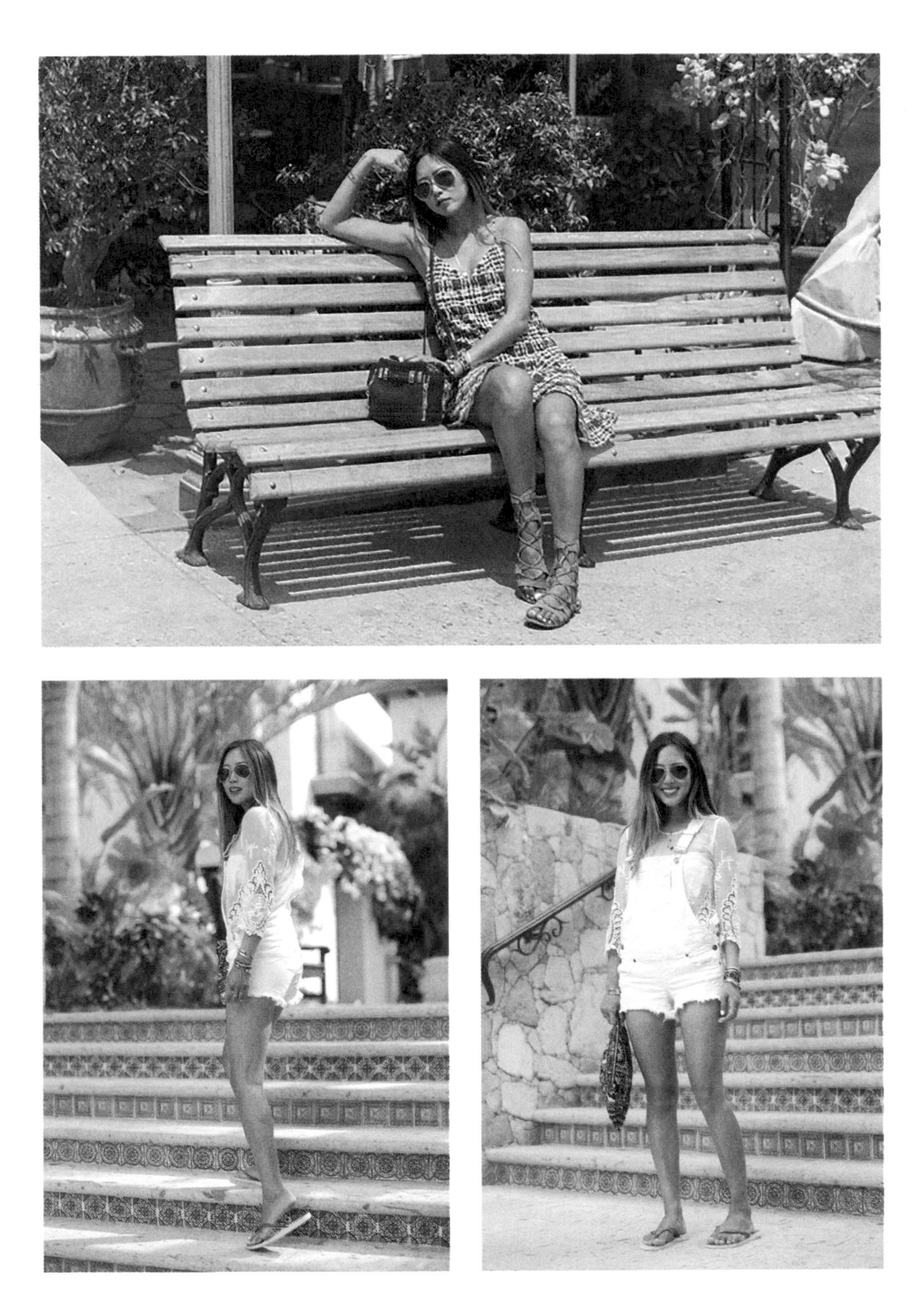

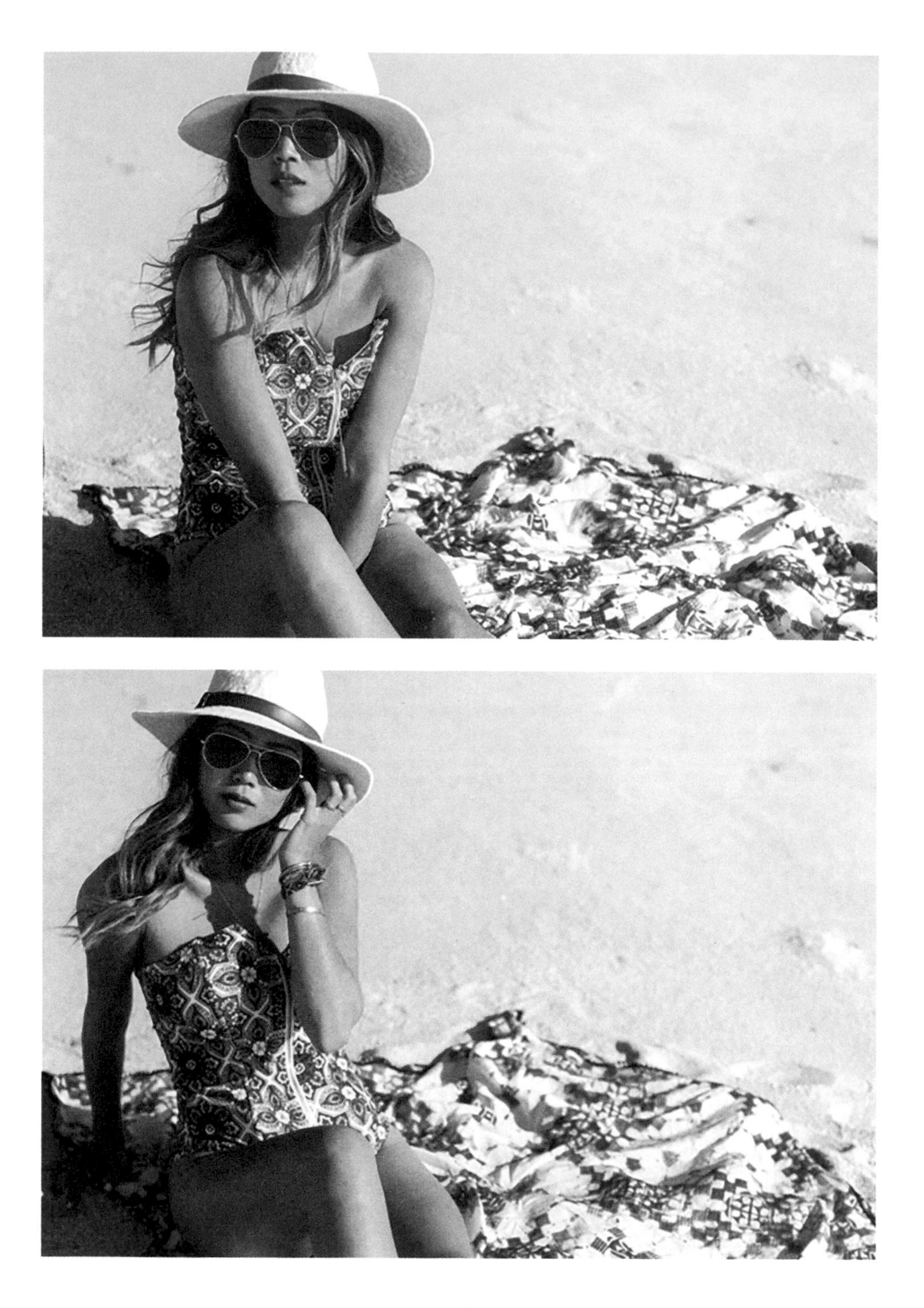

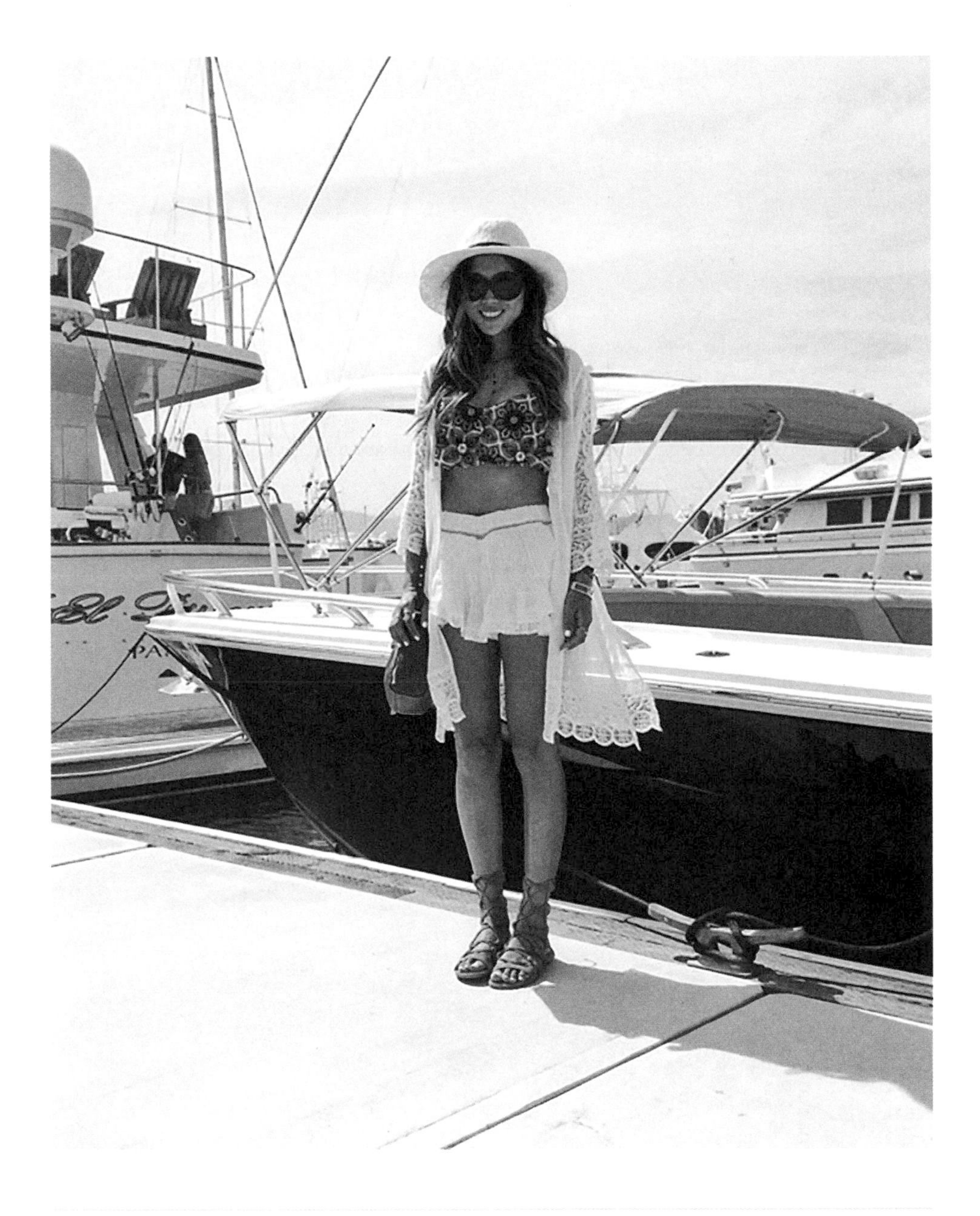

ABOVE *Schutz sandals.* **OPPOSITE** Looking back at these photos, it makes me laugh that I ever used a beautiful scarf by Greek-born, London-based designer Athena Procopiou as a beach towel. Props to my younger self! *Beach Riot swimsuit.*

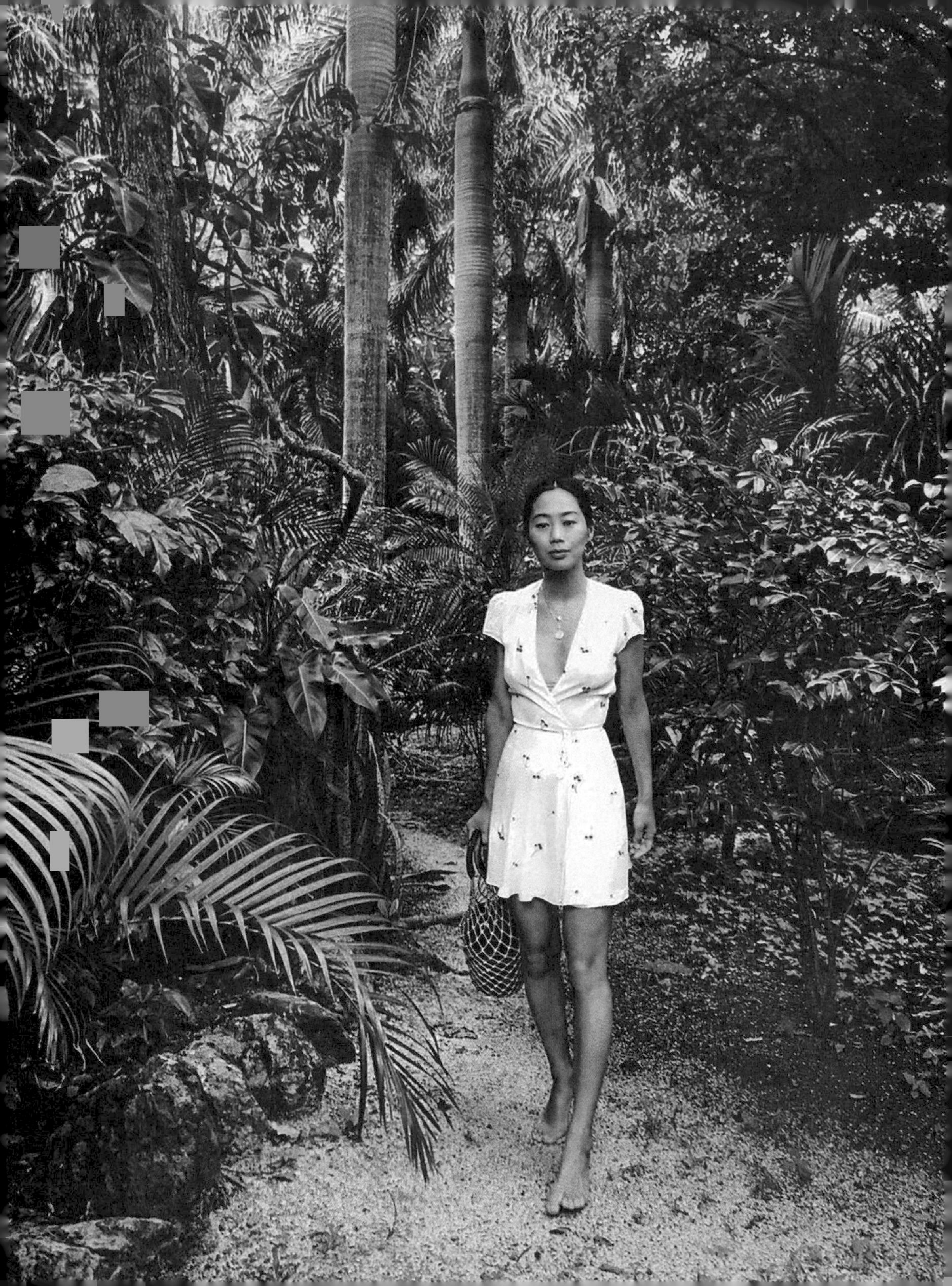

COSTA RICA

How fun is it to travel with friends? I'm so lucky that I have people in my life who I truly love getting out of town with—a lot of whom live outside of L.A. and are always down to meet up somewhere fun. The summer of 2017 I planned a little beach vacation in Costa Rica so I could surf and relax, and I invited Dani and our friend Jared, a N.Y. boy I met a few years back at MTV when we worked together on a Cover Girl commercial. A lot has changed for both of us since then, but he's become one of my really good friends and even stays with me whenever he's in L.A. All three of us had very different ideas about what "vacation" should be, and luckily because we're all so close I was able to run around and do activities while Jared just relaxed at the hotel. (Dani didn't care either way—she's so chill that she's happy doing whatever.) Like any relationship, a trip with friends who have varying interests requires great communication. Because Jared and I discussed what we wanted out of the trip before we went, we were able to coexist harmoniously and not resent each other for being lazy or, in my case, annoyingly energetic (those waves don't ride themselves!). Pro tip: Travel with friends who you're comfortable talking to in a real way; otherwise you could end up wasting precious time and money on a trip that's less than ideal.

OPPOSITE Reformation wrap dresses also make great surf cover-ups. Who knew?

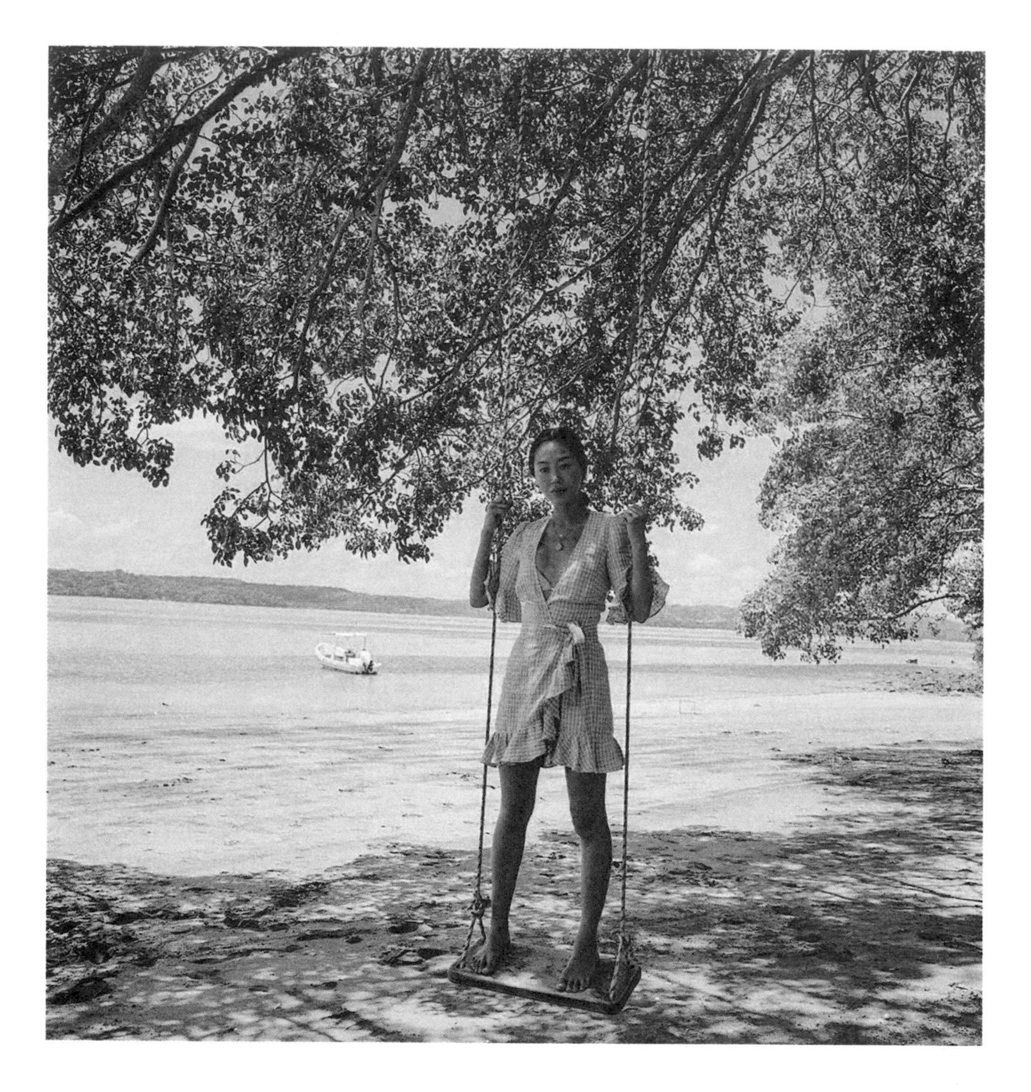

ABOVE Right before jetskiing, one of the most fun things we did as a group on the entire trip. *Reformation wrap dress.* **OPPOSITE (CLOCKWISE FROM TOP LEFT)** Central American beach towns are typically driven by surfers. *Dodo Bar Or skirt; Nomah Project bag I got as a gift in the Hamptons on a work trip right before Costa Rica* • Despite cleaning my plate, I didn't love this fish taco and plantain feast. *Gentle Monster x Song of Style sunglasses, Reformation dress* • Stares into space on a surfboard; thinks about next meal. • You know this is the end of the trip because I have a nice tan going on (despite slathering on copious amounts of Promise Organic SPF from CVS). I'm wearing Reformation, again. I think I went on a Reformation binge right before I left for this trip.

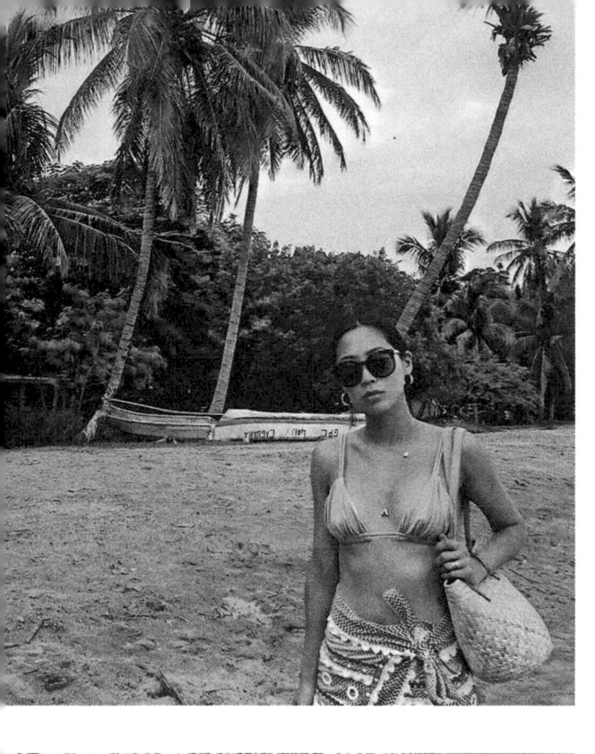
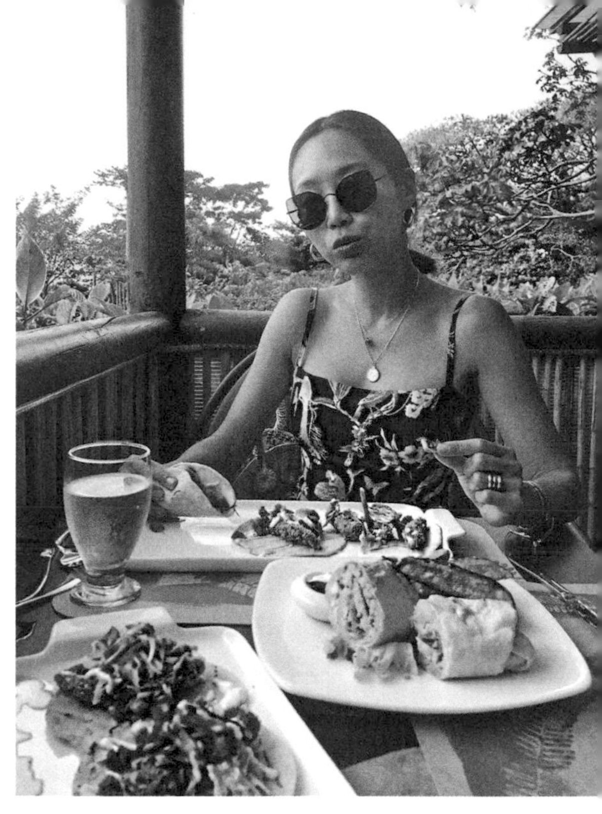
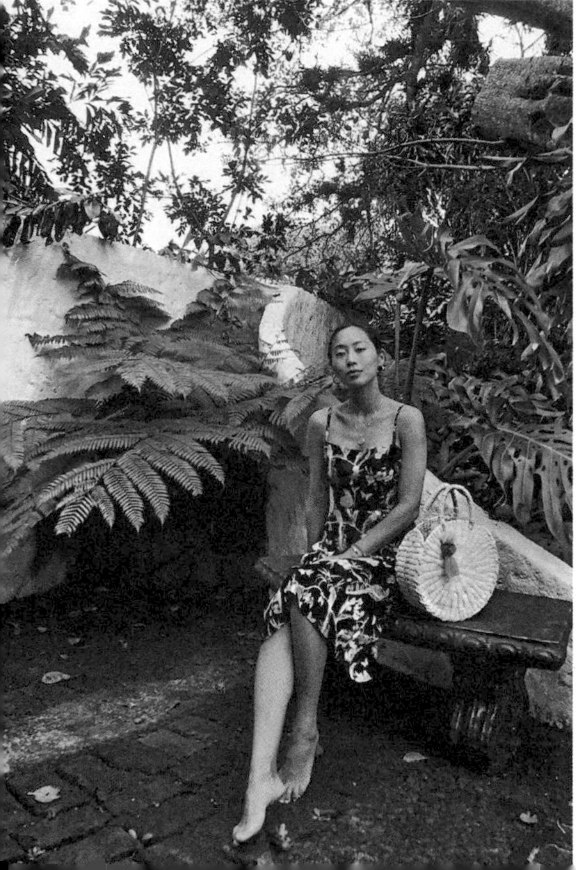
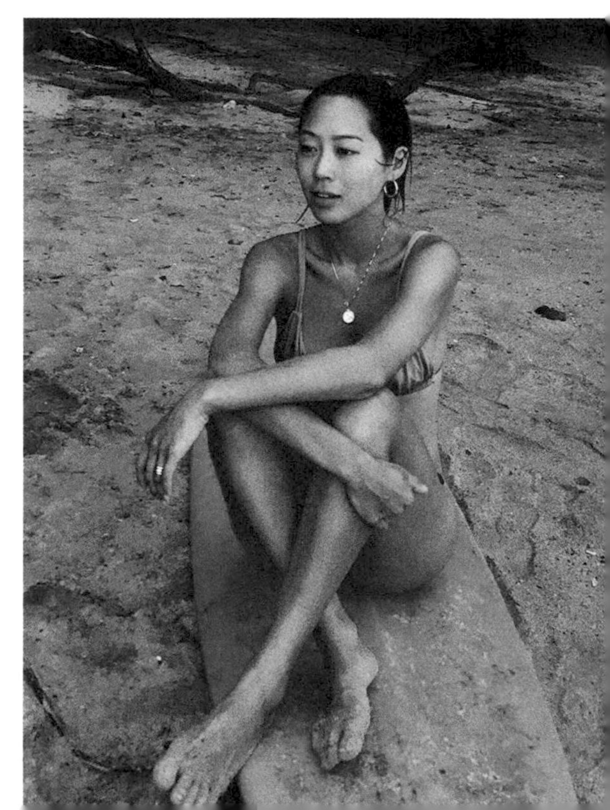

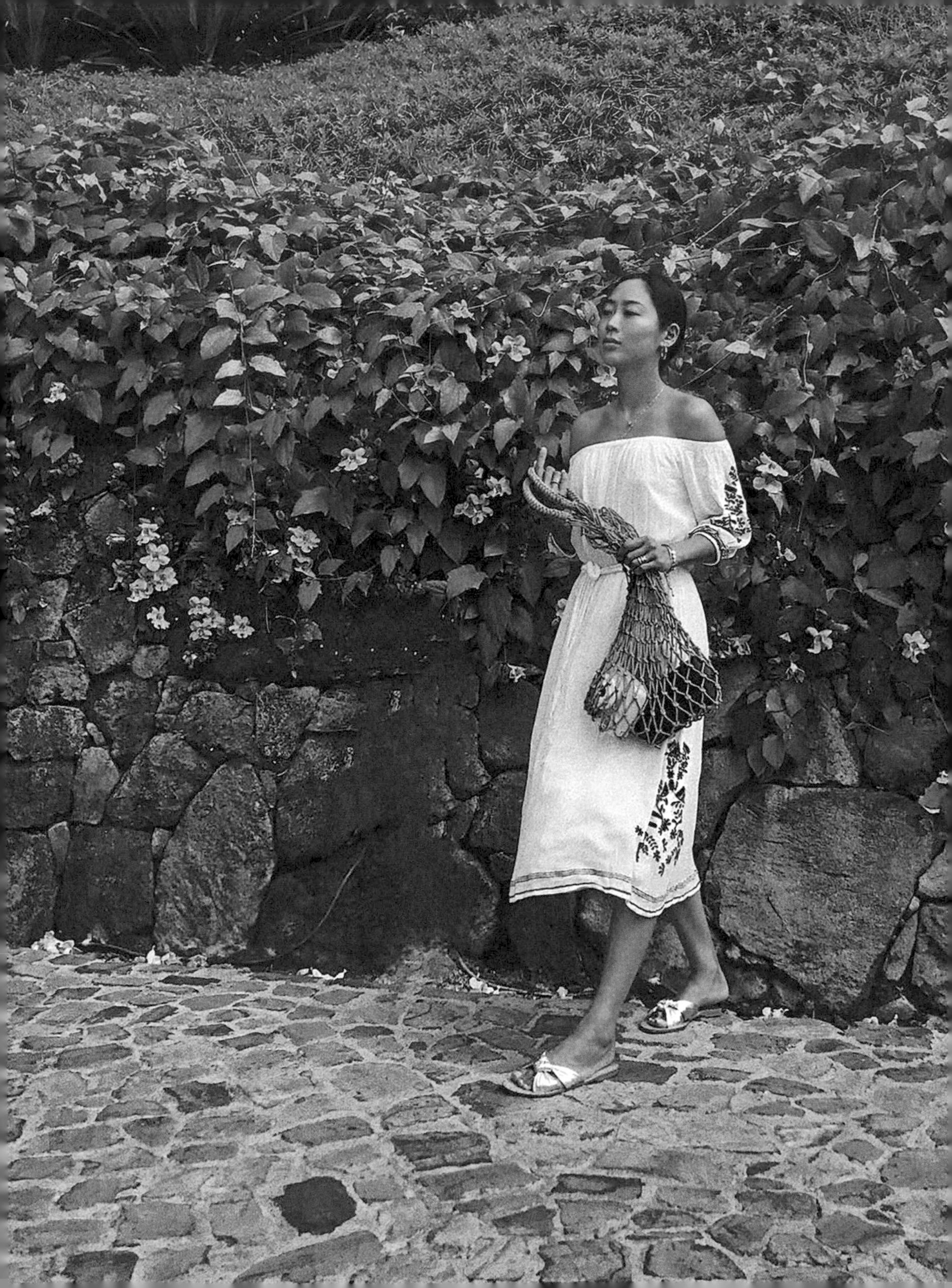

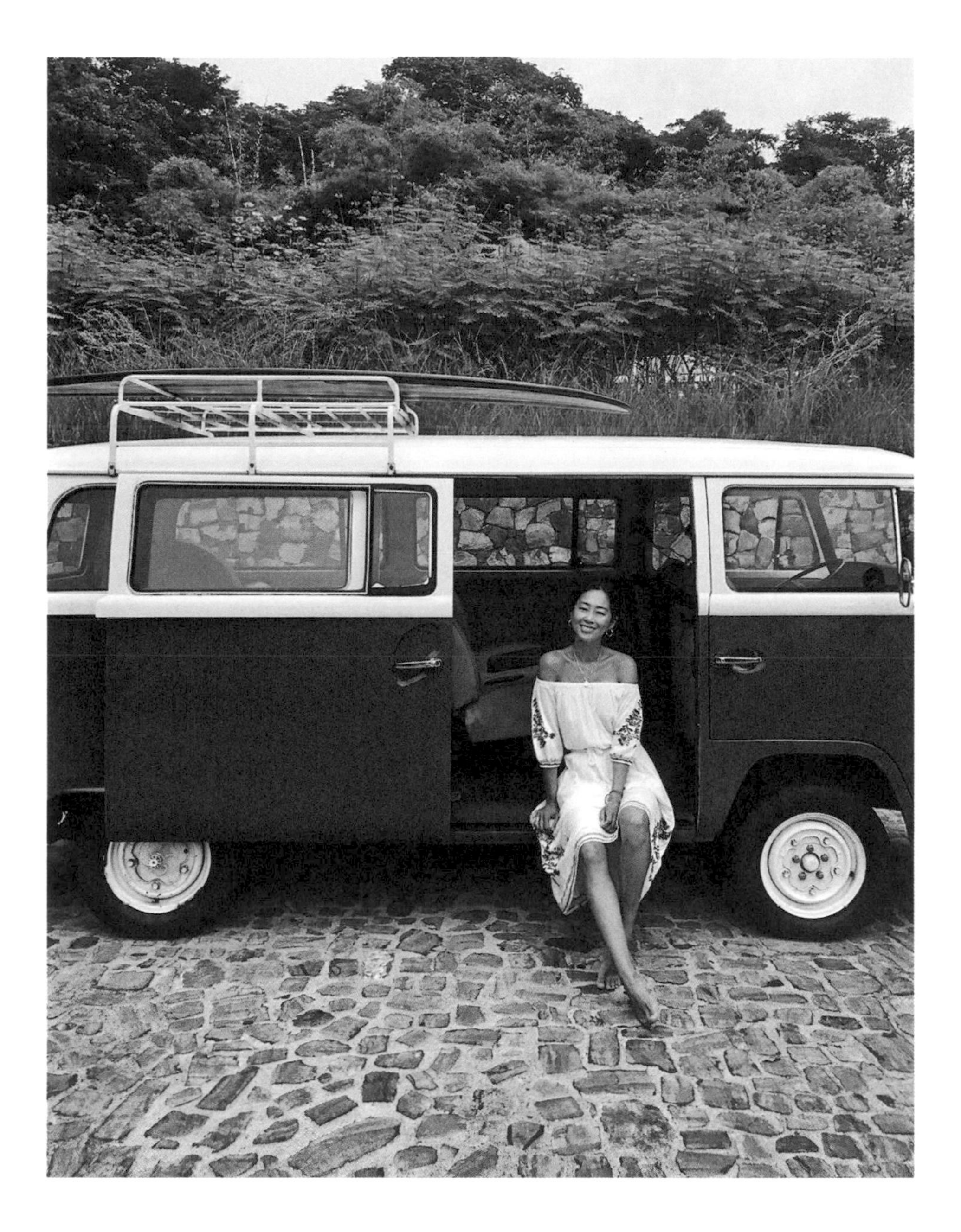

Tularosa dress.

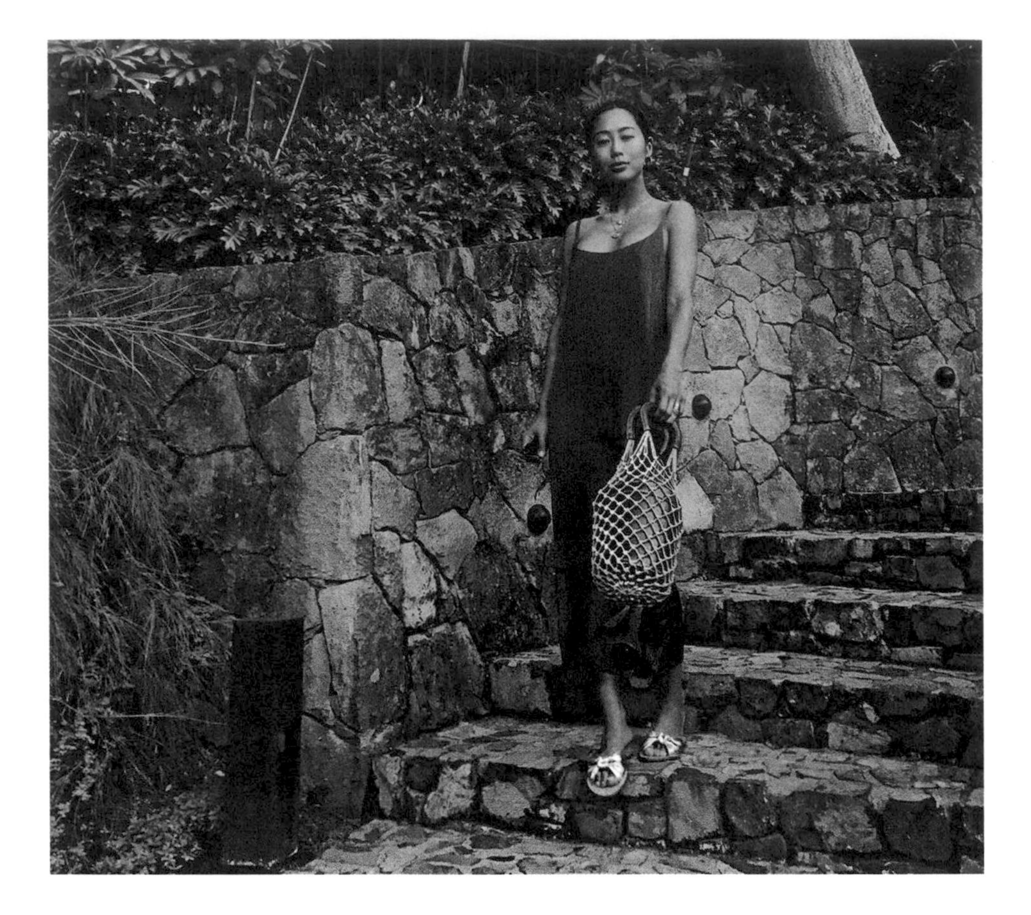

ABOVE *Asceno nightgown as a dress (yes, really!); Staud bag; Loeffler Randall shoes.* **OPPOSITE (CLOCKWISE FROM TOP LEFT)** We had an outdoor shower in our hotel room in the jungle. I felt like I was in really great shape here and was really proud of all the hard work I had put toward getting fit before I left. I even committed to doing Whole30, and I was cooking a lot (something I rarely have time to do). Of course I started feasting the second we landed in Costa Rica (think gallo pintos, rice 'n' beans, bowls of chifrijo, and—my favorite—fried plantains). But I felt strong and confident there. • This was Aimee day—so we did activities. I had to drag Dani and Jared out of the hotel room to zip-lining in the rainforest. *Two Songs T-shirt; J Brand jeans; Chloé backpack; Nike sneakers* • Hanging by the pool at the hotel (we did a lot of that). • Because it rained a lot on this trip, I spent a lot of time indoors reading. I finished *A Little Life* by Hanya Yanagihara, which made me sob. It's such a long book but it was so good and compelling—a coming-of-age story following four friends in New York, and one of them has a dark story that really touched me. Reading that alone in a jungle was a very cathartic experience.

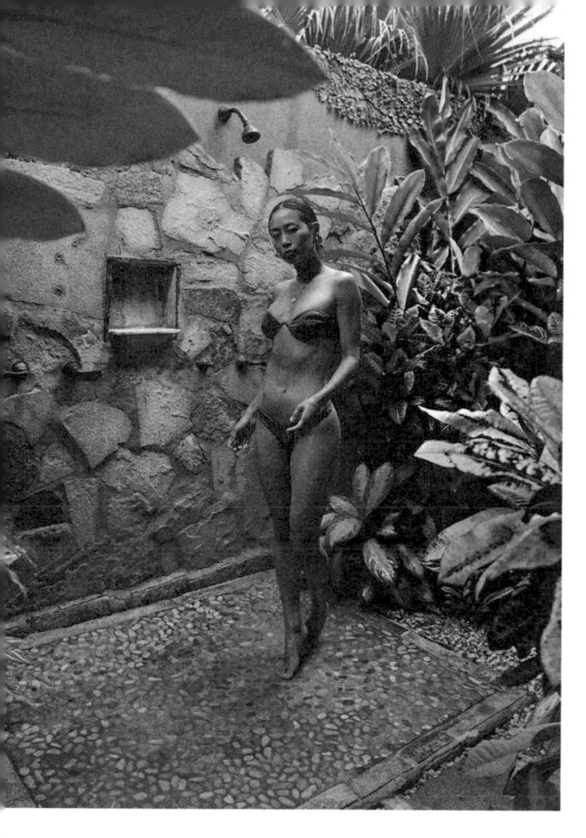
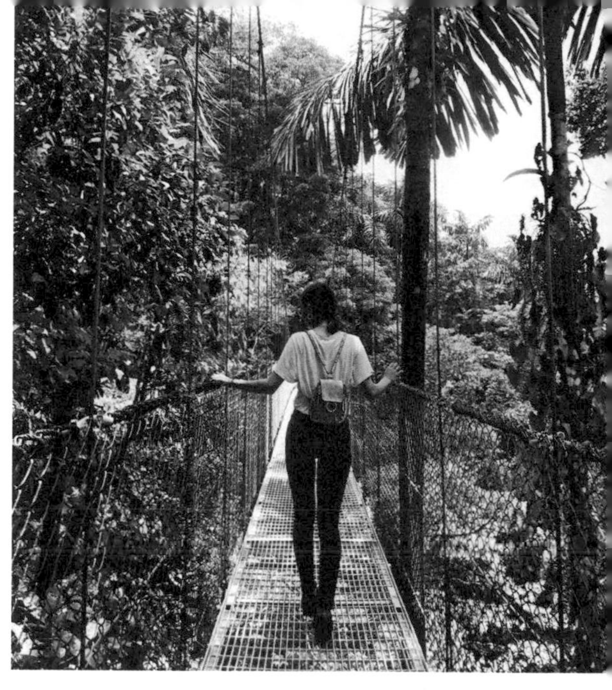
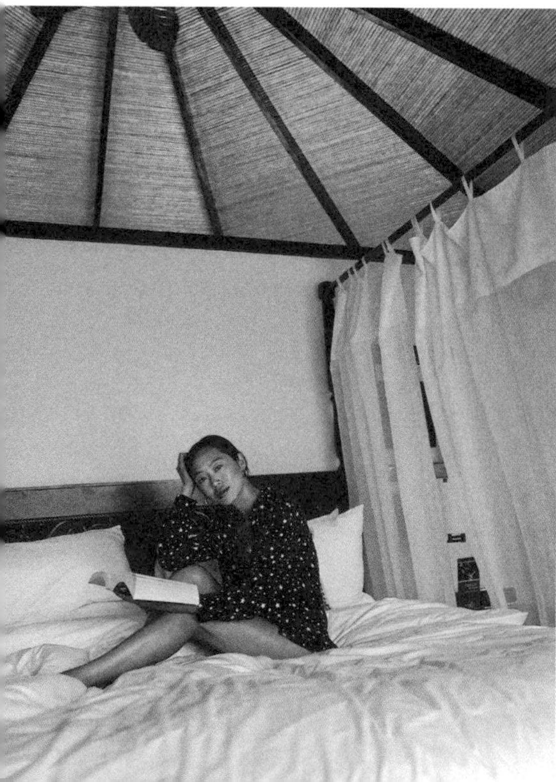
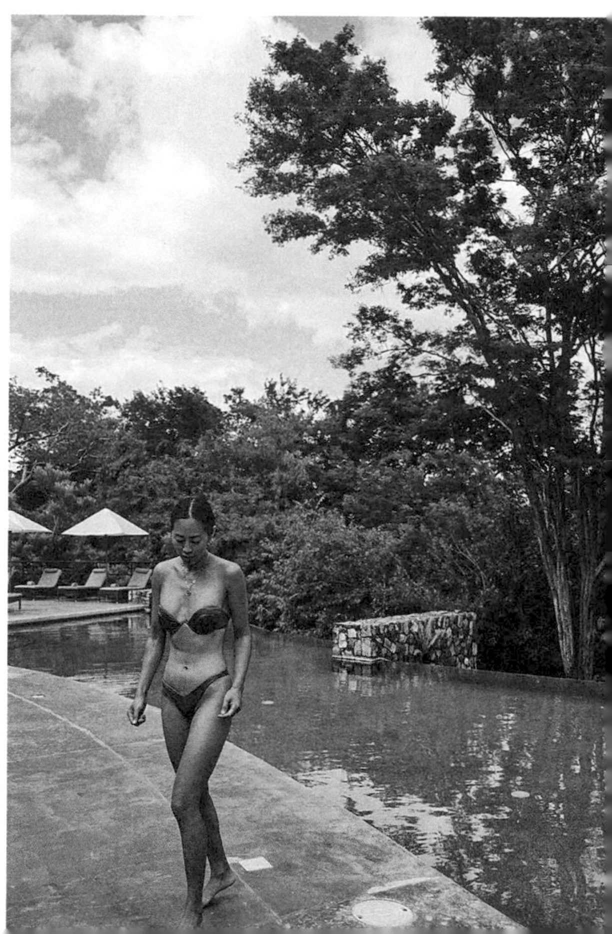

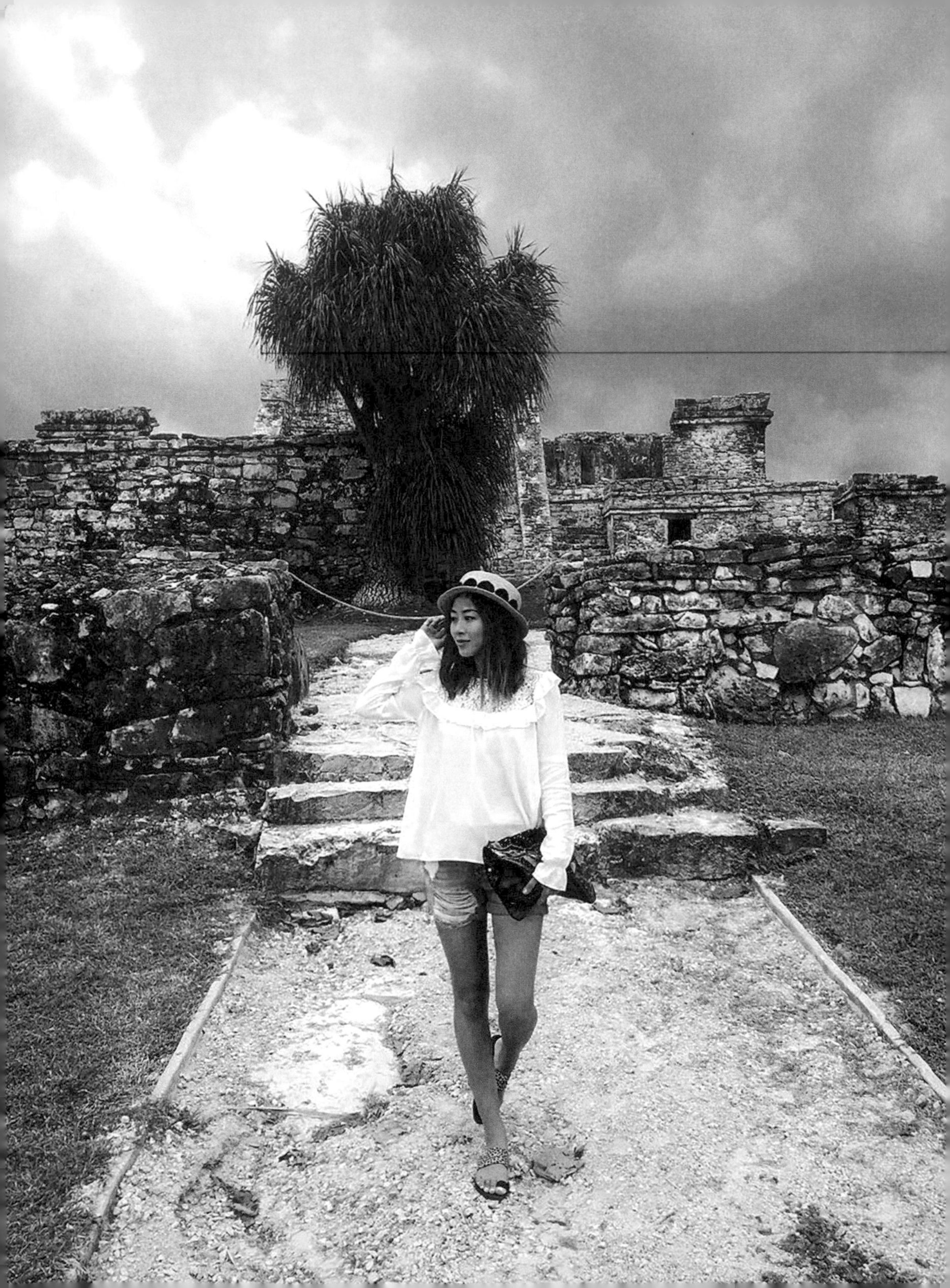

TULUM & NAYARIT

Mexico is such a beautiful country, and we here in America are so lucky to have it so close to us. So close, in fact, that it was a no-brainer to spend my birthday in Tulum in December 2015 with Dani, my best friend Jenny, and my Jacopo. I'd always wanted to go, so we pulled the trigger, and the trip is one we'll all remember forever—mainly because everyone got food poisoning except for me (as you all know, I have an iron stomach). Poor Jacopo had to drive us to the airport complete with a pale face and blue lips, and I felt so guilty that I was the only one not excruciatingly sick. But as soon as I got home, I got *E. coli* from Chipotle. You win some, you lose some.

The following year Revolve threw a New Year's gathering in Nayarit, a state on the western side of Mexico. It was a smaller Revolve crew than usual. Dani brought her best friend Carol, and Jacopo was able to join, so it was a perfect, special group. On our last full day, I surfed with the boys at sunset, and we all sat on our boards watching one of the most magical sundowns I've ever seen while the waves lapped up around us. It was a magical way to ring in a new year.

OPPOSITE Visiting ruins in Tulum.

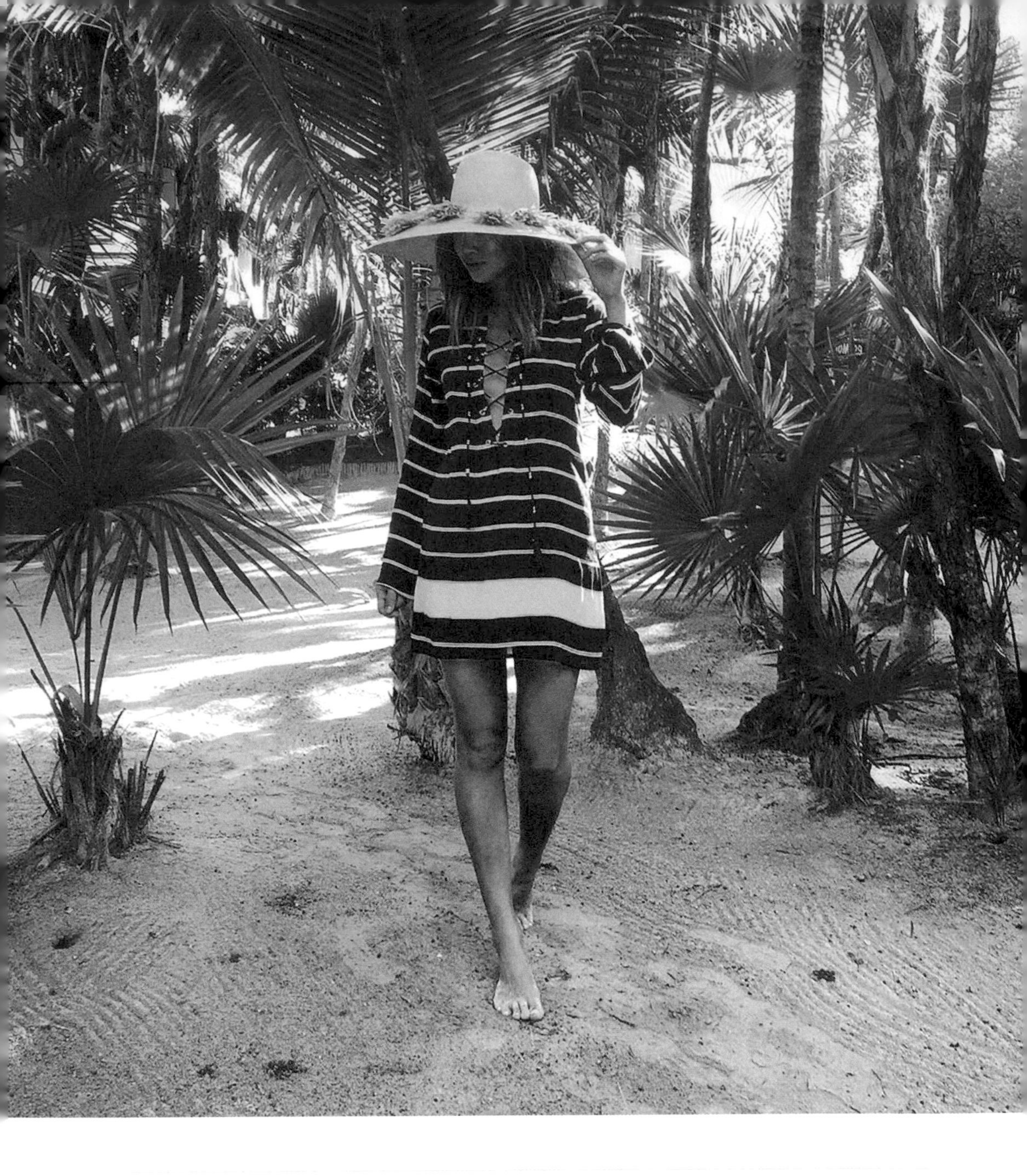

ABOVE *Faithfull the Brand dress.* **OPPOSITE, TOP** The hotel we stayed at had bikes, so Jacopo and I biked around while Jenny and Dani hung out at the beach (as they do). **OPPOSITE, BOTTOM ROW** In Tulum at our hotel, Coqui Coqui, a gorgeous boutique property that has since shuttered.

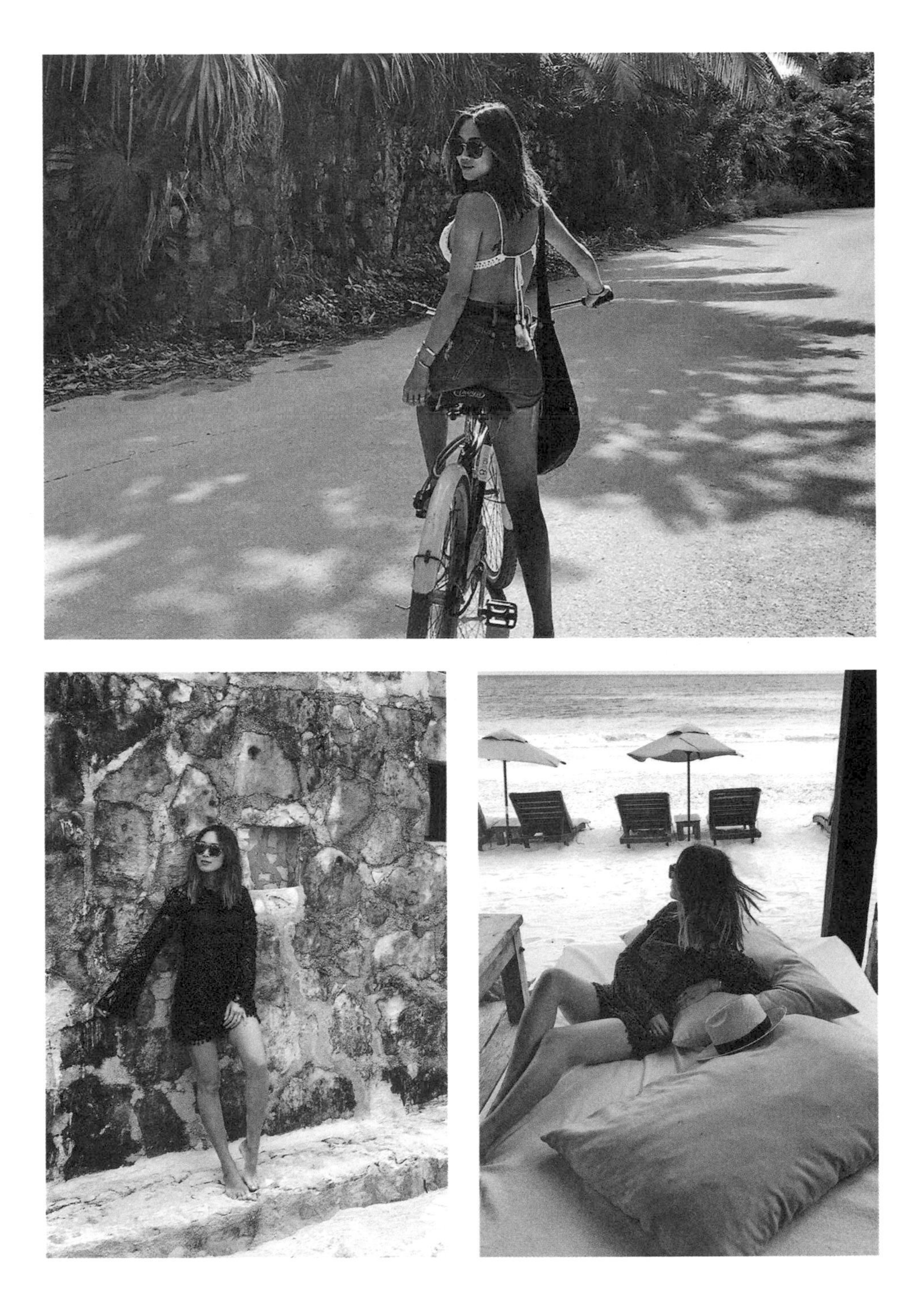

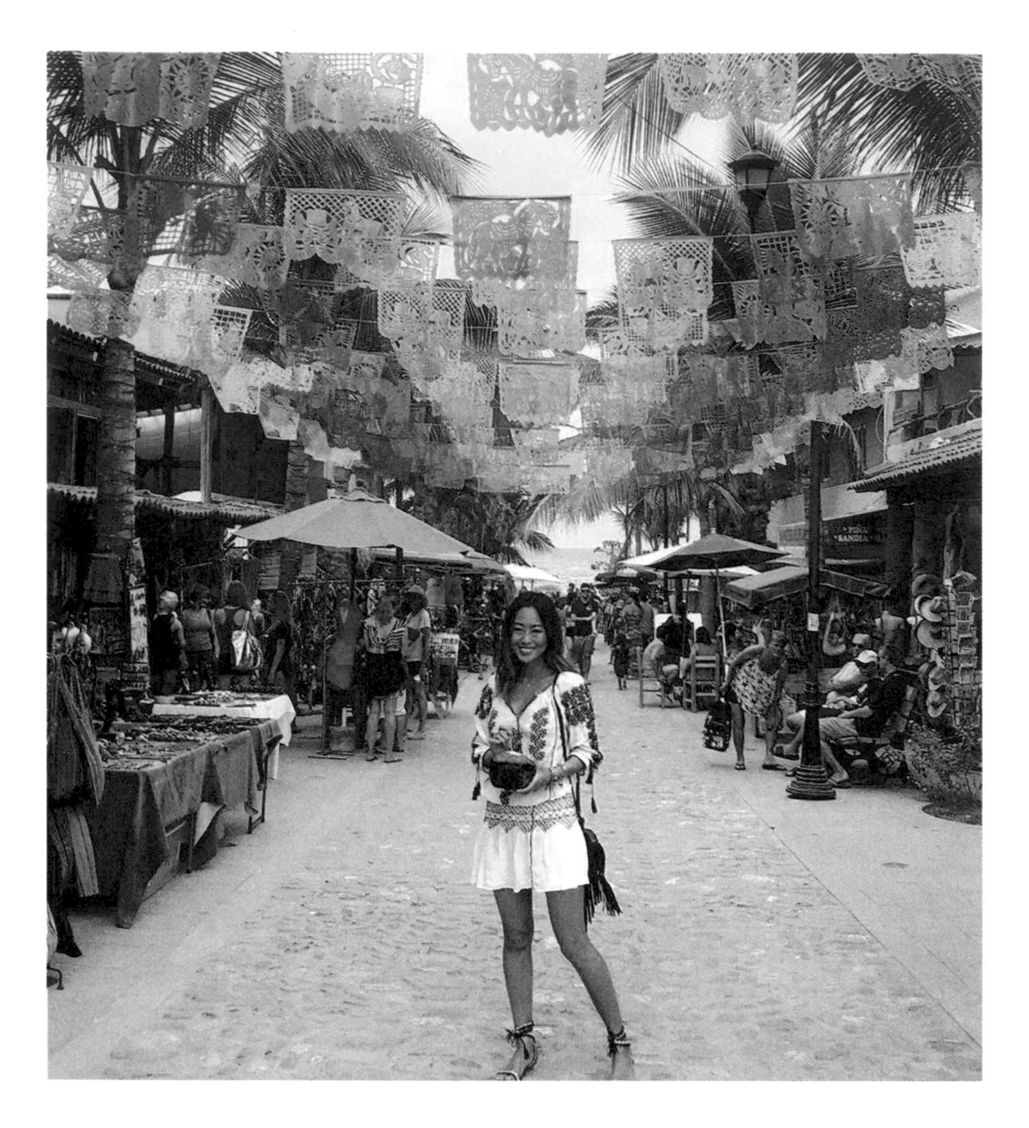

ABOVE We went to the markets in Nayarit and I found a hand-carved artisanal skull that was super expensive and too heavy to be carried home. I settled for a ton of friendship bracelets and coconut water instead. *Ulla Johnson dress; Schutz sandals.* **OPPOSITE (CLOCKWISE FROM TOP)** Twinning moment with Dani. *Jetset Diaries rompers* • New Year's Eve, right before dinner at our house. That night we ended up celebrating with Kevin Systrom, the cofounder of Instagram, because he just happened to be staying at the property next door. It was super random. We all ended up hanging out together, talking about how weird the universe is. • *Indah Clothing romper.*

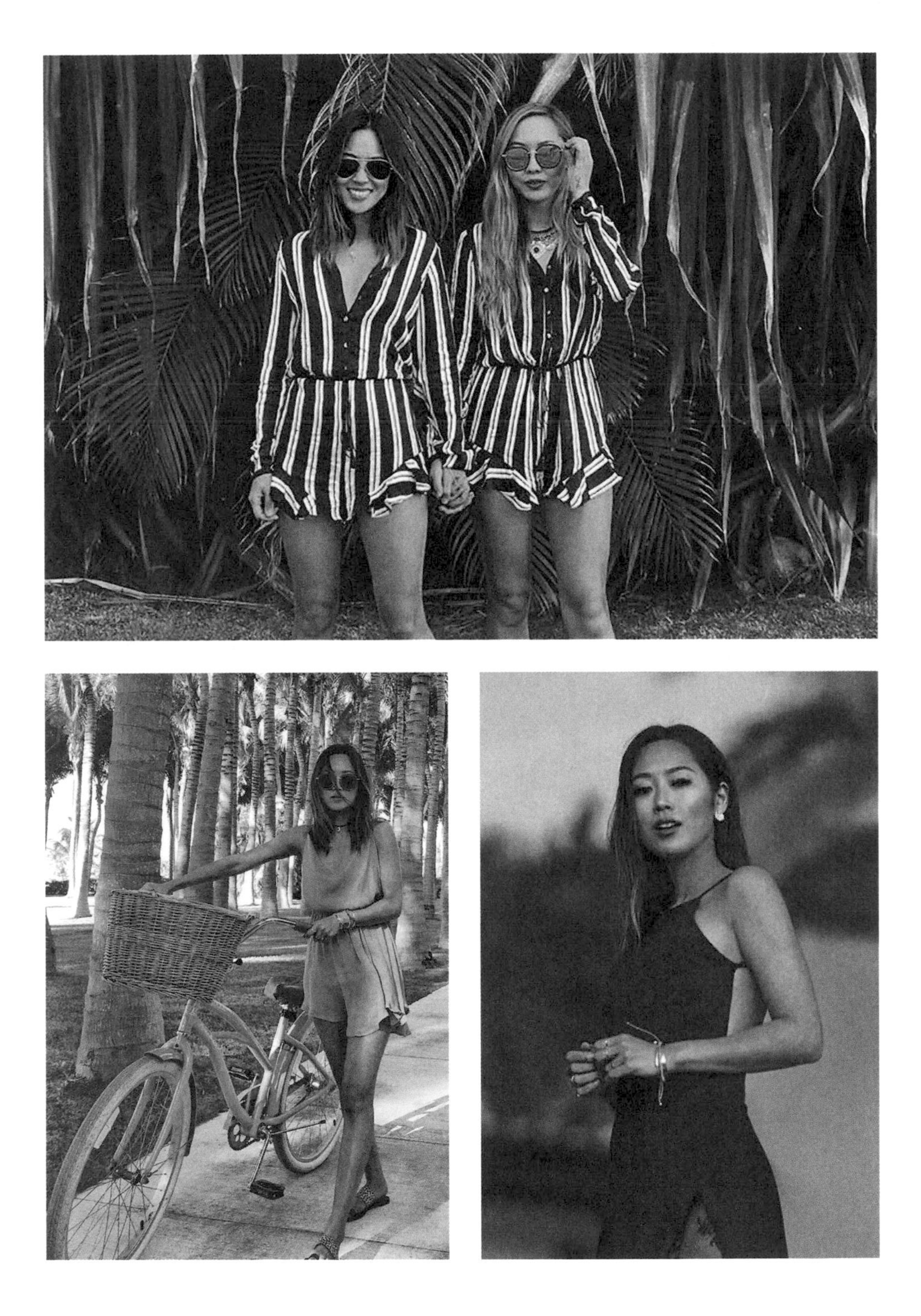

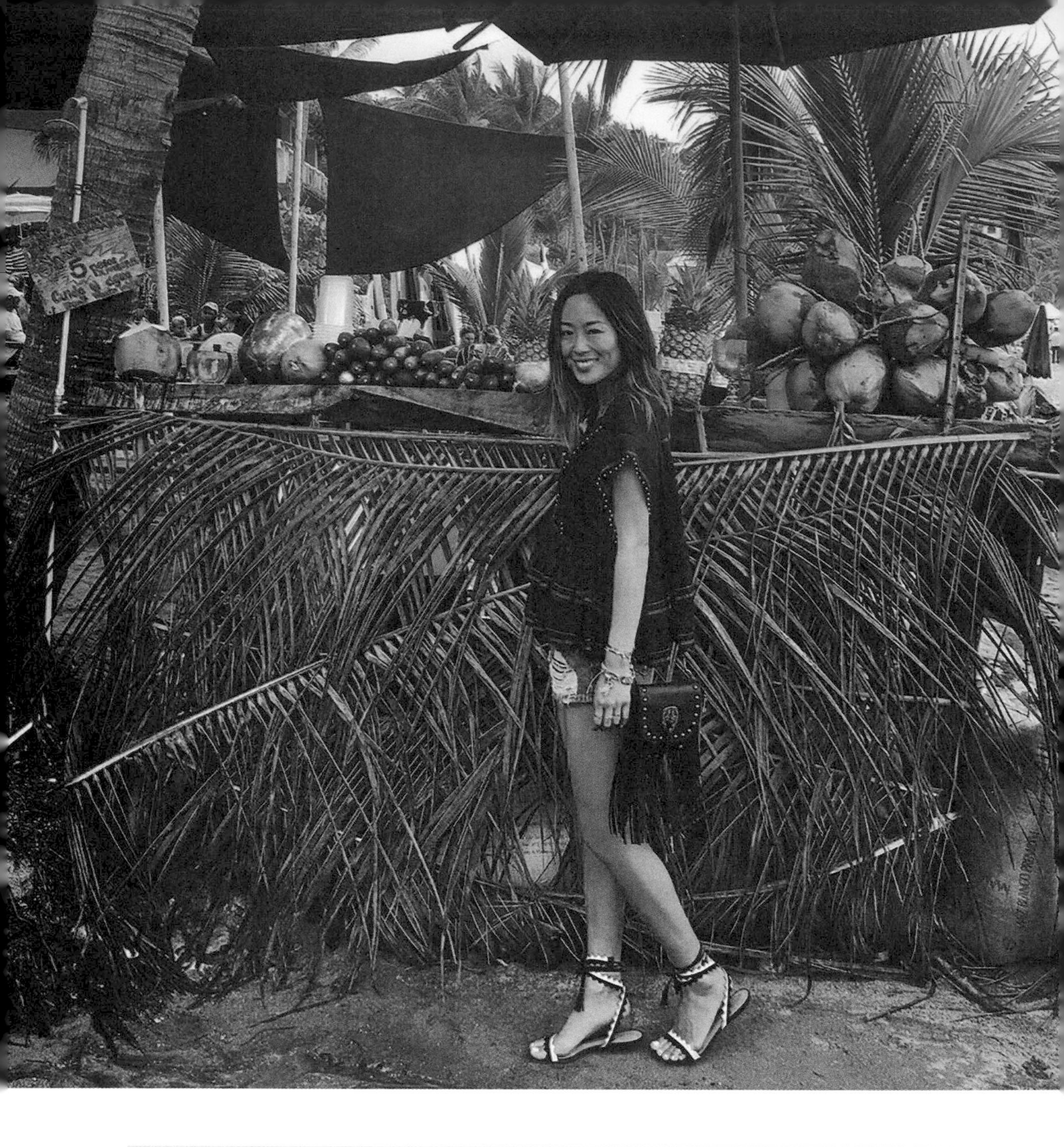

ABOVE There are so many coconut stands on the beach in Nayarit, and we all know how much I love a good coconut. *Isabel Marant top; Levi's shorts; Schutz sandals; Anarchy Street bag.* **OPPOSITE (FROM TOP)** One day Jacopo and I left the house and walked along the beach. This was someone else's property, but they had such a gorgeous hammock that I couldn't not trespass. I ended up buying one on the trip and taking it back to L.A. Dani has since stolen it. *Lovers and Friends dress* • *Tularosa top.*

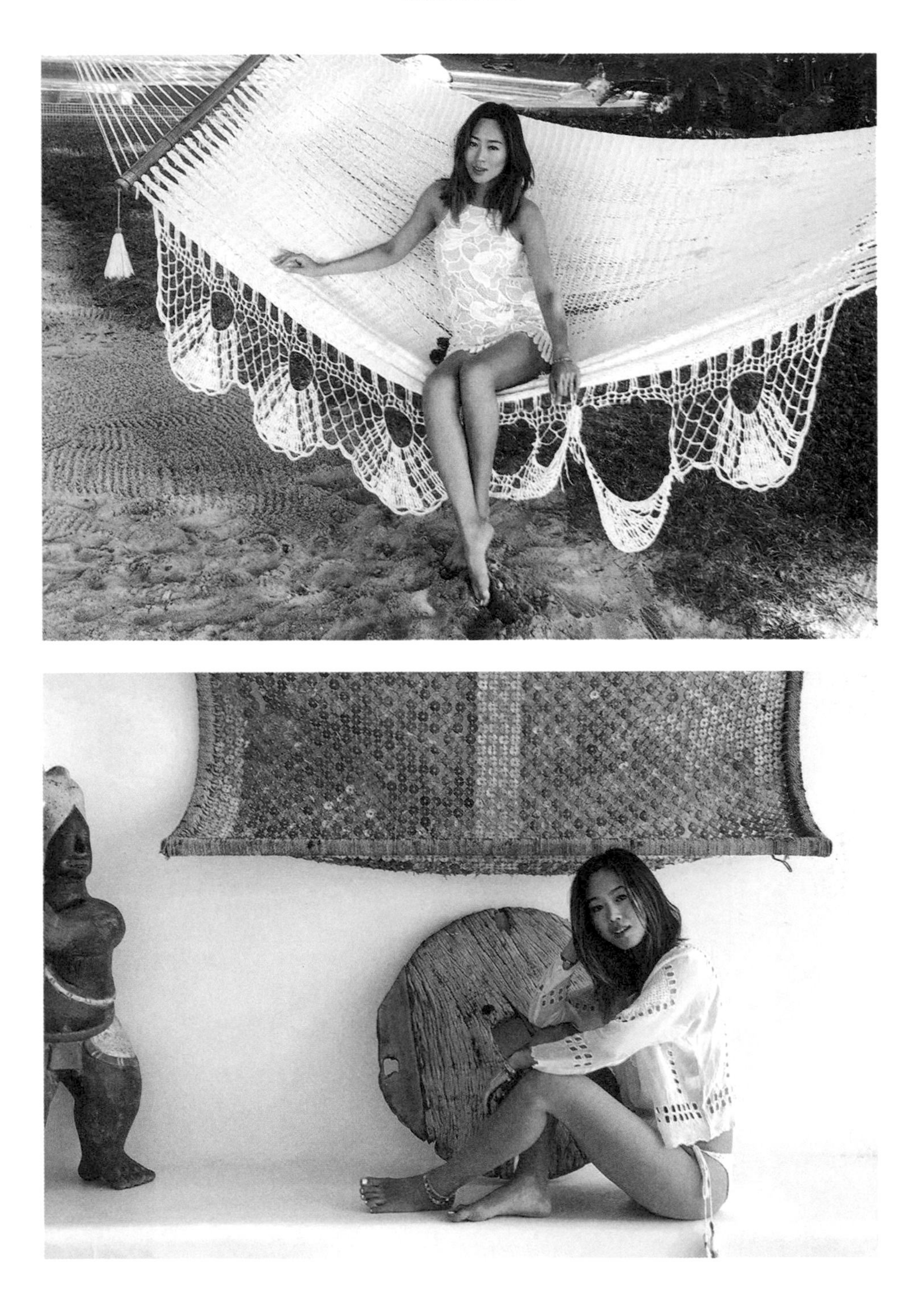

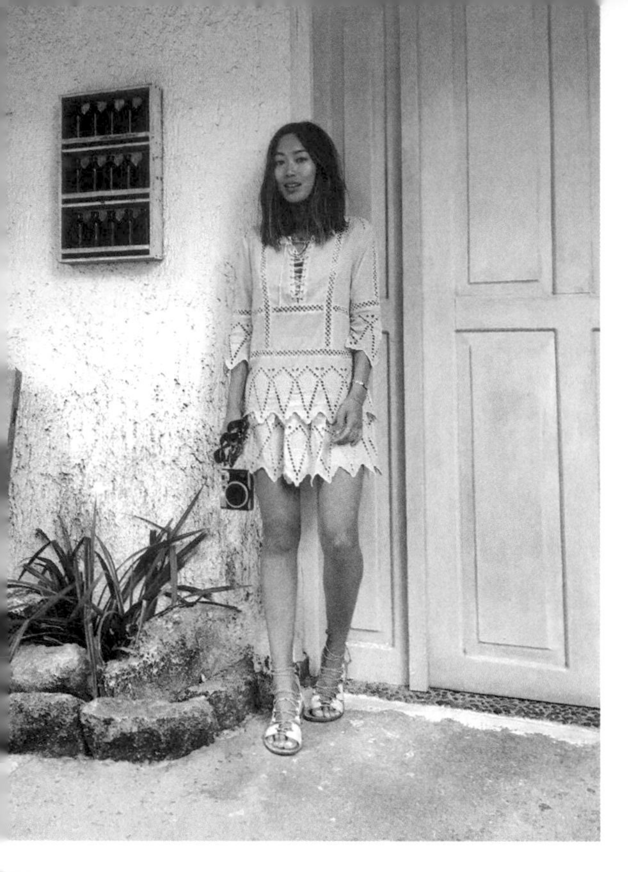

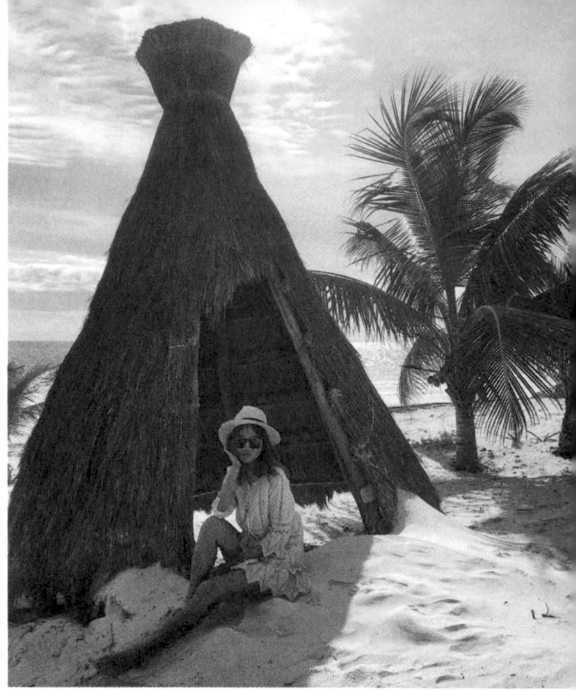

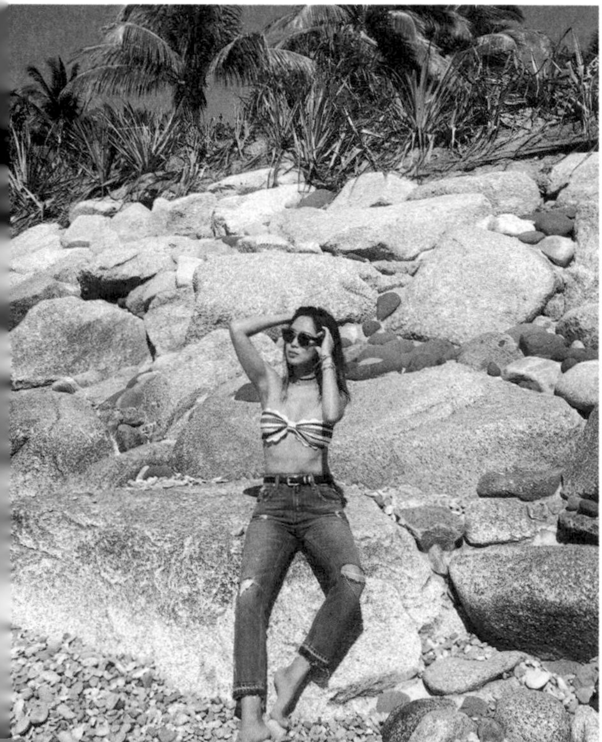

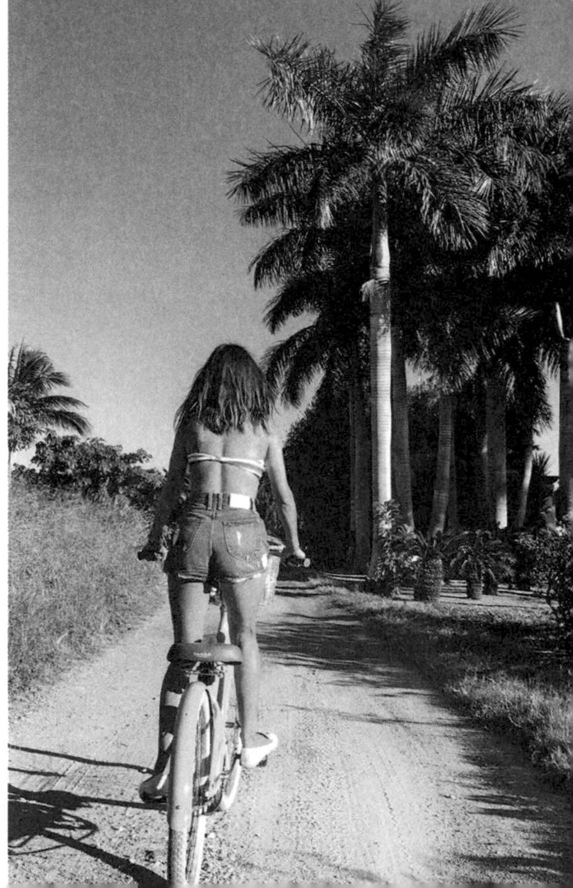

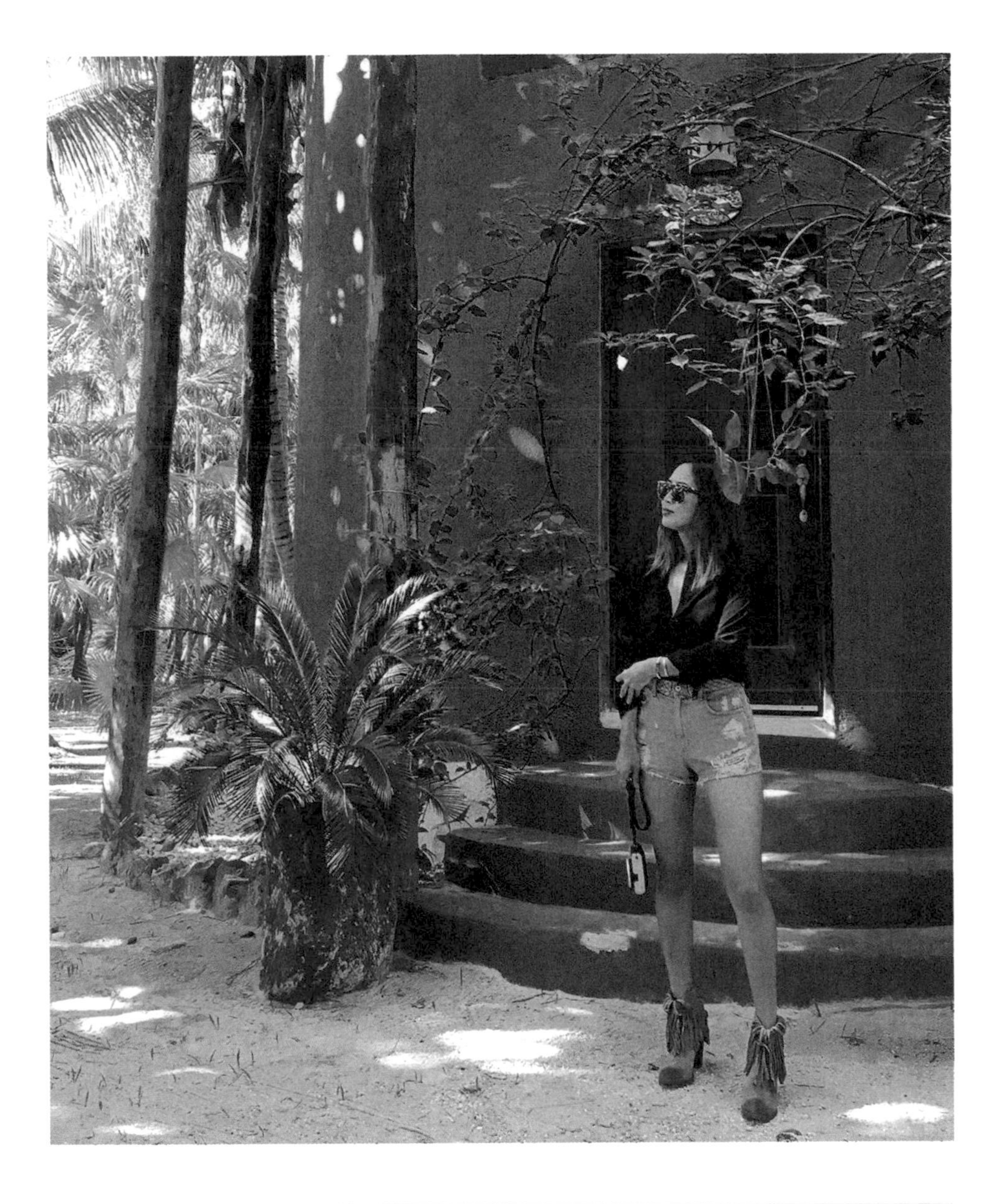

ABOVE In town before the dreaded food poisoning—a day none of us will ever forget. *Tularosa shorts; Frye boots.* **OPPOSITE, TOP ROW** We had lunch by the hotel and spent a ton of time walking—even though we had a car. Gotta get in those steps! **OPPOSITE, BOTTOM RIGHT** Lots of bike riding, even on vacay. **OPPOSITE, BOTTOM LEFT** *Marysia Swim bikini top; Tularosa jeans.*

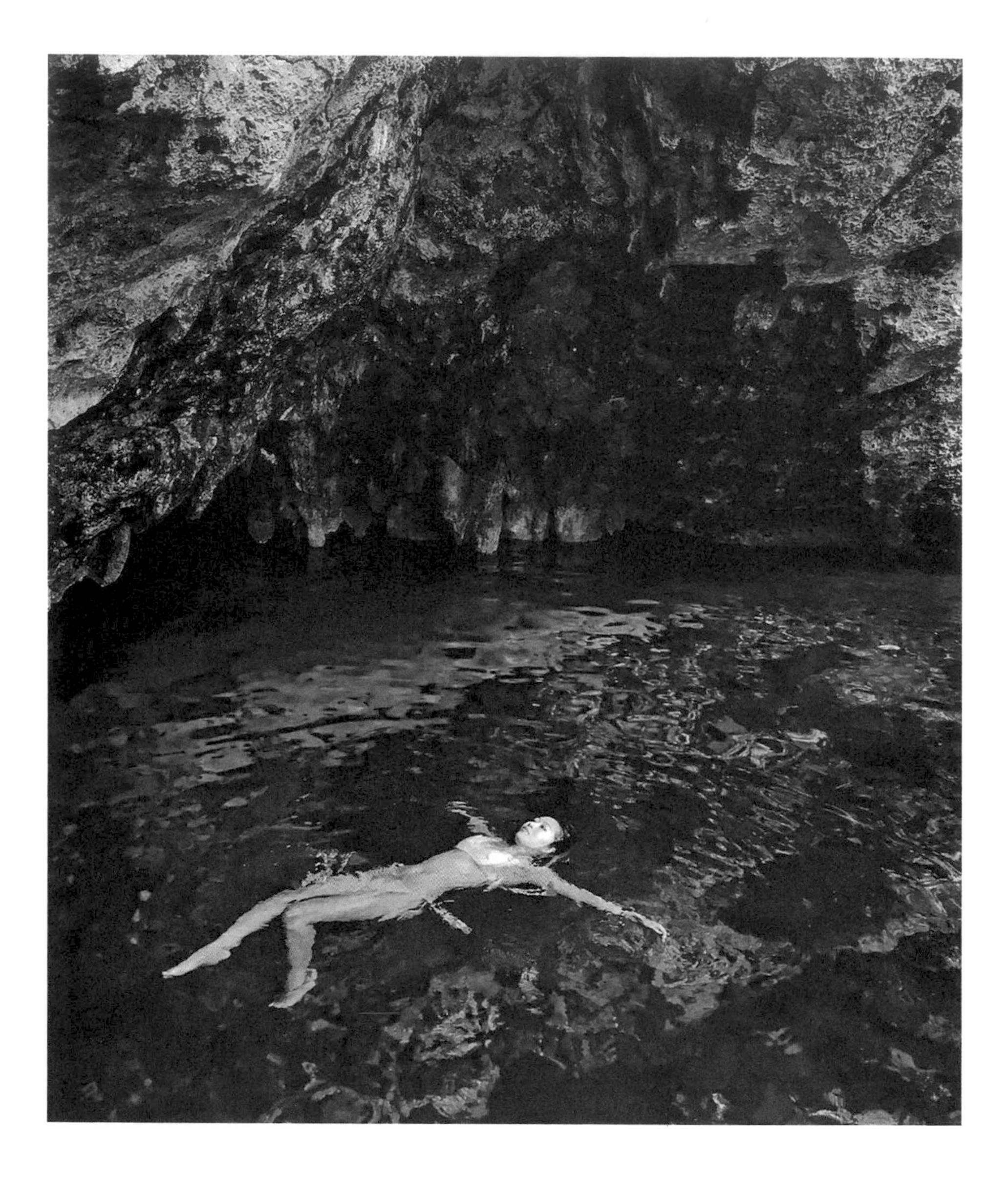

ABOVE Cenote (that's "say-no-tay" for all of you who took French in high school) is derived from the Mayan word for "well." It's a swimming hole, and Mexico has a ton of epic ones. You're asked not to wear harsh SPF to keep the environment maintained, so I just took a quick dip—despite the frigid water. **OPPOSITE (CLOCKWISE FROM TOP)** Chillin'. • I did not surf on this Chanel surfboard. I just posed with it. • A yacht day. *Acacia Swimwear swimsuit; Tularosa shorts.*

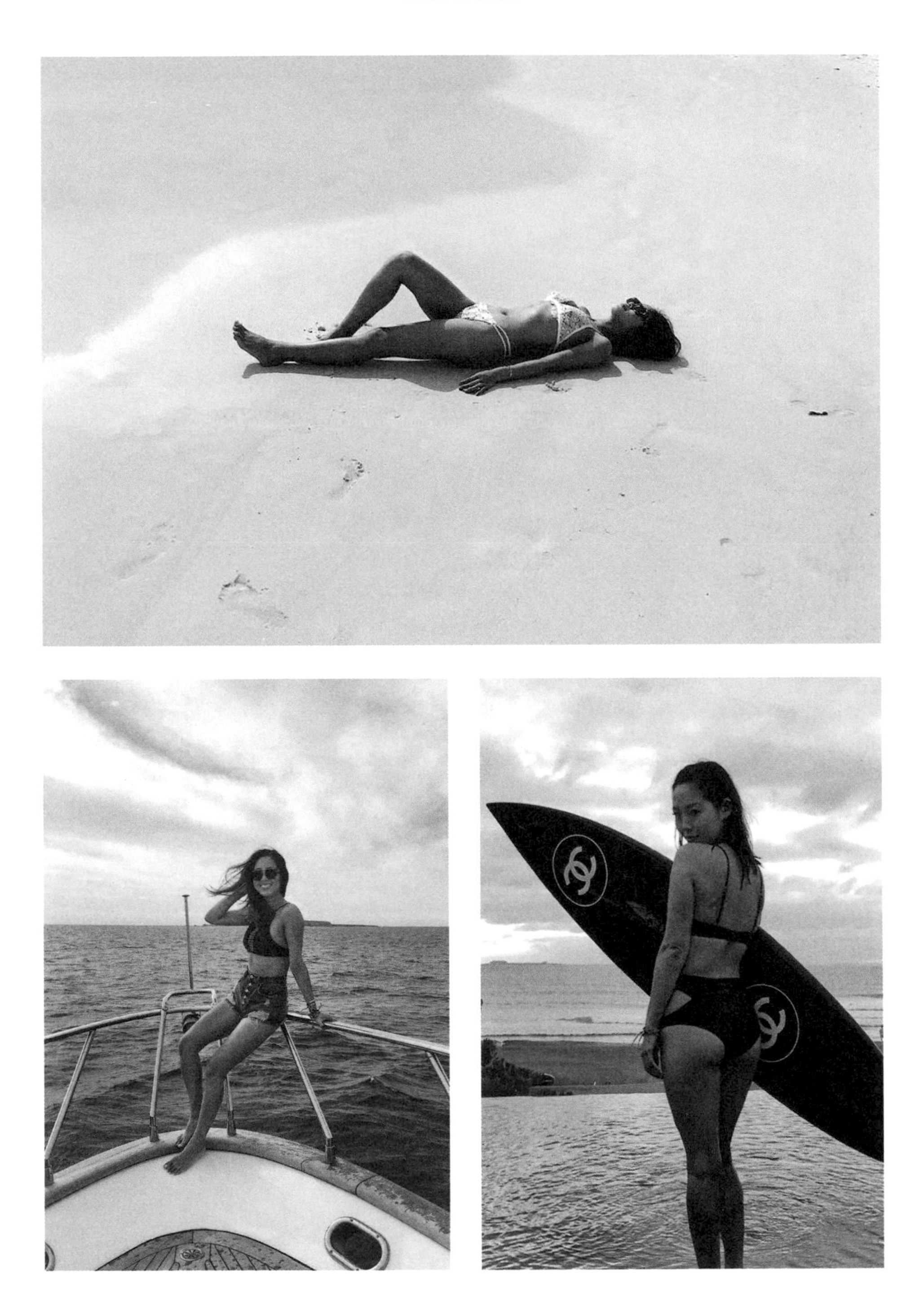

EUROPE

Antwerp

Capri

Croatia

The French Riviera

Ibiza

Iceland

London

Milan

Paris

Sicily

Switzerland

Venice

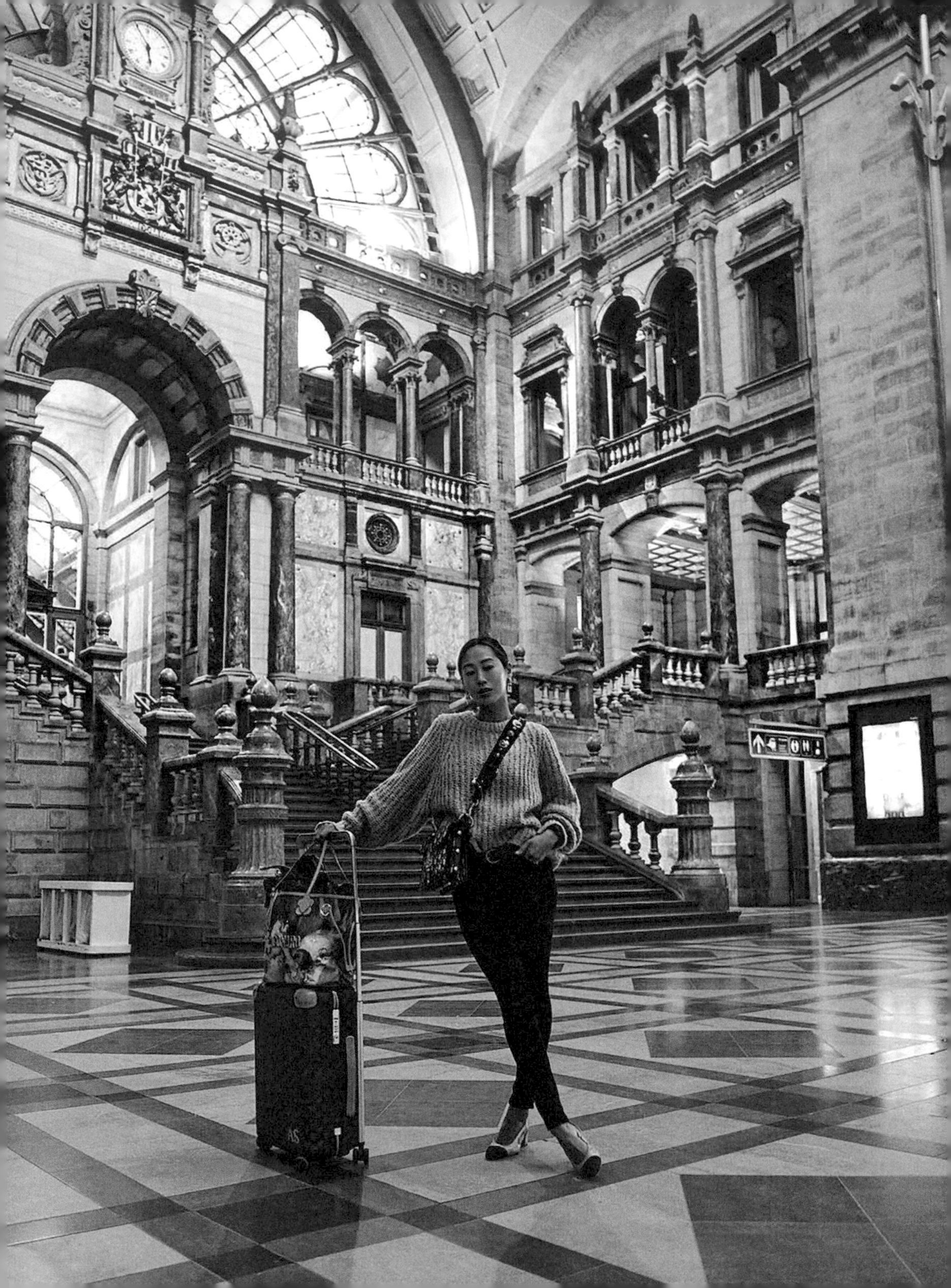

ANTWERP

As I mentioned earlier, in October 2017 Tiffany & Co. gave me the opportunity to learn about its business and the sustainability practices that go into mining and finishing its diamonds during an amazing two-part trip that began in Antwerp and continued to Mauritius. While the Mauritius portion focused on discovering the ways Tiffany & Co. taps into the local economy to mine and refine its stones, Antwerp is where I learned about the Belgian city's storied jewel heritage, and why it's been considered the diamond capital of the world for more than five hundred years.

The vibrant Dutch-speaking, Flemish city was the perfect place to spend four days exploring, and I discovered a charming, manageable city that has a thriving art and design scene, gorgeous medieval architecture and—importantly—amazing thick-cut French fries with mayo, a local specialty. The weather in Antwerp, especially in autumn, is known for being gloomy at best, but while I was there I was so lucky to experience sunny days that allowed for perfect on-foot exploration. I fell madly in love with this special place.

OPPOSITE I flew out of Paris before the Mauritius leg of this trip, so I got to experience a classic European-style high-speed train ride from Brussels to France—the first time I'd ever ridden a train in Europe. (The on-board snacks had nothing on South Korea, but I loved the experience nonetheless.) *Club Monaco sweater; Louis Vuitton trolley suitcase.*

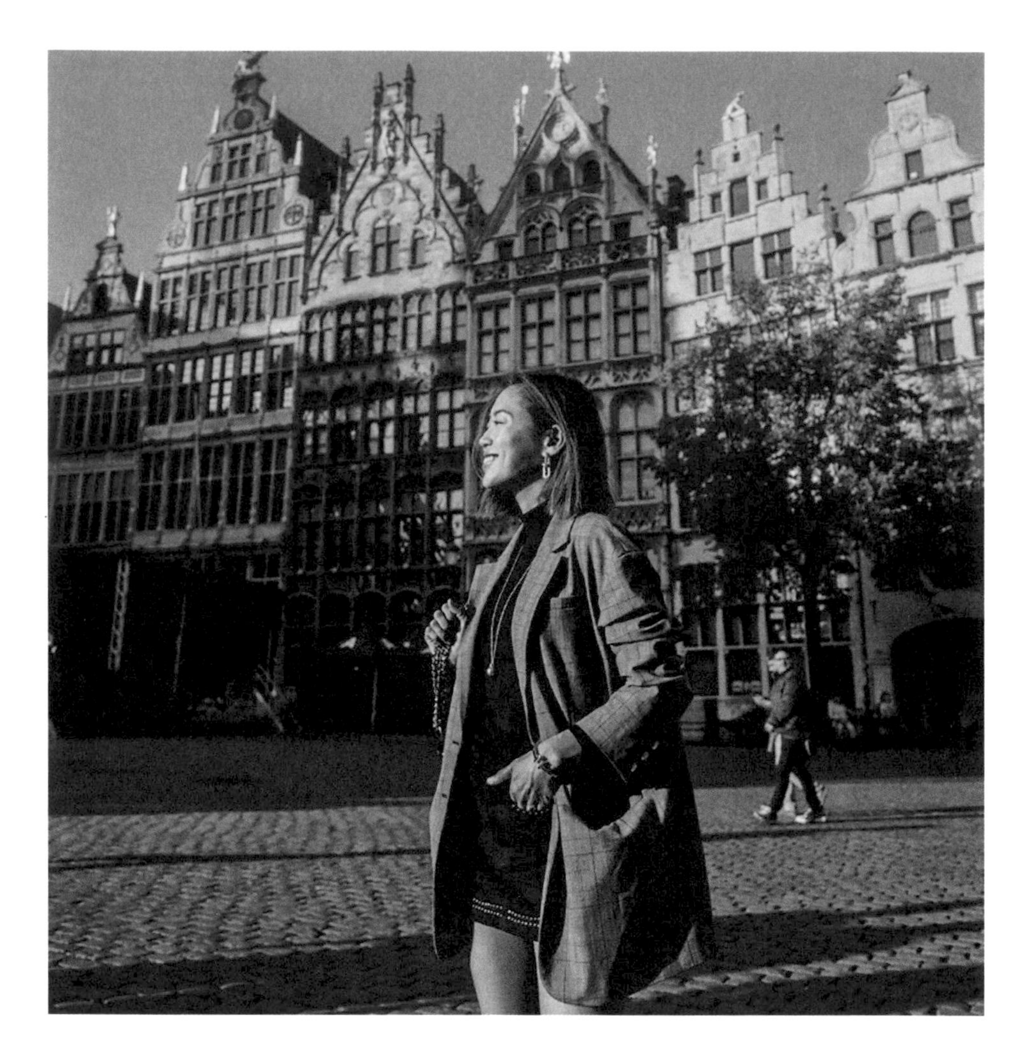

ABOVE Exploring by foot on a rare warm, bright day. We had the weather fates on our side for sure. **OPPOSITE (CLOCKWISE FROM TOP LEFT)** At Graanmarkt 13, one of the most beautiful concept stores I've ever seen (and I've seen a lot of them). We ate at the basement restaurant before getting a tour of a private, minimalist-luxe, shop-attached apartment upstairs—which is available for rent. How cool is that? *Self-Portrait jumpsuit; Tiffany & Co. jewelry* • The private apartment at Graanmarkt 13. Moving in, ASAP. • Day one, during a walking tour of the city with Jacopo. *Tibi blazer, Chanel bag* • Our hotel had the sweetest little courtyard, where we had breakfast each morning of the trip and totally felt like we were hanging out at someone's house. *Self-Portrait jumpsuit; Amanda Wakeley shoes.*

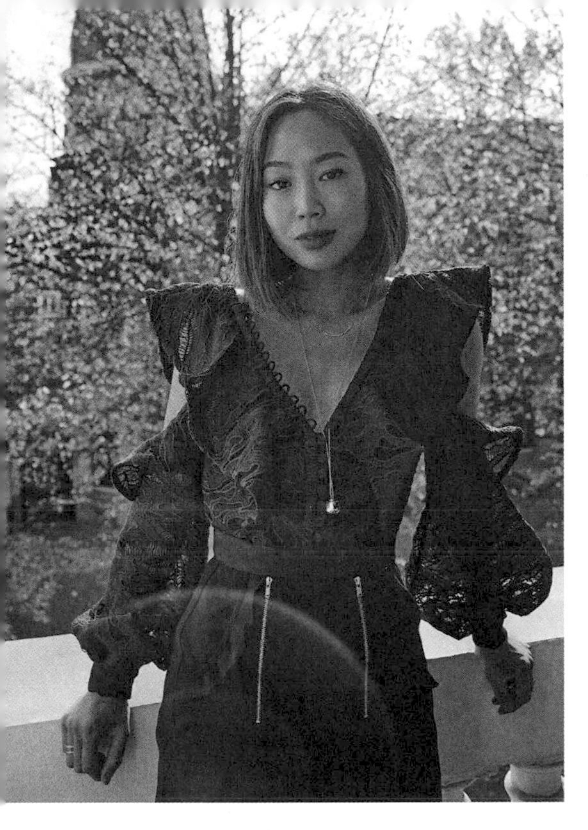

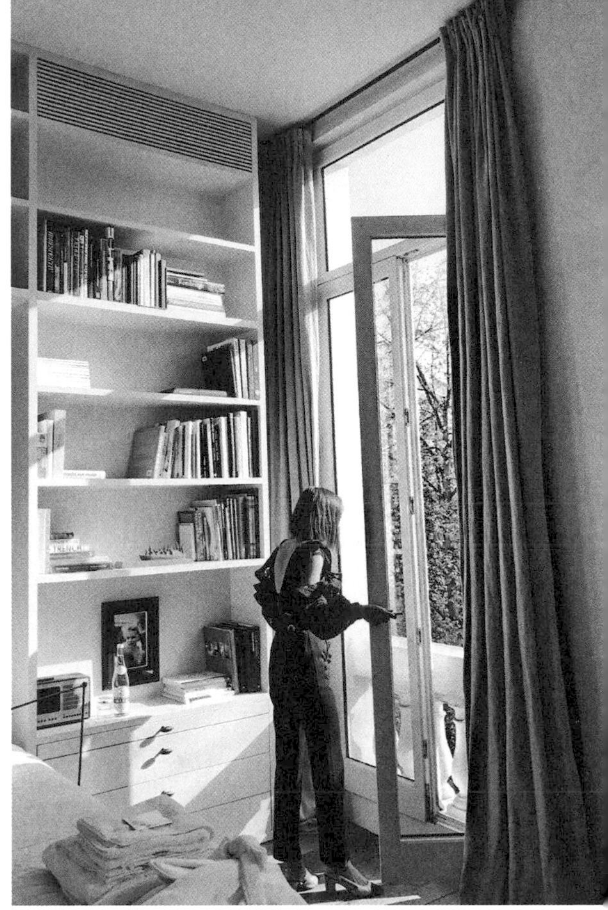

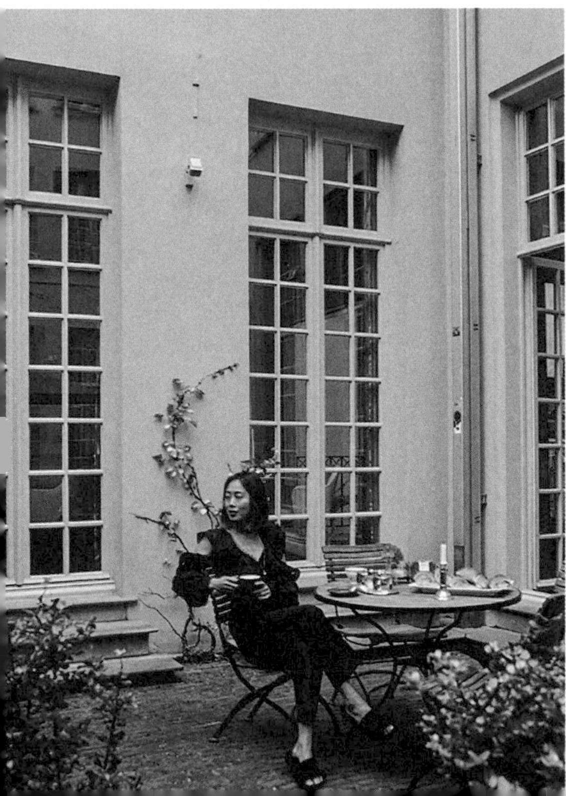

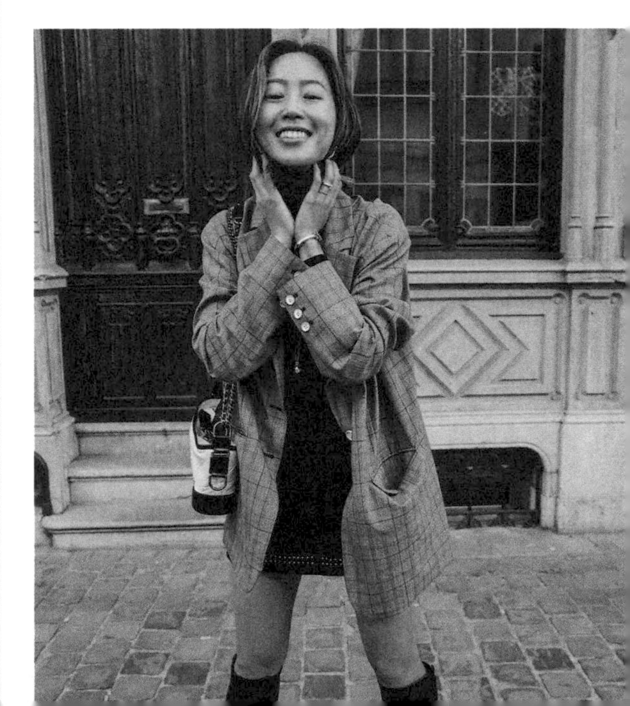

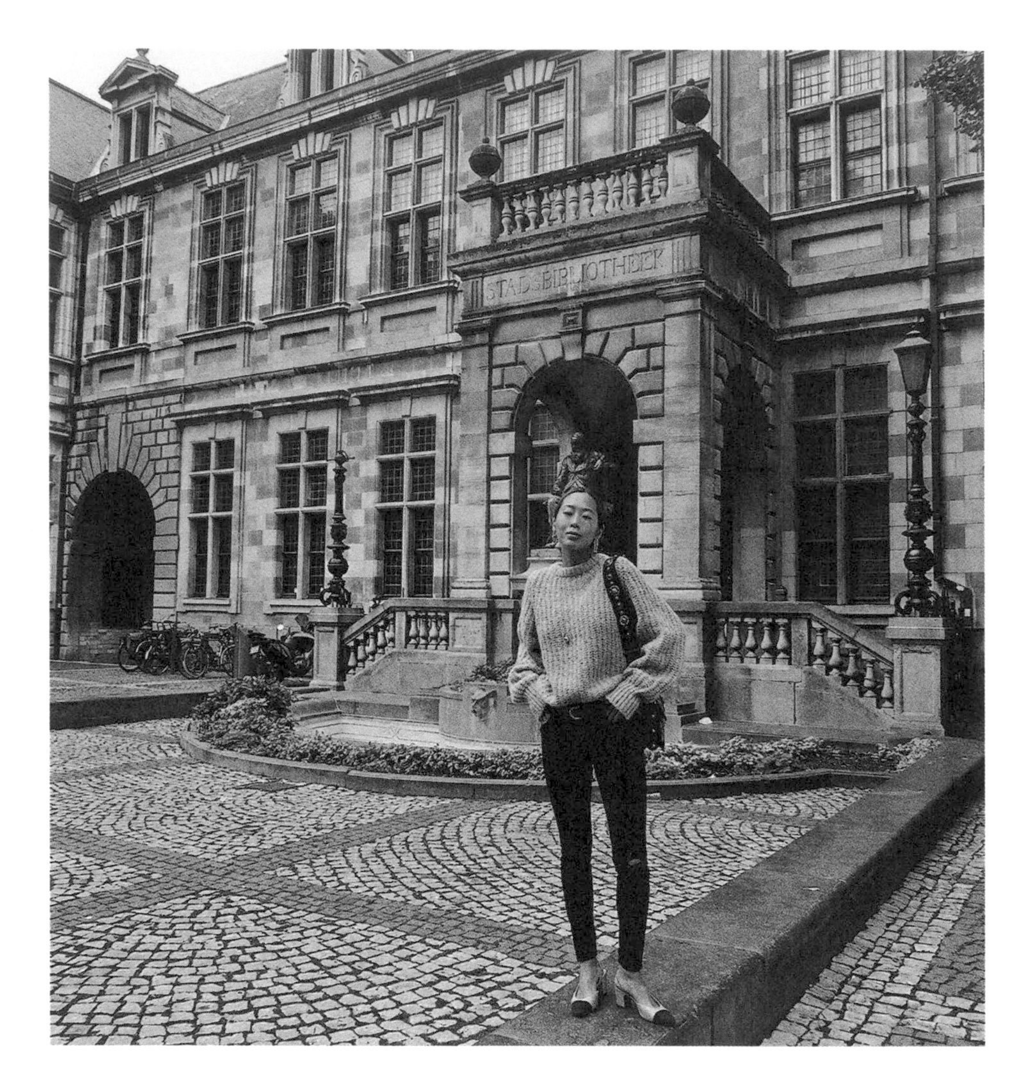

ABOVE Our last day in Antwerp. The Tiffany team and I went sightseeing with a man who I'm convinced is the best tour guide in the city. I have no other reference point, but he had so much passion for his town and we learned so much that I feel qualified to give him that title. **OPPOSITE (FROM TOP)** Each room at the cozy, eclectic Hotel De Witte Lelie—where we stayed—is completely different. While waiting for the rest of the group to go to dinner, Nathan from the Tiffany & Co. team was kind enough to take a photo of Jacopo and I on the most incredible leopard-print sofa, using his iPhone. I art directed, obviously. *Self-Portrait lace top; Frame leather pants* • Another hotel shot. So eclectic and cool.

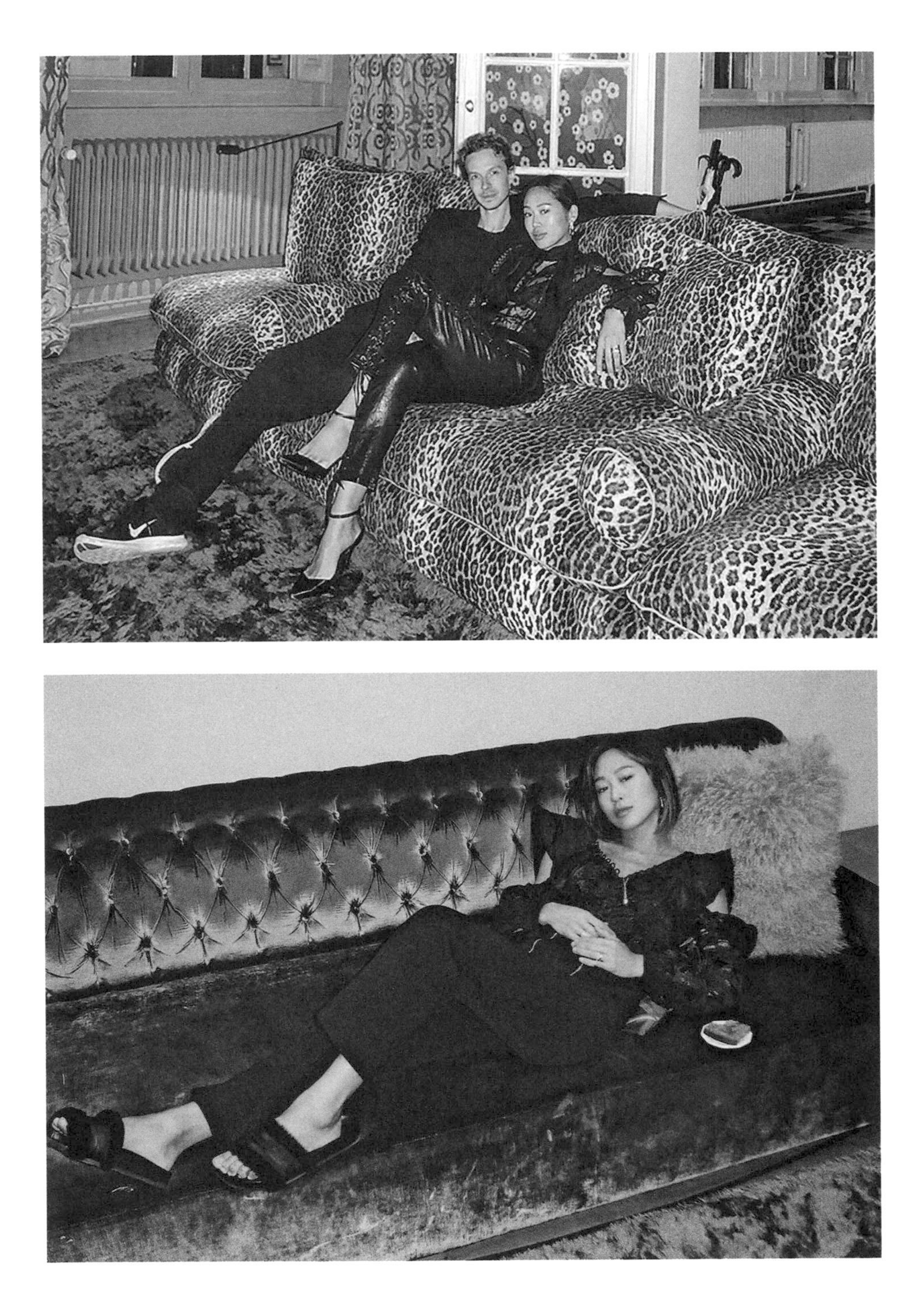

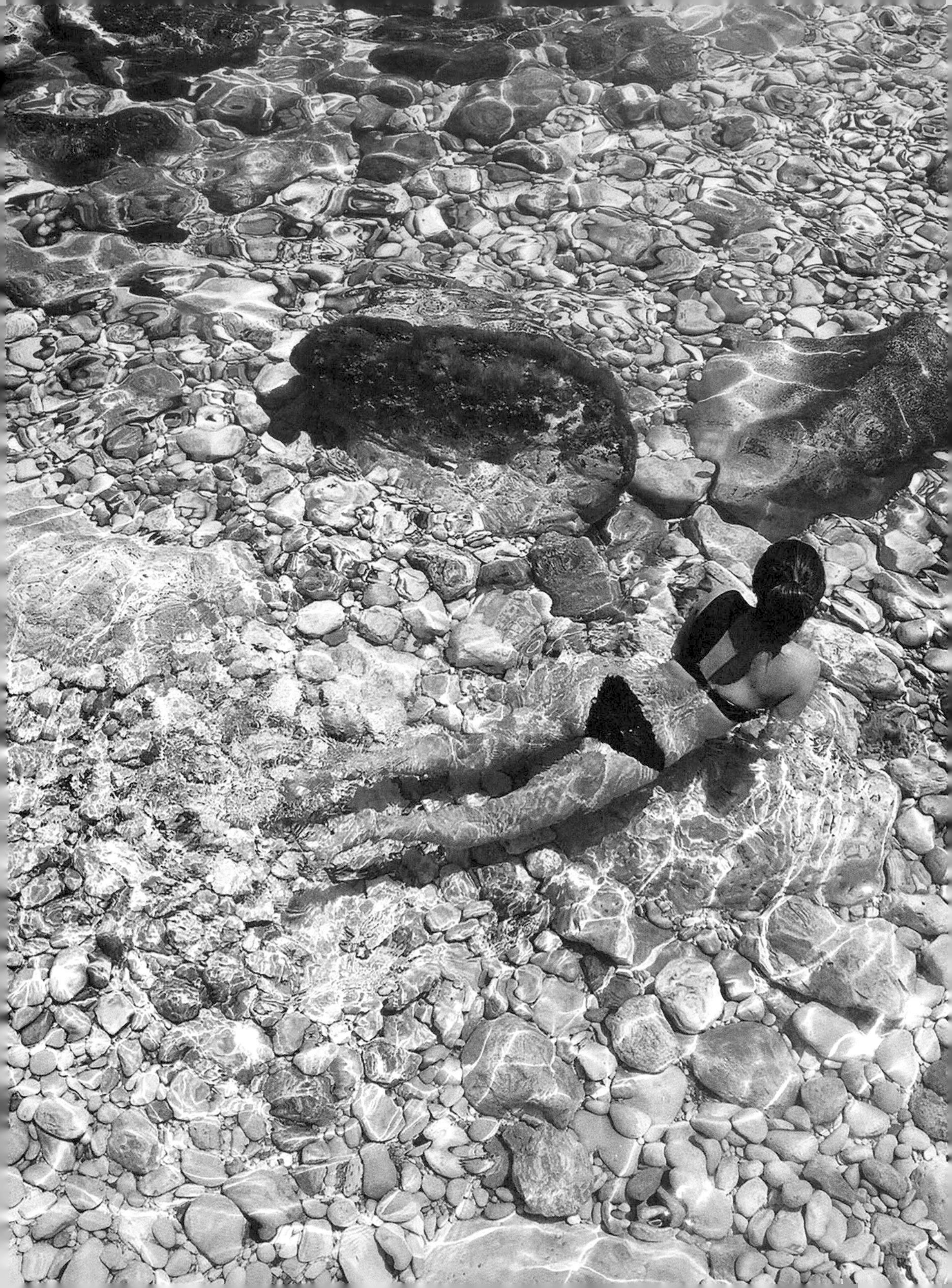

CAPRI

Jacopo and I have an amazing time together wherever we are (chillin' at home very much included), but Capri in June 2016 is one of my favorite trips I've done with him, hands down. We started in Milan and I had these outlandish ideas of what Capri would be like from movies and TV shows—glamour, yachts, and Jackie O. Then Jacopo took me on a ferry from Naples to Capri, on which everyone seemed to be getting motion sickness (definitely not the luxe Capri of my daydreams). I was so mad at him, and he was only trying to show me an authentic version of how real Italians travel. I didn't get over my anger until we arrived and I saw the beauty of our surroundings, and I felt such immense gratitude not only for being in such a gorgeous place, but for having Jacopo with me. We made up and ended up having a perfectly lovely, relaxing vacation together. True amore.

OPPOSITE We rented a small boat and day-tripped to a few little beaches to swim. Jacopo shot this at one of those out-of-the-way spots.

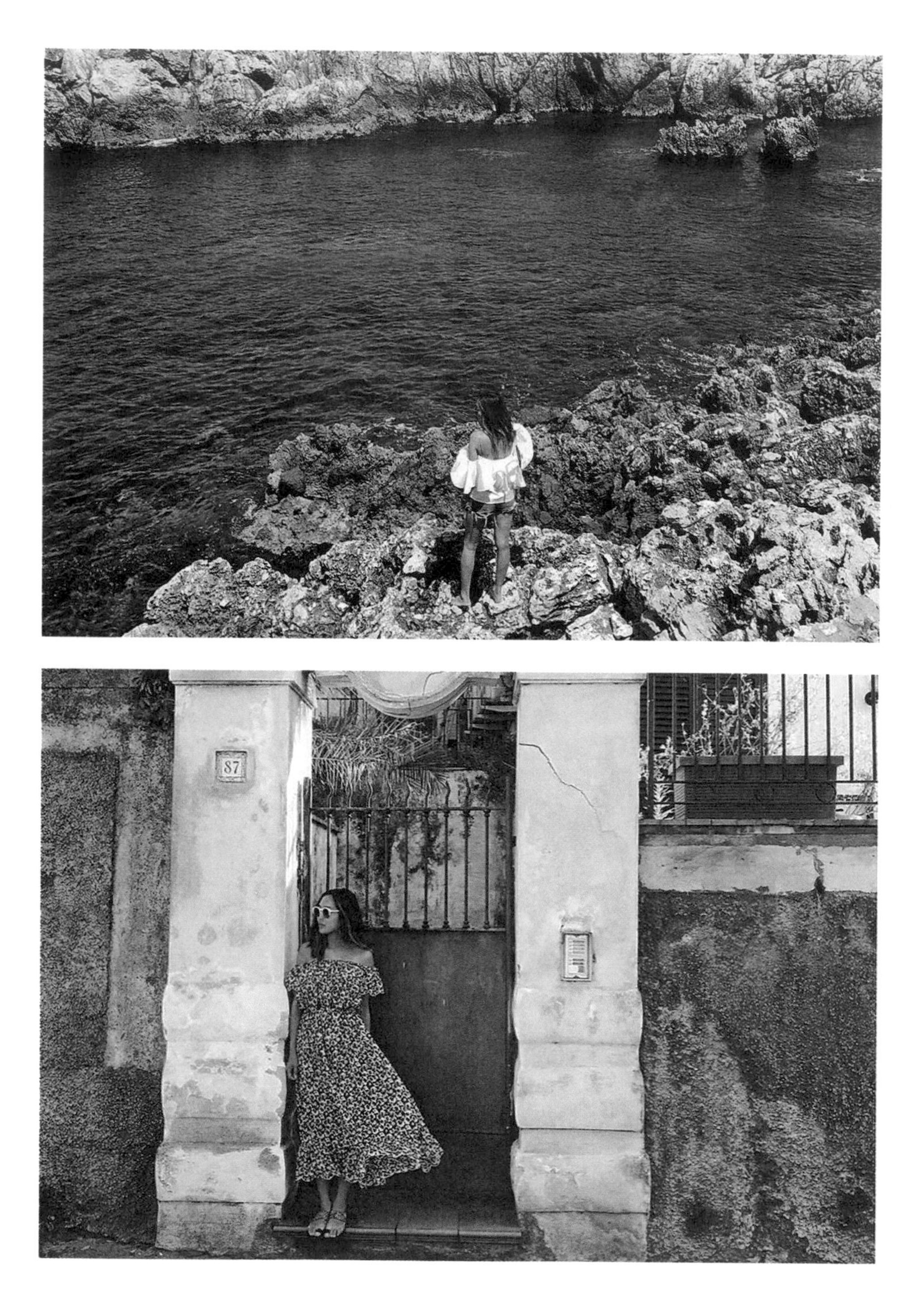
87

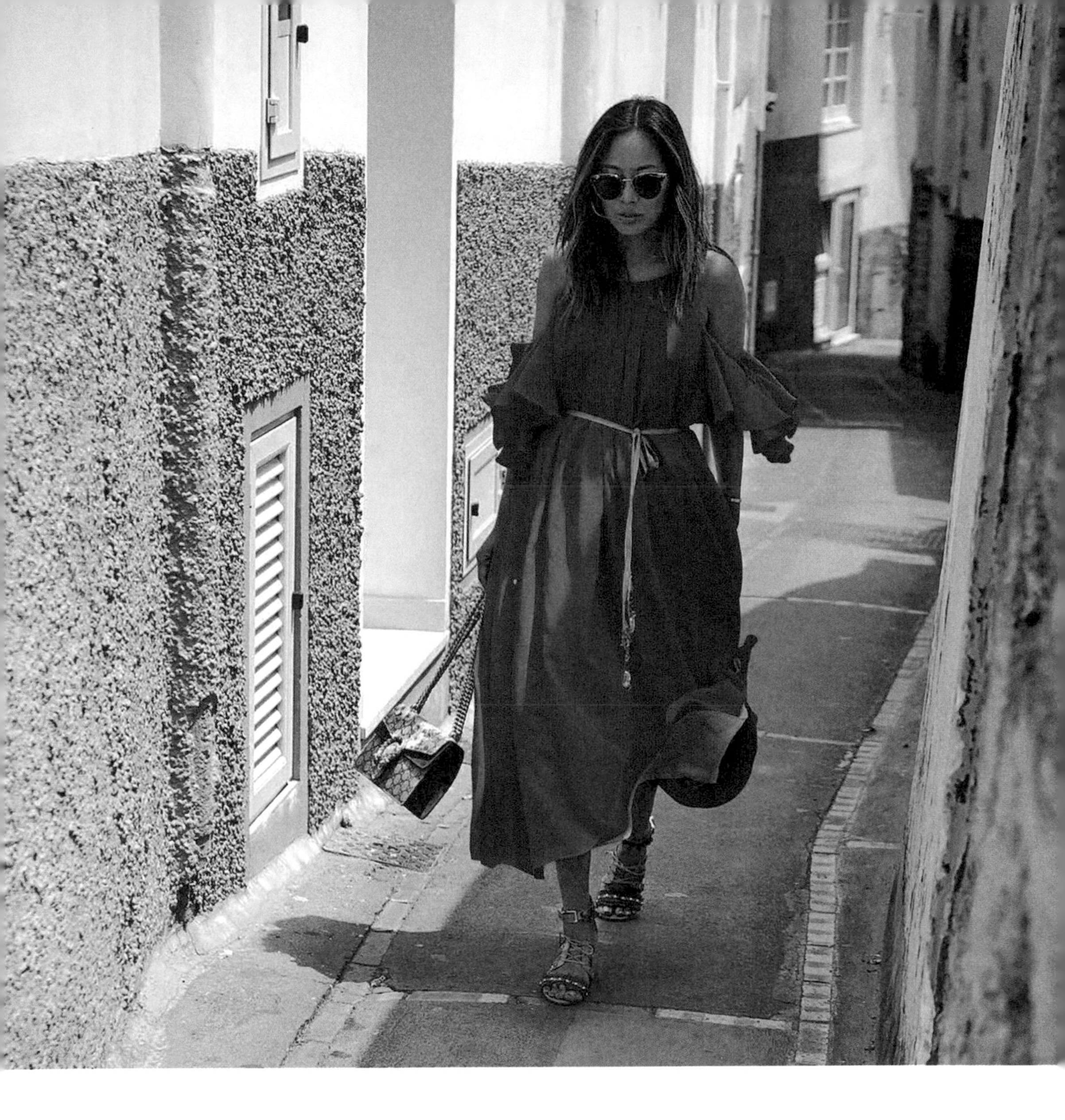

ABOVE We did Capri in a way that felt very down-to-earth (you can do it the opposite way, too). We definitely partook in touristy things, but nothing was super over-the-top or too glam. We took ferries, walked everywhere, and hung out with Jacopo's friends who live there. It all felt very "Italian," and I so enjoyed how real everything felt and not like a magazine editorial, as is the case sometimes when I travel for work. **OPPOSITE (FROM TOP)** If we weren't walking in Capri, we were on a scooter. *Caroline Constas top • Marysia Swim cover-up; Raye sandals.*

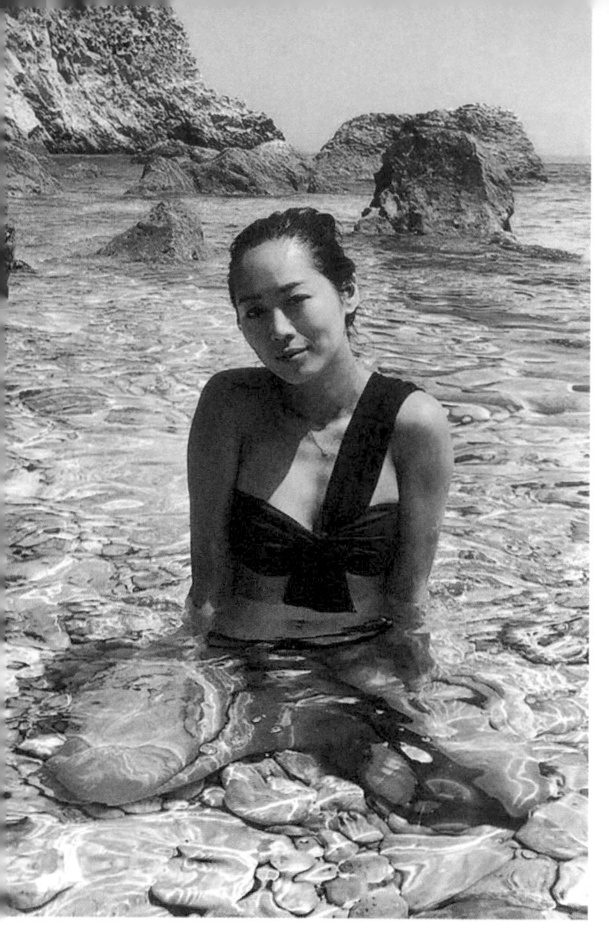

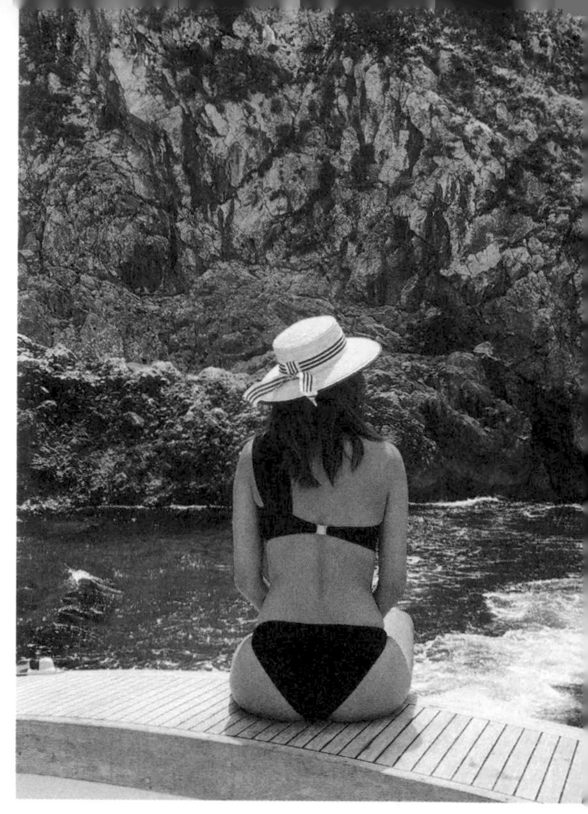

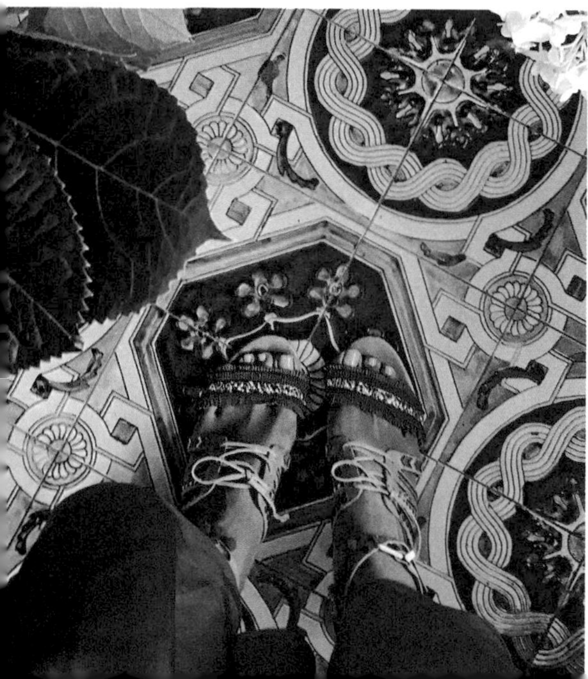

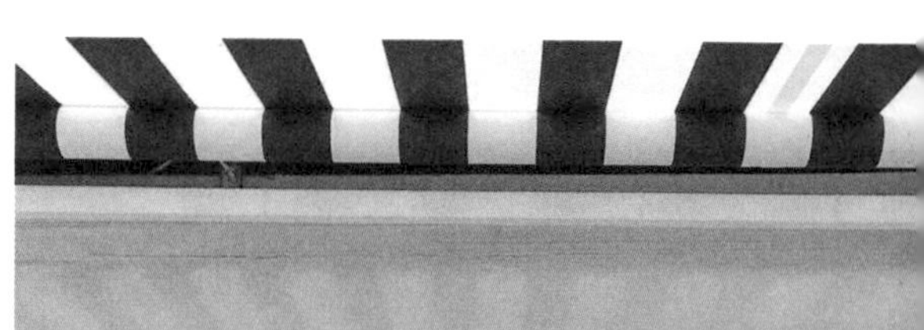

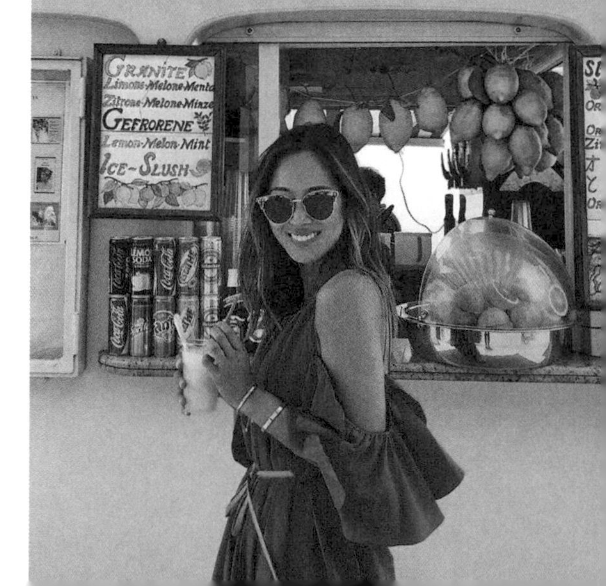
GRANITE
Limone-Melone-Menta
Zitrone-Melone-Minze
GEFRORENE
Lemon-Melon-Mint
ICE~SLUSH

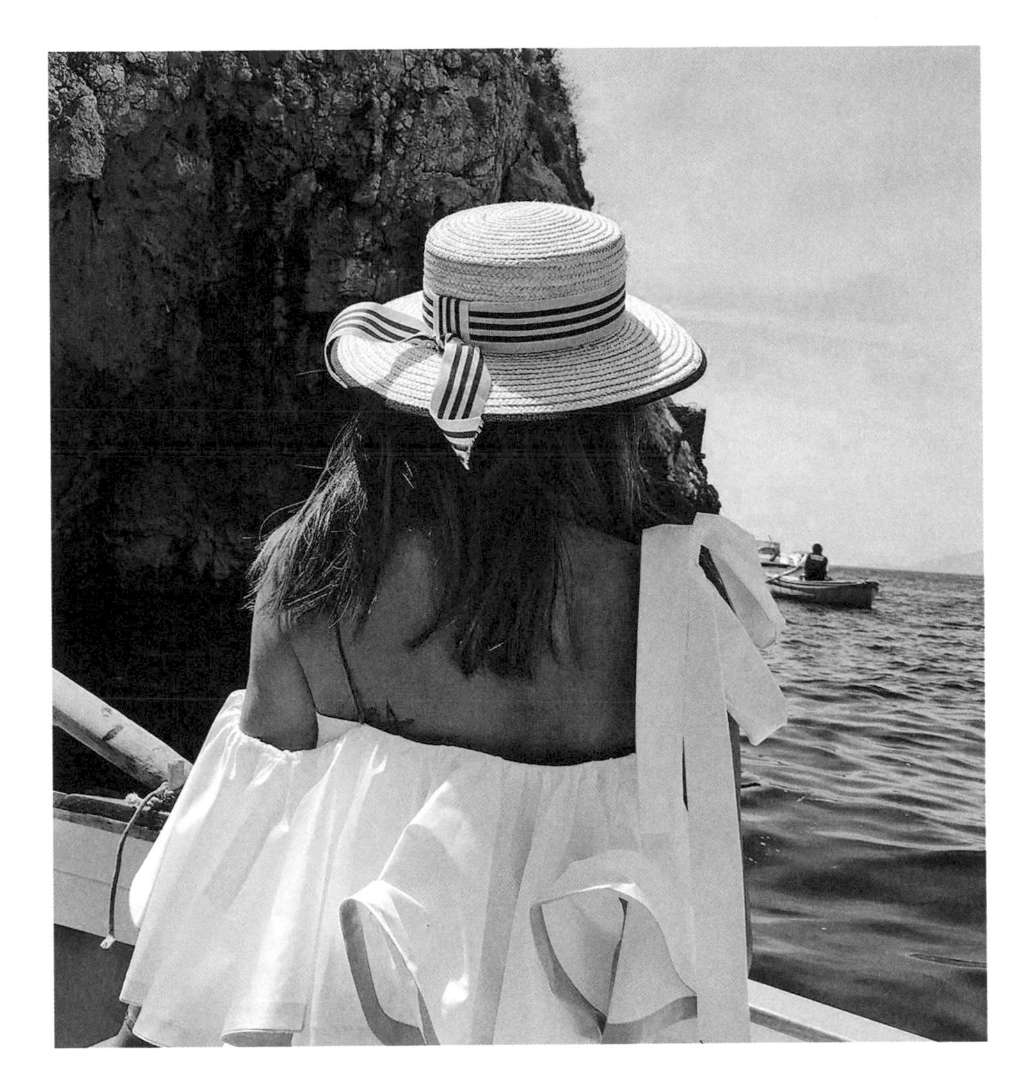

ABOVE The water in Capri is such an interesting shade of turquoise blue that is feels almost luminescent. We took a boat ride to a famous cave called Grotta Azzurra (which literally means "blue cave") and as an added bonus our "captain" sang to us on the way. *$10 Venice street hat; Anna October dress.* **OPPOSITE, TOP ROW** *Marysia Swim swimsuit.* **OPPOSITE, BOTTOM RIGHT** Every day I felt like I was in an old Italian film (or like I was Aziz Ansari in *Master of None* season two), with my Italian lover. This is me getting a lemon granita. *Anna October dress.* **OPPOSITE , BOTTOM LEFT** Same dress, same day. Everything there feels like it's a sea of orange, blue, and green—especially as far as gorgeous hand-painted tiles are concerned. And as we all know, #IHaveThisThingWithFloors. *Schutz sandals.*

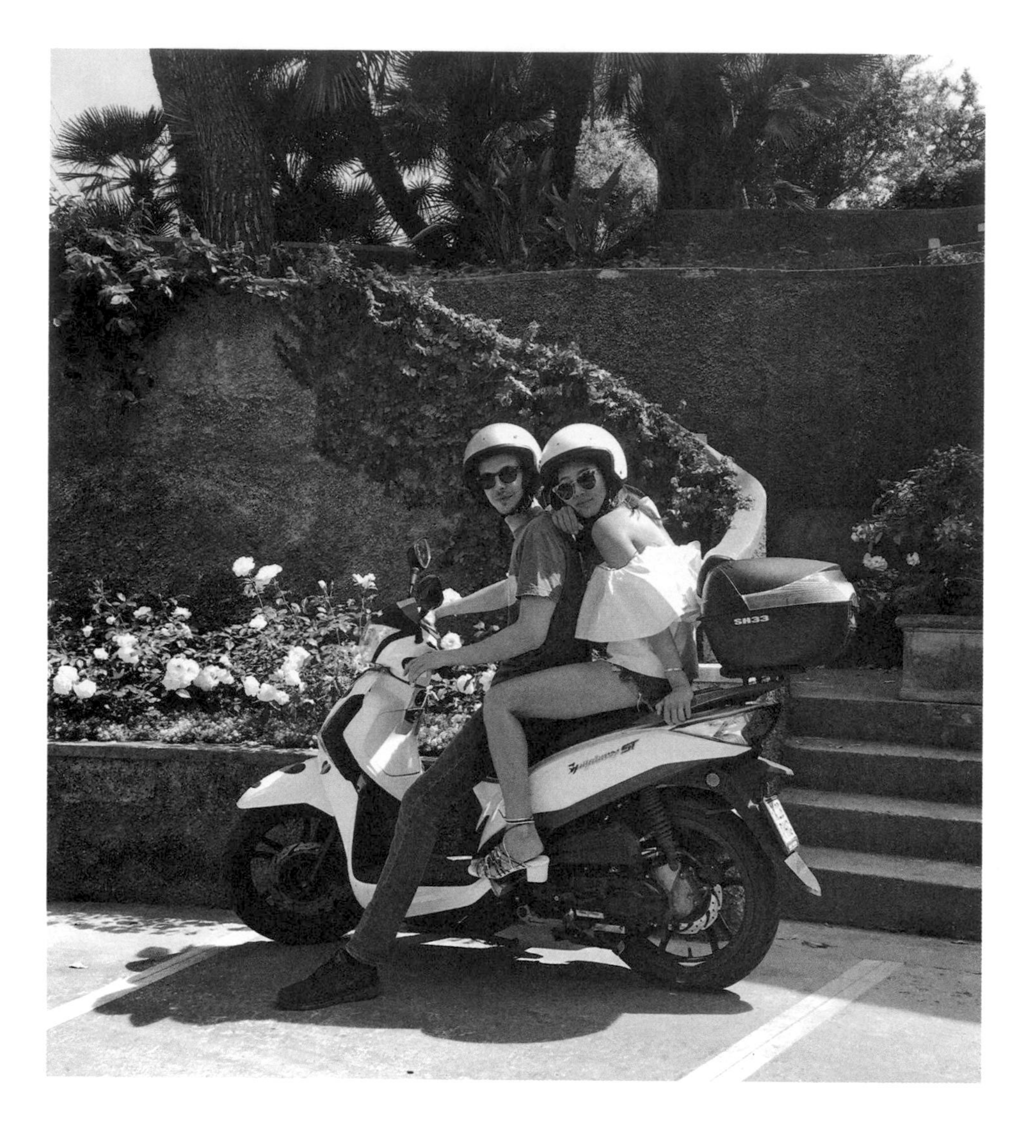

ABOVE It's hard to get a photo with Jacopo when we're traveling—someone needs to be behind the camera, right? The staff at our hotel was nice enough to shoot us right before we took off on a scooter tour. **OPPOSITE (CLOCKWISE FROM TOP)** We were in Capri for almost a week, so there was a lot of hanging by the water and relaxing. We'd explore during the day and swim before dinner. This is then. *Kiini swimsuit; Levi's shorts* • Back then I used to take a lot of these through-the-sunnies-shots. I don't do them a lot anymore, but I always thought it was cool to see the scenery through my shades. *Gentle Monster sunglasses* • Right across from where the ferry (yes, *the* ferry) docks, we ate pizza and walked around. *Caroline Constas top.*

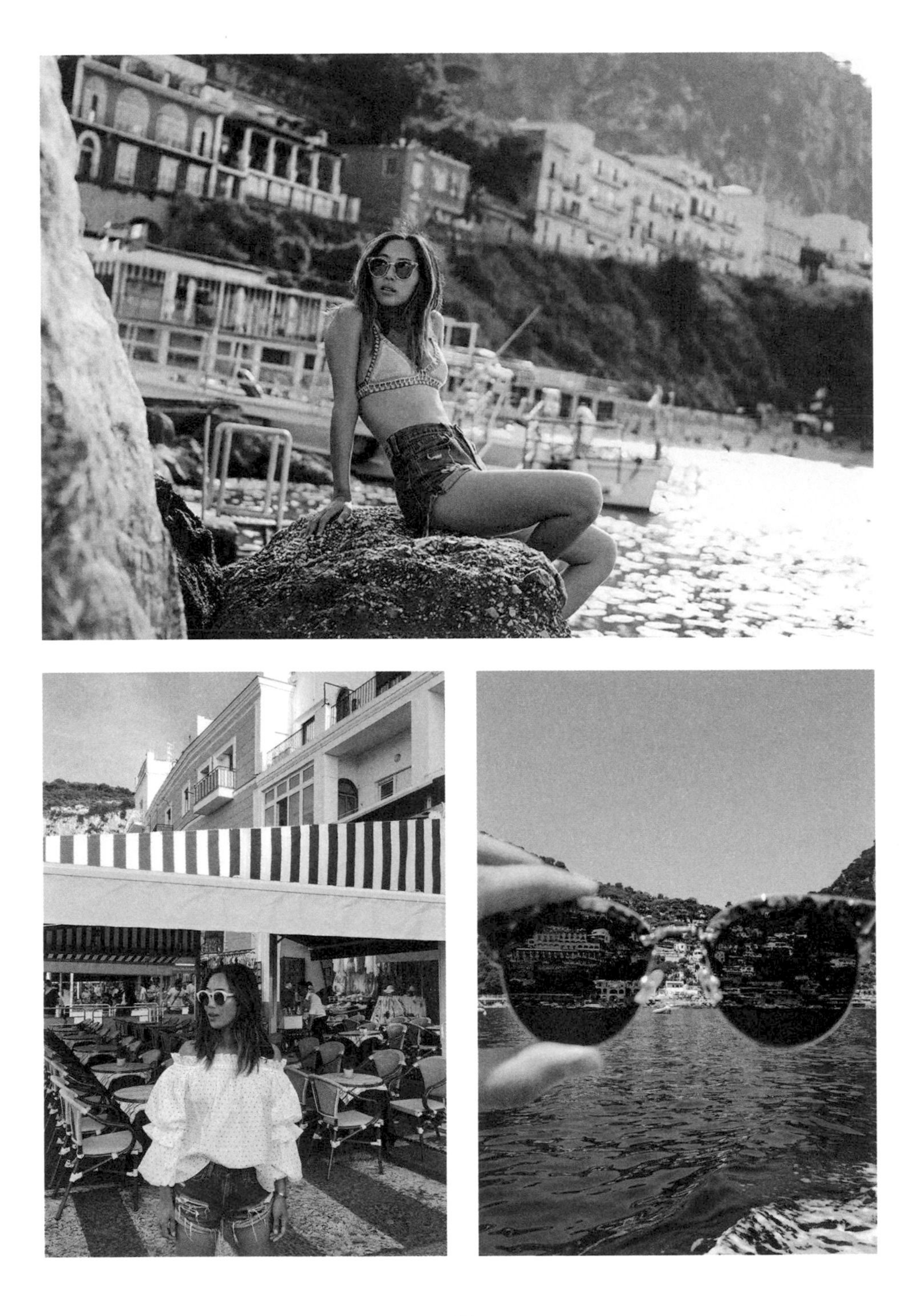

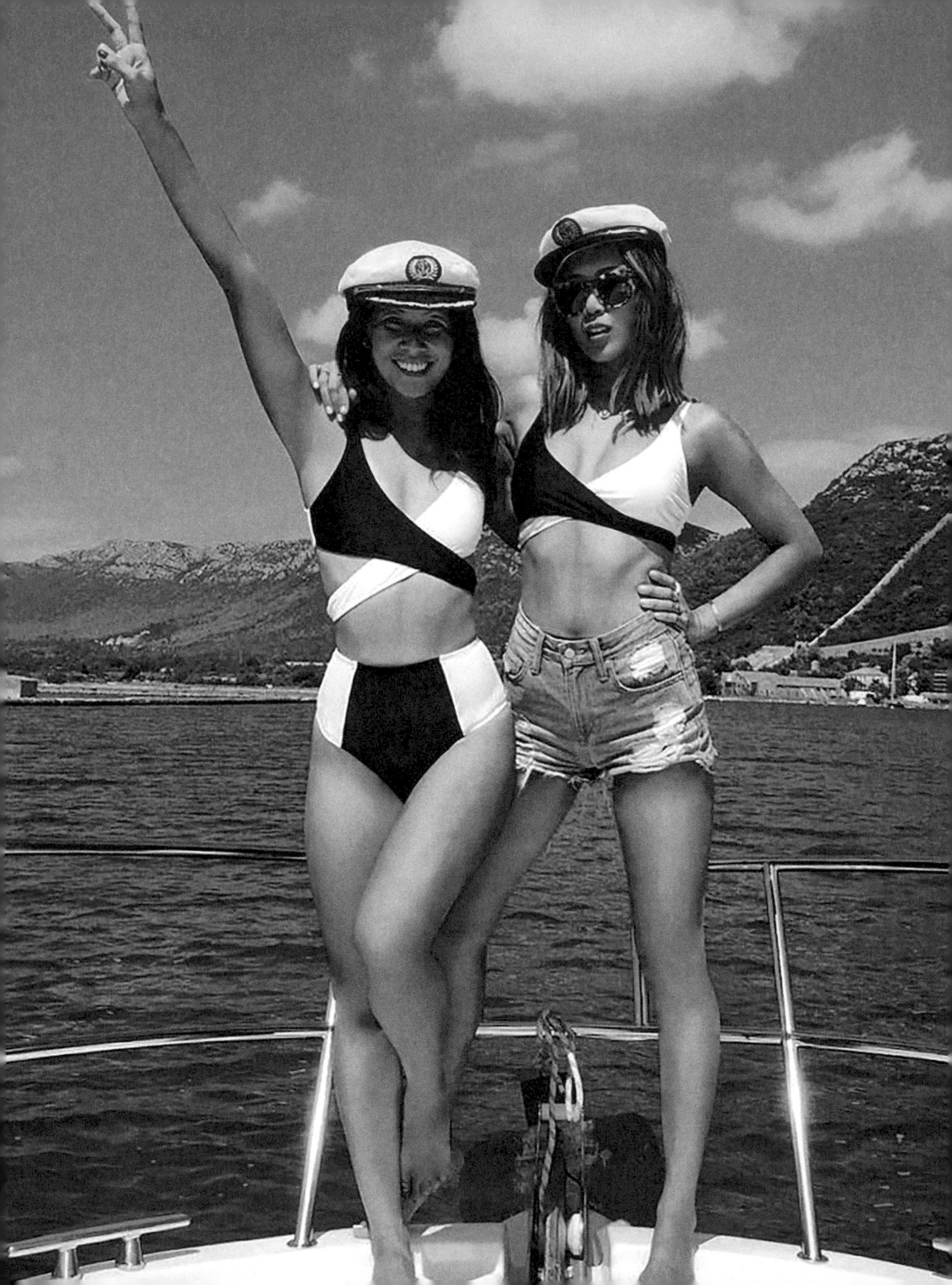

CROATIA

In August 2015 Revolve hosted its first-ever #RevolveAroundTheWorld in Dubrovnik, Croatia. Jacopo and Dani came with me, and I was so lucky that I knew all of the other bloggers on the trip, too. I love these trips because when you're in a house with a group of people for a week, you get to connect on a different level and end up making lasting friendships. We still all go on these trips together, and we're still all connected.

OPPOSITE Of course, when you're on a boat all day, there has to be multiple outfit changes. I'm here posing with Raissa Gerona, Revolve's chief brand officer. She's such a girl's girl and has become a dear friend—she genuinely likes to bring powerful women together to help each other shine. I've known her for years, and the way she manages her team and offers them encouragement is very inspiring to me as I grow my business. *Lovers and Friends swimsuit.*

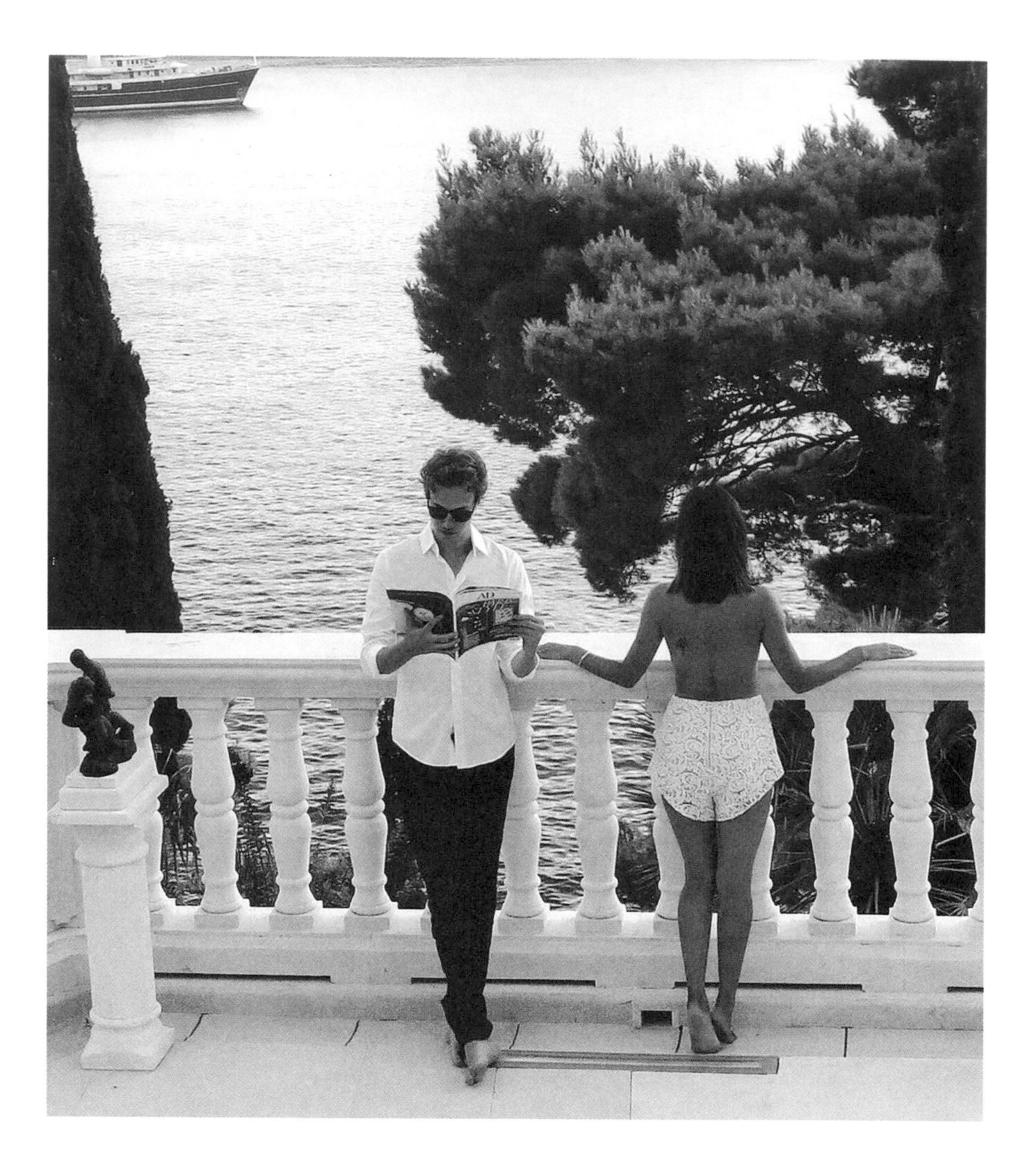

ABOVE The balcony of our house. I wanted to re-create a famous Slim Aarons photo with my Jacopo (Dani took the shot). **OPPOSITE, TOP** Soaking everything in. With its castles, Croatia looked like *Game of Thrones*—but with bloggers. **OPPOSITE, BOTTOM ROW** Dani got in trouble on this boat because she jumped off while it was moving and we almost got sent home. There was an hour of negotiation with the captain, and in true Dani fashion she was able to convince him to let us stay on the boat. By the end, they were even hugging. *Anarchy Street jewelry; Lovers and Friends swimsuit.*

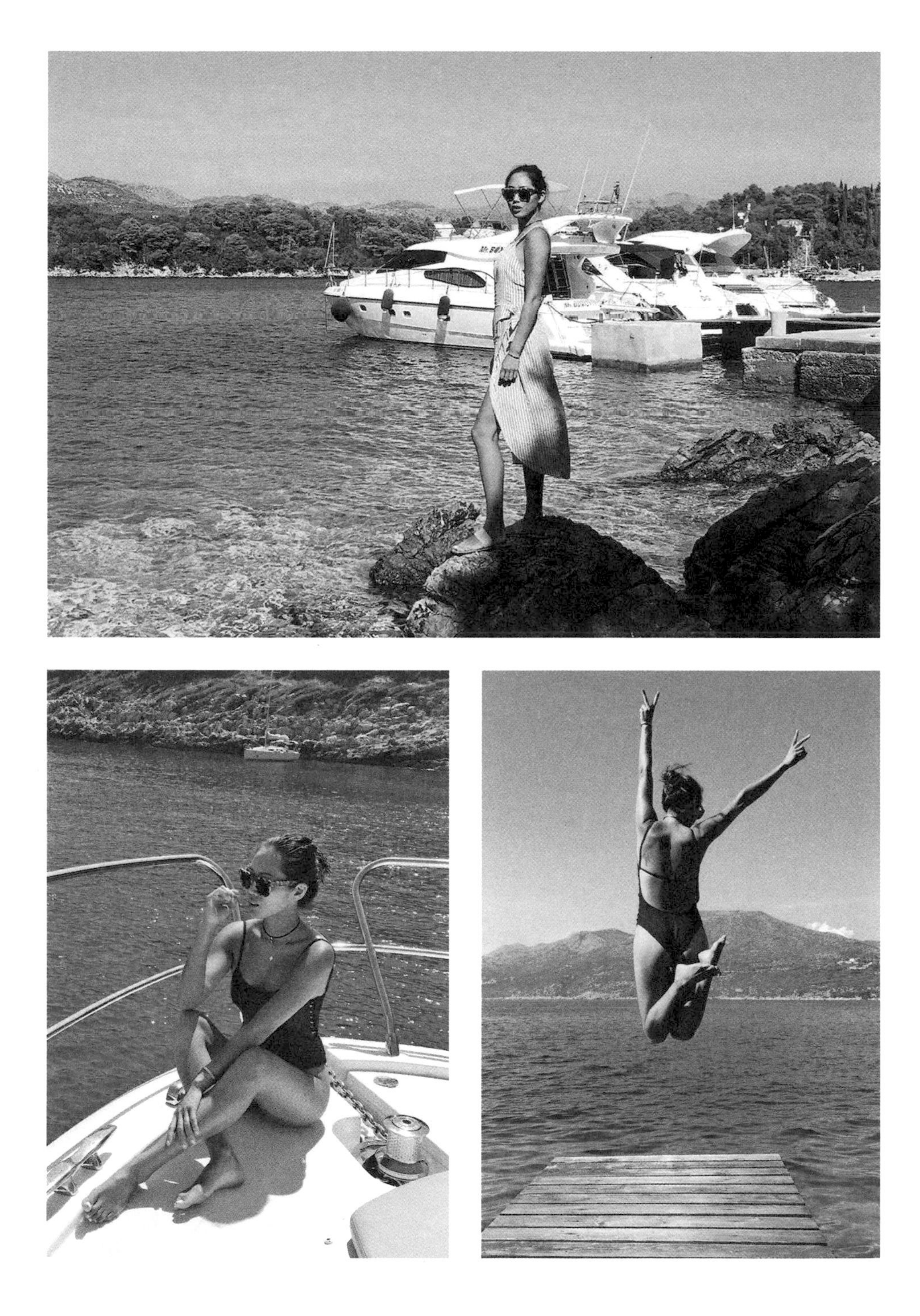

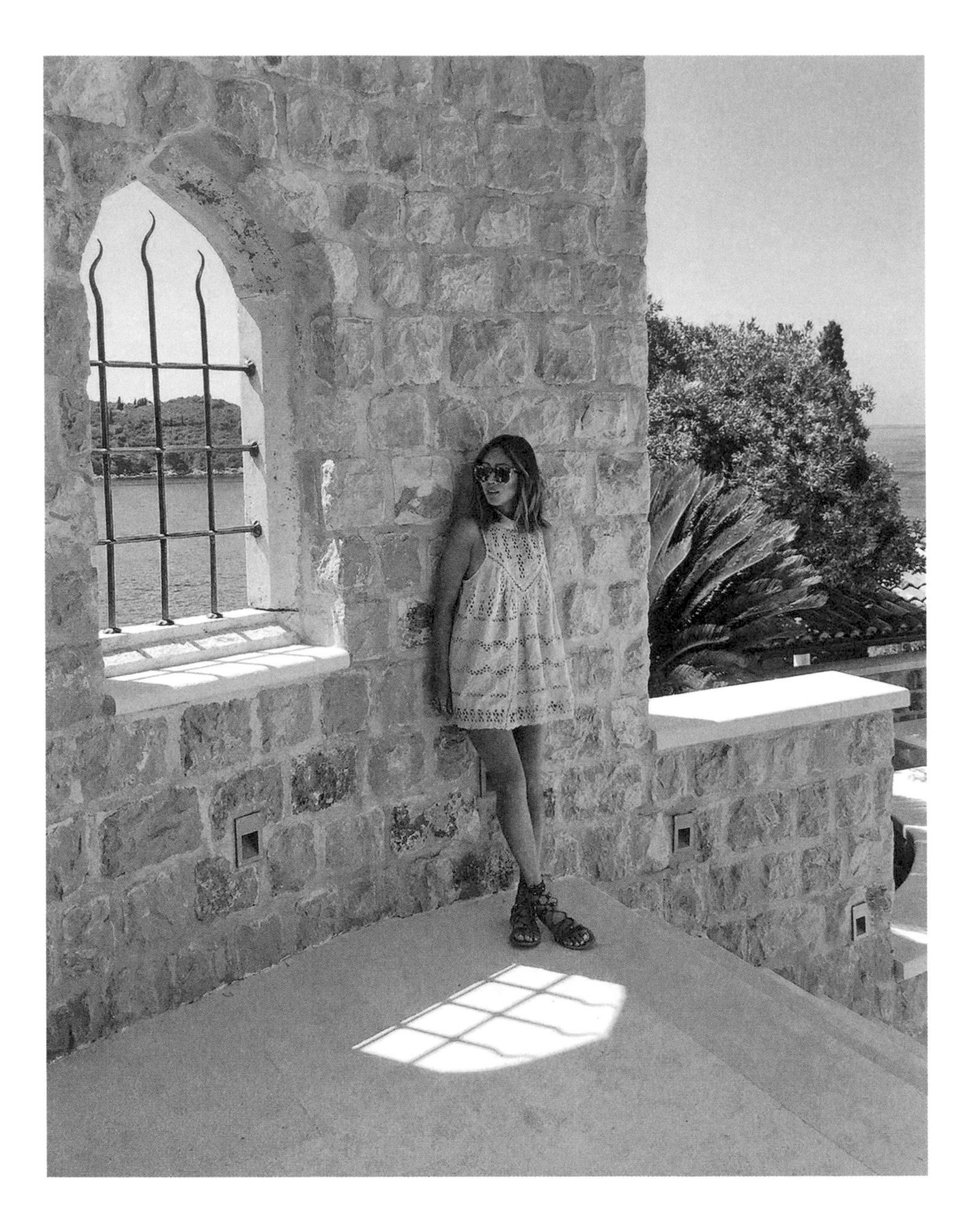

This is the house we were staying at (yes, really).

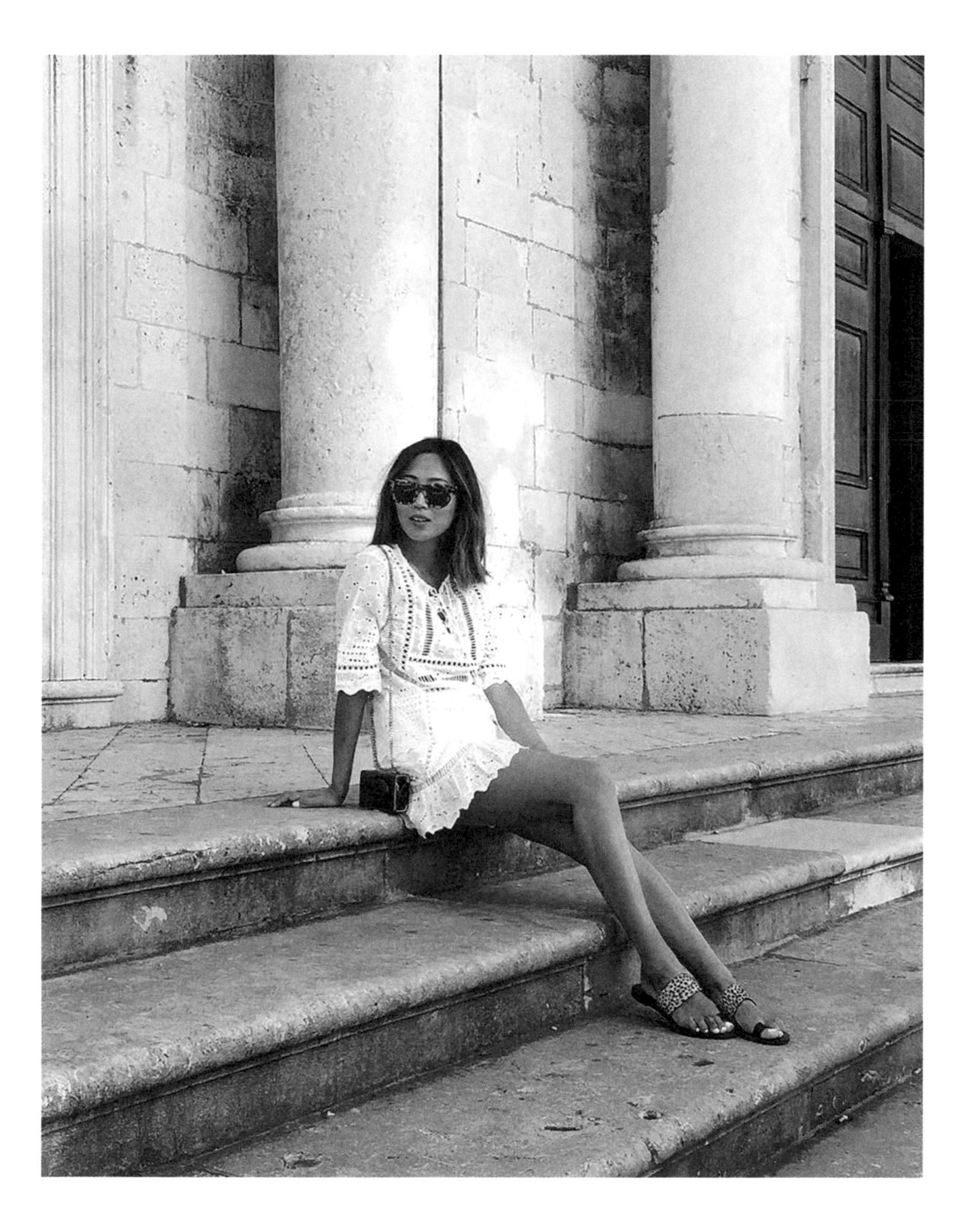

We walked around Dubrovnik and explored. Or rather, all the girls explored and got ice cream while the bloggers' boyfriends did their own thing. *Ministry of Style dress; Raye sandals.*

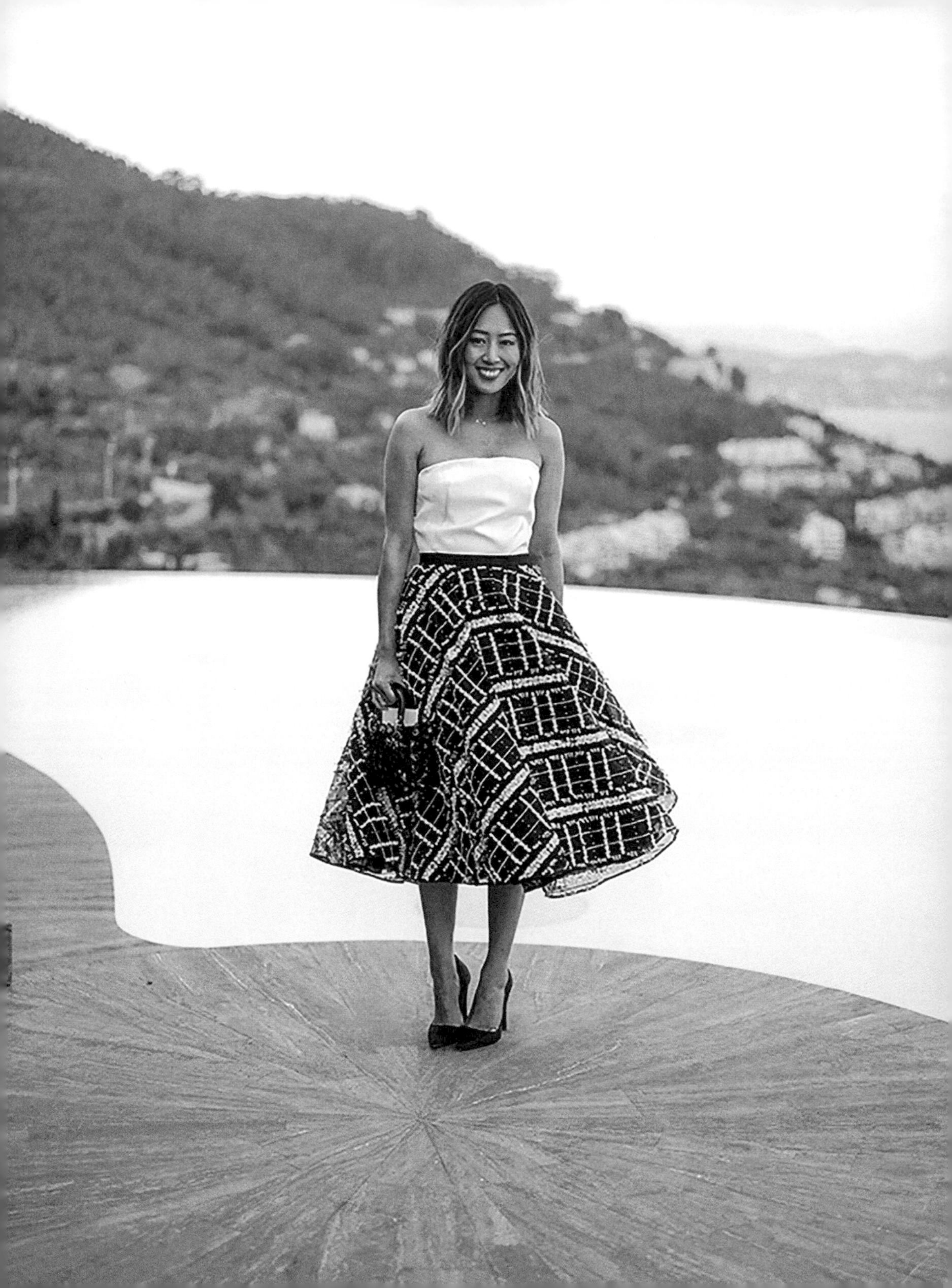

THE FRENCH RIVIERA

Once upon a time (in 2014 to be exact), I was in Sicily with my sister when a very cute Italian boy happened to text me. "I'm in the South of France," he wrote. This is the same cute Italian boy who I met on a press trip in Morocco a few months before, and I happened to have just gotten out of a long-term relationship. "Let's hang out," he continued. Uh, #WhyNot? I sent Dani home by herself, changed my flight, and decided to go see about a boy. The rest, as they say, is history. The guy ended up happening, and I've since been back to the Côte d'Azur a number of times for the Cannes Film Festival and other insanely cool work opportunities that I never thought would be possible. I love going to this glamorous part of the world so much, and I'm so lucky to have only happy memories from here. Pro tip: When something unexplainable inside of you makes you feel like you're being pulled toward something that sounds a little crazy, say yes. There could be a cute Italian waiting for you, too.

OPPOSITE In May 2015 Dior held its cruise show at Pierre Cardin's famed Palais Bulles house in a cliffside municipality called Théoule-sur-Mer. Not only was the space insane (its name literally means "bubble palace"), but the collection was done while Raf Simons was still at Dior's creative helm. This was also my first cruise show in a different country, which has become somewhat of a badge of honor among the fashion pack (I still get shocked when I get invites to these things—really!). *Dior head to toe.*

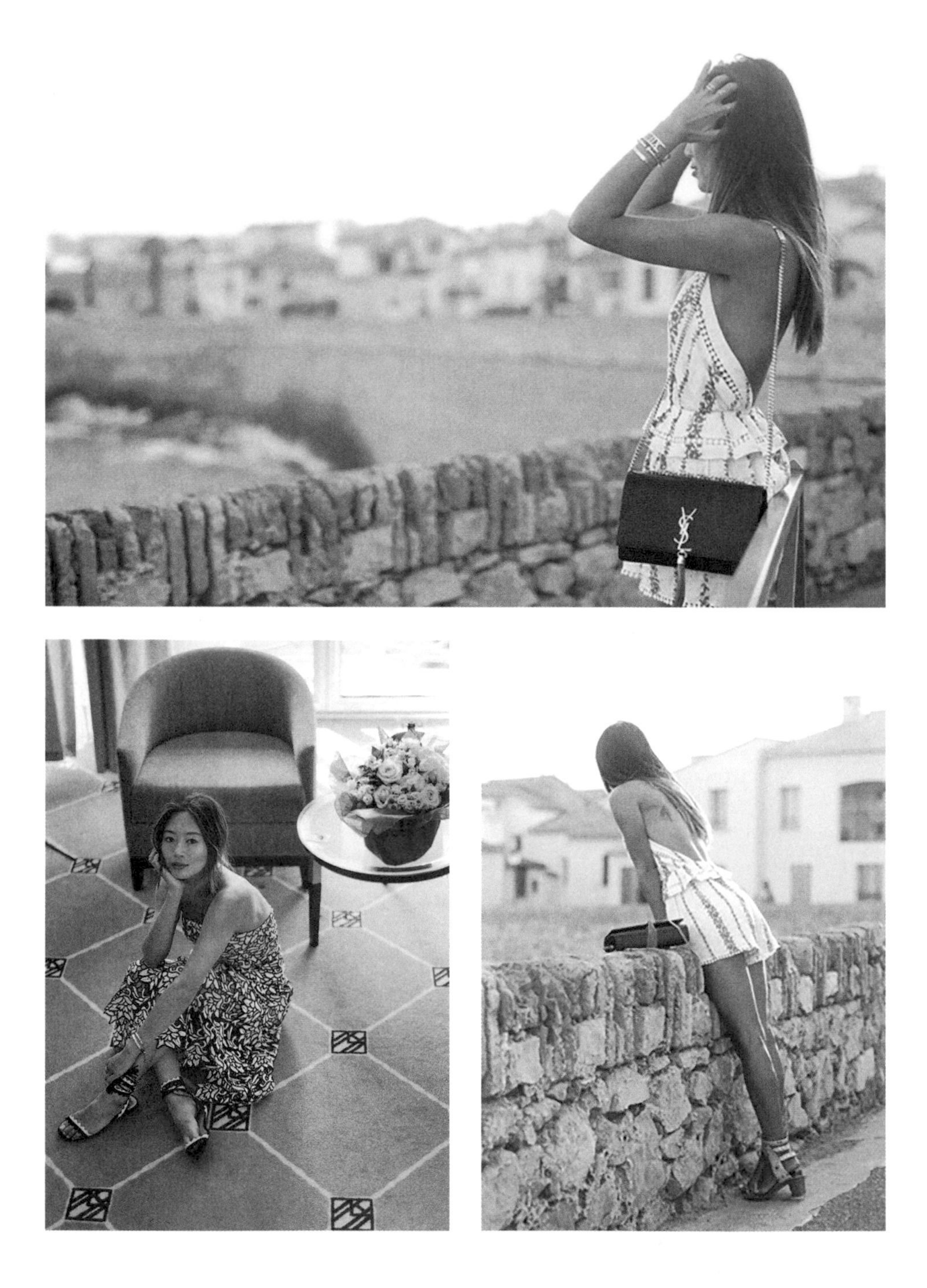

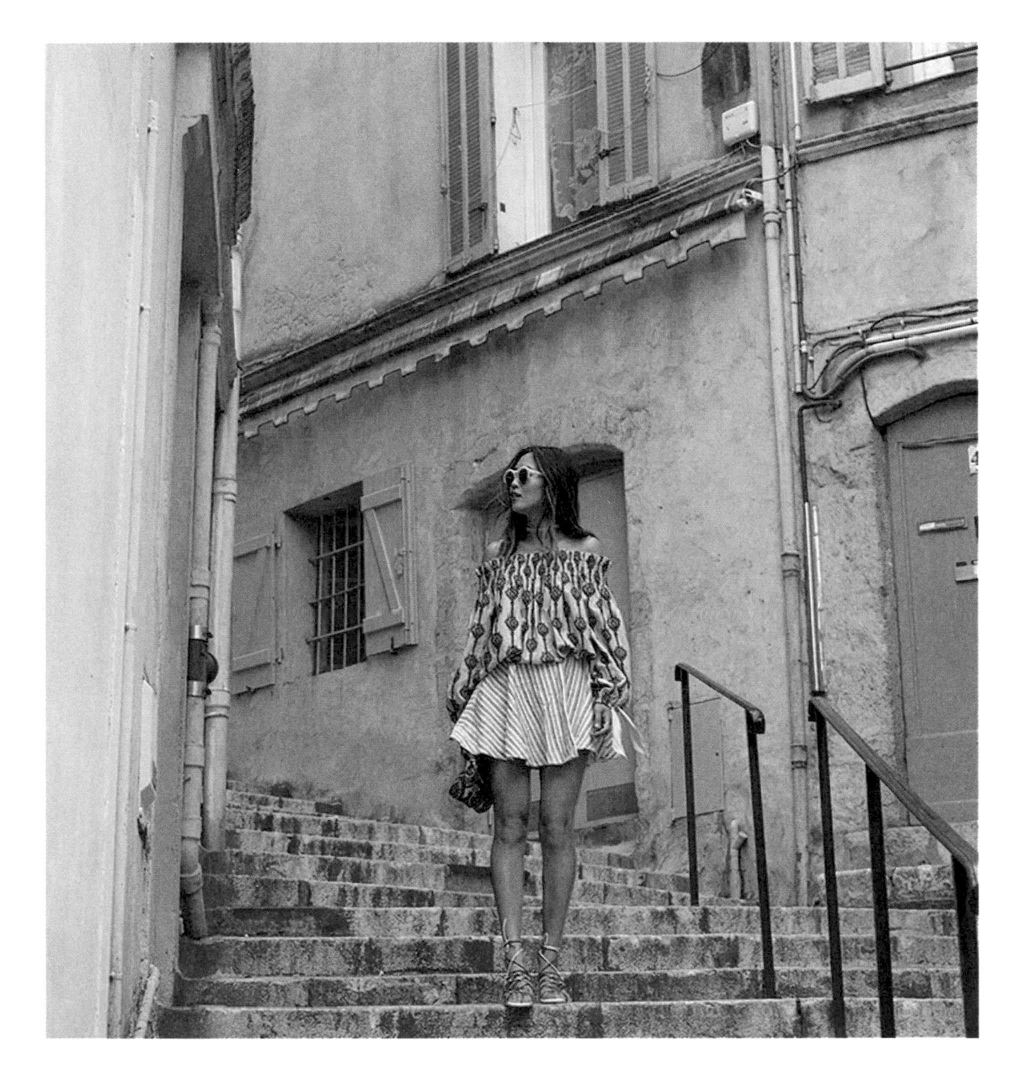

ABOVE During the film festival, exploring Nice. *Caroline Constas top; Tularosa skirt and shoes.* **OPPOSITE, TOP AND BOTTOM RIGHT** On that first trip when I went to see Jacopo, it was super nerve-racking to ask a guy I barely knew, let alone one who was an amazing professional photographer, to snap my photo (in 2014 people were still learning about what bloggers were in the first place). But, YOLO. He thought the whole thing was a little nuts and he probably didn't love the detailed directions I was barking at him to ensure he got the shot I wanted. Or maybe he did, as he's still my favorite lensman (and I still direct the shots). *Zimmermann dress; Isabel Marant shoes.* **OPPOSITE, BOTTOM LEFT** *Keepsake dress; Schutz sandals.*

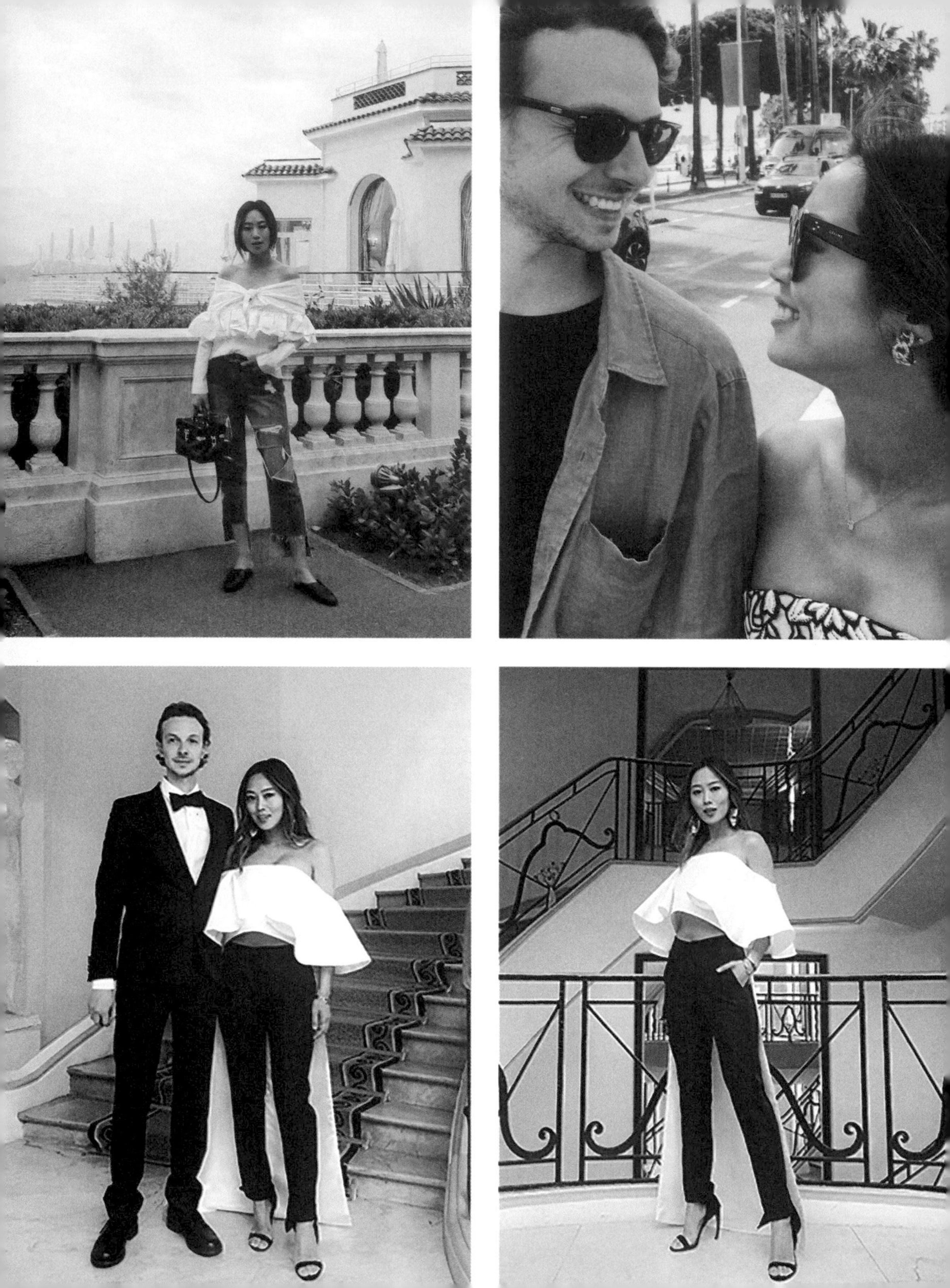

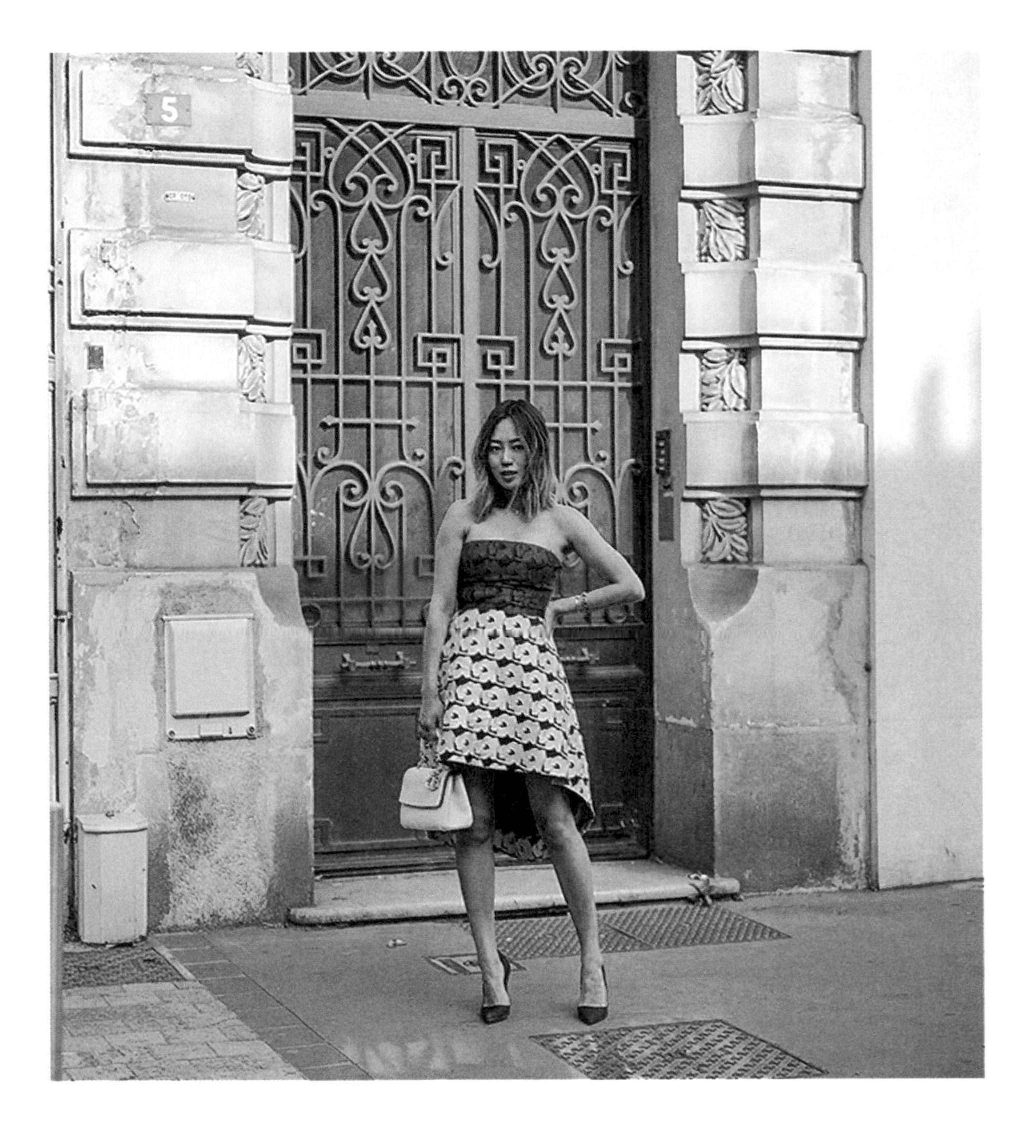

ABOVE Wearing Dior for a lunch. **OPPOSITE, TOP LEFT** At the famous Hôtel du Cap-Eden-Roc in Antibes. Dani and I were there with Louis Vuitton so we could learn about how the brand's perfumes are made. Talk about magical. *Johanna Ortiz top; SJYP jeans; Stella McCartney shoes.* **OPPOSITE, TOP RIGHT** Cannes stroll with my Jacopo. **OPPOSITE, BOTTOM ROW** Jacopo and I attended a black-tie party hosted by the perfume brand The Harmonist. Jason Derulo performed, and no one at the party seemed to know who he was—except me, of course. I was right up in front of him dancing like crazy and singing along. It was so much fun.

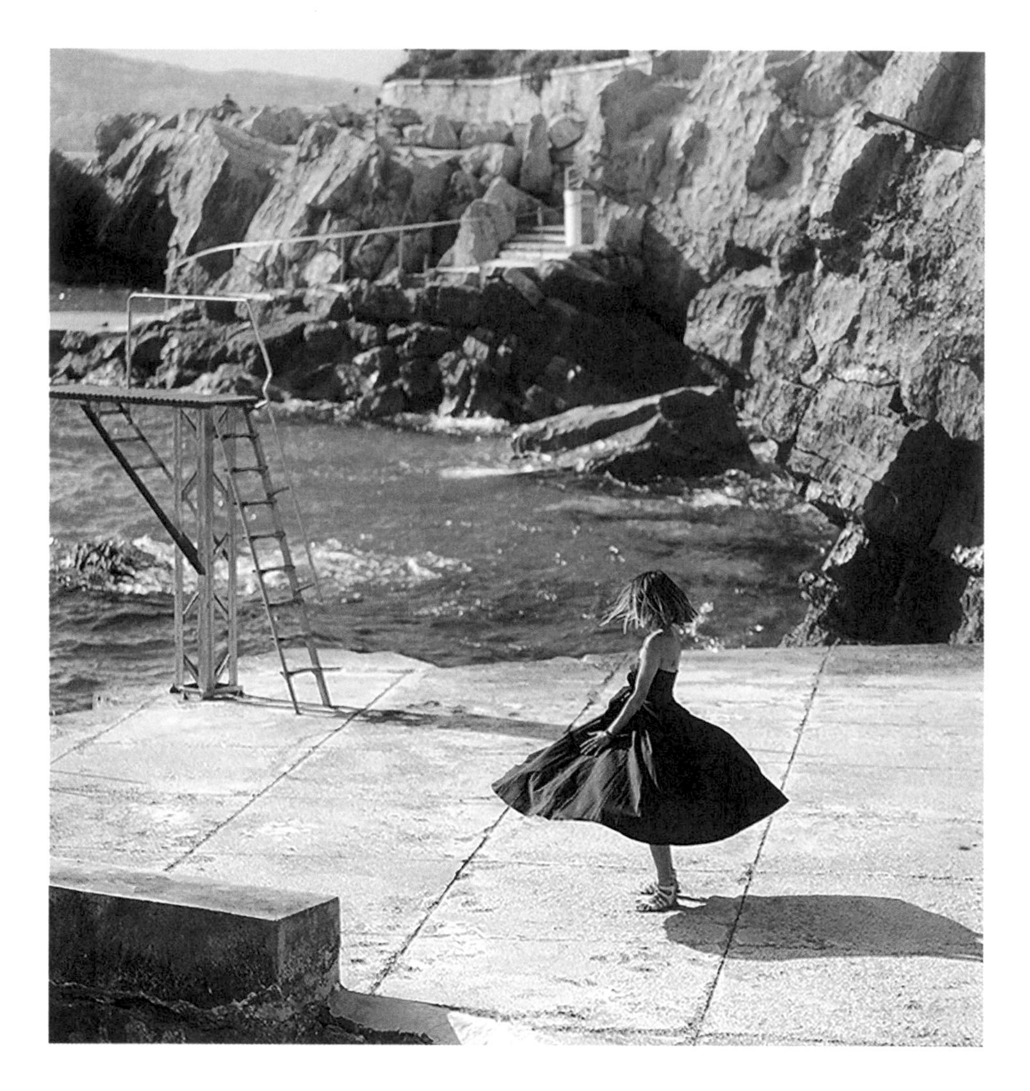

ABOVE I prepped so hard for my Grace Kelly moment during Cannes in 2016, and this diving board that just happened to greet Dani and me before this shoot was the *To Catch a Thief* moment we needed. *Tibi dress.* **OPPOSITE (FROM TOP)** My first time at the Cannes Film Festival in May 2016. If your hotel had an amazing rooftop and you didn't do a mini photo shoot on it, did your trip even happen? I think not. *Anna October dress, Proenza Schouler shoes* • People are so formal at Cannes, always (I'm talking evening gowns at breakfast). So even though I wasn't doing premieres or red carpets, I felt like this dress was appropriate for the vibe and the scenery. I didn't feel overdressed, but rather simple. It's an easy-to-wear piece for something that has such a distinct point of view. *Anna October dress.*

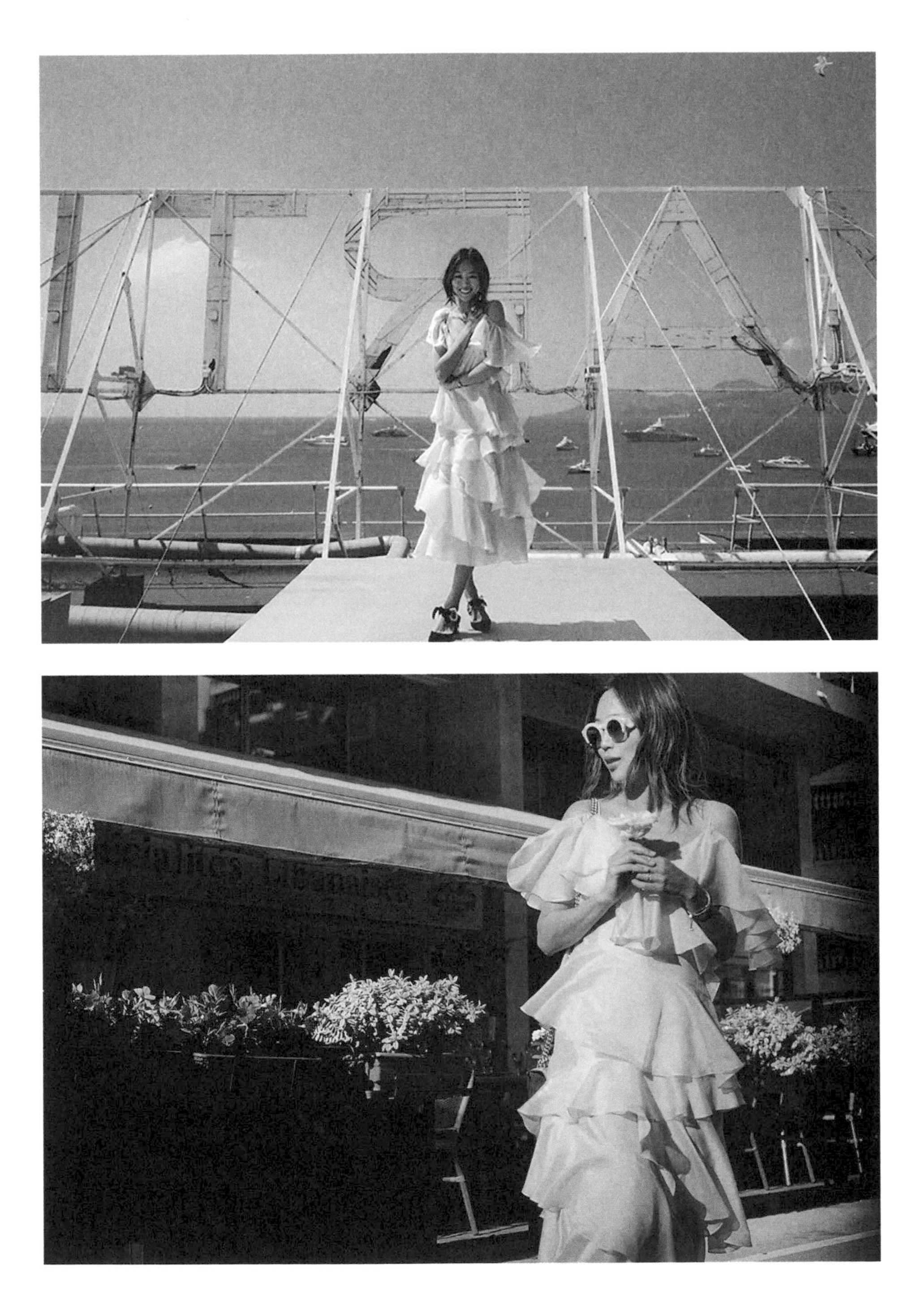

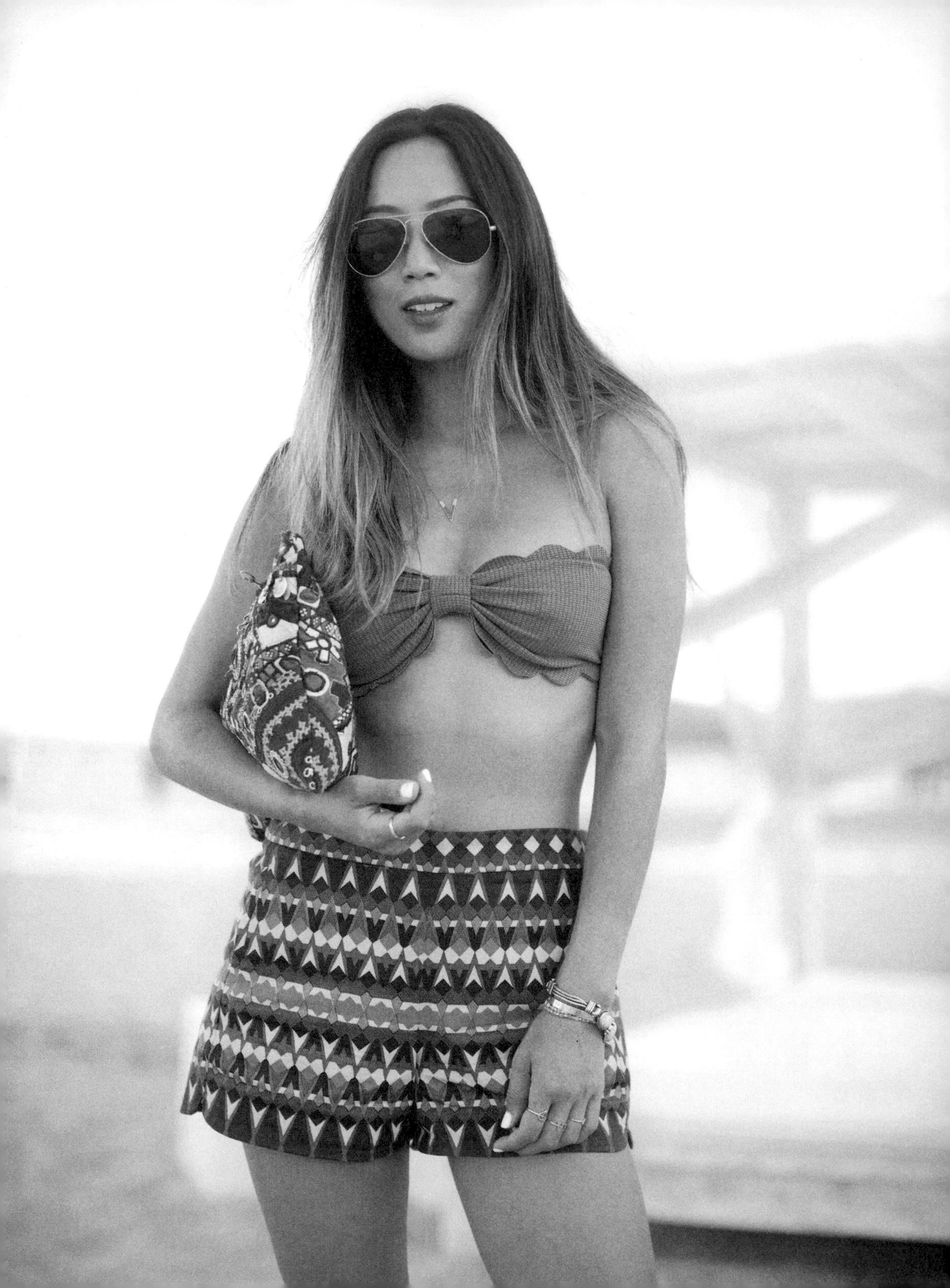

IBIZA

There are two very distinct ways to do Ibiza, the picturesque Spanish island town in the middle of the Mediterranean Sea—P. Diddy "white party" style and, uh, everyone-else style. In 2014 I actually got to experience both ways of doing Ibiza during the same trip. Dani and I went with Skin Inc., a skin-care brand that invited us to experience a hotel spa they were working with. Skin Inc. definitely provided the P. Diddy vibes (okay, it's not like we ran up a $75,000 bar tab or anything—we just stayed in a fancy hotel and had a driver). And we so enjoyed the energy of the city that we decided to extend our trip a few days. I felt kind of like Cinderella—one second we're being driven around and eating lunch on yachts, the next we're renting bikes and taking the public ferry (which we totally missed and, as luck would have it, we were offered a lift home by a club owner who happened to have extra seats on his yacht). The experience proved that one doesn't need a major bank account to be able to have adventures that you remember and cry laughing about, still, four years later.

OPPOSITE *Marysia Swim top; J. Crew shorts; Simone Camille bag.*

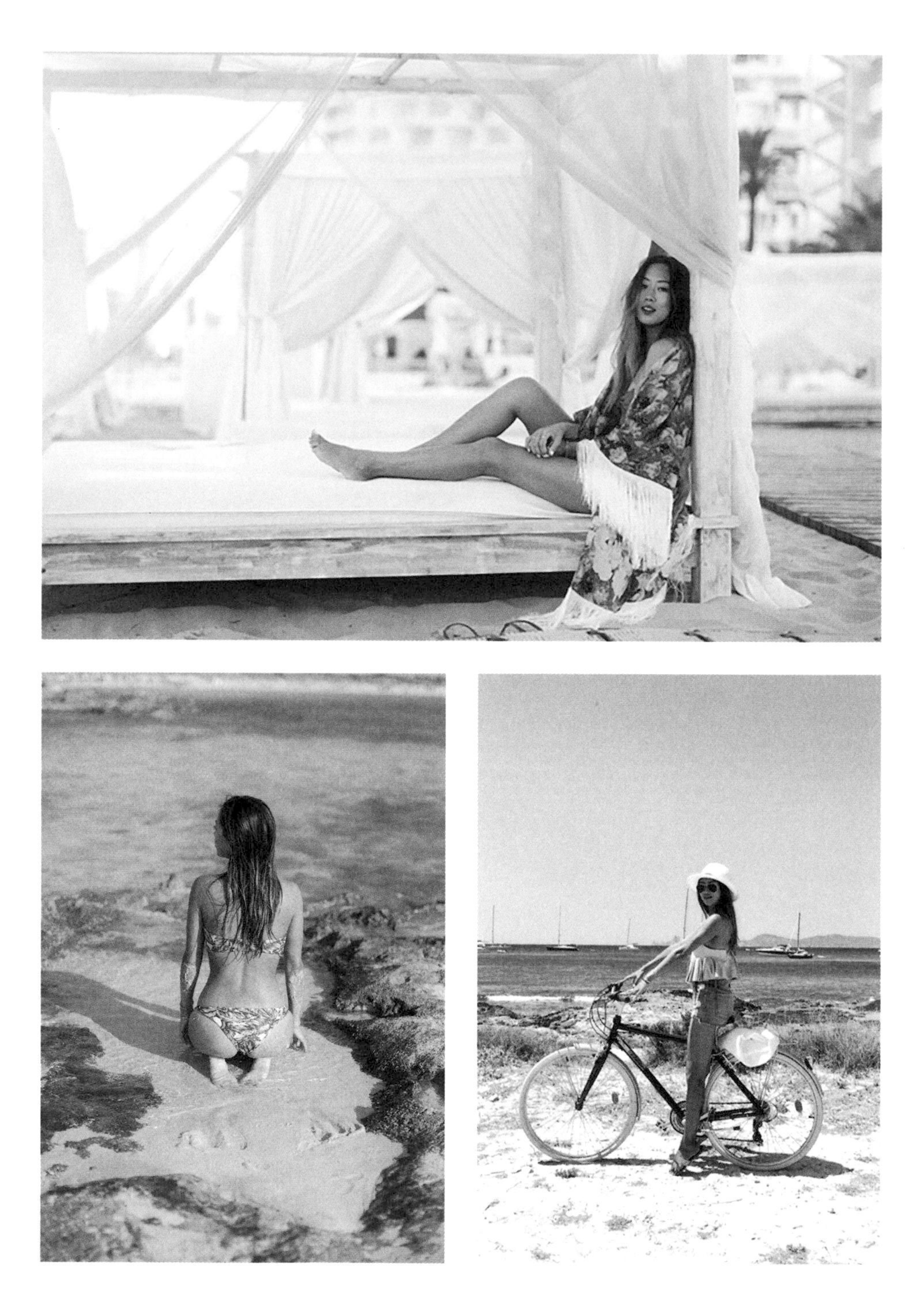

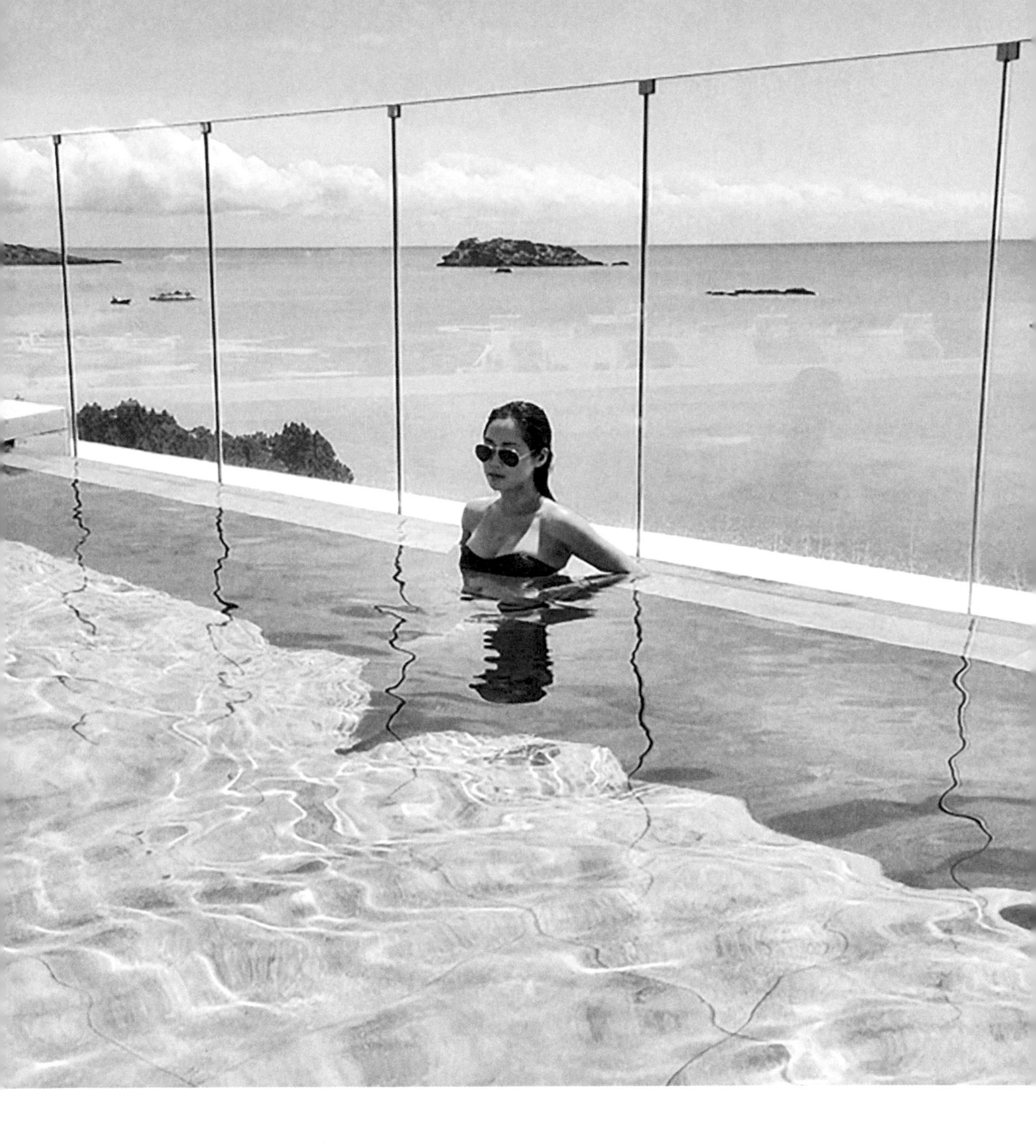

ABOVE Me at the hotel pool. **OPPOSITE (CLOCKWISE FROM TOP)** *Athena Procopiou kimono* • We took a ferry to Formentera and rented bikes. • *Mikoh Swimwear* in Formentera.

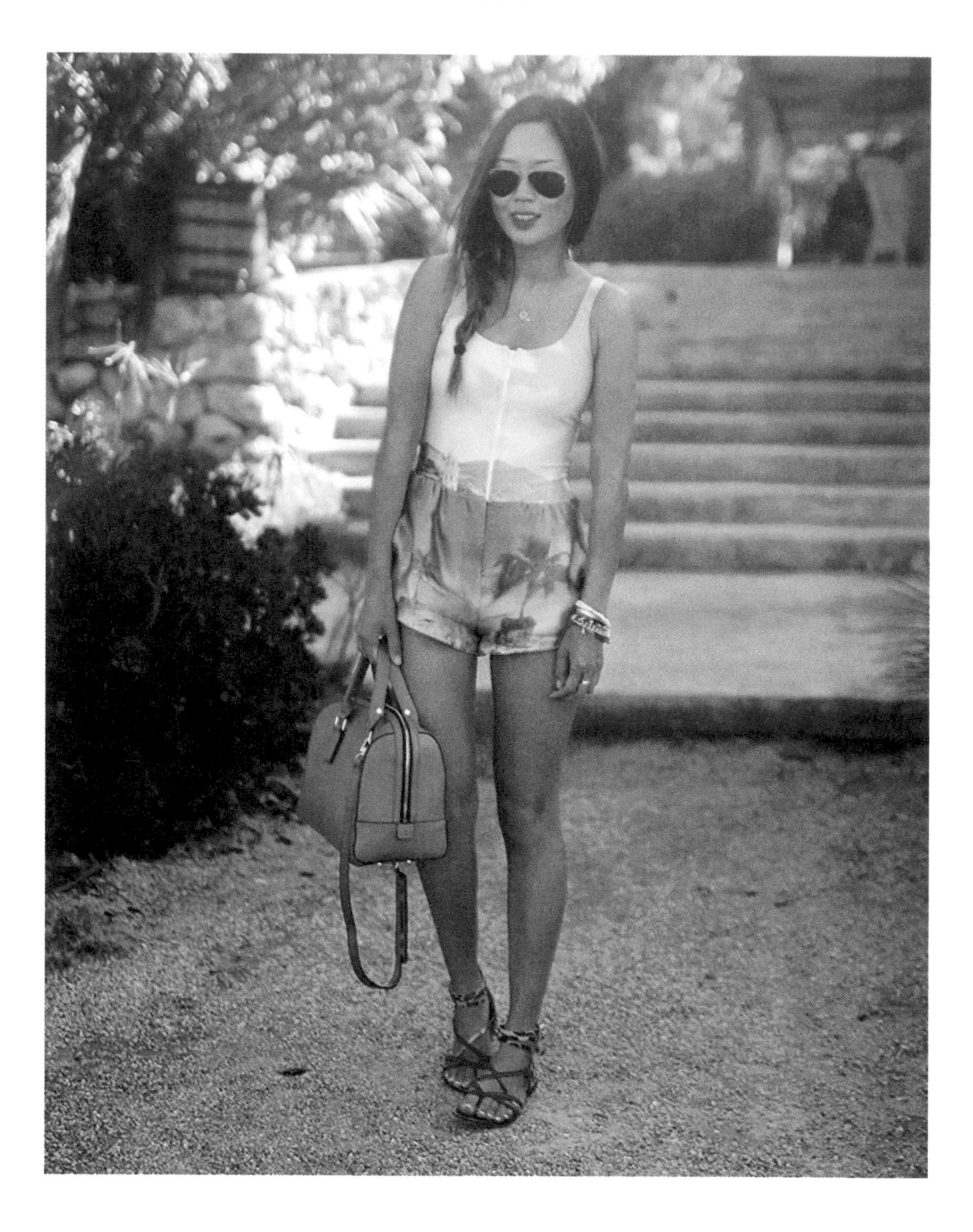

ABOVE First time in Ibiza in 2012. *We Are Handsome bathing suit; Prada shorts; Sam Edelman sandals.*

OPPOSITE (FROM TOP) Cameo denim dress in 2012. • At Playa Cala Bassa.

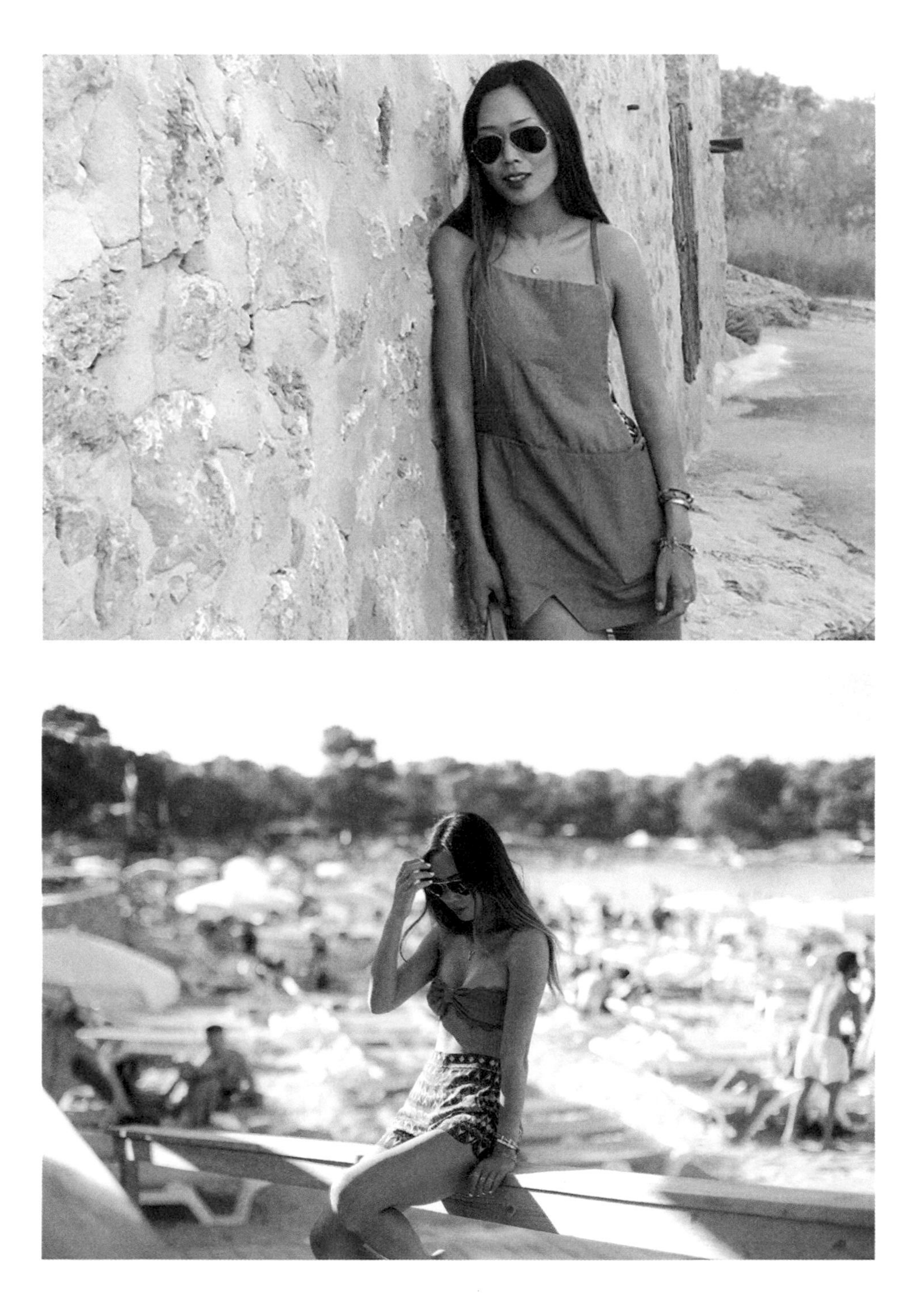

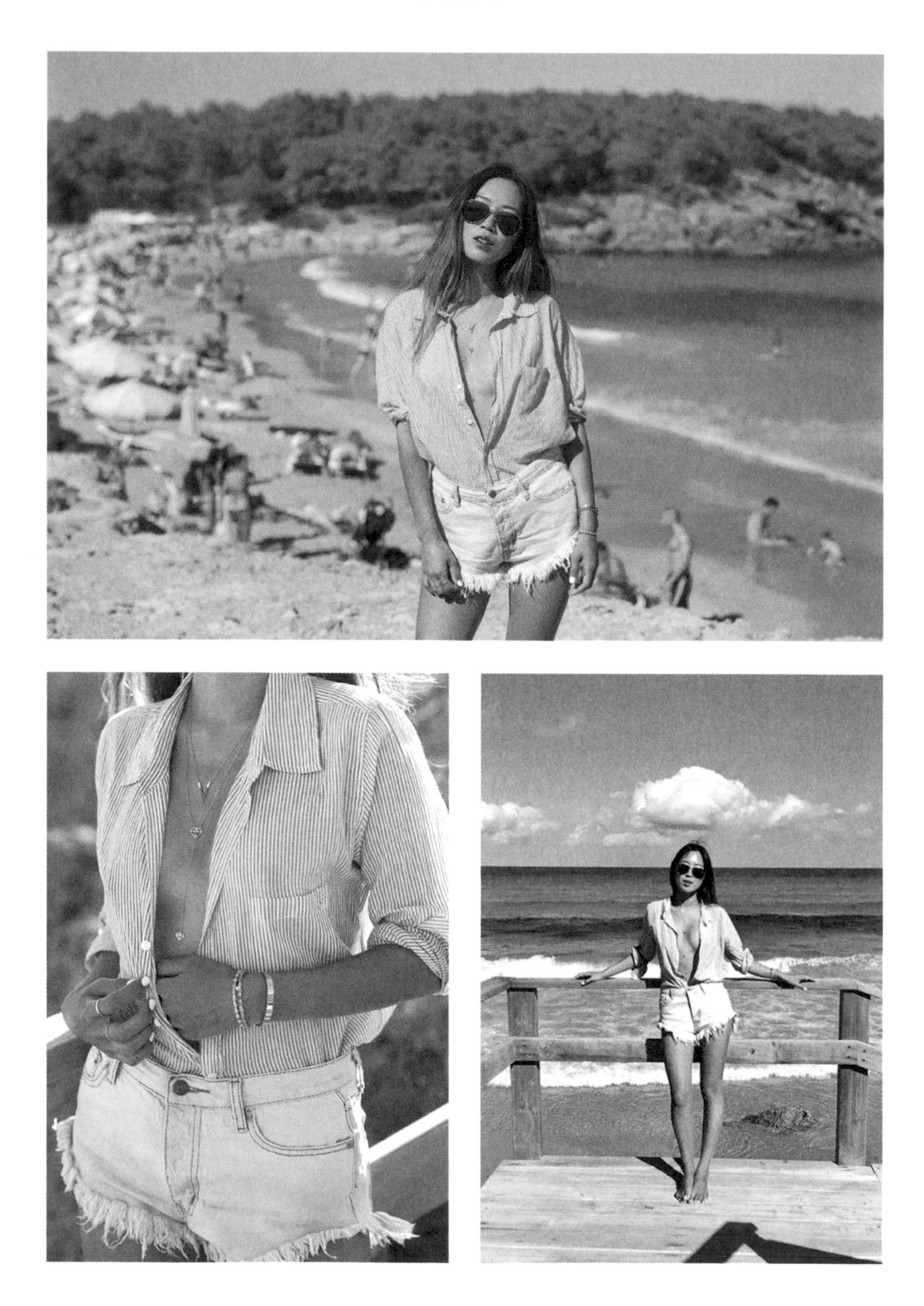

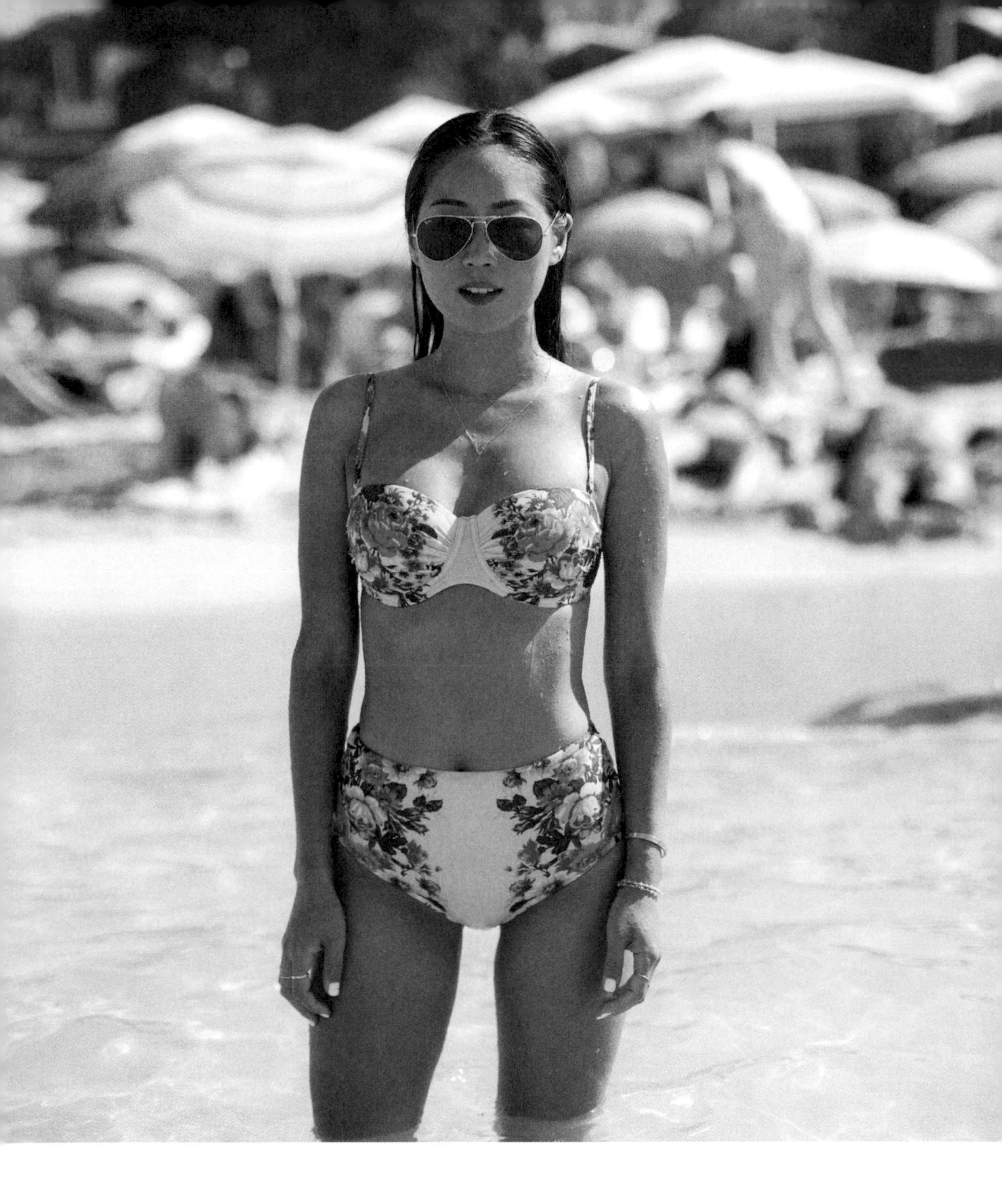

ABOVE Seafolly bikini in Playa Cala Bassa. **OPPOSITE** *Sundry striped shirt; Dani's ripped shorts.*

ICELAND

Iceland is the most mystical place I've ever visited. It's remote, wild, and unlike any country I've ever seen before—think thermal pools that appear in the middle of nowhere, vividly pink skies at 2 A.M., and black sand beaches. You can be road-tripping the country without music for hours (which Jacopo and I did when we went together in the summer of 2015) and not get bored for even a second, because the landscape seems to transform into something totally different and even more special every hour.

In April 2017 I had the opportunity to go back to Iceland for work, and while I was incredibly excited for my return, it was a tumultuous time for the Song women. Dani had just gone through a horrible breakup and canceled on being my trip companion at the last minute, and I was also reevaluating my life and how I was spending my time. I ended up bringing my friend Cubby on the trip with me, and the combination of his warmth and wisdom with the gorgeous Icelandic landscapes, endless daylight, and the silica- and sulfur-filled hot springs made me feel so good. Literally the sun "sets" at midnight and rises at 2 or 3 A.M. during the summer—it's wild, and we kept forgetting to eat dinner because we never felt like it was nighttime! The nature I saw made me realize and remember just how small the things inside my head are in relation to our huge, vast world—another reason why travel is amazing: it puts things in perspective.

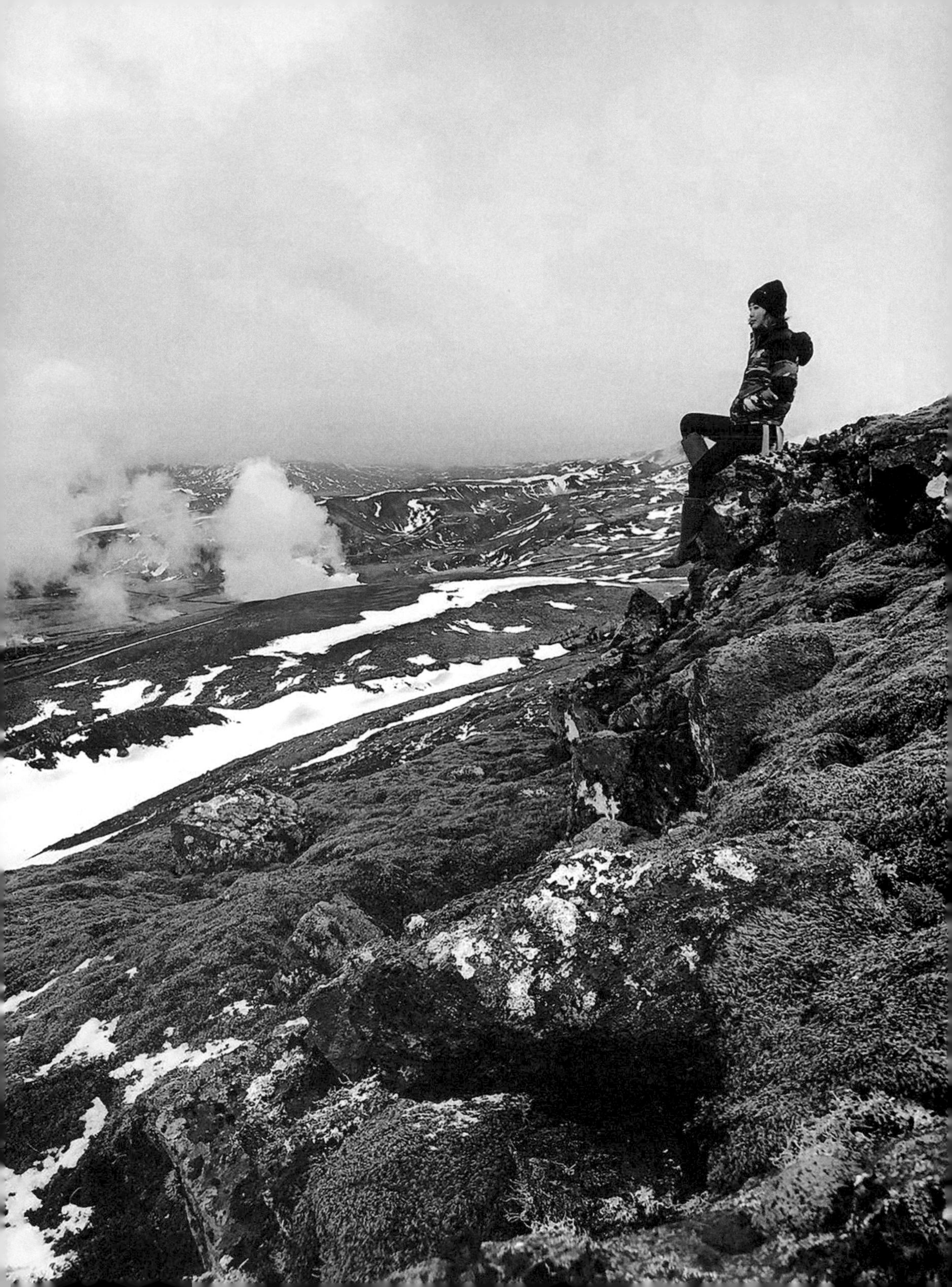

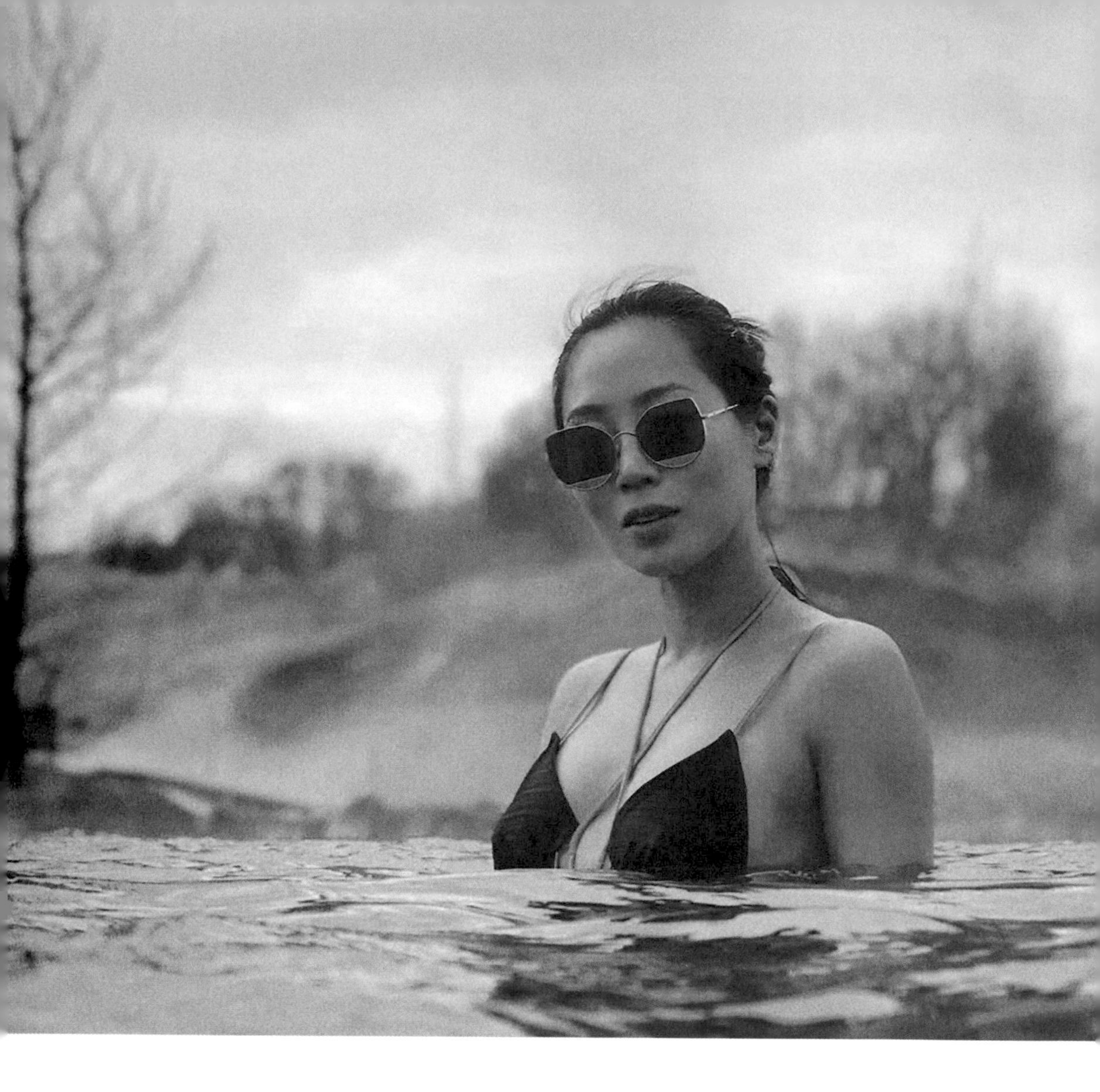

ABOVE Soaking in a secret lagoon. *Gentle Monster x Song of Style sunglasses.* **OPPOSITE (CLOCKWISE FROM TOP)** In front of our hotel. The scenery was insane—it looks like you're on a different planet. • By the waterfalls, where I got soaking wet. I was somewhat prepared in my rain boots, thankfully, and didn't follow my normal trend of wearing horrible vacation footwear that isn't even close to suitable for the elements and gets completely destroyed. #winning. • The black sand beach, which I'd Googled before the trip so I knew what it looked like. And I knew that for my photo moment, I wanted to wear a contrasting outfit that would offset the dark sand, which is why I chose the blue coat. *Mackage coat; Tibi scarf.*

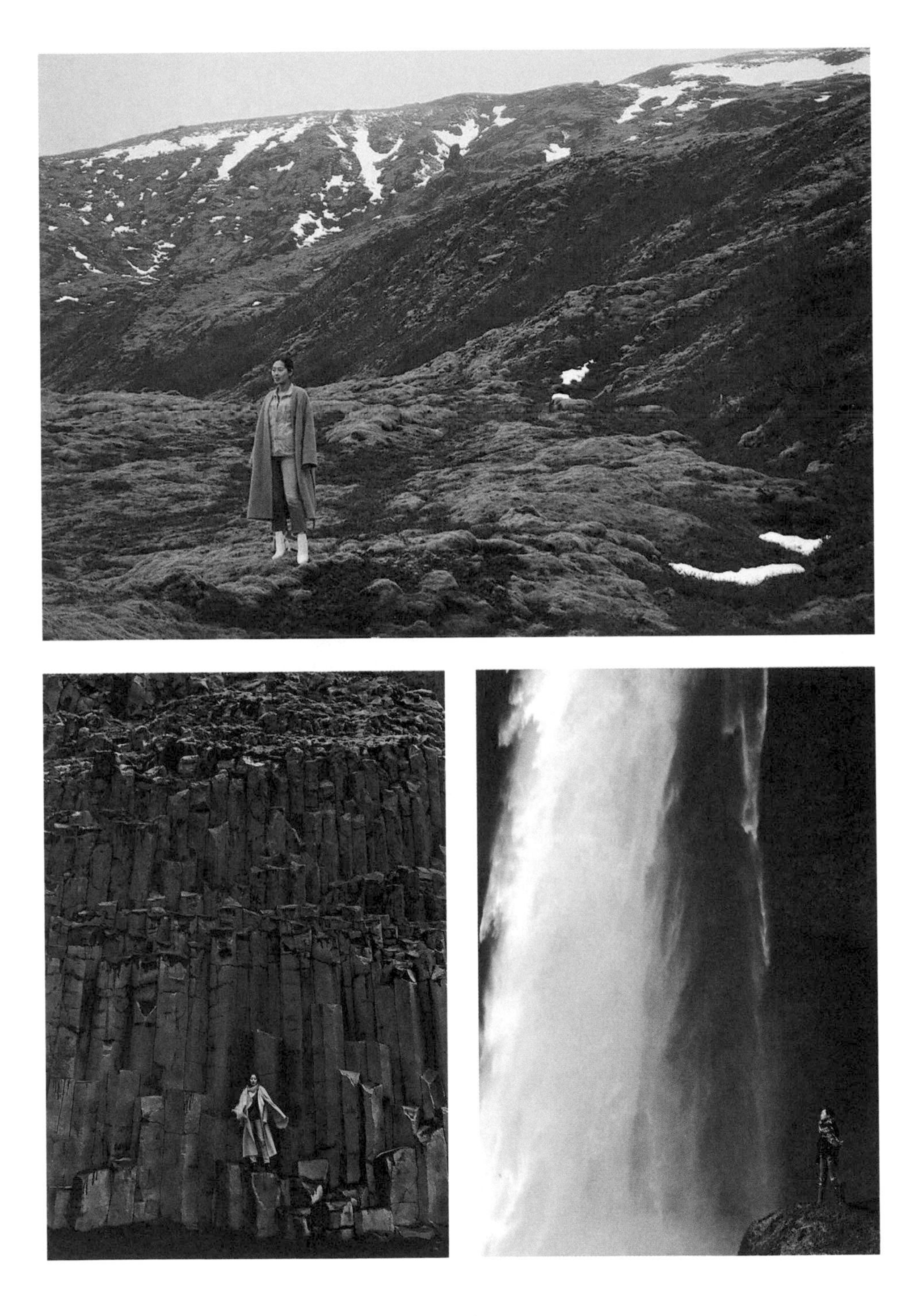

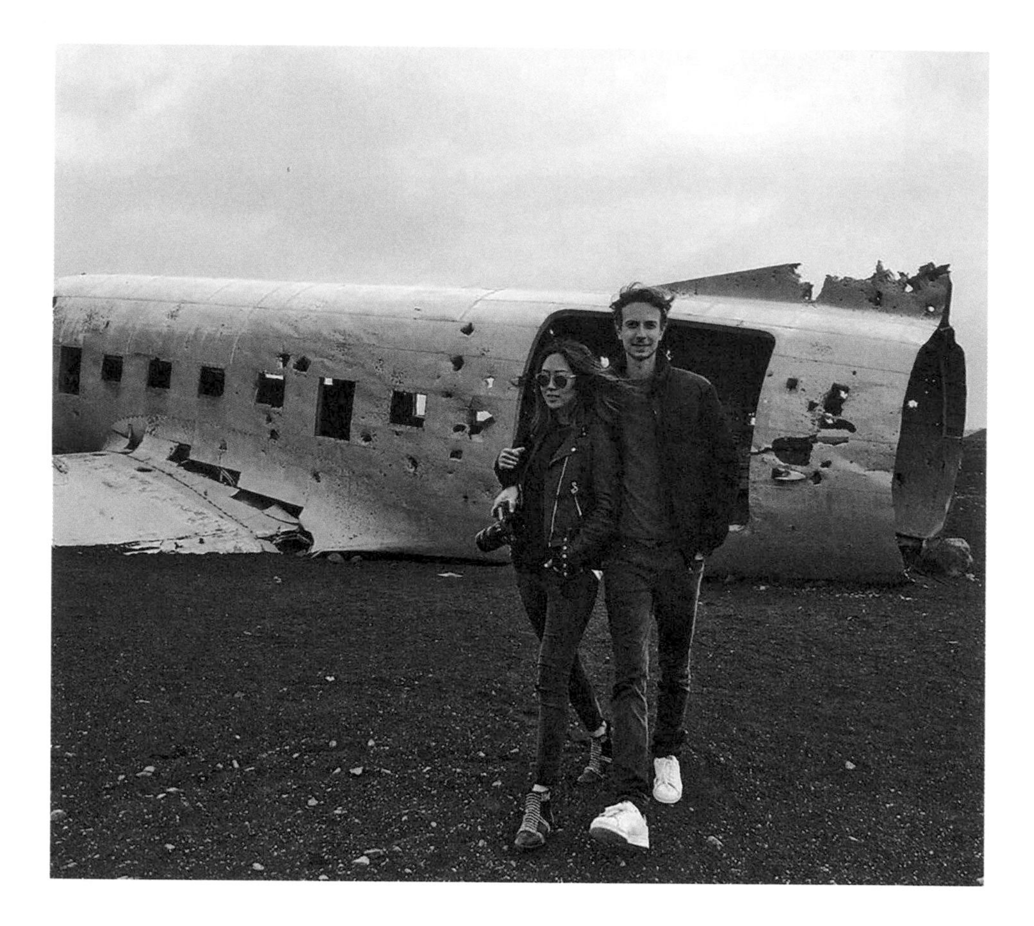

ABOVE In 1973 a US Navy plane crashed in Sólheimasandur in South Iceland (thankfully everyone on board survived!). The wreckage is still there on a black sand beach, and it has since become a major tourist attraction (Justin Bieber even shot a video here). I got a lot of negative feedback for posting this photo on Instagram because people accused me of "making light of a bad situation." Again, a great reason to travel is to learn about new cultures and historical events, which I always try to bring to my posts. We made new friends with Croatian hitchhikers, who took this photo of us. **OPPOSITE (CLOCKWISE FROM TOP LEFT)** The giant monster vans that we drove to sightsee with the Ole Henriksen team. It was so cold that I wore leggings under my jeans. This trip wardrobe was all about layering—denim jacket, thermal, the works. *Jimmy Choo snow boots* • My 2015 trip with Jacopo. He took this with an iPhone before vertical Instagram shots were a thing. RIP, waterfall. • The day we went to see a secret lagoon. *Mother shearling jacket* • A hot thermal pool at our hotel. Cubby loves taking photos and is an amazing storyteller—I learn so much from following him on Instagram. He took this from his room above while I was hanging at the pool.

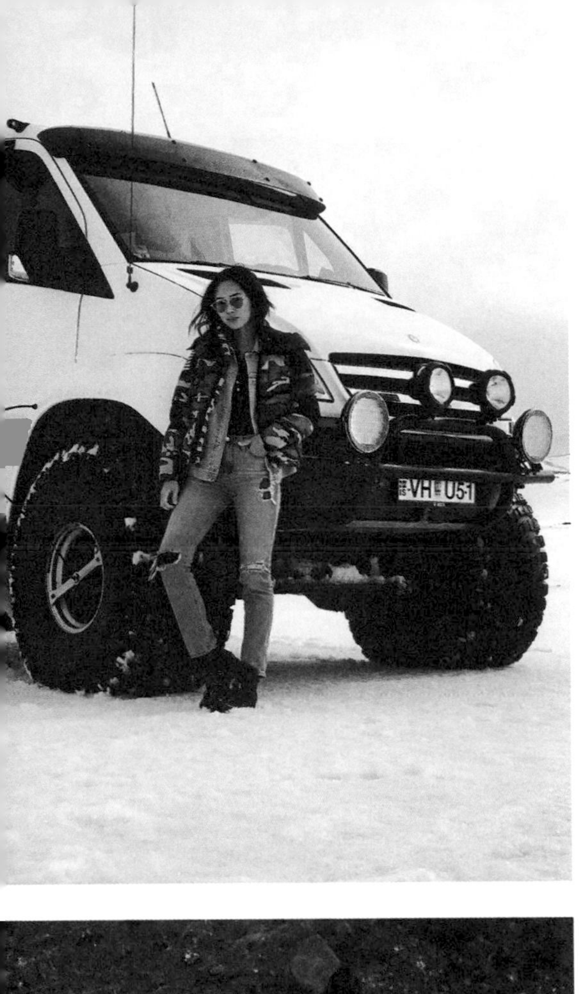

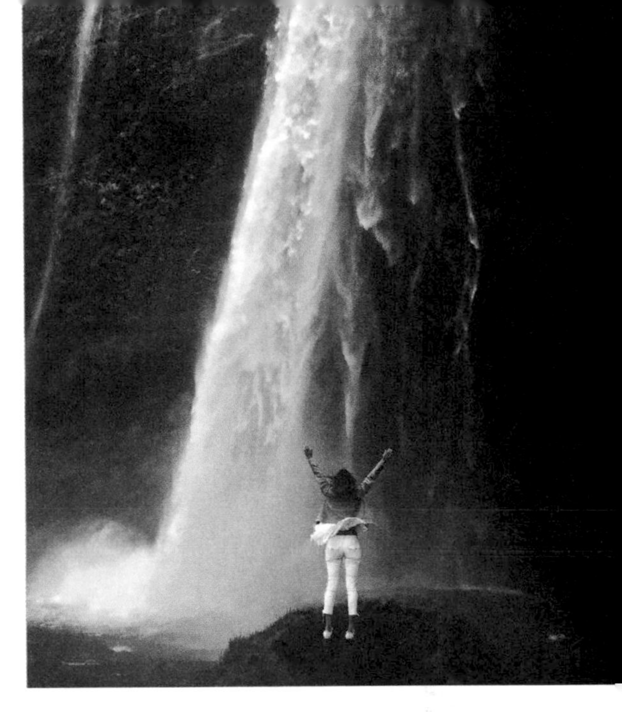

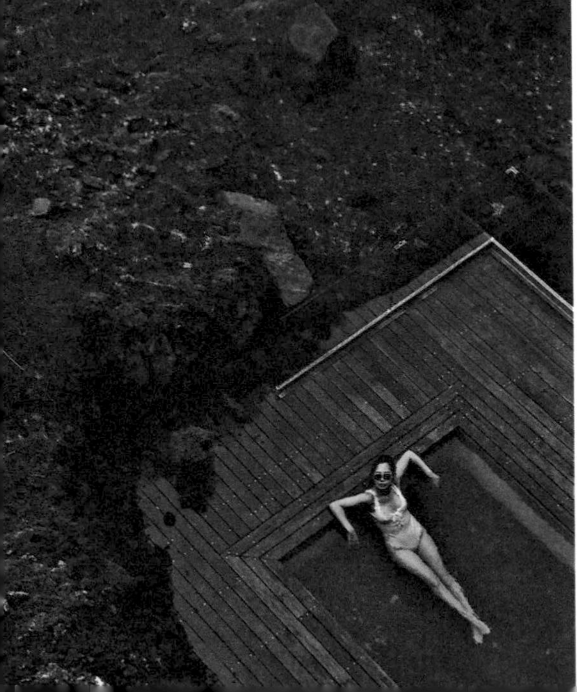

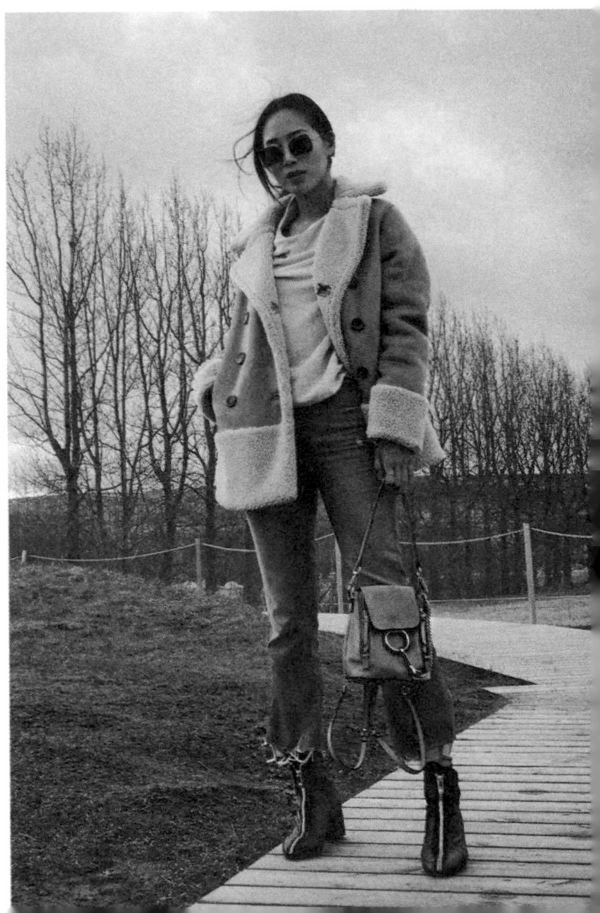

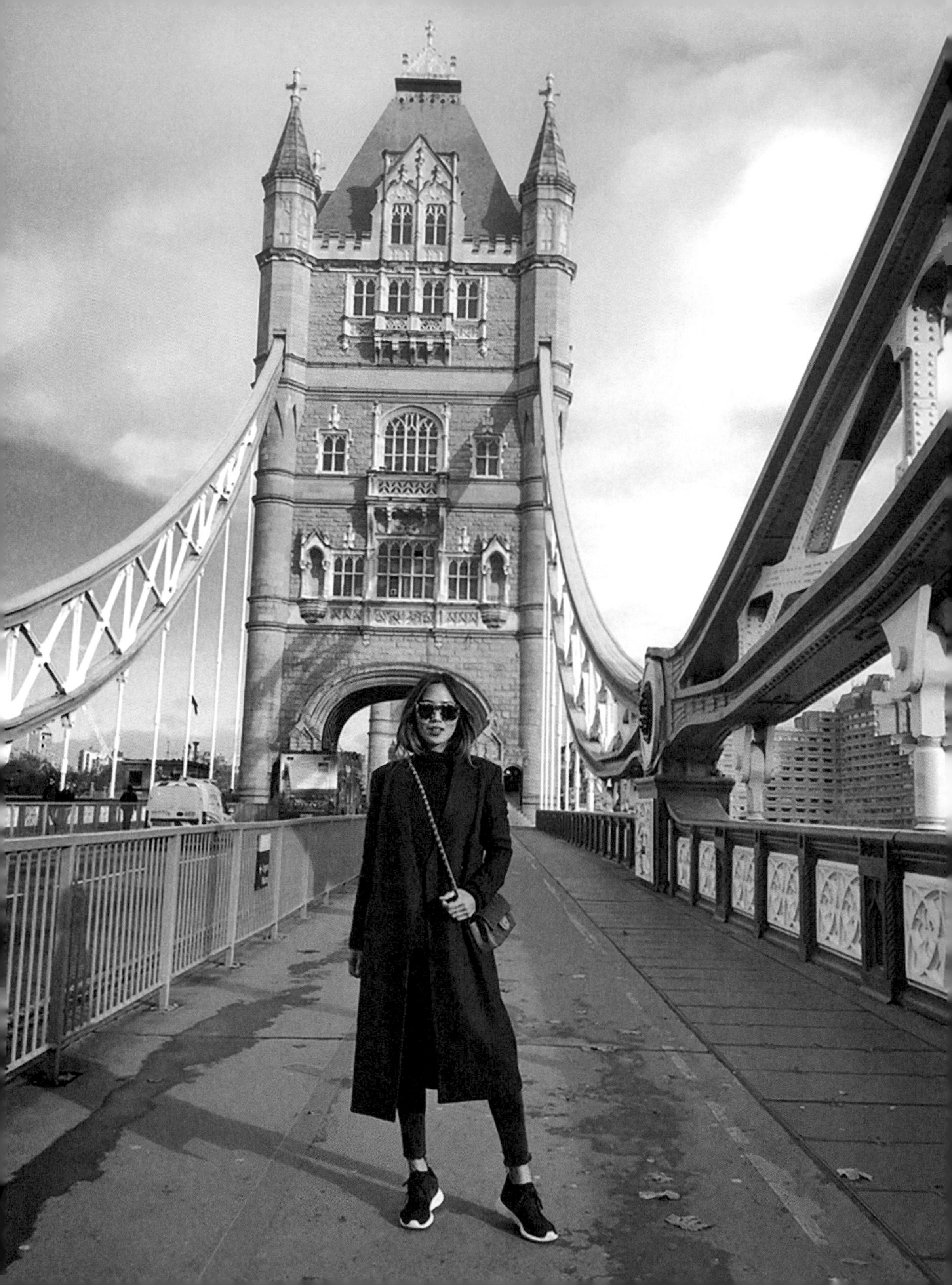

LONDON

The first time I ever visited London was in March 2014, when I went on a Harrod's press trip with Dani. I completely fell in love with the pastel townhouses and pristine landscapes of Notting Hill (imagining myself standing inside Hugh Grant's bookstore didn't hurt, either) and was so inspired by Iranian-born, Paris-based designer India Mahdavi's pink-saturated redesign of Mayfair restaurant Sketch that I modeled my own colorful marble chevron floors after the ones I saw there. Unsurprisingly, Dani fell in love with Shoreditch's grittier, street art–festooned buildings (and the tattooed guys who seemed to live there). I've been to London too many times to count since but that first trip was super special because of a fateful dinner, during which a man approached us in the middle of our meal and said, "You wear my dresses." I had no idea what he was talking about until a minute later, when he introduced himself as Han Chong, the mastermind designer behind one of my favorite British labels, Self-Portrait. We ended up hanging out on that trip and we're still friends today (and his dresses still always work for me, no matter which side of a city I find myself in).

OPPOSITE In 2015, being a tourist en route to a Jimmy Choo shoot in Switzerland. I only had two days—one on the way to Switzerland, and one on the way back—but I packed in a ridiculous amount of *National Lampoon's Vacation*–style sightseeing: Big Ben, Buckingham Palace (sans any Prince Harry sightings, sadly), the London Eye, Liberty London, and the Tower Bridge—where this shot was taken. *Tibi coat; Chanel bag; Nike sneakers.*

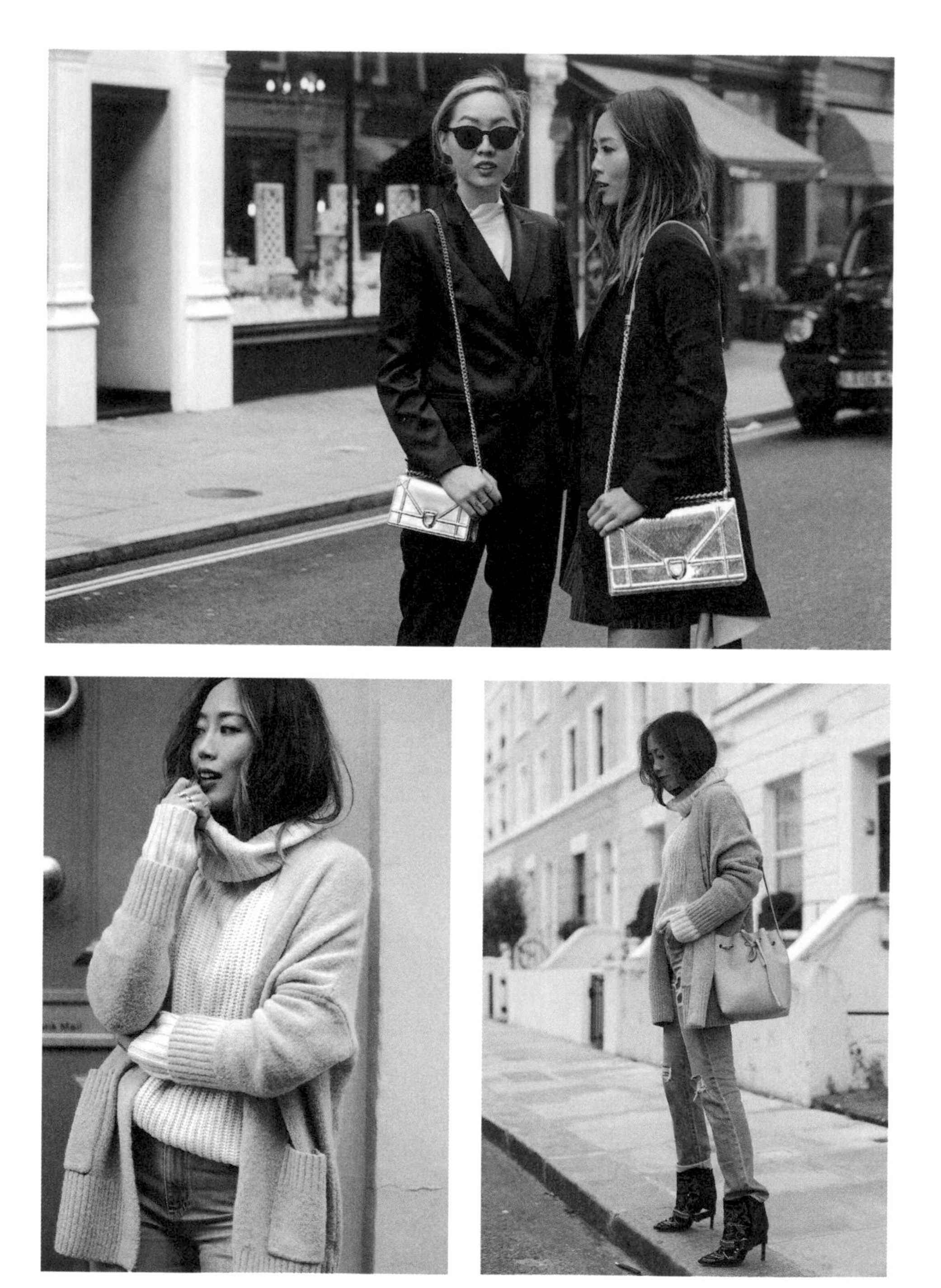

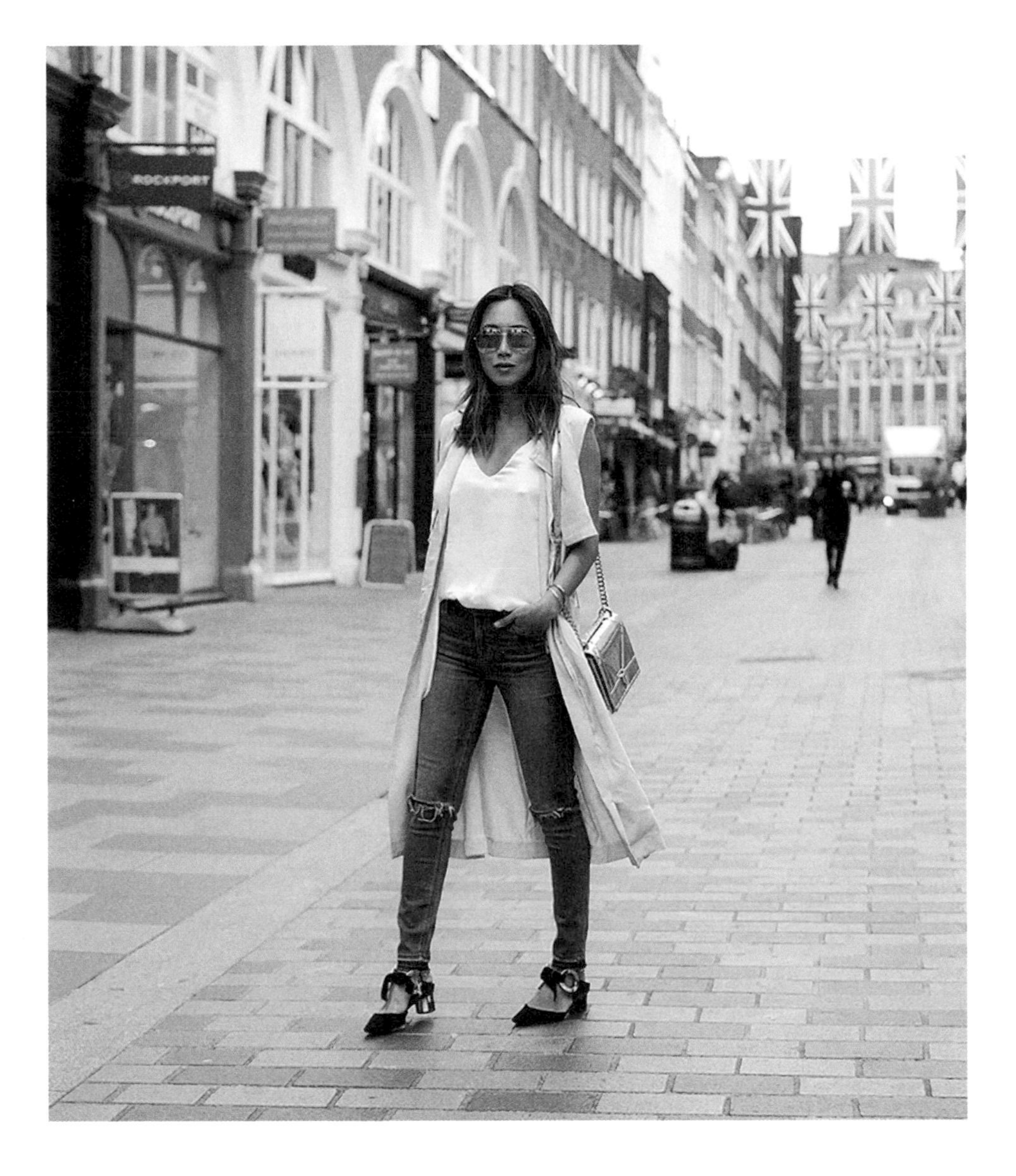

ABOVE In May 2016 I had the opportunity to go to the Dior cruise show with Dani at Blenheim Palace, a gorgeous country estate outside of London that was built in the early 1700s (fun fact: It's also where Winston Churchill was born). This was the beginning of the trip, before the fashion festivities. *Two Songs coat; Dior bag and sunglasses; Proenza Schouler shoes.* **OPPOSITE, TOP** Brad Goreski took this photo of Dani and me. *Both in Dior.* **OPPOSITE, BOTTOM ROW** Glorious Notting Hill. When can I move?

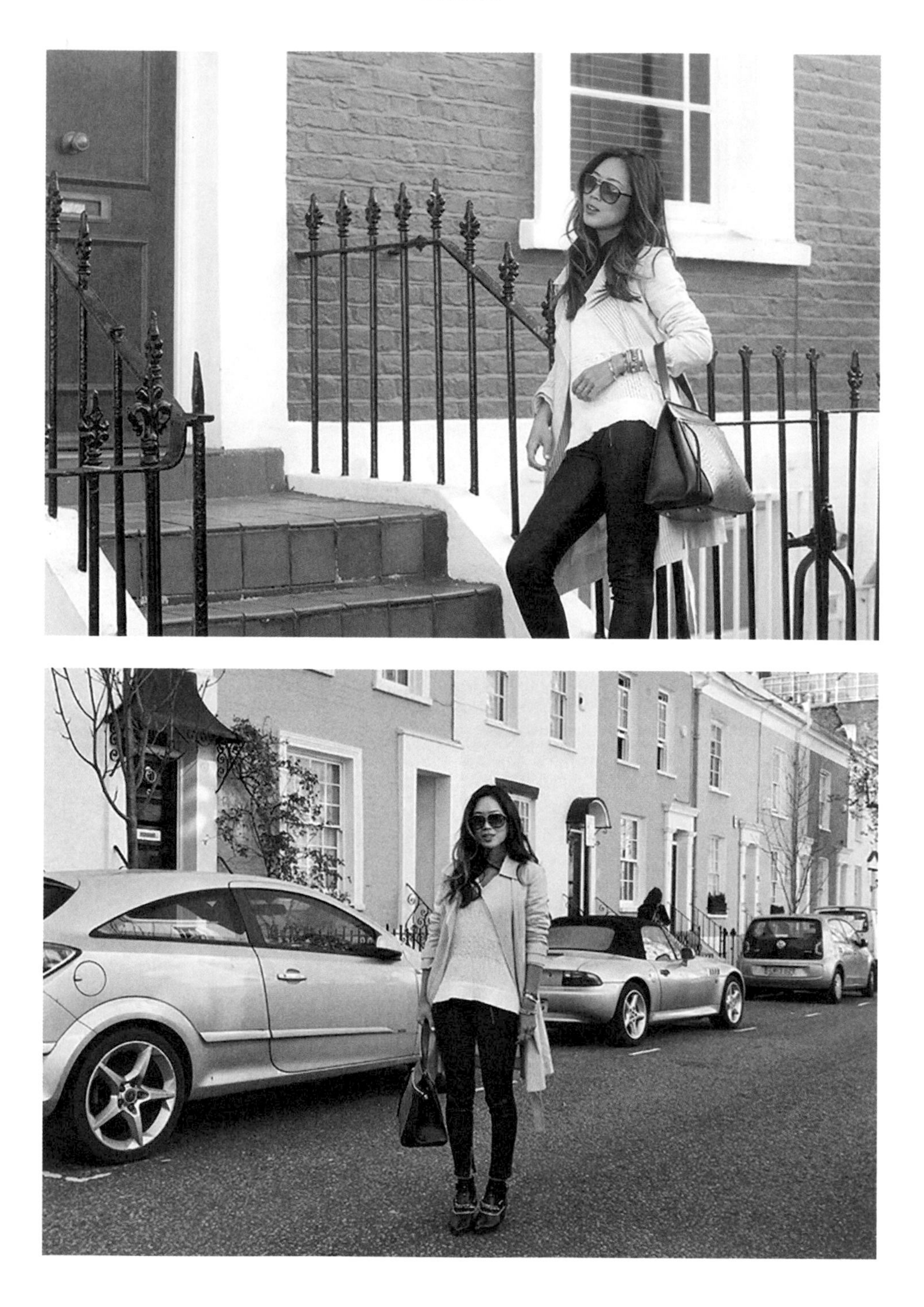

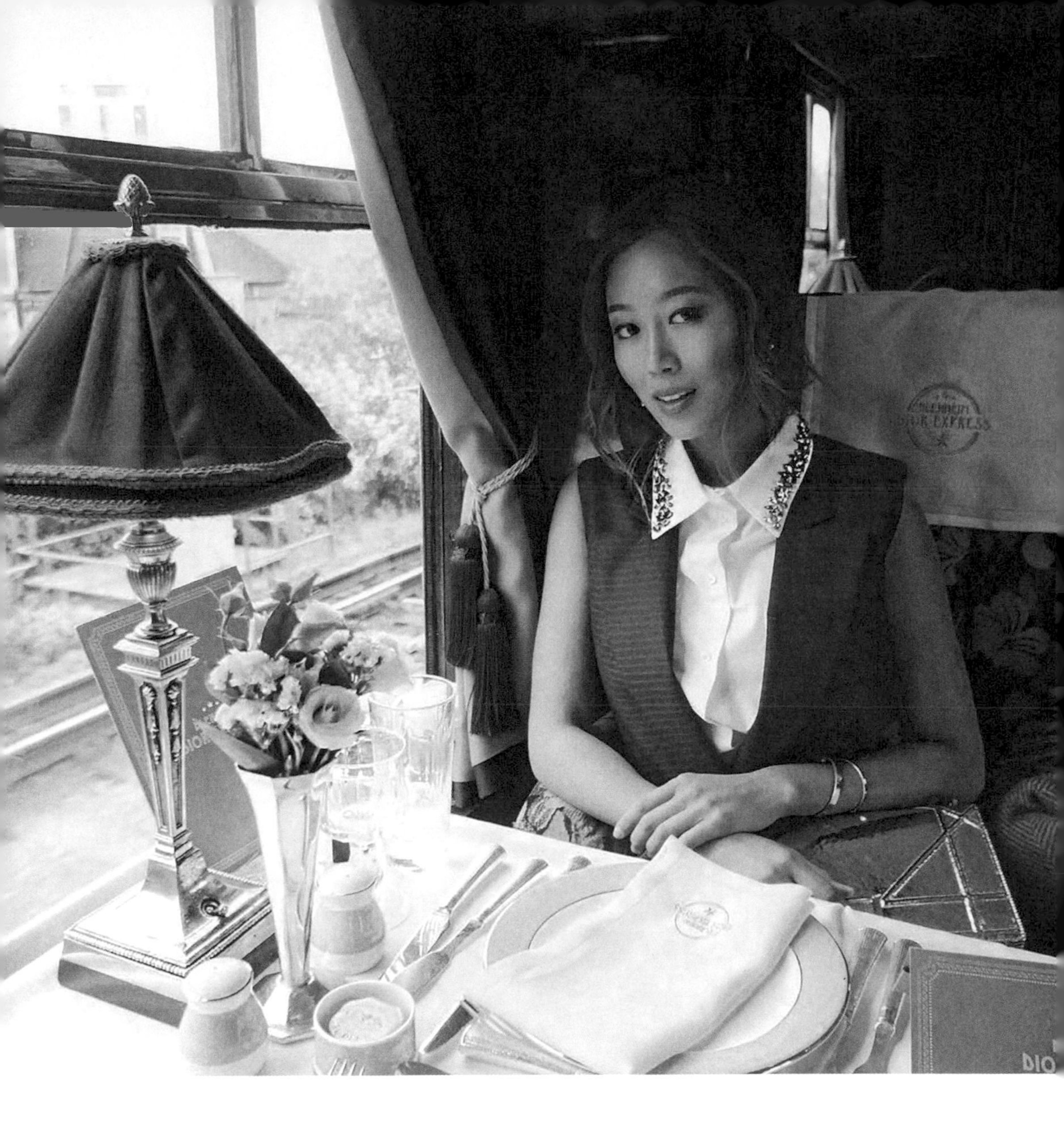

ABOVE Aboard the "Dior Express" to Blenheim Palace for the cruise show, which was actually the Orient Express—an incredibly famous, luxury Art Deco–inspired train that travels throughout Europe. It was insane—complete with a multi-course lunch and Dior napkins and china. One of the most special experiences I was lucky enough to have in recent memory. **OPPOSITE** Notting Hill in 2014. Back then I loved bigger bags, and now you will very rarely catch me putting anything bigger than a mini-cross-body in my suitcase—they're so much easier to travel with. *Céline bag.*

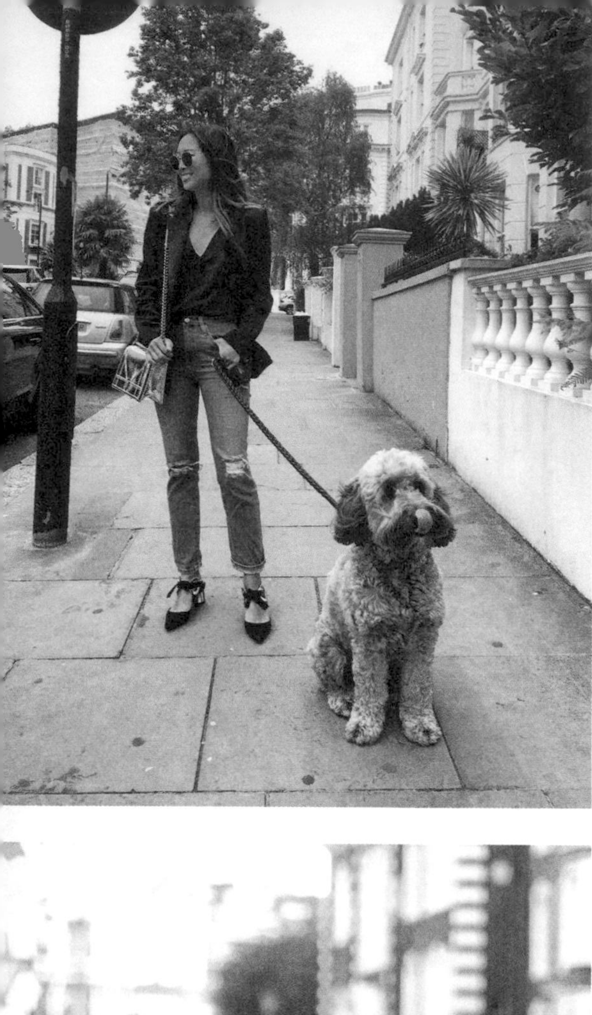

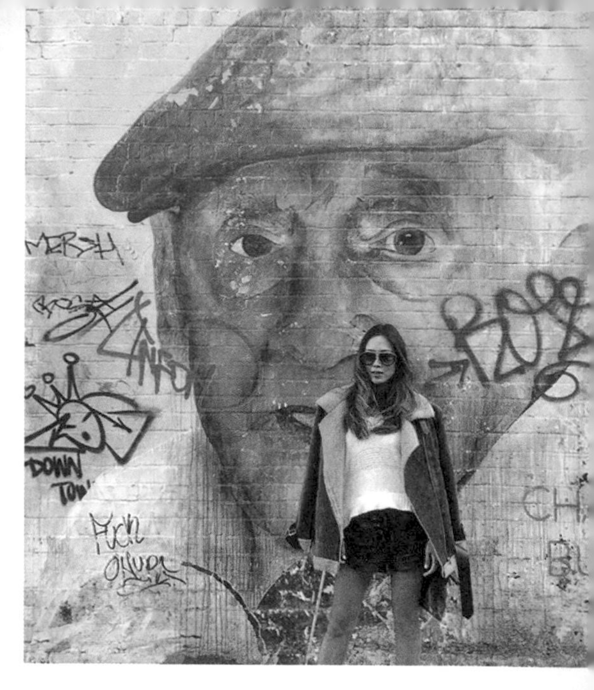

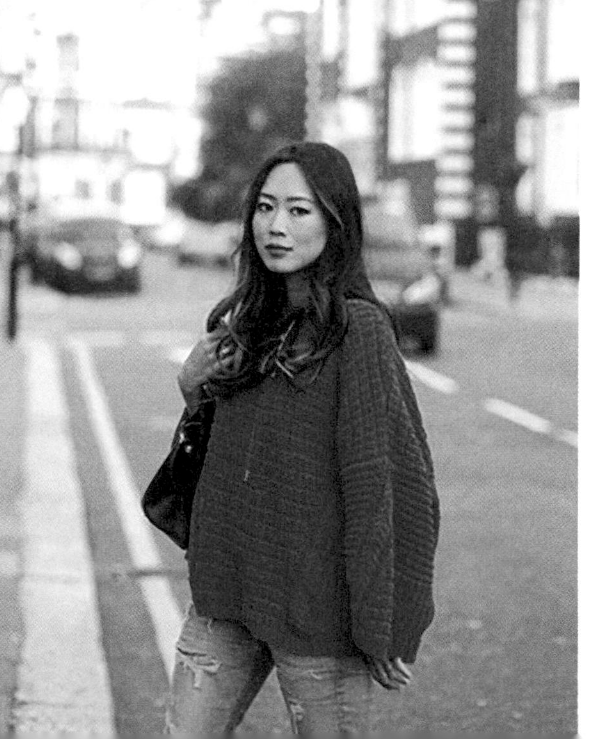

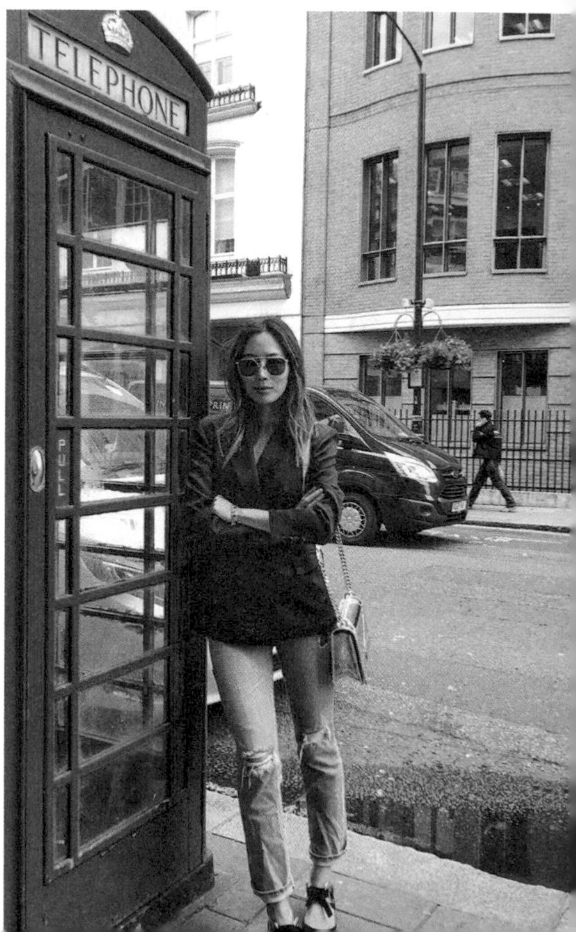
TELEPHONE
PULL

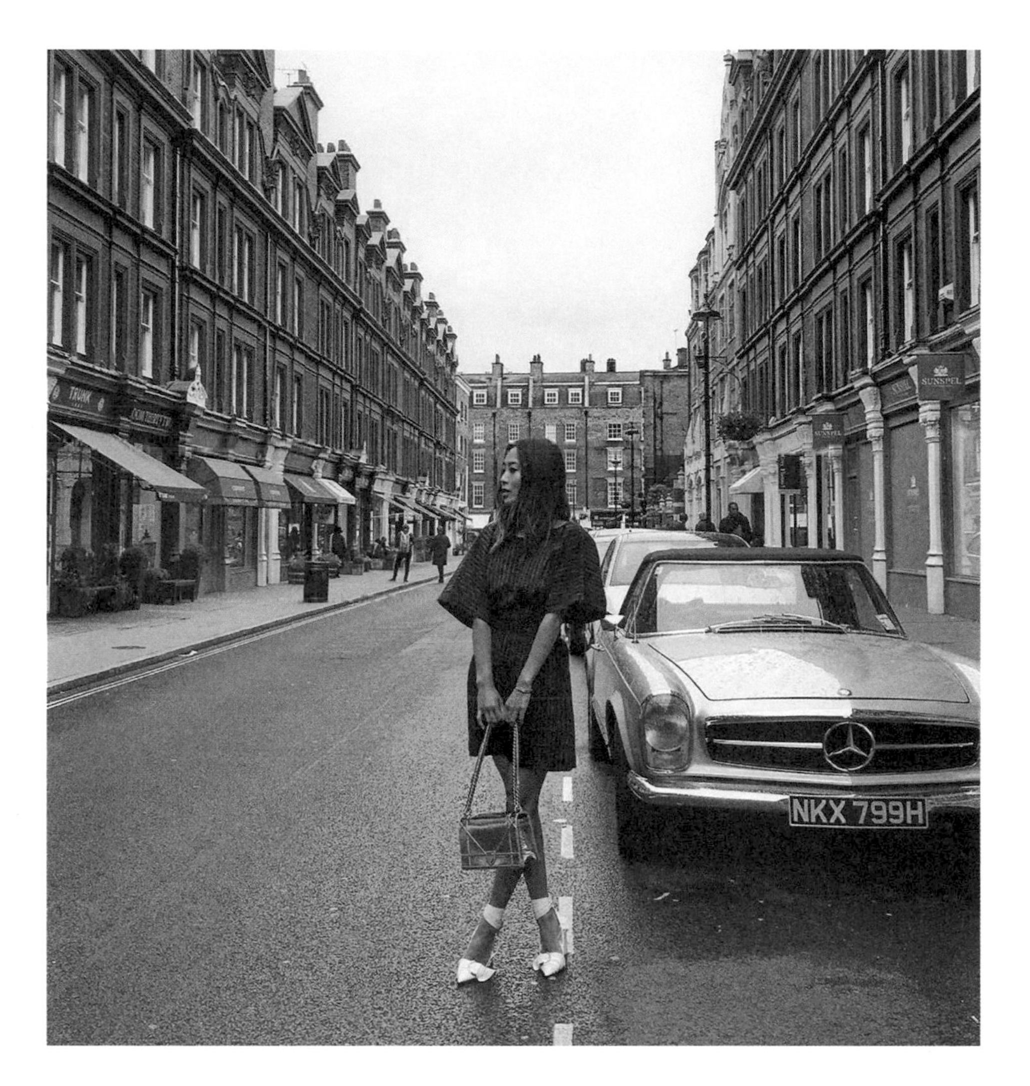

ABOVE Dani took this photo right before we stopped to eat lunch. **OPPOSITE (CLOCKWISE FROM TOP LEFT)** Before leaving for the Dior show, I wanted to see my British friends Matt and Eleanor—and Eleanor's incredible dog. • Dani's favorite neighborhood, East London. We walked around and people recognized us, which was crazy. We were more than happy to stop to chat, if only to hear their amazingly beautiful accents. • If you go to London and don't snap a photo next to a red phone booth, were you ever really there? • In front of our hotel, enjoying the amazing weather that I know never, ever appears. I've always had good luck with the weather in London—fingers crossed that my streak continues.

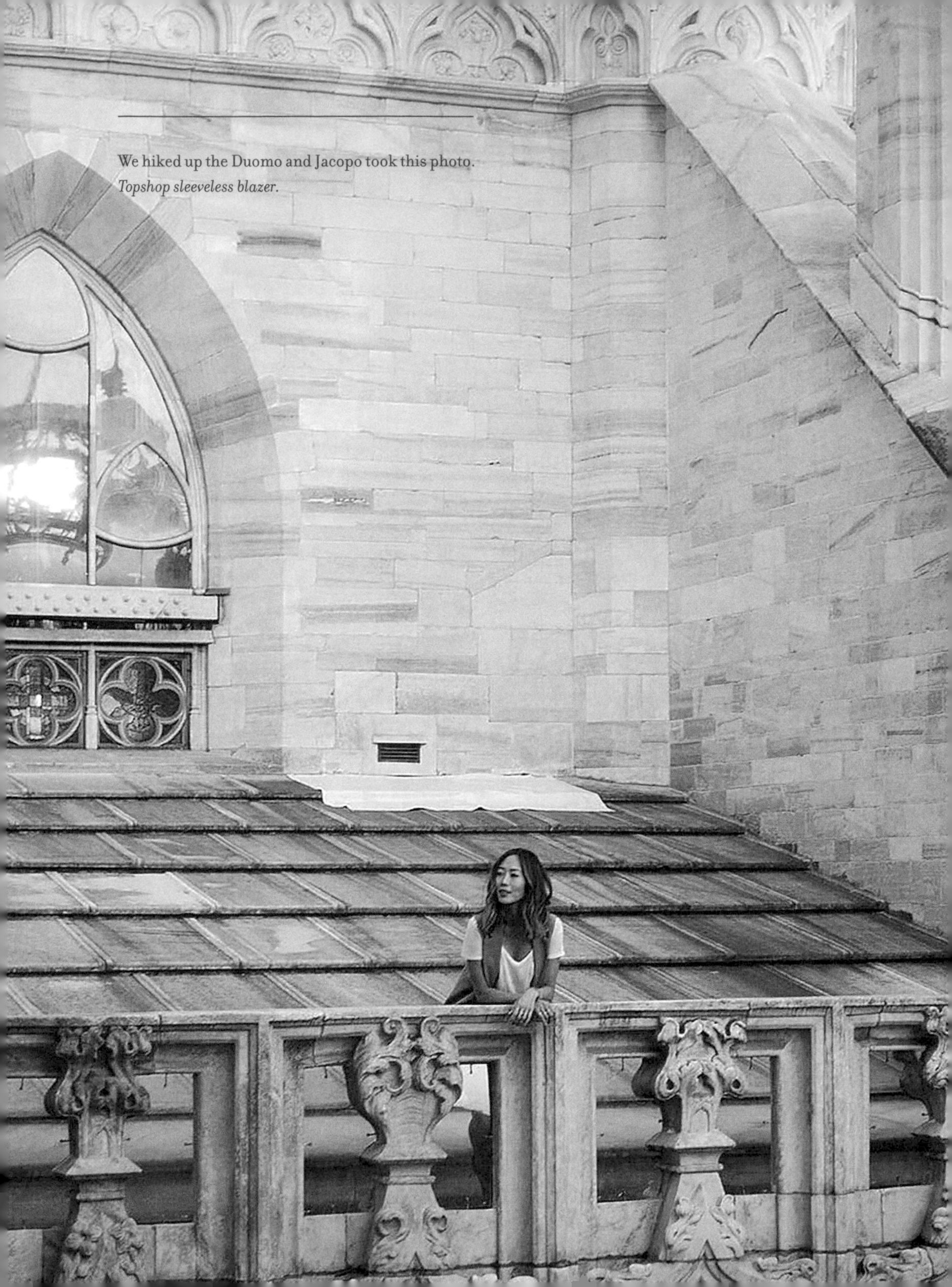

We hiked up the Duomo and Jacopo took this photo.

Topshop sleeveless blazer.

MILAN

The first time I ever went to Milan was in 2014 for Milan Fashion Week. I traveled with my friend Aureta Thomollari, a luxury consultant who had a blog, and we stayed with Scott Schuman, who is better known as the Sartorialist. I also met up with Jacopo on that trip. He and I weren't official yet, but he grew up in Milan and his family lives there so we had a really fun, chill time sightseeing together.

The most recent time I went to Milan was in February 2017, when I had the incredible opportunity to walk in Dolce & Gabbana's fashion show. (I. Know.) It was so special and I totally felt like Carrie Bradshaw in that *Sex and the City* episode—I'm so obviously not a supermodel, and I wasn't a celebrity kid like so many of the other catwalkers. I felt insecure (not a fun feeling when you're about to hit a runway) and just not like myself. But soon Pat McGrath was doing my makeup and Domenico Dolce was helping me pick an outfit that made me feel like "me" while Stefano Gabbana kept telling me to "be you!" Everyone was so warm and welcoming, and I quickly found my footing and was able to get through the show and have a great time in the process. Sometimes you just need some encouragement and gentle reminding of how hard you've worked for your opportunities to feel like you really do indeed belong.

MILAN MUST-EATS

There are many reasons Jacopo gives me all the feels, and the fact that he just happened to grow up in Milan and therefore knows all the best places to eat proper risotto Milanese is only one of them. These are some of our favorite places to go HAM on carbs (plus one vegan option for when my pants stop fitting). When in Milan . . .

Pizzeria Geppo
pizzageppo.it

Langosteria
langosteria.com

Giacomo Bistrot
@giacomo_milano
giacomobistrot.com

Trattoria del Pescatore
@trattoriadelpescatore
trattoriadelpescatore.it

Mantra Raw Bar
mantrarawvegan.com

Pasticceria Marchesi
@pasticceriamarchesi
pasticceriamarchesi.com

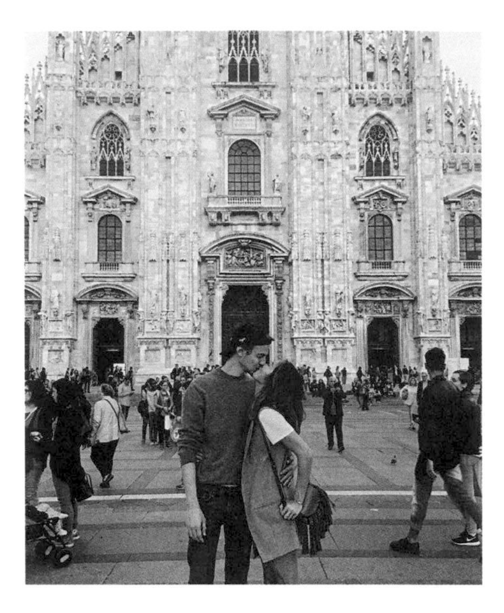

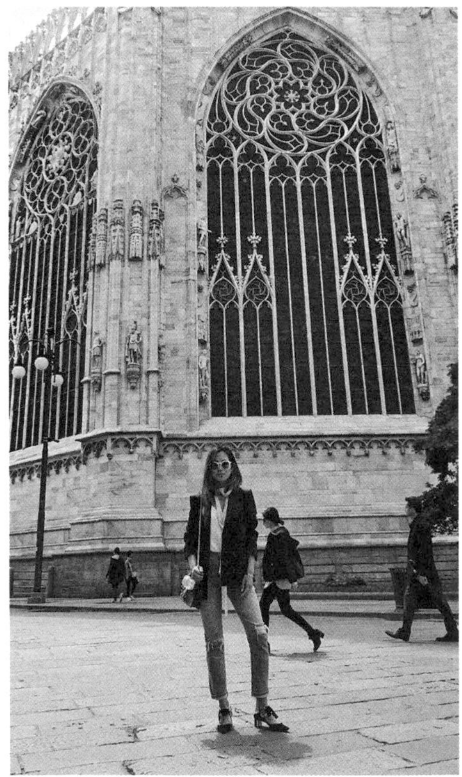

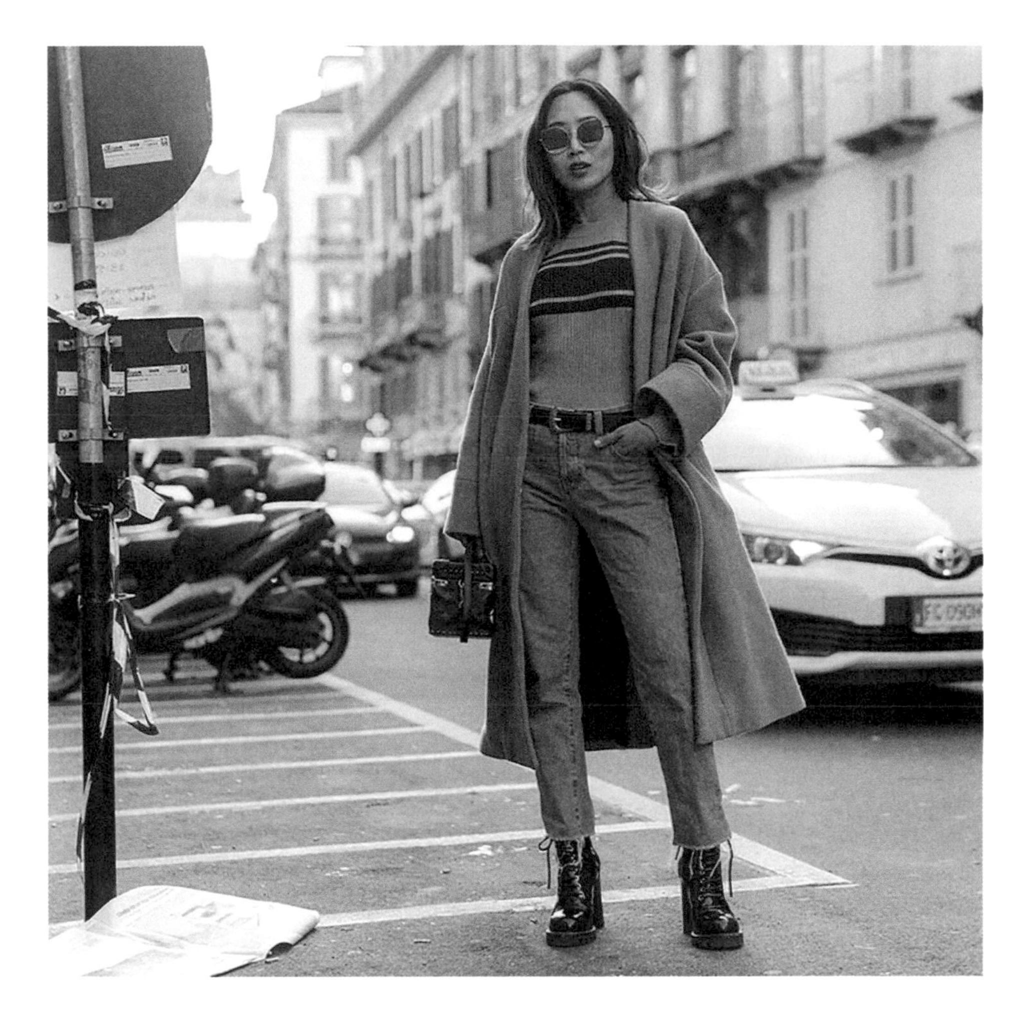

ABOVE The day I got to Milan for my D&G show. The day before the show, we did a walk-through—I was the last person to be fitted, and my fitting partner was Daniel Day-Lewis's son Gabriel. I actually felt intimidated because I was one of the few non-model models who wasn't famous offspring, and it was Domenico Dolce who comforted me and helped me pick out a look that made me feel like "me." *Gentle Monster x Song of Style sunglasses; IRO coat; Self-Portrait top; Citizens of Humanity jeans; Christian Louboutin boots.* **OPPOSITE (FROM TOP)** At the Duomo. I saw a cute couple trying to take a photo, so I offered to take their picture and asked them to take ours in return. I thought I was going to break my neck because Jacopo is so tall. • Jacopo has an apartment near the Piazza della Repubblica, so he and I played tourist and headed to the Duomo after eating at his favorite pizza place. *AG Jeans; Proenza Schouler shoes.*

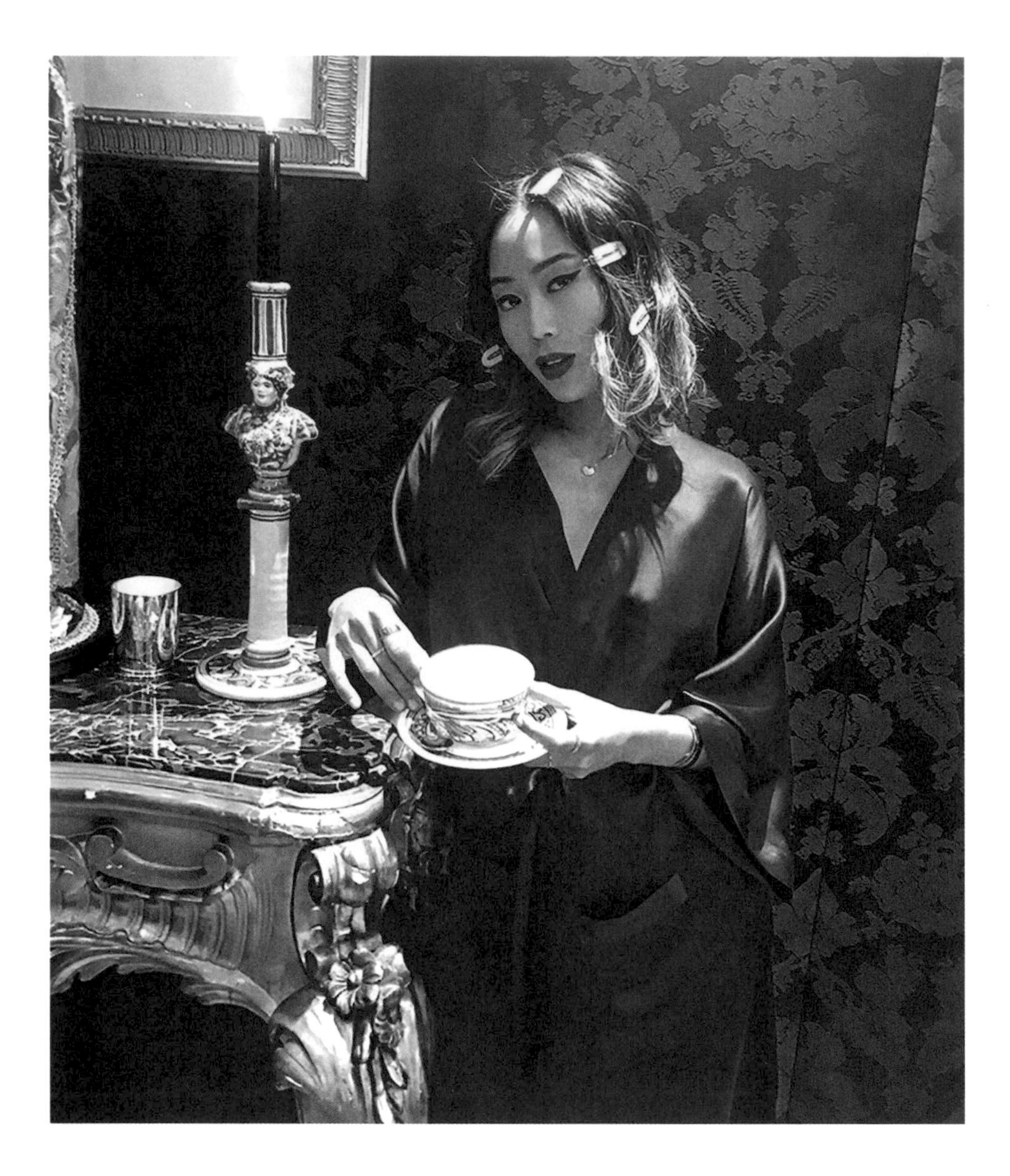

ABOVE This is the day of the D&G show. We were up super early in the morning for hair and makeup, and there was a ton of time to hang out. Despite the backstage chaos around me, I wandered around and took pictures because there was so much waiting and I didn't know what to do with myself. Resulting photo shoot, here. **OPPOSITE** The after-party. I got to sit on a throne and we partied with D&G on the dance floor. Wearing D&G, naturally.

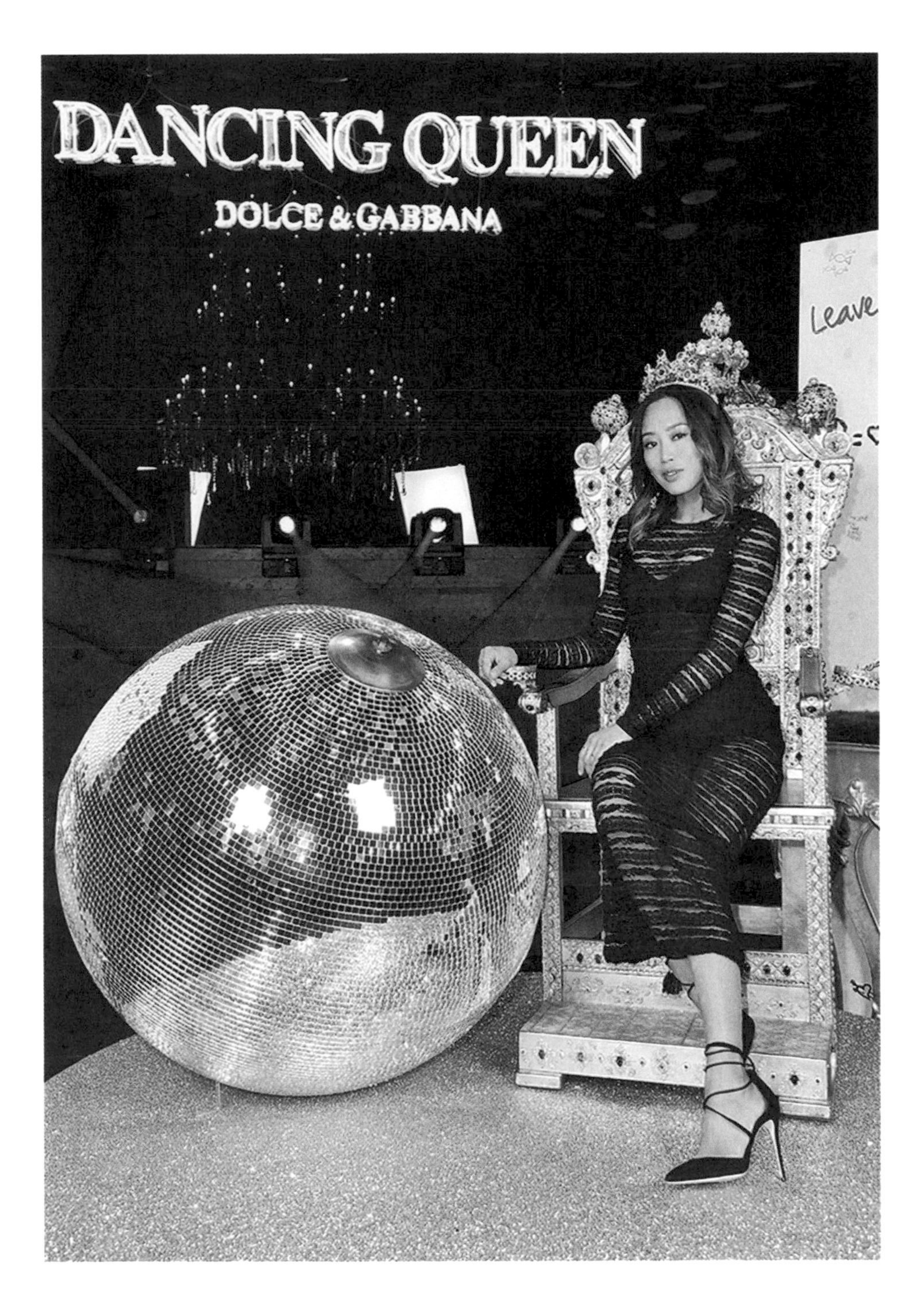
DANCING QUEEN
DOLCE & GABBANA
Leave

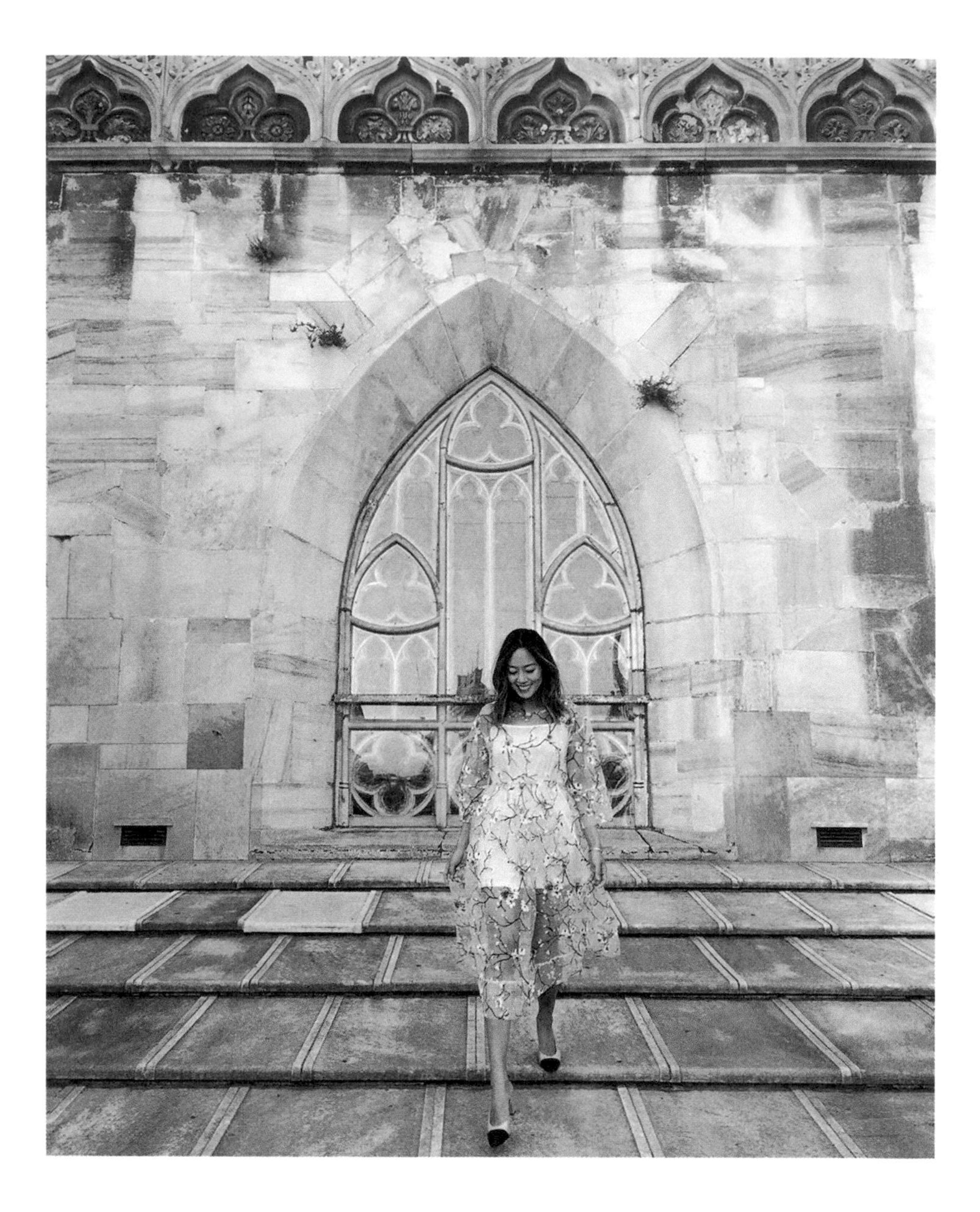

The top of the Duomo on a different day. Chanel shoes and yes, I did walk up the many flights of stairs to the top in Chanel slingbacks without incident (unless you count people staring at me in my gown and heels an incident). No matter. I needed my moment with my Italian, and I got it.

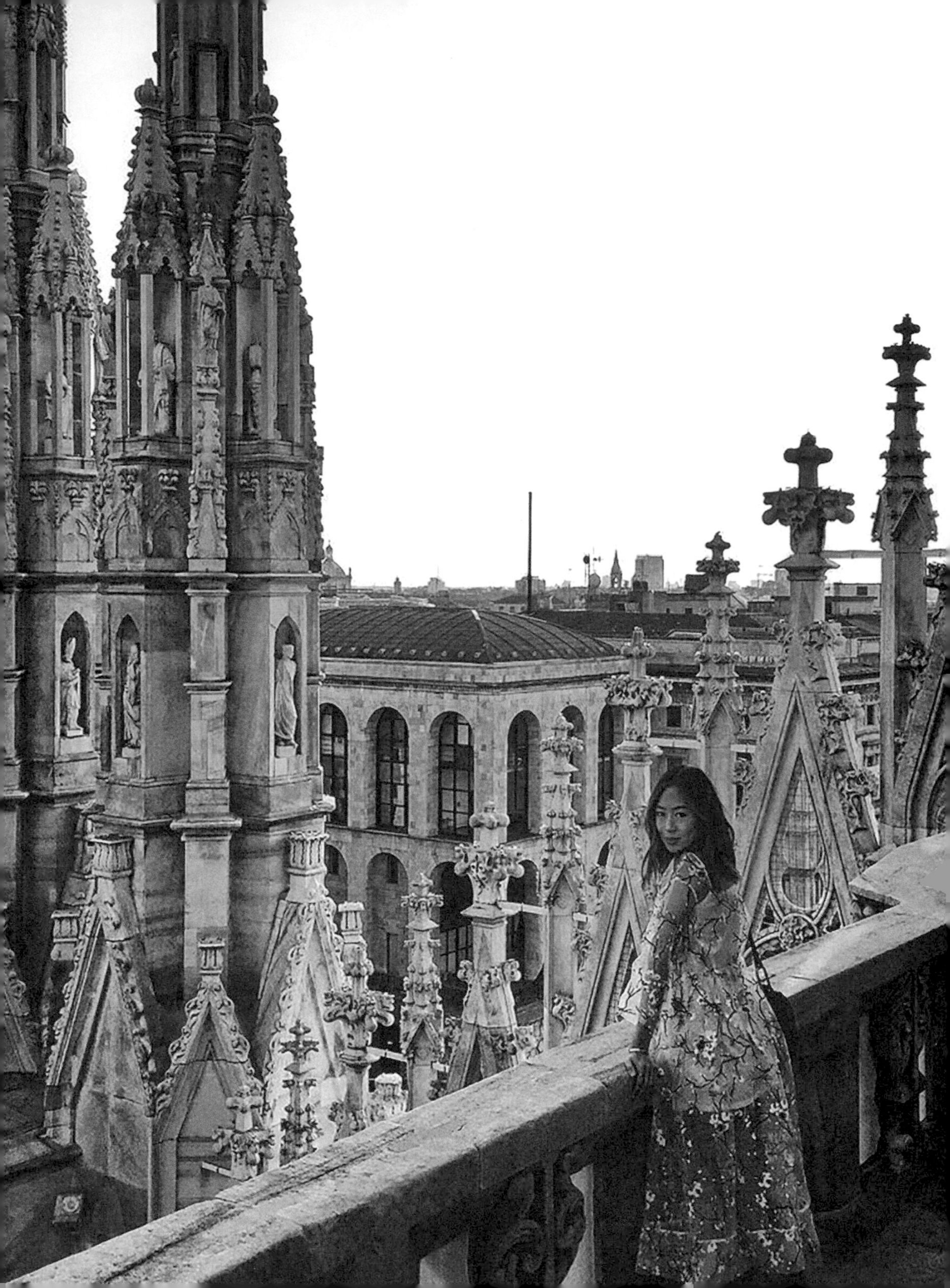

Long before I started *Song of Style*, I always used one getting-dressed-trick to help me pick outfits: taking photos. I find it so much easier to look at photos of myself in something instead of looking in a mirror, and it's still my go-to move—especially if I'm at Paris Fashion Week and have multiple outfit options that need comparing. *Dior dress.*

PARIS

Now that I'm in Paris roughly four times a year for work, it's crazy to think that my very first visit was only a mere five years ago, in 2013.

I always had such an idea in my head of what the City of Lights would be—romance, incredible food, and gorgeous fashion, of course. And similar to my daydreams about visiting Venice with a handsome love by my side (which I'll get into more a bit later), I always hoped for a Parisian fairytale if I was ever lucky enough to visit the dreamy city. I still can't believe that I've been able to experience all those things (though lost luggage, torrential downpours, and broken umbrellas are only a few ways the fairytale bubble has been burst over the years), and now I really do feel comfortable and at ease whenever I have to navigate my way on the Métro, recommend brunch options to friends, and find the prettiest off-the-beaten-path garden to breathe in for a second between shows (another amazing reason to travel: feeling like a local on the other side of Earth).

I know that some of my experiences in Paris aren't what you'd call, uh, *normal* per se (dinner in the Louvre and signing copies of my first book, *Capture Your Style*, at famed boutique Colette aren't exactly everyday occurrences). But Paris is a city where you can grab an inexpensive pastry and a coffee and literally wander the streets for hours, getting lost in the architecture and sounds of the motorbikes, and have an experience that you will remember forever. It's true: Paris has that je ne sais quoi, and it's *magnifique*.

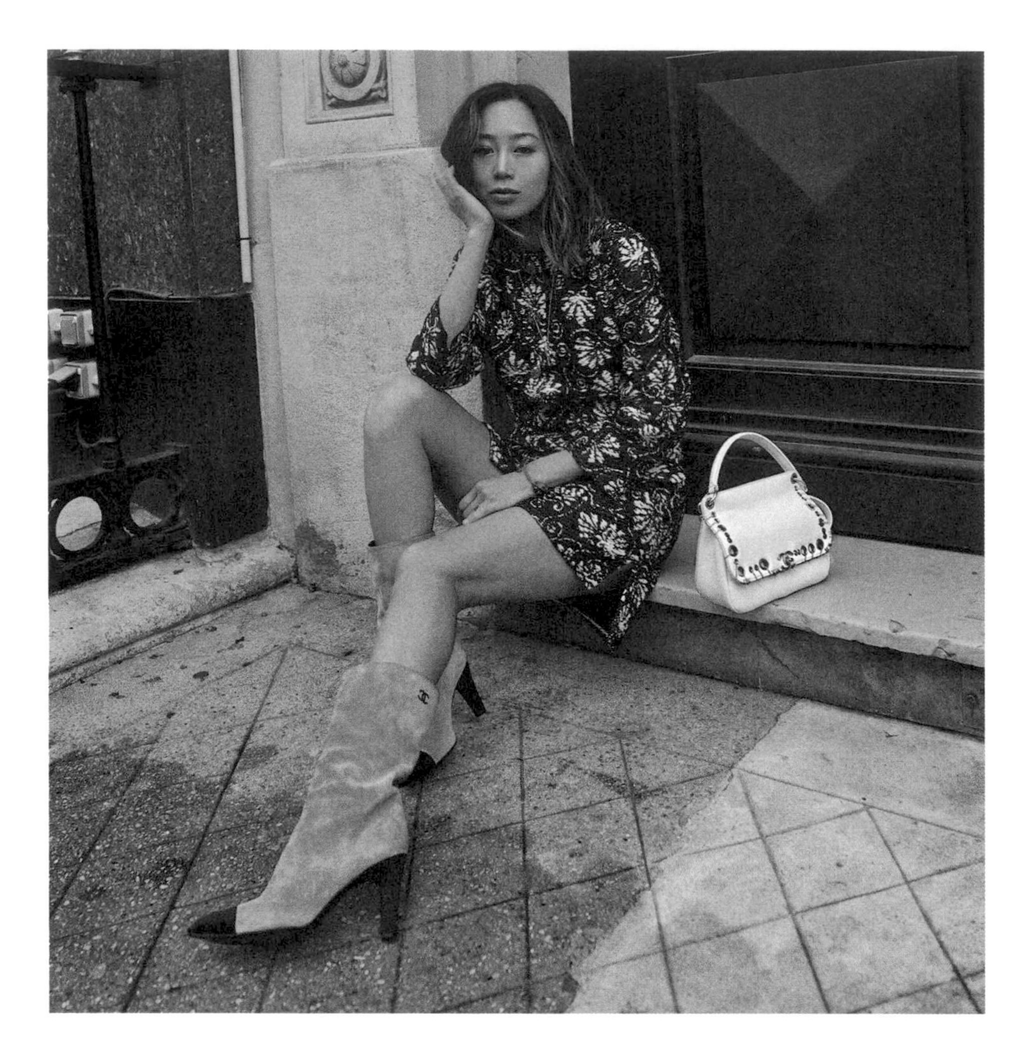

ABOVE This was that one time during the couture shows when my suitcase hadn't arrived. But Chanel was dressing me for its show, and my lost clothes were definitely not as good as the backups I was so kindly provided. There are worse times for your luggage to be lost, I suppose. **OPPOSITE, TOP AND BOTTOM RIGHT** After my trip to Munich with Louis Vuitton I headed back to Paris to celebrate the collection launch with a dinner inside the Louvre, which was held on a Tuesday when the museum is closed to the public. The experience of eating dinner in the world's most famous museum next to the *Mona Lisa* was so unreal that I barely noticed when Jennifer Aniston walked by me and said hi. I was too in awe of the art! **OPPOSITE, BOTTOM LEFT** This is what it really looks like when I get dressed. Mess everywhere, trying to figure out what shoes to wear while eating a bag of chips.

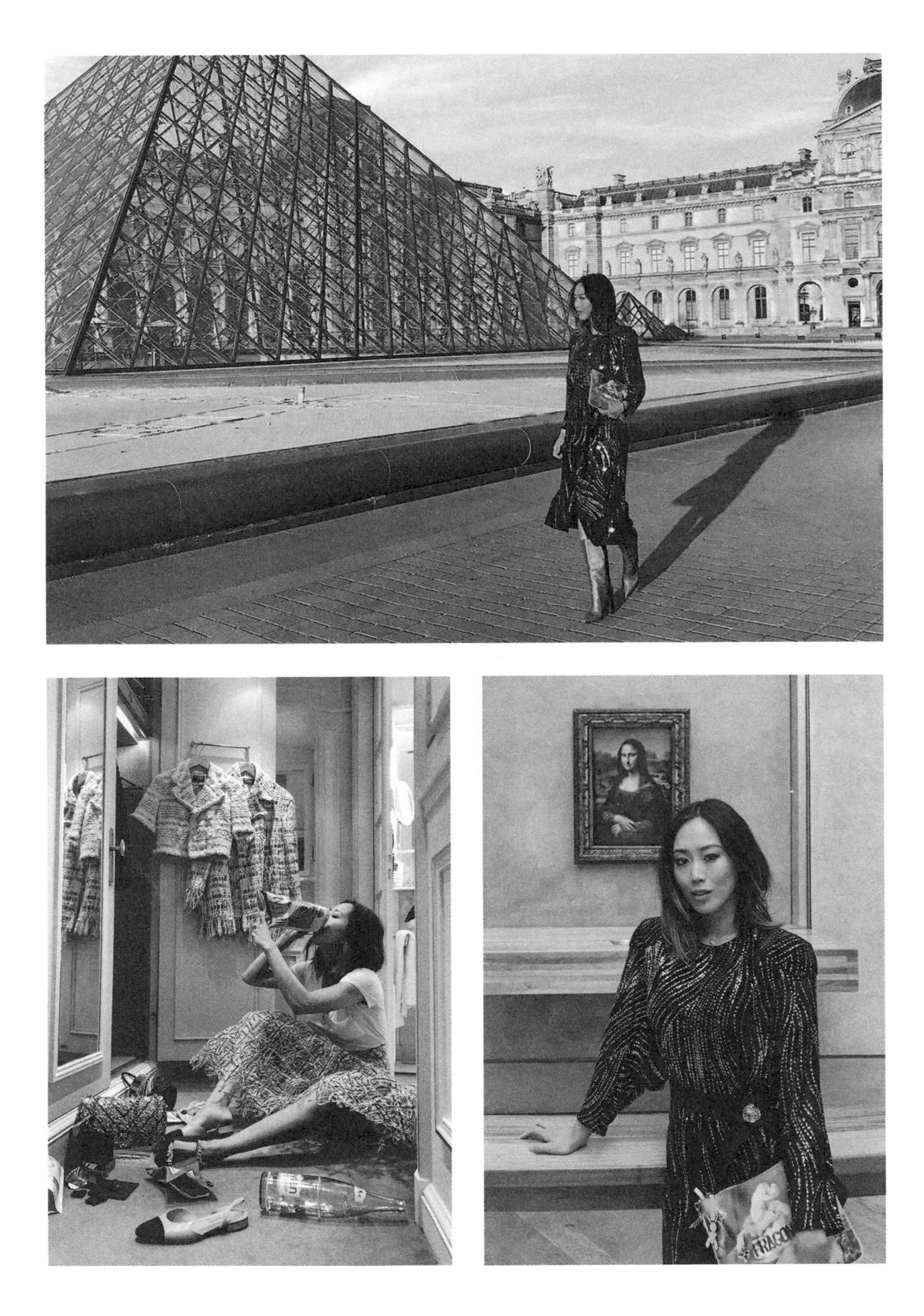

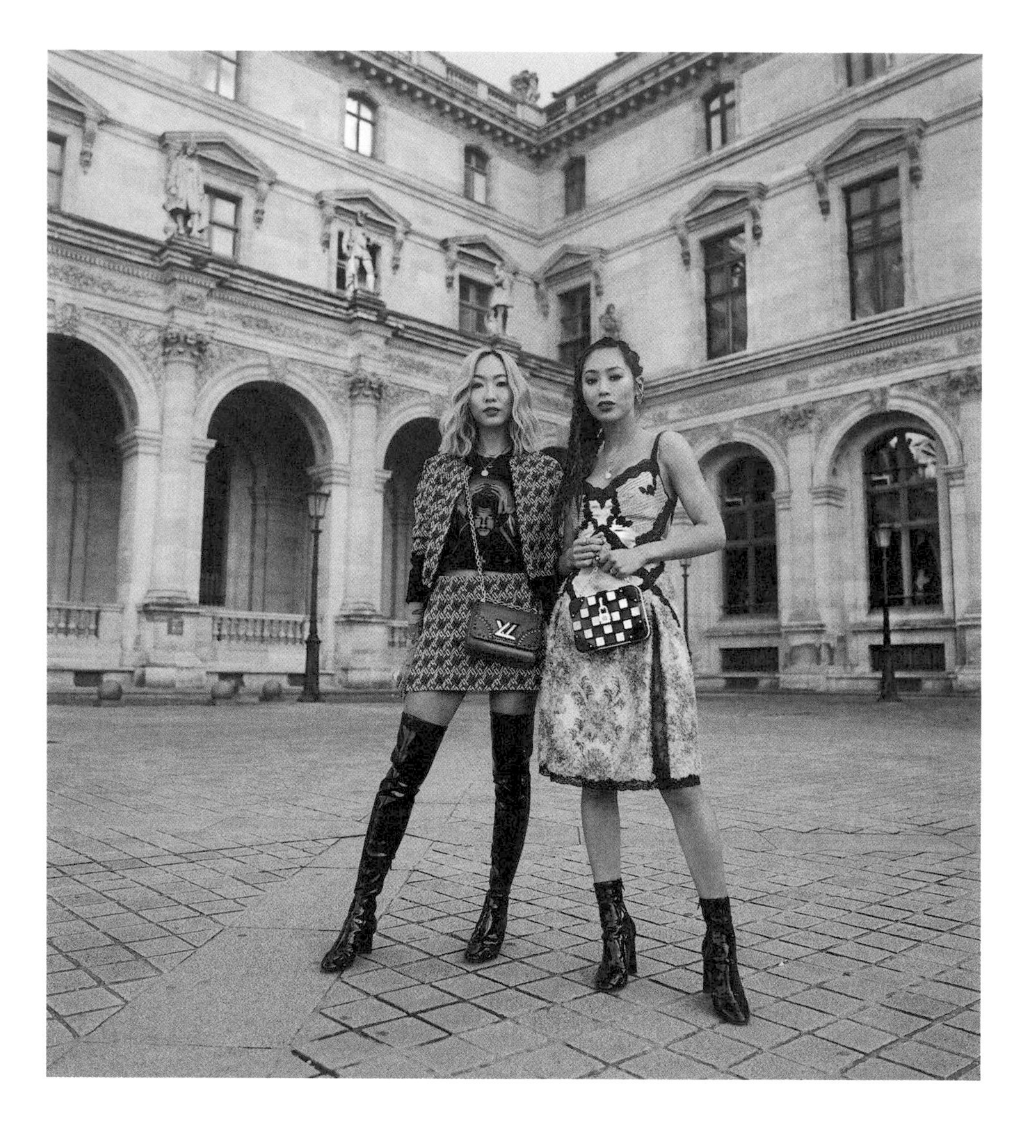

ABOVE Dani surprised me one season and showed up in Paris completely unannounced. I was so excited that I almost cried when I saw her. This is us before the Louis Vuitton show. **OPPOSITE (FROM TOP)** How gorgeous is this chandelier at Versaille? • I'm so lucky that I get to go to Paris three or four times a year for work, and I get so inspired there every single time. If I have a free day I try to go to Versailles, which is less than an hour from the city and features some of the most gorgeous French architecture in existence. On this trip in 2015 my friend Benita joined me. She had never been to the palace before, so we decided to go early one morning to beat the crowds. *Johanna Ortiz top; Ellery jeans.*

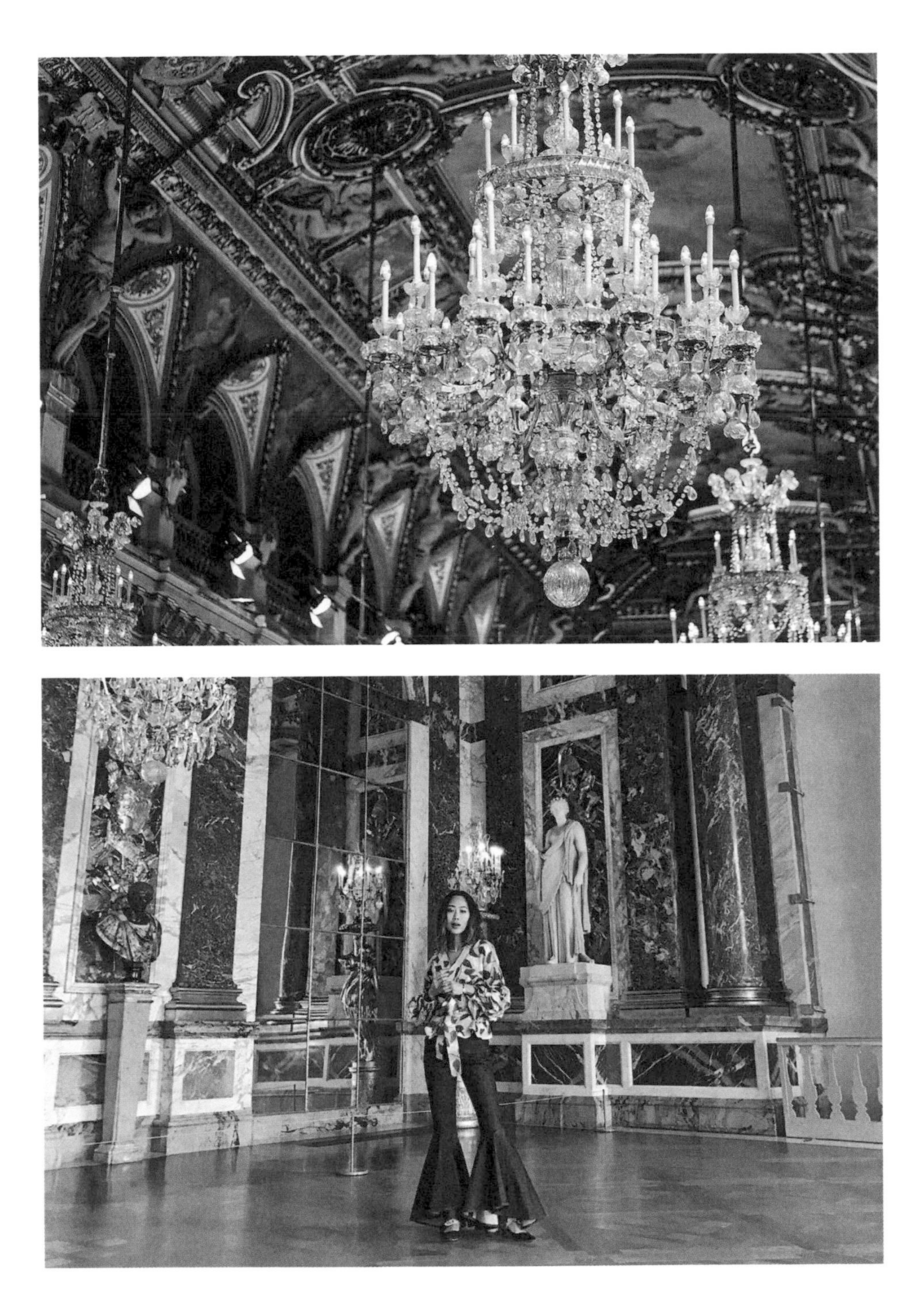

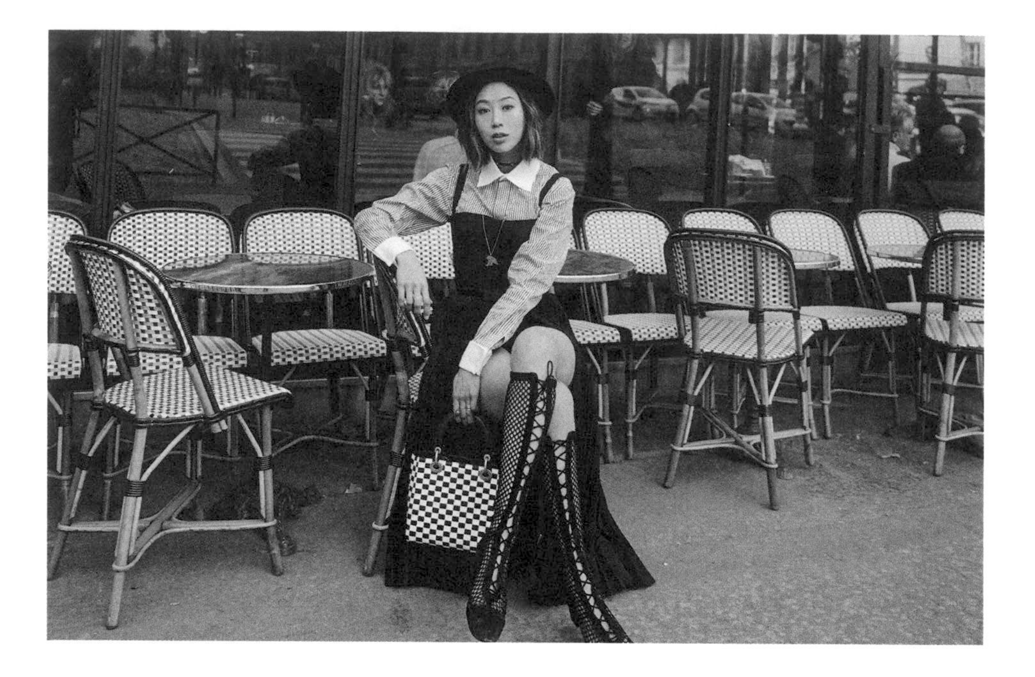

ABOVE When your Dior outfit matches a Parisian café. **OPPOSITE (CLOCKWISE FROM TOP LEFT)** Louis Vuitton asked me to help launch their Masters Collection, a really cool bag collaboration with contemporary artist Jeff Koons. Each piece in the collection was inspired by an Old Masters painting, so I had the opportunity to shoot photos of an LV bag featuring Jean-Honoré Fragonard's *Girl With a Dog* in front of the actual 1770 painting at Munich's Alte Pinakothek—a museum that has one of the most famous collections of Old Masters masterpieces in the world. This photo was taken when I landed in Paris before the German leg of my trip. Can you tell I'm excited? • Right before the Acne Studios show during Paris Fashion Week in March 2017, when it was raining and freezing! A few weeks before Paris Fashion Week started, *Business of Fashion*, one of my favorite fashion news websites, launched its #TiedTogether initiative to promote equality and inclusion, asking members of the fashion industry to wear a white bandanna during the shows. I made sure to wear mine as much as possible so it would get photographed and keep the conversation of togetherness and human unity moving forward. • For its Paris Fashion Week show in March 2017 Balmain wanted to dress me head to toe. But mixing-and-matching is much more my thing. *Balmain jacket; IRO top; Isabel Marant leather pants; Stella Luna heels* • When I first started coming to Paris Fashion Week years ago I stayed at an Airbnb with my team and my friends, which always made the experience so warm and fun (of course, bubble baths in five-star hotels have their pluses, too; but nothing beats laughing with your besties in a Parisian flat). In 2015 my friends Benita and Cubby joined my assistant Nicholas and me in a huge twenty-five-hundred-square-foot apartment in the sixth arrondissement, where we bought groceries, made "family" dinners, and pretty much had slumber parties every night. The best.

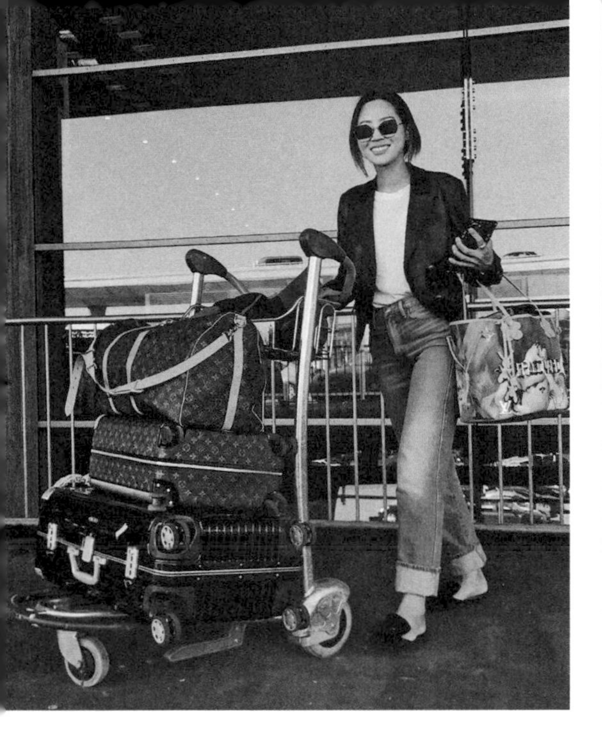

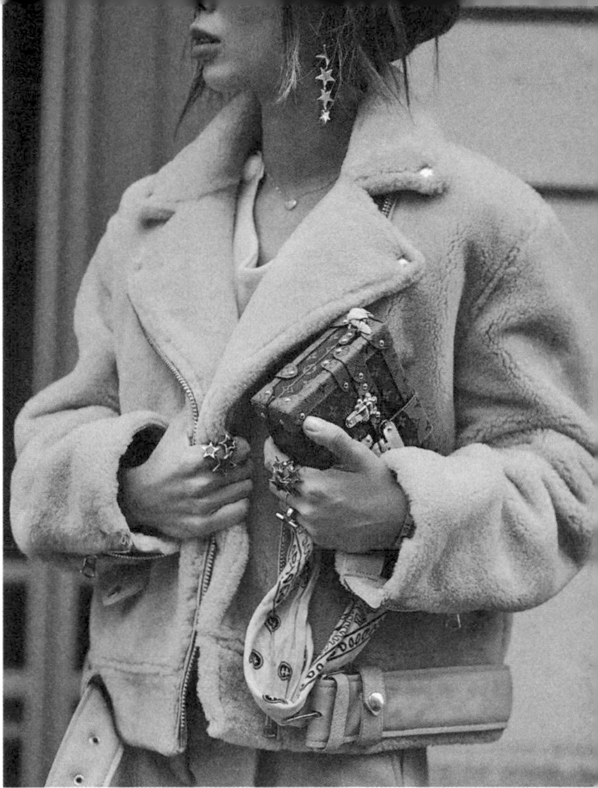

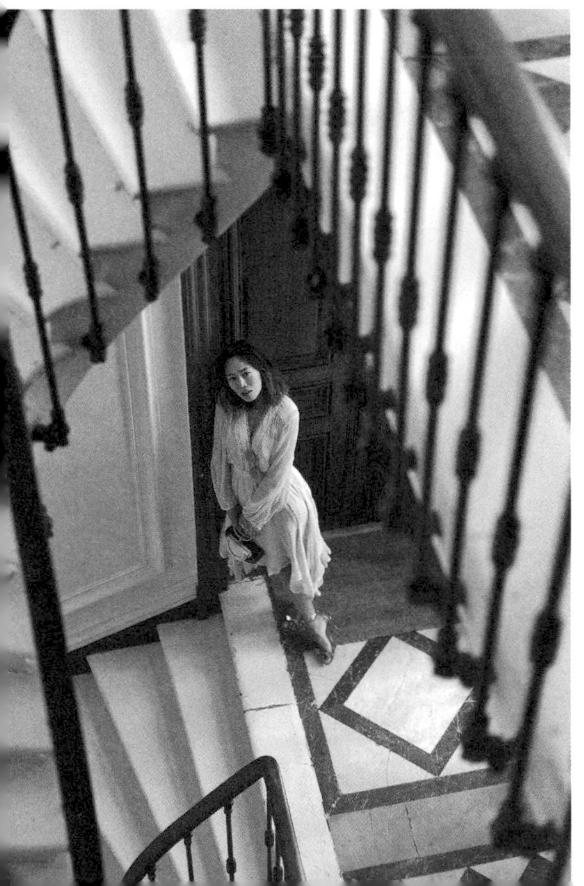

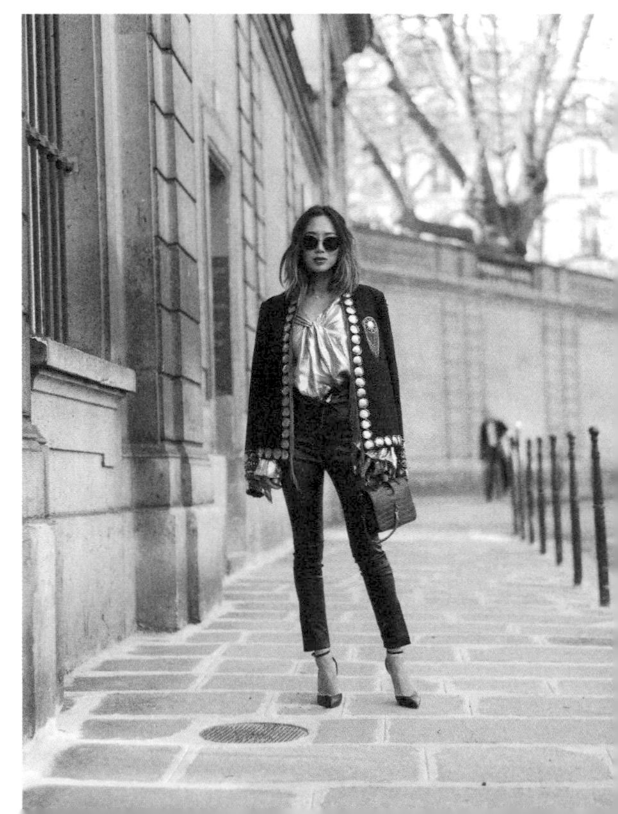

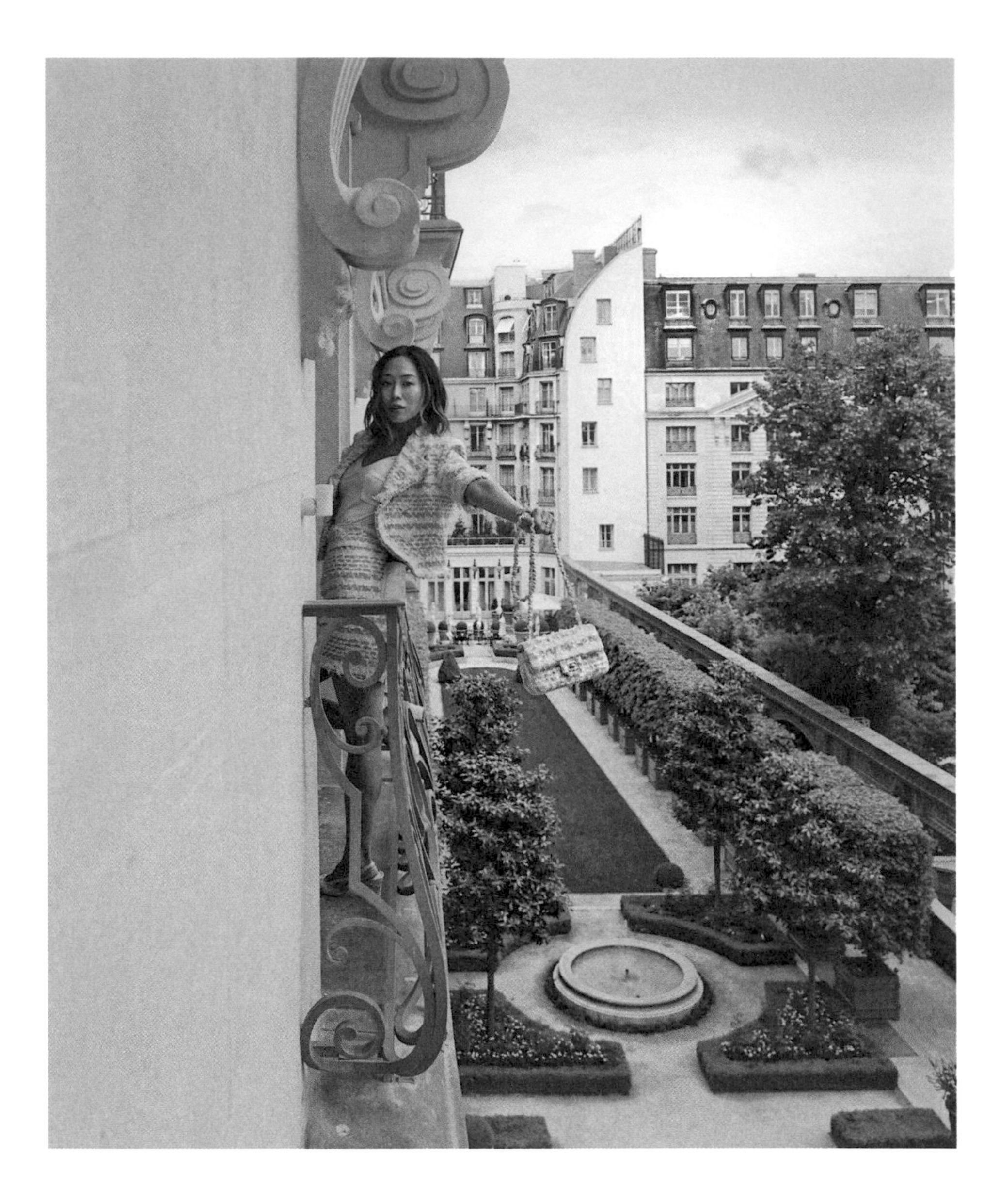

ABOVE My best friend Jared joined me at the Chanel Cruise show in May 2018. He art directed this epic photo that looks a lot scarier than it actually was. **OPPOSITE** My trip with Jared in May 2018 is probably one of my favorite Paris trips because the weather was so beautiful. We walked all over and stumbled upon a flea market, where I scored a vintage Gucci doctor's bag and Burberry jacket for Jared.

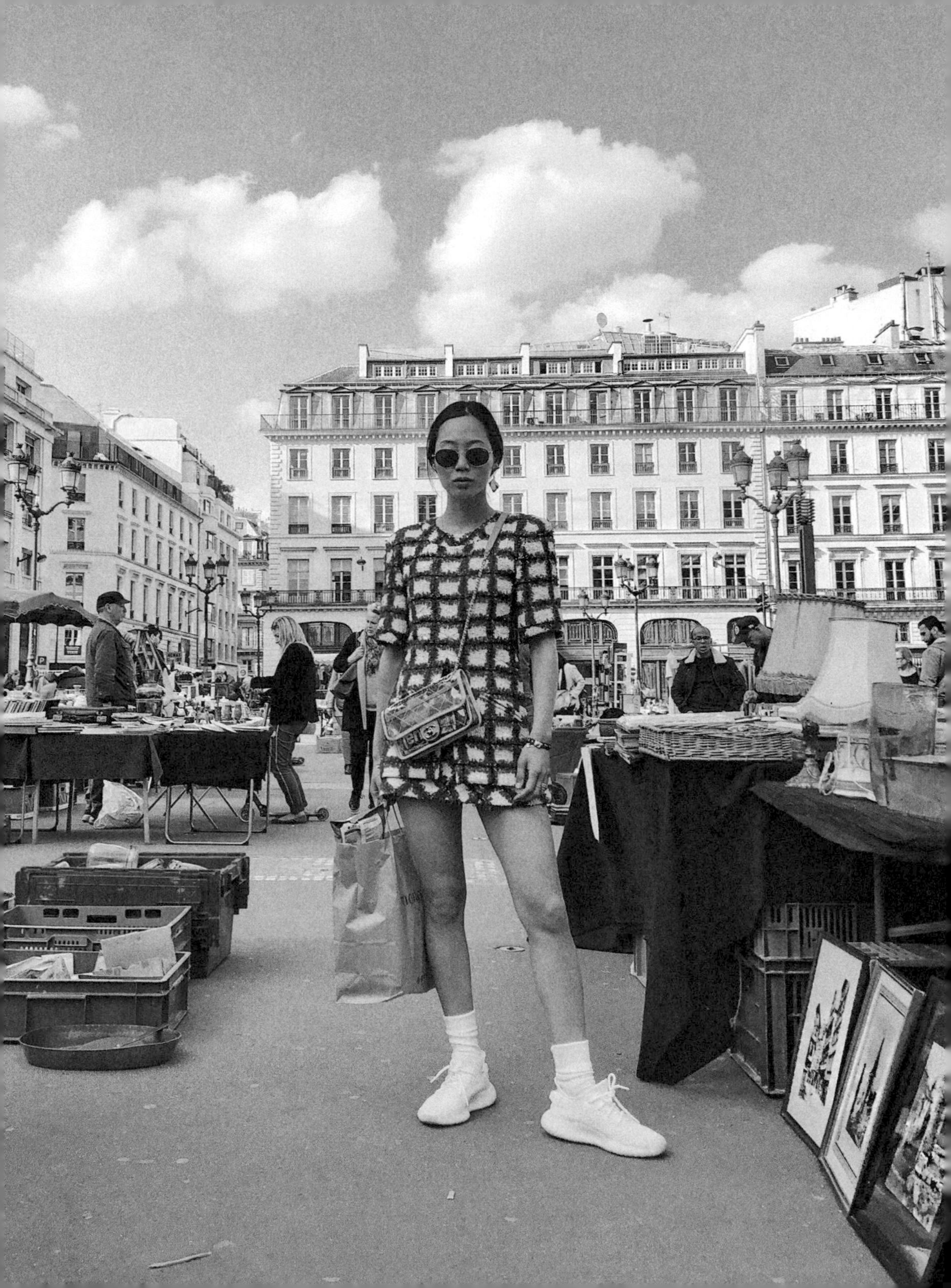

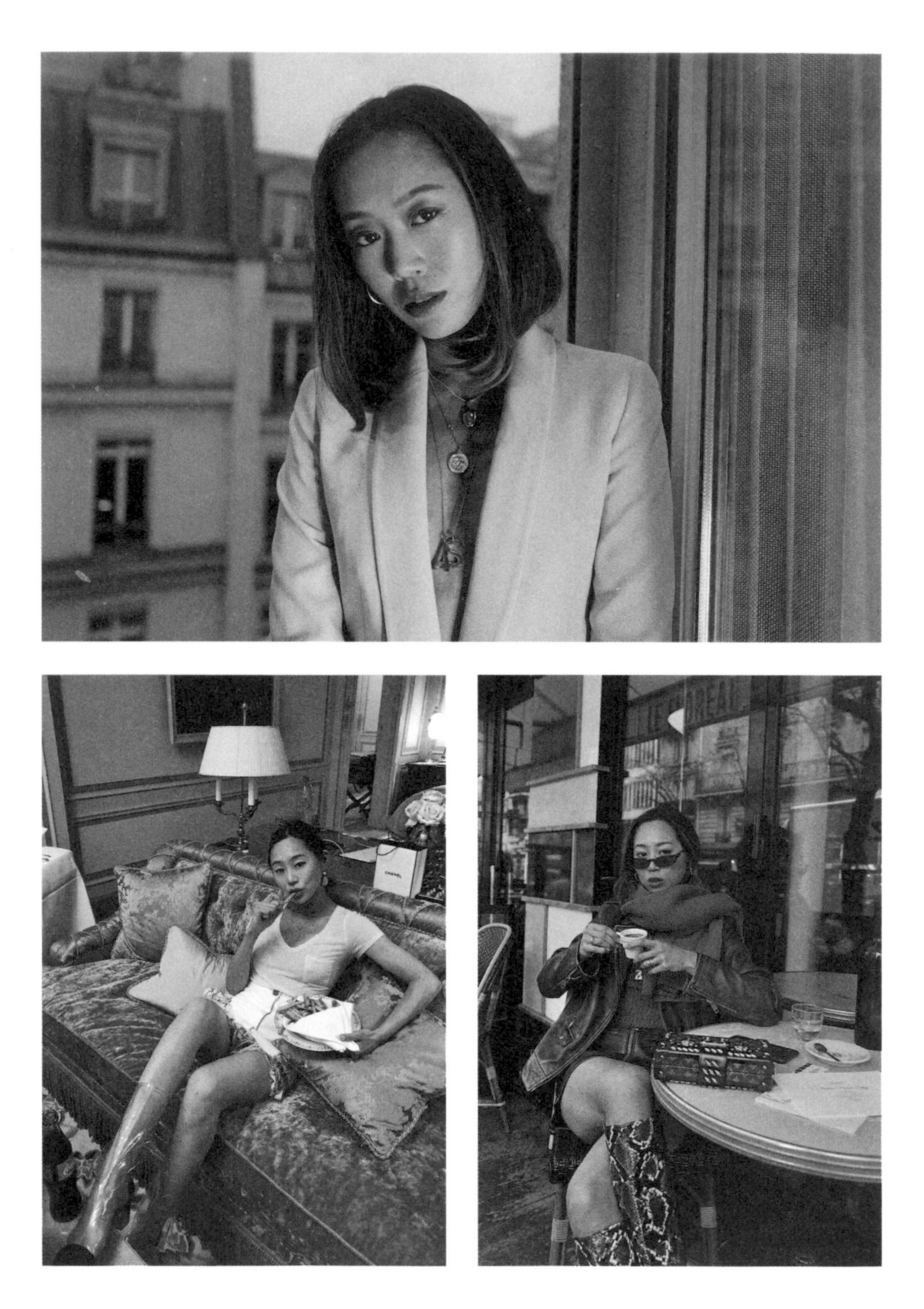
CHANEL

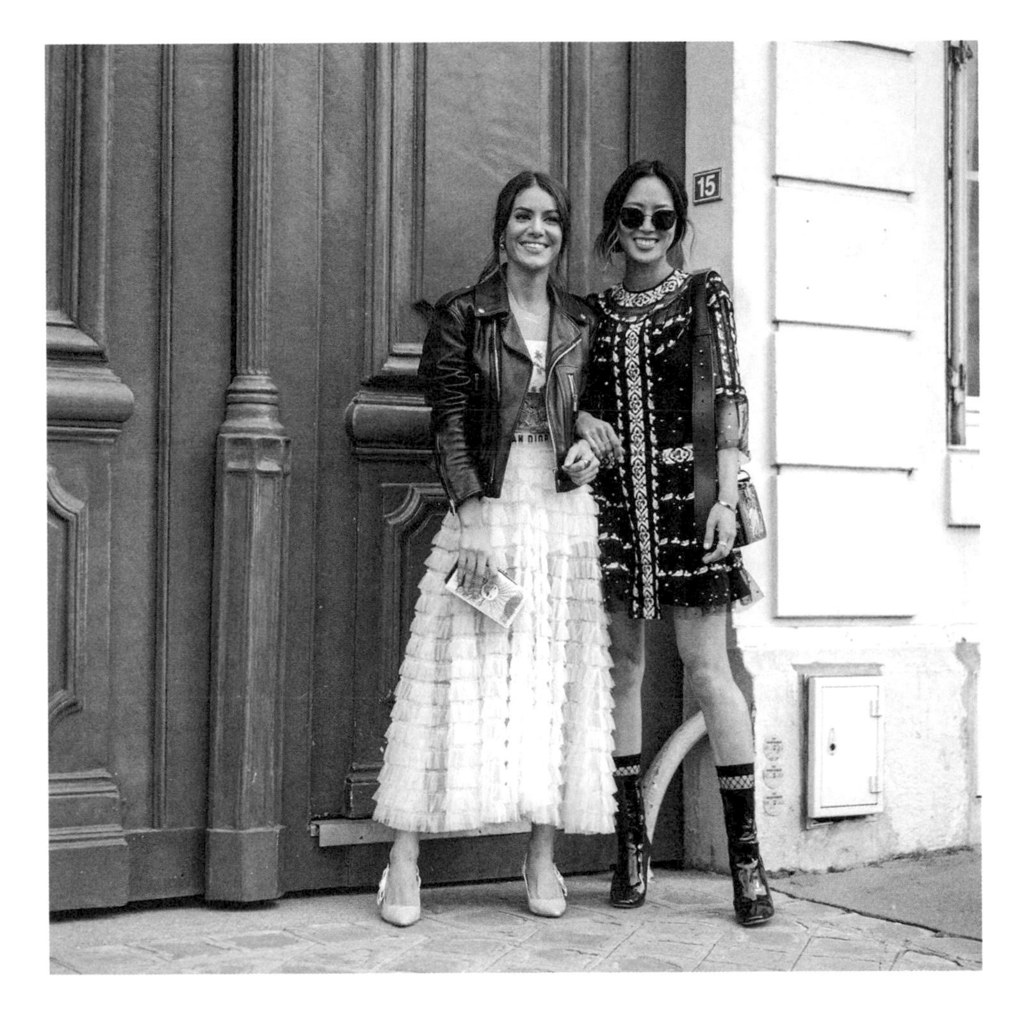

ABOVE In 2012 I met fellow blogger Camila Coelho at a house party. I didn't know anyone at the party and felt like everyone there was trying really hard to be "cool," except for Camila. We started talking and realized that we both felt out of place, and our energies immediately aligned. Camila lives in Boston, but we kept in touch and started running into each other at New York Fashion Week. Since we quickly realized how much we both love to travel, we've met up in Japan, in Anguilla, in Austin, and at Coachella. And now I can honestly say that Camila has truly become one of my best friends, and I feel so lucky that we've been able to support each other in our careers and in our personal lives. Here we are in Paris, probably talking about what we want to eat after the next fashion show. *Dior dress.* **OPPOSITE (CLOCKWISE FROM TOP)** Right before leaving for an Armani event. *Armani blazer* • People watching, aka my favorite Parisian pastime. • Three A.M. room service game was strong.

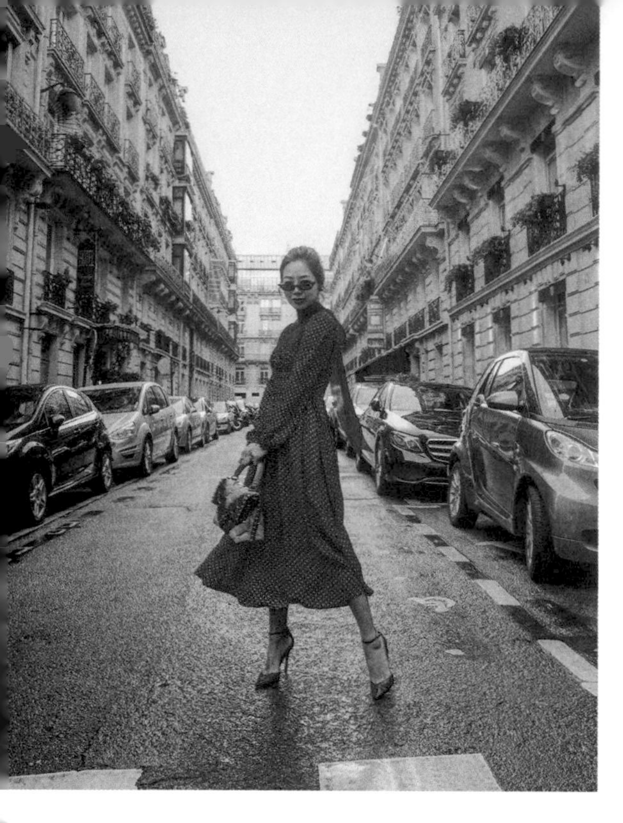

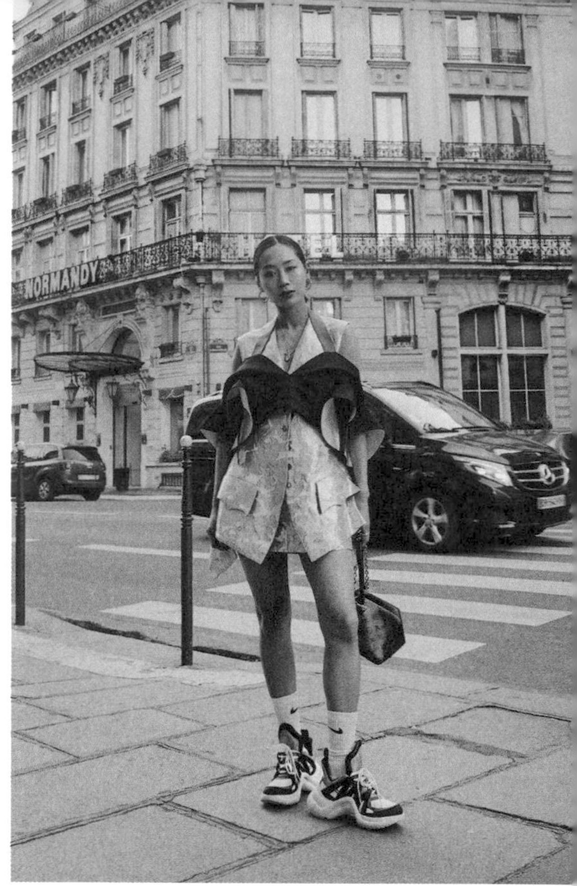
NORMANDY

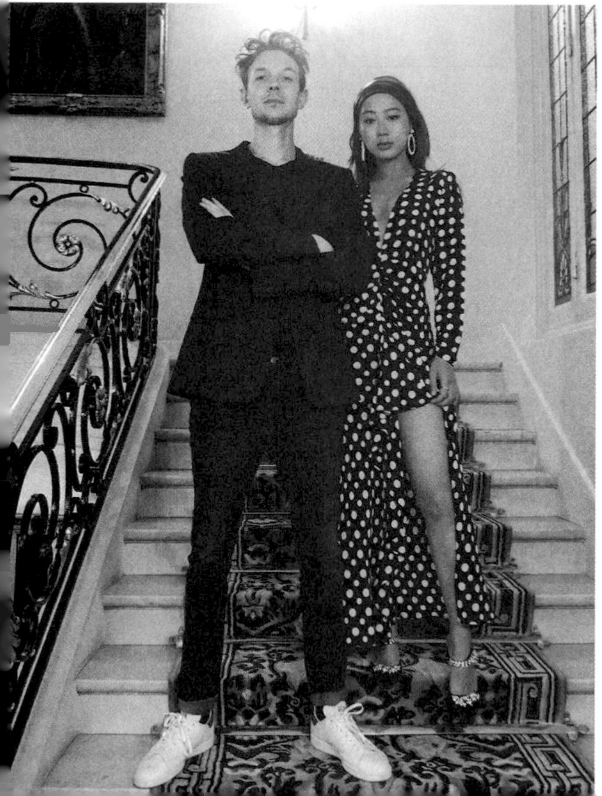

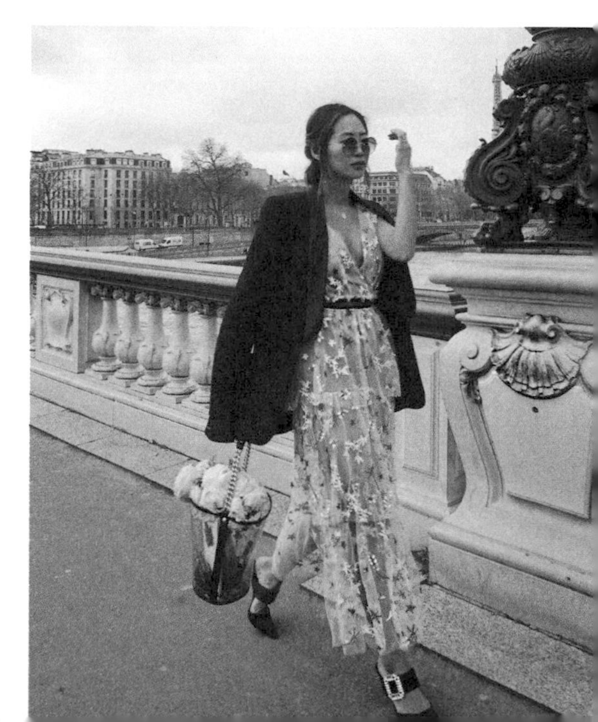

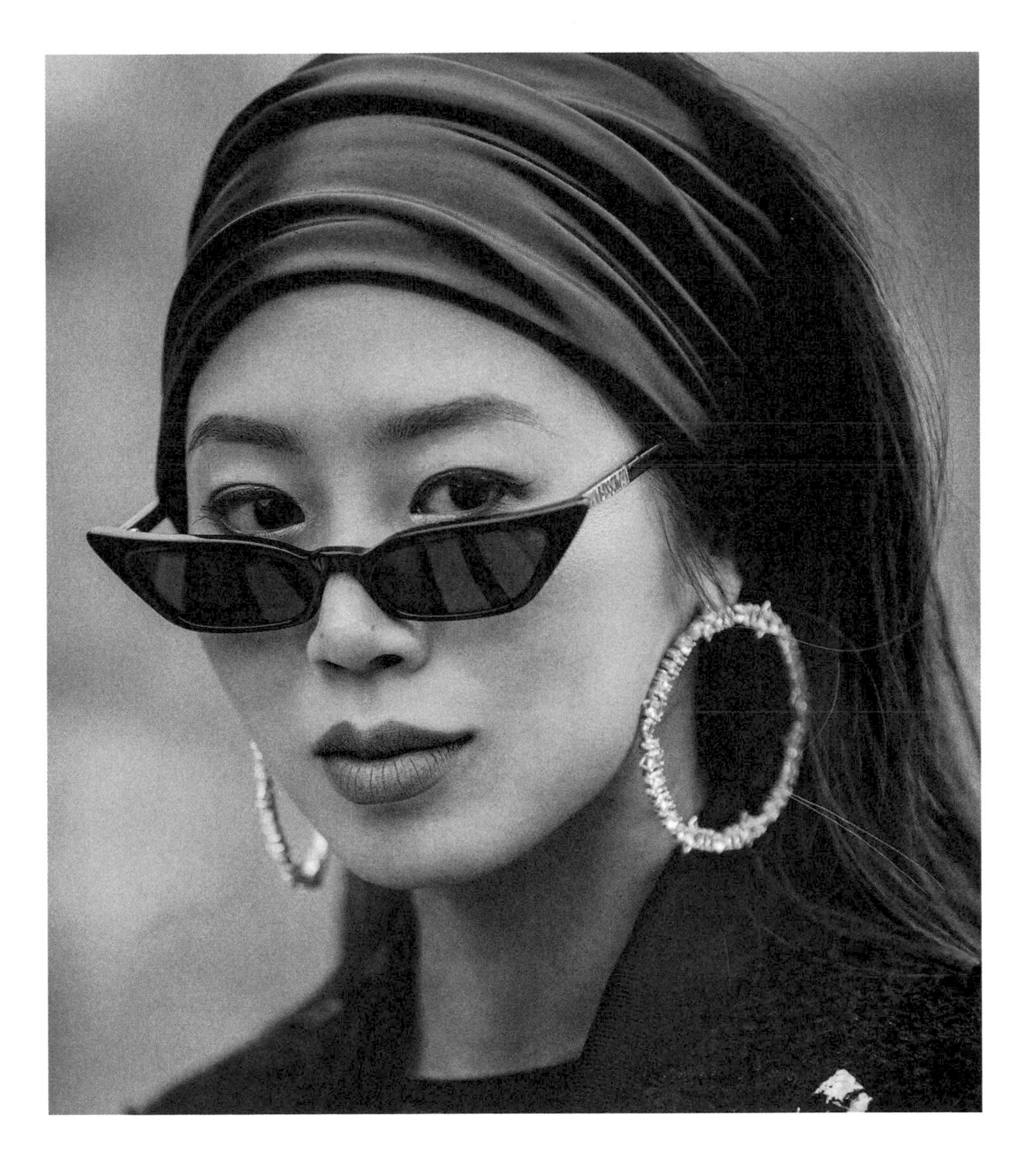

ABOVE This season my skin freaked out—these mini sunglasses from Poppy Lissiman made me feel more confident and somewhat protected. **OPPOSITE (CLOCKWISE FROM TOP LEFT)** *Poppy Lissman sunglasses; Valentino dress and bag; Stella Luna heels* • Right before the Louis Vuitton show at the Louvre. *Louis Vuitton head to toe* • Post-Chanel. *Black blazer and clear bucket bag by Chanel; Self-Portrait dress; Roger Vivier heels* • I was lucky enough to have my hair stylist Anh with me on this trip, and he gave me killer hair extensions—which I kept in for date night with Jacopo. #WhyNot.

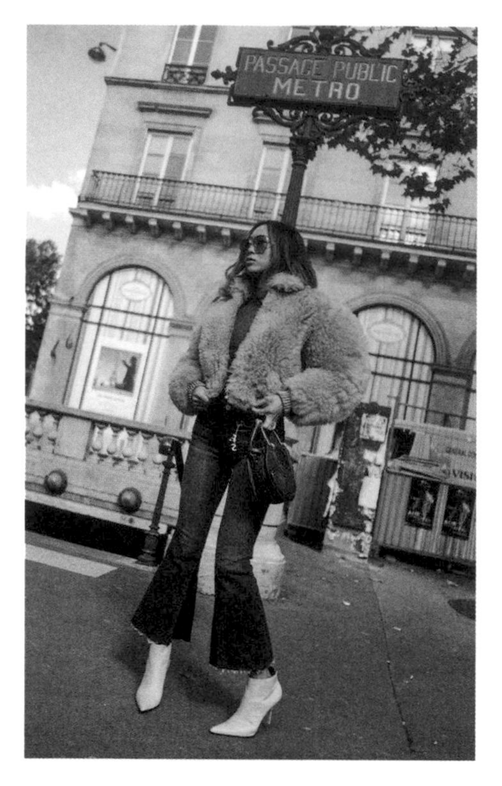

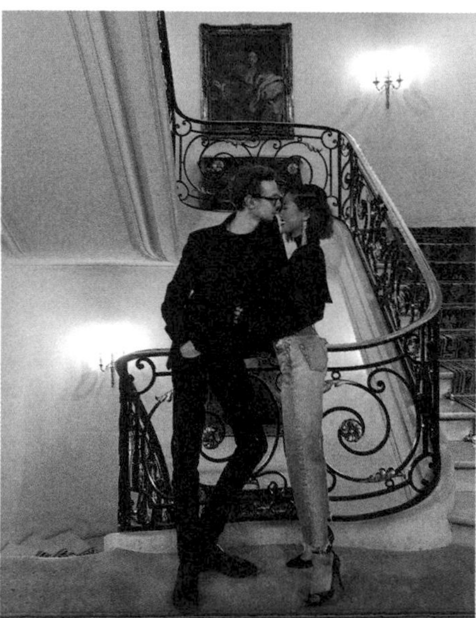

PARIS MUST-EATS

In addition to Paris's traditional delights, the city has a slew of vegan, Asian, and Italian options in beautiful settings that I happen to love. Bon appétit.

Pink Mamma
@bigmammagroup
bigmammagroup.com

James Bun
james-bun.com

Fragments
@fragmentsparis

Season
@seasonparis
season-paris.com

Peonies
@peoniesparis
peonies-paris.com

Soon
@restaurantsoon
restaurantsoon.com

Siseng
@siseng
siseng.fr

Jah Jah by Le Tricycle
@letricycle

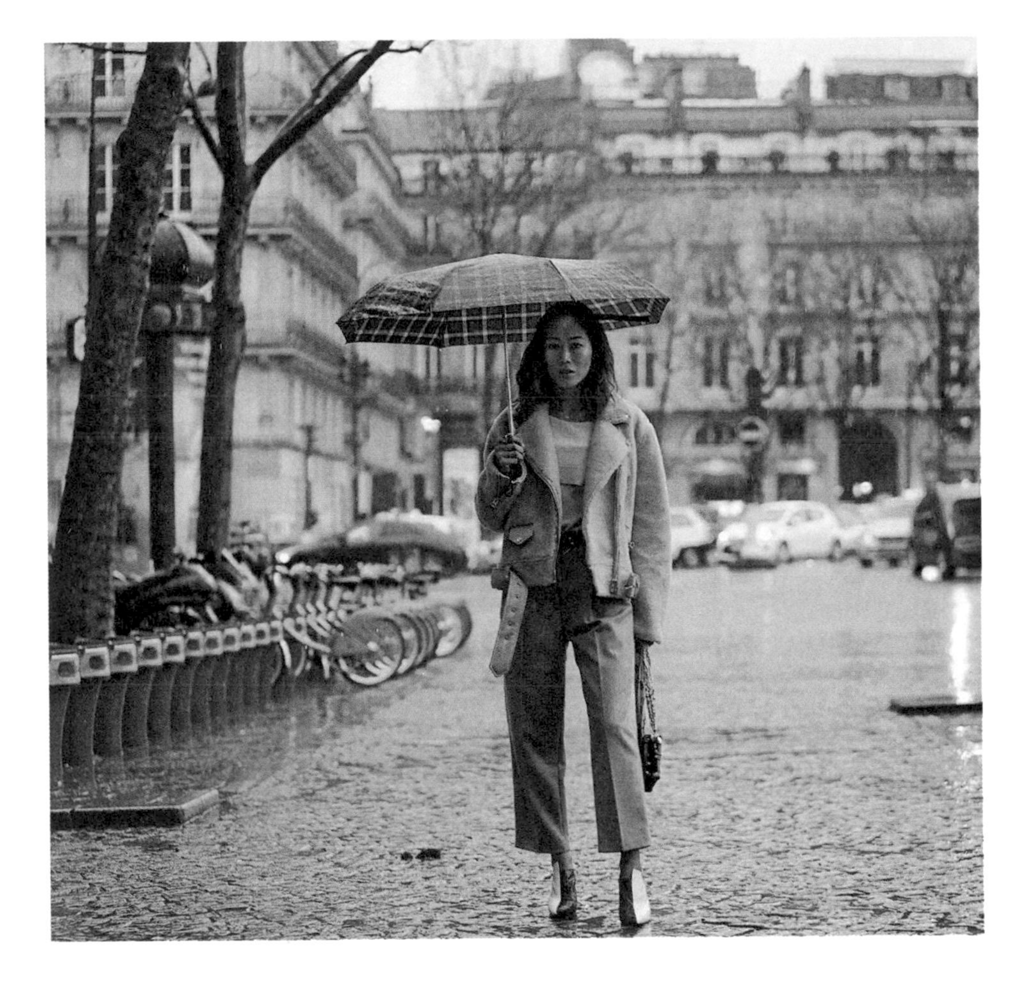

ABOVE The weather can be unpredictable in Paris. After the Acne Studios show in March 2017 it started to pour. I was already running around when the rain started, so I had to buy an umbrella from the first seller I saw. Right after this photo was snapped, the umbrella broke! Note to self: Always pack a sturdy travel umbrella and don't leave the hotel without it! *Acne Studios coat; Louis Vuitton bag; Elie Saab jewelry.* **OPPOSITE (FROM TOP)** At the Acne Studios Paris Fashion Week show yet again, only this time in September 2017. The weather was much better this season, but this day happened to be chilly. I broke out a teddy bear jacket, which happened to match the background and made for prime picture taking. I loved that my orange sweater matched the Paris Métro sign and that my shoes and jacket picked up the building facade, so I obviously had to stop for a photo—even though the show was starting in just a few minutes! *Acne Studios jacket* • I love when Jacopo gets to join me during Paris Fashion Week. This is us at our hotel, the Hôtel Plaza Athénée.

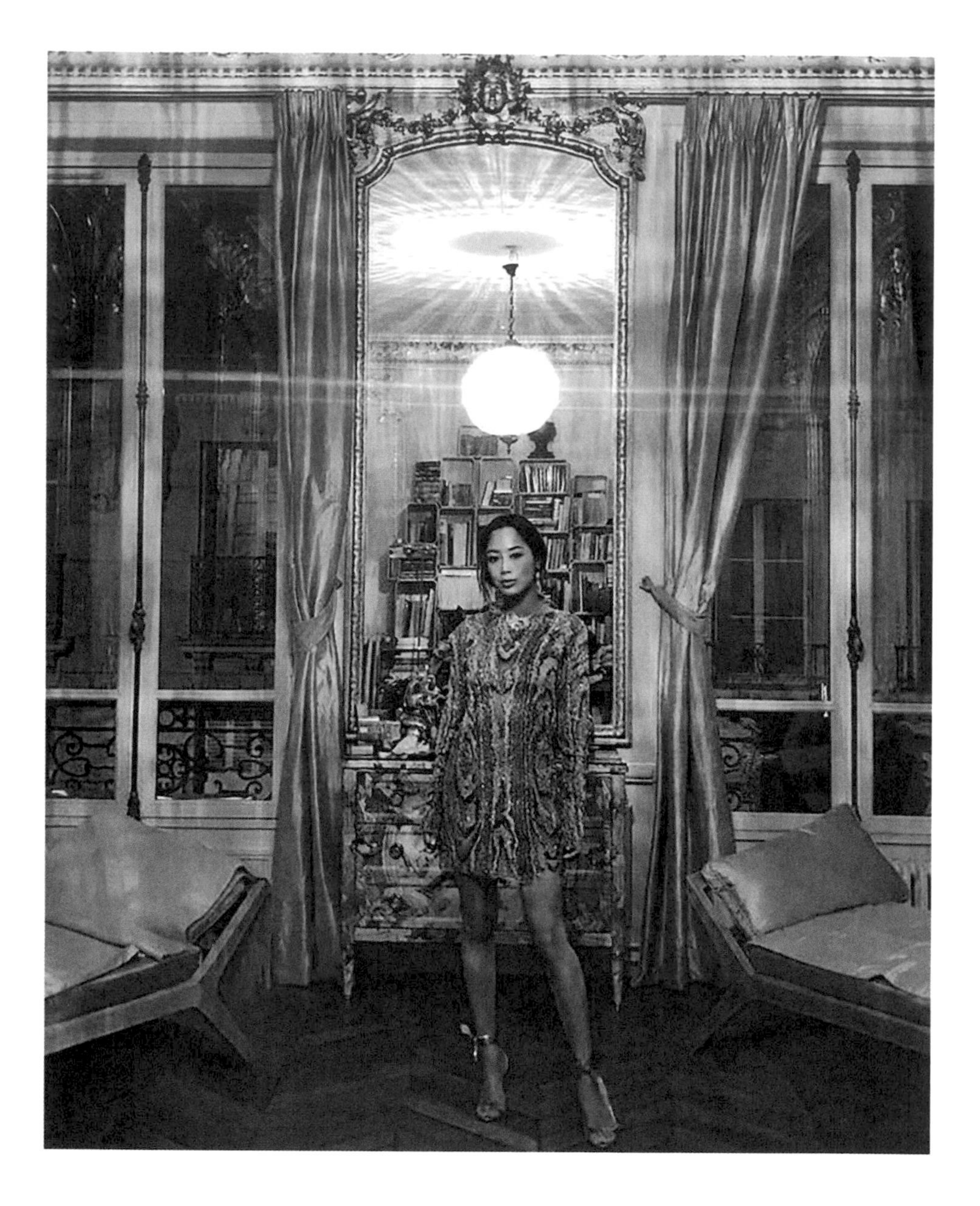

My beloved Airbnb in the sixth arrondissement. There is just something about the light in Paris that isn't like anywhere else, and I believe that one must always take full advantage of good lighting when it presents itself.

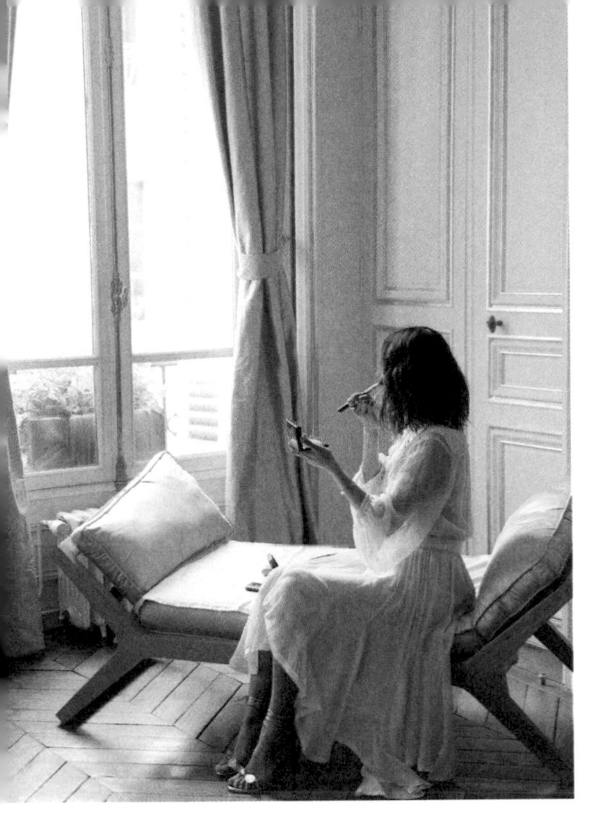

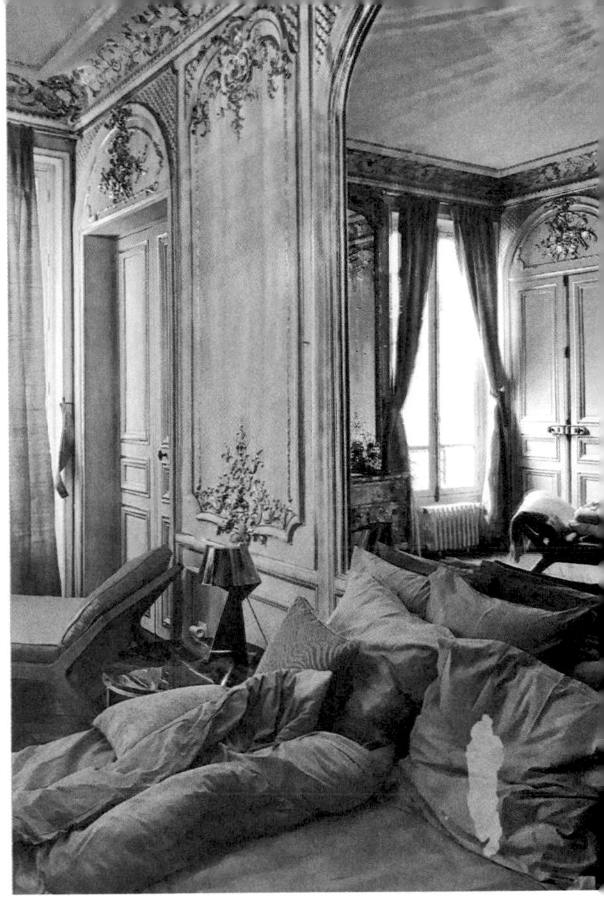

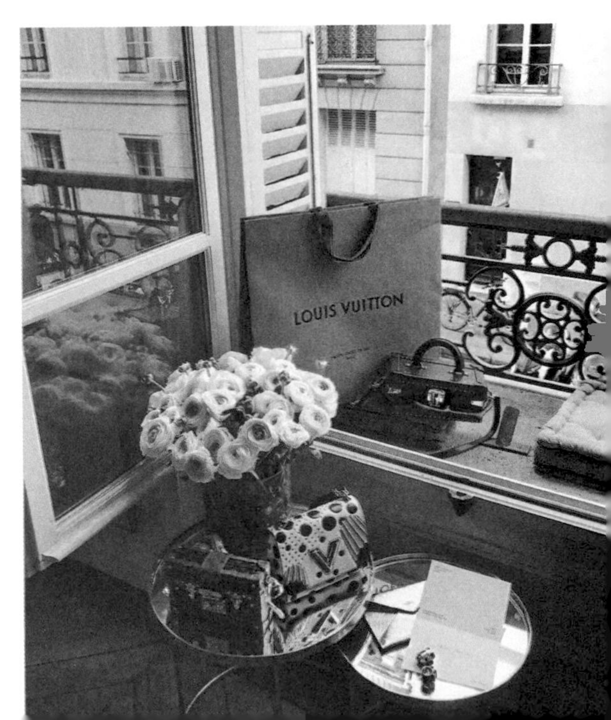
LOUIS VUITTON

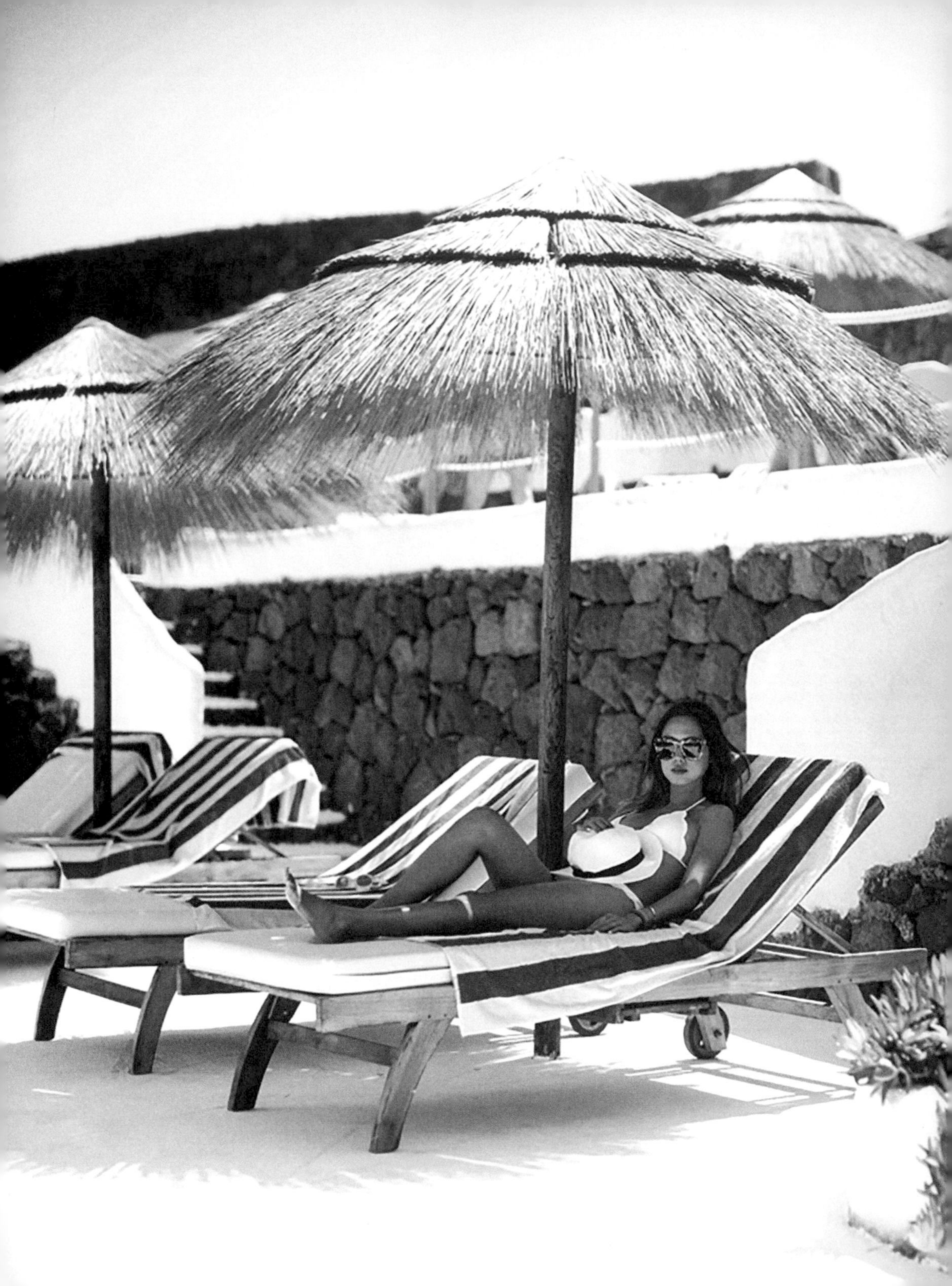

SICILY

In 2014 Dani and I went to Sicily. And to this day, we've never fought as hard and as much as we did on this trip. I'm not going to even pretend to remember what we fought about, but I know there was a good few-hour period where we gave each other the silent treatment. That is, until we rode ATVs to a volcano and Dani had to hold on to me for dear life. By the time we got to where we were going, our surroundings were so gorgeous that we forgot about the fight and acted like nothing had ever happened.

OPPOSITE We stayed at a beautiful, relaxing resort called Therasia. *Marysia Swim swimsuit.*

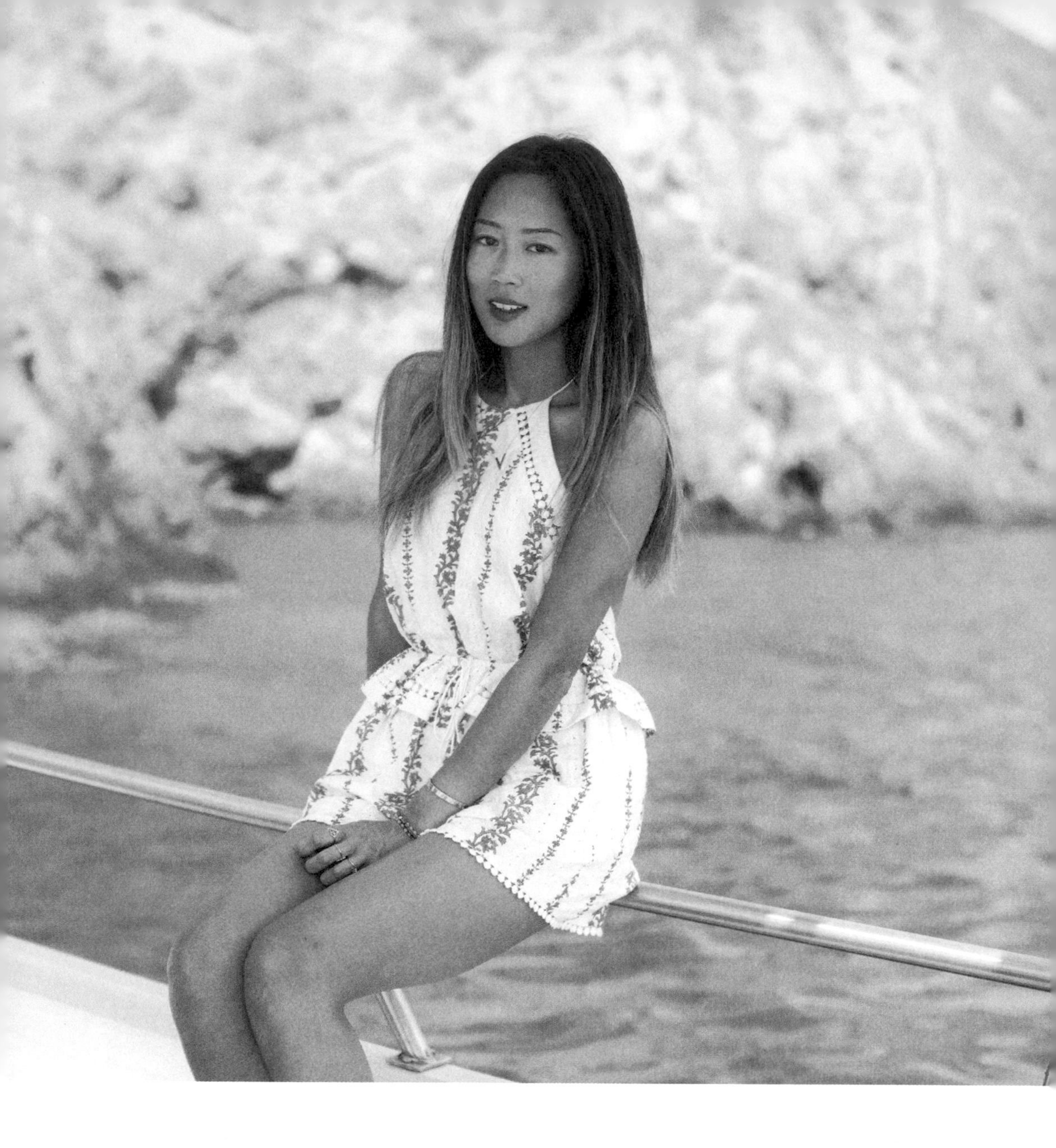

ABOVE *Zimmermann romper.* **OPPOSITE (FROM TOP)** Dani and I rented bikes, explored, and found a random stranger who proposed to me (I politely declined). Dani had braided my hair earlier in the day and things seemed to be chill between us—until we rode up the hill and got into another fight. This photo is pre-fight. *Zimmermann romper* • The scene of the proposal, which occurred as this photo was being snapped.

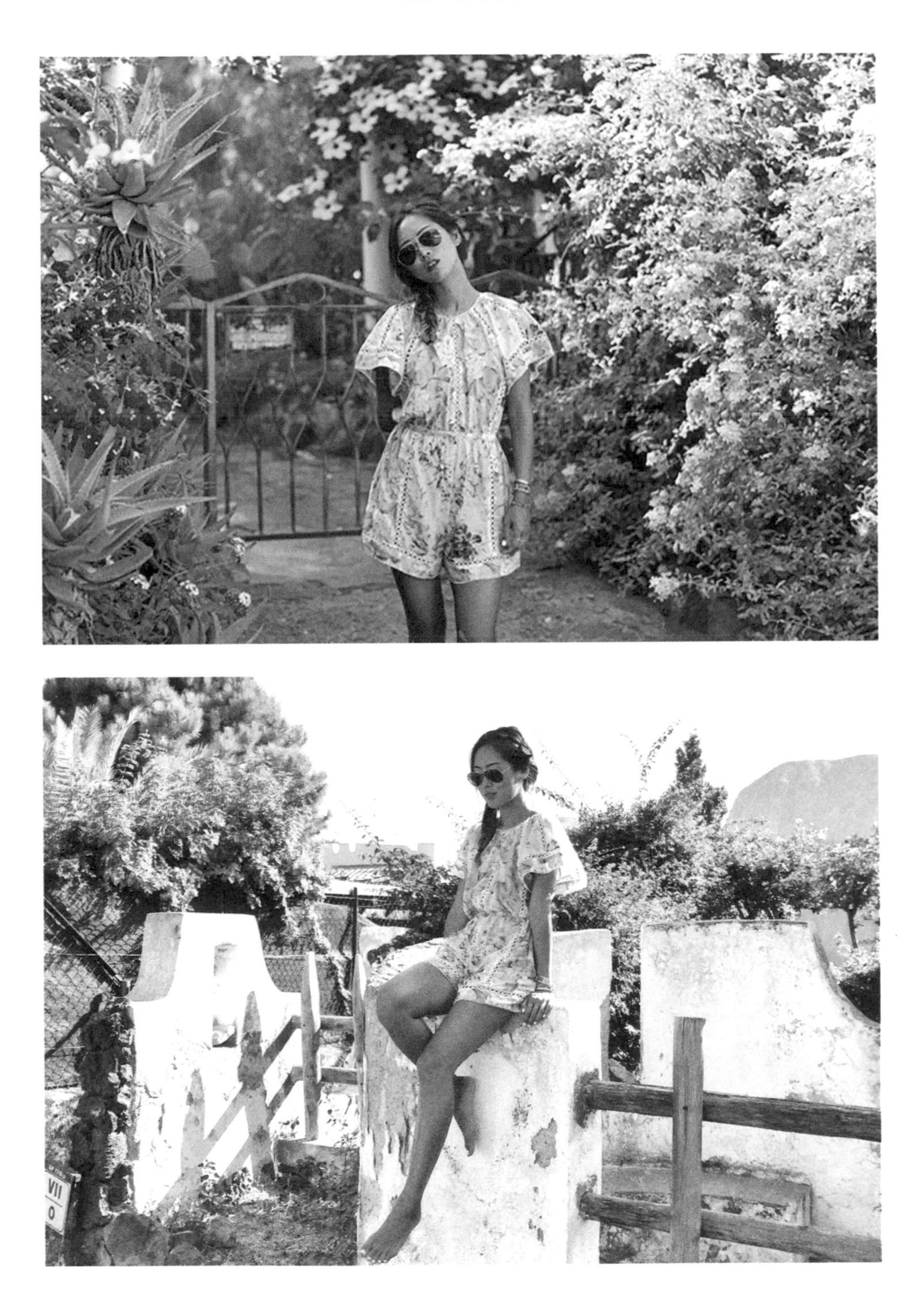

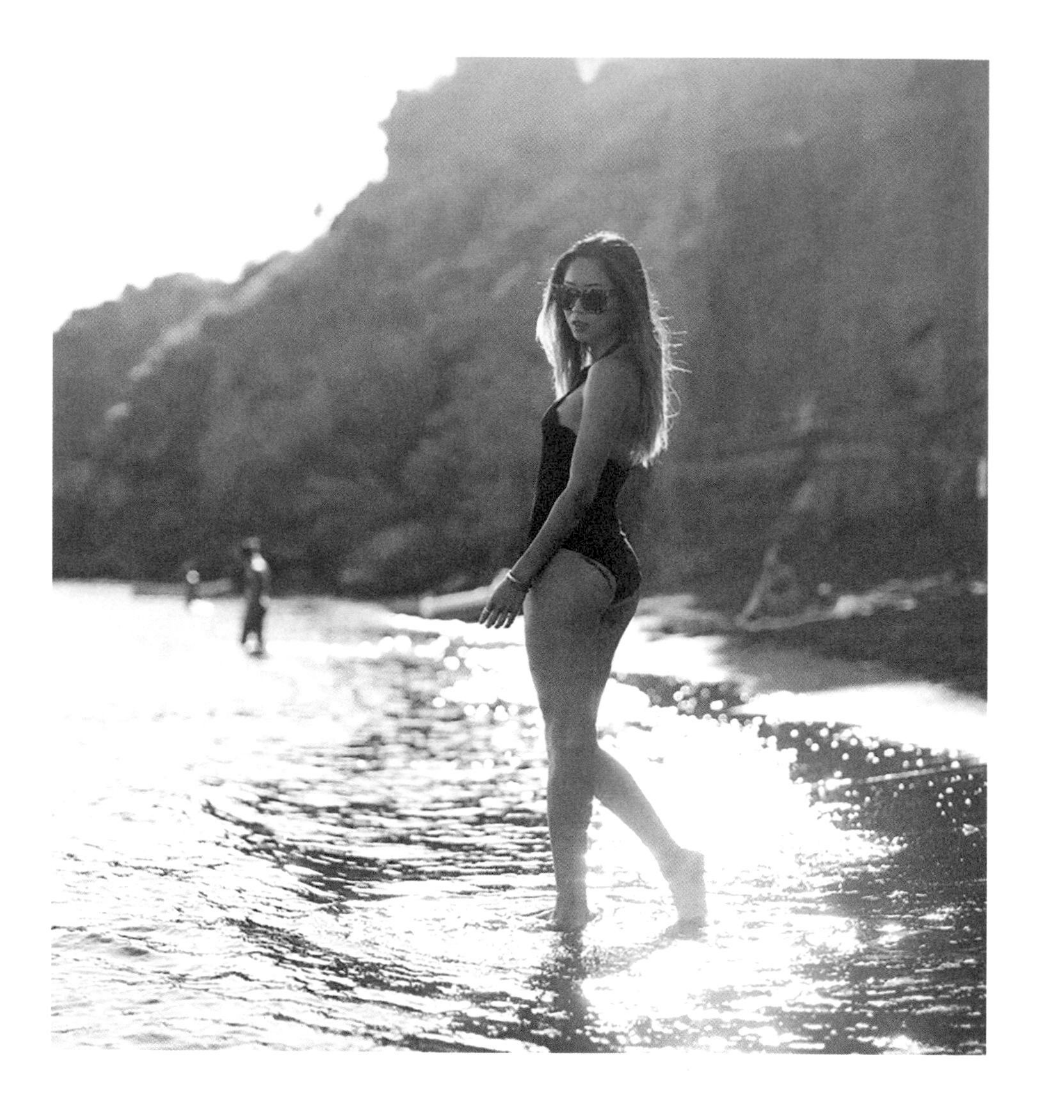

ABOVE AND OPPOSITE, TOP At the black sand beach, called Spiaggia dell'Asino, in a black bathing suit by Marysia Swim (I planned that). **OPPOSITE, BOTTOM RIGHT** At the resort, we wanted to do something touristy—but there weren't a ton of typical touristy things to do because the island is so small. So we rented a small boat that happened to have a couple aboard, and I got stung by something sinister while we were out to sea. Studies show that the acetic acid in lemon sooths the pain from jellyfish stings, a fact that—lucky for me—our captain knew when he poured lemon water on my sting and left me feeling good as new. *Seafolly swimsuit.* **OPPOSITE, BOTTOM LEFT** My James Bond–girl moment at the cliffs.

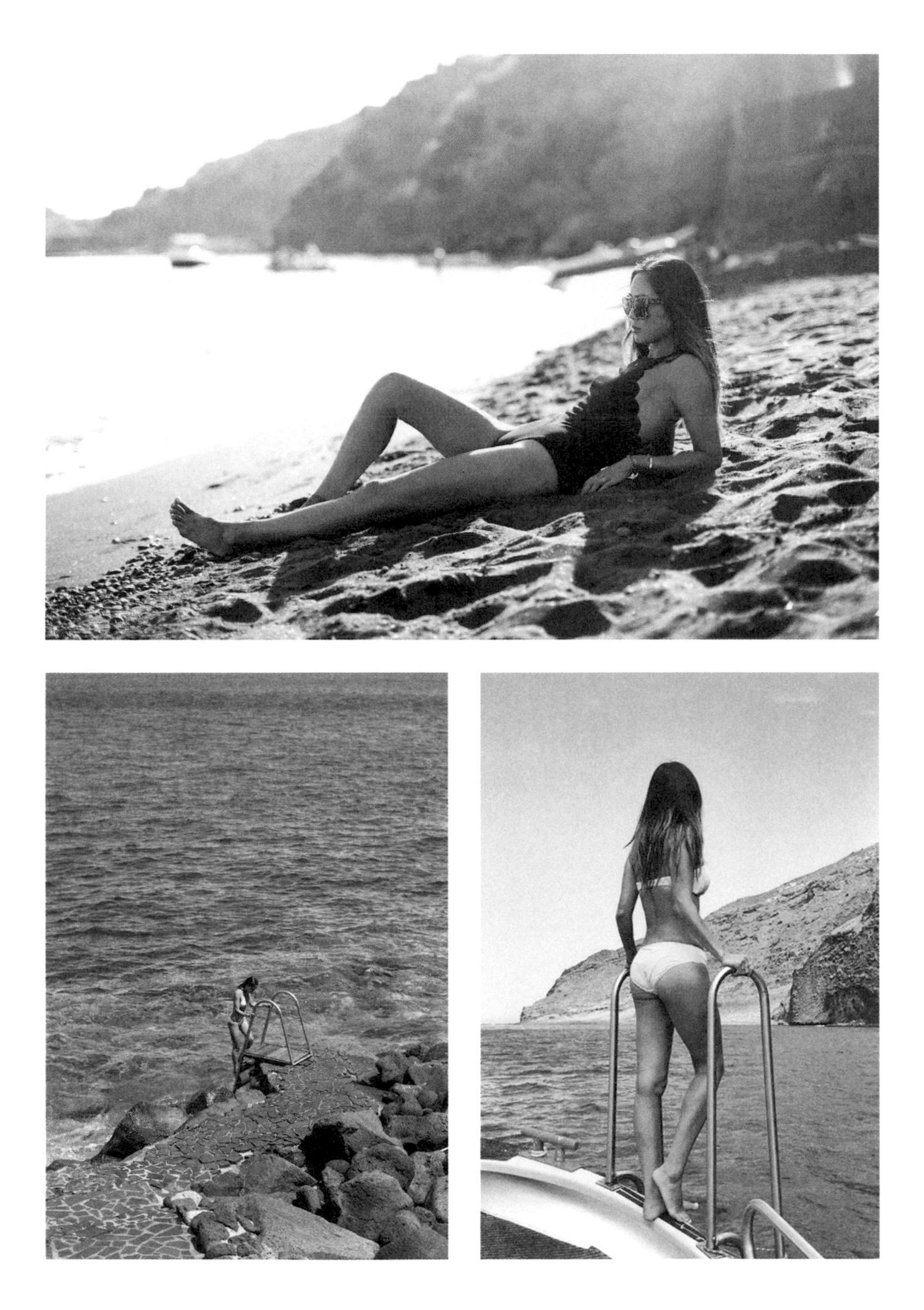

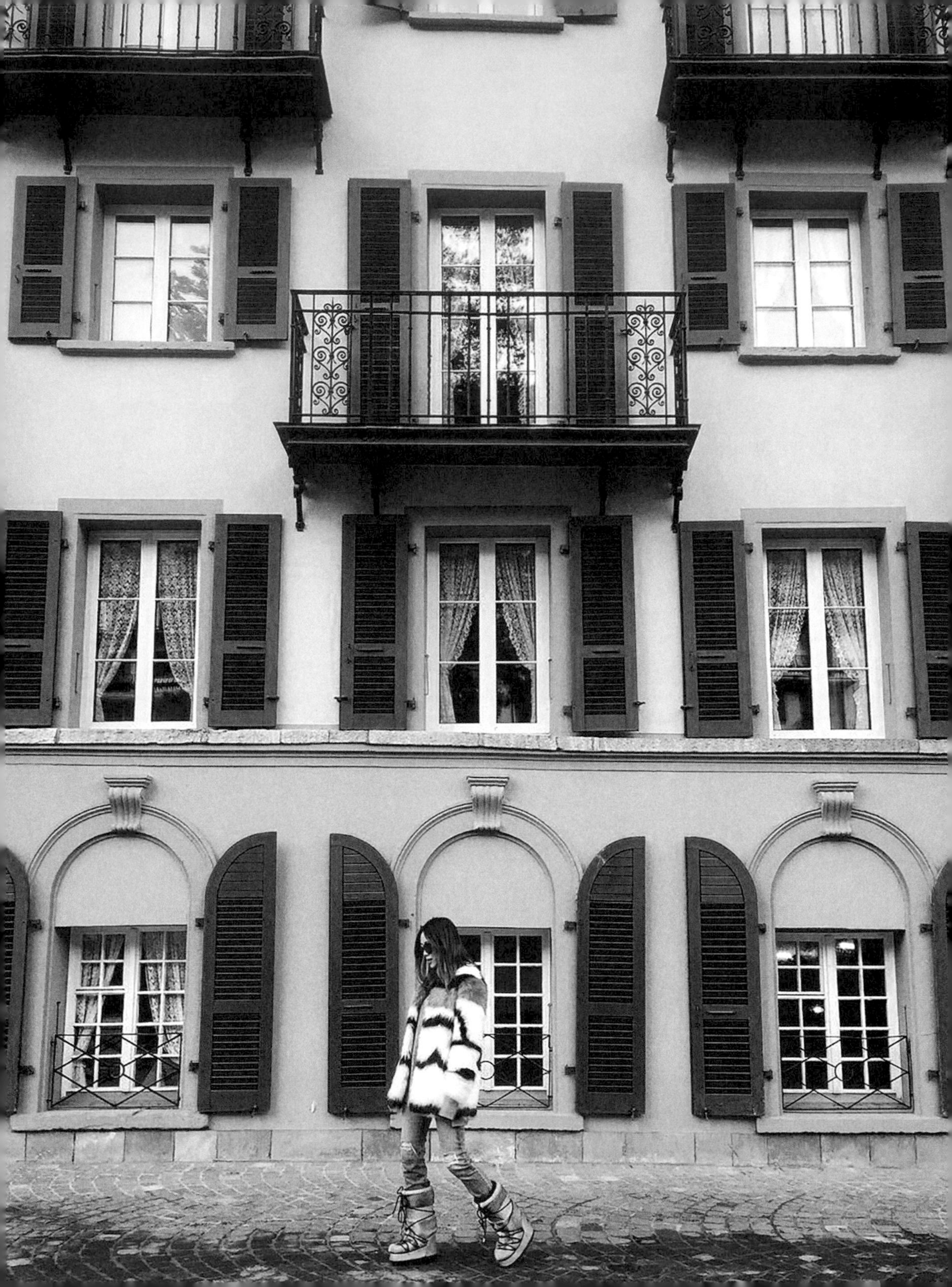

SWITZERLAND

Though I very much appreciate sweater weather, I'm not typically a cold-weather girl. I love the freedom that the mild Los Angeles weather brings and how easy it is to gallery hop, eat lunch in a beautiful courtyard, and see flowers blooming in the middle of winter. And when I travel, it's usually to warm-weather destinations. So I was excited and also somewhat nervous to go to Zermatt, Switzerland, in November 2015 to shoot a digital campaign with Jimmy Choo. The backdrop of the small Alpine village—which is home to the actual Matterhorn on which my favorite Disney ride is based—was nothing short of spectacular. Outside the clean, crisp air and the scenery, one of my favorite things about Zermatt was the town's commitment to ecofriendly transportation. The village has been car-free for years, with residents getting from points A to B via horse-drawn carriage—a method of public transportation that still exists today. More common than the horses, however, is the town's stable of electric buses, which are built at a family-owned workshop in southern France's Rhône Valley. Places such as Zermatt that are working to preserve their clean air and quality of life for future generations inspire not only hope but action at home. I loved seeing the innovation coming out of this small village.

OPPOSITE *Jimmy Choo boots.*

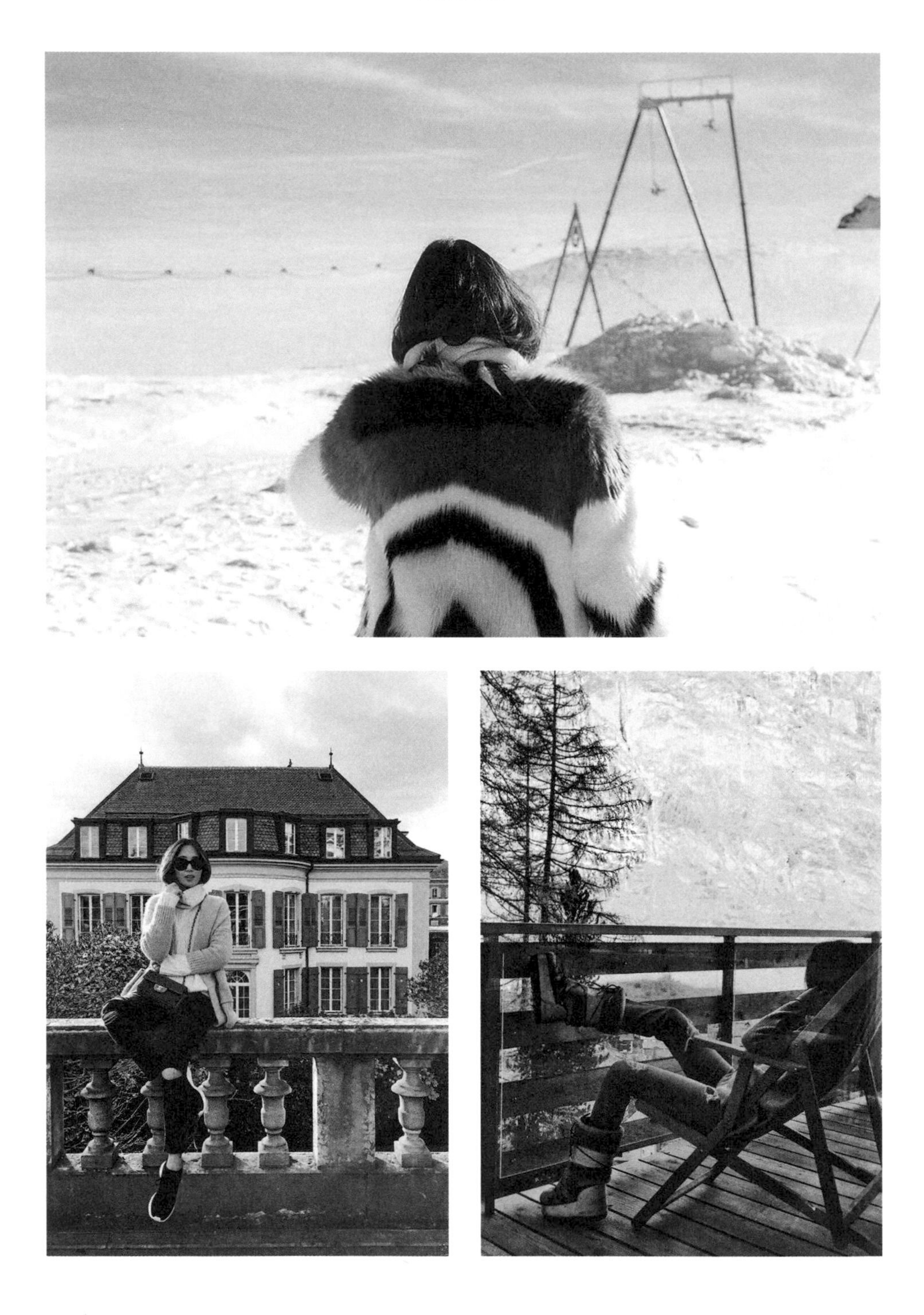

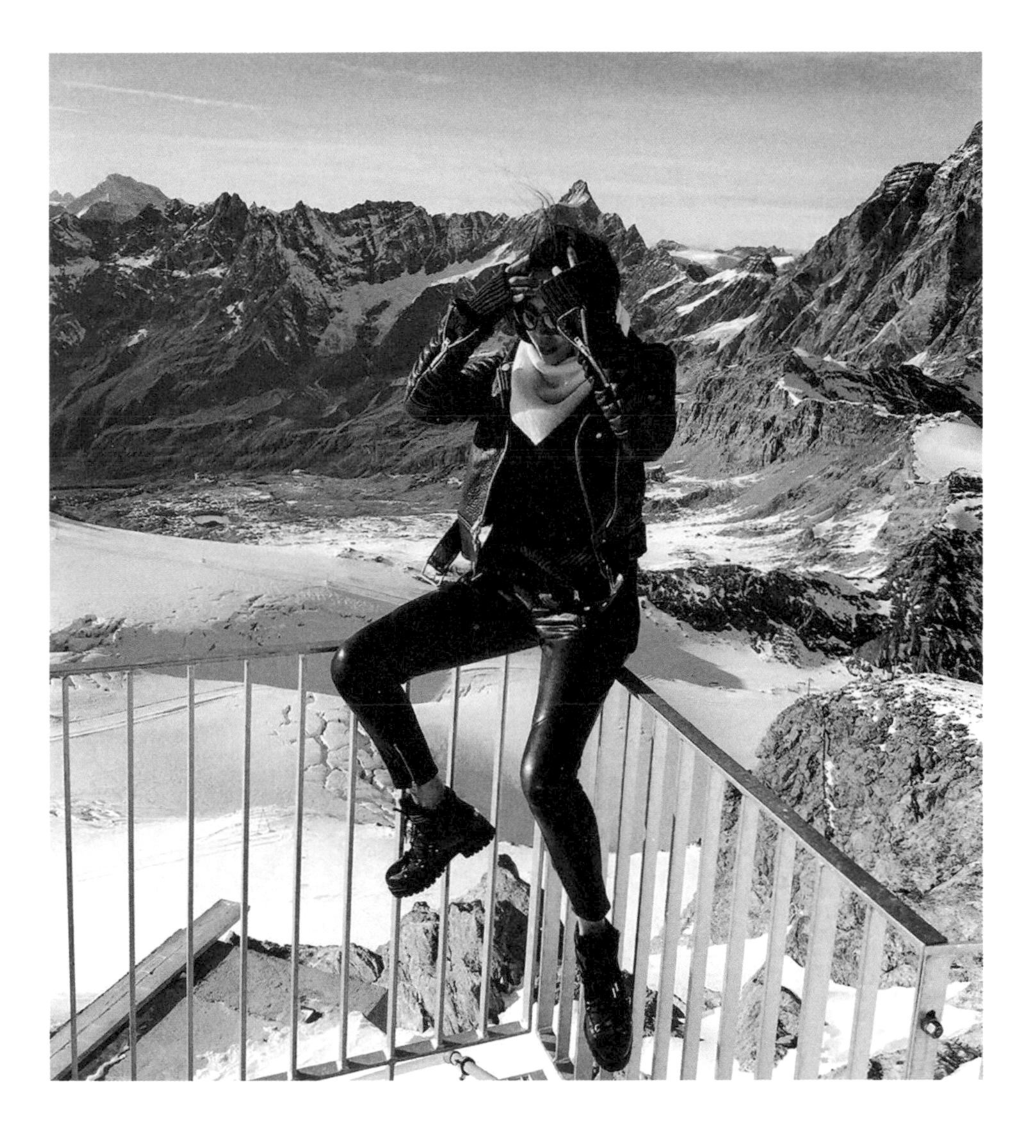

ABOVE This balcony was off the hair-and-makeup room at the chalet where we were shooting (yes, really—talk about #officeview). *The Arrivals leather jacket; J Brand leather pants; Jimmy Choo shoes.* **OPPOSITE (CLOCKWISE FROM TOP)** This is the day of the Jimmy Choo shoot. There were some other girls shooting content as well, so while they were working I went outside in the cold and, surprisingly, survived. *Scotch and Soda faux fur jacket* • On the balcony off my hotel room. *Jimmy Choo boots* • We had to fly into London before Zermatt, and this is my travel outfit for that leg of the journey. *J Brand jeans; Nike shoes.*

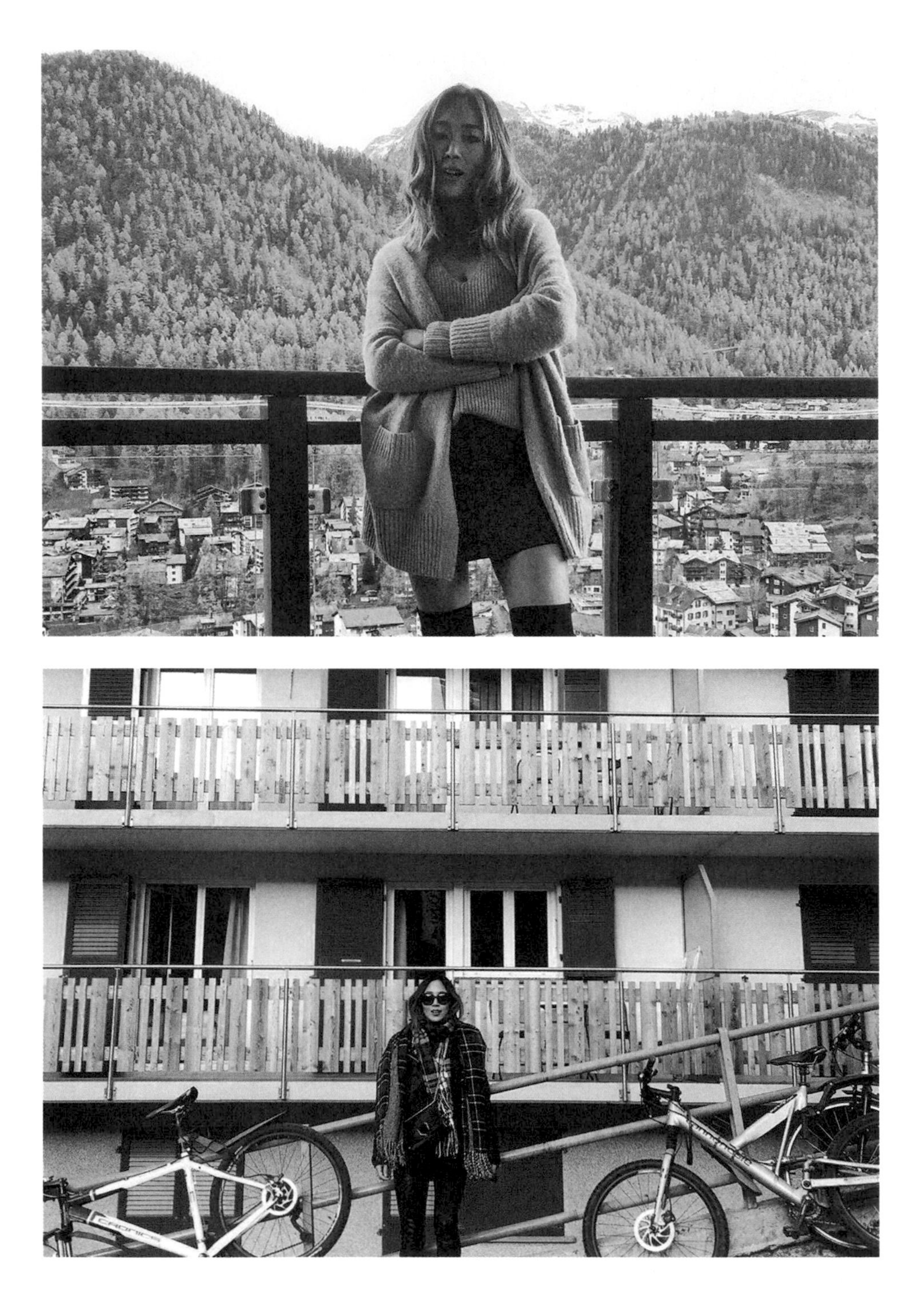

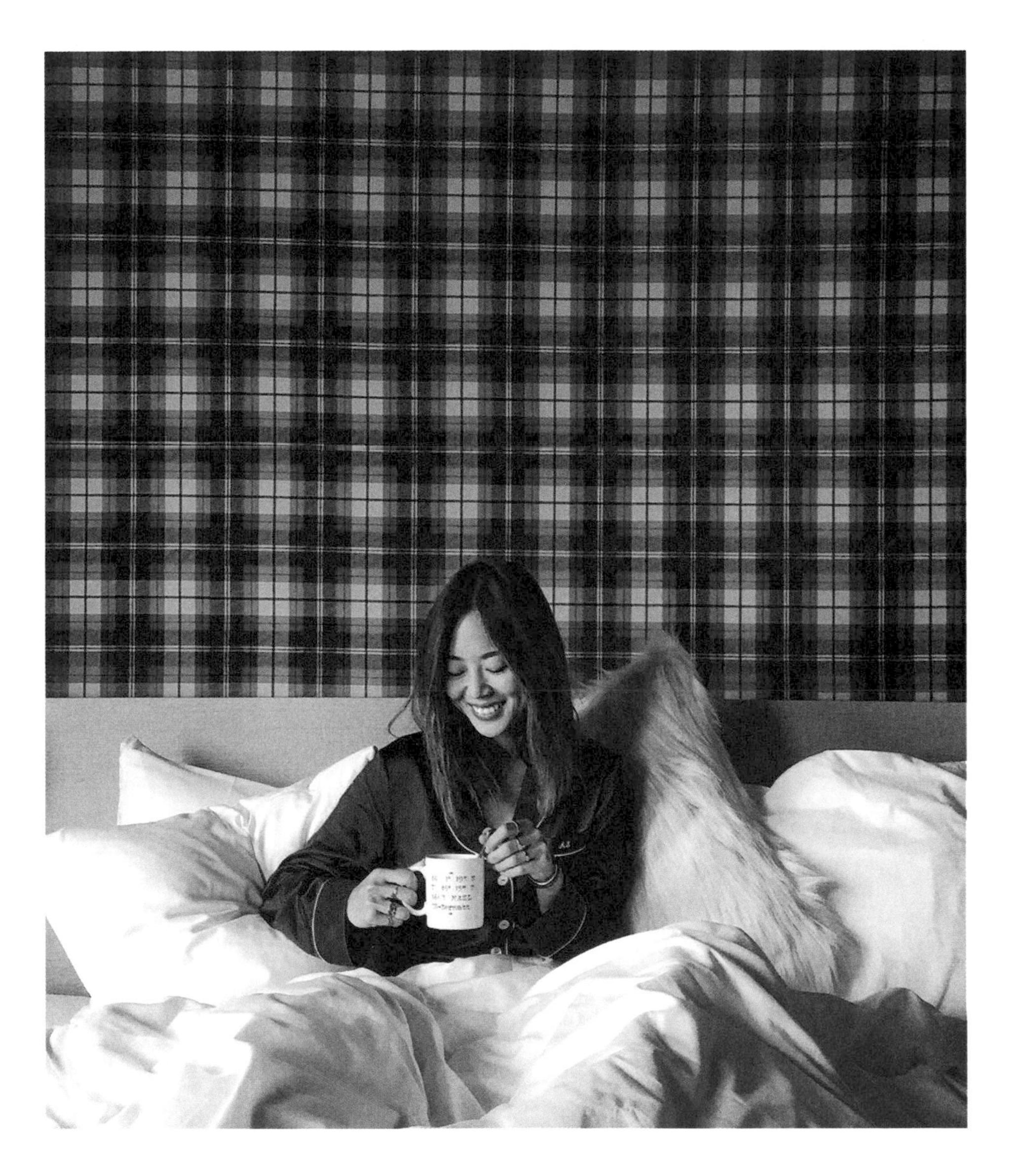

ABOVE At the hotel. The Jimmy Choo team got us pajamas from Olivia von Halle with our initials, which I still wear. **OPPOSITE (FROM TOP)** We shot at two locations: on the mountain and at a gorgeous chalet. This is the latter. *Vince sweater; Zara cardigan* • The day after the shoot, walking around Zermatt. It's such a small town, so I walked a ton—and yes, I'm wearing two scarves because it was so cold (blame my thin Cali blood).

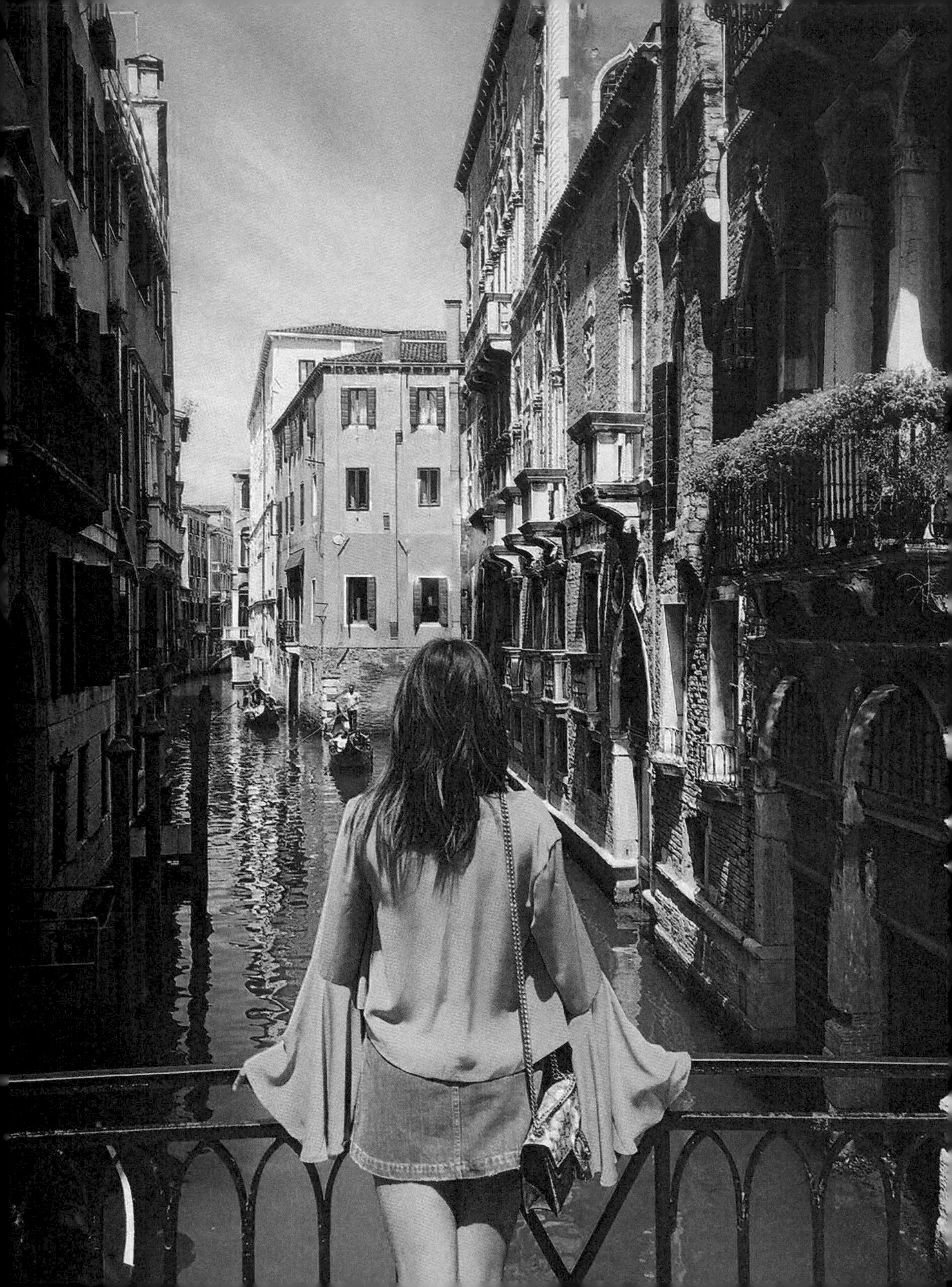

VENICE

I'd wanted to go to Venice forever because my dad had a painting of the canal-lined city in his office when I was a kid, and I always dreamed of going there with someone special so I could have a romantic time. And I got my wish in June 2016, when Jacopo and I were able to take a week-long holiday for fun after Milan. We took a two-and-a-half-hour train ride there (which of course bored me to tears, so I made Jacopo film a YouTube tutorial for me to pass the time). It was romantic and then some—there was beauty at every turn (not to mention insane history), and I can't imagine having spent my first time there without Jacopo by my side. It was all much better than the painting and proved yet again that you can indeed manifest most anything you want.

OPPOSITE *C/MEO top; Topshop skirt; Gucci bag.*

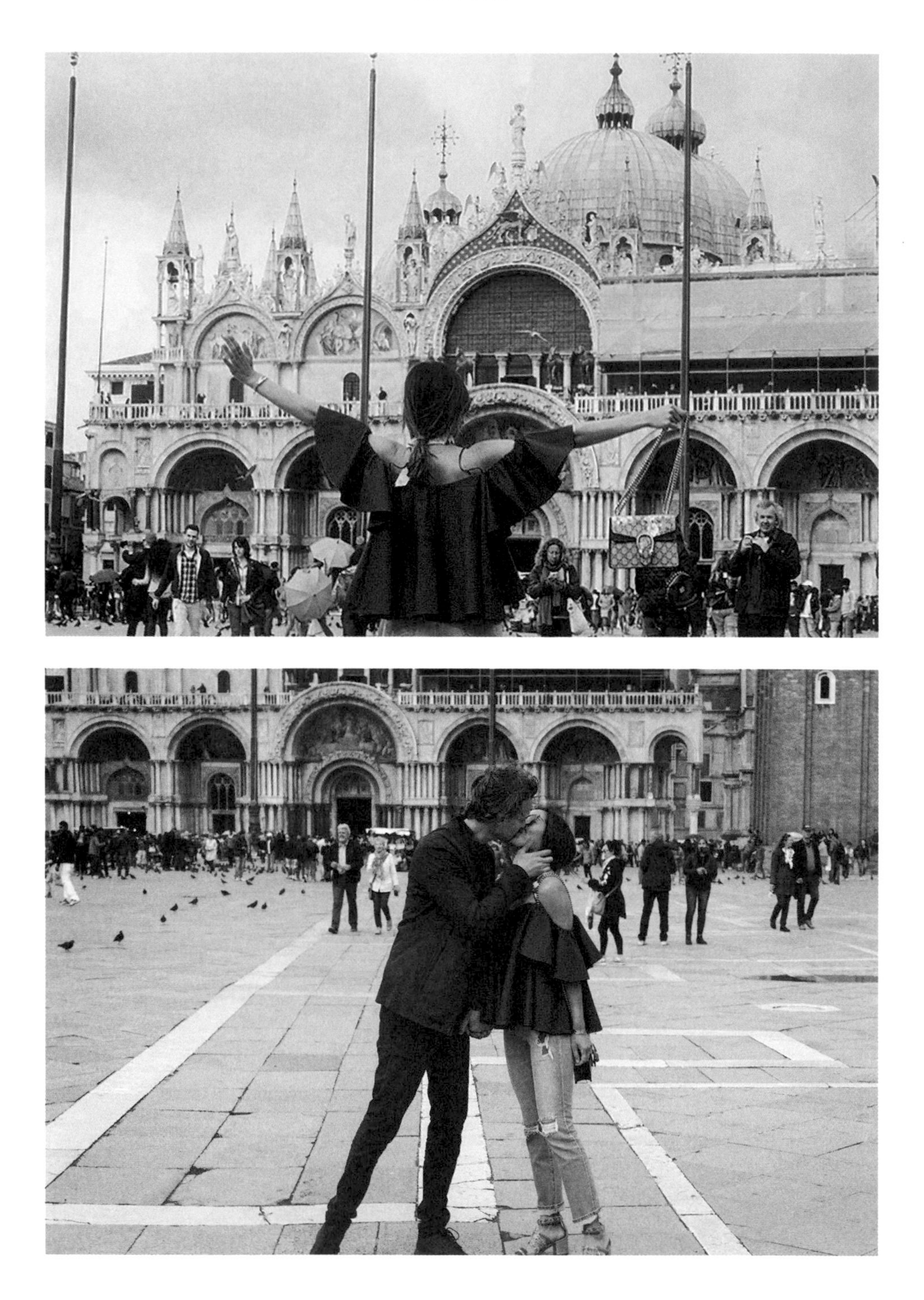

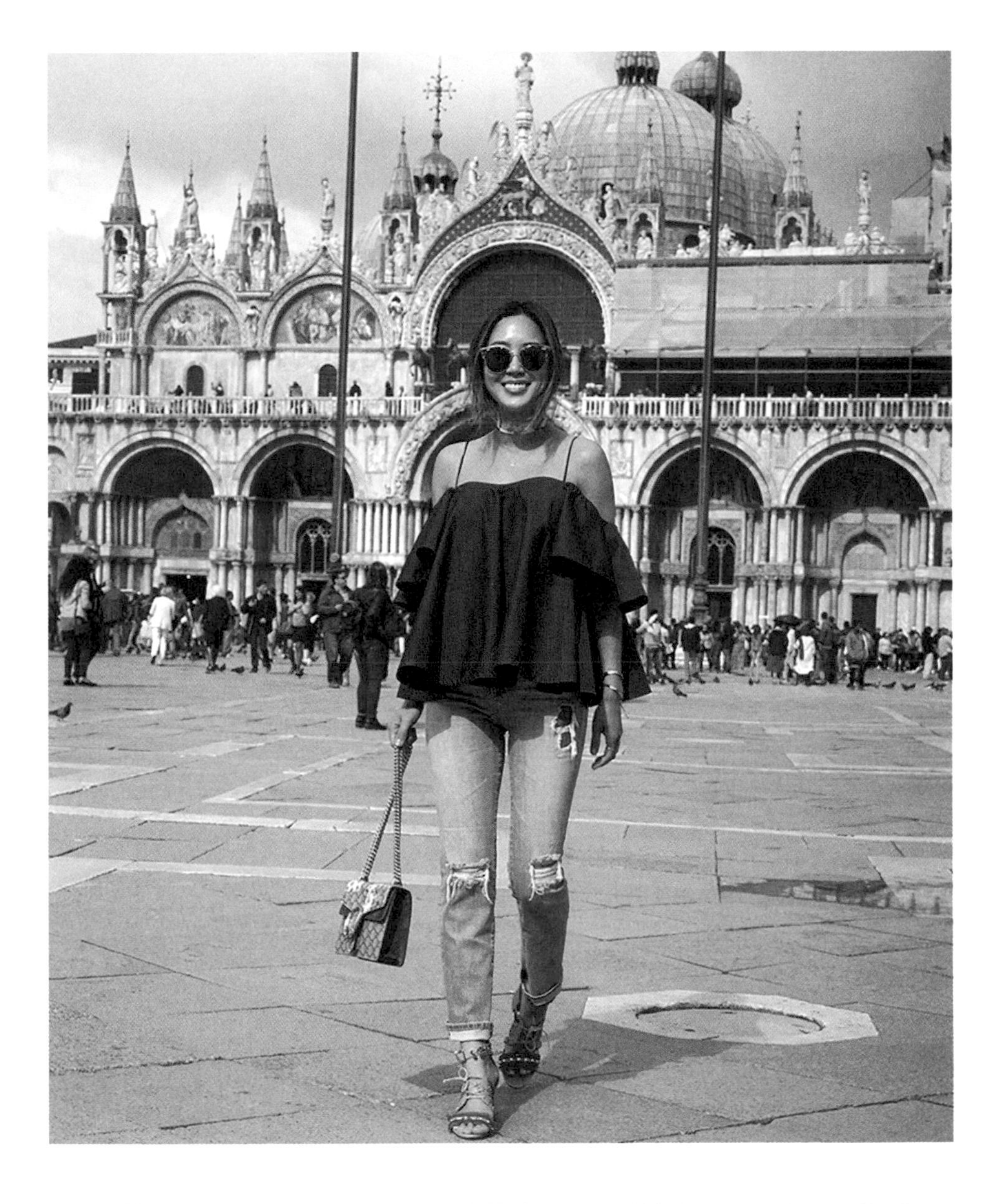

Being present and soaking up every ounce of the Venetian magic I was experiencing. Jacopo was shooting my solo shots, of course, and I asked a very kind tourist to capture one of us together—which she did in the most perfect way. *Anna October top; AG Jeans; Gucci bag; Schutz sandals.*

MUST-SEE MUSEUMS AROUND THE WORLD

One of my favorite things to do when I'm traveling is visit a museum (or three). I've always loved art, and seeing it in person leaves me with new knowledge and inspiration—two things I can always get behind. These are some of my trusty favorites around the globe, and they never get old.

ANTWERP

MoMu
@momuantwerp
momu.be

The Royal Museum of Fine Arts
@fineartsbelgium
kmska.be

LOS ANGELES

The Broad
@thebroadmuseum
thebroad.org

Hammer Museum
@hammer_museum
hammer.ucla.edu

Los Angeles County Museum of Art (LACMA)
@lacma
lacma.org

Norton Simon Museum
@nortonsimon
nortonsimon.org

NEW YORK

The Met
@metmuseum
metmuseum.org

MoMA
@themuseumofmodernart
moma.org

New Museum
@newmuseum
newmuseum.org

NICE/SOUTH OF FRANCE

Fondation Maeght
www.fondation-maeght.com/en/

Musée Masséna
nice.fr/fr/culture/musees-et-galeries/
musee-massena-le-musee

PARIS

The Louvre
@museelouvre
louvre.fr

Musée d'Orsay
@museeorsay
musee-orsay.fr

Musée Picasso
@museepicassoparis
museepicassoparis.fr

Petit Palais
@petitpalais_musee
petitpalais.paris.fr

SAN FRANCISCO

The Contemporary Jewish Museum
@jewseum
thecjm.org

de Young Museum
@deyoungmuseum
deyoung.famsf.org

SEOUL

Korea Furniture Museum
@koreafurnituremuseum
kofum.com

Leeum, Samsung Museum of Art
@leeum_official
leeum.samsungfoundation.org

VENICE

Doge's Palace
@visitmuve
palazzoducale.visitmuve.it

Palazzo Grassi
@palazzo_grassi
palazzograssi.it

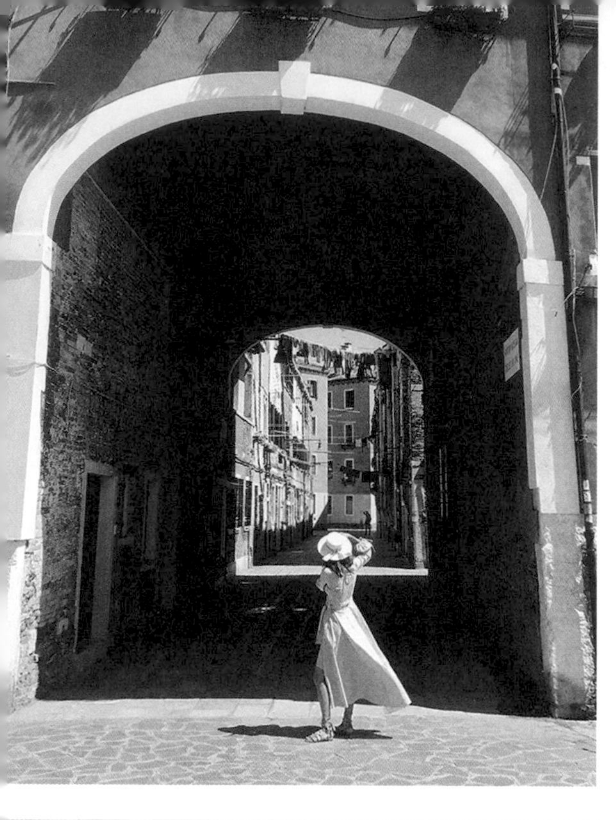

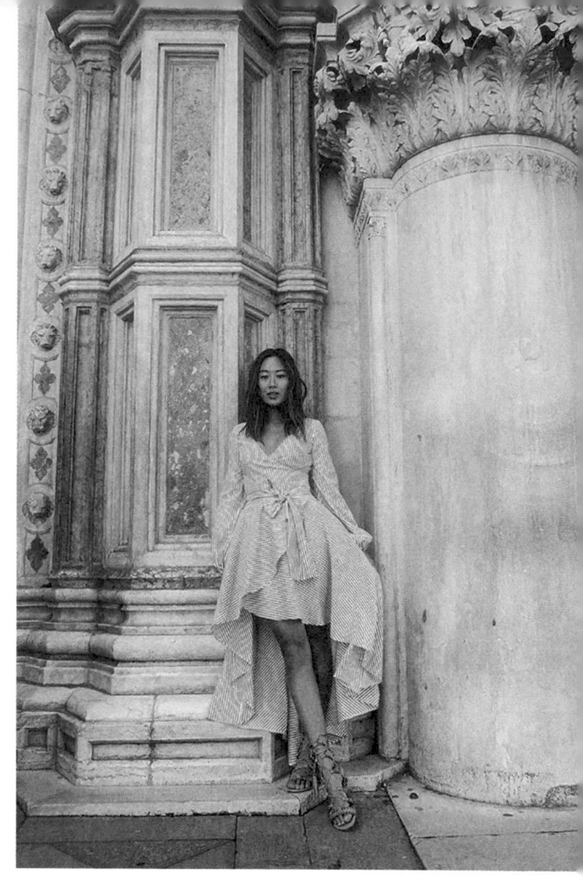

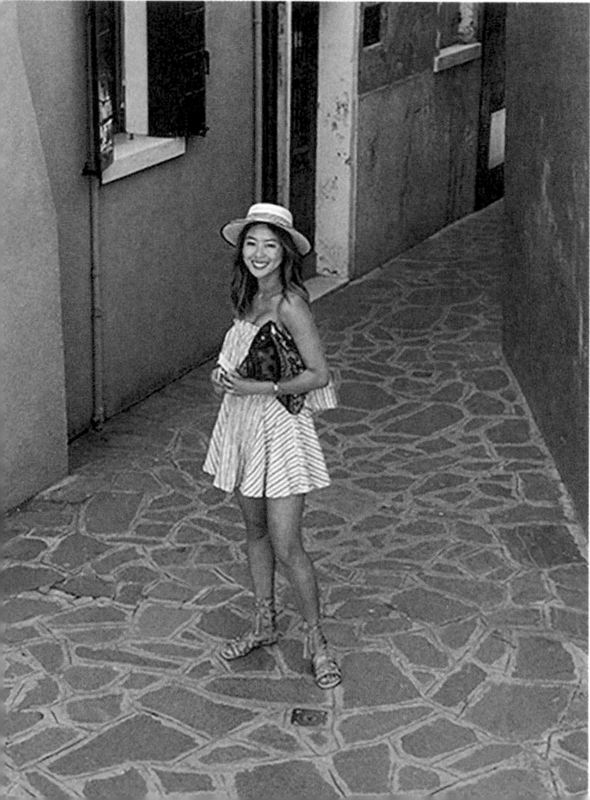

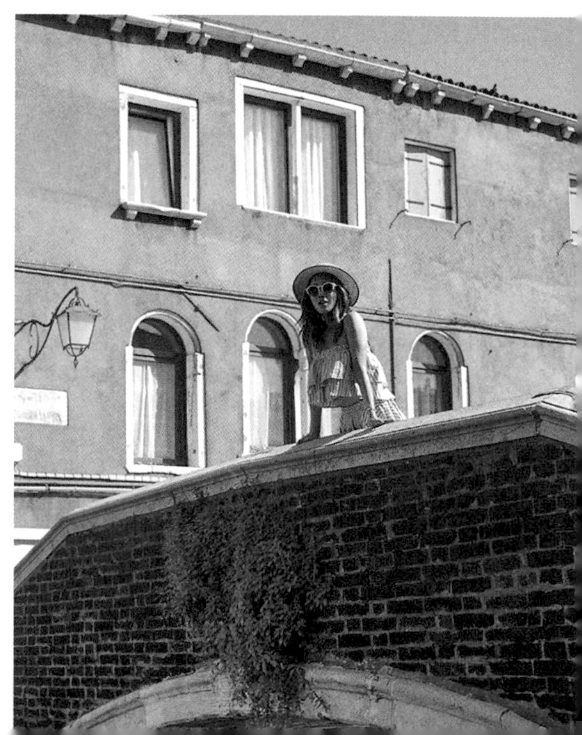

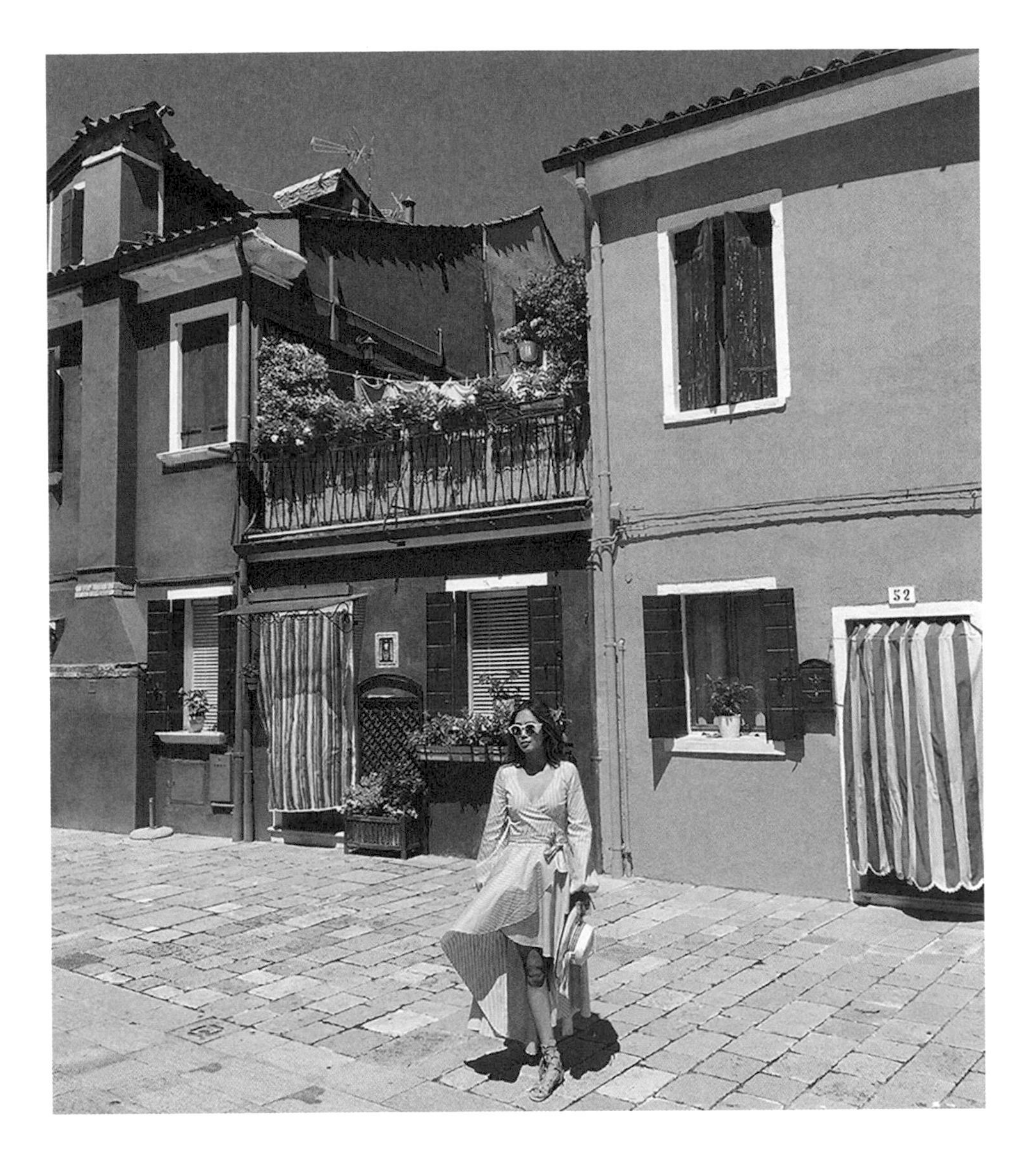

ABOVE AND OPPOSITE, TOP ROW *Caroline Constas dress.* **OPPOSITE, BOTTOM RIGHT** Outside of the city lie two towns—Burano and Murano—and we explored them both. We took a taxi boat there and ended up eating two meals at the same restaurant in Burano because the octopus and squid-ink spaghetti was so bomb. *Privacy Please top and bottom.* **OPPOSITE, BOTTOM LEFT** I picked up this hat from a street vendor because it matched my outfit (which was dreamy, if I do say so myself) and I have since worn it to death.

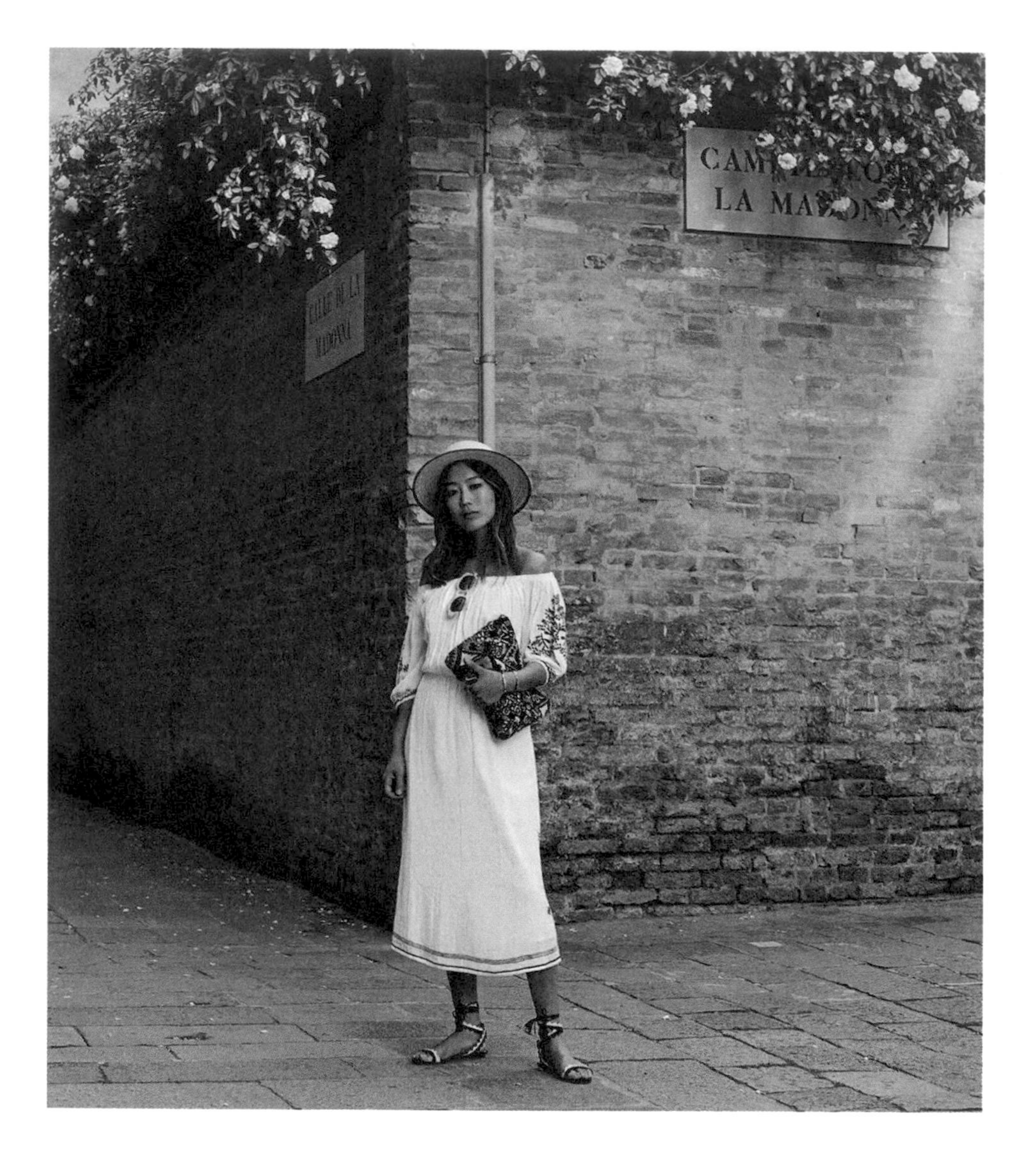

ABOVE We walked a ton in Venice. We purposely got lost (which I highly recommend when you're in another country—especially with someone who speaks the language) and ended up stumbling upon one of the best restaurants we experienced—eating all of the fish and pasta like a local really made me feel like I lived there. *Tularosa dress; Schutz shoes.* **OPPOSITE (FROM TOP)** You can't not ride a gondola in Venice, obviously. So we did. • More exploring. Everywhere is picture-perfect. Locals were drinking water out of the fountain—Jacopo included. *C/MEO dress; Raye sandals.*

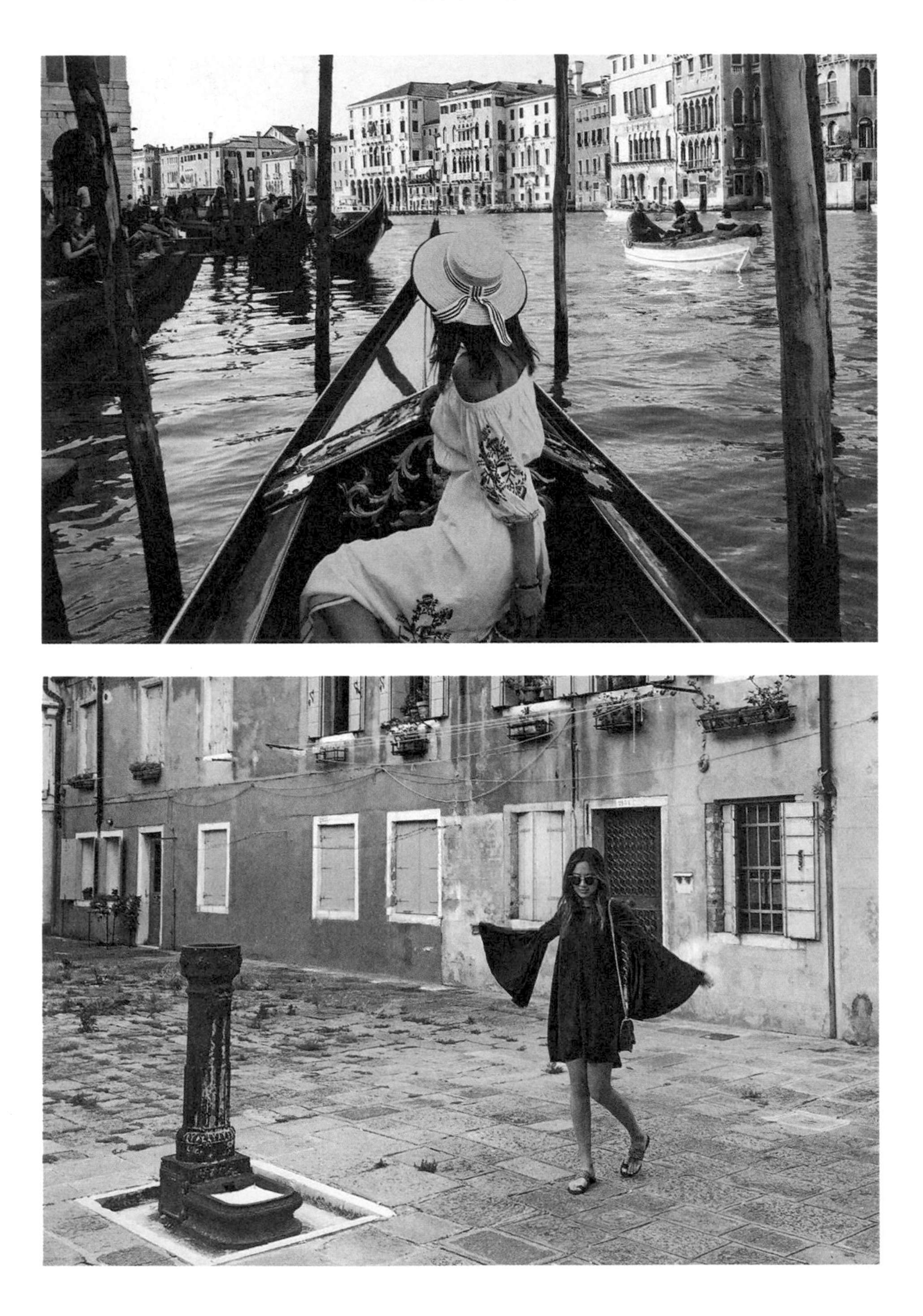

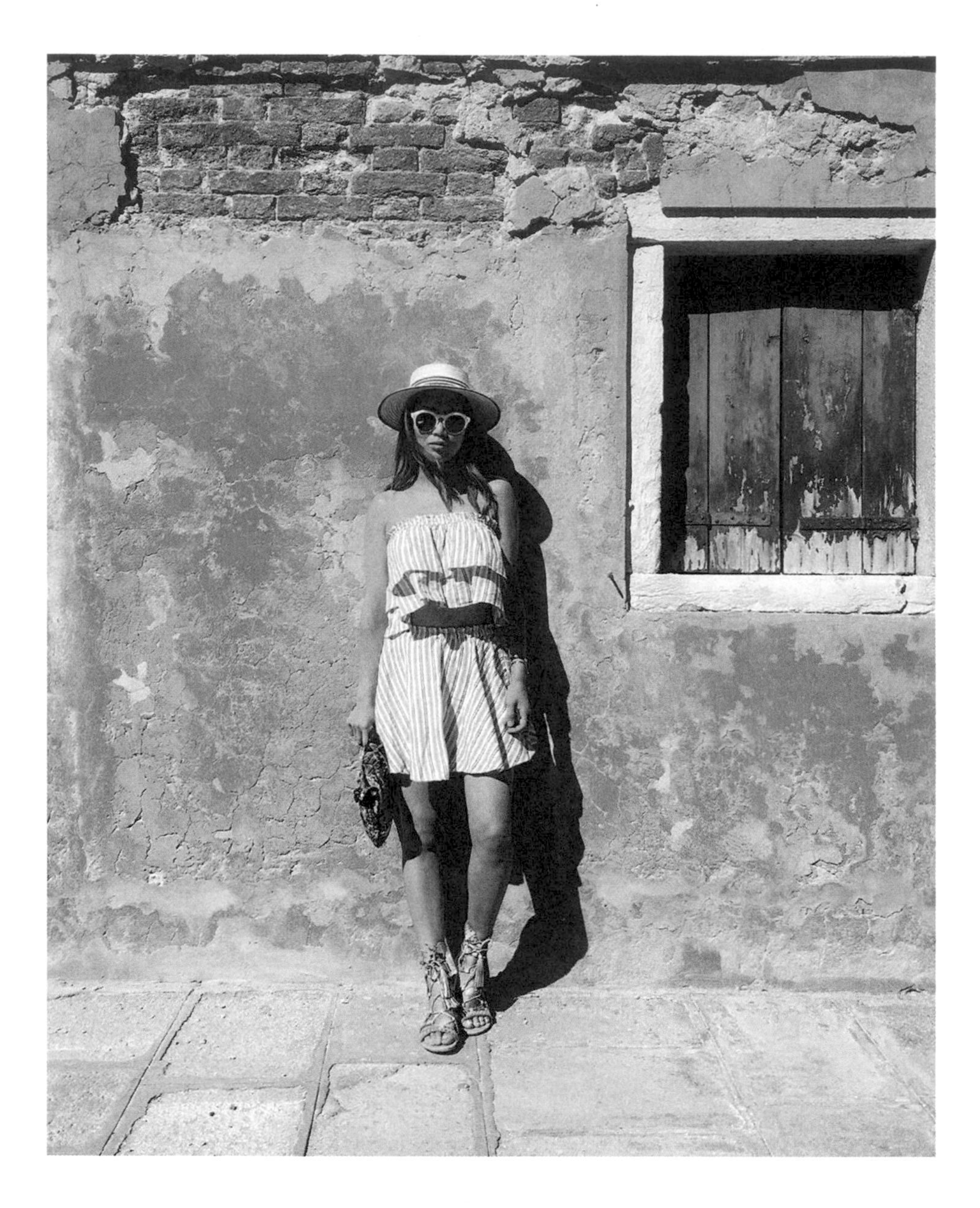

ABOVE *Privacy Please top and bottom.*

OPPOSITE One of the last days exploring. Peace out, Venice. *Two Songs top; Topshop skirt.*

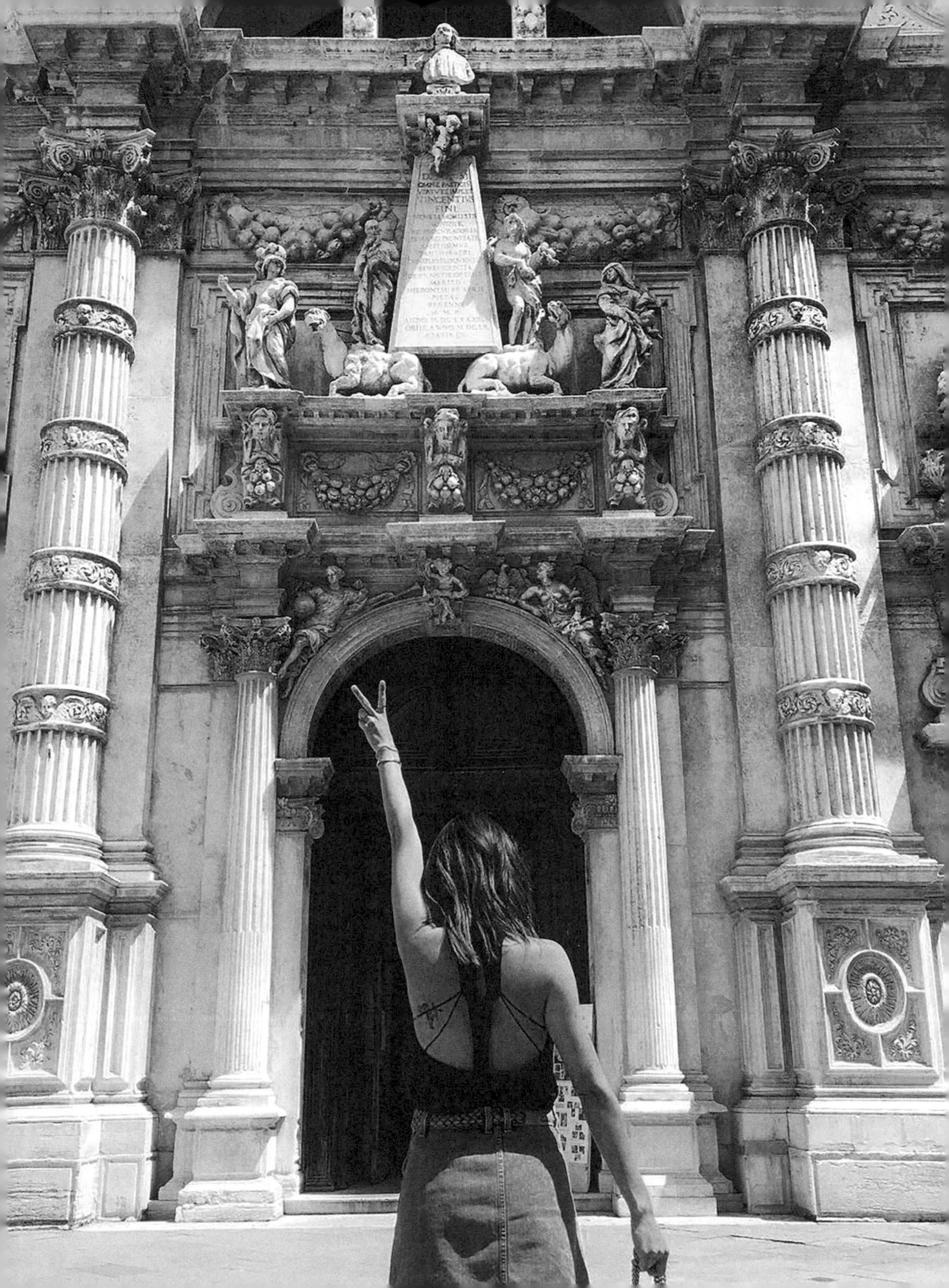
FINI

ACKNOWLEDGMENTS

Throughout the last ten years of my blogging career I went through countless air miles, cameras, and iPhones but only two boyfriends—so thank you to my Jacopo Moschin for your invaluable support and endless shoulder and head massages. You're also not such a bad photographer; I can totally see a future in photography for you.

I loved working with Erin again to write this second book. Although, I think that if we chatted less about boys and horoscopes we would have finished this book much sooner.

Thank you to my manager, Vanessa, for always reminding me to submit my notes and drafts to the editor. Sorry I always left your messages unread and blamed the poor Wi-Fi service—I lied.

Thank you to team SOS for putting up with me and helping me gather images for the book!

Thank you to my favorite mom (I only have one) for my wild childhood. Last book, you got upset that there weren't any photos of you, so I made sure there was at least one in this book. It's on page 158.

Thank you Dad for taking care of my dogs while I travel—even though I have to remind you to refill their water bowl, like, every day.

Thank you to my one and only sister, Dani. Every day I thank god that I have you. Even in my lowest moments the thought of your existence and the fact that you're my sister gives me energy. You're my favorite Song.

Thank you to my sweet new editor, Rebecca. I'm so happy you came on board. Thank you for your patience and for your love for abcV.

Also, on behalf of Instagram's one billion users, I'd like to give a special shout-out to @kevin for creating it.

Thank you avocados, raw bars, and chocolate coconut balls for staying up late with me while writing this book.

And last but not least, thank you to my incredible followers, from every corner of the globe, who continue to join me on my journeys. Your comments, likes, and messages have inspired me, encouraged me, and helped with my self-esteem. I hope that wherever in the world you are, you're happy, and you don't unfollow me.

PHOTOGRAPHY CREDITS

Page 27 © Fossil
Page 71 © Xin Wang
Pages 83 and 95 © Grant Legan
Pages 112 and 113 © Ikwa Zhao
Page 169 © Shimpei Mito
Page 323 © Anastasija Je